Facts and Inventions

Pencil sketch of James Boswell, by Sir Thomas Lawrence (1791). Courtesy of the Beinecke Rare Book and Manuscript Library, Yale University.

Facts and Inventions

SELECTIONS FROM

THE JOURNALISM OF

JAMES BOSWELL

Edited by
Paul Tankard
*With the assistance
of Lisa Marr*

Yale UNIVERSITY PRESS
NEW HAVEN & LONDON

Published with assistance from the Annie Burr Lewis Fund.

Published with assistance from the foundation established in memory of Philip Hamilton McMillan of the Class of 1894, Yale College.

Yale University Press books may be purchased in quantity for educational, business, or promotional use. For information, please e-mail sales.press@yale.edu (U.S. office) or sales@yaleup.co.uk (U.K. office).

Designed by Nancy Ovedovitz and set in Adobe Caslon type by Newgen North America. Printed in the United States of America.

ISBN: 978-0-300-14126-9 (cloth)

A catalogue record for this book is available from the Library of Congress and the British Library.

This paper meets the requirements of ANSI/NISO z39.48-1992 (Permanence of Paper).

10 9 8 7 6 5 4 3 2 1

Talking of Mr. [George] Steevens, he [Samuel Johnson] said he was a great writer in the newspapers. I thoughtlessly asked, "What pleasure can he have in that?" "Nay," said Mr. Johnson, "*you* can best tell that."

—James Boswell
(Journal, Friday April 14, 1775;
Ominous Years, 146)

Contents

2. EXECUTION INTELLIGENCE, 72

4. THE LIVES OF JOHNSON, 222

5. ESSAYS AND LETTERS, 289

List of Illustrations

Frontispiece. Pencil sketch of James Boswell, by Sir Thomas Lawrence (1791). Courtesy of the Beinecke Rare Book and Manuscript Library, Yale University.

Figure 1. Boswell's MS index to his essays in *London Chronicle*, 23 (1768). Courtesy of the Beinecke Rare Book and Manuscript Library, Yale University, xxvi.

Figure 2. The Amphitheatre, "Stratford Jubilee," Samuel Ireland, *Picturesque Views on the Upper, or Warwickshire Avon* (London, 1795). Courtesy of the Alexander Turnbull Library, Wellington, New Zealand, 22.

Figure 3. "James Boswell, Esqr, in the Dress of an Armed Corsican Chief," at Shakespeare Jubilee, engraving by J. Miller from a portrait by Samuel Wale, R.A., *London Magazine*, 38 (September 1769). Courtesy of HathiTrust, 29.

Figure 4. "Joseph Thayendaneken, the Mohawk Chief: From an Original Drawing in the Possession of James Boswell Esqr," *London Magazine*, 45 (July 1776). Courtesy of the Beinecke Rare Book and Manuscript Library, Yale University, 61.

Figure 5. Edinburgh Tolbooth Jail. "Heart of Midlothian: Taken Down 1817," Daniel Wilson, *Memorials of Edinburgh in the Olden Time* (Edinburgh, 1848), 1: facing p. 71. Courtesy of the University of Otago Library, Special Collections, Dunedin, New Zealand, 86.

Figure 6. "The Rev'd James Hackman: From the Original Drawing by Mr. Dighton," mezzotint, by R. Laurie (May 18, 1779). © Trustees of the British Museum, 94.

Figure 7. "Miss [Martha] Ray: Engraved from the Original Picture [by Nathaniel Dance, 1777]," engraving by Valentine Green (May 1779). © Trustees of the British Museum, 94.

Preface

The aim of this book is to present to a modern readership a large sample of a fascinating and overlooked body of writing by a major canonical author. Most of this material by James Boswell was last published more than two centuries ago in newspapers and magazines, and few people, even specialists in eighteenth-century British history and literature, will have seen any of it before. Old journalism is writing of a kind (or kinds) that—if it is found, read, and used at all by later readers and writers—is usually confined to the footnotes to other works. And, in fact, most of the 133 articles in this book have not yet risen even to that dignity. To read these pieces in a body of some kind is to have a clearer appreciation of them as sources of many kinds of potential usefulness and fascination, and to enable contemporary readers to do this has been my aim in presenting them not as context but as text.

Unlike his private diarizing, for which he has more recently become known, Boswell's journalism was—like all journalism—very public: there was nothing of a specialist nature about it; and, jostling for attention with other paragraphs, letters, advertisements and essays in the crowded columns of the periodicals, it was intended to be engaging and entertaining. However, it was—again, like all journalism—addressed to audiences for whom every item was immediately perceived to have a place in some familiar and ongoing discourse or narrative. To make these Boswellian texts accessible to modern and not necessarily specialist readers has seemed to me to require more (and a different kind of) intervention than would an edition of some single classic work.

In arranging, introducing, and annotating these articles, I initially had far more knowledge to acquire than to impart. It remains the case that this is not a textbook about eighteenth-century British politics, the American Revolution, the life of Boswell, or the history of journalism. People who know more than I ever will about those subjects—not to mention riots, executions, masquerades, the bottle conjuror, the Cock-Lane ghost, the Gentlemen Supporters of the Bill of Rights, and the history of rhubarb—will, I hope, appreciate Boswell's contributions to these subjects and use them for their own purposes. Less expert but curious and more general readers will find, as I have, a great deal to inform, amuse, and interest them.

Paul Tankard

Acknowledgments

I first hit upon the idea for this project in 2004, in response to Professor Jocelyn Harris advising me (as a new member of her department) that it would be a good idea career-wise to apply for a research grant. I thought that an edition of Boswell's periodical writings would be an extremely plausible academic task: that it would fill an obvious gap in the literature and would be clear and achievable. I am more than ever convinced of the former, however naive I may have been at first about the latter. As the deadlines have passed and my footnotes have accumulated, the extent and precise configurations of the knowledge I needed to acquire have become more apparent, and I see now that it more resembles one of those tasks that scholars enthusiastically project in mid-career and accomplish only after retirement.

Samuel Johnson famously observed that "[k]nowledge is of two kinds. We know a subject ourselves, or we know where we can find information upon it" (*Life*, 2:365). For much of my research on this project, I have relied on knowledge of the second kind. In addition to more traditional text-based research, I have tracked down via the Internet and approached via email a great many scholars in order to avail myself of their expertise. Most have been courteous, curious, and enthusiastically forthcoming with answers, advice, and simply good wishes. For any errors and gaps in my commentary that are the result of misreading, misinterpretation, and sheer ignorance, I am of course responsible—and will welcome gentle correction. The brief summaries that I have been obliged to give of complex historical realities have sometimes touched on matters that are subject to dispute among professional historians. In a work containing 133 texts and 1,343 footnotes on a great many different subjects, the opportunity for making errors large and small is quite remarkable. But, as Johnson also said (in the preface to his *Dictionary*), "In this work, when it shall be found that much is omitted, let it not be forgotten that much is likewise performed."

The following institutions have supported my labors. The University of Otago, Dunedin, New Zealand, where as a latecomer to my vocation as a scholar I have for ten years been happily employed, and in particular the Division of Humanities and the Department of English have provided much—well, some—of the time, resources, and professional impetus for this work. I am grateful for various small research grants and travel grants that have enabled me to work for months at a time in Melbourne, Australia, and for a pleasant morning in Wellington, New Zealand. These bodies have in particular funded the dedicated research assistance of Lisa Marr, which I have had for this project from start to finish and which is appropriately and gratefully signaled on the title page. I am also thankful for departmental funds that enabled me to call on the tenth- and eleventh-hour assistance of the learned and eagle-eyed Austin Gee. In 2007 I was honored to be a recipient of the Frederick A. and Marion S. Pottle Fellowship in Eighteenth-Century British Studies, awarded by the Beinecke Rare Book and Manuscript Library, Yale University, which enabled me to travel to and spend a month in New Haven, Connecticut, and to work with Yale's wondrous collection of James Boswell's papers. I hope the Pottles would have enjoyed this book. I am particularly grateful to Naomi Saito at the Beinecke for her attention during my visit and since. I am especially thankful for having, during my month at Yale, and subsequently, been adopted as a fellow-laborer by Gordon Turnbull and Jim Caudle, respectively the general editor and associate editor of the Yale Boswell Editions; these two scholars know more about Boswell than he did himself, and I am grateful for their ready and ongoing help, counsel, correction, and encouragement. During periods of leave in Melbourne, my use of the resources of two university libraries was facilitated by the heads of departments of English, John Frow at the University of Melbourne and, at Monash University, my former teachers and colleagues Clive Probyn and Alan Dilnot. I am grateful to the Rare Books section of the Matheson Library, Monash University, and its dedicated personnel (particularly Richard Overell) for many professional courtesies. Mention of Monash University reminds me that it was there in 1992, in a class called "The 'Age of Johnson'?" taught by Kevin Hart, that I first knowingly read any of the texts in this book (some of the paragraphs now in Chapter 4). I thank him for sparking my curiosity, and supervising the dissertations that led to my becoming a scholar of both Johnson and Boswell. I have been encouraged in my work by the Johnson Society of Australia, in particular Bryan Reid, who, like Boswell, is a journalist and a Johnsonian.

Scott Dawson, the product manager of Gale Digital Collections, kindly gave me repeated and extended "trial" access to the 17th–18th Century Burney Collection Newspapers, an amazing Web-based resource that I am pleased the University of Otago Library has subscribed to, in time for me to use it for revision and proof-checking. The office of the *Oxford Dictionary of National Biography* facilitated my contact with various *ODNB* contributors, if I couldn't track them down otherwise. I must also record my thanks to three models of modern scholarly communication, the electronic mailing lists C18-L (the Eighteenth-Century Interdisciplinary Discussion), H-Albion (the H-Net List for British and Irish History), and SHARP-L (the electronic forum of the Society for the History of Authorship, Reading, and Publishing). Members of these lists have been happy to share knowledge, intuitions, and suggestions on many obscure topics.

For their hands-on help in first cracking the "Rampagers," as well as for their week-by-week good cheer and continuing friendships, I am pleased to thank my ENGL 476 "Grub Street" class of 2008, the Grubblings: Barry Allen, Ruth Ballantyne, Flora Feltham, Jen Jewell, and Shapelle McKenzie. I thank Professor Wallace Kirsop and Meredith Sherlock, who gave me invaluable practical assistance when certain bureaucrats at Monash University Library forgot what university libraries are there for. Thanks to Patrick Spedding for advice and other favors, and to Paul Sorrell, who spent an afternoon helping me find an essay in my notes toward an introduction.

A number of eminent scholars have kindly read through the portions of the "Rampager" section relating to their own areas of expertise. All the following were strangers to me who generously offered guidance and correction simply in an effort to protect the work from error: John Cookson, Stephen Farrell (on Rockingham), Marie Peters (on Pitt), John Sainsbury (on Wilkes), Karl W. Schweizer (on Bute), and, in particular, Harry Dickinson of Edinburgh, who read the whole section, correcting misapprehensions major and minor. The two anonymous academic readers to whom my work was submitted (and resubmitted) by Yale University Press treated the manuscript to almost embarrassingly careful scrutiny and have contributed substantially to the quality of the finished text in terms of both style and substance. I will have no doubt failed to interpret some situations to the satisfaction of the learned, but I hope to have committed no factual errors. My esteemed colleagues at Otago, Chris Ackerley and Keith Maslen, read through whole sections and gave much valuable advice and encouragement on matters both specific and general.

For many instances of advice, assistance, information, or encouragement, which it would be laborious to describe and which the individuals concerned have probably forgotten, I wish to record my thanks to Arlene Allan, Peter Anstey, Peter Appleyard, Joel Berson, Lance Bertelsen, the late O M Brack Jr., Miles Bredin, David Brewer, Jenny R. Brooks, Henry Buehner, Miriam Burstein, John W. Byrne, John Cannon, Robert DeMaria, Ann Digby, Peter Durrant, John Finlay, Bob Folkenflik, Alexander Gourlay, John Hale, Jon Hall, David S. Hewitt, Joyce Ippolito, Nicky Jones, Megan Kitching, Paul Langford, Helen Leach, Nigel Leask, Tony Lee, Jack Lynch, Gregor Macaulay, Liam McIlvanney, Tom McLean, Emma MacLeod, Duncan Macmillan, Jackie McMillan, Brian McMullin, Marion Mertons, Jerry Morris, John Moulden, Holly Faith Nelson, Iain Old, Ruth Perry, Charles Pigden, John Preston, John Radner, Susan Rennie, Paul Rice, Nicholas Rodger, John R. Rodgers, Pat Rogers, Shef Rogers, Adam Rounce, Paul T. Ruxin, Peter Sabor, Ann Saunders, Terry Seymour, Rick Sher, Guy Spielman, Barbara Stone, John Sullivan, Roey Sweet, Peter D. G. Thomas, Lyn Tribble, Greg Waite, Jessica Warner, Pat Wheatley, Ilka White, and John Wiltshire. My inquiries to various institutions fell into the hands of the following helpful people: Julia Kate Harrison and Bruce Gorie (Court of the Lord Lyon), Donald Kerr (Special Collections Library, University of Otago), Sandy Leishman (Royal Highland Fusiliers Museum), Julia Muir-Watt (Whithorn and District Business Association), Kevin O'Hara (Northumberland Wildlife Trust), Anthony Tedeschi (Dunedin Public Libraries), Eve Watson (Royal Society of Arts), and Joseph Wisdom (Library of St. Paul's Cathedral, London). To anyone I have overlooked, my apologies.

I want finally to thank my wife, Tanya, for mostly cheerfully enduring trans-Tasman relocation and the increasing inseparability of her husband's work and after-hours activities, for her love and interest, and in particular for spending three days reading the multivolume *Epistles of Erasmus*, with no further result than personal edification.

PT

Introduction: Keeping the Newspapers Warm

BOSWELL AND HIS REPUTATION

For over two centuries, James Boswell has been well known—and still remains best known—as the author of *The Life of Samuel Johnson* (1791), the earliest and best of modern biographies and one of the world's most-loved books. Surprisingly, in these postliterate times, Boswell's *Life of Johnson* not only has a following among literary scholars, but still attracts the dedication and enthusiasm of nonprofessional readers. And while Johnson's own writings are studied by a large and growing scholarly community, the *Life of Johnson* and its predecessor, Boswell's *Journal of a Tour to the Hebrides with Samuel Johnson* (1785), remain the focus of the popular cult of the quotable and anecdotal Johnson. Since the 1950s, Boswell himself has become increasingly known to literary readers, not only as a biographer but as an exceptionally dedicated diarist and a vivid chronicler of everyday life. His extensive private journals, correspondence, and other manuscripts, suppressed by his family and long believed lost, were recovered in the early twentieth century, and the publication of the journals in a general or "trade" edition (1950–89) has given him a reputation as a self-fashioner of a surprisingly contemporary sensibility. For contemporary readers, the journals provide a vivid depiction of Boswell's own day-to-day life, his loves, interests, and activities, in London, Edinburgh, and Europe in the second half of the eighteenth century; for scholars of those times and places they are a rich source of social history; and students of human character, amateur and professional, are drawn to Boswell for his curiosity about other people as well as his all-but-comprehensive self-revelation.[1]

---

1. For Boswell and self-fashioning, see, for example, Nussbaum, "Manly Subjects," 103–26. For psychoanalytic readings of Boswell, see Newman, *James Boswell*.

These two categories of material, published biography and private papers—as extensive as they are—represent only part of what Boswell committed to paper in his lifetime. His first literary success was his history and travel book about the island nation of Corsica and its heroic nationalist leader: the *Account of Corsica, Journal of a Tour to that Island, and Memoirs of Pascal Paoli* (1768). His campaign on behalf of Corsica through this and other publications earned him among his contemporaries the characteristically eighteenth-century sobriquet "Corsica Boswell." His later literary coups, his two Johnsonian works, brought him a reputation as the "Great Biographer," but did so only a disappointingly few years before his death.

But there is a further and very extensive category of Boswellian writing, for which this book is intended to find a place in the canon. Before, after, and between his early and late literary triumphs, for thirty-five years, Boswell was—in the interstices of an Edinburgh legal practice and the management of his Ayrshire estate—a busy professional writer, with an almost constant presence in the British press. His work, over a great variety of subjects and styles, was published in numerous magazines and newspapers. Six hundred or more such items have been identified by scholars. However, almost the only use made of this material since its original publication has been by bibliographers, for whom it poses tantalizing puzzles and provides fuel for minor scholarly controversies, and biographers, for whom the list of Boswell's writings constitutes a scaffold for his doings, movements, and preoccupations. This material has never before been gathered or selected for publication under Boswell's name.

Boswell was from his youth attracted to newspapers and magazines, to their immediacy and heterogeneity, their unique and unprecedented ability to draw one imaginatively into the engine room of culture and society. Like many young writers, his earliest literary ambitions and compositions were poetical (although he also wrote theater criticism in Edinburgh, in his late teens); but from at least his second visit to London, as a young man of twenty-two, he seems to have appreciated that the poetry of the metropolis was the news. We sense him beginning to feel himself a citizen when, after being in London for a week, he writes in his journal, "I walked into the City and . . . then breakfasted at Child's Coffeehouse, read the political papers, and had some chat with citizens" (Nov. 27, 1762; *Lond. Journ.*, 51). A few months later, he wrote of his landlord that "regularly every day does he bring home *The Public Ledger*, which is most duly served up to me" (Feb. 9, 1763; *Lond. Journ.*, 184). The papers were still part of his breakfast routine thirty years later:

> Breakfasted at the Chapter Coffee-house and read the file of the *Morning Post* since August, and found various squibs against me. Read also a

file of Edinburgh [*Advertiser?*] for the same period. (Nov. 2, 1792; *Great Biographer*, 191)

His early attitude to the press is expressed in a digression in his *Account of Corsica*, where he remarks enthusiastically that

> an English news-paper is the most various and extraordinary composition that mankind ever produced. An English news-paper, while it informs the judicious of what is really doing in Europe, can keep pace with the wildest fancy in feigned adventures, and amuse the most desultory taste with essays on all subjects, and in every stile. (*Account*, ed. Boulton and McLoughlin, 121)

In this passage Boswell not only foreshadows the aspect of his career illustrated in this collection, but also seems to signal an early or incipient awareness that, within the newspapers, one might confound "what is really doing" with "feigned adventures." The manuscript of the *Account of Corsica* reveals that in this passage Boswell originally referred not to "an English news-paper" but specifically to the "London Chronicle" (*Account*, 121 n. 51). This was the paper to which, immediately after he left Corsica, he sent paragraphs about the country (and its distinguished visitor, himself), which were printed as he instructed, and which he later marked in his own bound volumes of that newspaper, helpfully indicating which were "fact" and which "invention" (Figure 1).

BOSWELL: LIFE AND WORK

A career as a London writer was not what Boswell's father, Alexander Boswell, Lord Auchinleck, had in mind for his eldest son.[2] Lord Auchinleck was the eighth hereditary laird of the Boswell family estate, Auchinleck in Ayrshire, and a judge of both the highest civil and criminal courts in Scotland. James, born in 1740, was a delicate and somewhat mystical child, who in adolescence recovered from his early timidity and became outgoing and ambitious for social distinction and literary fame. Sent to university at Edinburgh, he became distracted by the life of the theater, and his father had him transferred to the more dour environment of Glasgow. Rather than acquire Presbyterian seriousness, in March 1760 Boswell ran away to London. On this short visit, his hunger for experience found him exploring a vocation as a Catholic monk, living in a social

---

2. Boswell has been the subject of a substantial two-part scholarly biography: by Pottle (*Earlier Years*) and Brady (*Later Years*); for the more general reader, there is Martin, *Life of James Boswell*. Gordon Turnbull's long article on Boswell in the *ODNB* is a model of scholarly breadth and concision and has been a convenient source for much of what follows.

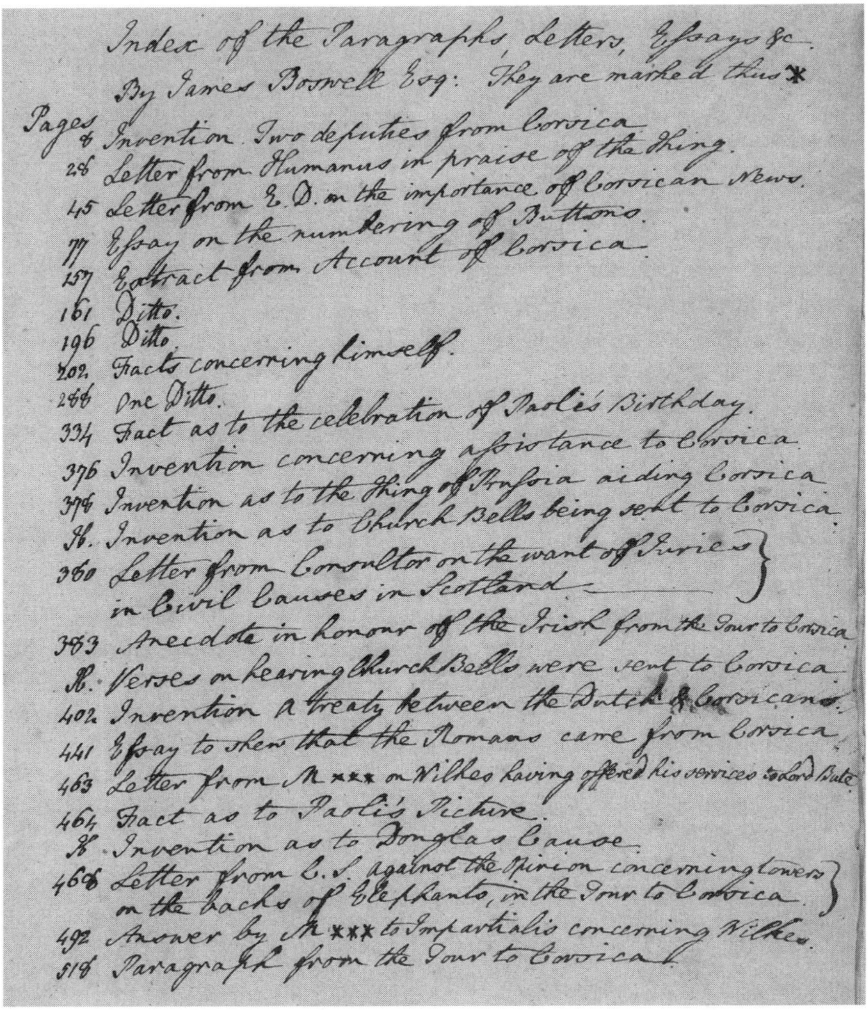
Index of the Paragraphs, Letters, Essays &c.
By James Boswell Esq: They are marked thus *

Pages
4 Invention. Two deputies from Corsica
28 Letter from Humanus in praise of the thing.
45 Letter from E. D. on the importance of Corsican News.
77 Essay on the numbering of Buttons.
157 Extract from Account of Corsica.
161 Ditto.
196 Ditto.
202 Facts concerning himself.
288 One Ditto.
334 Fact as to the celebration of Paoli's Birthday.
376 Invention concerning assistance to Corsica.
378 Invention as to the King of Prussia aiding Corsica
Ib. Invention as to Church Bells being sent to Corsica.
380 Letter from Consultor on the want of Juries in Civil Causes in Scotland
383 Anecdote in honour of the Irish from the Tour to Corsica
Ib. Verses on hearing Church Bells were sent to Corsica.
402 Invention a treaty between the Dutch & Corsicans.
441 Essay to shew that the Romans came from Corsica.
463 Letter from M*** on Wilkes having offered his services to Lord Bute
464 Fact as to Paoli's Picture.
Ib. Invention as to Douglas Cause.
468 Letter from C. S. against the Opinion concerning towers on the backs of Elephants, in the Tour to Corsica.
492 Answer by M*** to Impartialis concerning Wilkes.
518 Paragraph from the Tour to Corsica.

Figure 1. Boswell's MS index to his essays in London Chronicle, *23 (1768).*
Courtesy of the Beinecke Rare Book and Manuscript Library, Yale University.

whirl with literary, theatrical, and sporting types, acquiring a lifelong addiction to illicit sexual encounters, and craving a career as an officer in the Guards. After three months, his father had him return to Edinburgh and study the law. By this time he had begun to keep a private journal. After passing his law examinations, he left again for London in late 1762, this time with his father's grudging permission to seek a commission in the Guards. He rapidly made a succession of new and amusing acquaintances, including, in May 1763, the pre-eminent English man of letters of the time, Samuel Johnson. Looking around for an opportunity to get his name into print, he hit upon the idea of polishing and publishing the gossipy, extravagant, and shamelessly self-conscious correspondence between himself and his Edinburgh friend Andrew Erskine, which duly appeared as *Letters between the Honourable Andrew Erskine, and James Boswell, Esq.*, much to the chagrin of his father. The journal of this busy period was found in the early 1930s and in 1950 was published to great acclaim as *Boswell's London Journal, 1762–1763*.[3]

By August 1763, Boswell had given up his military ambitions, and his father allowed him to leave England to study the law at Utrecht in Holland, after which he would be permitted to tour Europe on the condition that he return to undertake a legal career in Scotland. He studied diligently at Utrecht and diverted himself by conducting a romance with a beautiful aristocrat and intellectual, Isabella van Tuyll van Serooskerken ("Belle de Zuylen"—later famous as the writer Madame de Charrière), whom for some years he considered marrying. He began his continental travels in June 1764, visited a number of German courts, and was introduced to many eminent people. His greatest triumphs were reserved for Switzerland, where he secured interviews with Rousseau and Voltaire. With Rousseau's encouragement, he determined to go to Corsica to seek an audience with Pasquale Paoli, the leader of the freedom fighters. Passing through Italy he consolidated his friendship with exiled English radical politician John Wilkes (a major character in this collection; see Chap. 3, n. 22 and ff.). He spent six adventurous weeks in Corsica, October–November 1764, met the illustrious General Paoli, and recorded his conversations. Before returning to Britain, he ensured that Corsica, its general, and its young British visitor were noticed in the London press by sending a series of reports, marked (falsely) as to date and location, to John Wilkie, publisher of the *London Chronicle*. Boswell continued by means of this campaign to keep Corsica in the news, until his *Account of Corsica* was published in February 1768.

After returning to Edinburgh, he studied for examinations in Scottish law and became an advocate. He remained a practicing lawyer for the rest of his life, but all his most genuine ambitions were elsewhere. He became an enthusiastic

---

3. In 2010 the *London Journal, 1762–1763* was reedited for the Penguin Classics series by Gordon Turnbull. I have consulted the elaborate annotation of this edition but, for the majority of my references to the text, have preferred the more widely dispersed edition by Frederick Pottle (1950). In any case, my citations of this text (and many others) include a date from within the text, to allow easy referencing across different editions.

partisan in a celebrated legal case of the 1760s, "the great Douglas Cause" (as he always called it; see "The Shorthand Reporters" in Chap. 1), and his short allegorical account of the case, *Dorando: A Spanish Tale* (1767), was very popular. After the *Account of Corsica* appeared, he went to London to enjoy its success and renewed his efforts to obtain British sympathy, aid, and intervention on behalf of Corsica. For the rest of his life, Boswell tried to make an annual extended visit to London, usually at least during the spring court recess, renewing and developing his friendships, in particular with Johnson and his circle. Paoli, who came to London in September 1769 when the Corsican resistance was defeated by the French, was welcomed by Boswell and remained his friend until he returned to Corsica in 1790. In November 1769, Boswell married his cousin Margaret Montgomerie. He was sincerely in love with her and remained so all his life, despite innumerable fleeting carnal liaisons and a number of serious love affairs.

He was firmly established in Edinburgh as a lawyer and family man, but kept up his London connections through correspondence and by reading and writing for the newspapers. He was visited in Scotland by Paoli in September 1771 and escorted him on a Scottish tour, of which his report for the *London Magazine* is included in this collection (Chap. 1). In late 1773, he hosted Johnson on a three-month visit to Scotland, during which time they toured the Highlands and the Inner Hebrides, both writers gathering materials for books. Johnson's *Journey to the Western Islands* was published the following year. As the 1770s proceeded, Boswell's family and legal practice grew. He was elected to Johnson's dining society, the (Literary) Club, in 1775. In 1774 and 1777 he did not manage his jaunt to London, though in the latter year he made a special trip south to spend two weeks in September at Ashbourne in Derbyshire, where Johnson was staying with an old friend. All this time Boswell kept his journal very carefully and contributed to the London press, in particular with his two series of essays, under the pseudonyms the "Hypochondriack" and the "Rampager" (which latter series this book reprints for the first time). In August 1782 his father died, making James Boswell the ninth laird of Auchinleck. Later that year, with his wife and their five children, he moved from Edinburgh to Ayrshire. This seems to have stimulated his active involvement in local Scottish political activity, through writing, seeking political appointments, and electioneering. For most of May and June 1784, he was in London, during which time he accompanied Johnson on a trip to Oxford. He was in Edinburgh when Johnson died, at the age of seventy-five. Boswell was well known to have long been collecting biographical materials about his friend and was immediately solicited by London publishers to write his life. The journal he had kept of their Scottish tour had been carefully written at the time, and, with the assistance of Shakespearean scholar Edmond Malone, he was able to revise it for publication on October 1, 1785, as *The Journal of a Tour to the Hebrides with Samuel Johnson, LL.D.*

In 1786 Boswell at last did as he had long wanted and moved his family to London, with the intention of being admitted to and practicing at the English bar. He also set to work, again with the encouragement, advice, and practical help of Malone, on his biography of Johnson. In early 1788 his years of intermittent political maneuvering paid off when he was elected recorder of the city of Carlisle, as the candidate of the wealthy political manipulator James Lowther, earl of Lonsdale. Boswell came to regret this appointment almost immediately: it was hardly an important post, and his patron was bullying and capricious. Furthermore, Margaret Boswell's health had been poor for some time, and in May that year the family moved back to Auchinleck. Boswell continued mostly in London, working on the *Life of Johnson*, but he was attending to Lonsdale's demands when news arrived of his wife's deteriorating condition. He and his sons hastened to Scotland, but she died before they arrived, on June 4, 1789. In October, Boswell returned to London, with four of his five children, and, having made arrangements for their schooling and accommodation, he resumed work on the *Life of Johnson*. In July 1790 he resigned his recordership and gave up the connection with Lonsdale.

The *Life of Johnson* was published in two large quarto volumes on May 16, 1791, and, in spite of its length and expense, it was immediately successful. Boswell remained mostly in London, enjoying (and orchestrating) its celebrity. He attended to his social, parental, and estate obligations, but he was getting no legal work and was depressed and frequently idle. He pursued various new schemes, marital, literary, and political, but none of them came to much. He spent a month in Cornwall in August–September 1792, with his daughters Veronica and Euphemia, visiting his oldest friend, W. J. Temple (see Chap. 3, n. 248), vicar of St. Gluvias. In November 1792, after the first edition of the *Life* had sold out, Boswell recorded with satisfaction receiving a sum in excess of £1,500 from the booksellers (*Great Biographer*, 201). He prepared a much-revised second edition, which was published in July 1793. He spent from June 1794 to January 1795 at Auchinleck, with three of his children, attending to his various responsibilities, but no longer keeping a journal and regretting that he had not made more of a mark in the world of politics or the law. He returned to London, and, at a meeting of the Literary Club, he became suddenly ill with kidney failure, presumably related to his lifelong recurrent bouts of venereal disease and his recent particularly heavy drinking. After five weeks in pain, Boswell died on May 19 at his house in Great Portland Street.

BOSWELL'S PERIODICAL WRITING

A biographical sketch such as this fails to represent undramatic but important and ongoing aspects of the subject's life and character: in Boswell's case, his lifelong friendships, his energetic socializing, his melancholia, his political activities, his pleasure in his ancestry and pride in his heritage, and (as Frederick A. Pottle, the twentieth century's foremost Boswell scholar, emphasizes) his "natural and almost constant power of being agreeable to others ... [his] charm, his affableness, his good humour, his genuine good will" (*Earlier Years*, 268–69). Similarly, brief accounts of Boswell's literary work will record his publishing milestones but fail to deal with the constant stream of material that he published in periodicals. Pottle, in his bibliographical account of Boswell's literary career, remarked that he considered "the most important" part of his book to be the section dealing with Boswell's journalistic articles, "which, if collected, would surprise us by their bulk" (*Lit. Car.*, xxiii).

There have always been writers of the more literary kind who have made regular or occasional contributions to the periodical press. If they have a decent-sized book-buying readership, and they write enough such pieces, they might gather up and repackage this material to form a readily recognizable kind of book: a collection of essays. Writers from Daniel Defoe to Virginia Woolf, George Orwell to Umberto Eco and Susan Sontag, have swelled their bibliographies with books of short prose texts that appeared first in newspapers and magazines. Whether described as columns, reviews, essays, or (increasingly) as "nonfiction," such collections are books for which there is only a small market, and publishers are usually interested in a writer's essays only if the writer is well known for other species of writing, such as fiction or poetry. Some important writers, like Charles Lamb, G. K. Chesterton, or Joan Didion, have been happy to be regarded primarily as essayists. But for most modern-day professional writers of books, journalistic work is a sideline, even if it is for some a more reliable source of day-to-day income than their long-form works. When such material—often book reviews or commentary on the arts and society—is collected into a body, it becomes (for its second audience) valued mainly as a commentary on the writer's major and more literary work.

A browse through this collection will quickly show that Boswell's contributions to the press do not, on the whole, have this character. His "Hypochondriack" essays, published in a collected edition in 1928, clearly belong to the traditions of Johnson's *Rambler* and *Idler* essays, and the *Spectator* and other series by Addison and Steele. His "Rampager" letters are far less traditional. Most of his periodical work was not only published without the now-conventional para-

textual element of the writer's name, but was, in fact, genuinely anonymous—in
the eighteenth century, for an author to be unnamed was not always the same
thing as to be unknown; only since the recovery of his private papers have many
of these writings been identified as Boswell's. Therefore, any value or function
that this material may have had as implied commentary on himself or his reputation derives only from the fact that Boswell was often enough his own explicit
subject matter. Boswell's collected nonfiction would look very different from,
say, Samuel Johnson's. Although Johnson apparently took some pleasure in regarding himself as a citizen of Grub Street and a journalistic gun-for-hire, his
items in the periodical press are, on the whole, things intended, even in their
ephemeral settings, to be rereadable, of permanent value and interest. Johnson
is not known to have sent to the press news reports, paragraphs, or even signed
letters, but far more dignified and generically formal pieces. He wrote elegant
essays, long reviews, lives of distinguished persons, histories and translations,
stately prefaces, and political tracts dealing with issues of high principle. Even
when Johnson wrote *down*, his writings had an *upward* tendency. But it is precisely because Boswell was not, in the main, contributing to the press in his
capacity as the public man, James Boswell, or as a literary man of any kind, that
he exploited a far broader range of the kinds of writing that were hosted by the
periodicals.

For similarities to Boswell's journalistic work, we need to look not so much
to major or literary writers, as to writers whose work was more topical and repu-
tations more ephemeral. We do not need to look far. On May 24, 1763, only a
week after first meeting Johnson, Boswell called by invitation on journalist and
wit Bonnell Thornton, who was at that time writing for the *Public Advertiser*, in
which he had favorably reviewed the Erskine–Boswell *Letters*. On that occasion
Boswell met other members of the "Nonsense Club," Charles Churchill and
Robert Lloyd, and was introduced to John Wilkes; he congratulated himself
that he had "just got into the middle of the London Geniuses" (*Lond. Journ.*,
266). In various combinations, this group, who met regularly from the mid-
1750s to 1764, was responsible for a great deal of satirical poetry and journalism,
including the essay series *The Connoisseur* (1754–56) conducted by Thornton and
George Colman (whom Boswell had met only a few weeks earlier), with contributions by other members. Pottle suggests that this collaboration was in fact
a model for the Erskine–Boswell *Letters* (*Earlier Years*, 116). A few weeks later,
Boswell mentioned this paper to Johnson, who "said it wanted matter"; when
reporting this in the *Life*, Boswell commented, "No doubt it has not the deep
thinking of Johnson's writings. But surely it has just views of the surface of life,
and a very sprightly manner" (1:420). The dissolute and charming Wilkes, who

later was to become a close friend of Boswell, was at the time of this first meeting involved with the satirical poet Charles Churchill in writing the scurrilous essay series the *North Briton* (1762–63), in mockery of the administration of the prime minister, Lord Bute. This series—with other facetious and polemical political essay-sheets, such as the *Monitor* (1755–63), Arthur Murphy's *Auditor* (1762–63), and many others—is likely to have been on Boswell's mind when he commenced his own political commentaries as the "Rampager."

A more literary writer, particularly if his authorship were always to be known, would take more care to write things of substance and repute. Yet when Boswell finished a serious political pamphlet, *A Letter to Lord Braxfield* (1780), he—unusually—went to some trouble to keep secret its authorship;[4] nevertheless, he derived a great deal of satisfaction simply from ushering these opinions into the public sphere. He recorded in his journal, "I said to [fellow advocate, William] Nairne that if I had a pamphlet to write every day, I should be happy" (April 27, 1780; *Laird*, 207). Boswell enjoyed simply being known *to himself* as a shaper of opinion, and for him the convention of anonymity was in fact an incitement to publish. He was, nevertheless, known among his associates to be a frequent contributor to the press, although this proclivity was not universally approved of. In February 1775, Johnson wrote to him, "Your love of publication is offensive and disgusting, and will end, if it be not reformed, in a general distrust among all your friends" (*Ominous Years*, 63–64; *Letters SJ*, 2:178 n. 9). Johnson was admittedly using the term "publication" in a broad sense,[5] but for Boswell, appearing in print was one means of making the private public.

A complete collection of Boswell's journalism would not be possible; for a start, we do not know how much of his work is (and will likely remain forever) unidentified. Furthermore, the prospective collector or editor is challenged not only by the sheer quantity of the identified material but also by the variety of subjects, the variety of *types* of material (journalism not being a genre, exactly), the greatly varying length and significance of the items, the lack of titles, and the close resemblance of many of them to each other. Some items (such as the extended news stories and the celebrity interviews) were in their original settings self-contained reading experiences; others most emphatically were not:

4. The addressee of the *Letter to Robert Macqueen, Lord Braxfield* succeeded Boswell's father as a judge in the High Court of Justiciary, and Boswell may well have felt that the *Letter*'s censure of the behavior of judges would have been weakened had his authorship been known (see *Laird*, 7–13).

5. In his *Dictionary of the English Language*, Johnson defines "to publish" in its primary sense as "to discover to mankind; to make generally and openly known."

they are more like contributions to an ongoing conversation or installments of a novel or a series of Internet-mediated micro-blogs. While I have long found the Periodicals section of the bibliography of Boswell tantalizing and thought much of the actual material (when located and read) to be extremely interesting, it seemed to me to require a considerable degree of editorial intervention to make its interest apparent to a modern reader.

Boswell was a lively and versatile writer who honed his skills in the press. He taught himself not only to sketch characters and craft anecdotes, but to allude and suggest, to affirm and to deny, to inform and mislead, through the forms or genres made available to him by the structures and practices of the eighteenth-century press. The newspapers in particular suited the needs of an expanding literate public of hurried, curious browsers, flipping from paper to paper—each with its own loyalties—in search of not so much *the* truth as some purported "intelligence" that was new or telling. This is not what is expected by readers accustomed to the twentieth-century "journals of record," which are the products of highly efficient information-gathering networks, with a global reach and staffed by committed and trained professionals. But it is perhaps an increasingly familiar scenario to twenty-first-century readers, adapting and re-adapting themselves to a rapidly expanding and evolving media environment. In the eighteenth century, as in the twenty-first-century "blogosphere," opinion and purported news circulated like gossip, temporarily catching the eye and the interest, to be replaced the next day with something new. Boswell remains one of the few major British writers to have appreciated intuitively the potentials of the conditions under which journalistic writing was conducted and to have developed a variety of ways to exploit these regimes. One day when as a young lawyer he had been much oppressed by his professional writing, he noted in his journal that he "Had been accustomed too much to make the law easy, and write papers like essays for a newspaper, without reading much" (February 21, 1767; *Search*, 32–33). The ephemerality of journalism was to him not a frustration but an opportunity, to write easily, spontaneously, conversationally, sometimes mischievously.

But to Boswell, the habitual accumulator and recorder of his own disparate experiences, his journalistic output presented the challenge of collection and arrangement. It is not surprising that such a chronicler of day-to-day life should archive his press cuttings. Using Boswell's archived cuttings, now in the Beinecke Library at Yale University, one sees the great biographer intermittently pursuing different systems of classification, a situation with which every researcher or untrained archivist can identify. For the period in which he contributed frequently and almost exclusively to the *London Chronicle*, he marked his contributions in his own bound volumes of the paper, but this method posed obvious retrieval and storage problems. For identifying his contributions, his handwritten indexes to these volumes are useful, as far as they go. He usually marked his own writings with a distinctive symbol. However, after his return to London from Corsica, he was more like a conduit than writer of the Corsican news, and his marginal crosses against certain items in later volumes seem to indicate an interest or involvement that renders differentiation impossible. When he spread his contributions to more publications than he could subscribe to or keep copies of, he took to snipping out cuttings. Some of these he put in envelopes or wrapped in paper bands or pasted onto cards, writing the dates and publication details on most but not all. It seems to me that the fact of Boswell's having cut out some particular piece, pasted it on card, and written its publication details is strong prima facie evidence of his authorship. That being said, I cannot guarantee that all of the texts here are Boswell's, and one feels that, although he was intermittently concerned to leave in his files evidence for later readers, on some occasions he was not altogether sure himself.

This invites the question: what were Boswell's filed cuttings for? Any answer is, of course, guesswork, but they appear to me to be—in the main—not a collection of items from the papers that simply interested him, such as many people collect, but (like his letters and journals, with which they were archived) part of the record of his own life and times. In a manuscript notebook (mostly dated 1785), Boswell made a note to himself: "Collect your essays out of the P.A. so far as you have them."[6] *Collect* may mean no more than gather up and archive them, as he did; all but four of the twenty "Rampagers" from the *Public Advertiser* have been carefully kept in his files. The fact that he made manuscript corrections to eleven of those cuttings may simply indicate a pride in his work, or it may indicate a half-formed intention to republish them as a collection, as he intended to do with his "Hypochondriack" essays, as he discussed with Johnson (*Life*, 4:179).

There are, in this collection, not just those twenty installments of his (other) column, but essay-length news reports, interview-based celebrity profiles, signed letters about himself and his affairs, advertisements, reflective essays on a range of subjects, letters to the editor on public issues, and (an unfamiliar category) many news paragraphs. This collection will, for most readers, add considerably to their appreciation of Boswell as a writer, but it will, I hope, be of equal value

6. As I am informed by James J. Caudle (personal communication).

and interest as a précis—albeit an idiosyncratic one—of British periodical culture from the 1760s to the 1790s.

THE PERIODICALS

When modern scholars and readers deal with writings of the past that were first and are still published as (or in) books, we immediately and on the whole correctly appreciate important things about those texts. *Rasselas, Gulliver's Travels, Pride and Prejudice*, and the *Life of Johnson* were books when they first appeared, and they are, for most readers, books still; in reading them today, we far more closely replicate the experience of their first and intended readers than we ever can with reprinted periodical items. In dealing with texts that were written for the periodical press, a detailed and accurate sense of context is vital to understanding what they are for and what they mean. Like periodicals today, the eighteenth-century publications in which Boswell's articles appeared have themselves particular characters, political outlooks, and intended readerships: is the *St. James's Chronicle* more like the *New York Times* or *Hello!* magazine? To understand the essays and articles, it helps to know, for instance, who owned the paper and what their politics were, when and where it appeared, who and how many people read it, and what they expected.

Each particular issue of a newspaper also has a very particular historical meaning: reading the articles now and outside of that context, we need to know when the paper came out, what was going on at the time, and what was in the issues of the paper on the days before and the days after. Even the particular page or part of the paper will show the item in relation to other items that would for the original readers have contributed to its meaning. There is a great deal of difference between an item appearing as the lead article on page one and being tucked away in an obscure corner of the second last page after the shipping news; and was it among the news, the letters, or the advertisements? Information of this kind is usually missing from even the most scrupulous bibliographies.

There were newspapers of a kind in the sixteenth and seventeenth centuries, often printed in connection with times of war or political disturbance, when information was contested or at least hard to come by, or what was reported was likely to have public ramifications. Governments and authorities quickly saw the need to control presses as a means of controlling the spread of information and ideas, and put in place licensing systems for printers and stationers. Conditions in early eighteenth-century Britain—a stable monarchy, an increasingly party-based political system, a rapidly growing metropolitan capital, an increasingly

literate and leisured middle class, a lively artisan class, and a thriving urban coffee-house culture—set the stage for the more or less genteel exchange of ideas
and information through newspapers that, in this period, became recognizable
as the predecessors of the press today.

In 1760, with the launch by John Newbery of the *Public Ledger*, there were
four daily newspapers in London; by 1783, there were at least nine (Werkmeister, *London Daily Press*, 2–3; Aspinall, *Politics and the Press*, 6 n. 4). During the
1760s, under a variety of pressures, the daily newspapers were transformed from
"print vehicles dedicated mainly to advertising and news to representations of
variegated cultural strata and sometimes radical opinion" (Bertelsen, "Education
of Henry Sampson Woodfall," 153). In practice, this meant the contents of the
papers became more miscellaneous and entertaining; as a means of fulfilling
this ambition, the *Public Advertiser* invited its readers to become co-creators
of the paper, by sending in for publication their comments, essays, and letters.
The paper itself described the new function of the daily paper to be "a *Magazine for the Day*" (*Pub. Adv.*, Mar. 14, 1763; quoted in Bertelsen, "Education,"
153). If newspapers were no longer just for information but for reading, they
would necessarily become of more immediate and practical concern to people
who, like Boswell, were interested in writing. Thus we find, among the news,
advertisements, poems, and satires, frivolous material meant not to inform but
to entertain, and particularly to entertain by looking *as if* it is meant to inform.
New media, as always, play host to new genres.

As well as the dailies, there were papers that appeared once, twice, or three
times a week (many of these called themselves *Chronicles*); during the 1780s,
there were "eight tri-weekly, and approximately nine weekly papers in London
at any time" (Aspinall, quoted in Barker, *Newspapers, Politics, and Public Opinion*,
23). These papers, rather than the dailies, were intended to circulate also in the
provinces and would thus include more provincial news.

It is not easy briefly to explain—or, indeed, to discover—the policies and
characteristics, the ownership and editorial arrangements, the print runs or cir-
culations, or even the fundamental publishing details of many old periodicals.
The papers changed names, and the names are often confusing—sometimes
deliberately so. They were mostly owned by groups of shareholders, who were
frequently printers and booksellers; some owners or shareholders had political
agendas, and some individual shareholders were more actively involved than
others. Journals and papers were said to be "conducted" (rather than edited) by
someone who may have been an owner, printer, or employee, who may have had
a hand in shaping policy, or may have had a purely practical role. Very little of
this information about the papers was actually *in* the papers, or, at least, not in

any systematic way. The political character of the papers is also important, but it was complex, ever-changing, and (of course) secretive: part of the point of propaganda being that it is not known to be propaganda. Early in the century, the state authorities had tried to manage the papers by the imposition of various taxes; in the latter part of the century—particularly at the time of crisis in the late 1780s, when the king became temporarily unable to fulfill his duties—the parties and factions of government (and opposition) turned instead to paying subsidies in return for favorable treatment. The *Public Advertiser*, which published Boswell's "Rampagers," with their mildly satirical attitude to the policies of the ministry, supported the opposition during the 1770s and changed in 1784 to supporting the government of the younger Pitt (Werkmeister, *London Daily Press*, 83).

These matters seem of little concern to Boswell, who was not a politician or a political thinker. He was on familiar terms with many of the printers, proprietors, conductors, and editors—not that these roles were always distinct—of these organs. The purposes for which he used the periodicals were entirely his own, and he was very skilled at it. He remarked, "in the time of the Corsican war, . . . I used to keep the newspapers constantly warm with paragraphs about the brave islanders" (Mar. 26, 1772; *Defence*, 67).[7] His success in such an enterprise consisted simply in ensuring that the issues that concerned him remained in the public consciousness. Indeed, the comment above from his journal about his Corsican paragraphs was made as he recorded with some satisfaction finding that a fiction he had put into print many years earlier had apparently become a received belief.

Pottle traces items by Boswell in nineteen newspapers and four monthly magazines; some of these were publications based in Edinburgh. The following are the publications represented in this collection:[8]

London Papers

The *Public Advertiser*, which was described as Boswell's "favourite newspaper" by his biographer Frank Brady (*Later Years*, 463), is the paper in which the highest number (forty-three) of the individual items in this collection first

7. He used the same expression in his "Memoirs" to describe his campaign in 1767 for the Douglas Cause, saying that he "took care to keep the newspapers and other publications incessantly warm with various writings" (*Lit. Car.*, xxxv).

8. The following details about the various publications are drawn from the sources named at specific points, as well as, for the London newspapers, the headnotes that are intermittently supplied in the online Burney Collection Newspapers.

appeared, even if we exclude the twenty "Rampagers." Many of these items are short news paragraphs. The paper commenced with this name in 1752, with Henry Woodfall as the printer, but it continued the numbering of the *London Daily Post and General Advertiser* (*NCBEL*, 1328) which had commenced publication in 1734, making it when Boswell began contributing the second oldest London daily paper still being published. Woodfall's son Henry Sampson Woodfall became the conductor in 1758 and raised the paper's profile by printing the anonymous letters of the political controversialist "Junius" (see Chap. 1, n. 98). A contemporary estimate was that in the 1780s it sold 3,000 to 4,500 copies a day (Archenholz, *Picture of England*, 65).

The *London Chronicle* (*NCBEL*, 1333) was a tri-weekly paper started in 1757 by Robert Dodsley and William Strahan, bookseller-publishers associated with Johnson, who wrote an introduction for the first issue. Boswell says that it was "the only news-paper he [Johnson] constantly took in" (*Life*, 2:103). It was printed as a small folio with eight pages per issue. The editor was Griffith Jones. This paper received the greatest number of Boswell's periodical contributions; Pottle identified almost two hundred—almost a third of his identified journalistic output. These contributions began in 1765 with the series of semifictitious news paragraphs sent from Corsica to the publisher of the *London Chronicle*, John Wilkie (*Earlier Years*, 266). Boswell's bound biannual volumes for the period January 1767 to December 1775 are at Yale, and in the first three of these eighteen volumes he carefully marked and indexed his contributions. Brady observes that Boswell "acted as the *London Chronicle*'s occasional correspondent in Edinburgh" (*Later Years*, 16). There are twenty items from the *London Chronicle* in this collection, mostly news and essays.

The *St. James's Chronicle* (*NCBEL*, 1333) was a triweekly evening newspaper, started in 1761 by printer Henry Baldwin, whom Boswell would come to know well as the printer of his *Tour to the Hebrides* and *Life of Johnson*. It was printed as a large folio in four pages, each with four columns. Nathaniel Thomas was employed as editor. In 1787 and 1790, while Boswell was preparing the *Life*, Baldwin helped him out financially (*Later Years*, 359, 415). Nine of Boswell's contributions to the *St. James's Chronicle* are included here, most of them concerning the lives of Johnson. Its other proprietors included Boswell's acquaintances Bonnell Thornton, actor-manager David Garrick, and later Shakespearean scholar George Steevens (see Chap. 4, n. 2).

The daily *Morning Post* (*NCBEL*, 1335) was established in 1772, part-owned by auctioneer James Christie and bookseller John Bell, with controversial and pugnacious clergyman Henry Bate (later, Bate Dudley) as editor, until 1781.

Bate Dudley, setting out to amuse as much as inform, published much scurrilous gossip and political material of a very abusive nature (Werkmeister, *London Daily Press*, 5). In 1778 he claimed to have reached sales of 5,000 copies a day (Barker, *Newspapers, Politics, and Public Opinion*, 23). In 1787, the paper's "interest in literature was limited to a steady abuse of James Boswell" (Werkmeister, *London Daily Press*, 92). Boswell's five contributions here are all from 1789–90 and concern the lives of Johnson. Scottish-born Peter Stuart was the editor at this time.

The remaining London newspapers excerpted in this book are represented by only one item each.

The *Gazetteer and London Daily Advertiser* commenced as the *Daily Gazetteer* in 1735 (*NCBEL*, 1328), but was descended from London's oldest daily paper, the *Daily Courant* (*NCBEL*, 1321). It was conducted 1783–90 by James Perry and James Gray, whom Boswell knew: he dined in company with them, August 28, 1790 (*Great Biographer*, 105).

The *General Evening Post* (*NCBEL*, 1327) was a triweekly, established in 1733 and from 1775 printed by Mary Say, London's only female master printer, who also printed the *Gazetteer*.

The last three London papers here were all late starters:

The *World* (*NCBEL*, 1336) was a daily started in 1787 by Edward Topham and John Bell, with Rev. Charles Este as editor, succeeded by Robert Merry. It folded in 1794 and was distinguished by a strong interest in fashion and the theater.

The *Star* (*NCBEL*, 1337) was London's first daily evening paper, started in 1788 by Peter Stuart (who later went to the *Morning Post*) and later conducted by Scottish-born poet John Mayne.

The *Diary: or, Woodfall's Register* (*NCBEL*, 1337) was an evening paper conducted by William Woodfall, younger brother of Henry Sampson Woodfall; it ran for only four years, 1789–93.

Edinburgh Papers

The *Caledonian Mercury* (*NCBEL*, 1375) was started in 1720 and was published three times a week, at first by Robert Allen, with William Rolland as editor. From 1729 to 1772, it was owned and run by Thomas Ruddiman and his family, before being taken over by John Robertson (Craig, *Scottish Periodical Press*, 24), with whom Boswell dealt. For half a century all official advertisements in Scotland were confined to the *Caledonian Mercury* and the *Edinburgh Courant* (Aspinall, *Politics and the Press*, 133). Boswell's eight contributions given here are mainly letters to the editor.

The *Edinburgh Advertiser* (*NCBEL*, 1375) was founded in 1764 and was published twice a week, on Tuesdays and Fridays, by John Reid and bookseller and printer Alexander Donaldson, who was a good friend to Boswell; this partnership had also published Boswell's early leaflets of verse. Donaldson's Edinburgh bookshop was a literary meeting place. His son James took over the *Edinburgh Advertiser* in 1774 (Craig, *Scottish Periodical Press*, 24). Five short items of news, mostly bogus, by Boswell are included here.

Magazines

The monthly *London Magazine* (*NCBEL*, 1297) was established by a group of booksellers in 1732, in opposition to the *Gentleman's Magazine*, under the editorship of Isaac Kimber and from 1755 his son Edward. Booksellers such as Charles Dilly and Robert Dodsley were shareholders; in Boswell's time it was printed by Henry Baldwin (*Defence*, 131), and its proprietors were probably Edward Dilly, John Rivington, and Richard Baldwin Jr. Boswell purchased a sixth share of the *London Magazine*, October 14, 1769 (*Search*, 336; *Earlier Years*, 436), from which time until shortly before it folded in June 1785 he was a part-owner and regular contributor. It was the natural venue for his essays of substance, including his "Hypochondriack" series; eight of his contributions are in this collection. Boswell records attending the monthly supper meetings of the proprietors and taking immense pleasure in the deliberations (*Defence*, 103–4, 170).

The *Gentleman's Magazine* (*NCBEL*, 1295), established in January 1731 by Edward Cave, was the original *magazine* in its literary sense. Begun as a monthly book-length compilation of London news, it rapidly became immensely popular and soon included original material and literary items. Samuel Johnson made his start in literature working for Cave on the *Gentleman's Magazine*, from 1738 until around 1744. By Boswell's time, the *Gentleman's Magazine* was something of an institution, and he seems to have regarded it as an appropriate repository for literary items and discussion about literature; four such items are included here.

The *Scots Magazine* (*NCBEL*, 1371) was "the one magazine published continuously in Scotland between 1750 and 1789" (Craig, *Scottish Periodical Press*, 33). Started by two booksellers in 1739 on the pattern of its two London predecessors, it was edited by scholar-printer William Smellie, 1759–65. Although

Scottish contributions were encouraged, it mainly relied on London papers for its supply of foreign and domestic news. By Boswell's time, it was more a repository for essays and belles-lettres than for news, publishing early works of philosopher James Beattie, dramatist John Home, "Ossian" poet James Macpherson, and Boswell—including the three items reprinted here.

Various characteristics of the eighteenth-century periodical press have been alluded to already, but it might be as well to mention directly some in particular. As regards their contents and format, the magazines are less unfamiliar to us than the newspapers, but both employ what is to modern readers the disconcerting practice of anonymity.[9] Today we tend to associate anonymity in the media with deception and scurrility. In eighteenth-century periodicals, anonymity was the rule and named authorship the exception. Indeed, it could be said that part of the understood function of the periodical press was to be a venue for anonymous discourse. Elements of this convention remained in place in the world of journalism for a very long time. For most of the twentieth century, a newspaper's senior writers on political or economic subjects might have had a journalistic "byline," but, on the whole, journalism was anonymous, pseudonyms were commonly allowed to letter-writers, and authority and responsibility were understood to reside in each particular newspaper as an entity. Until 1974, all reviews in the *Times Literary Supplement* were anonymous. This convention has, in the print media, been pretty comprehensively abandoned, and the least items of original reportage—apart from those from syndicated sources—have the name of a reporter attached. Could eighteenth-century British readers see this, they would regard it as possibly fetishistic and certainly as a derogation of the role of the editor or conductor and an outrageous limitation on press freedom. Of course, the older newspapers could manipulate the convention by presenting editorial opinions in the form of letters from readers. But the invitation to contribute to the press anonymously or pseudonymously, as Hannah Barker observes (*Newspapers, Politics, and Public Opinion*, 38), made the papers an oddly class-free zone, in which both the high and the low could involve themselves in public affairs and contribute their opinions. And for the writers themselves, anonymity, whether the exception or the rule, enabled them to achieve something very different to named authorship. If one is writing anonymously, one is not under pressure to care for one's reputation. One is not writing with half an eye to the volume of miscellaneous essays in one's Collected Works.

9. See Tankard, "Anonymity and the Press: The Case of Boswell," forthcoming in *Eighteenth-Century Life*.

The short unsourced snippets of news or "paragraphs" commonly found in late eighteenth-century newspapers, and which appear in Boswell's bibliography (and perhaps that of no other writer worth a bibliography), warrant particular notice. They are misrepresented by their appearance in a book like this. Here they are presented (mainly in the "Lives of Johnson" section) in relation to other texts on the same topic and by the same author, but this sense of coherence was not apparent in the context of their original newspaper venues, where (for instance, in the *St. James's Chronicle*) the fourth and final page was devoted to strings of paragraphs of unsourced observations and anecdotes on a variety of matters. In their original context, they are found simply listed in series, presumably in the order in which they came to the hand of the printer, with only a paragraph break between them, and without any familiar paratextual devices such as titles or the names of authors. They are, in fact, a form of journalism that persists in newspapers to the present day, usually in columns conducted by particular figures, named or frankly pseudonymous, in which are gathered unsubstantiated reports and rumors. Sometimes the conductors present themselves as embedded in a particular professional or social milieu: as (for instance) a Washington or Whitehall or Hollywood "insider." Such material is a marginal element in modern newspapers, which strive to be authoritative. In eighteenth-century newspapers, there was no endorsement from the printer (nor expectation on the part of the readers) of the accuracy of this material; it was simply a collection of what was being circulated around the town.

These paragraphs were not by any means all scuttlebutt or malicious rumor, and the contents were extremely miscellaneous. But there is clearly a sense that they are to be read as communications from people with "an interest." Werkmeister says that, in the case of Bate Dudley's *Morning Post*, "by 1780 there was hardly a 'paragraph' in the newspaper that was not paid for by someone" (*London Daily Press*, 7); Boswell, however, is unlikely to have had to pay to use the columns of the *St. James's Chronicle* to (in effect) publicize books that were to be printed by the printer of the *Chronicle*. In a letter of 1785 to the *St. James's Chronicle*, a contributor (probably George Steevens) articulates what must have been the commonly understood distinction; in offering gratuitous advice to Johnson's future biographer, he says:

Let Puffs [for the *Life of Johnson*] be restrained within their proper Channel, the News. From Paragraphs we may learn, almost every Day, who wishes to be thought of as the "confidential Friend" of Johnson; but let not the sober Biographer degrade himself by taking such a Task out of the Hands of the Poor, the Shallow, the Interested, and the Vain, who strive, by Means like these, to suggest themselves into Notice to which they have no Pretensions, except their Necessities and their Wishes. (Jan. 11, 1785, 4)

Steevens implies that the News (which includes "puffs": "an extravagantly laudatory advertisement or review," says the *OED*) are at the very least informative; by contrast, the contents of the "Paragraphs" are simply not reliable.[10] (Boswell's response to Steevens's advice opens Chapter 4.)

The reliance on anonymity and short unsourced contributions meant that newspapers evolved a style represented in formulae such as "a correspondent is of the opinion" or "we hear that" or "a correspondent observes." Such formulae have the effect—contrary to what might seem to be the intention—of giving readers a sense that the contributors' identities are part of the story. And the fact that this tone pervades the papers leads to the people who are the subjects of the stories often being referred to in similar allusive ways. In a private letter of 1785, politician Charles James Fox discussed the various methods of spreading political opinions in the press: "Subjects of Importance should be first treated gravely in letters or pamphlets. . . . It is not till a subject has been so much discussed as to become almost threadbare that *Paragraphs which consist principally in allusions* can be generally understood" (quoted in Barker, *Newspapers, Politics, and Public Opinion*, 44; my emphasis). This seems to me exactly the style employed by Boswell not only in his paragraphs but in his "Rampagers," in which he deals allusively with Subjects of Importance. The allusive style invites readers to appreciate and interpret current events simply on the basis of their own experience as readers of literature, pamphlets, and the newspapers. If the newspapers—and ephemeral publications in general—are any guide, the literate classes in the eighteenth century were *more* literate than most literate people today. Advertisements were complex and respectfully phrased; satire and parodies were witty and allusive. Eighteenth-century newspapers seem to constantly and explicitly call their readers to acts of interpretation, in contrast to the mass media of today, which aim to employ a style of diction that appears to be transparent.

As a correspondent to the periodical press, Boswell adopted various strategies for naming himself. In the letters "to the Printer" of a paper, he would

10. See the *OED*, s.v. "paragraph": "Journalism. A short article without a headline in a newspaper or periodical, usually consisting of an item of local news or gossip, or forming one of a regular series of notes on a particular subject. Hence: an item of news." In Sheridan's play *The School for Scandal* (1777), 4.3, when Joseph Surface tells Sir Peter Teazle that "People would talk," Sir Peter replies, "Talk,— . . . They'd paragraph me in the newspapers, and make ballads on me."

include his name if it suited his particular purpose; more often, he would use a pen name—particularly if he wished, implicitly or explicitly, to take issue with something concerning or contributed by James Boswell, or simply wished to disguise the fact that it was James Boswell alone (and not half a dozen different people) who was pushing some issue. He seems not to have used any name consistently—unlike, say, the famous political controversialist "Junius"—as his aim was not to draw attention to his anonymity but simply to fuel public debate.

THIS EDITION

Attribution

The identification of potential materials for this edition is based almost wholly upon the work of the undisputed *primus* of all things Boswellian, including bibliography, Frederick A. Pottle. It has not been my objective to either add to or subtract from Pottle's work, although I have done the former on occasion. For every item there is a reference to either or both of Pottle's bibliographies of Boswell, *The Literary Career of James Boswell, Esq.* (1929) (*Lit. Car.*) and the entry on Boswell that he contributed to *The New Cambridge Bibliography of English Literature*, ed. George Watson, vol. 2 (1971) (*NCBEL*). Because on these questions I am as one under authority, and so as not to add a further annotative layer to a text that general readers already may find sufficiently complex, this information is presented in an appendix.

Selection and Arrangement

To present these articles in a chronological sequence would be to depict them as mainly (or only) relevant to Boswell's biography; to present them organized by publication, as in a bibliography, would be to erect a purely scholastic system that would defeat any attempt to understand them in context. Boswell obviously took care over what kind of material he sent to which publication, but these decisions were purely pragmatic, and most of the time he was addressing an ideal reader who (like himself) reads *all* the papers. As Pat Rogers has astutely observed, with regard to the *Life of Johnson*, "What is most individual about the way Boswell processes 'matter of fact' is his sense of the value of temporal precision, and of minute attention to the *sequence* of events" ("Boswell and the Diurnal," 108); this sense is apparent in all his writings. The only way, I decided, for an editor to represent this reality, and to shape out of these disparate materials a book for reading rather than consultation, was to identify a number of thematic categories and present each category of material as a sequence—or, at least, a self-contained and consecutive reading experience. This approach would result, agreeably in my view, in a book of potential general interest: not unlike a magazine. However, this procedure still left to one side much material that is interesting precisely because it is so miscellaneous.

Thus, I have aimed at some compromise: while identifying subjects or themes that particularly engaged Boswell's pen and that will, I hope, attract readers interested in particular subjects (executions, the "Rampager," and Samuel Johnson), I have equally wanted to gather material that illustrates the variety of Boswell's interests and give a sample of what one finds in eighteenth-century newspapers; both of these aims are represented in the two generically organized sections ("Reports and Interviews," "Essays and Letters"). Some of the topics or individual items in those two sections may well be thought by some readers to be the most important or amusing. Other categories of material that could have been presented—if time and space had permitted—include Corsica, the Douglas Cause, the theater, literature and literary subjects (reviews, but also literary gossip), Scottish politics, the law, and many news items of which the subject is James Boswell, Esq. I dealt with these materials only to exclude them, partly because the resulting book would be impractically (and unpublishably) large, but also because I wanted the book to be—within its limits—comprehensive rather than representative, so that its five sections would contain all the Boswellian journalistic material to which their headings apply.

My aim was also that the book would read like a series of narratives and not simply as a collection of disparate items to be consulted for reference purposes. Some of this sense of narrative inheres in the chronological relationship between one item and the next (particularly in the section on Johnson); in the series of "Rampager" columns, the narrative had to be augmented from contemporary history and supplied editorially; in the generic sections, the narrative belongs not to the sections as a whole, but to the individual items, and was mostly to be found in and extracted from the newspapers. Those sections invited not a discursive section introduction but more extensive headnotes to individual items. The "Rampager" letters, by far the most complex section of the book, seemed to require both.

Boswell's remark about "keeping the press warm with paragraphs" supports my own feeling that these items would be best understood and presented serially, in the context of each other. Boswell sent many paragraphs to the papers simply to keep a topic alive in the public consciousness, and I decided to extend this treatment to the collection as a whole. I hope thus to have presented each section as a discrete reading experience, with its own intrinsic narrative and readerly pleasures. Three articles here were not properly journalistic pieces but pamphlets or broadsides, which I have included for the sake of a comprehensive coverage of a subject. It did not seem reasonable to exclude such texts solely on account of the method of publication. For similar reasons, although Boswell's uncollected verse seems to me a distinct body of material requiring separate treatment, a number of sets of verses appear here.

Texts

I have attempted to give as exact a representation as is practical of the texts as they first appeared. Most of these items have not reappeared in print after their first publication, and contemporary reprintings are mostly a result of the newspapers borrowing one another's materials, so it seems unlikely that, unless there is in specific instances evidence to the contrary, any differences between contemporary versions in different papers represent any authorial intention; therefore such versions have in general not been sought out or variations noted.

The text here attempts to preserve various eighteenth-century typographical and paratextual practices, such as the use of small capitals and italics, which Boswell's file copies show to have been in accordance with his preferences and expectations. I have corrected occasional typographical errors but have not modernized or regularized the varied and occasional eccentric practices of either Boswell or his printers (readers will notice that with regard to capitalization and other matters, the practices of some periodicals are more modern than those of others). I know of manuscripts for very few of these texts and have made no great effort to locate them, but it is clear from the manuscript corrections that Boswell made on occasion to the copies of published versions preserved in his files that he ascribed meaning to these practices. Where Boswell has on a file copy made a manuscript correction to a published version, it has been incorporated into the text (and the variation from the published text noted in the textual headnote), but all variations from the printed texts are carefully given in the Textual Notes at the end of the book.

Annotation

It is my aim and hope that this book will be of interest to an audience wider than various kinds of scholarly specialists, such as Boswellians and Johnsonians. But in order to be read, even by specialists, the texts collected here have required a great deal of annotation. In fact, these writings cover so many fields that there are no specialists who would be particularly qualified to read all of them with understanding—or, indeed, to annotate them. Some knowledge of various contexts has been required, including literature; British political and military history of the period; Boswell's own life, interests, and circumstances (a subject for which the documentary materials are of almost unparalleled— and ever-increasing—complexity); as well as a knowledge—not necessarily very deep—of hundreds of minor topics, texts, and personalities. This situation is complicated by two particular features of the material: its ephemerality and its allusiveness.

Not all that is reported or discussed in newspapers becomes history. This is particularly the case in a period when the material contributed to papers came not from professional journalists but from more or less interested parties, and attempts to report or record the major public events of the day were not systematic. Boswell himself was seldom at the center of public affairs but, rather, on the fringes; yet, in the intimate societies of eighteenth-century London and Edinburgh, he was familiar with many major players in public affairs and delighted in reporting or hinting at amusing sidelines to the news, making unexpected connections between the public and private, the important and the trivial. Much of this detail is unknown to historians, and I have a number of times had the experience of consulting living experts, such as biographers of particular people whom Boswell mentions, to find that the rumors, sayings, and daily comings and goings that he records or alludes to do not otherwise appear in the public record. Furthermore, his allusive style has necessitated numerous identifications of minor details that would have been everyday knowledge to his original readers, but which again are not the types of information that make their way into traditional works of reference.

It has been my aim that readers should be able to follow the text and, in particular, each of the five chapters without resort to some other book; thus I have aimed to provide sufficient editorial assistance and guidance to enable the reader to sense something of a narrative. Each chapter has its own short introduction, contextualizing the material. As I have worked, more and more individual items have seemed to me to require their own headnotes. This particularly is the case in the two generically focused chapters, "Reports and Interviews" and "Essays and Letters," in which almost every item deals with a new topic. The most tightly themed chapter, "The Lives of Johnson," has a longer introduction and subsequently fewer headnotes.

No reader is going to use this book in place of a biography of Boswell, a history of British newspapers, or an account of the American war. For all such matters, I have been prepared to rely on authoritative secondary sources: it is for the Boswellian texts themselves that this book will be read. Footnotes give other information that seems necessary to assist an educated general readership. Prominent among my sources are, of course, the volumes that constitute "The Yale Editions of the Private Papers of James Boswell," of which since 1950 there have been twenty-nine published (depending on how one counts), and there could be as many yet to come. I can recall very few instances in which I have had any reason to question their scholarship. I have relied on standard reference works, in particular the *Oxford Dictionary of National Biography* and the *Oxford English Dictionary*. In general I have not attempted to solve problems that have hitherto baffled specialist scholars. Unless otherwise noted, all references to the *ODNB* will be to the biography of the person who is the central concern of the particular note or sentence in which the reference occurs.

I have (whenever possible) provided vital dates and thumbnail descriptions for all people who appear by name or allusion at their first appearance in Boswell's text. A few people are thus identified after they have already been mentioned editorially. Cross-references are kept to a minimum, and readers should assume that where information, such as vital dates, is missing from an annotation, the information has already been given, and the index will direct them to other relevant places in the book.

Every individual article is immediately preceded by a note on its source. With regard to page numbers in the sources, there will be some inconsistency of citation style, as some periodicals were paginated by volume, some by issue, and some not at all. A further category of annotation is the headings or titles that I have provided for each item. Few of these texts, particularly those in the newspapers, had titles of their own when first published, and those they had were frequently formulaic, giving merely a genre-description ("letter" or "essay," etc.) and purported place of origin; usually, no attempt was made to give the item a distinctive discursive name that summarizes the contents. At the risk of anachronism, I have given each item a title or headline, partly in order to enhance the readability of the collection and partly in order to stress the origins of these texts by linking them with modern newspaper conventions. If there was a heading in the printed source, it has been included with the text.

Where on occasion there is already a footnote in the original published source, I have preserved the original note marker and placed the original note (in quotation marks) within a note of my own, following it with the source name in brackets and when necessary providing annotation.

Short Titles and Abbreviations

AV: *Authorized* ("King James") *Version* of the Bible

Ann. Reg.: *The Annual Register*, 1758–63.

Applause: *Boswell: The Applause of the Jury, 1782–1785*, edited by I. S. Lustig and F. A. Pottle. London: Heinemann, 1981.

Bailey: James Boswell, *The Hypochondriack: Being the Seventy Essays by the Celebrated Biographer James Boswell, Appearing in the London Magazine from November, 1777, to August, 1783, and Here First Reprinted*, edited by Margery Bailey. 2 vols. Stanford, CA: Stanford University Press, 1928.

Boswelliana: *Boswelliana: The Commonplace Book of James Boswell*, edited by Charles Rogers. London, 1874.

Brewer's Dict.: *Brewer's Dictionary of Phrase & Fable*, edited by Camilla Rockwood. 18th ed. Edinburgh: Chambers, 2010.

Cat. Yale: Marion S. Pottle, Claude Colleer Abbott, and Frederick A. Pottle, *Catalogue of the Papers of James Boswell at Yale University: For the Greater Part Formerly the Collection of Lieut.-Colonel Ralph Heyward Isham*. Vol. 3. Edinburgh: Edinburgh University Press; New Haven: Yale University Press, 1993.

Corres. 1: *The Correspondence of James Boswell and John Johnston of Grange*, edited by Ralph S. Walker. London: Heinemann, 1966.

Corres. 2: *The Correspondence and Other Papers of James Boswell Relating to the Making of the "Life of Johnson,"* edited by Marshall Waingrow. 2nd ed., corrected and enlarged. Edinburgh: Edinburgh University Press; New Haven: Yale University Press, 2001.

Corres. 3: *The Correspondence of James Boswell with Certain Members of the Club, including Oliver Goldsmith, Bishops Percy and Barnard, Sir Joshua Reynolds,*

Topham Beauclerk, and Bennet Langton, edited by Charles N. Fifer. London: Heinemann, 1976.

Corres. 4: *The Correspondence of James Boswell with David Garrick, Edmund Burke, and Edmond Malone*, edited by Peter S. Baker, Thomas W. Copeland, George M. Kahrl, Rachel McClennan, and James M. Osborn, with the assistance of Robert Mankin and Mark Wollaeger. London: Heinemann, 1986.

Corres. 5: *The General Correspondence of James Boswell, 1766–1769*, Vol. 1: *1766–1767*, edited by Richard C. Cole, with Peter S. Baker and Rachel McClellan, with the assistance of James J. Caudle. Edinburgh: Edinburgh University Press, 1993.

Corres. 6: *The Correspondence of James Boswell and William Johnson Temple, 1756–1795*, Vol. 1: *1756–1777*, edited by Thomas Crawford. Edinburgh: Edinburgh University Press; New Haven: Yale University Press, 1997.

Corres. 7: *The General Correspondence of James Boswell, 1766–1769*, Vol. 2: *1768–1769*, edited by Richard C. Cole, with Peter S. Baker and Rachel McClellan, with the assistance of James J. Caudle. Edinburgh: Edinburgh University Press; New Haven: Yale University Press, 1997.

Corres. 9: *The General Correspondence of James Boswell, 1757–1763*, edited by David Hankins and James J. Caudle. Edinburgh: Edinburgh University Press; New Haven: Yale University Press, 2006.

Defence: *Boswell for the Defence, 1769–1774*, edited by W. K. Wimsatt and F. A. Pottle. London: Heinemann, 1960.

Earlier Years: F. A. Pottle, *James Boswell: The Earlier Years, 1740–1769*. London: Heinemann, 1966.

Experiment: *Boswell: The English Experiment, 1785–1789*, edited by I. S. Lustig and F. A. Pottle. London: Heinemann, 1986.

Extremes: *Boswell in Extremes, 1776–1778*, edited by C. McC. Weis and F. A. Pottle. New York: McGraw-Hill, 1970.

Fasti Scot.: Hew Scott, *Fasti Ecclesiae Scoticanae: The Succession of Ministers in the Church of Scotland from the Reformation*. 7 vols. Edinburgh: Oliver and Boyd, 1915–28.

Gent. Mag.: *The Gentleman's Magazine*, 1731–1907.

Grand Tour 1: *Boswell on the Grand Tour: Germany and Switzerland, 1764*, edited by F. A. Pottle. London: Heinemann, 1953.

Grand Tour 2: *Boswell on the Grand Tour: Italy, Corsica, and France, 1765–1766*, edited by Frank Brady and F. A. Pottle. London: Heinemann, 1955.

Grant: James Grant, *Cassell's Old and New Edinburgh: Its History, Its People, and Its Places*. 6 vols. London, 1881–88. http://www.oldandnewedinburgh.co.uk.

Great Biographer: *Boswell: The Great Biographer, 1789–1795*, edited by Marlies K. Danziger and Frank Brady. London: Heinemann, 1989.

HLP: Hester Lynch Piozzi.

Holland: *Boswell in Holland, 1763–1764: Including His Correspondence with Belle de Zuylen (Zelide)*, edited by F. A. Pottle. London: Heinemann, 1952.

JB: James Boswell.

Laird: *Boswell, Laird of Auchinleck, 1778–1782*, edited by J. W. Reed and F. A. Pottle. New York: McGraw-Hill, 1977.

Later Years: Frank Brady, *James Boswell: The Later Years, 1769–1795*. London: Heinemann, 1984.

Letters JB: *Letters of James Boswell*, edited by C. B. Tinker. 2 vols. Oxford: Clarendon, 1924.

Letters SJ: *The Letters of Samuel Johnson*, edited by Bruce Redford. 5 vols. Princeton, NJ: Princeton University Press, 1992–94.

Life: *Boswell's Life of Johnson, together with Boswell's Journal of a Tour to the Hebrides and Johnson's Diary of a Journey into North Wales*, edited by G. B. Hill, revised by L. F. Powell. 6 vols. Oxford: Clarendon, 1934–50; vols. V and VI. 2nd ed. Oxford: Clarendon, 1964.

Lit. Anec.: John Nichols, *Literary Anecdotes of the Eighteenth Century*. 9 vols. London, 1812–15.

Lit. Car.: F. A. Pottle, *The Literary Career of James Boswell, Esq.: Being the Bibliographical Materials for a Life of Boswell*. Oxford: Clarendon, 1929.

Lond. Chron.: *The London Chronicle*, 1757–1823.

Lond. Journ.: *Boswell's London Journal, 1762–1763*, edited by F. A. Pottle. London: Heinemann, 1950.

NCBEL: *The New Cambridge Bibliography of English Literature*, edited by George Watson. Vol 2. Cambridge: Cambridge University Press, 1971.

ODNB: *Oxford Dictionary of National Biography*, edited by Brian Harrison and Lawrence Goldman, founding editor Colin Matthew. Oxford: Oxford University Press, 2004–10.

ODQ: *Oxford Dictionary of Quotations*, edited by Elizabeth Knowles. 7th ed. Oxford: Oxford University Press, 2009.

OED: *Oxford English Dictionary Online*.

Ominous Years: *Boswell: The Ominous Years, 1774–1776*, edited by Charles Ryskamp and F. A. Pottle. London: Heinemann, 1963.

P + number: reference to "Printed matter" in vol. 3 of *Cat. Yale* (see above).

Parl. Hist.: *The Parliamentary History of England from the Earliest Period to the Year 1803*. 36 vols. London, 1806–20.

Pol. Car.: Frank Brady, *Boswell's Political Career*. New Haven: Yale University Press, 1965.

Pub. Adv.: *The Public Advertiser*, 1752–94.

St. James's Chron.: *The St. James's Chronicle; or, British Evening-Post*, 1761–1866.

Scots Mag.: *The Scots Magazine*, 1739–1817.

Search: *Boswell in Search of a Wife, 1766–1769*, edited by Frank Brady and F. A. Pottle. London: Heinemann, 1957.

SJ: Samuel Johnson.

SJ Dict.: Samuel Johnson, *A Dictionary of the English Language: In which the Words are Deduced from Their Originals and Illustrated in Their Different Significations by Examples from the Best Writers*. 2 vols. London, 1755.

Tour: Boswell's *Journal of a Tour to the Hebrides*. References are to vol. 5 of the *Life* (see above) unless otherwise indicated.

Reports and Interviews

This first chapter presents a topically diverse range of texts, here grouped together because they represent one important subgenre of journalism: the work of a reporter. Telling stories to people about events at which they were not present is a practice as old as language, and telling readers the "five Ws" (who, what, when, where, and why) remained the basic role of newspapers until well into the twentieth century, when the immediacy of radio forced newspapers to find other things to do. Yet in the eighteenth century and despite the popularity of newspapers, the people who wrote news reports for the papers were regarded with suspicion, indeed, as "a semi-criminal class" (Clarke, *From Grub Street*, 7). The need to fill up the columns of papers day after day, whether anything important had happened or not, and the competition between different media outlets to attract an audience required (and continues to require) a ready supply of stories. Where there are such pressures, the lines between hunting down stories and embellishing them and manufacturing them must always be blurry—and were no doubt blurrier when most reporting was anonymous, and neither the papers nor the reporters were under any obligation to vouch for the truth of what was published.

Samuel Johnson, who was a dedicated observer of and commentator upon the periodical culture of his day, regarded the newspapers rather skeptically:

> No species of literary men has lately been so much multiplied as the writers of news. . . . To write news in its perfection requires such a combination of qualities, that a man completely fitted for the task is not always to be found. . . . To these compositions is required neither genius nor knowledge, neither industry nor sprightliness, but contempt of shame, and indifference to truth are absolutely necessary. He who by a long familiarity with infamy has obtained these qualities, may confidently tell to-day what he intends to contradict to-morrow; he may affirm fearlessly what he knows that he shall be obliged to recant, and may write letters from Amsterdam or Dresden to himself. (*Idler*, no. 30, Nov. 11, 1758; *Idler and Adventurer*, 2:94)

Johnson's "Idler" essays were written originally for publication in a weekly newspaper, the *Universal Chronicle*, so this passage is a bit of a joke at his own expense or that of his host. And as the succeeding paragraphs of the essay show, he is mainly thinking of news from foreign parts (his lazy reporter doesn't leave home), particularly concerning wars (in 1758, Britain was in the early stages of the Seven Years' War). Indeed, it sometimes seems that part of the attraction of the news in an eighteenth-century paper is that readers cannot and do not expect to be sure about its reliability. In a letter—or a text presented as a letter (the story it tells is a fiction, in any case)—in another newspaper, a writer claims to have overheard two men discussing crimes they had committed; he has them apprehended, at which point one of them tells him:

> "Lord, Sir, you are certainly out of your senses, or strangely mistaken in the nature of our conversation. We commit robberies and murders—no, no, Sir,—we only commit them with pen and ink. We are paragraph-makers, and we were merely telling each other in our usual way, what inventions we had used to gratify the curiosity of the public, during the last week, with extraordinary intelligence. Here to convince you," continued he, pulling out a parcel of papers from his pocket, full of robberies, murders, adulteries, rapes, impositions, political squibs, theatrical puffs, broken bones, and inferior casualties. (*Say's Weekly Journal*, Apr. 25, 1767, quoted in Clarke, *From Grub Street*, 7)

Boswell's intentions when writing "inventions" for the press were seldom libelous or even (in themselves) very serious. He did not want or expect to change the course of events, or even to be believed. His inventions function either to sustain public notice of subjects in which he has an interest (such as his books on Corsica or Johnson), or simply to provide other people with amusing material for conversation. In the four short "inventions" of March–May 1767, given in this chapter, no serious issues are raised, no identifiable causes promoted, and—arguably—no harm done. In the headnote to this clutch of texts, I quote Pottle's speculations on their purpose. Here I might add that what, it seems to me, Boswell learned from reading and writing news paragraphs is that a certain sort of story is more (or, perhaps, only) entertaining if it is thought to be true: this is, after all, the essence of the attraction of anecdotes, *ana* (or table-talk), and apothegms (witty retorts)—three essentially minor species of composition that Boswell was later to make the foundations of his own monumental achievement in the *Life of Johnson*.

Boswell also sent a clutch of amusing inventions to the press regarding the Douglas Cause (see "The Shorthand Reporters," below), of which—despite his own strongly partisan views on the topic—the only practical function was to keep the case in the news. And although, as F. A. Pottle points out, some of Boswell's fictitious Corsican reports were apparently taken seriously by later historians, and the Douglas Cause paragraphs were at least part of the reason that the Edinburgh newspaper editors were cited for contempt of court, there is nothing libelous or partisan in his inventions (*Earlier Years*, 307, 331). They are not *accurate*, but they read as if they might be:

which is (in some ways) just as good—or just as bad. Samuel Johnson knew a lady who "implicitly believed every thing she read in the papers; and that, by way of curing her of her credulity, he fabricated a story of a battle between the Russians and the Turks, then at war" (*Johnsonian Miscellanies*, 2:391). Hester Piozzi identified the lady as her own mother, Mrs. Salusbury, and explains that Johnson "could not endure . . . [h]er superfluous attention to such accounts of the foreign politics as are transmitted to us by the daily prints" (ibid., 1:235; Betty Rizzo located and gives the texts of Johnson's seven "inventions," which were in the *Public Advertiser* in 1770). The issue is not simply that the news is "implicitly believed" by people who (unlike Boswell and Johnson) do not appreciate the ways of printers and news-writers, but that the news impels such people to give "superfluous attention" to subjects that they do not properly understand, are irrelevant to their own lives, and of which the "news" may therefore as well be false as true, for all the good it does anyone. In short, the response to any disquiet about reports of this kind is: they are only paragraphs in the newspaper.

However, Boswell was not merely a "paragraph-maker": he was a serious journalist, and, when he reports at greater length on serious topics, we have no reason to think that his accounts of riots, mutinies, or interviews are any less reliable than his scrupulously accurate private journals. As Anthony Smith has noted, in those days a "journalist was not yet a man who went to *look*, though occasionally he might by chance *see*" (Smith, "Long Road to Objectivity," 160; Smith's italics). In the articles here, Boswell reports opportunistically, as someone who happens to be on the scene. With the exceptions of a series of plays he reviewed in the *Edinburgh Chronicle* in 1759 and the trip to Corsica that really began his career as a reporter, there is no sense of his ever going to "cover" some situation that he thought might be newsworthy. The issues, events, and person-alities about which Boswell writes in this chapter cover a wide range, and he writes here more disinterestedly than in his other contributions to the press. In this way, too, he more closely resembles a journalist, as we would understand the term, rather than a professional writer who chooses to write occasional pieces for the newspapers. In his choice of subjects, he exhibits a real newsman's instincts, recognizing when there is a "story" in some person or event that crosses his horizon.

Once he gets an idea for a story in which the public might be interested, he de-liberately pursues opportunities for gathering material. After he met—quite by acci-dent—the Abyssinian explorer James Bruce, he immediately wanted to learn more about his "most curious travels," and, as he wrote in his journal, "I was quite impatient to hear him talk. I . . . set out to try what I could do to get an appointment made to dine or sup in a tavern" (Edinburgh, Aug. 9, 1774; *Defence*, 272). When at a social occasion in London he met the Mohawk chief Theyendanegea, he again sensed that there was something here he could make use of, and "upon my proposing to pay him a visit, he [that is, Theyendanegea's traveling companion, Gilbert Tice] said he would be glad to see me any morning to drink tea with the Chief and him at the Swan with Two Necks in Lad Lane" (Apr. 18, 1776; *Ominous Years*, 342). These are appealing and familiar sce-narios: Boswell, like many reporters since, meets and interviews informants in taverns, for stories which he sends to the *London Magazine*; on both occasions we may imagine Boswell making clear the purpose of his interest and perhaps even taking notes.

Because of the variety of subjects treated in the items in this chapter, any further necessary background will be supplied in the headnote to each new topic.

1767

Riot in the Edinburgh Theater

[Edinburgh's Canongate Theatre opened as the Canongate Concert Hall in 1746 and was reorganized in 1752 when John Lee, the leading actor at London's Drury Lane Theatre, was invited to come to Edinburgh to establish a professional theater company. Lee's management raised the quality and reputation of the theater, but failed to make a profit or to otherwise satisfy the upper-class group of owners—nor did that of the other managers who followed him. (See Campbell, *Playing for Scotland*, chap. 3.)

The following piece records an incident that occurred after the popular actor George Stayley, who had upset the theater management, was not re-engaged for the 1767 season. J. C. Dibdin writes that when the theater opened on January 24, Stayley's supporters were in attendance, and "a peremptory demand was made for an apology from the management. This was refused; so, after the ladies had been allowed to leave the building, the audience proceeded to wreck the house.... Benches were torn up, candles were thrown about, scenes smashed, and everything destroyed that could be" (*Annals of the Edinburgh Stage*, 140–41).

The tone of Boswell's report suggests that he was present and active in the riot and a partisan of the rioters. The pages of his journal covering January 17–February 3, 1767, are unfortunately missing (*Search*, 21 n. 6).]

London Chronicle, February 14–17, 1767, 168

Extract of a Letter from Edinburgh.

The spirit of Liberty is beginning to be really felt in our northern climate.[1] Liberty is a plant not altogether natural to this soil; but it seems now to thrive

---

1. Some of the language used by JB in this piece alludes to contemporary events leading to the American Revolution. The "Liberty Tree" was an old elm in Boston, Massachusetts, which in Aug. 1765 became a gathering point for activities to protest against the British government's imposition of a stamp tax in the American colonies. The "Sons of Liberty" (also known as "Liberty Boys") were groups of mainly young men that formed in various American cities and attempted to impede the Stamp Act by public protests as well as by sabotage and rioting.

among us, as well as when fostered by the warmer sun of England. The theatres of London are always considered as sacred to the dominion of the people. There the *Vox Populi* is truly the *Vox Dei*, and must not be resisted.[2] There the bold and rough spirit which the cold-blooded sons of order cannot bear, has full room to play.[3] The Edinburgh theatre is at last beginning to enjoy the same freedom. Poor *Lee* had the direction of our stage for some time.[4] He was turned away with more severity than we would wish others to do to us, by an association of gentlemen who purchased the property of the theatre, and have since employed a variety of people under them. *Love*, who now plays Falstaff in Drury Lane was our manager a good while.[5] But he very wisely obtained a settlement under his friend *Garrick*. Of late we have been shamefully off for managers. It would be tedious to tell you all the story; but so it is, that our present managers with a fellow of the name of A——n, and some more of their strollers, have been impertinent to the town.[6] Upon which a party was formed, a riot ensued, and the playhouse was as compleatly demolished as your's was some time ago in Covent-Garden.[7] The gentlemen proprietors have made a great noise upon this

2. *Vox populi . . . vox dei*: "The voice of the people [is] the voice of God"; an ancient and proverbial warning (see *ODQ*).

3. The "sons of order" (as opposed to the "Sons of Liberty") suggests the Presbyterian elders of Edinburgh.

4. John Lee (1725–81) began his first season at the Canongate in mid-1752, with an ambitious program of productions, touring, and theater renovation. The owners did not support the increasing debt, and, after a complex period of legal dispute, Lee was on Feb. 23, 1756, arrested in mid-performance. His house and property were seized and sold off, and he was jailed for two months. JB's early stage idol West Digges (see Chap. 5, n. 133) was then appointed manager (*ODNB*).

5. James Love (the stage name of James Dance, 1721–74) succeeded Digges as manager at the Canongate in 1759. He too had difficulties with the proprietors, and by Sept. 1762 he was, by David Garrick's invitation, at Drury Lane, where he went on to great success in the role of Falstaff.

6. "A——n" is completed by JB in his file copy to "Aicken." James Aickin (c. 1736–1803) was engaged as an actor to replace Digges in 1759 and became the head of the company of actors. Aickin supported the management in the decision over George Stayley (*ODNB*, s.v. "Aickin, James"). The "impertinence" to which JB refers was probably the management's retraction of an earlier promise to reemploy Stayley, made after his supporters had disrupted a performance on Saturday, Jan. 10. The theater management then published a handbill announcing the suspension of entertainments until further notice, and Aickin's name was at the head of the list of signatories, and thus when performances recommenced on Jan. 24, he was a particular target of the riot. He was taken on at Drury Lane in Nov. 1767 and remained there for the rest of his life. *Stroller* was a disrespectful term for an itinerant actor.

7. The stage at London's Covent Garden Theatre was stormed during a performance of Thomas Arne's opera *Artaxerxes* in Feb. 1763, in protest at a change to the old policy of

occasion, and threatened to prosecute the Liberty Boys, which made a young fellow of some humour say the other day, that he thought *Liberty* and *Property* were going together by the ears.[8] As, however, this vengeance was taken on the insolence of the servants of the publick, by a considerable body, some of whom are young gentlemen of the highest rank from England, and others members of the respectable body of the law, it is thought the proprietors will see that they would only make themselves ridiculous in a court of justice. *Solvuntur risu Tabulæ.*[9] The sages of the law laugh, and think that they will be very glad to pocket the affront, and take better care in time coming, how they dispose of their property. We hope this little tumult will put an end to our present disgraceful theatre, and that the gentlemen who have thought it high time to demolish the old blind blackguard house, will procure us the rational and elegant entertainments of the stage, under the sanction of a royal patent."[10]

FOUR INVENTIONS

[In the following items and those in the next group, we have some of the clearest instances of Boswell in the role of what Pottle describes as "the anonymous irresponsible writer for the newspapers who delights in the coarsely indelicate, the broadly ludicrous, the unsubtly fantastic" (*Earlier Years*, 306). In these four pieces, unlike "The Shorthand Reporters" following, and the as-yet uncollected inventions for the *London Chronicle* concerning the adventures of Signor Romanzo, the Corsican envoy (see *Earlier Years*, 305), Boswell is "writing with no thought of promoting anything." For

---

allowing admission to a play during the third act at half-price. The benches in the boxes and pit were torn up, the linings in the boxes were cut to pieces, and the glass and chandeliers were broken. The damage amounted to £2,000, and four people were arrested; see *Ann. Reg.* (1763), 57–58.

8. The "young fellow of some humour" is possibly JB. "Liberty and property" was a slogan chanted by those who gathered under Boston's Liberty Tree and marched in procession to the colonial governor's mansion, on Aug. 14, 1765. It is found as "life, liberty, and property" in the Oct. 1774 "Declaration of Colonial Rights," which was a resolution of the First Continental Congress. To *go together by the ears* is "to fight; to scuffle; to quarrel" (*SJ Dict.*).

9. *Solvuntur risu Tabulae*: "the case is dismissed amid laughter" or, more colloquially, "the prosecution is laughed out of court"; Horace, *Satires*, 2.1.86 (the final line). The context has to do with the dangers of writing satire and provoking the ire of people in power. JB also uses the line at *Life*, 4:129 (June 4, 1781).

10. The proprietors of the theater had applied for a Royal Patent; when this was granted, the new owner, David Ross—an experienced Covent Garden actor and manager—had a new theater built as the Theatre Royal, which opened on Dec. 9, 1767 (Jackson, *History of the Scottish Stage*, 72–73). The poetic prologue for the occasion was written by JB and, as Pottle notes, "appeared in most of the periodicals of the day" (*Lit. Car.*, xxxvi n. 1).

speculation as to Boswell's motives in contributing squibs such as these, we can do no better than to quote Pottle again:

Did Boswell enjoy seeing himself in print so much that he got satisfaction out of sheer publication, whether recognized as his or not? Was his object to set traps for the unwary, his satisfaction coming when people repeated the paragraphs in his presence as facts, he laughing inwardly? Did he relish the sense of manipulating others so much that he was willing to descend to the level of gratuitous misinformation? Did he like the reputation of writing widely for the newspapers, a masked and Protean figure whose hand might be anywhere? Was it all just a part of his wish to write so that people would have to read him, not merely people of literary sophistication but also people whose reading never got beyond the news? Were the inventions a compensation for the sacrifice of fancy demanded by judicious habits of mind and responsible sticking to the facts? One can only speculate, but in the really important matter we are left in no doubt. Instead of dulling Boswell's perception of fact, the fictions sharpened it. (Ibid., 306)]

Two Sailors

London Chronicle, March 31–April 2, 1767, 320

Extract of a Letter from Newcastle, 25 March.

"A very whimsical accident happened here the other day. Two jolly Tars purchased a four-wheeled post chaise in London,[11] which they had got a Painter in Long-acre to ornament with anchors, and masts, and cannon, and a crowd of sea objects.[12] In this chaise they would needs be driven post with six horses down to Alnwic, where their mistresses live.[13] They came the greatest part of the way like smoak as the phrase is.[14] But at the stage before this,[15] they were so impatient to get along, that they would not wait to have the wheels of their

11. *Tar* was a common and inoffensive slang word for a sailor (coal tar was used on ships for waterproofing clothes and fabrics, and sailors ended up smelling of it). "Jolly tars" was a commonplace expression, from the lyrics to David Garrick's popular song "Heart of Oak" (see n. 112, below). A *post-chaise* was a closed-bodied horse-drawn carriage, used for carrying mail and passengers.

12. *Long-acre*: a street in central London, known for coach makers.

13. *Post*: at the speed or with the urgency characteristic of a postal courier. Alnwick is a small market town in Northumberland. It was a staging post on the Great North Road between London and Edinburgh.

14. *Like Smoak* [i.e., smoke]: very rapidly, quickly (*OED*).

15. *Stage*: a regular stopping place on a stagecoach route, where horses are changed and travelers taken up and set down (*OED*).

machine greased, crying, damn it, she has had tar enough for all the voyage, so off they came full speed; but just as they entered this city their wheels took fire, and the chaise was all in a blaze about them. They hallood most prodigiously till a number of the populace gathered round, and threw pailfulls of water upon them, which extinguished the fire: but the poor Tars, what with being singed and what with being drenched, made a most ludicrous and piteous spectacle. They however got their machine repaired, and took the road again next morning by break of day."[16]

Mad Officer Murders Bride

London Chronicle, April 7–9, 1767, 344

Extract of a Letter from P———n in L———e,[17] *dated March 31.*

"A very melancholy affair happened here lately.[18] An officer on the recruiting service, a young man of most engaging manners, and who was said to be the eldest son of a gentleman of considerable family and fortune in the West of England, made his addresses to a young lady of this town, who consented to marry him. The morning after their marriage the Captain seemed on a sudden to be in great emotion. He looked at his young wife with eyes flashing with indignation, calling out, 'What, my dear, you have got black hair, have you? I'll soon cure that,' and immediately drawing his sword, he stabbed her three times in a most barbarous manner, so that she expired in a few minutes. The family alarmed by the noise, came into the room, and found the unhappy gentleman tearing his hair, and crying bitterly over the body of his wife. He was instantly put under

16. In JB's file copy, he has added "NB" at the end of the article and, at the bottom of the page, the MS note, "N. B. My Lord Dumfries believed this story of the Tars, and told it often & often." The Dumfries were near neighbors of the Boswells in Ayrshire; see *Corres.* 7, 191 n. 2. William Dalrymple-Crichton, fourth earl of Dumfries (1699–1768); see *Earlier Years*, 306.

17. Preston in Lancashire, in the west of England, was a site of considerable Jacobite sentiment. (Jacobites were those dedicated to the restoration of the House of Stuart to the British monarchy; from *Jacobus*, for King James II and VII, deposed in 1688.) In 1715 the Battle of Preston concluded with a defeat that ended the first Jacobite rebellion; it was the last major battle on English soil. In Nov. 1745, the invading Highland army of Prince Charles Edward Stuart (see Chap. 3, n. 352) passed through Preston, and was enthusiastically welcomed, on its way to its furthest point south, at Derby (see below, n. 48); on their retreat a fortnight later, the army rested in Preston. No other Boswellian connection with Preston has been established.

18. JB's own younger brother, John Boswell (1743–98), was from 1762 a lieutenant in the army. From his late teens, he was subject to bouts of mental derangement.

confinement, and has continued raving mad ever since. The Lieutenant Colonel of his regiment has written a most polite and humane letter to the father of the young lady, condoling with him on his affliction, and acquainting him that the poor Captain was subject to violent fits of lunacy, one of which has been the sad occasion of the mournful accident. This may serve as a warning to young ladies in country towns, not to yield too hastily to their passion for a stranger, however agreeable, but to wait till they are fully informed of his character and situation."

Drunken Capuchin Monk

London Chronicle, May 9–12, 1767, 456

Extract of a Letter from Utrecht, April 28.[19]

"We have been not a little amused with a strange adventure which happened here last week. A French refugee who was formerly a capuchin at Paris, but having run off from his convent, has skulked for several years in this city,[20] was making merry at our tavern called the Old Castle of Antwerp,[21] and having got himself much intoxicated with liquor, he took it into his head that he was still a capuchin, and nothing would serve him but a procession. He accordingly sallied forth into the street, carrying a couple of large lighted candles, and bellowing some of his popish anthems. He was accompanied by the landlord and by one G——e, a limping preacher of the reformed communion,[22] both of whom were so well refreshed, that they joined in the chorus. They proceeded in this manner till they came opposite to the Gaanse market,[23] where they were met by Counsellor Vander Huvel Rucher, the Professor of Civil Law, and Rambonet, one of the Ministers of the French church,[24] who being shocked at so absurd

19. JB lived in Utrecht and studied law from Aug. 1763 to June 1764.

20. In Utrecht, JB was acquainted with a former Capuchin monk, a Monsieur des Essar, who seems a partial model for this character. In his private notes at the time, JB described him as "extravagantly French" and says that he "ran away twice from his monastery," after which he "came into Holland like other good Huguenots" (Pottle's translation of JB's French, c. Mar. 31, 1764; see *Holland*, 198).

21. The Old Castle of Antwerp was the name of a hotel in Utrecht (Het Kasteel van Antwerpen) that JB visited soon after his arrival in Utrecht in 1763 (*Holland*, 6 n. 2).

22. Another of JB's friends in Utrecht was Charles de Guiffardière (c. 1740–1810), a protestant ("reformed") minister, whom he considered an example of "young preachers who liked good living" (*Holland*, 187). The two corresponded; Guiffardière's "levity always shocked Boswell" (ibid., 48 n. 2).

23. The Ganzenmarkt (or Goose Market) in Utrecht is still a shopping precinct. Originally, a goose market was a place for modest traders of small livestock.

24. Gerhard Christian Rücker (1722–80) was one of the professors of law at Utrecht (*Holland*, 24 and n. 1). After hearing the opening lectures of Rücker and two other professors,

a profanation, endeavoured to lay hold of the rioters. This occasioned a scuffle, and a very hearty drubbing match went on; the capuchin laying about him most powerfully with the candlesticks. By this time the whole town was alarmed, and two of the Burgomasters came with a strong body of the trained bands,[25] and not knowing who had begun the disturbance, carried all parties to prison till they should cool. Next morning Count Nassau the Grand Bailiff,[26] took cognizance of the affair, and after thanking the three last gentlemen for their very proper interposition, gave a severe reprimand to the capuchin, and his drunken companions."

Canal to Link Dumfries and Ayr

[On May 5, 1767, Boswell went on a ride with James Bruce, the overseer of the Auchinleck estate, to inspect the Dalblair farm that he had purchased the previous month (*Earlier Years*, 325). He noted that it was "difficult riding" (*Search*, 70), but that they reached the top of Wardlaw and took in an "Immense prospect: Ayr, Ailsa, Ben Lomond, Jura, Galloway Hills, Cairnsmore, Clydesdale Hills." Wardlaw is a hill of 1,630 feet, some miles north of Dalblair. Some days later, on May 11–12, he went on another excursion, traveling with his father on judicial duties to Dumfries, and, falling into hypochondria, felt the vanity of all things: "judges, chaises, men, and horses" (ibid., 72). Between noble landscapes and hard riding, he could well have been moved to think of canals.]

London Chronicle, May 14–16, 1767, 472

Letters from Edinburgh say, that the project of a magnificent navigable canal between the firths of Clyde and Forth being laid aside for this year,[27] a good

---

JB decided to attend the lectures of Christian Heinrich Trotz (c. 1703–73) on civil law (ibid., 24, 42–43, 166). JB and Trotz became friends and saw each other socially (ibid., 166, 272). Jean-Jacques Rambonnet (d. 1768) and another minister, Daniel Theodore Huet (1724–95), are mentioned in a letter to JB as "wearisome and mournful personages" whose church is "no longer anything but a *church-yard*, I mean a cemetery" (ibid., 348); see also *Corres. 5*, 82 n. 18.

25. *Burgomaster*: "chief magistrate of a Dutch or Flemish town, nearly corresponding to the *mayor* in England" (*OED*). *Trained* (or *train*) *band*: "A trained company of citizen soldiery, organized in London and other parts in the 16th, 17th, and 18th centuries. Also occas. applied to similar forces in other countries, e.g. the French *arrière-ban*" (*OED*).

26. Jan Nicolaas Floris, Count of Nassau (1709–82), was Utrecht's chief magistrate or "Grand Bailiff" (*Holland*, 141); while in Holland, JB frequently socialized with him.

27. The proposal by engineer and inventor John Smeaton (1724–92) to build a canal to link these two firths, on the west and east, respectively, across the narrowest part of lowland Scotland, was subject to much debate about the route and rival schemes. On Apr. 3, 1767,

many gentlemen of the western and southern counties of Scotland are immediately to make application to parliament to have a small canal opened between Dumfries and Ayr,[28] which will be of considerable advantage to trade, and can be executed at a very moderate expence by the assistance of the rivers Nith and Lugar, and several lakes.[29]

THE SHORTHAND REPORTERS

[This series of japes is a perfect instance of Boswell's mixing "fact" and "invention" in his efforts to maintain what we would call a public profile for issues he was pursuing. In early 1767, as a young lawyer, Boswell became vitally interested in a celebrated case in Scottish civil law that was then toiling its way through the courts. The Douglas Cause was a complex and long-running case in which the right of thirteen-year-old Archibald Douglas to inherit his uncle's estate and title as Duke of Douglas was, in 1762, challenged on behalf of other claimants, the (young) Duke of Hamilton and his brother. The Hamilton case was that Archibald was not the child of the duke's sister, Lady Jane Douglas, but a French child who had not been legally adopted and had been obtained by deception. By early 1767, both sides had finished pleading and had presented voluminous summaries of their evidence, and a judgment was expected. Boswell, though not engaged professionally, was deeply engaged on an emotional level, particularly by the central issue, the principle of *filiation*: that a man was who his parents said he was. Despite the many mysteries and improbabilities attaching to the Douglas side, he became an enthusiastic partisan. He wrote, prepared, and published a range of texts, in prose and verse, long and short, serious and frivolous. It was on this subject that he later confessed or boasted that he had taken "care to keep the newspapers and other publications incessantly warm with various writing" (*Lit. Car.*, xxxv).[30]

In May, he finished his transparently fictionalized novella *Dorando* (published on June 15), which was an allegory of the Douglas case, and followed it up with numerous paragraphs, reports (spurious and otherwise), anonymous self-reviews and extracts, ballads, and other items in the papers. The following short series of fantasies

---

it was decided that a bill before the House of Commons for building the canal should be delayed to allow a discussion of the rival "great" and "small" schemes (*Scots Mag.*, 29 [1767], 177–90). JB's friend Sir Alexander Dick (see n. 106, below) was much involved with the project (*Corres. 5*, 142–43, 163), and it is likely that this invention was intended to tease him.

28. Between these two towns in the southwest of Scotland, Dumfries on the Solway Firth and Ayr on the Firth of Clyde, is a distance of approximately sixty miles.

29. Dumfries is at the mouth of the River Nith; the Lugar Water is a small river flowing into the Ayr, at the mouth of which is the town.

30. This statement was in the anonymous "Memoirs of James Boswell, Esq.," which JB published in the *European Magazine* in 1791, to celebrate the author of the newly published *Life of Samuel Johnson*. The text is reprinted in *Lit. Car.*, xxix–xliv.

quickly if briefly took on a life of its own. Its precise purpose is difficult to fathom, unless we credit Boswell with a very prescient understanding that, in a modern media environment, all publicity is good publicity. The pieces, which have been described as "one of Boswell's most elaborate and entertaining inventions" (*Search*, 74), display his talent for sketching characters—real or invented—and they keep the Cause before the minds of his readers. Unfortunately, no journal of Boswell's is known for this period, in which he was particularly busy with literary work (ibid., 74). The case was decided by the Court of Session for the Hamiltons in July 1767. Boswell continued his advocacy through his books *The Essence of the Douglas Cause* and *Letters of Lady Jane Douglas* (both November 1767) and rejoiced when the earlier decision was overturned by the House of Lords, on appeal, in February 1769.[31]]

London Chronicle, May 16–19, 1767, 480

A letter from Edinburgh says, "We hear that at the determination of the great cause of Douglas, the Lords Judges of the Court of Session are to sit for that day in one of the large rooms of the Royal Palace of Holyrood house;[32] and that scaffoldings are to be erected as in Westminster Hall at the trial of Earl Ferrers:[33] To defray the expence of which, as well as to raise a contribution for the Royal Infirmary, all who are admitted, except the Members of Court, are to give half a guinea each."[34]

No less than five eminent writers of short hand are preparing to set out for Edinburgh, in order to take the reports of the Scots Judges upon the Douglas Cause.[35]

31. For an accessible account of the Douglas Cause, focusing on Boswell's interest and activity, see Ruxin, "*Dorando* and the Douglas Cause," 79–94. Also see *Earlier Years*, 311–17.

32. The Court of Session is the supreme civil court of Scotland; the judges use the title "Lord" (and now "Lady"). Holyroodhouse is a royal palace, first built in 1521 on the site of a twelfth-century Augustinian monastery and substantially rebuilt in the 1670s; ("Bonnie") Prince Charles Edward Stuart held court there during the 1745 second Jacobite uprising. Pottle notes that this paragraph "was probably intended to tease the Hamilton party, the Duke of Hamilton being Hereditary Keeper of the Palace" (*Earlier Years*, 330).

33. Laurence Shirley, fourth Earl Ferrers (1720–60), was tried by the House of Lords in Apr. 1760 for the murder of his steward. Despite evidence of his history of periodic insanity, he was convicted, sentenced to death, and hanged on May 5 at Tyburn (JB was in London at the time: see *Earlier Years*, 489). He is the last member of the House of Lords to have been hanged. Westminster Hall is the oldest remaining part of the Palace of Westminster (which includes the Houses of Parliament) and was the venue for important trials, including state trials and impeachments.

34. The Royal Infirmary of Edinburgh was founded in 1729, as a hospital for "the Sick Poor." Originally, Edinburgh physicians donated their services, and it was funded by donations from churches and wealthy citizens.

35. At the time, it was not legal to report the speeches of the Lords of Session. Pottle says that this second paragraph "may have been designed to tease the Lord President [of the

Edinburgh Advertiser, June 12–16, 1767, 381

Extract of a letter from Berwick,[36] dated Monday, June 15.

"The decision of the Great Douglas Cause being fixed by your Court of Session for Tuesday the 23d, there passed through this town, from London, Messrs. Cust, Garnet, Tracy, Selwyn, and Burridge,[37] all allowed to write the short-hand better than any in England.[38] I passed an evening with them, and several gentlemen here, and I never was better entertained, as their art has enabled them to lay up a treasure of all the curious and interesting anecdotes they have heard in private conversations, as well as every important speech in all the public assemblies in the island. Their merit is so great, that your friend Mr. —— the bookseller has contracted to give them 300 guineas for a correct report of the Scots Judges upon the Douglas Cause. In my next you shall have more particulars."

Edinburgh Advertiser, June 16–19, 1767, 390

Extract of a letter from Berwick, dated Thursday, June 18.

"In my last, I wrote how much I had been entertained with the famous Stenographers, who are come from London to take down, in short-hand, the report of the Scots judges upon the great Douglas cause. Having stayed longer with us than they intended, I am now able to give you much fuller information concerning them. Mr. Cust is said to be a distant relation of the S——er of the H—— of

---

Court of Session, Robert Dundas (1713–87)], but probably originated in sheer impishness" (*Earlier Years*, 330). Further, see n. 55, below.

36. Berwick, or Berwick-upon-Tweed, is a northern English town on the coast of Northumberland, only two and a half miles south of the Scottish border. It was an important center for trade, and until 1482, when it was captured by the future English king Richard III, its rule changed frequently between England and Scotland. It nevertheless continued to retain a certain degree of independence, and pro-Scottish sentiment remains strong to this day. Berwick was the hometown of JB's lifelong friend and correspondent William Johnson Temple. Although by this time Temple was the rector of Mamhead, in Devon, during the period of this series of inventions, he was in Berwick to arrange his marriage (see *Corres. 6*, 186–208), though their letters make no mention of the shorthand reporters.

37. The names of the reporters are elaborated upon in the notes to the next item.

38. *Allowed*: i.e., acknowledged. In JB's daily memoranda in London in 1762–63, he occasionally deployed shorthand strategies derived from a system invented in the seventeenth century by Thomas Shelton (Boswell, *London Journal*, ed. Turnbull, lvii). He told SJ and others that he himself did not use "what is called stenography, or short-hand, in appropriated characters devised for the purpose" (Apr. 10, 1778; *Life*, 3:270), referring to *Stenography* (1758) by John Angell; SJ subscribed to this book and knew the author. In *Hypochondriack*, no. 66, "On Diaries," JB gives a comical account of an early attempt to write in a cipher which he could not later decode (Bailey, 2:262).

C——.[39] Mr. Garnet is own sister's grand-nephew to Father Garnet, the Jesuit, who was executed for the Gunpowder-plot.[40] Mr. Tracy is a gentleman of good family in Gloucestershire.[41] He has had an university education, and has made the tour of Europe. By extravagant living with the late D—— of H——, and many of the first nobility, he has dissipated a very fine fortune: But having very remarkable talents for writing the short-hand, it is believed that he is now richer than ever.[42] He said very pleasantly t'other night, that as he had spent his estate with D—— H——, he hoped his Grace's heir would enable him to get back a little;[43] and indeed, as I am informed, the Report of your judges will not sell for less than a thousand guineas. Mr. Selwyn has a great look of the ingenious gentleman whose good sayings have made so much noise.[44] But we cannot venture to affirm that it is he. Mr. Burridge is the most extraordinary personage among them:[45] He wears a brown coat and a cut wig,[46] and looks as grave as a parish

39. Sir John Cust (1718–70) became Speaker of the House of Commons in 1761. He was not well suited to the role, and under his chairmanship the House became very disorderly. JB was acquainted with his chaplain, Rev. Richard Palmer (Aug. 31, 1769; *Search*, 284). A "Mr. Cust" is one of "three different West Indian gentlemen" (i.e., gentlemen with West Indian interests) who, in a paragraph JB contributed to the *Pub. Adv.*, Mar. 16, 1791, was said to have written JB's own anonymous poem *No Abolition of Slavery* (1791).

40. *Own*: "chiefly used in relation to terms of kinship, to distinguish a close blood relationship from some other kind, as *an own brother* = a full brother as opposed to a half-brother or brother-in-law, etc." (*OED*). Henry Garnett (1555–1606) was a Jesuit priest and convicted Gunpowder Plot conspirator. The Garnets would have been very long-livers, if the reporter Garnet was the Jesuit's sister's "grand-nephew." Garnett had three sisters, of whom only Anne did not become a nun.

41. The Tracys were a leading family in Gloucestershire, of whom Richard (d. 1569) was known as a protestant extremist.

42. The "late D—— of H——" probably represents James Hamilton, sixth duke of Hamilton (1724–58), father of the nominal plaintiff in the Douglas Cause. John Tracy, also John Tracy Atkyns (1706–73), was a note-taker in the Court of Chancery during the lord chancellorship (1737–56) of Philip Yorke, first earl of Hardwicke. Tracy later sought Hardwicke's permission to publish his notes, which was refused, despite Tracy's reputation for accuracy. After Hardwicke's death, his son granted permission, and the notes were published, as *Reports of Cases Argued and Determined in the High Court of Chancery in the Time of Lord Chancellor Hardwicke*, 3 vols. (London, 1765–68).

43. The heir of the "late D—— of H——" was his young son, James Hamilton, the seventh duke (1755–69) and the nominal plaintiff in the Douglas Cause; see *Search*, 75.

44. JB alludes to politician George Augustus Selwyn (1719–91), an MP, but better known as a club-man and wit.

45. Richard Burridge (fl. 1670–1750), poet and pamphleteer, wrote *Hell in an Uproar: Occasioned by a Scuffle that Happened between the Lawyers and the Physicians* (1700) and was in 1712 tried for blasphemy.

46. A "cut wig" is a type of scratch-wig (see Chap. 4, n. 77): a small, short, plain wig.

clerk; yet, over his bottle, he has the most drole and ludicrous sallies; and, when he turns that cut-wig of his, you would laugh for a whole evening. His life has been one continued scene of strange adventures. He is a Cornishman by birth, and lived a good while among the miners.[47] He has been a proselyte to all sects of religion. He was long an attendant at the Popish-chapels in London. He next went over to Pennsylvania, and joined the Quakers; and, on his return to England, he commenced Methodist. He has large books of lectures and exhortations, with [a] variety of curious dialogues, all picked up from the different sectaries. In the year 1745, he was employed as a spy by the government, and by letting himself down a chimney at Derby, and keeping himself concealed, he, with the help of a dark lanthorn, wrote down many secrets of the Rebel Chiefs.[48] In one place, where none but ladies were admitted, he went in properly dressed, and with a fountain-pen, in the shape of a fan, he took down with white ink, on the bottom of a French song, the whole conversation, without so much as being perceived by those about him. It would be endless to recount the many entertaining anecdotes of these gentlemen. Besides, you are to see them soon; as you will also the Bishops of ——, and ——,[49] with many of the nobility, and some of the first lawyers.

It will be in vain to think of excluding the short-hand men, from your Court. They will appear like men of the highest rank, and quality. Nay they have often been known to dress themselves in women's cloaths, and as they have much depending upon the great Douglas cause, you may be sure they will greatly exert themselves."[50]

We just now hear, that the above gentlemen, are actually arrived in the Canongate.

Edinburgh Advertiser, June 23–26, 1767, 405–6

Extract of a letter from Berwick, dated Thursday, June 25.

"I am not a little disappointed about this D—— cause. My friends, the short-hand men, complain heavily. I cannot give you a better idea of it, than by sending you the following short letter, which I have just received from one of them.

---

47. The county of Cornwall in the southwest of England was from ancient times mined for tin.

48. On Dec. 4, 1745, the army of Prince Charles Stuart made camp at Derby. It was the furthest point south the Jacobite army reached in its attempt to conquer England. A dark-lantern (or lanthorn) has a shutter by which to conceal the light, but the term is also slang for a "servant or agent that receives a bribe at court" (*OED*).

49. If two bishops in fact attended the Douglas Cause proceedings, they have not been identified.

50. The line following the foregoing "extract" purports to be a "stop-press postscript, ostensibly added by the editor" (*Earlier Years*, 331).

Edinburgh, June 24, 1767.

Dear Sir,

'We arrived safe here, and went to the court on Tuesday; but, instead of the Cause, we had only the examination of a witness, at whom they were going to ask a parcel of *French* and *Dutch* questions in cookery,[51] which would have played the Devil with us, as our short hand will do for nothing but English. However, luckily for us, she kept to her mother-tongue, and is now put off till Tuesday the 7th of July. This is really hard. Cust says he would rather have half a dozen of his teeth drawn, and Garnet swears he would sooner engage in another gunpowder Plot. For my part, I am determined to make the best of it. It is impossible for us to remain here; for we cannot set out our heads but we have a whole mob at our heels, and messages from idle ladies every hour in the four and twenty. We set out to-morrow (disguised like English riders), on a jaunt to Inverary,[52] and other parts of the Highlands; so as to be back by the great day; for, a thousand guineas is well worth looking after. Till then, believe me very much yours, &c.

NOEL BURRIDGE.

"P.S. You shall hear again from us when we are in better humour."

Edinburgh Advertiser, July 3–7, 1767, 13

Extract of a letter from Berwick, dated July 6.

SIR,

"Inclosed is a letter I have had from my friends the short-hand men, to whom I beg leave to refer.

Inver. July 1, 1767.

Dear Sir,

"As poor Burridge has sprained his thumb, he desires me to write to you that we are all very well pleased with our jaunt here, not only with seeing this country,

---

51. JB wrote to Temple on June 22: "The Lords are to examine tomorrow Isabel Walker who was one of Lady Jane Douglas's Maids, & is the only Person now alive who has been accused as an Accomplice in the alleged crime of Partus Suppositio [i.e., procuring false children]" (*Corres. 6*, 189). For more on Walker, see *Corres. 7*, 92 n. 7. JB may be alluding to the claim of the Hamilton case, that a French child had been "cooked" up by Walker and Lady Jane Douglas, using *cook* in the sense of "to manipulate, 'doctor,' falsify, tamper with" (*OED*), and perhaps to Walker's married name, Mrs. Glass: Hannah Glasse (1708–70) being the writer of a famous cookbook.

52. *Riders*: i.e., commercial travelers. Inverary is a town in Argyle, in the west of Scotland, and Inverary Castle is the seat of the Duke of Argyll. JB visited there with SJ, Oct. 24–27, 1773, and wrote in the *Tour*, "I had reason to think that the Duchess of Argyle

but particularly on account of a very important discovery we made in finding out one Donald Maquire, who has the second-sight: What we have learnt of this man is really astonishing.[53] Formerly we were infidels with regard to the second-sight, but now believe it as we do our creed. We have wrote down a number of d—— curious anecdotes with regard to this affair, which we design to publish when we get back to London: Every part of it is more wonderful than the history of the Patagonians.[54] I am, &c.

ALGERNON CUST."[55]

1769

THE STRATFORD JUBILEE

[The Shakespeare Jubilee was a three-day festival staged in September 1769 at Stratford, where William Shakespeare was born in 1564. Under the supervision of David Garrick, the foremost actor and theatrical manager of the day, it was the first event of its type and the beginning of modern bardolatry. Stratford was at the time a small market-town, and, although occasional visitors came seeking Shakespearean sites, little effort had been made by the inhabitants to capitalize on the connection. Indeed,

---

disliked me, on account of my zeal in the Douglas Cause" (*Life*, 5:353); the Duchess, Elizabeth Campbell, was by her first marriage the dowager Duchess of Hamilton, and her son was the rival claimant in the Douglas Cause.

53. *Second-sight*: "a supposed power by which occurrences in the future or things at a distance are perceived as though they were actually present" (*OED*); from the late seventeenth century, it was much reported and discussed in Scotland, and SJ enquired into it on his Scottish tour with JB. Pottle describes Donald Maquire as a "Highlander invented by JB" (*Earlier Years*, 596). A Donald Macleod was the author of *A Treatise on the Second Sight* (Edinburgh, 1763).

54. From early in the sixteenth century, the region of Patagonia in southern South America had been rumored in Europe to be home to a race of giants, and this rumor was fueled by some accounts of the voyages of Magellan and Drake. The story was revived when the *Dolphin*, under Commodore John Byron, returned to London from a global circumnavigation and made its way into print in the *Gent. Mag.*, May 1766, from which it was reprinted in other papers. The official account of Byron's voyage, published in 1773, denied the rumors.

55. There are no further pieces in the series, as the publishers of four Edinburgh newspapers were at this point cited by Lord President Robert Dundas for contempt of court, for publishing material prejudicial to the case: mainly the above paragraphs, and reviews— mostly also by JB—of JB's *Dorando*. The publishers were defended by JB, whose defense succeeded to the extent that the publishers were let off with a rebuke. (On the day this item was published, the court began to deliver its decision in the Douglas Cause. This took a

what are now called heritage values were so little regarded that the mulberry tree that Shakespeare himself was supposed to have planted in the garden of his own house was chopped down by its owner in 1756,[56] and the house itself demolished in 1759. In 1764 the bicentenary of Shakespeare's birth had passed by without any commemoration. When in 1767 the Stratford Corporation decided to rebuild the decrepit Town Hall, it was suggested that extra finance could be found by approaching Garrick, whose devotion to Shakespeare was well known.

David Garrick went to London in 1737 with his former teacher Samuel Johnson, and made his name and fortune with Shakespeare, starting when he appeared as Richard III in 1741. By 1767 he had played nineteen Shakespearean roles (Deelman, *Great Shakespeare Jubilee*, 91), owned the Drury Lane Theatre, and had become the richest working man in England (ibid., 82). Accordingly, a letter came to Garrick from the Stratford Corporation cannily inviting him to provide a bust of the Bard— and a portrait of himself—for the Town Hall and offering him the freedom of the borough. This letter landed on fertile ground; by May 1769 Garrick had decided not simply to accept the invitation, but that these events should be celebrated with a public occasion at Stratford, at the end of the summer. The modern chronicler of the Jubilee says, "The Stratford Festival was the explicit culmination of a campaign to popularise Shakespeare which Garrick had been waging since the start of his career" (ibid., 89).

Garrick planned an elaborate program to cover three days and used the resources and personnel of Drury Lane to prepare performances, music, costumes, and indoor and outdoor decorations. Oddly, there was no performance of any work of Shakespeare's. It is difficult to exaggerate how much space in the papers in the weeks and months beforehand was devoted to discussion of the Jubilee, announcing details of the program, advertising various accoutrements, reporting progress, speculating about its form, and attacking it. When Boswell came down to London from Edinburgh in late August 1769, he had (so he told himself in his journal) "resolved not to go" to the Jubilee; "But as I approached the capital I felt my inclination increase, and when arrived in London I found myself within the whirlpool of curiosity, which could not fail to carry me down" (*Search*, 286).

The "whirlpool of curiosity" drew in many from fashionable society, and there were seven hundred people at the dinner on the first day. "Two Dukes . . . , at least half a dozen Earls, . . . and many, many more of the lower ranks of Peers and Peeresses" attended the Jubilee (Deelman, *Great Shakespeare Jubilee*, 177), as did a great many people involved in the London theater, including the dramatists Hugh Kelly,

---

week. By the casting vote of the Lord President, the judgment went to the Hamilton side. Immediately, an appeal was made to the House of Lords, which considered the case in Jan.–Feb. 1769. When the Lords, by a unanimous decision, reversed the Scottish judgment, JB took a prominent part in the celebratory riots in Edinburgh.)

56. For more on this subject, see Chap. 4, nn. 160–62 and text.

George Colman, Samuel Foote, and Arthur Murphy, with whom Boswell took the opportunity to become better acquainted (*Search*, 301). Although the festival itself was (as Boswell reports) rather a washout, Garrick salvaged some of the materials by successfully presenting his pageant of Shakespeare's characters as an afterpiece at Drury Lane (*Earlier Years*, 427). See also note 82, below.]

An Account of the Stratford Jubilee

Public Advertiser, September 16, 1769, 1–2 (lead article); with Boswell's MS corrections

Mr. WOODFALL,

ALLOW me amongst many others to describe Shakespeare's Jubilee at Stratford upon Avon. Upon such Occasions it is exceedingly difficult for those who are present to convey to People at a Distance a just Account of what is going on. There are few whose Heads are strong enough to be in the midst of gay Company and a variety of Entertainments, without having their Spirits put into such a Fermentation as to be incapable of settling to write; and they who can in these Circumstances be quite calm, and Masters of themselves, are for the most part of Feelings so dull, that we cannot expect from them but a heavy and inanimate Picture.

For my own part I am now returned to London, and I flatter myself that, after being agitated as much as any body, I have recovered my Tranquility, and am in Condition to give you a few Remarks on this celebrated Jubilee, which I am persuaded will engage the Attention not only of all Ranks in this Island, but of the Learned and Ingenious in every Part of Europe. For what was the Stratford Jubilee, not a Piece of Farce and Rhodomantade,[57] as many of the envious Foes of our Roscius attempted to make us believe,[58] but an elegant and truly classical Celebration of the Memory of Shakespeare, that illustrious Poet whom all Ages will admire as the World has hitherto done. It was truly an antique Idea, a Grecian Thought, to institute a splendid Festival in Honour of a Bard.[59] My Bosom glowed with Joy when I beheld a numerous and brilliant Company of

57. *Rhodomantade* (one of three spellings): "boastful or inflated language; extravagant boasting or bragging" (*OED*).

58. *Our Roscius*: i.e., David Garrick (1717–79; see headnote), called so after ancient Roman actor Quintus Roscius Gallus. JB uses this popular learned nickname for Garrick in his journal (e.g., Jan. 21, Apr. 6, 1763; *Lond. Journ.*, 163, 234).

59. JB perhaps has in mind the Athenian Panathenaic festival, which, though celebrated in honor of Athena, was the festival at which a competition in recitation of Homer (and Homer only) was held.

Nobility and Gentry, the Rich, the Brave, the Witty, and the Fair assembled to pay their Tribute of Praise to Shakespeare; nor could I help thinking that they at the same Time paid a very just Compliment to Mr. Garrick, the Steward of the Jubilee, who has done so much to make our Nation acquainted with the inestimable Riches of their own Stage in possessing so illustrious a dramatic Author with such amazing Variety and wonderful Excellence as Shakespeare. Garrick may be called the Colourist of Shakespeare's Soul.—He

> ———Dame Nature's Pencil stole
> Just where old Shakespeare dropt it.[60]

Let conceited and disappointed Authors and Players vent their Spleen against him, he may assure himself that his Fame will last for ever.[61]

The Morning of the first Day was ushered in with a pleasing Serenade by the best Musicians from London in Disguise.[62] The Jubilee began with an Oratorio in the great Church at Stratford; the Subject the Story of Judith; the Words by Mr. Bickerstaff; the Music by Dr. Arne.[63] It was a grand and admirable Performance. But I could have wished that Prayers had been read, and a short Sermon preached. It would have consecrated our Jubilee to begin it with Devotion, with gratefully adoring the Supreme Father of all Spirits, from whom cometh every Good and perfect Gift.[64] The Procession with Music from the Church to the Amphitheatre, led on by Mr. Garrick, had a very good Effect. The Amphitheatre was a wooden Building, erected just on the Brink of the Avon, in the Form

60. This particular couplet, from JB's own "Corsican Verses" (following), is no doubt quoted because, as JB records in his journal, when he read the poem to Garrick at the Jubilee, Garrick remarked on it as "both a fine poetical image and a fine compliment" (*Search*, 300).

61. There were numerous parodies and attacks on the Jubilee by Garrick's theatrical and literary rivals, prominent among whom were satirist Samuel Foote and irascible scholar George Steevens, who later claimed that he wrote at least forty such pieces. See Deelman, *Great Shakespeare Jubilee*, 116–24, and some excerpts in Stochholm, *Garrick's Folly*, 36–42.

62. The Serenade was performed by "musicians and singers from the Drury Lane Theatre, who were disguised as waiters with their faces smeared with dirt" (Stochholm, *Garrick's Folly*, 51 and ff.).

63. The oratorio *Judith* by Thomas Arne (1710–78), with a libretto by Isaac Bickerstaff (1733–1808?), was very successful when first performed at Drury Lane in Feb. 1761. The story, based on the Old Testament apocryphal book of Judith, has no Shakespearean connection.

64. JB's description of *Judith* and his pious remarks (he quotes James 1:17) are misleading, as he did not in fact arrive in Stratford until after noon on the first day (*Search*, 297).

of an Octagon, with eight Pillars supporting the Roof. It was elegantly painted and gilded. Between the Pillars were Crimson Curtains very well imitated as hanging over each Recess. In this Amphitheatre was a large Orchestra, placed as it used to be formerly in Ranelagh.[65] Here the Company dined exceedingly well between Three and Four. Between Five and Six the musical Performers appeared, and entertained us with several of the Songs in Shakespeare's Garland composed for the Occasion.[66] *Sweet Willy oh*, tender and pathetic. *The Mulberry tree*, of which the Chorus is very fine. *Warwickshire*, a Ballad of great Merit in it's Kind, lively, spirited, full of witty Turns, and even delicate Fancies. Mr. Garrick's Words, and Mr. Dibdin's Music, went charmingly together, and we all joined in the Chorus.

I shall not follow a regular Method of narrating the Proceedings exactly, but just mention what made Impression upon myself; that is the best Rule for every Man to follow if he wishes to entertain.

The Performance of the Dedication Ode was noble and affecting: It was like an Exhibition in Athens or Rome.[67] The whole Audience were fixed in the most

65. Garrick interspersed the main events of the Jubilee program with a number of processions; they were "planned and prepared . . . [but] had an almost impromptu atmosphere" (Deelman, *Great Shakespeare Jubilee*, 196). A band played, and songs were sung. The procession stopped at Shakespeare's birthplace en route to the Amphitheatre, which was a large wooden structure, with room for an audience of 1,000, built for the Jubilee on the banks of the Avon and modeled on the large decorative rotunda at Ranelagh Gardens, the fashionable public pleasure gardens at Chelsea (see Figure 2).

66. The light public songs that Garrick prepared for the Jubilee were published in *Shakespeare's Garland: Being a Collection of New Songs . . . Performed at the Jubilee* (1769). This book was available with other Jubilee publications, such as Garrick's dedication *Ode*, at a shop set up at Shakespeare's birthplace, by the official publisher to the Jubilee, Thomas Becket (Stochholm, *Garrick's Folly*, 58). The tunes were commissioned from a variety of composers, including William Boyce and Charles Dibdin (see Deelman, *Great Shakespeare Jubilee*, 152 ff., 314; Stochholm, *Garrick's Folly*, 153). Of the three songs JB names, the texts of "Sweet Willy O" and "Warwickshire, a Ballad" were appended to this article in the *Lond. Chron.* "Warwickshire," by Garrick and Dibdin (from which JB goes on to quote three lines), was played and sung a number of times at the Jubilee and was later much performed in London. The tune was later adopted as the regimental quick-march of the Royal Warwickshire Regiment.

67. Garrick's *Ode to Shakespeare* (1769), with music by Arne, was a vital part of the Jubilee as Garrick envisaged it. A combination of declamation and singing, it was performed by Garrick, with chorus and musicians conducted by Arne, in the Amphitheatre at noon on the second day, despite the cancellation of the preliminary Pageant owing to the inclement weather. Its purely poetical qualities were later criticized, but, at the time and in the circumstances, all agreed with JB that the performance was a triumph (see Deelman, *Great Shakespeare Jubilee*, 213–25).

Figure 2. The Amphitheatre, "Stratford Jubilee," Samuel Ireland, Picturesque Views on the Upper, or Warwickshire Avon *(London, 1795). Courtesy of the Alexander Turnbull Library, Wellington, New Zealand.*

earnest Attention, and I do believe that if any one had attempted to disturb the Performance, he would have been in Danger of his Life. Garrick in the Front of the Orchestra, filled with the first Musicians of the Nation, with Dr. Arne at their Head, and inspired with an aweful Elevation of Soul, while he looked from Time to Time at the venerable Statue of Shakespeare, appeared more than himself. While he repeated the Ode, and saw the various Passions and Feelings which it contains fully transfused into all around him, he seemed in Extacy, and gave us the Idea of a Mortal transformed into a Demi-god as we read in the Pagan Mythology.

I can witness from my own Hearing what did great Honour to Lord Grosvenor as well [as to] Mr. Garrick.[68] After the Ode his Lordship came up to the Orchestra, and told Mr. Garrick that he had affected his whole Frame, shewing him his Veins and Nerves still quivering with Agitation. What truly delighted me was to observe the warm Sincerity of Mr. Garrick's Enthusiasm for his immortal Bard throughout the whole Suite of Entertainments. While the Songs were singing he was all Life and Spirit, joining in the Chorus, and humouring every Part with his expressive Looks and Gestures. When he sung

68. Richard Grosvenor (1731–1802), Lord (from 1784, first Earl) Grosvenor, politician and landowner; he was known also for his interests in womanizing, art patronage, and horse-racing.

> Warwickshire Thief,
> He's the Chief,
> The Thief of all Thieves, &c.

his Eyes sparkled with Joy; and the Triumph of his Countenance at some Parts of the Ode, it's Tenderness at others, and inimitably sly Humour at others, cannot be described. I would not for a great Sum give up the Recollection which my Mind possesses of that wonderful Recitation. I know not whether it may be a Compliment to Mr. Garrick, but I must say that his Ode greatly exceeded my Expectations. I knew his Talent for little sportive Sallies, but I feared that a Dedication Ode for Shakespeare was above his Powers. What the Critics may say of this Performance I know not, but I shall never be induced to waver in my Opinion of it. I do say it is a Work of superior Merit, well suited to the Occasion by the Variety of it's Subjects, and containing both poetical Force and Elegance. It would be unpardonable should I omit acknowledging the Pleasure which I received from Dr. Arne's Music, which was truly fine; nor must I neglect thanking the whole Orchestra for their Execution.

As you have such a Number of Letters concerning this famous Jubilee, I would wish to avoid Repetition; I would wish not to go over the same Ground with others, though perhaps it may be with Description as it is with Farming, where different Persons going over the same Ground will make it have a very different Appearance, just from their different Methods of dressing it. When the Ode was finished, Mr. Garrick made a very genteel Address to us in Prose, modestly expressing how much he thought himself unequal to the Task he had undertaken, and assuring us, that he found it quite another Thing to speak in Public, supported by the great Genius of Shakespeare, from what he found it to speak in Public, supported only by his own feeble Genius; but he hoped we would shew him the same kind Indulgence as is usually shewn to those unfortunate Gentlemen who appear for the first Time in a Character. His Epilogue to the Ladies was very lively, and very well expressed. I hope he will favour us with it in print.[69] When Mr. Garrick had done, he invited any of the Company to speak if they were so disposed. Upon which Mr. King, the Comedian, got up to the Orchestra, and gave us a smart ironical Attack upon Shakespeare in the Character of a modern refined Man of Taste.[70] This might have done very well on some other Occasion; but, in my Opinion, it had better have been omitted at

69. Garrick's speech and epilogue ("to the ladies") appear never to have been included with the *Ode* in an edition of Garrick's plays or poetical works.

70. Thomas King (1730–1805), whose scripted interruption in the character of an effete, unpatriotic dandy was intended to give Garrick an opportunity to rebuff his critics, was well

this noble Festival: It detracted from it's Dignity; nor was there any Occasion for it. We were all enthusiastic Admirers of Shakespeare. We had not Time to think of his cavilling Critics. We were wrapped into Wonder and Admiration of our immortal Bard; and the Levity of the fine Gentleman disturbed the Tone of our Minds. I must be forgiven too for observing that this Exhibition looked so like a Trap laid on Purpose, that it displeased me; and I was angry to find any Notice taken of the venomous Insects who have shot their Stings in the Newspapers against the Jubilee, and particularly against Mr. Garrick. It had the Appearance of a Soreness unworthy of our Lord High Steward. If the Gnats at any Time slightly pierce his Skin, let him drop a little of the Oil of good-humoured Pleasantry upon the Place, and give himself no farther Trouble. This is my Receipt founded on Experience, *Probatum est.*[71] I must however do Justice to Tom King, and allow that he played his Part exceedingly well. I got acquainted at the Jubilee with this ingenious Comedian, and found him a genteel, agreeable Companion, and for all the shining of his *Brass**[72] upon the Stage, a very modest Man in private Society. I am surprized that your Correspondents who have so justly praised Mr. Angelo's Fireworks, have not mentioned the Pictures on the Bank of the Avon, fronting the Amphitheatre.[73] There we beheld Time leading Shakespeare to Immortality, Tragedy on one Side and Comedy on the other,

---

known as a favorite comic actor at Drury Lane, where he was Garrick's deputy and close friend. JB here met King for the first time (*Search*, 299), and he skipped the dinner on the second day to dine privately with him. Some weeks later, Oct. 13, JB breakfasted with King in London (ibid., 336).

71. *Receipt*: "prescription of ingredients for any composition" (*SJ Dict.*). *Probatum est*: "It is proved."

72. "* 'Mongst Drury's Sons he comes, and shines in *Brass*." (BOSWELL)

This comes from the passage concerning King in Charles Churchill's *The Rosciad* (1761), line 344, a satirical poem with passages on various actors. King "scored his first success with London audiences in 1759, playing Brass in Vanbrugh's *The Confederacy*, 1705" (Churchill, *Poetical Works*, 13 n. 463).

73. Fireworks, planned for the three evenings of the Jubilee, were by Domenico Angelo (1717–1802), fencing master and Garrick's versatile technical assistant at Drury Lane. Angelo devised a great number of new effects for the Jubilee. "Two Waggon Loads of Fireworks" and other devices were sent from London (*St. James's Chron.*, Aug. 26, 1769). Although the London papers reported a pyrotechnic display on the first night, it was in fact postponed because of the threatening weather until Thursday, when relentless drizzle ruined it completely. Some surviving fireworks were ignited before a very small crowd at 9:00 p.m. on the Friday. Angelo also arranged for the lamps that lit up the Stratford streets at night and which illuminated the "transparencies"—paintings on large, framed silk screens—that depicted well-known Shakespearean characters Lear, Caliban, Falstaff, and Pistol, as well as the opening words of *Henry V*, "Oh for a muse of fire."

copied from the fine Ideas of Sir Joshua Reynolds.[74] Behind these Pictures were placed a Number of Lamps, which gave them a most beautiful Transparency. In the same Style were five Pictures in the Windows of the Town Hall: In the Middle Shakespeare, in the Attitude of exclaiming,

"Oh! for a Muse of Fire!"

On the Windows on one Side of him, Lear and Caliban: On the Windows on the other Side, Sir John Falstaff and Ancient Pistol. In the same Style too was a Piece of Painting hung before the Windows of the Room where Shakespeare was born, representing the Sun breaking thro' the Clouds. Whether Inspiration poetical hath impregnated his Mind, Time must determine. I had a serene and solemn Satisfaction in contemplating the Church in which Shakespeare lies.[75] It is a large old Building, and has been a Kind of Cathedral, or a Church, belonging to some religious Society, for it has a regular Choir in which the Bard reposes. His Grave Stone is a good deal sunk below the Level of the Floor; but nobody will ever put a Hand to it, for his Epitaph is,

"Good Friends, for Jesus Sake, forbear
To dig the Dust enclosed here.
Blest be he that spares these Stones,
But curst be he that moves my Bones."

At one End of his Grave some pious Hands had placed a Garland of Flowers, Bays, Laurels, and other Ever-Greens; and there were also Festoons of Ever-Greens put on the Monument which is erected on the Wall next his Grave. The Monument is not very excellent. The warlike Music of the Warwickshire Militia, and the Discharge of Artillery, added considerably to the Grandeur of our Jubilee. We all wore, hung in a blue Ribband at our Breasts, a Medal of Shakespeare, very well cast by Mr. Westwood of Birmingham.[76] On one Side was the Head of Shakespeare, and round it this Inscription,

74. Sir Joshua Reynolds (1723–92), foremost British portrait painter, great friend of SJ; JB met him Sept. 25, 1769 (*Search*, 327), and dedicated the *Life of Johnson* to him. The painting is Reynolds's *David Garrick between Tragedy and Comedy* (1760–61), which shows the actor torn between two female figures, the stern figure of Tragedy and the beguiling and coquettish Comedy, as a tribute to his dramatic versatility.

75. Shakespeare's grave, with its famous inscribed warning, is in the chancel of Holy Trinity Church. It had been decorated earlier, as JB describes, by Garrick's wife, Eva-Maria (see n. 88, below), and one of the singers (Deelman, *Great Shakespeare Jubilee*, 170).

76. The design of these souvenirs was supervised by Garrick. The medals were available in solid gold, silver, or copper (Deelman, *Great Shakespeare Jubilee*, 184), all bearing the line from *Hamlet* (1.2.188). John Westwood (1744–92) was a Birmingham engraver.

WE SHALL NOT LOOK UPON HIS LIKE AGAIN.
And on the Reverse,
J U B I L E E
AT STRATFORD,
IN HONOUR,
AND TO THE
MEMORY OF
SHAKESPEARE,
SEPTEMBER 1769.
D. G.
STEWARD.

We also wore Favours called Shakespeare's Favours.[77] Ladies, Gentlemen, even Servants and Peasants wore them. Every human Being had, or seemed to have, an Idea of the classical Festival. Taste beamed a Ray on the Lively and the Stupid, on those who felt it, and on those who felt it not. The very Shop Bills upon this Occasion were Pieces of Genius. Mr. Jackson, from Tavistock-street, London, gave about the following one,

SHAKESPEARE'S JUBILEE.

A Ribband has been made on Purpose at Coventry, called the *Shakespeare Ribband*: It is in Imitation of the Rainbow, which uniting the Colours of all Parties, is likewise an Emblem of the great Variety of his Genius.

"Each Change of many coloured Life he drew."
JOHNSON.[78]

I dare say Mr. Samuel Johnson never imagined that this fine Verse of his would appear on a Bill to promote the Sale of Ribbands. Since I have mentioned this illustrious Author, I cannot but regret that he did not honour Shakespeare's Jubilee with his Presence, which would have added much Dignity to our Meeting.[79]

77. The "favours" were a variety of sashes and rosettes made of a decorative silk ribbon by John Jackson, haberdasher and warehouseman, of Tavistock Street (see the *Pub. Adv.* for Mar. 17, 1777, where he is listed as a bankrupt), who was also engaged to set up a temporary shop supplying masquerade costumes.

78. From the "Prologue Spoken at the Opening of the Theatre in Drury-Lane, 1747," written for Garrick to declaim at the first performance at the theater under his management, by Samuel Johnson (1709–84), preeminent British man of letters, from 1763 JB's friend and the subject of his best-known book, the *Life of Johnson*. See Johnson, *Poems*, 87–90 (line 3).

79. When JB called at SJ's London home to see him before leaving for (indeed, before deciding to go to) the Jubilee, SJ was with Henry and Hester Thrale and family (see

The Masquerade Ball was one of the best that has been in Britain.[80] There were many very rich, elegant, and curious Dresses, many beautiful Women, and many Characters well supported. All the Papers have already been pretty full on this Subject, so I need say little; only I must observe, that a Masquerade is an Entertainment which does not seem much suited to the Genius of the British Nation. In warmer Countries, where the People have a great Flow of Spirits, and a Readiness at Repartee, a Masquerade is exceedingly agreeable: But the Reserve and Taciturnity which is observable amongst us, makes us appear aukward, and embarrassed in feigned Characters. Many of our Stratford Masks seemed angry when one accosted them.—The Race at the Jubilee was neither better nor worse than other Races; nor indeed could it be expected to be any how extraordinary, except, as an ingenious Lady observed, we could have procured a Race of Pegasuses in Honour of our Poet.[81] It was much to be regretted that bad Weather prevented us from having the Pageant, upon which Mr. Garrick had bestowed so much Time in contriving, and so much Expence in furnishing.[82] It was to have been a Procession of allegorical Beings, with the most distinguished Characters

---

Chap. 4, n. 15) at Brighton. SJ had no aversion to sentimental commemorations, but the Jubilee was perhaps too theatrical, musical, and fashionable for his scholarly tastes. Also, having published his edition of Shakespeare four years before, he could claim that he had done his part for the Bard's reputation, but it is also likely that he felt no impulse to appear in a setting in which he would inevitably play second fiddle to his former pupil. His conspicuous lack of interest may have driven a wedge between the fans and scholars of Shakespeare and kept away other members of his circle, such as Goldsmith, Reynolds, or Burke (see Deelman, *Great Shakespeare Jubilee*, 123, 139, 180, 226). JB reiterates his remarks here in the *Life* (Aug. 1769; 2:68–69), adding, "Upon this occasion I particularly lamented that he had not that warmth of friendship for his brilliant pupil, which we may suppose would have had a benignant effect on both."

80. The masquerade was held on the evening of the Thursday. In his 1774 *London Magazine* "Essay on Masquerade" (see Chap. 5), JB expands on the following general remarks about this form of entertainment.

81. The horse race on the Friday was held in atrocious conditions; it had rained all the previous night, the Avon burst its banks, and the horses were knee-deep in water (Stochholm, *Garrick's Folly*, 102–3). The "ingenious Lady" who made the remark about a "race of pegasuses" was Lady Sarah Archer, née West (1741–1801), wife of whig politician Andrew Archer (1736–78; Deelman, *Great Shakespeare Jubilee*, 256).

82. The Pageant, to have been performed outdoors in procession by 217 performers, was postponed from Thursday to Friday on account of the rain, then—as the rain continued— canceled. However, it was adapted and staged at Drury Lane (as JB hopes it might, below) from Oct. 14, as part of a presentation called simply *The Jubilee*; in this form, it ran ninety times in the first season, enjoying the longest opening run of the century (see *Corres. 4*, 69–70 n. 2; Deelman, *Great Shakespeare Jubilee*, 89). The text was not published until 1926, in *Three Plays by David Garrick*, ed. Stein.

of Shakespeare's Plays, with their proper Dresses, triumphal Cars, and all other Kinds of Machinery: But the heavy Rains made it impossible to have this exhibited without destroying the valuable Dresses, and endangering the still more valuable Health of the fair Performers, who might have been rendered incapable of appearing in public for a whole Season, perhaps for Life. Nature seemed to frown on a Jubilee in Honour of the *Thief* who had "robbed her of all she was worth."[83] But as no Cost has been spared on this Pageant, I hope Mr. Garrick will entertain us with it in the comfortable Region of Drury-lane.

Much Noise has been made about the high Prices of every Thing at Stratford. I own I cannot agree that such Censures are just: It was reasonable that Shakespeare's Townsmen should partake of the Jubilee as well as we Strangers did; they as a Jubilee of Profit, we of Pleasure. As it lasted but for a few Nights, a Guinea a Night for a Bed was not Imposition. Nobody was understood to come there who had not Plenty of Money. Towards the End of the Jubilee many of us were not in very good Humour, as many Inconveniences occurred, particularly there not being Carriages enough to take us away but in Detachments, so that those who had to wait long tired exceedingly. I laughed away Spleen by a droll Simile: Taking the Whole of this Jubilee, said I, is like eating Artichoke entire. We have some fine Mouthfuls, but we must also swallow the Leaves and the Hair, which are confoundedly difficult of Digestion. After all, however, I am highly satisfied with my Artichoke.

To conclude as I began,—I will always be of Opinion that Shakespeare's Jubilee at Stratford upon Avon is an Institution which does Honour not only to our immortal Bard, but to all who have contributed towards it; and I hope that every seven Years it shall be celebrated with equal Ardour of Enthusiasm as it has been in 1769.[84]

> I always am, SIR,
> Your very humble Servant,
> J. B.[85]

83. Garrick's song "Warwickshire" (verse 7), "Of all she was worth, he robb'd Nature; / He took all her smiles, and he took all her grief, / And the thief of all thieves, was a *Warwickshire* thief" (*Shakespeare's Garland*, 4).

84. In 1771, the Stratford authorities invited Garrick to assist them in conducting an annual Jubilee (*Life*, 2:68–69 n. 2). Although the anniversary of the Jubilee was for some time kept as a local celebration, there was not another festival at Stratford until the bicentenary of Shakespeare's death, in 1816. A succession of attempts was made, but nothing regular was achieved until after the Shakespeare Birthplace was bought and restored in 1847, and a permanent Shakespeare theater was built in 1879 (Deelman, *Great Shakespeare Jubilee*, 290–93).

85. In the *London Magazine* reprint, in which JB's name is given in full, this report on the Jubilee is immediately followed by the engraved portrait by J. Miller of JB "In the Dress

Figure 3. "James Boswell, Esqr, in the Dress of an Armed Corsican Chief," at Shakespeare Jubilee, engraving by J. Miller from a portrait by Samuel Wale, R.A., London Magazine, *38 (September 1769). Courtesy of HathiTrust.*

An Account of the Armed Corsican Chief at the Masquerade

London Magazine, 38 (September 1769), 455

An Account of the Armed Corsican Chief at the Masquerade, at Shakespeare's
Jubilee, at Stratford-upon-Avon, September 1769

ONE of the most remarkable masks upon this occasion was James Boswell,
Esq; in the dress of an armed Corsican chief.[86] He entered the amphitheatre
about twelve o'clock. He wore a short dark-coloured coat of coarse cloth, scarlet
waistcoat and breeches, and black spatterdashes; his cap or bonnet was of black
cloth; on the front of it was embroidered in gold letters, VIVA LA LIBERTÀ; and
on one side of it was a handsome blue feather and cockade, so that it had an
elegant, as well as a war-like appearance. On the breast of his coat was sewed a
Moor's head, the crest of Corsica, surrounded with branches of laurel. He had
also a cartridge pouch, into which was stuck a stiletto, and on his left side a pistol was hung upon the belt of his cartridge pouch. He had a fusee slung across
his shoulder,[87] wore no powder in his hair, but had it plaited at its full length,
with a knot of blue ribbands at the end of it. He had, by way of staff, a very
curious vine all of one piece, with a bird finely carved upon it, emblematical of
the sweet bard of Avon. He wore no mask; saying, that it was not proper for a
gallant Corsican. So soon as he came into the room he drew universal attention.
The novelty of the Corsican dress, its becoming appearance, and the character
of that brave nation, concurred to distinguish the armed Corsican chief. He was
first accosted by Mrs. Garrick, with whom he had a good deal of conversation.[88]
There was an admirable dialogue between Lord Grosvenor, in the character of

---

of an Armed Corsican Chief" (see Figure 3), which was based on a sketch (now lost) by
Samuel Wale, R.A., for which JB posed in London on Sept. 12 (*Search*, 307 and n. 2). The
portrait was followed in the *London Magazine* by the following item, "An Account of the
Armed Corsican Chief." For the use of the signature "J.B.," see Chap. 5, intro.

86. JB's first taste of fame was a result of his visit to Corsica in 1765 and his best-selling
Account of Corsica (1768). Having left his Corsican costume in Edinburgh, JB had to hur-
riedly get a substitute together. He had a new cap made on Saturday, Sept. 2 (*Search*, 288);
then on Monday, he records, "I walked about searching all over town for my necessary accoutrements. . . . Some I had made on purpose. Others I borrowed. But at last I got everything in order, and everything that I wanted went into such small bounds that I could carry
the whole in my travelling bag, except my musket and staff" (ibid., 291).

87. *Fusee*: a light musket or firelock (*OED*), hence fusilier.

88. Eva-Maria (Veigel) Garrick (1724–1822), Garrick's wife, was an accomplished ac-
tress, dancer, and singer. JB had met her at the Garricks' London home, Jan. 21, 1763 (*Lond.
Journ.*, 162).

a Turk, and the Corsican, on the different constitutions of their countries, so opposite to each other—despotism and liberty—and Captain Thomson,[89] of the navy, in the character of an honest tar, kept it up very well; he expressed a strong inclination to stand by the brave islanders. Mr. Boswell danced both a minuet and country dance with a very pretty Irish lady, Mrs. Sheldon, wife to Captain Sheldon of the 38th regiment of foot (Lord Blaney's); she was dressed in a genteel domino; and before she danced, threw off her mask.[90]

Mr. Boswell having come to the jubilee to contribute his share towards what he called a classical institution in honour of Shakespeare, being also desirous of paying a compliment to Mr. Garrick, with whom he has always been on a most agreeable footing, and never unmindful of the cause which he has espoused, he wrote the following verses, which it is thought are well suited to the occasion, while they at the same time preserve the true Corsican character.[91]

Verses in the Character of a Corsican at Shakespeare's Jubilee

Broadside (folio half-sheet), printed Stratford, September 7, 1769

VERSES
In the CHARACTER of
A CORSICAN

89. Captain Edward Thompson (?1738–86), naval officer, minor poet, and friend of Garrick, who dressed as a sailor. During the Jubilee, he wrote a poem, *Trinculo's Trip to the Jubilee* (1770), in which he comments on some of the characters at the masquerade:

> Vain Boswell here stood like a Corsican drest
> Distributing lines which he writ
> 'Twould have puzzled e'en Shakespeare, to say which were best,
> His poesy, hist'ry, or wit. (29)

90. Captain Thomas Sheldon (d. 1804) and his wife Margaret, née Blennerhassett (1740–1827); on the first night at dinner, JB met and was quite taken with Mrs. Sheldon (*Search*, 299); the following morning she made tea for him at breakfast, before dancing with him in the evening. He notes that he put aside his decorative weaponry before the country dance. The colonel of the 38th Regiment was Cadwallader Blayney (1720–75), ninth Lord Blayney. A *domino* is a kind of loose cloak, chiefly worn at masquerades, with a small mask covering the upper part of the face; occasionally, the half-mask itself (*OED*).

91. JB wrote the verses that follow in Stratford on the day of the masquerade, read them to Garrick, and had them printed as a broadside—however, not in sufficient time for him to distribute them as he intended. The proofs were brought to him at the masquerade at "about two in the morning" (*Search*, 300). The title below is from the broadside.

AT
SHAKESPEARE's JUBILEE
At STRATFORD upon AVON, Sept. 7, 1769.
By *JAMES BOSWELL*, Esq.

From the rude banks of Golo's rapid flood,
Alas! too deeply ting'd with patriot blood;[92]
O'er which, dejected, injured Freedom bends,
And sighs indignant o'er all Europe sends:
Behold a *CORSICAN!*—In better days,
Eager I sought my country's fame to raise;
When o'er our camp PAOLI's banners wav'd,
And all the threats of hostile France we brav'd,
'Till unassisted, a small nation fail'd,
And our invaders' tenfold force prevail'd.[93]

    Now when I'm exil'd from my native land,
I come to join this classic festal band,
To sooth my soul on *Avon*'s sacred stream,
And from your joy, to catch a cheering gleam.
To celebrate great *Shakespeare*'s wond'rous fame,
And add new trophies to the honour'd name
Of Nature's bard, whom tho' your country bore,
His influence spreads to ev'ry distant shore:
Wherever genuine feeling souls are found,
His "Wood-notes wild," with extasy resound.[94]

    Had *Shakespeare* liv'd our story to relate,
And hold his torch o'er our unhappy fate;
Liv'd with majestic energy to tell
How long we fought, what heroes nobly fell!
Had *Garrick*, who Dame Nature's pencil stole,

92. The Golo is the longest river in Corsica. On May 8–9, 1769, the Battle of Ponte Nuovo took place near the river, between French forces and the Corsican army.

93. The Corsican forces were led by Gen. Pasquale Paoli (1725–1807), who wrote the constitution for the Corsican Republic and was elected its president in 1755. His forces took all of Corsica except the fortified towns from the Republic of Genoa. Genoa called on France for aid, and the Corsican forces, fighting a guerrilla war, were heavily outnumbered. They were defeated at the Battle of Ponte Nuovu, the Corsican government collapsed, French forces took over the island, and Paoli left for his long exile in London.

94. *Wood-note*: "A natural untrained musical note or song like that of a wild bird in a wood" (*OED*); from Milton's *L'Allegro* (1645), "If . . . sweetest Shakespeare, Fancy's child,/ Warble his native wood-notes wild" (lines 132–34).

Just where Old *Shakespeare* dropt it, when his soul
Broke from its earthy cage aloft to fly,
To the eternal world of harmony——
Had *Garrick* shewn us on the tragick scene,
With Fame embalm'd our deeds of death had been;
If from his eyes had flash'd the Corsic fire,
Men less had gaz'd to pity—than admire.

      O happy *Britons!* on whose favour'd isle,
Propitious *Freedom* ever deigns to smile,
Whose fame is wafted on triumphant gales,
Where thunders war, or commerce spreads her sails.
I come not hither sadly to complain,
Or damp your mirth with melancholy strain;
In man's firm breast conceal'd the grief should lye,
Which melts with grace in woman's gentle eye;*[95]
But let me plead for *Liberty* distrest,
And warm for her each sympathetick breast:
Amidst the splendid honours which you bear,
To save a sister island! be your care:
With generous ardour make *us* also *free*;
And give to *CORSICA, a noble* JUBILEE![96]

Verses on Seeing the Print of James Boswell, Esq; in the Corsican Dress

London Chronicle, October 5–7, 1769, 344

Verses on seeing the Print of JAMES BOSWELL, *Esq; in the Corsican Dress*

    BOSWELL, thy figure, thus display'd
        In garb of Corsica array'd,
        So warlike and so bold,
    Seems like an herald from afar,

95. "* *Feminis lugere honestum est. Viris meminisse.* TACITUS." (BOSWELL)
JB's couplet translates Tacitus, *Germania*, 27: "Lamentation becomes women: men must remember" (170–71). This note was added in the *London Magazine*.

96. In the *Lond. Chron.*, this item is directly followed by a note: "To give our readers a clearer idea of the songs alluded to by Mr. Boswell in the foregoing letter, we have here introduced them for the entertainment of the public," after which are printed the texts of four of the songs from *Shakespeare's Garland*: "The Morning Address. To the Ladies" (1), "Warwickshire. A Song. By Mr. G" (2–4), "Sweet Willy O. A Song. By Mr. G" (5–6), and "To the Immortal Memory of Shakespeare" (15).

Come to proclaim a general war,[97]
Of which so oft we're told.

Would Draper thus to Junius come,
Tho' erst his placid Cambridge chum,[98]
He'd strike him with affright:
His pen so keen, so fraught with gall,
Would from his chilly fingers fall,
No more would Junius write.

But tell us, Boswell, why that crest,
That Moorish head upon thy breast,
So much expos'd to view?
Is it, that those, thy face who see,
May have a hot dispute, Which be
The blackest of the two?[99]

1771

An Authentick Account of General Paoli's Tour to Scotland, Autumn 1771

[With the title of general, Pasquale Paoli led the government and army of independent Corsica from April 1755. Boswell, on his European tour in 1765, visited the island nation and got to know Paoli, whose cause he subsequently publicized in

97. A "general war" is an armed conflict between major powers in which the total resources of the belligerents are employed and the national survival of a major belligerent is in jeopardy.

98. The *Letters of Junius* were a notorious and anonymous series of political articles published over three years in the *Pub. Adv.*, beginning Jan. 21, 1769, and later collected and much reprinted. Written by an extremely well-informed figure with a strong background in classics and the law, the best of the letters were masterpieces of polemic and from a whig angle attacked both the policies and personalities in the two successive "tory" administrations, two prime ministers, the Duke of Grafton and Lord North, eventually taking aim at the king. An early target of Junius's abuse was Sir William Draper (1721–87), who, after a distinguished military career, had the effrontery to reply in print and under his own name to the first letter of Junius and four times subsequently. Draper's final letter to Junius appeared in this same issue of the *Lond. Chron.* Draper graduated in 1744 with a B.A. from King's College, Cambridge, where, JB seems to think, he was a *chum* (i.e., "a chamber-fellow, a term used in the universities," *SJ Dict.*) of Junius; it is not known who JB is here suggesting Junius might have been.

99. JB makes an issue of his swarthy complexion.

England through his *Account of Corsica, British Essays in Favour of the Brave Corsicans*, and other publications. After the French invasion of Corsica and the defeat of his resistance forces, Paoli left the island under British protection. He arrived in England on September 18, 1769, and in London two days later. The following day he met the prime minister, Grafton, and the next, September 22, Boswell visited him at his new London residence in Old Bond Street. Boswell showed Paoli around the city in the following weeks and introduced him to most of his circle, including Johnson and Garrick. Paoli was received by the king and granted a generous Civil List pension, which enabled him to live in London like a gentleman.

Paoli visited Scotland in September 1771, and Boswell hosted him and the Polish ambassador, Count Burzynski, in Edinburgh, September 3–11. See *Defence*, 22–24, and *Later Years*, 22–24, where Brady says that this account describes the tour "as developing into a quasi-royal progress" (22). Boswell kept no journal at this time.]

London Magazine, 40 (September 1771), 433–34

An authentick Account of General Paoli's *Tour to* Scotland, *Autumn* 1771

THE illustrious Corsican chief was all along resolved since he arrived in Great-Britain to make a tour to Scotland, and visit James Boswell, Esq; who was the first gentleman of this country that visited Corsica, and whose writings made the brave islanders and their general be properly known, and esteemed over Europe.[100] Engagements of a serious and important nature prevented the general from putting his scheme in execution, till Monday, August 26, 1771, when he set out from London accompanied by his excellency Count Burzynski the Polish ambassador.[101] They passed some time with Lord Lyttelton at Hagley-park, and viewed with pleasure that fine place, where, as Thomson says, the muses have *reared a lodge* for their votary.[102] They arrived incognito at Edinburgh, on Tuesday, September 3, at Peter Ramsay's inn, and went that afternoon and viewed the

100. JB was in Corsica from Oct. 11 to Nov. 30, 1765. His *Account of Corsica* (1768) had by 1769 been translated into German, Dutch, French, and Italian; he also edited a volume of *British Essays in Favour of the Brave Corsicans* (1769). Paoli remained in exile in England until 1790, when he returned to Corsica, first as president of the Corsican department of revolutionary France and then as president of the British protectorate of Corsica. The French reconquered the island, and in Oct. 1795 Paoli again left Corsica for Britain, remaining there until his death.

101. Tadeusz Burzynski (c. 1730–73), former governor of Smolensk, was the Polish envoy extraordinary to the Netherlands and Great Britain, 1769–73 (*Corres. 4*, 38 n. 15).

102. George Lyttelton, first Baron Lyttelton (1709–73), writer and politician. From the 1730s, he devoted himself to developing a splendid landscape garden at his ancestral estate, Hagley Park, in Worcestershire. Literary friends, such as poets William Shenstone (1714–63) and Alexander Pope (1688–1744), came on visits: poet James Thomson (1700–1748)

castle, the abbey of Holyrood-house, and the other buildings of that city.[103] On Wednesday, September 4, they went in the forenoon and saw Duddingston the seat of Lord Abercorn, where his lordship has displayed his magnificence and taste both in building and laying out ground.[104] From Duddingston they had a fine prospect of the country around, the Firth of Forth, the grand mountain of Arthur-seat, the ancient castle of Craigmillar, where the beautiful Mary Queen of Scots passed some of her days;[105] Prestonfield, the seat of Sir Alexander Dick, bart. and Duddingston Lock belonging to that gentleman.[106] They dined at Edinburgh with Mr. Boswell, and supped with Dr. Gregory, to whom they brought a letter from the ingenious Mrs. Montague.[107] On Thursday, September 5, the general and ambassador accompanied by Mr. Boswell set out early in the morning for the west. They stopped to breakfast at Linlithgow, and viewed there the ruins of the ancient palace of the kings of Scotland.[108] They then proceeded on the Falkirk road, and viewed the great canal of communication between the

---

often stayed there and revised *The Seasons* during a visit in 1743. In Thomson's *The Castle of Indolence* (1748), canto 1, stanza 66, Lyttelton is addressed: "We then a lodge for thee will rear in Hagley-Park."

103. Peter Ramsay's inn was the "White Horse" in St. Mary's Wynd, Edinburgh; its chief business was its extensive stables (see Grant, 2:119), which JB used (*Defence*, 308). Edinburgh Castle is the ancient fortification, set on a volcanic rock, overlooking the city. The roof of the Holyrood Abbey Church collapsed in 1768 and has never been restored.

104. James Hamilton, eighth earl of Abercorn (1712–89), was in 1761–84 a representative peer for Scotland, in the tory interest. He purchased the Duddingston estate near Edinburgh in 1745 and had a splendid house built there in the 1760s, by eminent architect Sir William Chambers.

105. Craigmillar Castle, only three miles from the center of Edinburgh, was begun in the late 1500s and was abandoned early in the eighteenth century. Mary, Queen of Scots, stayed there for some weeks, Nov.–Dec. 1566, after the birth of her son, who became James VI.

106. Prestonfield House, by Duddingston Loch, was the seat of JB's good friend and correspondent, celebrated physician Sir Alexander Dick (1703–85). His property shared a boundary on Duddingston Loch with Lord Abercorn's estate, but the ownership of the loch was a subject of long-standing dispute between Sir Alexander and Lord Abercorn, upon which legal judgment had been pronounced in Sir Alexander's favor only two years earlier (*Laird*, 205 n. 8).

107. Dr. John Gregory (1724–73), physician and medical writer, appointed in 1766 professor at Edinburgh University. Count Burzynski stayed with him at his house in St. John St., Canongate, while Paoli stayed with JB in James's Court (Grant, 2:119; see *Ominous Years*, 29 n. 5). JB met writer and literary hostess Elizabeth Montagu (1718–1800), "the queen of the blue-stockings," in London, Apr. 14, 1772, at Paoli's instigation, although he "had seen her in Scotland at Dr. Gregory's" (*Laird*, 121).

108. Linlithgow is a town twenty miles east of Edinburgh. The palace, on the site of an earlier manor house and fortification, was commenced by James I, from 1425, and altered

eastern and western seas, which is without question one of the greatest works in modern times.[109] They then viewed the iron works at Carron, which are carried on at so prodigious an expence, and have diffused so much opulence, and such a spirit of improvement in that part of the country.[110] General Paoli had a peculiar pleasure in viewing the forge where were formed the cannon and warlike stores, which a society of gentlemen in Scotland sent to the aid of the brave Corsicans.[111] They were elegantly entertained at dinner by Charles Gascoigne, Esq; of the Carron company, and while they sat at table all the vessels at Carron-shore, which were just in their view, had their flags displayed, a circumstance which led the general to speak with his usual esteem of the British *hearts of oak*.[112] They went that evening to Glasgow. On Friday, Sept. 6, they walked about and viewed the beautiful and flourishing city of Glasgow without being known. But by the time they got to the university, the report went that General Paoli was in town, and then every body was in motion, crowding to see him. Their excellencies viewed the elegant printing and academy of painting, sculpture, &c. of the Scottish Stephani, the Mess. Foulis, who were transported with enthusiasm to see such visiters.[113] The university was not sitting; but there luckily happened to be there the professors Moor, Muirhead, Anderson, Trail, Wilson, Read, and Stevenson,

---

and extended for the next two hundred years. Mary, Queen of Scots, was born there in 1542. Prince Charles Edward Stuart stayed there in 1745, and the palace was burned out by the troops pursuing him and left floorless and roofless, as it remains.

109. For the Forth and Clyde Canal, see n. 27, above. The bill to approve the construction of the "grand" canal project was passed in Mar. 1768, and work commenced the following June. The thirty-five-mile canal was opened to traffic in 1790.

110. The Carron Ironworks was established near Falkirk in 1759; using local ore and the best new engineering knowledge, it soon became the most productive foundry in Britain. The canal was built mainly to serve the transportation needs of this business. The managing director, Charles Gascoigne (?1738–1806), was in 1786 recruited by the Russian government to take charge of foundries at St. Petersburg, where he remained for the rest of his life.

111. JB was the prime mover behind this scheme; as he wrote to his friend W. J. Temple (letter of Aug. 24, 1768), "by a private subscription in Scotland, I am this week sending £700 worth of ordinance. The Carron Company has furnished me them very cheap" (*Corres. 6*, 242).

112. "Hearts of Oak" is a metonym for the British navy and its oaken vessels, popularized in the patriotic song "Heart of Oak," written by Garrick for his ballad opera, *Harlequin's Invasion* (1759): "Hearts of oak are our ships,/ Hearts of oak are our men." Set to a tune by William Boyce, it is now the official march of the Royal Navy. JB reports a singing party among the Corsicans at Sollacaro, at which he sang "Heart of Oak" and improvised a translation of it into Italian (*Account of Corsica*, 188). See Brownell and Brownell, "Boswell's Ballads," 124–25.

113. The Foulis brothers, Andrew (1712–75) and Robert (1707–76), were booksellers and (from 1744) printers in Glasgow, publishing classical and academic authors in accurate and

who shewed the university to great advantage,[114] and entertained their excellencies, and a number of other gentlemen of distinction, with wine and sweat
[*sic*] meats in the library. The magistrates of Glasgow behaved with that dignity
and propriety, which might be expected from gentlemen of extensive commerce,
and consequently enlarged minds;[115] gentlemen of great fortunes, and consequently independent spirits: They considered it as an honour to their city to
shew every mark of respect to so distinguished and truly estimable a personage
as general Paoli, and to the representative of a crowned head. They therefore met
their excellencies at the cross,[116] as they understood they were just setting out for
Auchinlech,[117] and most politely asked the honour of their company to dinner
on Tuesday. The streets and windows of Glasgow were quite full of spectators,
and every body was happy at having an opportunity of seeing General Paoli. It
may be remarked to the honour of human nature, that although the Polish ambassador was certainly, according to political ideas, the greatest man of the two
at the time, yet people seemed to forget him; so much was their attention fixed

---

elegant editions. JB depicts them as British successors of the famous sixteenth-century
French father and son printers Henry and Robert Estienne, both known as Stephanus. In
1753–54, the Foulis brothers expanded their operations and established an Academy of Fine
Arts, built around a collection of paintings and sculpture imported from the Continent; it
failed to make money, and the brothers died leaving substantial debts.

114. The university in Scotland's second city was founded in 1451. JB had attended there
briefly, in 1759–60. These professors were an eminent group (they are all noticed in *ODNB*).
Dr. James Moor (1712–79) was professor of Greek and author of *On the End of Tragedy, according to Aristotle* (1763), which JB recommended (*Life*, 3:39 n. 2). George Muirhead (bap.
1715–73), professor of Latin, edited a number of volumes of classics published by the Foulis
press. John Anderson (1726–96) was professor of natural philosophy; in 1777 he called on
JB, and they agreed that SJ should write to rebut the fashionable skeptical philosophers
(*Life*, 3:119). Dr. Robert Traill (1720–75) was professor of divinity and a Church of Scotland
minister. Alexander Wilson (1714–86) was professor of practical astronomy. Thomas Reid
(1710–96) was professor of moral philosophy, whose *Inquiry into the Human Mind, on the
Principles of Common Sense* (1764) was a foundational text of the Scottish "Common Sense"
school of philosophy and was greatly admired by JB for what he saw as its successful rebut-
tal of David Hume (see *Grand Tour 1*, 27). Dr. Alexander Stevenson (d. 1791) was professor
of medicine. Professors Anderson, Reid, and Stevenson were also present at the university
when JB visited with SJ in 1773 and joined them for breakfast (*Tour*, Oct. 29; *Life*, 5:369).

115. Boswell's characterization of the "magistrates of Glasgow" as "gentlemen of extensive commerce, . . . enlarged minds . . . and . . . independent spirits" is intended as a pointed
contrast of the wealthy business leaders of Glasgow with the oligarchs of Edinburgh; see
Smout, *History of the Scottish People*, 381–90.

116. Glasgow Cross is a major junction of five streets that marks the medieval center
of the city.

117. Auchinleck (the usual spelling) is the house and estate in Ayrshire of the Boswell
family.

on one whom they knew to be a real great man, though he was now under misfortunes. The Polish ambassador, who is a young man of great rank, and at the same time of abilities and spirit, and a sincere admirer of the Corsican chief, was pleased himself to see such an honest tribute of applause payed to exalted merit. Mr. Boswell conducted their excellencies that evening to Auchinlech, the seat of his father, who was extremely happy to receive such guests.[118] They staid there Friday night and all Saturday, walked a great deal, and saw the place as much as they could do for the time. On Sunday, Sept. 7, they set out early in the morning, and breakfasted with James Campbell, Esq; of Treesbank.[119] They dined at Stewarton, where they were met by Mr. M'Dowal, sheriff-depute of Renfrewshire, and Mr. Logan, sheriff-substitute of Ayrshire,[120] and several other gentlemen of that county; who, with a detachment of the tenants of Auchinlech, convoyed their excellencies to the march of the shire.[121] That night they returned to Glasgow. On Monday, Sept. 9, they set out to view Loch Lomond.[122] They went up as far as Firkin Point, ascended a good way the mountains above it, and had an extensive prospect of the lake both to the east and west, with Ben Lomond and other hills. At night they came to Rosdoe, the seat of Sir James Colquhoun of Luss, bart. where they were most hospitably entertained.[123] Sir James's barge was ready on general Paoli's arrival, and carried him round one of the beautiful islands in Loch Lomond belonging to Sir James. In the course of this little sail,

118. JB's father, Alexander Boswell, Lord Auchinleck (1707–82), judge and landowner. Although he is said to have later described Paoli as a "land-louping scoundrel of a Corsican" (*Life*, 5:382 n. 2), there is no contemporary source for this remark. In a letter of Sept. 18, 1771, to David Garrick, JB wrote of "the joy of my worthy father and me at seeing the Corsican Hero in our romantick Groves" (*Corres. 4*, 38).

119. James Campbell (c. 1709–1776), of Treesbank, JB's brother-in-law and friend, whom JB usually addressed ceremoniously by his estate name only. JB and SJ stayed with him, Oct. 30–31, 1773 (*Tour; Life*, 5:372–73).

120. Stewarton is a largish town in East Ayrshire, about halfway between Ayr and Glasgow. In 1767, JB defended four men involved in a riot there against high food prices (*Corres. 5*, 160–61, 164–65). Charles MacDowal or MacDouall (d. 1791), of Crichen, was an advocate and sheriff-depute of Renfrewshire (*Extremes*, 132 and n. 6). Hugh Logan (1739–1802), of Logan, Ayrshire, was spoken of as "the 'Laird of Logan' and celebrated for his racy wit and extravagant hospitality" (*Corres. 7*, 197 n. 1).

121. The *march* is the shire boundary or border.

122. Loch Lomond, twenty miles northwest of Glasgow, is the largest freshwater lake in Britain. Firkin Point is at the north end of the loch's western shore; Ben Lomond, on the eastern side, is a mountain of 3,195 feet and is the most southerly of the Scottish peaks higher than 3,000 feet referred to as Munros.

123. Rossdhu is the mansion at Luss, further south on the eastern shore of the loch, built c. 1770 by Sir James Colquhoun (1714–86). JB and SJ stayed there with him, Oct. 26–27, 1773 (*Tour; Life*, 5:363–64). Sir James was depicted by Smollett in *Humphry Clinker* (1771), vol. 3.

his excellency saw the lake to great advantage, and was much delighted with it. On Tuesday, Sept. 10, they breakfasted at Dumbarton.[124] They had stopped there the day before, and the magistrates had presented them with the freedom of that town. This day the General viewed the castle of Dumbarton, with the situation of which he was much pleased, and from thence he had a prospect of the mouth of Clyde, and the sea-port towns of Greenock and Port Glasgow. Their excellencies dined at Glasgow at the Saracen's Head with the right honourable Colin Dunlop, Esq; lord provost, and the other magistrates; Lord Frederick Campbell, member for the city, and a number of other gentlemen of distinction, in all fifty-two at table; and after dinner their excellencies were presented with the freedom of the city, which they accepted in the politest manner.[125] That evening they went to Whitburn.[126] On Wednesday, Sept. 11, they got back to Edinburgh about noon, and honoured Mr. Boswell with their company all that day. The ambassador lodged at Dr. Gregory's: the General slept under the roof of his ever grateful friend. On Thursday, September 12, they set out on their return to England. During General Paoli and the ambassador's short stay at Edinburgh, they enjoyed the company of most people of distinction, learning, and genius, who were in town;[127] and, without any flourish or parade of words it may be truly said, That this visit to Scotland will be remembered in the most pleasing and honourable manner.[128]

124. Dumbarton is a town on the banks of the Leven, near where it flows into the Firth of Clyde, north-northwest of Glasgow. Dumbarton Castle is built on a steep plug of rock overlooking the town. The port towns of Greenock and Port Glasgow are across the water, south of the Clyde. JB and SJ visited Dumbarton, Oct. 28, 1773 (*Tour, Life*, 5:368).

125. The Saracen's Head in Gallowgate, Glasgow, was opened in 1755 as an inn with lodging for thirty-six people and stabling for sixty horses, and for some time it was the city's most fashionable resort. JB and SJ stayed there Oct. 28–29, 1773 (*Tour, Life*, 5:369). Colin Dunlop (1706–77) was provost (or chief magistrate), 1770–72. Lord Frederick Campbell (1729–1816) was an MP for Glasgow, 1761–80, and later for Argyll.

126. Whitburn is a town in West Lothian, about halfway between Edinburgh and Glasgow.

127. "Paoli's presence in Edinburgh was a magnet for the notable: Blair, Hume, Robertson, and the rising politician Henry Dundas, all came to dinner or supper" (*Later Years*, 23). These four are Hugh Blair (1718–1800), clergyman and rhetorician; David Hume, skeptical philosopher (see Chap. 4, n. 118); William Robertson, clergyman, historian, and principal of the university (see n. 212, below); Dundas, see n. 198, below.

128. As a postscript to this subject, we should note that JB wrote two letters, published anonymously in the *Lond. Chron.*, Oct. 24 and Nov. 28, 1771, attacking the Edinburgh authorities for not conferring the freedom of the City of Edinburgh on Paoli. The provost of Edinburgh at the time was John Dalrymple, brother of JB's mentor and friend David Dalrymple, Lord Hailes, whose relationship with JB was disrupted by these letters (see *Defence*, 23–24).

1772

Some Anecdotes of the Late Voyage of Mr. Banks
and Dr. Solander in the Northern Seas

[Joseph Banks established himself as a conscientious naturalist on an Admiralty expedition to Newfoundland and Labrador in 1766. A landed gentleman, he used his influence with the First Lord of the Admiralty, Lord Sandwich, to obtain places for a small self-funded scientific party on Captain James Cook's first voyage, 1768–71, in the *Endeavour*, to observe the transit of Venus from Tahiti and then (under sealed orders from the Admiralty) to explore the unknown southern lands of New Zealand and New Holland (the east coast of Australia). Banks and his assistant, Daniel Solander, were thus able to botanize in regions new to enlightenment science. The two explorers and naturalists returned to great fame in London. When Banks's party was excluded from Cook's second voyage, Banks immediately began arranging a voyage to the Hebrides, Iceland, and the Orkneys. They departed Gravesend aboard the *Sir Lawrence* on July 12, 1772. They spent seventeen days in the Hebrides, six weeks in the North Atlantic island nation of Iceland, and a week in the Orkneys. Banks and Solander left the ship when they arrived in Edinburgh on October 29 and returned by land to London.

Boswell met them both before the trip at the home in London of the president of the Royal Society, Scottish military physician Sir John Pringle, on March 22, 1772 (*Defence*, 56). When they passed through Edinburgh on their return from Iceland, Boswell dined with them on November 2 at Fortune's tavern (*Boswelliana*, 270), and also breakfasted with Solander (*Defence*, 146), on which occasions he presumably gathered the information for this article (he was not keeping a fully written journal at this time).]

London Magazine, 41 (November 1772), 508–9

Some Anecdotes of the late Voyage of Mr. BANKS and
Dr. SOLANDER in the Northern Seas

AN illustrious English writer of the present age observes, that "Curiosity is one of the permanent and certain characteristicks of a vigorous intellect. [. . .] This passion is perhaps regularly heightened, in proportion as the powers of the mind are elevated and enlarged. Lucan therefore introduces Cæsar speaking with dignity suitable to the grandeur of his designs, and the extent of his capacity, when he declares to the high priest of Egypt, that he has no desire equally powerful with that of finding the origin of the Nile; and that he would quit all the projects of the civil war for a sight of those fountains, which had been so long concealed. And Homer, when he would furnish the Sirens with a temptation, to which his hero renowned for wisdom might yield without disgrace, makes them declare, that none ever departed from them, but with increase of knowledge."[129]

Mr. Banks and Dr. Solander, to whom the world is already so much obliged for the additions which they have made to our stores of entertainment and utility, who, with the noblest heroism, have ventured into unknown seas, and amongst uncivilised nations,[130] having, to the disgrace of some in the highest departments, and perhaps of more than are perfectly known, been disappointed this year, in getting proper ships for another voyage into the Southern ocean,[131] have employed this interval in visiting Iceland, and some of the Scottish isles, accompanied by Dr. Lind, and Mr. Gore who has been thrice round the world.[132]

Still intent on great objects, though diligent observers even of the minutest circumstances of nature, they have in this late voyage applied themselves in a particular manner to the study of Volcanos; and although they do not seem to have carried their ideas upon this subject so far as Sir William Hamilton,[133] they

129. Johnson, *Rambler*, 4:184–85 (no. 103, Mar. 12, 1751); JB omits a passage, indicated by my ellipsis. This passage is also quoted by JB in the next essay (on James Bruce), where he goes on to quote the passage SJ refers to from Lucan's *Civil War*). In book 12 of Homer's *Odyssey*, the hero Odysseus is tempted by the Sirens.

130. Sir Joseph Banks (1743–1820), naturalist and (from 1778) president of the Royal Society. Daniel Solander (1733–82), Swedish-born botanist who trained under Linnaeus; from 1765, assistant librarian at the British Museum, where he met Banks, and subsequently Banks's secretary and librarian. The first of Captain James Cook's three voyages of exploration was in contemporary London usually spoken of as Banks's voyage, and, on their return to England in June 1771, he and Solander were more honored and fussed over by society, the court, and the newssheets than was Cook, whose achievement was at the time recognized only by the Admiralty, the Navy, and the Royal Society.

131. A second voyage to the South Seas was planned, but Banks seems to have overplayed his influence with the Admiralty, insisting on quarters for a larger party (which was to include a "valet" to Banks, who was actually a woman) and disputing Cook's choice of vessel. The Admiralty supported Cook, and the second voyage departed July 13, 1772, without Banks's party.

132. James Lind (1736–1812), a Scots physician, was an amateur astronomer and scientific observer; he twice traveled to China and later became a physician to the Royal Household at Windsor and was elected to the Royal Society. John Gore (?1729/30–90), who as master's mate in the *Dolphin* had already circumnavigated the globe, 1764–66, was the third lieutenant of the *Endeavour* on Cook's first voyage. He joined Cook's third voyage, as first lieutenant of the *Resolution*, and became commander of the expedition after Cook was killed in Hawaii in Aug. 1779.

133. Sir William Hamilton (1731–1803) held a diplomatic post in Naples, where he devoted himself to collecting art and antiquities and where JB met him in Mar. 1765 (*Grand Tour 2*, 54–55). Volcanoes were another of his enthusiasms, and he made vivid and detailed

have certainly made such discoveries, as very much to strengthen and enlarge the theory of the prodigious effects, which have been produced by fire in various parts of the terrestrial globe.

It is believed they are the first human beings who have been upon the top of mount Hecla in Iceland, that most extraordinary burning mountain, whose bowels are on fire while it is covered with snow, and which the Grecian or Roman mythologists could not have failed to fancy possessed by some being of a tremendous nature.[134] They found ashes of a pretty considerable depth all along as they ascended the mountain, yet when they reached the higher parts of it, there was a continual drizzling, the moisture of which fixed itself in their hair like hoar-frost, and when they were at the summit, the cold was intense in a most striking degree.

At Geisar in Iceland they found a monstrous *crater*, or as it may be called *cistern*, formed by a Volcano, which held a vast quantity of hot boiling water, and threw it into the air to a very great height.[135]

It is remarkable, that Iceland was one of the earliest seats of learning in Europe. They have long had printing among them, and their *Gymnasium* or college still flourishes.[136] Much of the ancient history of the northern parts of Europe, in particular of Sweden and Denmark, is preserved by them, and they have several hundred different books in their language, and some translations. *The Whole duty of Man* is translated into Icelandick.[137]

---

reports to the Royal Society of the eruption in 1767 of Mt. Vesuvius, accompanied by his own drawings, and shipped to London a large collection of volcanic specimens.

134. Mount Hecla or Hekla, an active volcano sixty-eight miles east of Reykjavík, was, from the Middle Ages, known throughout Europe and was described as an entrance to Hell, for its destructive power and dramatic appearance. The claim that they were the first to have ascended the mountain seems overstated: Banks's journal for Sept. 25 says more modestly, "No one was ever higher *of gentlemen*" (Rauschenberg, "Journals of Joseph Banks's Voyage," 223; my emphasis).

135. Geisar—the English *geyser*—is in Icelandic the proper name for the Great Geyser, its name derived from the Icelandic verb for *to gush*. The Great Geyser (which is no longer active) is one of a hundred or so hot springs in the Haukadalur Valley, about thirty miles northwest of Mount Hecla. The party visited the area on Sept. 21 (see Rauschenberg, "Journals of Joseph Banks's Voyage," 220–22).

136. The oldest gymnasium (secondary college) in Iceland, the Lærði Skólinn (Learned School), was established in Skálholt in 1056. Now known as Menntaskólinn í Reykjavík, it moved to Reykjavík in 1786.

137. *The Whole Duty of Man* (1658) was a famous English devotional work, published anonymously and frequently reprinted in the seventeenth and eighteenth centuries. It is now thought to be the work of the royalist and high-church scholar Richard Allestree

The inhabitants are much depressed by the inclemency of their climate and other causes, and have no encouragement to industry.[138] They are an honest, plain, pious race of men, unaccustomed to see strangers, and therefore not expert at entertaining them; but withal abundantly hospitable, and ready to do every thing to oblige them, so soon as the wants or wishes of strangers are made known to them.

Our travellers have in this late tour discovered one of the grandest natural curiosities in one of the western isles of Scotland called Staffa, a curiosity which it is amazing has never before been observed.[139] It is an immense aggregate of pillars of different sizes in a variety of regular forms, and infinitely superior to the celebrated *Giants Causeway* in the north of Ireland.[140] Besides, there is in Staffa, a cave of the same kind of work which goes back above a hundred feet, and is perfectly light even at the farthest end, having a dome of a magnificent elevation supported by tall pillars.

It is hoped that the publick will be favoured with a full account of this voyage.[141]

(1619–81). The Icelandic translation, *Skyllda Mannsens við Gvd, Sjalfann sig og Náungann* (Man's duty to God, himself, and his neighbour), by Jón Þorkelsson Vídalín, was published in 1744.

138. At this stage Iceland was a Danish dependency. The population and the economy were both declining, and the people were living in squalid poverty, because of a succession of natural disasters, the infertility of the land, and oppressive landlords.

139. Staffa is a small island off the west coast of Mull in the Inner Hebrides. In his journal, Banks records being told on Aug. 12 of this hitherto unreported geological wonder; a small party departed by boat and the following day viewed the spectacular cliffs and piles of basalt columns, including the sea cavern known as Fingal's Cave. Banks's journal gives an unusually full description and reflects, "Compard to this what are the cathedrals or the palaces built by man [?] Mere models or playthings imitations as diminutive as his works will always be when compard to those of nature" (Rauschenberg, "Journals of Joseph Banks's Voyage," 207).

140. The Giant's Causeway is a famous area on the coast of County Antrim, with volcanic formations of the same kind as those at Staffa, consisting of hexagonal columns, formed when molten lava is rapidly cooled by contact with water. It was brought to the notice of science in the late seventeenth century. On Oct. 12, 1779, JB tried to interest SJ in visiting the site (SJ said it was "Worth seeing, but not worth going to see"; *Life*, 3:410).

141. Banks never published his finding or the customary account of his voyage (his biographers remark on his reluctance to publish). The only publication arising from the expedition was Uno von Troil, *Letters on Iceland* (1780). Banks's own journal was first published in 1973, in the scholarly edition by Rauschenberg, referred to above.

1774

Some Account of the Very Extraordinary Travels of the Celebrated Mr. Bruce

[The renowned explorer James Bruce—who was a distant relation of Boswell's—returned to England in June 1774, having spent from June 1768 to March 1773 traveling in Egypt, Abyssinia,[142] and the Sudan. He had long since been presumed lost and returned to Europe to great acclaim, having penetrated (in disguise) mysterious and ancient kingdoms, passed through previously unknown or seldom-visited territories, eaten at savage courts flesh cut from living animals, discovered what he thought (or said he thought) was the source of the Nile, been made a provincial governor by the Abyssinian emperor, fought in battles against rebellious warlords, traversed deserts, suffered and recovered from illness and near-starvation, (perhaps) seen the Ark of the Covenant, and fathered a child with an Abyssinian princess. Bruce was a man of great size (six foot four and well built), energy, and curiosity, learned in history, languages, and medicine, and he brought back with him a great collection of drawings and scientific specimens, maps, journals, and manuscripts. For a time his celebrity eclipsed that of Banks and Cook; in a letter of July 10, 1774, Horace Walpole wrote, "Otaheite [i.e., Tahiti] and Mr Banks are quite forgotten" (Walpole, *Correspondence*, 24:21). Bruce's haughty bearing and temper, which served him well on his travels in feudal and highly stratified societies, made him few friends on his return to the metropolis. His credibility was questioned, on account of his more colorful claims; he did not publish his own account of his travels until 1790 (*Travels to Discover the Source of the Nile*, in 5 volumes).

Boswell was introduced to him in Edinburgh, at the Court of Session, on Tuesday, August 9, and, as he tells in his journal, "I was very desirous to be with him" (*Defence*, 272). He visited Bruce at his lodgings later that day, and his journal gives a good sense of the scene of the interview. He found Bruce "impatient, harsh, and uncommunicative" and confesses: "I at first felt myself feeble and awkward with him, owing in part to my consciousness how very ignorant I was of the very rudiments of the knowledge respecting the countries which he had been seeing. My curiosity and vanity united, were, however, sufficient to impel me, and as he grew more rough I grew more forward; so that I forced in a manner a good deal from him" (ibid., 272). After giving some samples of the manner of their discussion, he says, "information [was] dug from him, as from a flinty rock with pickaxes" (ibid., 274). Two days later, Boswell met him again, in the evening at the Assembly (a private society for dancing, held weekly during the winter season in Edinburgh, *Corres. 9*, 211 n. 4): "I tried him again a little, but with very small success" (*Defence*, 279). On Monday, August 15,

---

142. Abyssinia was from medieval times the English and European name for the territories including modern-day Ethiopia and its former empire.

Boswell discussed Bruce with David Hume and John Ord and afterward with his fellow advocate Andrew Crosbie (ibid., 283). He dictated the article the following day.

A few months later, Boswell was told that Bruce was annoyed by the article, particularly (and understandably) the reference to Polyphemus; in his journal he said: "I could see plainly that he did not like me; probably because I had given the public a good dish of his travels, better dressed than he could give himself. . . . Bruce is a rough-minded man, and has not such principles as that one would court him. I had seen him as a curiosity and extracted from him a good essay for the *London Magazine*; and there was enough" (*Ominous Years*, 45–46).]

London Magazine, 43 (August 1774), 388–91

Some Account of the very extraordinary TRAVELS of the celebrated

Mr. B R U C E,

Which at present engages the Attention of the Public

JAMES BRUCE, Esq. of Kinnaird, in the county of Stirling, in Scotland, a gentleman of a good family, and a handsome fortune, was for some time his Britannic majesty's consul at Algiers; but his curiosity and spirit of adventure prompted him to undertake a series of travels, which must be contemplated with astonishment.[143] Mr. Bruce was excellently fitted for travelling, both by his natural and acquired abilities; being above six foot high, of a size every way proportioned; a firm mind, a determined countenance, and a robust constitution; sagacious, observing, and a very good draughtsman.

The compiler of this sketch does by no means pretend to full or accurate information of what Mr. Bruce has brought home to enrich the curious stores of his country, to which such ample acquisitions have been made in the present reign. He waits with impatience for a compleat account from Mr. Bruce's

143. James Bruce (1730–94) was sent to school at Harrow in London; he then commenced law at Edinburgh University. His health was delicate, and he abandoned the idea of a legal career, devoting himself to private study and intending to set up in trade. After the death of consumption of his first wife, he embarked on a grand tour, and—his curiosity whetted by his studies of languages, history, art and architecture, the Bible, and astronomy—he developed a taste for travel. When in 1758 his father died, Bruce succeeded to the lairdship of the Kinnaird estate and contracted to supply coal to the rapidly expanding Carron Ironworks; this produced an income that financed his foreign adventures. Bruce was offered the post of consul general at Algiers, which he took up in Feb. 1763. Algiers was a perfect base for conducting expeditions. Bruce's personality was far from diplomatic, and he was relieved of his duties in Apr. 1765; he then set about preparing for his long-contemplated journey to Abyssinia. See Bredin, *Pale Abyssinian*, 250 ff.

own pen; but knowing what an ardent desire there is to know something, in the mean time, he hath collected a few striking particulars, for the entertainment of the readers of the London Magazine.

Mr. Bruce being master of a number of modern languages, particularly the Arabic,[144] he traversed Egypt with an ease, such as that with which a native of one kingdom in Europe traverses another. But Egypt only served to encrease his curiosity, and made him resolve to penetrate into Ethiopia, visit the kingdom of Abyssinia, and explore the sources of the Nile.

Abyssinia has become an object of interesting and pleasing attention in Europe, since the publication of Mr. Samuel Johnson's tale, called *Rasselas Prince of Abyssinia*, a work in which that eminent writer has displayed a rich fund of moral instruction, embellished with oriental imagery, and rendered interesting by a well conducted story, in the tissue of which several real facts concerning that country are interwoven.[145] It has been translated into many languages, and read with universal admiration.

The Portuguese jesuits, whose spirit cannot be enough admired, did by means of their missionaries make an establishment in Abyssinia, and civilized its people in a considerable degree.[146] One of these jesuits, *Pere Lobost*, has given us an account of Abyssinia in a quarto volume with a map of the country.[147] But what is very remarkable, the discovery of the origin of the Nile was, so far as we know, reserved for Mr. Bruce; at least no European before him has been said to have gone so high. *Lobost* has traced the Nile up to a large lake in Abyssinia, called *Dembea*, but there it was lost; as perhaps none of the Portuguese ventured

144. Bruce was a gifted linguist: he knew various modern European languages (French, Italian, Spanish, Portuguese, and Greek), ancient languages (Latin, Classical Greek, and Hebrew), and languages of the Near East, which he studied in Syria in preparation for his travels (Arabic, Chaldean, Syriac, Ge'ez, Amharic, and Tigrinya, the language of the Abyssinian court). See Bredin, *Pale Abyssinian*, 72.

145. SJ's "oriental tale," *The History of Rasselas: Prince of Abyssinia* (1759), was highly regarded on publication and has never been out of print; by the time of JB's article, it had passed through four London editions and had been translated into Dutch, French, German, Italian, Russian, and Spanish.

146. Portuguese Jesuits first went to Abyssinia in 1508, when, after some centuries of isolation, the Ethiopian emperor requested military help from Portugal.

147. Father Jerome Lobo (1593–1678), a Portuguese Jesuit assigned to India, conducted missionary work in Abyssinia, 1625–34. His account, taken from his more extensive memoirs (1710), was translated into French by the Abbé Joachim Le Grand, as *Voyage Historique d'Abissinie* (1728), which was anonymously abridged and translated into English by the young SJ in 1735. Lobo describes visiting the source of the (Blue) Nile in 1629, following his fellow Jesuit, Pedro Paez, who in fact appears to have been in 1618 the first European to have visited the area.

farther for fear of the crocodiles and alligators, and the savage people roaming about. Mr. Bruce advanced with intrepidity beyond the lake of Dembea, into which he perceived the Nile to flow, and ascending up the country along its margin, he at length reached three springs, which burst from under a mountain, and give birth to this wondrous river, the subject of so much enquiry, and of so much superstitious veneration.[148]

It is indeed not easy to account for the source of the Nile; mysterious to the ancients it certainly was: Mr. Johnson observes in the Rambler, No. 103, that "Curiosity is heightened, in proportion as the powers of the mind are elevated and enlarged."[149] Lucan introduces Cæsar speaking with dignity suitable to the grandeur of his designs, and the extent of his capacity, when he declares to the high priest of Egypt, that he has no desire equally powerful with that of finding the origin of the Nile, and that he would quit all the projects of the civil war for a sight of those fountains, which had been so long concealed. The passage in Lucan, alluded to by Mr. Johnson, is as follows:

> Sed cum tanta meo vivat sub pectore virtus,
> Tantus amor veri, nihil est quod noscere malim,
> Quam fluvii causas per secula tanta latentes,
> Ignotumque caput: spes sit mihi certa videndi
> Niliacos fontes; bellum civile relinquam.[150]

Mr. Bruce may exult in having attained to what imperial Cæsar so ardently wished for in vain.

148. As JB observes, the source of the Nile and its putative discovery had been a subject of mystery, speculation, and controversy since ancient times. According to his published account, Bruce arrived at the springs at Gish, above Dembea, on Nov. 4, 1770. What he "discovered" was one of a number of sources of only one of the main tributaries of the Nile, the Blue Nile. He knew of Lobo and seems to have been aware that Gish had been visited by Paez (*ODNB*), but neglects to mention them in his own account; furthermore, he saw, on his return journey, the confluence of the Blue Nile with the larger White Nile near the site of present-day Khartoum. After the second installment of this article was reprinted in the *Lond. Chron.* (Sept. 8, 1774), a letter signed "Philo" was published in a subsequent issue (Sept. 20), drawing to readers' attention the earlier claims of Lobo and Paez, as given in SJ's translation of Lobo and in Geddes's *Church History of Ethiopia* (1696), and putting the blame for the exaggeration not on Bruce, but his "injudicious encomiast."

149. For this passage from *Rambler*, no. 103, see n. 129, above. The next sentence is also taken from Johnson; the closing quotation mark should follow "concealed."

150. Lucan, *Civil War*, 10.188–92 (the words come at the end of a speech by Caesar): "But, though such intellectual vigour and love of truth flourish in my breast, yet there is nothing I would rather learn than the causes, concealed through such long ages, that account for the Nile, and the secret of its source. Give me an assured hope to set eyes on the springs of the river, and I will abandon civil war" (605).

He found the Nile in some places compressed between rocks, into such narrow bounds that he could leap over it. There is a large river in Northumberland of which the same remark has been made.[151]

The Portuguese jesuits having fallen into the common error of their society, engaging in political schemes, and the Abyssinians having discovered their design to subject the country to the pope, they were all put to death, with an indignation suitable to the ferocity of the Abyssinians, and for which it must be owned, there was but too good an apology. Since that time, the Abyssinians have relapsed into all their former barbarism, and it has been the established law of the country, that any Frank, by which name they call all Europeans, who should presume to enter it, should be cut off without mercy.[152] This was a formidable bar in Mr. Bruce's way; yet he persisted in his enterprize. He dressed himself as a Syrian, and proceeded into Abyssinia, as one of that nation, till he reached the residence of the king. His helmet one day unluckily fell off, and it was discovered that he wore his hair. This, and other circumstances, made it be strongly suspected that he only pretended to be a Syrian, and was in reality a Frank, upon which the people were going to stone him: but as the Europeans are much famed in Abyssinia for knowledge in physic, Mr. Bruce happily availed himself of this, and having before learned that the Abyssinians are much troubled with agues, he had taken the precaution to bring along with him a large quantity of bark,[153] which he administered with great success; so that those barbarians, from gratitude for the relief which they had received, or rather perhaps from the principle of attention to their own good, which actuates mankind in general to a kind of secondary benevolence towards others, preserved his life.

By degrees he acquired the language of the country, which has a considerable affinity with the Arabic; and being held in esteem, he got into the confidence of the king, who as a mark of distinction made him lie upon a skin at

151. Near Rothbury in Northumberland, the Coquet River passes through a narrow gorge called the Thrum.

152. Bruce was the first European to visit Abyssinia in 150 years and was allowed in partly because he was not a Catholic.

153. *Ague* means fever, especially malarial fever. The bark of various plants was used as treatment for pains and fevers: the white willow (*salix alba*) was known from ancient times. In 1763, in the *Transactions* of the Royal Society, Rev. Edmund Stone told of the "success of the bark of the willow in the cure of the agues (fever)"; he is thus credited with having identified salicylic acid, the active ingredient in aspirin. Shrubs of the *cinchona* species were introduced to Europe in the 1640s from Peru as a source of quinine. Bruce studied medicine in 1765, while he was consul general in Algiers, and later in Aleppo, Syria, under an English doctor, Patrick Russel, who taught him the treatment of tropical illnesses. Several times in his travels, his medical knowledge saved his life and enabled him to treat people he visited in return for protection, safe conduct, and other favors.

the door of his own chamber, and carried him along with him, when he went to war. The king was by no means a man of extraordinary abilities, but was of a most despotic disposition, for the exercise of which he had ample room in the government of Abyssinia.[154] The sovereigns of that country boast of as long a line as is that of the kings of Scotland, which Churchill has very well ridiculed in his *Prophecy of Famine*.

> That ancient seat, where majesty display'd
> Its ensigns—long before the world was made.[155]

The Abyssinians hold that their first monarch was the son of Solomon, by the queen of Sheba, at that interview which she had with him, so highly to her satisfaction; so that, according to the Abyssinian history, that princess did more than see his wisdom.[156] The Abyssinians, however, cannot vaunt, that Solomon's wisdom has been communicated to his descendents, who swayed the scepter over them; for besides the present king, whose capacity was but of an inferior kind, the king who reigned when the Portuguese jesuits pushed the extension of the papal authority, was so weak a man as to be persuaded to favour their scheme, on which account he was dethroned by his people.[157]

The universality of the feudal system may justly be held as a strong proof of its consonance to the nature of man; and of its universality the evidence is

154. JB does not have a clear impression of the admittedly complex political situation. The Abyssinian emperor (or "King of Kings") at this time was a fifteen-year-old boy, Tekle Haimanot II, but the real power in the region had long been Mikail Sehul (c. 1691–1779), Ras of Tigray, who had arranged the deaths of the two previous emperors and the installation of their successors; see Marcus, *History of Ethiopia*, 45–47, 51–52. Bruce bore letters of recommendation to Ras Mikail and the king, but when he and his party arrived in Gondar, the Abyssinian capital, on Feb. 15, 1770, they were out of town, leading an army against a neighboring province, and Bruce did not present his letters until Mar. 9. Having impressed them with his success in treating smallpox, his guns and marksmanship, his horsemanship, and his personal qualities, Bruce was made first a lord of the king's bedchamber, a commander of horse, and a provincial governor.

155. Charles Churchill, *The Prophecy of Famine: A Scots Pastoral, Inscribed to John Wilkes, Esq.* (1763), lines 161–62. The satirical poet Churchill (1732–64) was a friend and ally of Wilkes; JB met him, with Wilkes, on May 24, 1763 (*Lond. Journ.*, 266).

156. For the biblical account of King Solomon being visited by the Queen of Sheba, see 1 Kings 10:1–13. Bruce devotes almost all the second volume of his *Travels* to a translated history of the Abyssinian kings' descent from Solomon.

157. In 1624, Paez converted the Abyssinian emperor Socinios (or Susneyos), who submitted the church to papal authority. However, this brought to a head hostility toward Catholicism from the local Orthodox Christians, and in 1632 the succeeding emperor had the Jesuits banished or executed, and closed the country to European missionaries until 1702; see Marcus, *History of Ethiopia*, 39–40.

always encreasing. Mr. Banks and Dr. Solander found it in the islands of the South sea.[158] Mr. Bruce found it in Abyssinia, where although there are vassals of every gradation, there are no slaves. The rule of succession amongst this people, is lineal in all families without distinction of sex, except in the royal family: as to which, a rule similar to that of the Salic law in France obtains; so that males only are allowed to succeed.[159]

The territory of Abyssinia is extensive: it is very mountainous; but its mountains are not to be compared with the *Andes*, or the *Alps*, and are not even so high as some of the mountains in Scotland; yet their height is such, as to have effect in breaking the clouds, so as to produce a deal of rain, which lasts for six months in the year, when the people remain in a state of listless inactivity. During the other six months, their king leads them out to war, as they are in continual hostilities with their neighbouring nations. Their army is composed both of cavalry and infantry. The men and horses, as they are in other mountainous countries, are of a small size, but have much activity and spirit: their arms are bows and arrows, slings, guns, shields, and coats of mail of chain work. There is no money in the country, but they carry on a tolerable commerce by barter; their vallies being fruitful in grain, and their hills in vines, of the produce of which they make a strong red wine. They also make mead. They have black cattle and sheep in abundance; they can therefore afford to send out such a proportion of their commodities, as to procure themselves guns, shields, and coats of mail, which they get chiefly from Ispahan.[160] They have the art of making gunpowder, which is extraordinary, considering their rude state in other respects. They are remarkably dexterous in the use of the sling, with which they throw stones of a

---

158. JB was acutely sensitive on the subject of succession, owing to his protracted conflict with his father over the entail of the Auchinleck estate. Lord Auchinleck's scheme was to entail the estate on his heirs (regardless of gender) and thus possibly to pass over JB entirely. JB was devoted to the principle of male succession; see *Later Years*, 116–21. In Banks's account of the South Sea islanders, he wrote, "the subordination which takes place among them very much resembles the early state of the feudal laws, by which our ancestors were so long governed, a system evidently formed to secure the licentious liberty of a few, while the greater part of the society are unalterably immersed in the most abject slavery." See Banks, *Journal*, 176.

159. Salic Law was an important body of legal traditions, developed from the sixth century by the Salian Franks. From Shakespeare's mention of it in *Henry V*, it is best known for the regulation concerning agnatic succession—i.e., the rule excluding females from the inheritance of a throne. "Salic law" is often thought to be, as JB implies here, synonymous with agnatic succession.

160. Ispahan or Isfahan, a city in central Persia (modern-day Iran), was at different times the imperial capital and, by the seventeenth century, a great city with a population of c. 600,000.

great weight with very great force and with much exactness of aim. Their guns have only match-locks, so that the firing of them is a tedious and aukward operation, and they do not depend much upon the execution that is to be done by them.[161] The method of firing them is this: a man has a pole, into which hooks are fixed at different heights: he sticks this into the ground, and rests his gun upon one or other of the hooks, according to the altitude of the object, which he intends to hit; he then applys his lighted match to the motion hole, and so causes the explosion. Mr. Bruce had some guns with firelocks, and flints with him, which he recommended, but the king held them cheap, having observed that they once or twice missed fire, which guns with match-locks never can do. Match-lock guns made a considerable part of the arms used in Gustavus Adolphus's wars, and we find them as late as in the army of Lewis XIV.[162] Mr. Bruce was with the king of Abyssinia, one half of the year in war, and during the other half he had full leisure, which he employed, partly, in making drawings of such scenes of that country, as seemed best to deserve attention.[163]

London Magazine, 43 (September 1774), 429–31

The people of Abyssinia know little of the art of building: they live in huts, some of which are formed of the branches of trees, others of mud, and some of mud and stone together. There are villages, or collections of these huts, which contain a large number of inhabitants. What is called the capital consists of about twenty-five thousand souls.[164] The king has a large house or palace of stone, which was built by the jesuits. It has turrets, a square in the middle, and a gallery all around. It is of such size and strength, that the king might defend himself

161. A matchlock gun required a slow match or fuse (made from a cord) to be lit in order to ignite the powder; by the late sixteenth century, these weapons were mostly displaced by firelocks, in which the charge is ignited by a spark produced by a flint in the gun's lock.

162. Gustavus Adolphus "the Great" of Sweden (1594–1632) was a king and general, whose military success was attributed in part to the maneuverability of his infantry and the firing speed and accuracy of his musketeers. The armies of the French "Sun-King" Louis XIV (1638–1715) were at war more or less continuously, at first with the Habsburg Empire and then with Spain, from 1667.

163. Bruce could draw but also had with him on his travels an Italian artist, Luigi Balugani, who was recruited in Algiers in 1765 and died in Abyssinia in late 1770. Despite Balugani's usefulness and loyalty, Bruce seems to have felt that the presence of another European in his party would diminish his own achievements. He scarcely mentions him in his *Travels* and later tried to pass off Balugani's drawings as his own.

164. Gondar was founded in 1635 and by the end of the seventeenth century had grown to be a great center of national culture and religion, with a population of c. 60,000 people. It remained the national capital until 1855.

in it against all Asia, were it not that, by a strange inattention, its situation has been so chosen, that there is *no well* within it.

The colour of the Abyssinians is not, properly speaking, black, but rather a dusky, tawny, or copper colour; and some of them, who live under the line, are very fair.[165] The country is cold enough, for a part of the year, to require the use of fire; and the trees, which are scattered copiously over the kingdom, furnish plenty of fuel. The people, especially the lower sort, have very little dress, and not any have coverings on their heads, the king excepted.

Their religion is a kind of coarse Christianity, with a considerable mixture of Judaism. They have a great many monks, and their sacred establishment is a species of the Greek church dependent upon the patriarch of Alexandria.[166]

The light of the gospel beams upon them very faintly, for they are a fierce, and a cruel people: a strong instance of which is their manner of eating. Not satisfied with devouring raw flesh, their custom is to eat collops cut from live animals, which they tear to pieces with their teeth while warm, and palpitating with vital motion.[167] The flesh of an animal, after it is dead, is considered by them as quite unsavoury. The most expert butcher therefore amongst them is he, who can cut most flesh from a beast before it is deprived of its life; for doing which, the utmost attention and nicety is required, so as to avoid the great arteries, or those parts, the destruction of which will soon bring on death. A company of Abyssinians at dinner is a horrible spectacle: they are seated, each with a cake made of flour in his hand—live cattle are brought to the door, and the inhuman butcher cuts morsels off them, which are instantly carried in to the company, who lay them upon their cakes, and eat them directly, all bathed in tepid blood of the miserable animals, whose lowings and groanings, through violence of anguish, serve for a dinner bell, or music to the

165. *Under the line*: at the equator (*OED*).

166. The Christian faith of Ethiopia is an ancient branch of Eastern Orthodoxy, established in the country since the fourth century. It has a strong monastic tradition and observes Jewish practices such as the Sabbath, circumcision, and the veneration of the Ark of the Covenant. The Ethiopian liturgy is in the ancient language of Ge'ez, and its scriptures include texts not in the canon of other churches, including the Book of Enoch, of which Bruce brought the first manuscripts to Europe. (The Orthodox Church of Ethiopia became independent from the Coptic Orthodox Church of Alexandria, with its own patriarch, in 1959.)

167. Bruce claimed that in Jan. 1770, en route to Gondar, he had witnessed three travelers cut steaks from a live cow and that once in Gondar he partook of banquets in which a cow was kept alive while being butchered and eaten. Bruce seems to have told these stories from the time he arrived in London and attracted much notoriety and skepticism (see Bruce, *Travels*, vol. 3, chap. 11; Bredin, *Pale Abyssinian*, 100–102).

shocking barbarians. This *savage repast* puts one in mind of Virgil's description of the Cyclops:

> *Vidi atro cum membra fluentia tabo*
> *Manderet, et tepidi tremerent sub dentibus artus.*[168]

The learned Selden, in his book *De Jure Naturæ & Gentium*,[169] in which he takes occasion to treat of the ancient customs of the Jews, asserts, that the prohibition to eat blood, issued by GOD to Noah (Gen. ix. 4 "But flesh with the life thereof, which is the blood thereof, shall ye not eat") was to prevent a practice which had prevailed in the antediluvian world, of eating in the cruel manner that the Abyssinians now do. The words seem well adapted to counteract such a practice; and Selden illustrates his conjecture with that learning and ingenuity which distinguish his writings. It was wonderful that it should prevail in Abyssinia, as it is so adverse both to the Jewish and Christian systems.

After having remained above two years in Abyssinia, it may well be believed, that Mr. Bruce would be very desirous of leaving it. But this he found a still more difficult matter than getting into it; for he had become of importance to the king, who therefore seemed resolved never to part with him. One day, when the king was in more than ordinary good humour, he told Mr. Bruce, that he would grant him any thing that he should ask. Mr. Bruce seized this opportunity, and told the king, that as he did not keep his health in that climate, and was anxious to return to his native country, he hoped he should obtain permission to depart. The king seemed astonished at the request, and was at first in a furious rage; but recollecting himself, he, *for his oath's sake*, like Herod of old,[170] determined to give up his own inclination. Mr. Bruce had by this time collected a good many drawings, and a number of Abyssinian manuscripts. That people have long had the art of writing, and have a great deal of such history as they compose, for which materials cannot be deficient, as there are perpetual wars,

---

168. Virgil's description of the Cyclops is quoted from the *Aeneid*, 3.626–27; Achaemenides sees Polyphemus slaughter two of Odysseus's crew and then says, "I watched while he devoured their limbs, all dripping with black blood-clots, and the warm joints quivered beneath his teeth" (trans. Fairclough, 1:413, 415). This analogy was suggested to JB by his fellow lawyer John Ord (*Defence*, 283).

169. John Selden (1584–1654), jurist and scholar, in his book *De Jure Naturali et Gentium* ("Of the Laws of Nature and Peoples," 1640), identifies six moral duties required of all humanity by biblical and other traditions, as well as a seventh, "added after the flood . . . forbidding anyone to eat flesh cut from a living animal" (Rosenblatt, quoted in *ODNB*, s.v. "Selden, John"). Andrew Crosbie drew this passage to JB's attention (*Defence*, 283).

170. Herod Antipas, the tetrarch of Galilee in Jesus's time, is reported to have had John the Baptist beheaded for his stepdaughter Salome "for his oath's sake"; see Mark 6:26.

and as the king always carries a historian with him, to record the transactions of each campaign. Mr. Bruce having packed up his books and papers, and provided camels and servants to attend him on his journey, he quitted the capital of Abyssinia, giving out that he was to travel back to Egypt the way he came; but, being justly apprehensive that the king would change his mind after he was set out, and indeed having received intelligence, that there was a design to seize him and bring him back, he took a quite different course. Instead of travelling a great way in Abyssinia, he struck off directly for the desarts of Nubia, in getting at which, he was not long in the king of Abyssinia's dominions. He had a dreadful journey for thirty days, through sandy desarts, scorched with the intense heat of a glowing sun, and swept by winds of so pestiferous a quality, as to kill both man and beast, if their lungs are assailed by the noxious blasts.

In the course of this journey, Mr. Bruce lost all his camels, and all his attendants, except one man. During the whole peregrination, they did not meet with any wandering tribe whatever. Mr. Bruce, and his surviving attendant, being unable to carry the baggage, and reduced to an almost desperate state, he left his curiosities in the desert, and with his faithful attendant walked on they knew not whither, only keeping towards the East, and hoping that they should fall in with some inhabited place. His shoes very soon went in pieces, and he was then obliged to struggle along upon his naked feet through burning lands, and over rocky places, till his feet were prodigiously swelled, blistered, and lacerated. At the end of eight days, they reached the town of Siana, in the dominions of the grand signor.[171] There the aga or officer of the janissaries treated them with a good deal of humanity, altho' he often reproached Mr. Bruce very roughly on account of his being an infidel. Mr. Bruce begged to have camels and attendants to go back with him into the desert, that he might recover his books and papers. "Of what value are any books or papers that you can have, you infidel!" cried the aga. Mr. Bruce then told him, that he had several receipts for curing distempers, among his papers, which it was a pity should be lost. The aga listened to this, and allowed him camels and attendants, with whom he set off; and, as fortunately no wild wanderers had been at the place, he found his baggage just where he left it. He went and came in the space of four days upon a camel, that journey, which it had cost him eight days to come on foot, when worn out with fatigue and distress.

171. *Siana*: i.e., Syene, the Greek name for Aswan, the ancient trading city in southern Egypt, on the Nile. The *grand signor* presumably refers to Mustafa III (1717–74), sultan of the Ottoman Empire; *aga* of the janissaries is the chief military officer (a janissary is a troop of Turkish infantry).

One misfortune still awaited Mr. Bruce, of which he had no apprehension. There is in Nubia a species of gnat, such as is found in some parts of the West Indies, which, when it stings, deposits in the human body an egg, which becomes a worm of a spiral form, that screws itself deeply into the flesh.[172] One of these gnats had bitten Mr. Bruce in one of his legs; he scratched it, and it was more and more irritated: at last it was discovered that a worm was lodged. To those who are acquainted with the method of taking out these insects, nothing is more easy than gradually to unscrew them; but the person who attempted to relieve Mr. Bruce, broke the worm, (which is always attended with very bad consequences) and Mr. Bruce's leg was in so bad a state, that a gangrene was apprehended, and a French surgeon proposed amputation.[173] Mr. Bruce luckily opposed this being done. By degrees, the venom was removed, and he recovered perfect strength and soundness.

Mr. Bruce afterwards visited the interior parts of Africa, where he discovered the finest remains of Roman magnificence now extant.[174] The climate of that country is so fine, that there is neither rain nor frost; therefore the stone is not in the least discoloured, nor the carved work impaired. In one part, it is

172. Guinea worm disease (or dracunculiasis) is an infection, formerly prevalent throughout Africa and the Middle East, which is caused by drinking water containing fleas (which JB calls "gnats"), which themselves contain the larvae of the parasitic guinea worm. The water flea is digested, but the larva is not, and grows in the small intestine over a period of twelve to fourteen months to a worm two to three feet in length. The worm makes its way to another part of the body, usually the feet or legs, where it will cause a painful blister and emerge and release milky liquid containing larvae if it comes in contact with water, thus contaminating local water supplies. The worm itself is removed by winding, as JB describes, but much more slowly and carefully—usually over a period of weeks. See Bredin, *Pale Abyssinian*, 238, 241–42.

173. In his *Travels*, Bruce reports being infected by the guinea worm (5:428). In an appendix, he describes being treated, on his journey back to Britain, at the Lazaretto in Marseilles (5:60–61).

174. It was before, rather than after, his Abyssinian journey that Bruce visited the "interior parts of Africa" (i.e., the Roman sites along the northern African coast). He and Balugani made architectural drawings of Roman ruins, and Bruce eventually presented three volumes of them to George III, claiming the lot as his own work. Mauretania Caesariensis was a Roman province established in the first century, taking in present-day coastal Algeria. The amphitheater mentioned is at El Djem (Roman Thysdrus) in present-day Tunisia, about forty (not 400) miles from the major port of Sousse (the Roman Hadrumetum). Built in the third century, it seated 35,000 spectators and remained relatively intact until the seventeenth century. Parian marble was the particularly fine white marble that in Classical times was quarried from the island of Paros in the Aegean.

believed in the *Mauritania Cæsarensis*, he found an amphitheatre, better than that of *Nismes* in France, or *Verona* in Italy. It is all built of the finest white Parian marble, and must have been a work of immense labour; for there is no such marble in Africa, and it is situated above four hundred miles from any sea port; so that the marble of which it is built must have been first brought a great way in ships, and then transported above four hundred miles by land carriage. Some of the Roman remains in Africa discovered by Mr. Bruce, were a good deal buried, or covered by the blowing of sand, till he had them cleared; and it is hoped, that we shall have several curious prints from his drawings.

In the narrative now given, there is no intentional mistake: the compiler has omitted many particulars, as to which he was not sure of having received clear information. He shall think himself happy, if he can impart to others as much satisfaction as he himself had, from the recital of what he now chearfully communicates.

Some people have complained of Mr. Bruce, as being close and reserved since his return to Britain, and have represented him as

Nec visu facilis nec dictu affabilis ulli.[175]

But it should be considered, that a gentleman of fortune, and who has the *blood of Bruce* in his veins, is entitled to maintain a dignity of character.[176] He has travelled for his own instruction and amusement, and he is not bound to communicate his knowledge, but when and how he himself pleases. Besides, Mr. Bruce is above being made a show, or talked to, and stared at, as a strange man.[177] When teased with idle or ignorant questions, no wonder that he should repulse troublesome people; but when he meets with men of knowledge, and of classical enquiry, he is very ready to take the trouble of giving them the satisfaction of which they are worthy.

175. *Nec visu*, etc. (Virgil, *Aeneid*, 3.621): "In aspect forbidding, in speech to be accosted by none" (trans. Fairclough, 1:413); a rather unflattering description, considering that it is Virgil's description of the great Cyclops, Polyphemus. (In this text as quoted, JB or the printer gives *affabilis* rather than *adfabilis*: they are both acceptable variants of the word for affable.)

176. That is, Robert the Bruce (1274–1329), Scottish nationalist leader and, as Robert I, King of Scots, from 1306. James Bruce's ancestry is traceable to him through his mother's line. JB also was descended from Bruce, through his paternal grandmother (*Earlier Years*, 8).

177. JB's defense of Bruce's character here is in response to the skepticism that he was subjected to after the first glow of his return had faded and which was only exacerbated by his low tolerance of the many people he considered as his inferiors.

1776

An Account of the Chief of the Mohock Indians, Who Lately Visited England

[The Mohawk are a North American indigenous people, originally located in the Mohawk River valley in upstate New York and southeastern Canada. The Mohawk took the side of the British in the American War of Independence. Theyendanegea (also known as Joseph Brant) visited London in April 1776, and Boswell was introduced to him and his companion Gilbert Tice at a ball at the Haberdashers' Hall on Thursday, April 18 (*Ominous Years*, 341–42). Boswell was invited to call on them for breakfast, at the Swan with Two Necks, and appears to have done so, but his journal for this period survives only in rough notes (ibid., 343–44).]

London Magazine, 45 (July 1776), 339 (lead article)

An Account of the Chief of the Mohock Indians, *who lately visited* England.
(With an exact Likeness.)

It is well known that the chief of the Mohock Indians visited England in the reign of Queen Anne, and was very well received at the court of that princess. His picture is preserved in the British Museum.[178] At that time the Mohocks were a very rude and uncivilized nation. The periodical essays of the Augustan age of England, as Queen Anne's reign has been called, shew us that the very name of Mohock was then terrible in London; and we find many ingenious and entertaining remarks produced from speculating upon the visit of the wild American chief.[179] But somewhat more than half a century has made a very

---

178. In 1710, four *sachems* or tribal leaders of American indigenous people visited England. Although often known as the "four Mohock Kings," three were Mohawk and one Mahican. They came to request military aid against the French and religious instruction for their people. They were received in London as a diplomatic mission and were presented to Queen Anne. The most senior of the party was Tiyanoga/Theyanoguin, also known as King Hendrick (c. 1680–1755), whose full-length portrait (titled *The Emperor of the Six Nations*) by John Verelst is in the British Museum. As a result of the visit, a chapel was established at Fort Hunter, near Amsterdam, New York. See Bond, *Queen Anne's American Kings*, 58–60.

179. In London in early 1712, the "name of Mohock" was appropriated by (or applied to) supposed gangs of young rakes whose random and violent attacks were much discussed; they were mentioned by Swift, Pope, and others, though how much truth there was in the reports is unclear. In *Spectator*, no. 50 (Apr. 26, 1711), Addison gives fictitious extracts from the diary of a native American visitor, in order to satirize the religious observances, politics, and fashions of Londoners. In *Tatler*, no. 171 (May 11–13, 1710), a story is told about the Indian "kings" complimenting their upholsterer landlord.

great change upon the Mohock nation. They are now so well trained to civil life, as to live in a fixed place, to have good commodious houses, to cultivate land with assiduity and skill, and to trade with the British colonies. They are also converted to the Christian faith, and have among them a priest of the church of England, who regularly performs the sacred functions as prescribed in the Liturgy, which is translated into their language.[180]

The grandson of the chief who visited England in Queen Anne's reign is their chief at present.[181] He is in the prime of life, and has seen a good deal of service along with the late Sir William Johnson.[182]

The present unhappy civil war in America occasioned his coming over to England. He was solicited by both sides to give his assistance, and found himself perplexed amidst a contrariety of arguments upon a great subject, which he could not well understand. Before coming to a decisive resolution, he resolved to go himself into the presence of THE GREAT KING, as the British sovereign is styled amongst the American Indians. He accordingly came to London in 1776, accompanied by Captain Tice, an officer of English extraction born in America, and who has a settlement just in the neighbourhood of the Mohock nation.[183]

---

180. Rev. John Stuart (1740/41–1811) commenced his duties as the Anglican priest at Fort Hunter, New York, in Dec. 1770, under the patronage of Sir William Johnson; see Dictionary of Canadian Biography, s.v. "Stuart, John."

181. The visiting chief, Theyendanegea or Joseph Brant (1742–1807), was a step-grandson of another of the "four Mohock Kings," the sachem Sa Ga Yeah Qua Pieth Tow (or Sagayendwarahton or Peter Brant), not of Tiyanoga or King Hendrick, as JB seems to think. However, as Kelsay points out, "one Mohawk word for 'grandfather' could mean any of a grand-father's brothers or half-brothers" (*Joseph Brant*, 171).

182. Sir William Johnson (c. 1715–74), British colonial estate manager, who was appointed in 1746 by the New York governor as Northern Superintendent of Indian Affairs, successfully cultivating Indian loyalty to the Crown. His common-law wife was Brant's half-sister. Impressed by Brant's scholastic abilities, Johnson arranged for his schooling. Brant fought on the British side in campaigns in 1764 and, on his return from England, raised his own loyalist force of irregular volunteers.

183. In late Dec. 1775, Brant came to London, in the company of two of the sons-in-law of (the, by then, late) Sir William Johnson: the new Superintendent of Northern Indian Affairs, Guy Johnson, and Daniel Claus; their mission was to secure their own appointments by presenting themselves to the colonial secretary. The party of fifteen or more included Gilbert Tice (1740–91), the innkeeper at Johnstown, whom Guy Johnson had appointed to the rank of captain in the Indian Affairs Department. Johnson thought that some Indians in the entourage would be useful, and the Mohawks saw a chance to put their long-standing land grievances to the king. Brant and John Hill Oteronyente were, according to Indian custom with important business, sent as speaker and prompter, respectively (see Kelsay, *Joseph Brant*, 157–62).

By what mode of reasoning this chief was convinced of the justice of the demands of Great Britain upon her colonies, and the propriety of enforcing them, we have not been informed: but it is said, that he has promised to give his assistance to government, by bringing three thousand men into the field. He and Captain Tice sailed for America early in May.[184]

This chief had not the ferocious dignity of a savage leader; nor does he discover any extraordinary force either of mind or body. We have procured for the satisfaction of our readers, a print of him in the dress of his nation, which gives him a more striking appearance;[185] for when he wore the ordinary European habit, there did not seem to be any thing about him that marked preeminence. Upon his tomahawk is carved the first letter of his Christian name, *Joseph*, and his Mohock appellation thus, *Thayendaneken* (pronounced *Theandenaigen*) the *g* being sounded hard as in *get*. His manners are gentle and quiet; and to those who study human nature, he affords a very convincing proof of the tameness which education can produce upon the wildest race. He speaks English very well; and is so much master of the language, that he is engaged in a translation of the New Testament into the Mohock tongue.[186] Upon his arrival in London, he was conducted to the inn, called *The Swan with two Necks*, in Lad-Lane.[187] Proper lodgings were to be provided for him; but he said the good people of the

184. On Mar. 14, Brant had an interview with the colonial secretary, Lord George Germain; the government promised Brant and his people land in Canada in return for their loyalty against the Americans. (There is no evidence that Brant mentioned 3,000 warriors in his meetings with the colonial secretary; see Kelsay, *Joseph Brant*, 172–73.) Brant and John Oteronyente left London soon after a second meeting with Germain and set sail from Falmouth in early June (ibid., 174). While they were away, the thirteen united American colonies had declared their independence from Britain. On his return to New York, Brant recruited Indians as loyalists, and Brant's Volunteers participated in various attacks, including the Cherry Valley (New York) massacre in Nov. 1778 (*Later Years*, 126). He visited Britain a second time in 1785.

185. The print of Brant used as frontispiece in the *London Magazine* was based on a drawing (now lost) in the possession of JB. The rather handsome images of Brant in paintings made on this visit suggest it is not a good likeness (see Figure 4).

186. From 1772 to 1774, Brant assisted Rev. John Stuart in translating the Gospel of Mark, which was probably complete by this time, though not published until 1787, "as part of a new edition of the Mohock Prayer Book" (Kelsay, *Joseph Brant*, 671 n. 49). See Dictionary of Canadian Biography, s.v. "Stuart, John (1740/41–1811)."

187. The Swan with Two Necks was in Lad Lane, a street now gone: "it stood in the part of Gresham Street which runs between Wood Street and Milk Street," in Cheapside, close to St. Paul's (Besant, 468). Established in 1677, it was the largest of the coaching inns in London, so it was considered a place at which to stay on arrival in the city but not usually any longer.

*Figure 4. "Joseph Thayendaneken, the Mohawk Chief: From an Original Drawing
in the Possession of James Boswell Esqr,"* London Magazine, *45 (July 1776).
Courtesy of the Beinecke Rare Book and Manuscript Library, Yale University.*

inn were so civil, that he would not leave them; and accordingly he continued
there all the time he was in London. He was struck with the appearance of
England in general; but he said he chiefly admired the ladies and the horses.

1778

MUTINY AT EDINBURGH OF THE SEAFORTH HIGHLANDERS

[In an atmosphere characterized by rumors of war and invasion, the regiment of
Seaforth Highlanders was brought to Edinburgh in September 1778. The soldiers,

who had been newly recruited from the Earl of Seaforth's highland estates, came to believe, in the absence of any better explanation of their movements, that they were to be sold to the East India Company and sent overseas, in contravention of their contracts. They refused to embark at Leith and complained also of pay owed to them. Boswell records going to Castle Hill on the first day of the mutiny, Tuesday, September 22, 1778, at about noon, in fine weather. He saw there about one hundred mutineers. Later in the day, after the mutineers had occupied Arthur's Seat, the peak in King's Park at the other end of the town, he strolled by to take in the atmosphere and described himself as "wonderfully animated by this extraordinary scene" (*Laird*, 21). In his journal, Boswell records having written the first of these accounts over three days, and sending it off Thursday night, September 24 (*Laird*, 21, 22). Local sentiment was very favorable to the Highlanders, who conducted themselves with discipline and good cheer. Tactful negotiation resolved the standoff without violence, and a week later the Seaforth Highlanders took a ship at Leith to Guernsey and Jersey and thence to the Royal Naval Base at Portsmouth, in the south of England. In May 1781 the regiment was posted to the East Indies; illness on the voyage saw fewer than 400 out of 1,100 fit for service on arrival in Madras, and very few of them ever returned to the Highlands; see Stewart, *Sketches*, 2:197–98.]

Mutiny in Scotland

Public Advertiser, September 29, 1778, 2

MUTINY IN SCOTLAND.

Extract of an authentic Letter from Edinburgh, dated Sept. 22, 1778

OUR whole City is in an Uproar at present, occasioned by a Mutiny or Insurrection of a large Body of Lord Seaforth's Highland Regiment.[188] They were this Day to have been embarked in Transports at Leith, to be carried to Guernsey:[189] But a considerable Number of them alledging that their enlisting Money had

188. The 78th Regiment of Foot (or Seaforth Highlanders) was a regiment of about 1,000 men raised, mainly from his own highland estates, by Kenneth Mackenzie, first earl of Seaforth (1744–81), and first paraded in Elgin in May 1778. The regiment was known as "the Wild Macraes" because of the many soldiers of that surname.

189. Leith is the port of Edinburgh. Guernsey, in the Channel Islands, was a British military base. On Feb. 6, 1778, France and the fledgling United States signed treaties of friendship and alliance. After some months of military skirmishing between Britain and France—and public anxiety; see, for instance, Apr. 9, "Talked of French invasion," and Apr. 28, "our fears of invasion" (*Extremes*, 252, 319)—France declared war on Britain on July 10 in support of the American rebellion.

not been paid; that large Arrears were due to them, and that they had been enlisted on the Faith of serving only three Years, or during the War; whereas they understood they were now to be sent to the East Indies, from whence they could never get Home again,—absolutely refused to go. The Duke of Buccleugh's Regiment of Fencibles marched into the Castle this Day, in place of Lord Seaforth's Highlanders: But they were not ordered to interfere; and indeed the Consequences might have been dreadful.[190] The Highlanders had, it seems, been preparing for this for some Time, and were well provided both with Powder and Ball. In the Forenoon they patrolled the Streets in Arms, but without attempting any Hostilities against the Inhabitants, who indeed were universally upon their Side; at least, the Mob was; and the History of Captain Porteus [sic] proves what an Edinburgh Mob is.[191] About five Hundred of them assembled in a Field near Leith, from whence they marched to Arthur's Seat, a prodigious lofty Mountain, within the Royal Park, and not Half a Mile from the City, and there (now past Eight at Night) they are advantageously posted, and plentifully supplied with Bread, Cheese, and Beer, by the Bounty of Numbers of Wellwishers. What will be the Result of this no Mortal can say. Should they march in the Night, and get into the Highlands and excite Tumults, how terrible must be the Situation of this Country, at a Time when we are threatened with a French Invasion![192] Yet it is difficult to form a probable Conjecture how they can be brought into Subjection. What adds to the Agitation of the Day, is, that it is the Anniversary of his present Majesty's Coronation,[193] when the Cannon of the Castle and of the Ships in Leith Harbour, have been fired off; and to be sure, any Spirit of Mutiny in Scotland, and especially amongst Highlanders, is most alarming. It is truly astonishing what a Concourse of People is gathered around Arthur's Seat. The Highlanders fired several Shots at one of their Officers, who attempted to go up. In the Forenoon they had several Scuffles with their Officers, and a good many Wounds were received on both Sides.

190. Henry Scott, third duke of Buccleuch (1746–1812), raised his regiment of fencibles (volunteer part-time soldiers, for home defense) in 1778.

191. In Apr. 1736, Capt. John Porteous (c. 1695–1736) led the troops that had fired on a mob trying to free two smugglers from the gallows. He was tried for murder, but his execution was deferred. Hearing rumors that he had been granted a reprieve, on Sept. 7 a mob of about 4,000 or more came into town, broke into the Tolbooth prison, dragged Porteous out, and hanged him at the Mercat Cross in the Grassmarket.

192. The possibility of a French invasion was much in the air; see *Life*, 3:326, 360 n. 3, 365 n. 4. "A landing of a French force being expected near Greenock," but the foe never appeared (Grant, 4:307).

193. George III was crowned on Sept. 22, 1761.

P.S. *dated Sept. 23.*

My Letter of last Night was too late for the Post, and this Night no Post goes for London.[194] I am sorry that I cannot yet give any more favourable Account of the *Revolt.* We have had a Paper hawked through the Streets, entitled, "Authentic Intelligence from the new Camp on Arthur's Seat, commanded by a Party of Lord Seaforth's Highlanders, particularly the brave *Mac Craws*;" in which a very favourable Account is given of the Mutineers, who are said to want nothing but Justice to be done them.[195] I saw To-day Mr. *Bennet*, a very respectable Clergyman, whose Parsonage is at the Foot of the Mountain, and he told me that a Number of them came down to his House in the Morning, and seemed to be calm, reasonable Men; that he entertained them with a good hospitable Breakfast; and that they talked freely with him.[196] Their alledged Grievances are what I have mentioned in my Letter. Many People of Distinction have been up with them To-day: in particular, a young married Lady of Quality, who made them a Present of all the Guineas she had in her Purse; they were exceedingly polite to her Ladyship; formed themselves into Ranks to do her Honour, and spread Plaids upon the Ground that she might sit.[197] Supplies of Provision have been still sent up to them. The Lord Advocate of Scotland walked for some Time in the King's Park, near to the Camp, amongst other Gentlemen; and it was hoped that his Lordship, who notwithstanding one rash Expression (Starvation) is a humane as well as a sensible Man, would, in his Character of one of the high

194. After coming home from viewing the mutineers, JB "wrote some account of it in a great hurry for the *Public Advertiser*. But was too late for the post" (*Laird*, 21–22).

195. This paper seems not to have survived or been otherwise recorded.

196. Rev. William Bennet (1707–85) was the minister at Duddingston, next to Holyrood Park (*Fasti Scot.*, 1:20), the parish church of Sir Alexander Dick (*Laird*, 19 n. 8). JB met Bennet often at Dick's house at Prestonfield and, in particular, notes meeting him over dinner at Dick's on Wednesday, Sept. 23, when "we had much conversation about the men on the hill" (ibid., 22).

197. The "people of distinction" were probably spectators like JB himself, although he seems, from his account in his journal, not to have ascended to the Arthur's Seat encampment, but to have gone out after dinner and viewed the scene from "King's Park, where crowds were gathered. It was truly picturesque to see the Highlanders in arms upon that lofty mountain. Several people had been up amongst them, and bread and beer had been carried to them" (*Laird*, 21). By "a young married Lady of Quality," JB may be alluding to Harriet Powell (d. 1779), who, though she appears by this time to have been married clandestinely to Lord Seaforth, had earlier been his mistress and was formerly a courtesan. On Tuesday JB recorded in his journal, "It was offensive during the commotion to see Harriet Powell in the rear of Lord Seaforth's chaise with the coronet" (ibid., 21).

Officers of State for Scotland, have contributed to an agreeable Accommodation.[198] But I do not find that any Consultation has been held with him. Sir Adolphus Oughton, our Commander in Chief, and General Skene, who is next in Command, are happily two of the best Men in the World; so that every lenient Measure will be tried.[199] Had there been hot-headed Men in Command, we should probably have had a very horrible Civil War. For, if an Attack had been made on the revolted Highlanders, not only the Populace of Edinburgh, a large Proportion of whom are their Countrymen, would, it is to [be] feared, have joined them, but the Highlanders in general might have risen.

More News *of the* Mutiny *in* Scotland.
Extract of a Letter from Edinburgh, Sept. 24.

EVERY Friend to his King and Country must sincerely regret that several Negociations [*sic*] which were carried on Yesterday between General Skene and the revolted Highlanders, proved ineffectual. They continue in Arms upon their great natural Fortress, which they are able to defend against many Regiments. They have taken up their Ground in the most advantageous Manner, and their Sentinels and advanced Guards are placed very judiciously. They have Drums and Bagpipes, and keep up their Spirits with Musick and Dancing, and Variety of animating Exercises. The Weather has been uncommonly favourable for them, except that a little Rain fell last Night. Your People in England flock to see peaceable Camps, upon flat Heaths and Commons. How much nobler a Scene have we of Edinburgh, when we ascend the lofty Arthur's Seat, and behold a Band of brave Fellows actually in a State of Resistance to what they think Oppression. A Party of the Eleventh Regiment of Dragoons is come to Town,

198. The Lord Advocate of Scotland is the country's chief legal officer and was at this time, after the last Jacobite rebellion in 1746, the chief officer of government. Henry Dundas (1742–1811), from 1802 the first Lord of Melville, became Lord Advocate in May 1775, at the young age of thirty-three. JB knew Dundas from college days in Edinburgh; he admired his abilities but regarded his success with some jealousy, as he wrote in a letter to Temple, on May 22, 1775 (*Corres. 6*, 375). In the House of Commons, on Mar. 6, 1775, in a speech on American affairs, Dundas is said to have first used the word "starvation," and it became a nickname for him (*OED*); see *Life*, 2:160 n. 1.

199. Sir Adolphus Oughton (1720–80), a professional army officer, had succeeded to the rank of lieutenant general when he became commander of the forces in North Britain on May 29, 1778. He met SJ at dinner at Boswell's, Aug. 16, 1773 (*Tour; Life*, 5:43). His deputy, the adjutant general, was Maj. Gen. Robert Skene (d. 1787) of Halyards, Fife, who held a number of important army posts. JB was friendly with both of these men, and his journal of this period records him dining with each of them, and they with him.

but nothing offensive hath as yet been attempted on either Side.[200] This Forenoon two of the Officers of Seaforth's Highlanders, Mr. Mackenzie of Kilcowie, a Highlander, and Mr. Moodie, a Lowlander, both beloved by the Men, went up to them to endeavour to treat.[201] The Scene was truly similar to something in ancient Rome, as when the Commons made a Secession to the sacred Mountain.[202] The Officers were safely conducted to the Top of Arthur's Seat, and being placed on the highest rocky Summit, they harangued the Soldiers with a very earnest Warmth. Mr. Mackenzie, who spoke in Earse, seemed to be very eloquent. Some of the Men, who appeared as Leaders, were not less eloquent; and it was expected that an Accommodation would take Place upon Condition of their being paid every Shilling due to them, and obtaining Assurance that they should not be sent to the East Indies. But we are afraid that Things are yet in a very unsettled State; for the Magistrates have issued a Proclamation for the Inhabitants to keep within Doors when the great Alarm Bell, called the *Fire Bell*, shall be rung, as it seems the Highlanders have threatened to march through the City, and the Commander of the Troops has resolved to oppose them.

It is strange that we cannot get a distinct State of the Merits of the Case; and that this Body of Revolters have been now three Days *in actual Rebellion* in the Sight of our Metropolis, and of the Castle. One should think an End might have been put to the Affair before now. The Commanders have taken a great deal of Pains; and this Day being the Election of a Peer to Parliament, we have the Earls of Eglintoun and Loudoun here, who are General Officers, and very popular.[203] What a Noise must this make all over Europe! But how dismal

200. The 11th Regiment of Dragoons, commanded by Col. Ralph Dundas (d. 1814), together with troops from other regiments, was summoned to Edinburgh, to attempt to storm Arthur's Seat.

201. Colin Mackenzie (d. 1781) was from 1742 sixth laird of Kilcoy (or Kilcowie, on the Black Isle peninsula). Lt. Donald Moodie (1758–80) was born in Melsetter in the Orkneys: hence, not a "Lowlander"; see the Marquis of Ruvigny and Raineval, *Moodie Book*, 49.

202. JB uses the same analogy in his note on the mutiny in the *Tour* (Sept. 1, 1773; see *Life*, 5:142 n. 2). He alludes to an event in the early days of the Roman Republic, known as the Secession to the Sacred Hill, when in 494 B.C. the plebeians, under the leadership of Sicinius, left the city in a body in protest at the oppression and cruelty of the patricians and encamped on a hill, subsequently known as the Mons Sacer, about three miles from Rome. They intended to secede from the republic but were conciliated by a delegation of moderate patricians, including Menenius Agrippa, who recited to them the fable of "The Belly and the Members." They returned to the city after more equitable distribution of wealth and administrative power was agreed to. See Livy, *Ab urbe condita*, 2.32.

203. After the Scottish Parliament was abolished in 1707 by the Act of Union, only sixteen Scottish peers were entitled to sit at any time in the British House of Lords. This was

is it that I must conclude in Uncertainty. They talked To-day of marching for London.

Mutiny in Scotland, Fourth Day

Public Advertiser, October 1, 1778, 2

MUTINY *in* SCOTLAND.
FOURTH DAY.
Edinburgh, Sept. 25, 1778

LAST Night a long Negociation was carried on between the Revolters on Arthur's Seat, and the Earl of Dunmore, late Governor of Virginia, who went to them with Offers from Sir Adolphus Oughton and General Skene.[204] A great deal of warm Conversation passed, partly in English, partly by an Interpreter. But at length an Agreement was happily concluded, and they engaged to march down this Morning. Accordingly his Lordship went up to them this Morning; and about Eleven o'Clock they came down from the Mountains, in martial Array, with the Music of Drum, Fife, and Bagpipe, his Lordship with a drawn Cutlas marching at their Head. Near to the Abbey of Holyrood-house, they were met by General Skene; and their Meeting was announced to a wide Extent, by Joyful Huzzas, both from the Highlanders and the Crowds who accompanied the Procession. The General then took the Command of them, and marched them into that Division of the Royal Park called St. Anne's Yards. There he formed them into a Square; and standing in the Center, he addressed them in a manly, graceful, and conciliating Manner, hoping that they would henceforth behave like good Soldiers and true Highlanders. He read aloud to them the Articles of Agreement, which were: *First*, A general Pardon. *Secondly*, That all Bounty-money or Arrears due to them should be paid. *Thirdly*, That they should not be sent to the East-Indies. These Articles were signed by Sir *Adolphus Oughton*,

---

a by-election to fill a vacancy (*Laird*, 22 n. 1). Archibald Montgomerie (1726–96), eleventh earl of Eglinton, was a professional soldier and was in 1774 elected as a representative peer; he was Margaret Boswell's clan chief and the younger brother of JB's early mentor, the tenth earl (see Chap. 5, n. 9). John Campbell (1705–82), fourth earl of Loudoun, had twenty years earlier been an unsuccessful commander in chief of the British forces in America and was now governor of Edinburgh Castle (see *Laird*, 22 n. 8 and 23 n. 3). Both were "General Officers"—i.e., officers of high military rank.

204. John Murray, fourth earl of Dunmore (1730/31–1809). He was from 1770 governor of New York and from 1771 of Virginia as well. After being driven out by the colonists in 1776, he returned to Britain to take a seat in the House of Lords.

Commander in Chief, General *Robert Skene*, next in Command, the Duke of *Buccleugh*, and the Earl of *Dunmore*. The Highlanders shewed every Demonstration of Attachment to General Skene, and said they would go to the End of the World with him. The Articles were then read in *Earse* by Mr. *Fletcher*, who acted as Interpreter, and a Copy with the original Subscriptions was read to the Men.[205] General Skene was by Degrees attended by a large Company of Persons of Distinction, the Duke of Buccleugh, Earl of Dunmore, Colonel Scott of the Glasgow Regiment,[206] and many others, particularly some of the Officers of the 11th Regiment of Dragoons, and some of the Officers of the Seaforth Regiment. It was intimated to the Men, that a Court should be held next Morning, and all Complaints against their Officers fairly tried by Officers of other Regiments. The General then ordered the Soldiers to sit down, and a Quantity of Cheese, Loaves, and Beer was brought in the Square; with which, after Grace had been said in *Earse* by the Rev. Mr. Robertson, Minister of the Highland Church, they were heartily regaled.[207] Lord *Seaforth* came himself, some of the Men having signified their Wish to see him. And his Lordship assured them, that wherever they should be sent, he would accompany them.[208] He ate of their Bread and Cheese, and then mounted the Cart on which the Beer had been brought, drank to them in their Beer, the Men giving him several Cheers. The Duke of Buccleugh and General Skene did the same, and were also saluted with Acclamations. Never was there a more agreeable Transition from Hostility to festive Good-humour. The Men are billeted in the Suburbs, and will chearfully embark on Monday.

Thus has a very alarming Affair been happily settled, owing to the Patience and good Temper of our present Military Commanders; and it is hoped that the

205. Mr. Fletcher, who read the articles in Erse (i.e., Scottish Gaelic), has not been identified.

206. The 83rd Regiment of Foot (or Royal Glasgow Volunteers) was created in Jan. 1778. Lieutenant-Colonel George Scott of the 61st Foot was appointed colonel to the Royal Glasgow Volunteers in July 1778.

207. Joseph Robertson (d. 1801) was at this time the minister at the Gaelic Chapel-of-Ease in Castle Wynd, Edinburgh. See *Fasti Scot.*, 1:30. JB arranged a supper with him a few days after the end of the mutiny (*Laird*, 25).

208. As lieutenant colonel of his regiment, Lord Seaforth did indeed accompany his men on their subsequent postings. He traveled with them when they were posted, in May 1781, to the East Indies, but died suddenly on board ship before they reached St. Helena. His death was said to have had so depressing an effect on his loyal Highlanders that, combined with sickness, heat, and the conditions of the voyage, 247 of them died on the voyage, and of the 1,100 members of the regiment who had left Portsmouth only 390 were fit for service when they arrived in Madras in Apr. 1782.

Soldiers of this 78th Regiment will for the future live in that Harmony which is the Beauty of Subordination. The poor Fellows were of the wildest Highlanders, many of them *Mac Craws*, of whom Dr. Johnson gives so picturesque and curious an Account in his Highland Travels.[209] It is remarkable that not above three or four of the Men were at all the worse for having been three Days and three Nights exposed to the open Air upon a very high Mountain. Every Gentleman must feel for the Uneasiness which the Officers have suffered during this very strange Insurrection. It must not be omitted, that the Highlanders expressed great Loyalty to *King George*, and it is believed wish much to see him.[210]

1784

Burke Installed as Lord Rector of the University of Glasgow

[In 1782, Edmund Burke was paymaster to the forces—a particularly lucrative office—in Lord Rockingham's brief government and resumed the office in February 1783 in the Fox-North coalition. In November that year, "he was unexpectedly informed that he had been chosen Lord Rector of Glasgow University. This testimony of respect was less a matter of form than it has since become, and Burke was far from despising the honour conferred upon him by the unsolicited votes of the Scotch graduates" (Macknight, *History of Burke*, 3:75). The dismissal of the coalition ministry a few weeks after his election was "something of an embarrassment to the university, for the Lord Rector was expected to use his influence with the government on the university's behalf" (Lock, *Edmund Burke*, 51).

Boswell had a complex relationship with Burke, which is reflected in the *Life of Johnson*, his depiction in which has been described as "Eminent but indistinct" (*Corres. 4*, 81). While Burke was in power, Boswell "cultivated his acquaintance assiduously" and, despite their political differences, "had no inhibitions about asking him for assistance" in gaining some remunerative government appointment (*Pol. Car.*, 93). On August 8, 1783, Boswell wrote to ask Burke to recommend him for the high legal office of solicitor general—or "for some other appointment." When he was passed over, Boswell wrote on November 20 expressing his "resentment of the total neglect which I have had the mortification to experience," but also congratulating Burke on

209. In his account of the valley of "Glensheals," inhabited by the clan Macrae, SJ writes of a visit to the village of Aucknashiel (Johnson, *Journey to the Western Islands*, 32–33). JB's own account of the visit is in the *Tour* (*Life*, 5:141–43).

210. In the *Tour*, JB concludes his footnote on the mutiny by remarking that "Those brave fellows have since served their country effectually at Jersey [i.e., the Battle of Jersey, Jan. 6, 1781], and also in the East-Indies, to which, after being better informed, they voluntarily agreed to go" (*Life*, 5:142 n. 2).

his election to the rectorship and offering to entertain him at Auchinleck (*Corres. 4*, 136, 138–40). He did not receive a reply. On April 8, 1784, Boswell noted in his journal, "Heard Burke Glasgow. Resolved go" (*Applause*, 202). On the day of the installation the following Saturday, Boswell rode into Glasgow; on the way he had a "providential" escape from injury in a fall from his horse. He waited on Burke at his hotel, was cordially received, and joined him and other dignitaries at breakfast before attending the installation.]

Edinburgh Advertiser, April 13, 1784, 236

The Right Hon. Edmund Burke dined,[211] on Tuesday last, at Dr. Adam Smith's, with Principal Robertson, &c.[212] On Wednesday, he was entertained at dinner at Fortune's by the Directors of the Bank of Scotland.[213] On Thursday, he went to Hatton, the seat of the Earl of Lauderdale.[214] On Friday, he arrived at Glasgow, accompanied by Lord Maitland, and dined at Professor Millar's.[215] On Saturday, he was installed as Lord Rector of the University of Glasgow,[216] on which

211. Edmund Burke (1729/30–97), Anglo-Irish whig MP and political philosopher, orator, man of letters, and a founding member in 1764 of Johnson's Literary Club. JB first met him at dinner, through Reynolds, on May 6, 1772 (*Defence*, 138), although, as he later recalled, he had known of and admired him from his student days in Glasgow (see *Applause*, 204).

212. Adam Smith (bap. 1723–90), political economist and from 1751 professor of logic and moral philosophy at Glasgow, was a leading figure of the Scottish Enlightenment. He was one of JB's teachers at the university. The *Pub. Adv.* reported (Dec. 23, 1784), "Mr. Burke owes his dignity of Lord Rector of Glasgow University, to Dr. Adam Smith, with whom he once was candidate for a Professorship, and with whom he has since lived in habits of great friendship." William Robertson (1721–93), prominent historian and a leading figure in the Church of Scotland (moderator in 1763–64); he was principal of Edinburgh University from 1762 until his death.

213. Fortune's Tavern, in the Old Stamp Office Close, was "in the greatest vogue between 1760 and 1770" (Grant, 2:231). The Bank of Scotland, established in 1695, is the second-oldest surviving bank in Britain. After a clear-out of directors in 1770, fifteen new directors, including many private bankers, were appointed, identified in Saville, *Bank of Scotland*, 154.

214. Haltoun (or Hatton) House, set in a park near Ratho about ten miles west of Edinburgh, was the seat of the Lauderdales; the house was destroyed in the 1950s. James Maitland, seventh earl of Lauderdale (1718–89), was one of the directors of the Bank of Scotland appointed in 1770.

215. James, Lord Maitland (1759–1839), son and heir of the seventh earl of Lauderdale, was a Whig MP 1780–89 and, after his succession in 1789 as the eighth earl, a Scottish representative peer. He had studied at Edinburgh, Oxford, and Glasgow, and was taken to Paris by his tutor Dr. Andrew Dalzell (see n. 218, below); he later took part in the French Revolution. John Millar (1735–1801), from 1761, Regius professor of civil law at Glasgow; Adam Smith was instrumental in arranging his appointment.

216. By ancient tradition the rector is elected by the students for an annual term, which is followed usually automatically (as in Burke's case) by a second annual term. Since 1689

occasion he made an excellent speech, declaring he had that day received by much the greatest honour he ever had in his life.[217] He was then entertained at dinner, where were present, Lords Maitland and Daire, Professors Dalzell and Stewart of Edinburgh, Mr. Boswell, who came from Ayrshire to meet him, &c. &c.[218] His instructive and pleasant conversation was greatly admired. With that liberality of sentiment for which he is distinguished, he proposed the health of Mr. Dundas, who held the office of Lord Rector before him.[219] On Sunday he went to view Loch-Lomond. Yesterday he was to return to Glasgow, and he is expected at Edinburgh on Wednesday or Thursday.

---

the principal has been the effective head of the University of Glasgow, and the position of Lord Rector is mostly an honorary role. Eighteenth- and nineteenth-century rectors were usually senior political or legal figures.

217. Other accounts of Burke's address give a different impression: "Burke, having taken the oath of fidelity, rose and 'expressed his thanks for the honour done him—his regard for the learning and talent within the walls in which they were—and his esteem for the national character, by which, he confessed, he had been favourably impressed.' After this great orator had spoken about five minutes, he became suddenly confused, in consequence of the novel situation in which he was placed, and concluded by stating that he was unable to proceed, as he had never before addressed so learned an assembly" (Hay, *Inaugural Addresses by Lords Rectors*, 189). In his journal, JB says merely, "He made a speech of a few sentences," then his journal breaks off. But he also made rough notes of the speech (said by the journal editors to be "the only memorial of it thus far known"), which begin with sentiments similar to those given in this account: "By much the greatest honour I ever received" (*Applause*, 204, 205 n. 2).

218. Basil William Douglas, Lord Daer (1763–94), was a student of Dugald Stewart's at Edinburgh University and went on to become a supporter of the French Revolution and involved in various radical societies and movements before his early death. Andrew Dalzell (1742–1806), after serving as private tutor to the Lauderdale family, was from 1779 professor of Greek at Edinburgh. Dugald Stewart (1753–1828) was professor of mathematics and moral philosophy at Edinburgh. In his journal, JB said of this occasion, "I was a little flurried from the consciousness of my being in the midst of opposition" (*Applause*, 204); he presumably felt himself to be a lone tory in a company of whigs.

219. Henry Dundas was rector 1781–83.

2

Execution Intelligence

Under the cloak of anonymity, Boswell claimed (in the first essay, below) that he attended all the London public executions. Anonymous writers are licensed to exaggerate, but we certainly have records of Boswell attending a considerable number of executions, in both London and Edinburgh. It is also true that, despite his occasional efforts to disguise his interest, Boswell had in his lifetime a discreditable reputation as a habitual execution-goer. On October 25, 1769, he was at court and overheard three gentlemen discussing in wondering terms his presence at and interest in executions; he recorded hearing this with interest but not displeasure: "One said, 'There was he, Sir, on a triumphal car.' All wondered how people could go to see executions. Curious" (*Earlier Years*, 434). A few years later, in the purported correspondence of Martha Ray and James Hackman—whose story is told in this chapter—Boswell was alluded to as "Paoli's friend and historian" and was said to be known to "hire a window by the year, which looks upon the Grass-market at Edinburgh": the Grassmarket being a small square in the center of the city that was the site of the public gallows (Croft, *Love and Madness*, 103; Herbert Croft's novelization of the Hackman case went through seven editions). The twenty-year-old Charlotte Burney (a younger sister of Frances Burney, the novelist and diarist), meeting Boswell for the first time over dinner April 7, 1781, noted to herself, "They say Mr. Boswell has such a passion for seeing *executions* that he never misses one if he can help it; and he *seemed* as if he had all their terms by heart" (quoted in *Laird*, 312).

Anyone who attended all the London hangings would have been kept very busy. The eighteenth century was the high-water mark of the use of the death penalty in Britain. From 1761 to 1795, there were 1,170 executions from Old Bailey trials (Gatrell, *Hanging Tree*, 616). Public hangings were conducted eight times a year at the famous site of Tyburn, west of the city, or, from 1783, outside Newgate prison, and usually several felons were hanged on each occasion (ibid., 7). There were any number of capital crimes. Under what later commentators called "the Bloody Code," the number of capital offenses in England had grown from only fifty in 1688 to over 220 in 1832 (Potter, *Hanging in Judgment*, 4). However, a great many of the new capital offenses dealt with highly specific crimes and were rarely prosecuted, and the vast majority of those executed in the eighteenth century were executed under very old common law or statutory offenses (see Beattie, *Crime and the Courts*, 513–14). In 1832, after growing pressure culminated in the Punishment of Death, etc., Act, the law was comprehensively reformed, and the number of capital crimes was reduced by two-thirds.

Boswell was attracted to executions, but he should not be taken as necessarily approving of them or of death as a punishment so indiscriminately applied. A list that Boswell made of the capital crimes of those who died at the Newgate executions he attended on Wednesday, June 1, 1785, includes:

1 *George Ward* ⎫ assaulting a woman in Wigmore Street
2 *Thomas Conner* ⎰ and taking a basket of linens.
3 *George Mawley*: escaping twice from hulks.
4 *Henry Wood*: robbing Humphry Stokes, highway, of metal watch.
5 *Thomas Bateman*: assaulting a woman, Fleet Street, and taking gold locket.
6 *Patrick Daley*: stealing bars of iron out of barge on Thames.
7 *Thomas Scott*: robbing W. Thompson, Whitechapel Road, of silver watch, etc.
8 *William Harding*: burglary in the house of Robert Snow, and taking silver plate.
9 *John Hughes*: attacking James Braverling on highway in City of London and taking haberdashery.
10 *James Haywood*: burglary in house of John Veal, Whitechapel, and stealing gold pap-spoon, six silver tea-spoons, punch-ladle, and wearing-apparel. (*Applause*, 304–5 n. 8)

Even as one retypes a list like this, and no doubt as Boswell noted it down, the specificity and indeed triviality of the detail seem to contrast with the profound and terrible fate suffered by each of these carefully named individuals. The attention that he gives to executions suggests an attitude on his part that to take these deaths seriously, to attend them and to attend *to* them, is part of what is simply due to anyone who dies. (It is also possible that he simply made the list because he considered writing an article about these executions but did not get around to doing so. A month before the last two texts in this chapter, there was an account of this execution among the paragraph news in the *Public Advertiser*, June 2, 1785; it confirms most of Boswell's details, but there is no evidence that it is from his hand.)

Boswell attended his first execution not in London, but in Edinburgh. As a schoolboy, he certainly would have seen, if not executions, then the processions attendant upon them. His school was on the route from the Tolbooth to the Grassmarket gallows (*Earlier Years*, 17–18). The first known time that Boswell actually attended a hanging is indicated by an undated entry in the scrapbook assembled under the title *Boswelliana*; he was in the company of his older friend, the actor James Love.[1]

> At an execution in the Grass Mercat, Boswell was observing that if you will consider it abstractly there is nothing terrible in it. "No doubt, sir," replied Mr. Love, "if you will abstract everything terrible that it has about it, nothing terrible will remain" (*Boswelliana*, 308)

Boswell's private papers contain evidence of his attending at least twenty-one public executions, of which the following is a chronological list, with some detail of his involvement and the source in his papers. No doubt others will be added when his papers are fully explored, and there will be others that are unrecorded.

1758–62, Edinburgh; in company of James Love, but no other details (*Boswelliana*, 308).

May 4, 1763, London. With "a sort of horrid eagerness," Boswell went to Tyburn for the execution of Paul Lewis, Hannah Diego, and John Rice. On a visit to Newgate the previous day, he had seen the condemned and much admired Lewis, a highwayman, whose fate disturbed his sleep for the three nights following the execution (*Lond. Journ.*, 251–52).

January 22, 1765, Turin, Italy. Just as Boswell set out for Milan, he left his chaise to join a crowd running to see the execution of a thief and watched from "close to the gallows" (*Grand Tour 2*, 43).

March 25, 1767, Edinburgh. Robert Hay, whom Boswell had defended on charges of robbery and assault, was found guilty and condemned. He was hanged, though it is unclear if Boswell attended; for a three-day period he omitted to keep his journal (*Search*, 27–28, 30, 56 and n.).

February 24, 1768, Edinburgh. John Raybould, forger, another of Boswell's clients; Boswell went to see him before his execution, more (as he admitted) to dispel his own "gloomy imagination" than to console Raybould (*Search*, 139). He remarked how little he was disturbed by witnessing this hanging (ibid., 141).

March 23, 1768, London. Boswell attended the execution at Tyburn of James Gibson, forger, and Benjamin Payne, highwayman, and wrote an account for the *Public Advertiser*; see the letter from "Mortalis," below. He admired Gibson's "easy and steady resolution," which he said exceeded that of any others he had seen in the same position or what he could have hoped for himself (*Search*, 151).

October 18, 1769, London. At Tyburn, he witnessed the execution of six men, including George Low; two days later he discussed the subject with Johnson and reported his own attendance in a paragraph in the *London Chronicle*, October 24 (*Search*, 343; *Life*, 2:93); see below.

---

1. James Caudle, who has studied the Boswelliana MS, estimates the date as between 1758 and 1762, from its position in the scrapbook (personal communication).

May 30, 1770, Edinburgh. Another of Boswell's clients, William Harris, was condemned for forgery. Boswell visited him the evening before the execution, which he attended, and afterward wrote that he "was much shocked and [was] still gloomy" (*Defence*, 8–9; *Corres. 1*, 261).

September 25, 1771, Edinburgh. On October 20, 1771, Boswell wrote to his friend John Johnston of having last seen him "at the foot of the gallows," which suggests that the two friends had attended the execution in the Grassmarket of a convicted robber, William Pickworth (*Corres. 1*, 273 and n. 1).

March 24, 1773, Edinburgh. Boswell had attended parts of the trial of Alexander Murdison and John Miller, sheep-stealers, and witnessed their hanging, with John Watson, a housebreaker, in the Grassmarket; he noted that the "Effect diminished as each one went" (*Defence*, 156).

March 2, 1774, Edinburgh. Boswell defended a young woman, Margaret Adam, who, with her younger sister Agnes, was tried for murder. He successfully moved for separate trials, and Agnes was later reprieved. He briefly notes, "At M.A.'s execution" (*Defence*, 208).

September 21, 1774, Edinburgh. The legal case with which Boswell had involved himself most deeply was that of John Reid, sheep-stealer, whom he had successfully defended in 1766. Boswell wrote accounts of Reid's arrest and trial, a broadside stating his case, a letter urging that he be pardoned, and an account of the execution, which he attended (*Defence*, 349–50); all these texts are in this chapter.

April 19, 1779, London. Boswell interested himself in the celebrated case of James Hackman, for the murder of Martha Ray. He wrote an account of the trial and a letter of reflections on Hackman's fate for the *St. James's Chronicle*, and other items (given in this chapter), and attended his execution (*Laird*, 93).

June 23, 1784, London. Boswell "witnessed the shocking sight of fifteen men executed before Newgate" and afterward visited Johnson (*Applause*, 249; *Life*, 4:328).

April 28, 1785, London. He arranged to attend the hanging at Newgate of nineteen men (*Applause*, 287–88).

June 1, 1785, London. He attended the execution of ten men at Newgate and made the list quoted above of the malefactors and their crimes (*Applause*, 304–5).

July 6, 1785, London. Boswell took Sir Joshua Reynolds to see the execution for arson of Peter Shaw, former servant of Edmund Burke, with four others, and wrote an account for the *Public Advertiser*, published as "Execution Intelligence" 1, below (*Applause*, 318).

August 16–17, 1785, London. He arranged to attend the execution of seven men and a woman, including the siblings Elizabeth and Martin Taylor, for burglary. Boswell talked to some of the condemned beforehand and wrote "Execution Intelligence" 2, below, for the *Public Advertiser* (*Applause*, 337–38).

April 19, 1790, London. He was at Newgate by 5 a.m. for the execution of Thomas Masters and Antonio Marini. He spoke to the prisoners (both convicted of murder) in the press-yard beforehand (*Great Biographer*, 47).

May 19, 1790, London. "I this morning saw three men hanged before Newgate" (*Great Biographer*, 51).

Despite the implied censure, noted above, of Boswell's desire to be present at these arguably grisly and certainly profoundly unmodern public occasions, his interest in the spectacle was a taste he shared with many people. Executions were well attended, no doubt from a variety of motives. But Boswell was also aware that it was not seemly to attend so many with such enthusiasm and that among the better-off and better-educated classes to attend executions was seen as rather vulgar or prurient. He was annoyed at his habit being publicized in *Love and Madness* and pointedly quotes Johnson's censure of the book for "mingling real facts with fiction" (*Life*, 4:187; see *Applause*, 98 n. 2).

In late 1783, the place of execution in London was shifted from the ancient Tyburn gallows, in order to do away with the traditional public procession. In the *Life of Johnson*, Boswell reported Johnson's complaining about this "innovation" and arguing that "executions are intended to draw spectators. If they do not draw spectators, they don't answer their purpose. The old method was most satisfactory to all parties; the publick was gratified by a procession; the criminal was supported by it."[2] Boswell comments, outside the diegesis, "I perfectly agree with Dr. Johnson upon this head, and am persuaded that executions now, the solemn procession being discontinued, have not nearly the effect which they formerly had" (1783; *Life*, 4:188–89).

Despite his approval of the actual spectacle, Boswell wrote (below, in the letter signed "Mortalis") about the "cruelty" of English law, and later, when defending John Reid, complained of "those lesser crimes which are at present capital by law in England, and by practice in Scotland." As a young man, he rationalized his execution-going as a training in both sympathy and (somewhat illogically) philosophical detachment; in his journal for March 23, 1768, he writes:

> It is a curious turn, but I never can resist seeing executions. The Abbé du Bos ingeniously shows that we have all a strong desire of having our passions moved, and the interesting scene of a man with death before his eyes cannot but move us greatly. One of weak nerves is overpowered by such spectacles. But by thinking and accustoming myself to them, I can see them quite firmly, though I feel compassion. (*Search*, 150)

He rewrote this passage to become part of the essay published the following month.

Ten years later, after the execution of James Hackman, with whose case he strongly involved himself in an extra-professional capacity, it seems that he decided to at-

---

2. As G. B. Hill notes, SJ's "real opinion" is more likely to be the more compassionate view we find in *Rambler*, no. 114, in which he powerfully argues for the futility and injustice of using capital punishment for crimes of robbery (*Life*, 4:188 n. 3).

tend no more executions and came to consider his interest in them as something of a weakness or, as we might say, an addiction. Two men were to be hanged in Edinburgh at the Grassmarket, but, he writes, "I resolved to avoid it, as it always makes me gloomy for some time after" (May 10, 1780; *Laird*, 211). A few months later he notes that he "shunned" an execution, but nevertheless felt "dreary at night, thinking of the execution" (Aug. 15, 1780; *Laird*, 391). But on both occasions he also admitted to feeling "a strange inclination to go and see the execution *as usual*" (my emphasis) and to "feeling an inclination to see it." He told Johnson, "I used to go much [to executions], but I've cured myself of it." But he was apparently only in remission, and when after five years he relapsed, he did so seriously. In June 1784, he was part of what the *Gentleman's Magazine* called "an amazing concourse of people" to witness fifteen malefactors suffer for their crimes (*Gent. Mag.* [June 1784], 474). The following year he attended at least four executions, on each occasion not simply joining the crowd but carefully planning to do so and making arrangements in the preceding days with the Newgate authorities to go behind the scenes and see the full execution ritual. In this way he saw at close quarters at least forty-two people meet their deaths.

As a young man, Boswell came across a letter (signed "T. L.") in the *London Chronicle*, July 23, 1768, opposing capital punishment; he merely marked it (in the margin of his file copy) "!" His "Mortalis" essay (below) had been published in the *Public Advertiser* only three months earlier. When in May 1783 he republished this essay as part of one of his essays as "The Hypochondriack," he prefaced it by purporting to consider "whether society has a right to punish individuals, especially to the extent of death"; but he actually proceeds in the essay to take it for granted that "we are sure society could not exist without such a right" (no. 68; Bailey, 2:276). He concluded that executions should be free of cruelty or terror, but that "death, simple death, when slowly and solemnly inflicted, will be fully sufficient to answer the purposes of publick punishment" (ibid., 284). But hanging was not, at the time, necessarily simple or free of cruelty and terror: before the mid-nineteenth century, when the standard drop was introduced, death from the short drop resulted not from breaking the neck but from strangulation and could take up to twenty minutes. As complex as Boswell's motives for his interest in executions may be, and as disturbing as it might be for a modern audience, a charitable view might be that Boswell's attention to the ends of these individuals is a recognition of the magnitude of what they are required to suffer. When he visited Johnson, after attending the multiple execution of June 23, 1784, he "said to him that I am sure that human life is not machinery, that is to say, a chain of fatality" (*Applause*, 249). He subjected himself to these events, despite the terror and gloom they often caused him, at least partly in an effort to confer upon each condemned individual something of the dignity always due to a fellow creature and to the unique and unrepeatable particularities of experience that constitute each of us.

1768

The Executions of Gibson and Payne

Public Advertiser, April 26, 1768, 2; with Boswell's MS alterations

To the Printer of the Public Advertiser.

SIR,

THAT the People of England possess that Quality called *Good-Nature*, will not be denied by any Man whose Judgment is free from Prejudice, and whose Fancy is not fretted by real Ills, or clouded by fanciful ones. But it must also be acknowledged, that the People of England are, of all Nations in the World, the most desirous of seeing Spectacles of Cruelty.[3] Bull-baiting, Cock-fighting, and even Throwing at Cocks, were for many and many a Year the Delight of the English; and it is not long since Assemblies of *good-natured* People were deliberately held to see their Fellow Creatures beat, bruise, and sometimes actually kill each other.[4]

Though this Desire of seeing Spectacles of Cruelty has peculiarly prevailed in England, it has more or less been the Passion of Mankind in all Ages and Countries; hence the various Satires against it by Poets; hence the various Attempts to account for it by Philosophers. Lucretius, who was both a Poet and a Philosopher, refers it to Self-Love, as we may see from that celebrated Passage *Suave*

---

3. The English (i.e., not the Scots) were known for their attraction to blood sports, which was often remarked upon by foreigners. Puritans objected to these recreations, mainly because they took place on holidays associated with Catholic festivals and often involved gambling and drink. Most of them were suppressed by the Cruelty to Animals Act of 1835 (see Malcolmson, *Popular Recreations*, 6–14, 118–38, 158–59). As a young man in London, JB recorded, on Dec. 14, 1762, that, having "resolved today to be a true-born Old Englishman," he "went at five o'clock to the Royal Cockpit in St. James's Park and saw cock-fighting for about five hours to fulfill the charge of cruelty." He was repelled by the spectacle: the cocks were "mangled and torn in a most cruel manner," and the gamblers were indifferent to their suffering (*Lond. Journ.*, 86–87).

4. In *bull-baiting*, a bull was tied to a stake in a ring or pit, and trained dogs set upon it. *Cock-fighting* involves pitting two or more specially bred and trained roosters (with spurs) against each other in a cockpit, where they would fight often to the death. In *throwing at cocks* (or cock-throwing or cock-shying) a rooster was tied to a post, and people took turns throwing *coksteles* (special weighted sticks) at the bird until it was knocked down or killed; this sport was played particularly at Shrove-tide. The sport of boxing emerged in England early in the eighteenth century, in the form of bare-knuckle boxing or prize-fighting. Broughton's rules for the regulation of the sport were introduced in 1743.

mari magno, &c.[5] He thinks that Men love to behold Scenes of Distress, that we may hug ourselves in Security, and relish more our own Safety and Ease, by comparing ourselves with those who are suffering. Though I, as well as every rational and virtuous Man, must think that Lucretius is in general a very false and a very hurtful Writer; yet I must candidly own, that he is often ingenious and just in his Observations. In the present Case, he certainly has a great deal of Merit; though I would be for compounding his System with that of the Abbe du Bos, who accounts for our Desire of seeing Spectacles of Cruelty from the universal Wish that we all have to be moved, that is to have our Souls agitated;[6] for to be sure there is nothing so irksome to a Man of any lively Sensations as to have his Faculties thrown into a kind of a Torpor, so that in Shakespeare's Words,

"They cream and mantle like a standing Pool."[7]

5. This passage, from Lucretius, *De Rerum Natura,* 2.1–4, beginning, "Suave, mari magno turbantibus aequora ventis," was something of a commonplace:

> How sweet it is, when high winds trouble a great sea,
> to view from land the danger of another;
> not that there is joy in another's suffering,
> but that it is sweet to perceive evils from which you are free yourself.

Baxter Hathaway notes that "From Hobbes to Addison the Lucretian principle had played a part of some importance in the analysis of the source of tragic pleasure" ("Lucretian 'Return upon Ourselves,'" 678). By here citing both Lucretius and DuBos, JB is engaging in an ongoing critical debate, one that is continued by Burke and Hume. Hathaway quotes and discusses this passage from the *Hypochondriack* text (686 ff.).

6. Jean-Baptiste DuBos (1670–1742), French priest, diplomat, and historian. His *Réflexions critiques sur la poésie et sur la peinture* (1719) is described as "a potent force in literary criticism throughout Europe during most of the eighteenth century" (Hathaway, "Lucretian 'Return upon Ourselves,'" 680). DuBos gives public executions as an important instance of man's need not for serenity but activity: "That natural emotion, which rises, as it were, mechanically within us, upon seeing our fellow creatures in any great misfortune or danger, hath no other attractive, but that of being a passion, the motions whereof rouse and occupy the soul; nevertheless, this very emotion has charms capable of rendering it desirable, notwithstanding all the gloomy and importunate ideas that attend it. . . . We see crowds of people flock to one of the most frightful spectacles, that human nature can behold, that is, the public execution of a man upon a scaffold, where he undergoes the most exquisite torments inflicted by the law: . . . the groans of one's fellow creature, will make so deep and so forcible an impression, as not to be easily effaced; but the attractive of the emotion on those occasions, carries a greater weight with it than all the reflections and advice of experience" (*Critical Reflections,* 1:10). In the *Life,* 2:103, JB gives SJ's praise of the book.

7. *Merchant of Venice,* 1.1.89: "There are a sort of men whose visages / Do cream and mantle like a standing pond" (said by Gratiano).

This will more fully account for what I am endeavouring to explain, and will make Human Nature appear not so grossly selfish as Lucretius paints it.

Of all public Spectacles, that of a capital Execution draws the greatest Number of Spectators; and I must confess that I myself am never absent from any of them: Nor can I accuse myself of being more hard-hearted than other People. On the contrary, I am persuaded that nobody feels more sincerely for the Distresses of his Fellow Creatures than I do; or would do more to relieve them. When I first attended Executions, I was shocked to the greatest Degree: I was in a manner convulsed with Pity and Terror; and for several Days, but especially Nights after, I was in a very dismal Situation.[8] Still, however, I persisted in attending them, and by Degrees my Sensibility abated; so that I can now see one with great Composure, and my Mind is not afterwards haunted with frightful Thoughts, though for a-while a certain Degree of Gloom remains upon it. I can account for this Curiosity in a Philosophical Manner, when I consider that Death is the most awful Object before every Man, who directs his Thoughts seriously towards Futurity; and that it is very natural that we should be anxious to see People in that Situation which affects us all so much.[9] It is true indeed that none of us who go to see an Execution have any Idea that we are to be executed; and few of us need be under any Apprehension whatever of meeting with that Fate: But dying publicly at Tyburn, and dying privately in one's Bed, are only different Modes of the same Thing. They are both Death; they are both that wonderous, that alarming Scene of quitting all that we have ever seen, heard and known, and at once passing into a State of being totally unknown to us, and in which we cannot tell what may be our Situation: Therefore it is that I feel an irresistible Impulse to be present at every Execution, as I there behold the various Effects of the near Approach of Death, according to the various Tempers of the unhappy Sufferers; and by studying them, I learn to quiet and fortify my own Mind. I shall never forget the last Execution I saw at Tyburn, when Mr. Gibson, the Attorney, for Forgery, and Benjamin Payne for an Highway Robbery, were executed.[10] Poor Payne was a thin young Lad of Twenty, in a mean Dress, and a red Nightcap, with nothing

8. JB attended his first London execution on May 4, 1763, and describes his reactions in his *Lond. Journ.*: "I was most terribly shocked, and thrown into a very deep melancholy" (252). He spent the next three nights staying with friends, because he was "so haunted with frightful imaginations that I durst not lie by myself" (ibid., 254).

9. Gatrell contends that the "philosophical manner" in which JB purported to regard hangings illustrates that by the mid-eighteenth century curiosity was no longer a sufficient reason for genteel people to attend public executions (*Hanging Tree*, 251).

10. In his journal, JB recorded attending the executions of Payne and Gibson on the morning of Wednesday, Mar. 23 (*Search*, 150–51); that account formed the basis for this essay. Payne was tried on Feb. 24, 1768, on two counts each of theft with violence and highway

to discriminate him from the many miserable Beings, who are penitent and half dead with Fear. But Mr. Gibson was indeed an extraordinary Man.[11] He came from Newgate in a Coach, with some Friends attending him. I met the mournful Procession in Oxford-Road, and I declare that if I had not been told it, I should not have known which was Mr. Gibson. He was drawn backwards, and looked as calm and easy as ever I saw a Man in my Life. He was dressed in a full Suit of Black, wore his own Hair round and in a natural Curl, and a Hat. When he came to the Place of Execution, he was allowed to remain a little in the Coach. A Signal was then given him that it was Time to approach the fatal Tree. He took Leave of his Friends, stepped out of the Coach, and walked firmly to the Cart. He was helped upon it, as he was pinioned, and had not the free Use of his Arms. When he was upon the Cart, he [put on a white nightcap, &] gave his Hat to the Executioner, who immediately took off Mr. Gibson's Cravat, unloosed his Shirt Neck, and fixed the Rope. Mr. Gibson never once altered his Countenance. He refreshed his Mouth by sucking a sweet Orange. He shewed no stupid Insensibility; nor did he affect to brave it out like those hardened Wretches, who boast that they die hard. He appeared to all the Spectators a Man of Sense and Reflection, of a Mind naturally sedate and placid. He submitted with a manly and decent Resolution to what he knew to be the just Punishment of the Law.— [It was said that his Forgery was only a temporary expedient to stave off his credit, & that he meant no fraud in the end. This might make his mind easier though he was sensible that he suffered justly as the Law must judge by external acts.] Mr. Moore, the Ordinary of Newgate, discharged his Duty with much Earnestness, and a Fervor, for which I and all around me esteemed and loved him.[12] Mr. Moore seems worthy of his Office, which, when justly considered, is a very important one; if administering Divine Comfort to Multitudes of miserable Souls be important.—Poor Payne seemed to rely on that Mercy, which I trust has not been refused him.—Mr. Gibson seemed truly devout, and in short, from

robbery. He was found guilty and sentenced to death (Proceedings of the Old Bailey, Ref: t17680224–9).

11. James Gibson was tried on Jan. 16, 1766, for deception and forgery, and found guilty (Proceedings of the Old Bailey, Ref: t17660116–32). He was sentenced to death on Feb. 24, 1768 (ibid., Ref: 017680224–1). His case was described in a 1780 edition of the popular compilation of gallows stories, the *Newgate Calendar*. As a clerk to an attorney, Gibson was a gentleman and naturally attracts more of JB's interest and sympathy.

12. The ordinary—i.e., chaplain to Newgate—was at this time Rev. John Moore, who held the position from 1764 until his death in 1769. It was not the most attractive of ecclesiastical appointments, and ordinaries were held in some disrepute, in part due to the practice of supplementing their stipends by writing accounts of famous felons. JB, however, also spoke well of Moore's long-serving successor, Rev. John Villette (see *Life*, 4:329 and n. 3). See Linebaugh, "Ordinary of Newgate," 249.

first to last his Behaviour was the most perfect that I ever saw, or indeed could conceive of one in his unhappy Circumstances.——I wish, Sir, I may not have detained you too long, with a Letter on Subjects of a serious, but I will not say of a gloomy Cast, because from my Manner of viewing them, I do say that they become Matters of curious Speculation, and are relieved of their dreary Ideas.

I am, SIR,

Your constant Reader,

MORTALIS.

1769

Curious Mr. Boswell on Top of a Hearse at Tyburn

London Chronicle, October 21–24, 1769, 400 (postscript)

As a strong instance of strange curiosity, James Boswell, Esq; was observed last Wednesday at Tyburn, when six men were executed;[13] and in order to be as near as possible, where did he sit, but on the top of the hearse which waited to carry away the body of George Low, one of the malefactors.[14] *A man so various*, &c.[15]

Verses on Seeing Mr. Boswell on the Top of an Hearse at Tyburn

London Chronicle, October 24–26, 1769, 403

Verses on seeing Mr. BOSWELL *on the Top of an Hearse at* Tyburn; *by the Author of the Verses on seeing his Print in the* Corsican *Dress*[16]

13. This was Wednesday, Oct. 18, 1769. JB made no journal entry that day, but discussed the execution with SJ the day after (see *Search*, 343; also *Life*, 2:93).

14. George Low was sentenced at the Old Bailey on Sept. 6, 1769, for stealing money and goods from a peddler on Aug. 7. See Proceedings of the Old Bailey, Ref: t17690906–104.

15. John Dryden, *Absalom and Achitophel* (1681), lines 545–50; describing Zimri, who in the poem represents George Villiers, second duke of Buckingham:

> A man so various, that he seem'd to be
> Not one, but all Mankind's Epitome.
> Stiff in opinions, always in the wrong;
> Was Every thing by starts, and Nothing long:
> But, in the course of one revolving Moon,
> Was Chymist, Fidler, States-man, and Buffoon.

16. For the text of these anonymous verses by JB, published in the *Lond. Chron.* a few weeks before (Oct. 7, 1769), see Chap. 1, pp. 33–34.

WHAT! *Black* and all *Black*,[17] are you here,
    Again to rouse my verse?
The Moorish head's,[18] too pale, you fear;
    So now you try an hearse.[19]

Believe me, Sir, such swarthy sights
    May breeding females move;
And by and by our race of whites
    May arrant *tawnies* prove.[20]

For foreign service to suborn
    Is British laws to shock-O.
But you most sly—before they're born,
    List subjects for *Morocco*.[21]

1774

THE CASE OF JOHN REID

[Of the legal cases in which Boswell was professionally employed, that which most deeply engaged his sympathies was the case of John Reid, who was tried for his life in Edinburgh in 1774. Seven years earlier, in 1766, Reid had been Bos—well's first client in a criminal case; he was charged then with sheep-stealing, and Boswell successfully defended him, persuading the jury against the evidence—and the clear expectation of the judges. In early 1774, Reid was arrested again, on a similar charge. He was accused of having, in October 1773, either stolen or know-ingly received and sold nineteen sheep. When he first found he was suspected of the crime, he fled to England. He was arrested in March 1774 when he returned to his home. Boswell again took his case, assisted by Michael Nasmith as agent

17. This refers to both JB's clothing—the black of the Corsican dress, a dark coat, and black spatterdashes and cap/bonnet—and his swarthy complexion, which he frequently mentions as a matter of his own curious interest (see *Earlier Years*, 434, 463).

18. The heraldic flag of Corsica, featuring a black Saracen's head on a white field, was sewn as a crest on the breast of JB's coat; it is still used today by Corsican separatists.

19. Hearses were traditionally black vehicles.

20. *Tawnies*: brown-skinned people; "tawny-moor"—as in the later *Morocco*—was a name given to the tawny or brown-skinned natives of northern Africa (*OED*).

21. The poem implies that by this public appearance JB would attract the ladies and thus—being "swarthy" himself—engender upon them children of Moorish aspect, who could in turn become soldiers for foreign service.

(solicitor).[22] On this occasion, the defense was weak, and the court implacable. Perhaps unwisely, Boswell insisted on basing part of his case for the defense upon revealing the prejudices of the bench, arising from Reid's earlier prosecution and acquittal (see n. 24).

After the trial, verdict, and sentence, Boswell campaigned in the press and through petitions to various authorities for a reprieve or pardon for Reid or for the commutation of the sentence to transportation. When all such avenues were exhausted, Boswell arranged for Reid's portrait to be painted (*Defence*, 296–97), attended him at his execution, and even briefly considered a plan, later abandoned, for his resuscitation (ibid., 304–5).]

John Reid Brought to Edinburgh

Caledonian Mercury, January 12, 1774, [2]

Last night was brought to town under a strong guard, and committed to prison, on a new accusation of sheep-stealing, the noted John Reid,[23] whose trial before the High Court of Justiciary in the year 1767 made so much noise,[24] and was afterwards made the subject of distinguished attention[25] in the great Douglas cause.[26]

22. Michael Nasmith (d. 1777), W.S.—i.e., Writer to the Signet (i.e., a solicitor with certain authority derived from the Scottish royal courts)—was engaged at JB's particular request (*Defence*, 247–48).

23. Reid (1725–74), a drover and flesher (butcher) who lived at Hillend, near Falkirk, Stirlingshire, about twenty miles west of Edinburgh, was charged with having, in Oct. 1773, stolen nineteen sheep from Alexander Gray, at Lyne in Peeblesshire, about thirty miles from Hillend.

24. In Sept. 1766 (not 1767), Reid became JB's first criminal client. On Dec. 15, 1766, JB defended him, successfully and against the evidence, on a charge of stealing 120 sheep (*Earlier Years*, 299, 308–9).

25. This "distinguished attention" would have stuck in the minds of few other than JB. The Lord Justice Clerk, Thomas Miller, Lord Glenlee (1731–1804), who (like other judges) had been severely disconcerted by JB's triumph in the first Reid case, had "shortly after, when delivering his opinion in the Douglas Cause, indulged in an *obiter dictum* attacking Reid's acquittal" (*Later Years*, 97). He was reported as having said: "We have indeed seen cases where there was a moral impossibility of the prisoner's innocence, and yet we have seen juries acquit such a one. Such a case was that of Reid, who was lately tried before the Criminal Court. A council [*sic*] at that bar, who likes to distinguish himself upon such occasions, patronized the prisoner's defence and notwithstanding the clearest and most positive evidence. . . . The jury acquitted the prisoner" (quoted in Ramsay, "Boswell's First Criminal Case," 316).

26. For the Douglas Cause, see Chap. 1, headnote to "The Shorthand Reporters." JB usually referred to the case as "the great Douglas Cause."

The Trial of John Reid

Edinburgh Advertiser, July 29–August 2, 1774, 77

Yesterday morning at eight o'clock, came on before the High Court of Justiciary here, the trial of John Reid butcher at Hillend, in Stirlingshire, accused of sheep stealing, or for receiving sheep knowing them to be stolen. After pleadings on the relevancy, the court found the libel relevant, if proved, to inflict the highest punishment.[27] The jury were then sworn in, and the witnesses both for and against the prisoner examined, which continued till about three o'clock, when the Lord Advocate summed up the evidence very ably against the prisoner,[28] as did Mr. James Boswell on the other side, in a very masterly and pathetic manner, which did him great honour both as a lawyer, and as one who wished for a free and impartial trial by jury. The jury were enclosed about five o'clock, and this day at two returned their verdict all in one voice, finding the pannel *guilty* of the theft libelled.[29] Mr. Boswell moved the court to delay pronouncing sentence for a few days, as he would endeavour to show, that a capital punishment should not be inflicted. The court unanimously over-ruled this motion, and sentenced Reid to be executed in the Grass-market, on the 7th of September next.

The Mournful Case of Poor Misfortunate and Unhappy John Reid

[After the trial (August 1) and verdict of guilty, a sentence of death was unanimously agreed by the judges (see *Defence*, 268). Boswell immediately set about pursuing as many judicial and extra-judicial avenues as he could think of to keep Reid from the gallows. On September 2, he was notified that Reid had been granted a respite of fourteen days (ibid., 306). On September 7, as he writes, "a curious thought struck me that I would write the case of John Reid as if dictated by himself on this the day fixed for his execution. I accordingly did it, and hit off very well the thoughts and style of what such a case would have been." It was printed as a single-sided broadsheet, "that it might be hawked about the streets this very night" (ibid., 319–20).]

27. In Scots legal terminology, a *libel* is the part of an indictment that states the grounds for a prosecution. *Relevancy* refers to the correctness of the indictment in a criminal action.

28. The Lord Advocate of Scotland, 1766–75, was James William Montgomery (1721–1803), Member of Parliament, 1766–74.

29. The *panel* (usual spelling) is the accused in a criminal action. *Libel*, as a verb, is to institute criminal proceedings by filing a libel.

Figure 5. Edinburgh Tolbooth Jail. "Heart of Midlothian: Taken Down 1817," Daniel
Wilson, Memorials of Edinburgh in the Olden Time (Edinburgh, 1848), 1: facing p. 71.
Courtesy of the University of Otago Library, Special Collections, Dunedin, New Zealand.

Broadsheet (folio half-sheet), printed Edinburgh, Saturday, September 10, 1774

THE MOURNFUL CASE OF POOR MISFORTUNATE AND UNHAPPY
JOHN REID, Now lying under sentence of death in the Tolbooth of Edinburgh,[30]
taken from his own mouth on Wednesday night,[31] *the 7th of September 1774,*
being the day fixed for his execution

30. Reid's trial took place on Monday, Aug. 1, 1774. As full an account of the trial as
can be constructed, from JB's trial papers and other contemporary documents, is given
in *Defence*, 249–64. The jury brought in a guilty verdict, and the sentence of death was
pronounced the following day, to be carried out on Wednesday, Sept. 7 (ibid., 267). The old
Edinburgh Tolbooth was built c. 1590, in the Lawnmarket west of St. Giles' Church, in
what was said to be a Franco-Scottish style (see Figure 5). Having ceased to be used for its
original purpose, it was used in JB's day as a prison. It was demolished in 1817, and its site is
marked by brass plates in Parliament Square.

31. JB noted that the words "taken from his own mouth" were "a lie" and were added
by "old Robertson," the father of John Robertson, the printer; JB was told that Reid was
angry about this (*Defence*, 332). For comments on this and the document in general, see

This is the very day on which I was doomed to die; and had it not been for the mercy of our most gracious Sovereign,[32] whom GOD long bless and preserve, I should by this time have been a miserable spectacle, and my last speech crying dolefully through the streets of this city.[33] O! listen then unto me, while I am yet in the land of the living, and think that it is my GHOST speaking unto you!

Much cry has been made against me by small and great.[34] And how can a poor man like me withstand it? But before I go hence and be no more, I trust you will hear the words of truth, and peradventure your minds may be changed.

I am condemned because some of these sheep were found in my flesh-house and I could not bring downright probation of him from whom I came by them.[35] But I say now, as I told my lawyer, who said it unto the Lords and will say unto the end, that William Gardner, and none else, was the man, and he is now a transported thief,[36] though he was loose when I was seized and caused him for

---

Rawlings, *Drunks, Whores, and Idle Apprentices*, 6, 8; and Ramsay, "Boswell's First Criminal Case."

32. Reid's wife Janet (Clarke) Reid asked JB to petition the king on his behalf. Although JB told Reid that he thought this "would have no effect" (*Defence*, 276), on Aug. 20 JB sent a petition with a covering note to Henry Herbert, tenth earl of Pembroke, who was at the time a lord of the bedchamber to George III (ibid., 289–90). A fourteen-day respite was granted Aug. 26, and JB was notified about it on Sept. 2 (ibid., 306 and n. 1).

33. "Last speeches" or "gallows speeches" were often published as broadsides or pamphlets, and sold by peddlers at executions, not unlike theatrical programs. JB noted that the plan for this text was that it be "printed and cried, to conciliate the lower populace" (*Defence*, 332). In most cases, such "last speeches" were not written or even dictated by their subjects; they would usually satisfy public curiosity with a description of the offenses of the criminal and, unlike this text, satisfy moral authority with a confession of guilt. See Gatrell, *Hanging Tree*, chap. 5.

34. Another provocative allusion to Lord Justice Clerk Miller. JB and Michael Nasmith continued to think that the judges were prejudiced against Reid on account of the earlier case and that by their having "taken some striking liberties with poor John's character . . . all mankind were authorized by the Court to hold him guilty" (Michael Nasmith to JB, Sept. 6; *Defence*, 316).

35. *Flesh-house*: (obsolete) a place where meat is killed or sold; a butcher's shop; shambles (*OED*).

36. In the "declaration" read at his trial, Reid declared that the sheep found hanging in his flesh-house and others pastured near his house, which he was accused of having stolen, had been brought to him by William Gardner, a cattle dealer (*Defence*, 259). Gardner and Reid were fellow tenants of Reid's neighbor, William Black, and Gardner lived "within thirty yards of John" (ibid., 311). Gardner was at this time himself in prison at Stirling, under sentence of transportation for stealing from a shop. JB did not introduce Gardner at the trial, for fear Reid would end up convicted of "reset [i.e., receipt] of theft" (i.e., receiv-

to be taen,[37] that he might answer therefor and I not be the sufferer. John Brown the messenger in Linlithgow can attest this; and many an honest man has no witnesses present when he receives goods.[38] But I see that my being tried two times before, though cleared by juries, many of whom, now alive, can bear testimony for me, has made me be thought guilty at all events.[39]

I hope none of you shall by malicious report of enemies be brought to trial, since it is all one whatever is the fate thereof.

What will you say when Gardner's conscience smites him in America and he owns that I got the sheep honestly from him, and I am gone and cannot be recalled?[40]

May all good Christians, then, charitably pray that as the King's heart is in the hand of the Lord, and he turneth it whithersoever he will,[41] it may please him to save me from an ignominious death, which can do harm to no man.

A Pardon Urged for John Reid, Condemned to Be Hanged for Sheep-Stealing

London Chronicle, September 17–20, 1774, 276

To the PRINTER of the LONDON CHRONICLE.

Edinburgh, Sept. 13.

SIR,

The rigour of our present penal laws has been long the subject of complaint. It is to be hoped that the Legislature will at last see fit to relax it.[42] In the mean time, the utmost care should be taken, that there should at least be full evidence

---

ing stolen goods), but after the trial took steps to contact him. A Writer to the Signet at Stirling, acting at JB's request, asked Gardner if he "had given or sold Reid any sheep, and he declares to me he never did" (ibid., 275). Reid steadfastly stuck to his story.

37. *Taen*: taken. One of JB's slight attempts to make this sound as if it is the voice of Reid himself.

38. John Brown was the "messenger" or agent of the court who arrested Reid and, at the same time, arrested Gardner on his separate matter (*Defence*, 311, 318).

39. As well as the trial in 1766 at which JB previously defended him, Reid had also been tried at Glasgow in 1753 for stealing two cows and acquitted (*Defence*, 298).

40. JB notes, "Nasmith suggested the idea of Gardner confessing in America" (*Defence*, 320).

41. "The King's heart is in the hand of the Lord . . . and he turneth it whithersoever he will" (Proverbs 21:1, *AV*).

42. JB sent this letter to the papers when other avenues of appeal had been exhausted. He hoped that it might be seen by someone of power and influence (hence, the signature, "a Royalist"); but it was in fact sent too late and "did not appear until the evening of the

against an unhappy man before he is dragged to a violent death, for theft, or any of those lesser crimes which are at present capital by law in England, and by practice in Scotland.[43] We have at present in this city a remarkable man lying under sentence of death, being convicted of the theft of a few sheep. His name is John Reid. He is remarkable, because he was formerly tried and acquitted by a very worthy Jury, notwithstanding which some persons in high office publicly represented him as guilty. In particular one great man of the law exclaimed against him, in his speech in the great Douglas cause. This is a striking specimen of what goes on in this narrow country.[44] A strong prejudice was raised against him, and now he was condemned upon circumstantial evidence, which several impartial Gentlemen of very good skill were of opinion was inconclusive. He has uniformly affirmed that although the sheep were found in his possession, he had obtained them by a fair and honest bargain from another man. His case is very much similar to that of Madan, who was lately in the cart at Tyburn just going to be turned off, as guilty of a robbery, upon circumstantial evidence, when Merrit appeared and confessed that he was the man who had committed the crime.[45] But the man from whom Reid got the sheep has not as yet been so conscientious as Merrit. He has maintained an obstinate denial; but having been transported for housebreaking, he will probably confess in America.

A respite for fourteen days was sent to Reid from the office of Lord Rochford, from whence Madan's respite also was sent.[46] But, according to my information, an opinion from Scotland was desired upon the case: an opinion from that very

---

day before the execution, when not even the King himself could have got a pardon to Edinburgh in time" (*Ominous Years*, xv).

43. This is awkward, unless JB means the reverse of what he says—i.e., "by law in Scotland and by practice in England": England had many more penal statutes than Scotland, and Scots law was less severe in terms of capital punishment (John Finlay, personal communication).

44. The disparagement of the Lord Justice Clerk, Thomas Miller, here and in the paragraph following, led to JB's being challenged to a duel by the judge's nineteen-year-old son, William Miller (1755–1846). From Oct. 6 to 18, JB and his wife were much agitated by this; under advice, JB wrote a letter to young Miller, and the matter was settled without fatality (see *Ominous Years*, 11–25).

45. "Amos Merritt came forward at Tyburn on 19 August 1774 and declared that he himself had committed the crime of highway robbery for which Patrick Madan was about to be hanged. Madan was reprieved and later pardoned; he was present to bid farewell to Merritt when the latter was hanged for another crime on 10 January 1775" (*Defence*, 293 n. 2). (When Merritt was tried on Sept. 7 for the earlier crime, he was acquitted; Proceedings of the Old Bailey, Ref: t17740907–62.)

46. William Henry Zuylestein, fourth earl of Rochford (1717–81), at this time a secretary of state and member of North's cabinet, signed the respite for Reid (*Defence*, 306 n. 1).

man who exclaimed in the Civil Court against a man acquitted by a Jury in the Criminal Court, when his life was staked upon the issue.[47]

The determination of the Sovereign is expected here with anxiety. I wish to avoid strong expressions. I would turn my mind only towards mercy. This will reach you on Saturday. It is intreated that you may insert it directly; as it may perhaps have influence in some manner that we cannot exactly foresee, and an express with a pardon, or with another respite till there can be time to hear from America, will prevent what I am afraid would have a wretched appearance in the annals of this country. I am, Sir,

Your constant Reader,
A ROYALIST.

Death of John Reid

London Chronicle, September 24–27, 1774, 302

This day John Reid, for sheep stealing, was executed in the Grass-market, the respite which his Majesty was pleased to grant being expired.[48] This unfortunate man all along denied his being guilty of the theft for which he was condemned upon circumstantiate evidence.[49] He uniformly persisted in averring, that of the crime laid to his charge he was totally innocent, having got the sheep without suspicion from one William Gardner, who was afterwards convicted of house-breaking, and is now transported.[50] When upon the ladder, with the rope about his neck, just as he was turning over, and dropping into eternity, his last words were, "Mine is an unjust sentence."[51]

47. *That very man*: i.e., Lord Justice Clerk Miller. In fact, as JB was later informed, the respite from Lord Rochford was conveyed via the Lord Justice Clerk, who had the option to deliver it or not (*Defence*, 306 n. 1).

48. This paragraph was probably sent to London as an interim measure, while JB was preparing the longer piece (following) for local publication, which appeared in London a few days later. Reid was executed on the afternoon of Wednesday, Sept. 21. JB's account is given in *Defence*, 343–52.

49. Note the word *circumstantiate*, which *SJ Dict.* gives only as a verb, "to place in particular circumstances"; *OED* has *circumstantiate*, adj. = *circumstantiated*, adj. (now chiefly Scots). This unusual word is used also in the article following.

50. JB records that Reid "persisted in denying the theft for which he was condemned," despite JB pressing him on the issue a number of times that very day (*Defence*, 345).

51. "Just as he was going off, he made an attempt to speak. Somebody on the scaffold called, 'Pull up his cap [i.e., the hood covering his face].' The executioner did so. He then said, 'Take warning. Mine is an unjust sentence.' Then his cap was pulled down and he went

Account of the Execution of John Reid

[Immediately after Reid's execution, Boswell and Michael Nasmith "agreed that a recent account would make a strong impression" and notified the papers that "there would be a paragraph tonight giving an account of the execution." Boswell wrote the paragraph over dinner and "made two copies of it, and, both to the printer of *The Courant* and *Mercury*, subjoined my name to be kept as the authority" (*Defence*, 350). He also arranged for it to be republished, with introductory and concluding paragraphs added, in the *London Chronicle*, which for the sake of the extra paragraphs is the text used here.]

London Chronicle, September 27–29, 1774, 311

Extract of a Letter from Edinburgh, Sept. 23.

"THE execution of John Reid, in this place, on Wednesday last, for the alleged crime of sheep-stealing, has made more noise than any thing that has happened of a long time in Scotland. The uncommon rigour of an execution after respite, for a single act of theft, must have been owing to some extraordinary cause, which time will discover.[52] But the case is more deplorable, when it is considered that, according to all human probability, now that with his latest breath he hath given an awful testimony, [he] suffered wrongfully. The following account of him appeared in all our Newspapers:

'This day John Reid was executed in the Grass-market, the respite which his Majesty was pleased to grant being expired. We have good authority to assure the Public, that this unfortunate man all along denied his being guilty of the theft for which he was condemned upon circumstantiate evidence. The utmost pains were taken to obtain the whole truth from him; and he uniformly persisted in averring, that of the crime now laid to his charge he was totally innocent, having got the sheep without suspicion from one William Gardner, who was afterwards taken up, convicted of house-breaking, and is now transported. This forenoon, in particular, every effort was used to make him confess if he really was guilty: He was again and again told, in the most solemn manner, that he could not hope for mercy, if he went into the other world with a lie in his mouth; but he still declared his innocence, while, at the same time, he was,

---

off. . . . To me it sounded as if he said, 'just sentence'; and the people were divided, some crying, 'He says his sentence is *just.*' Some: 'No. He says *unjust.*' Mr. Laing, clerk to Mr. Tait, one of the town clerks, put me out of doubt, by telling me he had asked the executioner, who said it was *unjust*" (*Defence*, 349; see also xviii).

52. The "extraordinary cause" to which JB is alluding was the alleged prejudice of the Bench.

to all appearance, most sincere and fervent in his devotions, and in penitence for the sins which he acknowledged. He walked to the place of execution decently dressed in white linen cloaths with black ribbands;[53] and was attended by the Rev. Doctors M'Queen and Dick of this city.[54] His calmness and resignation were remarkable when upon the scaffold, where he again adhered to what he had formerly said. When upon the ladder, with the rope about his neck, just as he was turning over, and dropping into eternity, his last words were, "Mine is an unjust sentence."

There was last night a meeting of the Jury, who brought in the fatal verdict against him. What was the result of their serious deliberations, may perhaps be laid before the Public."'[55]

1779

THE HACKMAN CASE

[On the evening of Wednesday, April 7, 1779, the Covent Garden Theatre emptied at around 11:15 p.m., after a performance of the comic opera *Love in a Village*. As they were about to get into a carriage, two women in the crowd were accosted by a young man who stepped into the street from a nearby coffeehouse. Brandishing a pistol, he shot one of the women in the head; she died instantly. He then pulled out a second pistol and attempted to shoot himself, but this second shot only grazed his brow; he collapsed to the ground, "beating himself about the head [with his pistol], endeavouring to kill himself and crying, 'Oh! kill me, kill me! for God's sake, kill me!'" (*London Evening Post*, Apr. 8–10, 1779). He was arrested immediately after the shooting and put up no resistance.

Crimes of passion were and are common enough, but the character and connections of all involved in this case made it sensational from the start. The murdered woman, Martha Ray, was a talented singer, but she was better known as the long-

---

53. Talking with JB on Aug. 31, 1774, Reid "said his wife was resolved that he should die in white; that it was the custom in his part of the country to dress the dead body in linen, and she thought it would cost no more to do it when he was alive" (*Defence*, 302). Gatrell cites this passage as an example of the concern of felons, and their families, for "the body's integrity" (*Hanging Tree*, 86–87).

54. Rev. Daniel Macqueen, an Edinburgh minister (*Defence*, 288), and Rev. Robert Dick both attended Reid at his execution (ibid., 347–49). JB says that they both told him they believed Reid to be not guilty (ibid., 339–40, 344). JB dined with them both the following Wednesday (Sept. 28; *Ominous Years*, 7), and again on Oct. 3 (ibid., 10).

55. It may be that JB hoped to prepare an account of the jury deliberations himself; in any case, no such account has been reported.

term mistress of a senior political figure, John Montagu, fourth earl of Sandwich; her murderer, James Hackman, was a twenty-six-year-old former soldier who had been ordained as a clergyman only weeks before. Hackman had met Ray four years earlier, when he was invited by Lord Sandwich to his country seat while on regimental business in Huntingdon. Sandwich was serving in his third stint as the First Lord of the Admiralty and was admired (if also distrusted) for being well educated, skillful, and hard-working; he was also a patron of music. Martha Ray, at thirty-five or so, had been his mistress for eighteen years and had borne him nine children, of whom five had survived.

Hackman was a handsome young man of otherwise impeccable character; it is possible that Ray, concerned perhaps at the lack of security in her position, had at one stage thought of leaving Sandwich in order to marry him—or else to pursue a career as an opera singer. In any case, whatever relationship there may have been between them had apparently cooled off, on her side, but Hackman had become besotted with her. A few days before the shooting, he had received a letter from her, asking him to abandon "his pursuit"—though, in a statement negotiated between his and Sandwich's lawyers, he claimed not to have spoken to her since the beginning of 1776. Hackman claimed that on the night of the shooting he had followed Ray to the theater intending only that she witness his suicide and that he killed her in "a momentary phrensy"; indeed, the suicide note found on him instructed his brother-in-law to care for her, if in some way he could. Nevertheless, Hackman intended at first to plead guilty; but, before the trial began on April 16, he was persuaded by his lawyer and family "to avail himself of the plausible plea of temporary insanity" (*Morning Post*, Apr. 12, 1779, quoted in Brewer, *Sentimental Murder*, 27).

Like most of fashionable London, Boswell was fascinated by the proceedings. In the nine days between the murder and the trial, he visited various people connected with the principals, including Hackman's brother-in-law, Frederick Booth, to satisfy his thirst for information and arranged (among other things) to attend the trial. He was to travel to court with Henry Howarth, one of the prosecuting lawyers, but the coach was full, so he took a hackney. At the door of the court, he spoke with Booth, who did not attend the proceedings. The courtroom was packed for the trial, with many people wanting to be close to this scene of passion and tragedy, including Boswell, who sat at the defending counsel's table.

The case has inspired book-length treatments, of varying degrees of reliability; see Dawes, *Case and Memoirs of James Hackman*; Croft, *Love and Madness*; Levy, *Love and Madness*; and Brewer, *Sentimental Murder*. The notes below as to the facts of the case are taken from the quasi-official Proceedings of the Old Bailey.]

Hackman's Trial for Murder, and His Speech to the Court

[After the trial—and as he recorded in his journal for April 16 (*Laird*, 85–86)—Boswell called on Woodfall, the printer of the *Public Advertiser*, to offer him an account but found that one had already been commissioned, from "a blackguard being"

Figure 6. "The Rev'd James Hackman: From the Original Drawing by Mr. Dighton,"
mezzotint, by R. Laurie (May 18, 1779). © Trustees of the British Museum.
Figure 7. "Miss [Martha] Ray: Engraved from the Original Picture [by Nathaniel Dance,
1777]," engraving by Valentine Green (May 1779). © Trustees of the British Museum.

(possibly George Steevens). He sought out Booth and gave him an account of the trial (as is related in the third item following). He returned to the rooms he was leasing in the town house of the bookseller Charles Dilly and "wrote paragraphs and [a] letter about [the trial]"—that is, the news reports following and the "Reflections"—then called successively on Henry Baldwin and Nathaniel Thomas, who ran the *St. James's Chronicle*. After going to a meeting of the Club and giving news of the trial, he again called on Thomas "about the letter concerning Hackman" (ibid., 86).]

St. James's Chronicle, April 15–17, 1779, 3

Yesterday Morning came on at the Old Bailey, the Tryal of the Rev. Mr. Hackman, for the wilful Murther of Miss Ray.[56] The Culprit pleading not guilty to the Indictment, several Witnesses were examined to prove the Mur-

56. James Hackman (1752?–79); Martha Ray (1742?–79); see Figures 6 and 7. The trial at the Old Bailey began at 9:30 a.m. on Friday, Apr. 16; see Proceedings of the Old Bailey, Ref: t17790404-3.

ther; on his Side none.[57] But when called upon for his Defence, he read a Speech from a written Paper, which he held in his Hand, after which the Jury consulted upon their Verdict, and brought him in Guilty.

The following is a Copy of the Paper read by him on the above Occasion.[58] It was delivered with all that Energy of Expression which the particular Feelings of the Culprit would allow.

"My Lord,

I Should not have troubled the Court with the Examination of Witnesses to support the Charge against me, had I not thought that pleading guilty to the Indictment gave an Indication of contemning Death, not suitable to my present Condition, and was in some Measure being accessory to a second Peril of my Life; and I likewise thought that the Justice of my Country ought to be satisfied, by suffering my Offences to be proved, and the Fact established by Evidence.

I stand here this Day the most wretched of Human Beings, and confess myself criminal in a high Degree; yet, while I acknowledge with Shame and Repentance, that my Determination against my own Life was formal and complete, I protest, with that Regard to Truth which becomes my Situation, that the Will to destroy her who was ever dearer to me than Life, was never mine till a momentary Phrensy overpowered me, and induced me to commit the Deed I deplore.—The Letter which I meant for my Brother-in-Law after my Decease, will have its due Weight as to this Point, with good Men.[59]

Before this dreadful Act, I trust nothing will be found in the Tenor of my Life, which the common Charity of Mankind will not excuse. I have no Wish to avoid the Punishment which the Laws of my Country appoint for my Crime; but being already too unhappy to feel a Punishment in Death, or a Satisfaction in Life, I submit myself with Penitence and Patience to the Disposal and

57. There were five witnesses: John Macnamara, a young man who was helping Ray into her coach when she was shot; Mary Anderson, a fruit seller, who had seen the shooting; Richard Blandy, the arresting constable; James Mahon, who had taken hold of Hackman; and a surgeon, Dennis O'Brien, who examined Ray's body at the inquest on the afternoon following the shooting.

58. This prepared statement was made available to the court, appeared in all the newspapers, and is included in the official transcript of the trial. Pottle says that it is "highly probable that Boswell wrote Hackman's speech" (*Lit. Car.*, 260); his visits to Booth and association with Hackman's defense would suggest this.

59. The letter Hackman mentions, to Frederick Booth (fl. 1775–1829), his sister's husband, was found in his pocket after the shooting. It had already appeared in the newspapers and is included in the transcript of the trial.

Judgement of Almighty God, and to the Consequences of this Enquiry into my Conduct and Intention."

Mr. Hackman was attended into and out of Court by his Friend Mr. Dawes, a Gentleman of the Bar, who has kindly attended him in his Confinement, and endeavoured to give him all the Counsel and Satisfaction in his Power.[60]

Mr. Hackman is a fine Figure of a Man, not 25 Years of Age.[61] His Head was bound up with a white Handkerchief,[62] and he received his Sentence with the utmost Composure of Mind. The whole Court were in Tears, and Judge Blackstone, who tryed him,[63] delivered himself to the Jury in a Manner that did equal Honour to his Heart as a Man, and his Abilities as a Judge, sitting on so awful an Occasion as that of distinguishing between Murther, as effected in a momentary Phrensy, and a previous Intention to kill with Malice aforethought.[64]

The convicted Prisoner is perfectly easy at his Condition; and as the Circumstance of his Case may gratify Curiosity, the Publick are requested to suspend their Opinion of it until it shall be laid before them, authenticated by his Friends, and uninfluenced by Prejudice, or unembellished by Partiality.

Reflections on Hackman's Trial

St. James's Chronicle, April 15–17, 1779, 4

To the Printer of the St. J. CHRONICLE.

SIR,

I Am just come from attending the Tryal and Condemnation of the unfortunate Mr. Hackman, who shot Miss Ray; and I must own that I feel an unusual Depression of Spirits, joined with that *Pause* which so solemn a Warning of the dreadful Effects that the *Passion of Love* may produce, must give all of us who have lively Sensations and warm Tempers. Mr. Hackman is a genteel young Man, not Five-and-twenty. He was several Years an Officer in the Army; but

---

60. Manasseh Dawes (d. 1829), barrister and writer, assisted Hackman's defense. The sympathetic treatment *The Case and Memoirs of James Hackman*, which was published within weeks of Hackman's execution and by June had reached its tenth edition, is attributed to him by Brewer (*Sentimental Murder*, 47, 74 ff.; see also Levy, *Love and Madness*, 211 n. 18).

61. Hackman was in fact at least twenty-six, having been baptized Dec. 13, 1752.

62. His head was bound because of his self-inflicted wound on the night of the murder.

63. Sir William Blackstone (1723–80), judge and legal scholar, author of the famous *Commentaries on the Laws of England* (1765–69).

64. As Brewer observes, "Blackstone, like most judges at the time, was strongly opposed to pleas of temporary insanity" (*Sentimental Murder*, 67).

having had his Affections engaged by Miss Ray, he quitted that Profession and took Orders, having Hopes that she would unite herself to him by Marriage. Let not any one too rashly censure him for cherishing such a Scheme. I allow that he was *dignus meliore flamma*, worthy of a more deserving Flame;[65] but she who could enchant for Years, in the Autumn of Possession too, the First Lord of the A——ty, a Nobleman so experienced in Women, might surely fascinate in the Blossom of Courtship, a young Officer, whose amorous Enthusiasm was at its Heighth.[66] There is in Love a certain Delusion which makes a Man think that the Object of it is perfect; and that even the Faults, which he cannot but know she has had, are purified and burnt away in the Fire of his Passion. Thus was Mr. Hackman lately situated; but whether from mere Change, to which Fancy is liable, or from Considerations of Prudence and Interest, he found that Miss Ray no longer showed the same Affection towards him as formerly. As his Manners were uncommonly amiable, his Mind and Heart seem to have been uncommonly pure and virtuous; for he never once attempted to have a licentious Connexion with Miss Ray.[67] It may seem strange at first; but I can very well suppose, that had he been less virtuous, he would not have been so criminal. But his Passion was not to be diverted with inferior Gratifications. He loved Miss Ray with all his Soul, and nothing could make him happy but having her all his own. Finding his Hopes blasted, his Life was miserable. He endeavoured to dissipate the Gloom, but it overpowered him; and the Consequences were told us To-day by himself, in a decent and pathetick Speech to Mr. Justice Blackstone, who presided at his Tryal. He was in great Agitation, and I was afraid would have been incapable of Utterance; but he collected himself, and read it with much Pathos and Energy from a Paper which he held in his Hand.

The Audience were affected in the tenderest Manner by this Speech, and by a Letter from the Prisoner to his Brother-in-law, which he intended should be delivered after he had fallen by his own Hands, and in which he prayed for Blessings upon his Mistress; and intreated his Brother-in-law, if ever it should happen that she should stand in Need of his Assistance, to give it for the Sake of his departed Friend. This Letter proved that there was certainly no antecedent Malice. But Sir William Blackstone very properly observed, that to constitute

65. *dignus meliore flamma*: JB's own translation follows immediately. See Horace, *Odes*, 1.27.20: *digne puer meliore flamma!* (boy worthy of a better flame).

66. The First Lord of the Admiralty, John Montagu, fourth earl of Sandwich (1718–92; see Hackman headnote, above), was twenty-four years older than Martha Ray, and Hackman, ten or so years her junior.

67. JB is representative of the contemporary commentators in describing Hackman as a man of virtue—not a violent and licentious man, but a man of sensibility, overpowered by love (see Brewer, *Sentimental Murder*, 51).

the legal Crime of Murther, it is sufficient if there be an Intention at the Time. Accordingly Mr. Hackman was found guilty, and Sentence of Death was pronounced upon him for Monday next.

I could not but admire the Candour and honourable Regard to Truth in Mr. Hackman, who acknowledged a Design in a Moment of Phrensy, tho' he knew that Death must be the inevitable Consequence, when he might with much Plausibility have said, that the Pistol which he meant to discharge at his own Head, in Miss Ray's Sight, took *by Chance* a Direction towards her Head, in the Confusion in which he was, when she suddenly turned round to him. But he disdained Falsehood or Evasion.

His Case is one of the most remarkable that has ever occurred in the History of human Nature, but it is by no Means unnatural. The Principle of it is very philosophically explained and illustrated in *The Hypochondriack*, a periodical Paper peculiarly adapted to the People of England, and which now comes out monthly in *The London Magazine*.[68] In the Thirteenth Number of that Paper, published last October, is this Passage:

"To return to the Passion of Love with all its feverish Anxiety, that being the principal Subject which I wish to keep in View in this Paper; it is to be observed that there is in it no Mixture of disinterested Kindness for the Person who is the Object of it. We have indeed many poetical Instances of an Affectation of this, where a rejected Lover prays for Blessings on his Delia, and hopes she shall be happy with a more deserving Swain.[69] But we may be certain that these are false Expressions; for the natural Sentiment in such a Situation is Hatred, and that of the bitterest Kind. We do not feel for her who is the Object of our amorous Passion, any Thing similar to the natural Affection of a Mother for her Child, of which so fine a Test is related in the Judgement of Solomon, where the true Mother, with melting Tenderness, intreated that her Child should be delivered to a Stranger, who contended with her for the Right to it, rather than it should be destroyed.[70] On the contrary, the Fondness for the Object of our Love is purely selfish, and nothing can be more natural and just than what Lucy in the

68. The anonymous "Hypochondriack" essays were by JB, but the fact of his authorship was not publicly known until a note by Edmond Malone to the posthumous third edition of the *Life of Johnson* (1799); see *Life*, 4:179 n. 4. Number 13 of the series, published Oct. 1778, was the last of three consecutive essays headed "On Love" (see Bailey, 1:190–97). There are no variations here from the *Hypochondriack* text.

69. Love poems to Delia—a name for a fictitious or idealized mistress, or the object of a young man's romantic love—are a commonplace in pastoral verse. Tibullus addressed poems to her, she is mentioned by Virgil in the *Bucolics*, and Samuel Daniel's cycle of sonnets called *Delia* (1592) was very popular.

70. For the judgment of Solomon, see 1 Kings 3:16–28.

Beggar's Opera says to her dear Captain Macheath, "I love thee so, that I could sooner bear to see thee hanged, than in the Arms of another."[71] The natural Effect of disappointed Love, however shocking it may appear, is to excite the most horrid Resentment against its Object, at least to make us prefer the Destruction of our Mistress, to seeing her possessed by a Rival. I say this is unrestrained Nature, and wherever Passion is stronger than Principle, it bursts forth into horrid Deeds. Not many Years ago a young Gentleman of very good Family in Ireland was executed for the Murther of a young Lady with whom he was in Love, whom he shot in the Coach with her Father, as she was on the Road to be married to another. And so strong was the Sense of untutored Mankind in his Behalf, that the Populace rose in a tumultuous Manner to rescue him from Justice, and the Sentence of the Law could not be fulfilled but by the Aid of a large Body of Soldiers."[72]

The Use to be made of so striking an Instance as that of Mr. Hackman, is to make us watch the Dawnings of violent Passion, and pray to God to enable us by his Grace to restrain it. "Think ye that those on whom the Tower of Siloam fell were greater Sinners than others? I tell you nay. But except ye repent ye shall all likewise perish."[73] These were the Words of the Saviour of the World; and in humble Allusion to them, I would say to all that are conscious that their Passions are violent, Think ye that this unfortunate Gentleman's general Character is in the Eye of Heaven, or of generous Men in their private Feelings, worse than yours [?]. No, it is not. And unless ye are upon your Guard ye may all likewise be

71. John Gay's immensely popular *The Beggar's Opera* (first performed in 1732), 2.3. As a young man, JB found Gay's Macheath (and West Digges, an actor who famously played the gallant outlaw) an attractive model for aspects of his own youthful personality; he records having "thought myself Captain Macheath" (*Lond. Journ.*, 264). One of the earliest executions he attended (May 4, 1763) was that of Paul Lewis, a highwayman, of whom he says, "He was just a Macheath" (ibid., 251). Redford suggests that "Gay's highwayman appealed so strongly to Boswell's imagination not only because of his dashing lawlessness, glamorous raking, and polygamy, but also because Macheath had been rescued on the verge of death in an extravagantly improbable reversal of plot" (Redford, "Boswell's Fear of Death," 109–10). See also *Earlier Years*, 111.

72. This has been sourced by Bailey (1:195 n. 11) to a story from Ireland reported in the *Ann. Reg.* (1761), concerning one John Macnaughton, who on Nov. 10 hired some men to kidnap from a coach a young woman to whom he claimed to be married; shots were exchanged and she was killed. At his trial in Strabane on Dec. 11, Macnaughton was distraught and called her his wife. The report does not in fact say that "the Populace rose in a Tumultuous manner to rescue him," but there was apparently some sympathy for him. See Bailey for other references.

73. See Luke 13:3, 4 (JB seems to quote the *AV* from memory). The use of "ye" in the sentences following is an attempt to keep up a solemn and quasi-biblical tone.

in his melancholy Situation. While Human Justice is to be satisfied, let us consider that his Crime was neither premeditated Cruelty, nor base Greediness. He is therefore an Object neither of Abhorrence nor of Contempt; and upon such an Occasion I could wish that the Royal Prerogative could transmute the Mode of Punishment from that which is common to mean Offenders, to what would better suit the Character of the Sufferer.[74] This, however, is but a slight Consideration, on which it does not become us to dwell, while we should be employed on what is of infinitely greater Importance. Let us unite our fervent Prayers to the Throne of Heaven, that this our Brother may obtain Forgiveness through Jesus Christ, and be admitted in another State of Being to everlasting Happiness.

I am, Sir, your's, &c.

J. B.

Hackman at His Trial: Boswell's Account to Mr. Booth

Public Advertiser, April 19, 1779, 3

   Mr. Booth, of Craven-street, Brother-in-law to the unfortunate Mr. Hackman, is as genteel and amiable [a] Man as lives.[75] The Letter from Mr. Hackman to him proves what might be expected from his Feelings and Generosity. He was too much agitated to be present in Court during Mr. Hackman's Trial; but remained without near to Newgate. Mr. Boswell, who left the Court as soon as Sentence was pronounced, was the first Person who informed him of the Fate of his Relation and Friend.[76] Upon being told that he was found Guilty, and that, from the Circumstances of the Case, it could not be otherwise, Mr. Booth eagerly asked, How Mr. Hackman had behaved?[77] Mr. Boswell answered, "As

74. A judicial verdict could not be changed by the monarch, but a punishment could be mitigated by a royal pardon, either conditional or unconditional.

75. Frederick Booth was an attorney. JB appears to have sought his acquaintance in the week after the murder. Craven St. is south off the Strand, just east of Charing Cross. JB called on Booth twice on Sunday, Apr. 11 (*Laird*, 75–76), and again on Tuesday, Apr. 13 (ibid., 78). After the visit described here, JB seems to have tried through Booth to see Hackman himself; he called at Newgate on Saturday, Apr. 17 (ibid., 91), but did not find Booth there, and on Sunday, Apr. 18, he left there a note for Booth (ibid., 92).

76. In his journal, JB wrote that, after leaving the trial, he "Met Booth, *mains serrées*" (with "clenched fists"; *Laird*, 85).

77. The focus of JB's interest, and that of most other contemporary observers, was not Hackman's guilt or otherwise, or the legal questions, but Hackman's behavior—at his trial and sentencing (and later at his execution): how he "performed" love, honor, contrition, remorse, resignation (Brewer, *Sentimental Murder*, 67–68).

well, Sir, as you, or any of his Friends, could wish; with Decency, Propriety, and in such a Manner as to interest every one present. He might have pleaded that he shot Miss Ray by Accident; but he fairly told the Truth, that in a Moment of Phrenzy he did intend it."——"Well, said Mr. Booth, I would rather have him found Guilty with Truth and Honour, than escape by a mean Evasion."——A Sentiment truly noble, bursting from a Heart rent with Anguish!

Dr. Johnson, the great Moralist of the Age, mentions, in his Rambler, that Dr. Boerhaave never saw a Criminal led to Execution, but he thought, "Perhaps this Man is, upon the whole, less guilty than I am."[78]—Let those whose Passions are keen and impetuous consider, with awful Fear, the Fate of Mr. Hackman. How often have *they* infringed the Laws of Morality by Indulgence. *He*, upon one Check, was suddenly hurried to commit a dreadful Act.

Boswell Did Not Attend Hackman to Tyburn

[Hackman's execution took place on April 19. A report appeared that day in *Lloyd's Evening Post* (Apr. 16–19, 1779; for the text, see *Laird*, 93–94), and was reprinted in the *Public Advertiser*, April 20, and *St. James's Chronicle*, April 17–20. The report magnified Boswell's prominence in the proceedings, giving him more notoriety than even he preferred. Boswell sought advice from various friends, including Edmund Burke, about how he should respond and records submitting "a good paragraph in <tone of> waggery" to Woodfall, the printer of the *Public Advertiser* (*Laird*, 95).]

Public Advertiser, April 21, 1779, 4

It was not Mr. Boswell,[79] but the Rev. Dr. Porter of Clapham, who so humanely attended the late unfortunate Mr. Hackman.[80] Mr. Boswell had for a

78. Herman Boerhaave (1668–1738), Dutch medical scholar. The anecdote is in Johnson, *Rambler*, 4:242 (no. 114).

79. The report mentioning JB was probably (as Pottle suggested, quoted in *Corres. 3*, xciv) by George Steevens (see Chap. 4, n. 3); there was obvious animosity between them: Steevens had been present at the Club after the trial, when JB felt himself "a man of consequence" for being able to report what had transpired (*Laird*, 85), and was also present in the press-yard before the execution, where JB found him "disagreeable [when] unrestrained by Johnson" (ibid., 93). Steevens may also have been the "blackguard being" who was commissioned ahead of JB for the account in the *Pub. Adv.* (ibid., 85). JB was "vexed" and "uneasy" about his name appearing in such a context (ibid., 93, 94). (There was a correspondence about this report and the corrected version in *Notes and Queries* in 1863; the writers had not seen this paragraph of JB's.)

80. Moses Porter (bap. 1735–91), a lecturer and curate of Holy Trinity church, Clapham, and a close friend of Hackman.

Day that Praise, which is so justly allowed to generous Tenderness; but he has taken Care that it shall be enjoyed by the worthy Person to whom it is due.[81]

1785

EXECUTION INTELLIGENCE

[By publishing the following two articles under this heading, the *Public Advertiser* looked to be presenting—and promising to continue—an original category of news. Boswell appears to have taken the initiative, but little is known about the circumstances of their publication. Lucyle Werkmeister suggests (*Jemmie Boswell*, 7) that he may have written the first in payment for the *Public Advertiser* printing puffs for his forthcoming political pamphlet, *A Letter to the People of Scotland* (1785). There seems no evidence for the tantalizing assertion of Peter Martin that Boswell became "a regular correspondent for the *Public Advertiser*, covering Newgate trials as well as executions" (*James Boswell*, 476). The series was not continued by Boswell or any other reporter, and it may be that the subject was regarded as unworthy of detailed consideration by the newspaper reading public.]

Execution Intelligence 1

[In his journal for July 6, 1785, Boswell described having taken Reynolds to see that day's executions at Newgate (see Figure 8) and records having "given a particular account of it in the *Public Advertiser*" (*Applause*, 318). Lustig and Pottle comment that the first paragraph in the published version (below) is "incongruously affixed to Boswell's report," and must have been supplied by another contributor and grouped with Boswell's materials by the printer (ibid., 319, 338).]

Public Advertiser, July 7, 1785, 3

While a great concourse of spectators were assembled, the first person who appeared upon the scaffold yesterday morning was Mr. Boswell; *that* was nothing extraordinary; but it was surprising when he was followed by Sir Joshua Reynolds.[82]

---

81. When the *Lloyd's* report was reprinted in the *Lond. Chron.*, Apr. 17–20, Porter's name was substituted for JB's. In the *St. James's Chron.*, JB's waggish clarification was in the same issue as the uncorrected report.

82. In his journal, JB notes that the night before this execution, Reynolds expressed interest in attending with him. JB told him to be ready at 5:30 a.m., then called on William Herne (see n. 96, below), one of the under-sheriffs, presumably to make arrangements. The next morning, they were admitted to Newgate, heard the condemned at chapel, saw the

Figure 8. "The New Gallows at the Old Bailey," James Mountague,
The Old Bailey Chronicle *(London, 1788), 4: frontispiece. Courtesy of*
Special Collections, Diamond Law Library, Columbia University.

—"Evil communications corrupt good manners."[83]—It is strange how that hard Scot should have prevailed on the amiable painter to attend so shocking a spectacle.[84]

Peter Shaw, one of the five convicts who suffered yesterday for having robbed Mr. Stanhope's house, persisted to the last in denying that he had set fire to it.[85]

---

irons knocked off, and had some conversation with them; see *Applause*, 318–20. Reynolds wrote to JB the next day, thanking him for taking him; see *Corres. 3*, 199–200.

83. 1 Corinthians 15:33 (*AV*).

84. This paragraph, which testifies to JB's discreditable reputation as an execution-goer, also marks "the beginning in the newspapers of really malignant reflections on Boswell. For this he could no doubt blame the liberties he had taken in his *Letter to the People of Scotland*" (*Applause*, 319–20), as well as "the ridicule of Dr. Johnson and his trio of biographers [which] was a national sport from 1786 on" (Werkmeister, *Jemmie Boswell*, 12).

85. Peter Shaw was tried at the Old Bailey on May 11, 1785, for "feloniously stealing" from his employer on Apr. 4 (see Proceedings of the Old Bailey, Ref: t17850511–2). The *Gent. Mag.*, 55 (July 1785), 566–67, reports five malefactors executed at Newgate on July 6, 1785: "John Ivemay and John Honey, for robbing Edward Gray, Esq. on Ealing-Common, of a watch and two seals; Peter Shaw, for stealing in the dwelling-house of Edwin Francis Stanhope, Esq. in Curzon-Street, May-Fair, two gold boxes, six watches, a quantity of medals, &c.; and Joseph Brown, for breaking into the dwelling house of Mrs. Goddin, at

He behaved with a manly composure, and said it was the happiest day of his life; it was but going to Heaven a little sooner; only he regretted his wife and children. He had been some time servant to Mr. Burke, of whom he spoke to Mr. Boswell with great regard: "He is a worthy good gentleman—God Almighty prosper him. His brother, out of his own generosity, came to the Court, and gave me a character."[86] —Shaw was a tall handsome fellow, a native of Ireland; his long hair hung flowing down his back, and his manners were much above those of an ordinary servant. He never once changed countenance, or shewed either fear or affectation. One very extraordinary circumstance marked his possessing himself perfectly: While he stood under the fatal tree, and the awful moment was approaching, he observed Sir Joshua Reynolds and Mr. Boswell, two friends of his old master, Mr. Burke, placed by Mr. Sheriff Boydell;[87] upon which he turned round, and with a steady but modest look made them a graceful bow.

Ivemay and Horey [*sic*], the two highwaymen of yesterday's sad groupe, were good-looking young men, especially the former.[88] When they came upon the scaffold, Horey addressed himself to the people, saying, "Let *us* be an example; take warning by us." "Ay (added Ivemay) here's warning enough for you all."[89]

The ceremony of knocking off their irons just before taking the convicts out to execution, is the most striking circumstance of the whole. Horey affected a little too much spirit upon that occasion; for he called to his companion, "My boy, let's be glad we are *free* again." A momentary freedom; for in a minute after he was pinioned. It, however, put one in mind of Marcus, in Addison's Cato:

Hampstead, and stealing a quantity of wearing apparel, &c.; and Robert jackson [*sic*], for forging a letter of attorney from Benj. Bell, late a seaman on board the Carysford, with intent to defraud Samuel Danton, and Isaac Clementson. They were all young men, in the prime of life. What a pity!" They were all sentenced May 11, 1785 (see Proceedings of the Old Bailey, Ref: s17850511–1, which also gives the name as Honey, not *Horey*).

86. Shaw had been employed by Edmund Burke for five or six months. At the trial, Burke's brother, lawyer and political writer Richard Burke (1733–94), said of Shaw, "he was a remarkable good servant, and attentive, I had no reason to doubt his honesty then" (ibid.).

87. John Boydell (1720–1804), eminent engraver and printseller, known as Alderman Boydell, was active in public offices. He was sheriff in 1785 and later Lord Mayor (see also Chap. 4, n. 80).

88. Ivemay was tried with Honey on May 11, 1785, for theft with violence: highway robbery (see Proceedings of the Old Bailey, Ref: t17850511–1).

89. JB was not alone in being responsive to the undoubtedly theatrical elements of these occasions, in which even the sufferers would participate; note his description following of knocking off the irons (fetters) as a "ceremony" and his comment that Honey affected "too much" spirit; in the next article, he also calls the cutting down of the bodies from the gibbet a "ceremony."

> "Good morrow, Portius; let us now embrace;
> Once more embrace whilst yet we both are *free*."[90]

A number of Italian Noblemen and Gentlemen saw the execution yesterday from a window,[91] and we are sorry witnessed a superstition as weak as any in their own country [:] no less than four diseased persons, who had themselves rubbed with the sweaty hands of malefactors in the agonies of death, and believed this would cure them.[92]

Execution Intelligence 2

[In his journal, Boswell records calling on the Ordinary of Newgate Prison, Rev. John Villette, on August 16, 1785, in order to arrange his visit to Newgate the following day, before the executions described in this article. He intended to get up early for the execution but was woken late; nevertheless, he joined the crowd soon after 6 a.m. and was let into Newgate by the keeper, Richard Akerman. He spoke with the condemned, gaining some of the facts for this article. (See *Applause*, 337–38.)]

Public Advertiser, August 18, 1785, 4

Yesterday there was the greatest concourse of people ever remembered assembled before the door of Newgate,[93] to witness the melancholy exit of eight malefactors, seven men, and one woman.[94] Olive, the boy of 14, who was to have

90. Joseph Addison, *Cato: A Tragedy* (1713), 1.2.5–6. The quoted words are actually addressed to Cato's son Portius by Sempronius, a senator, not by Marcus, the other son of Cato. The original has "once" for "now" in the first line.

91. During this season in London, JB was living at the home of General Paoli (*Later Years*, 282), where he would regularly meet a variety of Italians. On July 1, he records arriving home to find present for dinner, among others, "Conte Carloucci and Conte Piazzi, two Cremona noblemen," and after dinner they were joined by "M. d'Ageno, Genoese Minister," and a number of Italian musicians (*Applause*, 316).

92. The touch of a hanged felon was believed by some to have healing qualities, in particular, to "cure tumours and warts" (Gatrell, *Hanging Tree*, 81). (When these paragraphs were given in the *General Evening Post*, they were followed by another four paragraphs on the event, by another hand.)

93. On Wednesday, Aug. 17, 1785, the *Lond. Chron.* reported, "The crowd was as great as ever known on the like occasion. . . . At four this morning it is supposed curiosity had drawn more than a thousand people into the Old Bailey" (Aug. 16–18, 1785; quoted in *Applause*, 338 n. 3).

94. According to the Old Bailey transcripts, the eight malefactors executed this day were James Lockhart (also Lockart), Richard Jacobs, John Rayboult (also Reboult) alias Prescot, Thomas Bayley, John Morris, James Guthrie, Martin Taylor, and Elizabeth Taylor; see Proceedings of the Old Bailey, Ref: s17850629–1. Those mentioned particularly by JB are discussed in notes below.

suffered with them, had obtained a respite through the humane interposition of that active and benevolent gentleman, Col. Erskine.[95] Both the sheriffs, Hopkins and Boydell, and Mr. Herne, one of the under sheriffs, were present, and were accompanied by a number of gentlemen.[96] The scene was a very different one from the last, where Peter Shaw and his fellow convicts behaved with so much intrepidity.[97] Several of the unhappy persons of yesterday appeared to be in terrible agitation, particularly Morris and Guthrie, two grenadiers of the guards.[98] They wept bitterly. Morris was a Shropshireman, Guthrie a Scotsman of the county of Fife: He was born at Dysart, and served his time to a shoemaker at Aberdeen. Morris had a lock of his sister's hair twisted round one of his fingers when he died. Taylor, who stabbed his wife dangerously when she came to see him after he was under sentence of death, was very penitent. His sister, who was placed next to him, and was concerned with him in housebreaking, was not quite eighteen years of age; she seemed very insensible.[99] Taylor was particularly anxious that their dead bodies should be taken care of. One Joseph Price had been engaged for that purpose; but he would not be satisfied till he saw that Price was there in readiness. So "Joseph Price! Joseph Price!" was called by the executioner, and echoed by the crowd, till he came near to the scaffold, and Taylor spoke to him. There was amongst these convicts a mulatto boy, who behaved very decently.[100] Taylor and his sister were in close conference, when suddenly the platform fell, and the whole line was launched into another state of being.[101]

95. George Olive, aged fifteen, was tried on June 29, 1785, for damage to property: arson. He was accused of having set fire to his master's house. He was found guilty and sentenced to death, but the prosecutor and jury recommended mercy on account of his youth (see Proceedings of the Old Bailey, Ref: t17850629–2). I found no further evidence of the involvement of Col. James Francis Erskine (1743–1806), second son of the Earl of Mar.

96. John Boydell, see n. 87, above; John Hopkins (bap. 1715–96), grocer, and William Herne (1745–1838), vintner, were aldermen of the City of London; Herne later served as sheriff and was knighted, and Hopkins served as mayor and was also knighted.

97. For Peter Shaw and the last executions, see the previous item.

98. John Morris and James Guthrie were tried on June 29, 1785, for theft with violence: highway robbery (see Proceedings of the Old Bailey, Ref: t17850629–60). Before the execution, JB conversed in particular with Guthrie, his fellow countryman (*Applause*, 338).

99. Martin Taylor and his sister Elizabeth Taylor were tried on June 29 for breaking and entering, and stealing (see Proceedings of the Old Bailey, Ref: t17850629–67). Of Joseph Price, who was to receive the Taylors' bodies (presumably to keep them from being sent to anatomists for dissection), nothing more is known.

100. The "mulatto boy" was James Lockhart (or Lockart), a young Indian, the servant of Ewan Bailey; he was tried on June 29 for stealing diamonds, pearls, and other jewels from his employer (see Proceedings of the Old Bailey, Ref: t17850629–61).

101. The *Lond. Chron.*, Aug. 16–18, 1785, reported, "The brother and sister kissed each other several times, both before and after the prayers upon the scaffold, and they went out

After hanging an hour, their bodies were cut down; the ceremony of which, though so often mentioned, is unknown to most of our readers. The executioner places himself under the body, which rests upon his shoulders, while the hands are brought over his reach. A man on each side also supports the body, and the executioner's man, mounted upon steps, cuts the rope. The body is then tumbled over upon a plank, which is in readiness, and is borne into Newgate to be carried away for interment as soon as may be convenient. These convicts all died very easily. A gentleman, who is an attentive examiner of shocking scenes, made Guthrie's cap be pulled up, when the body was stretched out in Newgate, and there did not appear any distortion in his countenance.[102] Poor Morris, the grenadier, said—I have made my peace with GOD as well as I can.

Sir Joshua Reynolds was *not* with Mr. Sheriff Boydell at yesterday's execution; at least was not seen. Mr. Boswell *was*.[103] Mr. Burke said once to Mr. Boswell—you have seen more life—*and more death*, than any man I know.[104]

---

of the world hand in hand, in which state they remained till they were cut down" (see *Applause*, 338 n. 1).

102. As may be guessed, this gentleman was JB. In his journal he says, "I made Guthrie's cap be pulled up and looked at his face, which was neither black nor distorted" (see *Applause*, 338).

103. The reference to Reynolds and JB alludes to the discreditable first paragraph added to the previous item, as described above.

104. When JB and Burke breakfasted together on Monday, Mar. 31, 1783, Burke "alluded pleasantly to my attending executions, and said, 'You have seen more life and more death than any man.' 'Well,' said I, 'and I hope I shall see immortality'" (*Applause*, 89–90).

The Rampager

In 1758, Henry Woodfall, the printer and editor of the successful daily newspaper the *Public Advertiser*, passed the responsibility for the paper on to his talented nineteen-year-old son, Henry Sampson Woodfall. Young Woodfall was not merely the heir to the property and experience of a prominent family of printers, he was an accomplished reader of the classics and on friendly terms with many writers and wits. Under his editorship, the *Public Advertiser* flourished. After the format was modernized in 1763, the paper was less narrowly devoted to news and advertising, and became a vehicle for culture and opinion (Bertelsen, "Education of Henry Sampson Woodfall," 153). By one estimate it was "the most important daily paper of the 1760s" (Clarke, *From Grub Street*, 88–90). Then, in 1769, the anonymous political writer who signed himself "Junius" made the paper the venue for his startling and well-informed anti-government invective. His highly controversial letters, published between once and three times a month until January 1772, signified the complexity of and the passions aroused by the issues and the allegiances of the contemporary political scene, and considerably boosted the sales of the *Public Advertiser*. Political essays were a prominent and much-discussed form of public writing, and Boswell seldom heard a conversation in which he didn't want to join.

Over a period of twelve years, Boswell wrote an intermittent series of essays in the form of letters for the *Public Advertiser*, signed with the name "Rampager." Published at intervals ranging from one week to seventeen months, the "Rampagers" are not truly "periodical essays" but *sporadic* essays; this sporadic character is probably one cause of the failure of the series to make any impression on the imagination of the public. Yet Boswell addresses each new occasion of publication with his characteristic gusto, writing as if he expects his name and persona to be recognized by his readers, and it looks as if he originally intended the essays to appear far more frequently and regularly than he was ever able to manage. The first four of the "Rampagers" appeared at monthly intervals in 1770; after that, he seldom managed to write more than two

a year. The period they span (1770–82) overlaps with his far more successful essay series, the seventy essays published under the name "Hypochondriack" (1777–83). Not
only did Boswell manage to write these latter essays regularly—ten a year for seven
years—but they are longer essays, far more considered and less topical. They are also
more traditional, on the model of the *Spectator* and *Rambler*—indeed, on the model
of Bacon—addressing abstract and perennial issues and employing a range of literary
and topical allusions. Indeed, lacking any playful or fictional elements, they may be
considered more serious and traditional than those classic series. The "Rampager" is
most emphatically not an essay series with this character and could not on any terms
bear comparison with the classic essay series of the eighteenth century. It is a series of
a different kind: from start to finish, the objects of the Rampager's attention are almost
exclusively topically political.

Boswell does not proceed by sober and serious analysis, but neither is his voice
that of passionate or principled commitment: the Rampager is most emphatically not
another Junius—nor a potential target for Junius. He has no private information to
impart or party-political point of view to express. His approach to the many issues he
addresses through the series is uniformly extravagant and frivolous. The "Rampagers"
show Boswell not so much out of his depth as quite out of sympathy with the professional and ideologically serious business that politics was becoming. What he most
makes fun of is politics itself. He treats politics as a game, a subset of Britain's social
life, a realm of personalities, promotion, and publicity, rather than of principles, policies, or even parties. Indeed, in an early unpublished essay that appears to have been
very much in the "Rampager" style, he compared changes in Lord Bute's administration to an alleged Scottish outdoor game he called "Hop-Romp." (He wrote this essay
on February 13, 1763, and sent it to John Wilkes for publication in his anti-government
newspaper the *North Briton*, but it was not used; see *Lond. Journ.*, 189 and n. 5.) The
"Rampager" letters are a commentary on what he reads in the newspapers, and in fact
he treats political activity as if it were, in essence, little more than a means of getting into the newspapers, no different from or more important than other forms of
public amusement; in "Rampager" no. 7, he links "News and Nonsense, Politics and
Play-houses," as "Subjects of Entertainment." Much of the imagery he adopts relates
to performance and theatricality. He depicts practicing politicians as musicians, the
contributors to the *Public Advertiser* as beasts in a menagerie, the king as a character
in a classic play, and the participants in the American war as embodying the titles in a
book catalogue: in other words, they are all playing a role.

Boswell's own "political career" has been carefully examined by Frank Brady; more
carefully, perhaps, than a career that "scarcely got off the ground" would seem to require (Fry, "James Boswell," 89). Brady says that Boswell's "central and most persistent
ambition . . . was to represent the County of Ayrshire in the House of Commons" (*Pol.
Car.*, 1). In a letter of Feb. 7, 1763, to Lord Eglinton, he wrote of his desire to make "a
distinguished figure in Parliament" (see *Lond. Journ.*, 181), and, when general elections
were held in 1774, 1780, 1784, and 1790, he hoped to be a candidate himself or worked

for candidates whom he hoped might favor him with some appointment (Fry, "James Boswell," 92–93). As much as anything else, he wanted to be an MP so that he could "reverse the proportions of his year (to live in London, and visit Scotland)," although, Gordon Turnbull emphasizes, he was also motivated by "a sincere disapproval of the way elections were arranged and controlled at this time" (*ODNB*). Brady argues that Boswell wanted to be in Parliament, not so much to advance any particular cause or serve a party, "but simply because being an M.P. was a respectable position, which would enhance the reputation of the Boswells of Auchinleck, and ensure that he spend part of each year in London" (*Pol. Car.*, 2).

Despite his various serious political writings, it is clear from his private papers, as well as the "Rampager" letters, that Boswell found it hard to take seriously the people for whom political activity takes precedence over every other aspect of public life; yet he envied their success and the prestige it brings. He is baffled—so he says—by the advancement of his high-flying university contemporary Henry Dundas; when Dundas became (at the age of thirty-three) the Lord Advocate of Scotland, Boswell wrote abusively of him in a letter to his lifelong friend and correspondent William Temple, calling him "a coarse, unlettered, unfanciful dog," and asked plaintively, "Why is he so lucky?" (May 22, 1775; *Letters JB*, 1:225). One is tempted to respond that perhaps being unlettered and certainly being unfanciful is actually a qualification for political success; this is virtually what Temple told Boswell in a letter almost twenty years later: "Had Dundas been ambitious of being a wit and an author, he would never have been Secretary of State" (Apr. 21, 1794, quoted in Fry, "James Boswell," 99).

But that plaintive question is actually rhetorical, or, at least, Boswell—who is one person of whom it cannot be said that he does not know his own weaknesses—came in time to appreciate the vital differences between himself and successful politicians. In his second *Letter to the People of Scotland* (1785), he contemplated Dundas's success and conceded, trying to maintain his dignity, "I am not so well fitted [as Dundas] for party exploits" (60). Michael Fry argues that Boswell did not simply lack application—as he certainly did—but also that he lacked the stomach for "the drudgery, frustration, risk, compromise—in other words, the *discipline*—of politics" ("James Boswell," 92). A more complex figure with whom to compare him (and with whom he compared himself) is Edmund Burke. As we see also in other chapters, Burke was for Boswell an attractive and troubling figure, someone whom—unlike Dundas—Boswell would try to emulate; he was something more than a party man: he was a philosopher and an orator, a man of letters, for whom politics was—among other things—a profound intellectual interest. In this, Boswell could not follow him. In May 1779, he advised Temple, "I must candidly tell you that I think you should not puzzle yourself with political speculations more than I do. Neither of us is fit for that sort of mental labour" (*Letters JB*, 2: 288). Certainly, he often confessed that abstract speculation on any subject was not one of his strengths, writing in one of his "Hypochondriack" essays (no. 53: "On Words"; Feb. 1782) that at times "intense inquiry" had "affected [him] even with giddiness and a kind of stupor, the consequence of having one's faculties stretched in vain" (Bailey, 2:150). He told Paoli that, presumably at university, "[I] had intensely applied myself to metaphysical researches, and reasoned beyond my depth, on such subjects as it is not given to man to know" (Boswell, *Account of Corsica*, 192), and had rendered himself melancholy; many years later, he noted that trying to read Hume's philosophy made him feel dreary and depressed (*Laird*, 387). He was not psychologically equipped to think through, from first principles, issues political or otherwise. Some weeks after writing his first "Rampager" (no. 11) on the American war, he confessed to Temple (Mar. 18, 1775), "As to American affairs. I have really not studied the subject. It is too much for me perhaps; or I am too indolent or frivolous. From the smatterings which Newspapers have given me, I have been of different minds, several times" (*Corres. 6*, 358).

Nevertheless, as he immediately continues (in a passage that closely echoes what he wrote in "Rampager" 10; see below), he has opinions:

> That I am a Tory, a lover of power in Monarchy, and a discourager of much liberty in the people I avow. But it is not clear to me that our Colonies are compleatly our subjects. . . . At any rate, the measures of Administration seem to have been ill digested & violent. I should hope that things may now take a good turn. (*Corres. 6*, 358)

He records having unwisely broached the subject of America with Johnson and enraged him when he "attempted to argue in favour of our fellow-subjects on the other side of the Atlantick. I insisted that America might be very well governed . . . by having a body of representatives, without whose consent money could not be exacted from them" (Sept. 23, 1777; *Life*, 3:205). The American war and topics connected with it are the main subject of the remaining "Rampagers," but Boswell deals with the subject almost exclusively by parody, finding ludicrous allusions and making jocular suggestions about arming the Jews and prescribing rhubarb. In his 1783 *Letter to the People of Scotland*, he claimed that he was "one of the few [in Scotland] who . . . ventured to oppose" the taxation of the American colonies "both as unjust and inexpedient" (4). But he could not have claimed that his opposition, such as it was, discomfited anyone or was even much noticed.

His political opinions are not doctrinaire or party-political, and are not developed in relation to a "political theory, or even to a large view of affairs . . . anything like a general strategy hardly entered his head" (*Pol. Car.*, 2). Attempting to have the best of both worlds—or figuring himself (to himself) as an ancient laird, superior to the unseemly business of canvassing, bribing, and voting—he described himself as "a tory with whig principles" (*Extremes*, 252; see Fry, "James Boswell," 97). In the "Rampager" essays, he only once uses either of these terms himself. Consistent with this attitude, the main avenue that he pursued for political advancement, aside from Ayrshire electioneering, was the venerable practice of seeking the acquaintance of and ingratiating himself with people in power and inviting their favor. Boswell is well known to have enjoyed making the acquaintance of prominent people, but his motivation was not simply snobbery or a psychological need to seek father-substitutes, but also the practical desire for promotion and employment. As well as Dundas and Burke, Boswell approached, cultivated, or sought favors from Wilkes, Lord Bute, both the Elder and Younger Pitt, Lord Mansfield, and James Lowther, Earl of Lonsdale. Indeed, it is remarkable how many participants in public life in London and Edinburgh were known to him personally.

But the political world of the eighteenth century was changing: in the recent past, most politicians were men who were already powerful, who formed loose and changing alliances in order to serve their own perceived interests. In the late eighteenth century, the profession of politics was becoming less a matter of personal connections than a matter of diplomatic skill and administrative experience, and interest in the sound management of the complexities of an expanding domestic economy, as well as of international affairs. Boswell's series of "Rampager" letters begins at a time when the political instability of the 1760s came to a head. After the long period of strong leadership and continuity under Sir Robert Walpole and his immediate successors, government was seen to be weak or at least in constant flux and subject to extraparliamentary influence. Political issues were debated heatedly in public rather than in the privacy of Parliament, through pamphlets and increasingly in newspapers; new organizations were formed and campaigns conducted to address or protest against particular issues or decisions. Boswell wanted to be part of this, but he also rather deplored it. He enjoyed the color and drama of the new arrangements but did not quite know what all the fuss was about.

But the "Rampager" letters are not a sport of nature: they are firmly within a journalistic tradition. We have noted in the introduction the continuities between aspects of Boswell's writing and such contemporary works as the satirical essay series the *North Briton*. Even today, hardly any newspaper is without some paid provider of humorous commentary on current events, with or without overtly serious implications. Frequently, such contributions are hosted on the editorial pages and more often than not are in the form of cartoons. Readers of the press in all political jurisdictions will be able to think of examples. The technique of creating humor by incongruously juxtaposing elements from two or more otherwise separate discourses—as Boswell does here, when likening the Parliament to an orchestra (no. 1), or finding references to the American war in a book catalogue (no. 15)—may seem somewhat juvenile or unsophisticated, but is precisely what Freud, in *Jokes and Their Relation to the Unconscious* (1905), identifies as the essence of wit.

But Boswell is well aware of his strengths and limitations and is frank with his readers about what he is doing. His choice of name and persona for these letters is a tribute to his relationship with George Dempster, one of his oldest friends (see n. 37 below). "'Rampaging' was one of Dempster's favourite terms" (*Corres.* 7, 153 n. 7), and the word and its derivatives seem to have formed part of Dempster and Boswell's private vocabulary. Dempster is the "rampageneous friend" whose relationship with Boswell is the starting point of the letter of November 25, 1771 (no. 7). He was a successful MP for twenty-eight years; he is usually viewed as a whig, but "[h]is insistence on speaking and voting in accordance with his conscience rather than with his party gained him a reputation for incorruptibility and independence, and the sobriquet Honest George" (*ODNB*). His independence would have appealed to Boswell, although the work and sacrifices required of him to maintain it might not have.

In these essays, Boswell frequently reminds his readers about what to expect from him, that the name "Rampager" is not chosen at random but signifies his "rampage-neous" disposition and procedures (nos. 7 and 9). In the second essay, sounding as if he is setting himself up to be a regular correspondent, he defines his outlook, saying that *to rampage* "signifies to indulge in joyous extravagant Merriment, free of all Care and all Malice." He also defined the term "To rampage (or to ramage)" in his incomplete and unpublished "Dictionary of the Scots Language": "To romp. To act or speak with violence" (Turnbull, "Boswell's 'Dictionary of the Scots Language,'" 39.) Again and again he explicitly emphasizes the deliberate extravagance and oddity of his humor, which is based on conceits and analogies: his fancy (that is, imagination), he says, "is apt to perceive remote Resemblances" (no. 20) and licenses him to "run from the Southern Provinces to the Northern, and from the Northern to the Southern" (no. 18), without any discipline or system. Serious folk are not to take him to task: "I do not think myself obliged to observe any Connection or Regularity in my Essays" (no. 7), "My Province in these Essays is not Business and Order. My Readers, therefore, must not expect any Thing like Accuracy" (no. 18). But he also insists on his impartiality: he repeats the assertion that his ridicule is "well-meant" (no. 9) and that his essays are distinguished by his "hearty Good-humour and sportive spirit" (no. 10).

In his surviving records, Boswell seems only once to mention the series, and the "Rampagers" were not known to have been of his composition until his private papers were recovered and drew attention to a substantial body of work that would not otherwise have been identified. His correspondent Temple was in on the secret and wrote to him (July 5, 1770), "Your Rampager's sometimes make me laugh" (*Corres. 6*, 279). In his journal, August 24, 1774, he describes a conversational fancy of his own and says, "I shall work up this into an essay for *Rampager*, the designation which I assume as a signature to all my lively essays in *The Public Advertiser*" (*Defence*, 291–92); he had only published his latest "Rampager" the previous week and did not pursue this subject when he next wrote one, the following March. Boswell valued the "Rampagers" sufficiently to make a file of cuttings—among his private papers now at Yale (*Cat. Yale*, P 152)—containing sixteen of the twenty known "Rampagers." In the cuttings, each essay has been marked by Boswell with a cross or a star; some he has marked as well with a hand-drawn *maniculum* or pointing hand. More interestingly, he has also noted for each essay the place of composition (in all cases, "written at Edinburgh"), occasionally summarized the contents, and on some he has made careful corrections and alterations. The text given here incorporates Boswell's emendations, and details of his annotations are given in the textual notes. This care would suggest that he at least half-intended to gather and reprint the series. But the fact that he embarked on a very different series while he was writing them might also suggest that he felt that the "Rampager" was going nowhere and that a more successful series would have to be in a different style and engage another aspect of his character.

Despite the invisibility of the "Rampagers," they (or Boswell) seem to have been valued by Henry Sampson Woodfall, as we can see from the fact that fourteen "Rampagers" were published by him as leading articles—that is, they were the first item in the paper, after the advertisements, and distinguished by a decorative capital within a royal crest. I have thought it useful to record this information at the head of the essays, given how much more vital such paratextual matters are to the appreciation of periodical publications than to that of books. Indeed, most of the articles in this collection belong more to newspaper culture than to literary culture; this applies in particular to the "Rampagers." Every one of the essays makes apparent the diligence with which Boswell reads the papers and the care with which he scrutinizes them, as many of his references could not be known from any other sources.

The text that follows is the first time the series has been gathered together: indeed, this publication is the first reprinting of any of the series since the eighteenth century. Each essay is here given a number in sequence and a brief title indicating the subject matter; the only heading in the original publication, "To the Printer of the *Public Advertiser*," has been in all cases omitted. As elsewhere in this collection, the titles on the individual essays (all except no. 6, the parody of Addison's *Cato*) are editorial summaries, although they have frequently been constructed from the essays themselves or the handwritten headings that Boswell intermittently supplied on his own file copies (which may be found in the textual notes).

Seeing them together—as no eighteenth-century readers ever did—we see that no one other than Boswell could have written them.

1770

No. 1: Recent Discord in the "Political Orchestra"

[In this first (and by far the longest) "Rampager," Boswell establishes his authority as a political spectator by surveying the national politics of the previous fifteen years (that is, beginning from when he was about fourteen). He treats politics not as a contest of policies or ideologies, but more like what would now be termed a soap opera, concentrating on personalities, and depicts the British Parliament during this period as a discordant orchestra, in which there is a continuous jockeying for the position of first fiddle (that is, what is now known as prime minister). While no politicians are named, Boswell's satire is clear enough to enable individuals to be securely identified. It is important to have a grasp of the political personalities on whom his attention is focused in this first "Rampager."

Sir Robert Walpole was the first occupant of the role now usually thought of as prime minister of Britain, for a period of twenty years (1721–42). After he resigned in 1742, Walpole continued to exert a powerful influence on the king, George II, and in 1743 his loyal supporter Henry Pelham was asked to form a ministry. Pelham's premiership was stable and relatively uneventful, and, when he died in 1754, his elder brother, Thomas Pelham-Holles, the Duke of Newcastle, succeeded him. By this time the old tory party had more or less disintegrated. The following fifteen years—the period covered in this essay and setting the stage for those that follow—was a politically tumultuous time, characterized by rapid changes in national leadership. In 1756, the war against the French in America spilled over into war in Europe, with the beginning of the Seven Years' War against France and other European powers. After the war, to help fund imperial defense, the taxation of the colonies was increased, exacerbating the tensions with America that a dozen years later would lead to the War of Independence. Political alliances were made and broken and made again. George II died in 1760 and was succeeded by his grandson, George III, who was hostile to the hitherto dominant Old Corps Whigs and soon loosened their long-standing grip on Parliament.

A brief comment is necessary on the eighteenth-century party labels *whig* and *tory*, as well as the term *prime minister*. *Whig* and *tory* do not refer to political parties as we understand them today and can be misleading; parties were simply loose groupings of MPs, who had no institutional party organization and seldom used these labels of themselves (indeed, both labels were originally terms of abuse). Nevertheless, the whigs, who were at this time a relatively new political force and were in the ascendancy through the century, represent those—at first, aristocratic families, but increasingly the wealthy merchants and industrialists—who would limit the political power of the Crown. They support free trade and lower taxes; in modern terms, they are republicans and classic liberals. The tories were originally the supporters of the Crown and the Anglican establishment; they tended to favor national isolationism, and the expansionist wars of the mid-eighteenth century left them outside the political mainstream. Although later historians often describe prime ministers Bute and North as tories, simply because they were closely identified with the king, they themselves rejected the label. The actual title "prime minister" had no legal standing until the twentieth century; the politician who is invited by the sovereign to form a ministry is effectively the prime minister, but, although the description was often used in the eighteenth century, Walpole, Grenville, and North denied the existence of such a position. The following chronological list of prime ministers (with the names Boswell uses for them here in italics) may be helpful.

1721–42	Robert Walpole
January 1742–July 1743	Spencer Compton, Earl of Wilmington
1743–54	Henry Pelham
March 1754–November 1756	Thomas Pelham-Holles, Duke of Newcastle: *Hurry Scurry*

November 1756–June 1757	William Cavendish, fourth duke of Devonshire
July 1757–May 1762	Newcastle again; however, William Pitt, later first earl of Chatham-*Furioso*, was secretary of state and the dominant figure under Devonshire and during Newcastle's second term
May 1762–April 1763	John Stuart, third earl of Bute: *Sawney*
April 1763–July 1765	George Grenville: *Gentle Shepherd*
July 1765–July 1766	Charles Watson-Wentworth, Marquess of Rockingham: *Yorkshire Farmer*
July 1766–October 1768	Pitt, now earl of Chatham; became PM at the king's invitation but was ill and ineffective
October 1768–January 1770	Augustus Fitzroy, third duke of Grafton: *Gravetone*
January 1770–March 1782	Frederick North, Lord North: *Auster*]

Public Advertiser, April 14, 1770, 2 (leading article)

SIR,

YOU Londoners, Mr. Printer, are very apt to imagine yourselves the ablest, if not the only Politicians in the Kingdom. It is true you are at the Centre of Politicks, by being placed in the Capital, so that you resemble the principal Performers in a Band of Musicians, who occupy the Centre of the Orchestra. Your Politicks, indeed, at present, cannot well be called a *Concert*; for there seems to be no *Harmony* amongst you. On the contrary, there is a continual *Discord*, every one trying who shall *play the first Fiddle*,[1] insomuch that whoever gets into that Place, let him play with ever so much *Skill*, you are perpetually jogging his Elbow, and *putting him out* of Tune. The Truth is, you have too many *Crotchets* in your Heads,[2] and are so fond of what you call the *free* Stile of Music, that there is no getting you to keep any of the *known Rules*. You are inclined to explode all *tying* of the Notes,[3] as *Chains* upon your Genius; though every sensible Musician must agree, that without *tying* the Notes, there can be no regular Piece, but only a Jargon of unconnected Sounds. For my own Part, I cannot boast any deep Knowledge of the Science of Music, nor have I ever yet performed in any *public*

---

1. *First fiddle*: traditionally, the position of the concertmaster of an orchestra; colloquially, *to play first* (or *second*) *fiddle* is to take a leading (or subordinate) position (*OED*). JB uses the expression in the *Tour*, Sept. 28, 1773; see *Life*, 5:264.

2. JB puns on the musical usage of *crotchet* (a quarter note), as well as "A whimsical fancy; a perverse conceit; a peculiar notion on some point (usually considered unimportant) held by an individual in opposition to common opinion" (*OED*).

3. In music, to connect notes by a tie or ligature, to indicate that the sound is to be sustained.

Concert; but I have studied it a little, can play on several Instruments, and am ready to be *engaged* as soon as I am offered a good *Salary*.[4] In the mean Time, let me divert myself with considering how the POLITICAL ORCHESTRA of GREAT BRITAIN has been conducted in my Time, who have been our *first Performers*, and with what Kind of Music we have been entertained.

The first, I remember, was HURRY SCURRY, a Fiddler of exceeding quick Parts, but so volatile, that he never could keep to one Tune.[5] Sometimes he would play you a serious Composition wonderfully well, but before you knew where you was, bounce he went to a Rigadoon, and then fall again to a Minuet.[6] He had a remarkable Turn for *Church* Music, and as he was withal a most luxurious Fellow, he was much beloved by *my Lords the Bishops*.[7] He, however, took a *Tremor* in his Nerves, owing to his having heard, or imagined he heard,[8] some *French Music* all *on Flats*; the Consequence of which was, he could play nothing but the most desponding and plaintive Airs, so that he was obliged to *resign* his Place.[9]

4. JB is here alluding to his lifelong hope for political advancement. As well as involvement in local Ayrshire politics, this ambition led him to seek preferment from a succession of notables, of which the only result was his being in thrall for a number of years to the appalling Earl of Lonsdale and being rewarded in 1788 with the Recordership of the city of Carlisle. However, JB was very fond of music: he could play the violin and flute; he knew a great many ballads and would frequently sing on social occasions (see Brownell and Brownell, "Boswell's Ballads," 119–21).

5. Thomas Pelham-Holles, Duke of Newcastle (1693–1768), succeeded his brother as whig prime minister in Mar. 1754 until Nov. 1756. Newcastle was a skilled manager of the "Old Corps" whig faction, preferments, and parliamentary tactics, with a reputation for energy and industry but little sense of policy. From July 1757, he governed in coalition with Pitt, who provided inspirational leadership in foreign policy. In a letter of 1735, Lord Hervey said of Newcastle that he "does nothing in the same hurry and agitation as if he did every thing"; see Coxe, *Memoirs*, 3:229.

6. A rigadoon is a lively and somewhat complicated dance for two persons; a minuet, a stately dance for two in triple time (*OED*).

7. Newcastle was an important patron and noted for his extravagant spending on entertainment. "After 1736 he extended his influence into the affairs of the Church of England . . . deeply interested in the church, he exercised his powers of ecclesiastical appointment to advance the careers of churchmen of orthodox theological views and whiggish political sensibilities" (*ODNB*).

8. Newcastle had a reputation as a hypochondriac.

9. The "*French music* all *on Flats*"—a flat marking the drop of a tone by a semi-tone— suggests that the news was all depressing. In America, British forces were defeated by the French at Louisburg, Cape Breton Island, in July 1755, while in Europe the elaborate arrangements and campaigns conducted by the British to avoid war fell to pieces and resulted in Austria, Russia, and France uniting against Great Britain and the so-called Seven Years' War. Newcastle resigned on Nov. 11, 1756, to allow William Pitt to take control of the war

After him mounted FURIOSO, a Musician of very extraordinary Talents[10]—
He gave us nothing but *martial* Music—*Britons Strike Home*—*Hearts of Oak
are our Ships*—and such other rouzing Compositions.[11]—He seemed *desperately*
fond of *American* Music, and put us quite mad with the *Indian War-hoop*,[12] professing, at the same Time, an utter Abhorrence at all *German* Compositions.—
So much, however, did his *Taste* alter, that he came to be more delighted with
German Music than any Performer we have ever had—He went so far as to
endeavour to persuade us, that all the *American Music* was composed upon *German Grounds*;[13] and he would therefore join in a *perpetual* Concert with the *King
of Prussia*, as one of the best Musicians of that Country.[14] He once, indeed, at-

---

effort; his place was taken by the Duke of Devonshire, but Newcastle returned in July 1757
with responsibility for domestic affairs and to use his influence with the old-guard whigs to
ensure parliamentary support for the war (*ODNB*).

   10. William Pitt (the Elder), from 1766 first earl of Chatham (1708–78), whig; although
denominated as a secretary of state, he was the dominant political figure, under Devonshire
(Nov. 1756–June 1757) and until he resigned before the end of Newcastle's second term (July
1757–May 1762). He was an eloquent orator, and, in the eyes of many of his contemporaries,
Britain's successes in its various campaigns were due largely to his abilities. JB met Pitt
in Feb. 1766, at his own request and within weeks of his return from Corsica, in order to
acquaint him with the Corsican situation (*Grand Tour 2*, 304–11).

   11. Pitt left responsibility for domestic affairs to Newcastle in order to devote all of his
energies to war. "Britons, Strike Home" is a stirring song from Henry Purcell's patriotic
opera *Bonduca: The British Heroine* (1695). For the song "Heart of Oak," see Chap. 1, n. 112.

   12. Pitt was a fierce opponent of taxation of the Americans by the British Parliament: in
Jan. 1766, he argued that since the "House of Commons did not represent North America"
it could have "no right to lay an internal tax upon America"; see Horn and Ransome, *English Historical Documents*, 748. For the word *hoop*, meaning "A cry or call of 'hoop'; a whoop,"
the *OED* cites a contemporary phrase, "the *war-hoops* of the Indians."

   13. In 1743, while in opposition, Pitt had called Hanover "a despicable electorate" and
opposed all continental connections. He had been openly against the Treaty of Westminster of Jan. 1756, under which Britain and Prussia had agreed to oppose the French, Aus-
trian, and Russian forces, saying he "would not have signed [the treaty] for the five great
places of those who had signed it" (*ODNB*); however, when shortly afterward he became
responsible for Britain's conduct in the war, he changed his view. In Feb. 1757, Pitt urged
Parliament to provide supplies to Frederick II of Prussia in order to fulfill the Treaty of
Westminster obligations. On Dec. 9, 1762, speaking against the peace negotiated by Bute,
Pitt told Parliament that "America had been conquered in Germany" (*Parl. Hist.*, vol. 15,
col. 1267). See Peters, *Elder Pitt*, 106, 142.

   14. In 1758, Pitt brought about a second Treaty of Westminster, under which Britain was
to subsidize Prussia and neither side was to make a separate peace with their joint enemies.
The Prussian king, Frederick II ("the Great," 1712–86; king from 1740), was in fact a talented
musician: a flautist and composer.

tempted to amuse the *King of France* with some of *Stanley's Concertos*, by Way of *Overtures*.[15] But Furioso's Music was, upon the Whole, such as had no Plan whatever but to make a confounded Noise, and he actually did not know how or when he should stop.[16] He pretended, therefore, that *the Rest of the Band* would not *play along with him*, and so he got rid of the Difficulty.

To him succeeded Sawney, the Scot,[17] a very honourable gallant Gentleman in private Life, and the *Ladies* will tell you, *a good Performer*, too;[18]—but a Performer by no Means fitted for the English Nation.— Sawney would not humour them, not he—He would play his own Tunes, and as long as he was

---

15. Hans Stanley (1721–80), MP and a lord of the Admiralty, was sent by Pitt to Paris in May 1761 as an envoy in an attempt to negotiate the cessation of hostilities—i.e., to make peace overtures. His mission failed, and he returned to London in September. He was not involved in the successful negotiations in 1762 but supported the peace and retained Pitt's confidence in subsequent appointments. JB seems to have met him in Paris in 1766 (see *Corres. 6*, 318 and n. 15).

16. On the accession of George III in Oct. 1760, the new king's friend and counselor Lord Bute (see following note) was admitted to the cabinet. Bute and Pitt were initially united in their opposition to George II's policy of favoring Hanover, but a permanent rift developed when Pitt changed his stance. Pitt was also heavily critical of the terms of the peace Bute reached with France, which eventually put an end to the Seven Years' War (*ODNB*). Pitt found himself isolated in cabinet, and in Oct. 1761, after his proposal for a declaration of war against Spain was rejected by all of the cabinet except his brother-in-law Temple, he resigned. (JB does not comment on Pitt's period in office as Earl of Chatham, 1766–68, during which he was seriously unwell and politically inactive and which ended with his resignation.)

17. John Stuart, third earl of Bute (1713–92), succeeded to office when Newcastle resigned as first Lord of the Treasury; he was the first prime minister to be (like JB) a Scot. Bute had been tutor to George III as a young man. (JB was from 1765 very friendly with Bute's eldest son, Lord Mountstuart, and traveled in Italy with him. However, he did not meet Bute himself until May 1781, when he wrote to him, then in retirement, and was twice received by him; see *Laird*, 339 ff.). *Sawney* was a derisive term for Scotsmen used by the English, particularly after the Jacobite rising of 1745–46. (JB recorded a similar fantasia on Bute's career in a conversation with Lord Eglinton, July 18, 1763 [*Lond. Journ.*, 309], and, in a memorandum written a few days later, he seemed to consider publishing some version of it [Boswell, *London Journal*, ed. Turnbull, 284, 516], although he is not known to have done so.)

18. Bute was known to have enjoyed staging amateur dramas at his family home, giving rise to insinuations such as "Lord Bute was fond of acting *Lothario*" (Wilkes, *Letters*, 155 n.: letter, supposedly from Wilkes, of Mar. 15, 1763). Lothario is a character in Nicholas Rowe's *The Fair Penitent* (1603), whose name has become a byword for a womanizer. Bute was rumored—almost certainly falsely—to have had an affair with George III's mother, Augusta, the dowager Princess of Wales.

conscious that he *played true*, he never minded, though the whole Nation should stop their Ears, and make Faces at him. *Fie on the Wars*, was his favourite Tune—But he was also fond of—*A Lass wi' a Lump o' Land*—*Clout the Caldron*—and other such pleasant Ditties.[19]—SAWNEY gave much Offence; for as he was very proud, he would strut with his blue Bonnet, and short Tartan Highland Dress, with his Bag-pipe under his Arm, and turn his bare Posteriors on the first People in the Kingdom.[20]—He was unlucky too in having about him two or three little conceited *Under-Musicians* from *Scotland*, some of them no better than *common Shepherds* in their own Country; but they would needs play Symphonies, and stand in the Way of capital Performers.[21]—While this went on, there

19. All three are traditional Scottish songs. "Fie on the Wars" dates from the late seventeenth century (Tytler, *Poetical Remains*, 226). Here the title refers to Bute's initial refusal to accede to Pitt's request to declare war on Spain and to his successful efforts in bringing the Seven Years' War to an end. The other two songs are found in the much-reprinted collection *The Tea-Table Miscellany: A Collection of Scots Sangs* (1723–27) by Allan Ramsay (1684–1758). "A Lass wi' a Lump o' Land," expressing a preference for a girl in possession of either cash or property, first appeared in the second volume (1726), 7. "Clout the Caldron," concerning a tinker who repairs pots and pans but is willing to "clout the cauldron" of a fair housewife, was in the first collected edition (1730), 105.

20. Despite withdrawing Britain from the wars with an advantageous peace, Bute was thought by his opponents to have given too much away to France and Spain and had by 1763 become deeply unpopular; he received death threats, was jostled in public, and was satirized and lampooned in the press. He was often caricatured in the way that JB describes, suggesting that his Scots heritage, and his pride in it, was the basis of his unpopularity in England. The blue bonnet was a traditional symbol of the Jacobites (see Chap. 1, n. 17). Bute was said by his political enemies, for the sake of public sport, to have been vain about his well-shaped legs.

21. Bute was a great dispenser of government positions to his many talented London-based compatriots. As Richard Sher points out, JB and SJ still thought this subject worthy of discussion ten years after Bute had left office ("Favourite of the favourite," 181); on Apr. 14, 1775, SJ remarked, "Lord Bute . . . showed an improper partiality to Scotsmen" (*Ominous Years*, 143–44). In particular they discussed John Home (1722–1808), a clergyman (a "common Shepherd") who in 1757 became Bute's private secretary and succeeded Bute as tutor to the Prince of Wales. He was the recipient of a number of pensions. There was considerable resentment about Home's access to and presumed influence upon Bute and his seeming lack of any particular qualifications or skill. Home was also a playwright, and his political eminence gave new impetus to his dramatic career. In 1757–60 he had three plays ("Symphonies") staged in London—although Garrick had rejected two of them some years earlier (*ODNB*)—and it could be claimed that his success was at the expense of that of better qualified Englishmen ("capital [i.e., London] Performers"), such as Charles Churchill, who abused Bute and Home in print, in the *North Briton*, no. 7 (July 17, 1762), and *The Prophecy of Famine: A Scots Pastoral* (1763). Some of JB's early writings had been published

started up *Jack* the *Squinting* Ballad-singer, who went about the Streets with a Parcel of Blackguard Songs, to the Number of *Forty five*,[22] all of such a Nature as to inflame the Populace against SAWNEY, in which the Rogue succeeded so well, as to persuade them that they were to be *fed upon Oatmeal*, and *yoked like Beasts*, as the Song call'd, *The Merry First of August*, says.[23] So to work they went, and pelted poor SAWNEY with rotten Apples, and Oranges,[24] to such a Degree, that he was glad to come down from the *Orchestra*, and has since gone to *Italy* to improve himself in Music.[25]—*Jack*, however, had no great Reason to boast; for the Fellow was detected in singing both *Bawdy and Blasphemy*, for which he was *banished* for some Time, and, on his Return, was committed to *Bridewell*.[26] It

---

in company with Home's (see *Earlier Years*, 60, 71), and JB records meeting him in 1760 (*Life*, 1:457), and at social occasions thereafter, in London and Edinburgh, as recorded in his journals. See also Chap. 5, n. 246, for David Mallet, who was appointed by Bute to a remunerative sinecure in 1763.

22. John Wilkes (1725–97), radical politician and journalist, who was often caricatured by his most distinctive feature, a squint. He entered Parliament unopposed at a by-election in 1757. He and Churchill were responsible for the essay series the *North Briton* (1762–63)—intended as a rival to Bute's *The Briton*—no. 45 of which (Apr. 23, 1763) was Wilkes's notorious response to George III's praise of the settling of the Seven Years' War: it spawned forty court cases against Wilkes and led to his arrest under a general warrant and brief imprisonment, Apr. 30–May 6, in the Tower. The number forty-five—with its echo of the year of the second Jacobite uprising ("the Forty-Five")—became a byword for liberty and free speech. JB met Wilkes on May 24, 1763 (*Lond. Journ.*, 266), and remained on good terms with him all his life; his account of introducing Wilkes to Johnson in May 1776 is a famous passage (*Life*, 3:64–79).

23. August 1 was the date of the accession of George I in 1714 and an occasion for celebration for all supporters of the house of Hanover. "[Glorious] First of August" is given as a "Whig Song" in *The Jacobite Relics of Scotland*, ed. James Hogg:

> Let those that detest all Popish priests,
> Remember the First of August,
> And those who abhor to be yok'd like beasts
> Give thanks for the First of August. (1:407)
> (The phrase "fed on oatmeal" is not in this version.)

24. Appropriate fruits, since Bute saw the passage of a cider tax through Parliament, with invasive powers given to excise men; oranges may allude to Spain and the peace negotiations.

25. Bute continued to influence George III until 1766, by which time the king had more experience of public administration. Bute traveled in Italy for three years, 1769–71.

26. After being released on the grounds of parliamentary privilege, Wilkes challenged the legality of the general warrant. However, on Nov. 15, 1763, before a legal decision could be made on this issue, the House of Commons resolved to expel him for seditious libel. At the same time, the scurrilous (and privately printed) *Essay on Woman* (1763)—of which

must, at the same Time, be acknowledged, that those who persecuted *Jack* were droll Geniuses enough. There was HURLOTHRUMBO, a very *rough* Musician, and by much too *general* in his Ideas.[27] He paid no Regard to *Bars*; played on *false Keys*; made *Opens* where there should be none, and piqued himself on *seizing*, at once, *any* Air, *warranting* his *Practice* to be *just*. There was also *Jemmy Twitcher*, a profligate *Catch* Singer,[28] and fat *Will*, Mr. *Pope*'s *noted* Parson, who played so many Solos on the *Jews Harp*, crying out, that the Music was *divine*, though his Performances rather tended to prove the contrary.[29]

Wilkes had written at least the annotations—was read in extracts in the House of Lords, where he was condemned for impious and obscene libel. Having lost all parliamentary support, Wilkes fled to France on Dec. 25. In his absence, he was expelled from the Commons in Jan. 1764 and convicted for the two libels in February. He remained in Paris for most of the next four years. In Feb. 1768, short of money and hoping for a pardon, he returned to London, and—rallying popular support, which he was always able to do—on Mar. 28 he stood successfully for the parliamentary seat of Middlesex. While Parliament was trying to decide how to deal with him, he was sentenced on the 1764 convictions and imprisoned in King's Bench Prison (i.e., not Bridewell, which was a palace on the banks of the Fleet, part of which was from 1556 used as a prison).

   27. *Hurlothrumbo: Or, the Super-Natural* (1729) was a burlesque opera by Samuel Johnson (1691–1773), a dancing-master from Manchester, which had a record-breaking run at the Haymarket Theatre when first performed (a copy is listed in the *Sale Catalogue* of JB's library, 44). JB may intend this to represent SJ, who was opposed to Wilkes, wrote the *False Alarm* (1770), and was "general in his ideas." Another candidate is politician Edward Thurlow (1731–1806) [i.e., T"hurlo"w], who assisted the prosecution of Wilkes, and in Mar. 1770 became solicitor general. "Rough music" is the use of domestic implements to make a racket around someone's home as a means of punishing or embarrassing them. For "general" warrants, see nn. 22 and 26, above. There are further allusions to prisons and the law.
   28. Lord Sandwich (see Chap. 2, Hackman case headnote and n. 66) had been an associate of Wilkes in the rakish Monks of Medmenham (or Hell-fire Club) and in the Beefsteak Club (at a meeting of which on Nov. 27, 1762, JB saw them both; see *Lond. Journ.*, 51). Sandwich had led the ministry's attack on Wilkes in the Lords in 1764 and thus acquired the nickname Jemmy Twitcher, after a character in John Gay's *The Beggar's Opera* who betrays a colleague. See Rodger, *Insatiable Earl*, 99–105. Sandwich held elaborate private concerts and enjoyed singing.
   29. Pope's close friend, theological adviser, and executor was William Warburton (1698–1779), who was from 1760 the bishop of Gloucester. He was of a large and spare build; "fat" is perhaps broad irony. In *The Duellist*, Churchill describes him as "Ripen'd by a long course of years,/He great and perfect now appears./In Shape scarce of the human kind" (*Poetical Works*, III.785–87); Cash mentions his "tall bony self" (*John Wilkes*, 151). His book *The Divine Legation of Moses, Demonstrated on the Principles of a Religious Deist, from the Omission of the Doctrine of a Future State of Rewards and Punishments in the Jewish Dispensation* (1738–41) generated much controversy. In the notes to the *Essay on Woman*, Wilkes parodied Warburton's pedantic style of annotation.

Next came the celebrated GENTLE SHEPHERD, who had a great deal of the *Theory* of Music in his Head, but very little *Execution*.[30]—He had a *violent* Inclination to regulate the *American* Concerts, so nothing would serve him but sending over a Number of People to *stamp* to them, by Way of making them keep Time.[31] In vain did the Americans undertake to keep perfect good Time, without such Superintendants—*Stampers* he would send, let the Consequence be what it might. This same GENTLE SHEPHERD, though reckoned plodding and dull, had nevertheless a strange Kind of Vivacity. He wanted to be another *Orpheus*, and make the *Woods* dance after him—

> *Vocalem temere insecutæ*
> *Orphea Sylvæ.*[32]

He *pitched* upon the *Apple-trees* as his select Followers, but he soon found that he had been bringing up Sticks wherewith to break his own Head.[33]

The next *first Musician* was a YORKSHIRE FARMER, who being averse to the Stile of the *Court*, begged Leave to entertain us with agreeable *Country* Music.[34]

---

30. George Grenville (1712–70), prime minister, 1763–65. He was an able parliamentarian and efficient economic manager but lacked political skill. He was nicknamed "Gentle Shepherd" because during the 1763 debate on the Cider Bill he asked rhetorically "where" else a new tax could be laid if not on cider; Pitt whistled the air of the popular tune *Gentle Shepherd, tell me where*, and the House laughed. See Lawson, *George Grenville*, 149.

31. Grenville is best known for his determination to tax the American colonies by introducing to Parliament the Stamp Act of 1765, which was to apply to all newspapers, legal documents, licenses, dice, playing cards, and official documents in the colonies. These measures raised the crucial question of taxation without representation, and this act was the first major measure in events leading to the imperial crisis.

32. Horace, *Odes*, 1.12.7–8: "Unde vocalem temere insecutae / Orphea silvae" (whence in confusion the trees followed after tuneful Orpheus, 34). In Greek mythology, the music of the poet Orpheus had the power to move inanimate things. *Woods* here is a metonym for America and its forests.

33. Grenville supported Bute's cider tax.

34. Charles Watson-Wentworth, second marquess of Rockingham (1730–82), prime minister, July 1765–July 1766 (and again in 1782). He was born in Yorkshire and inherited extensive properties. The terms *court* and *country* allude to ideological tendencies among parliamentarians, dating from the end of the previous century: the "Court" faction tended to support the king's chosen ministers and believed that frequent elections threatened the constitution; those of the "Country" persuasion believed that the power of the monarch and his ministers (the court) encroached upon the rightful role of Parliament and the House of Commons—in effect, they thought political power was best consolidated in the hands of independent landed gentry. The Rockingham whigs were influenced by "country" politics, although by this time this influence was waning.

But, alas! the good FARMER's Music would not do. For tho' he was very able to pipe it away to a Team of Oxen, when plowing a *Turnip Field*, he had not *Power* sufficient for a *public* Performer, and so he was obliged in his Turn to *resign*.[35] I own I regretted him; for though his *Instrument* was *feeble*, he played very pleasingly,[36] and had besides some Musicians along with him, whom I liked—in particular *George St. Andrews*, who has now betaken himself to the *East Indies*, where, I am told, he makes a considerable Figure as one of the *Directors* of their Concerts.[37]

The next *first Musician* was GRAVETONE, who, having a little Royal Blood in his Veins, somewhat resembled *Prince Henry* as described by SHAKESPEARE;[38]

35. By "plowing a turnip field" and "piping away to a team of oxen," JB is likely alluding to Rockingham's rural constituency and constituents, or at least implying that he was a country bumpkin whose skills were not sufficient to manage a national government. Furthermore, the king was well known for his interest in farming, and turnips were "associated with George III . . . as a result of a long-standing satirical tradition linking turnips with the Hanoverian kings. According to popular rumour, George I had been hoeing turnips in his garden at Hanover when he heard of Queen Anne's death" (Miller, "J. M. W. Turner's *Ploughing up Turnips*," 577). So the *plowing* and *piping* suggest conducting the king's business and giving directions to his loyal supporters, inherited from Newcastle. Rockingham faced difficulties in establishing his government because he refused to have Bute or Grenville or their supporters in his cabinet; he invited Pitt, who refused him; and he did not have the support of George III. He was interested in the development of his estates and preferred his family home and doing political business at horse races to spending time in Parliament. Rockingham did not resign but was removed after a disagreement with the king.

36. Rockingham regarded the stamp tax imposed on the American colonies as both unjust and unwise, and his major achievement was to see to the repeal of the Stamp Act and thus end the riots against it in America—although his hand was forced by the colonists' refusal to import goods from Britain, which caused the exports of British merchants and manufacturers to suffer. Rockingham was a nervous and very ineffective Parliamentary speaker, although fluent enough in private conversation; but JB is likely also alluding to his rumored impotence (*ODNB*; Farrell, "Practices and Purposes of Party Leadership").

37. JB's Scottish friend George Dempster (1732–1818), of Dunnichen, was from 1760 the MP for Perth Burghs, which included the town of St. Andrews; Dempster spoke frequently in Parliament and supported Rockingham, who as prime minister appointed him as secretary to the Order of the Thistle, though he was never a minister. Dempster was very active as a director of the East India Company. "[T]he evidence suggests they [JB and Dempster] had met in the late or even the middle 1750s" (*Corres. 9*, l). See also n. 181, below.

38. Augustus Henry FitzRoy, third duke of Grafton (1735–1811), whig prime minister, 1768–70, nicknamed "Royal Oak" (see n. 198, below; he was a fourth-generation descendant of Charles II). He was invited to form a government after Pitt (now Earl of Chatham) became ill and incapable. In Shakespeare's *Henry IV*, Parts 1 and 2, Henry V is depicted as Prince Hal, an irresponsible playboy who associates with the disreputable Sir John ("Jack") Falstaff, who also appears in *Henry V*.

for, like him, he had once kept very odd Company, such as *Jack*, the *squinting* Ballad-Singer.[39]—Then he would go and play "*Jockey*" at the *Newmarket* Meetings, and indulge himself in other Extravagancies.[40] But no sooner was he advanced to the Rank of *first Musician* than he appeared with quite a different *Air*; he led the Band like a Master, and played a very strong Bow.—He did not give the Satisfaction he ought to have done: For some absurd, riotous People wanted forsooth to have *squinting Jack* admitted into the Concert-Hall, though he had been *kicked down Stairs* no less than three Times; and they exclaimed against GRAVETONE for being firm against so ridiculous and shameful a Plan.[41] One of the most virulent Enemies of GRAVETONE was a Ballad-Singer, who used to ply in *Ivy-Lane*, *Pater-noster-Row*, disguised in *an old Roman* Dress—Nobody could tell who he was—Some took him for *a Man of Fashion*—others for an *Irish White Boy*. Every Thing he sung was quite *false*; but there was something so keen and lively in his *Manner*, that he passed with the Generality for a very good Singer.[42] Many People found Fault with GRAVETONE that he did not take

39. While Wilkes ("Jack, the squinting ballad-singer") was imprisoned in the Tower in spring 1763, a great parade of notable people, including Grafton, tried to visit him "to hear from himself his own story and his defence; and to shew that no influence ought to stop the means of every man's justifying himself from an accusation, even though it should be of the most heinous kind" (Grafton to Temple, May 3, 1763; quoted in Grafton, *Autobiography*, 191). (Later, during his exile in Paris, Wilkes made a number of secret visits to London in attempts to use his influence to gain a pardon. Grafton, now as First Lord of the Treasury, refused to help, and Wilkes in a fury wrote his abusive *Letter to the Duke of Grafton* [1767].)

40. Grafton was also known for being (with Rockingham) a founding member of the Jockey Club, which has run horse races at Newmarket since 1752. "Grafton was often referred to as 'a jockey' [i.e., a horse owner and rider] in the radical press, a term that neatly associated a disreputable love of the turf with womanising and a propensity for devious and fraudulent conduct" (Sainsbury, *John Wilkes*, 203). The "other extravagancies" may refer to the sequence of mistresses he was known to have kept.

41. After Wilkes's election as MP for Middlesex in Mar. 1768, he continued to provoke the ministry, and Grafton, who had supported him earlier—and despite his reluctance to inflame his followers—now supported his expulsion from Parliament in Feb. 1769. Wilkes was reelected a few weeks later, on Feb. 16, rejected by the Commons the following day as "incapable" of election, returned in a second by-election on Mar. 16, which was declared void, and when he won a third by-election on Apr. 13 the Commons declared his rival, a ministry nominee, to have been elected, although Wilkes won the vote by 1,143 to 296. Wilkes was in King's Bench Prison all this time, from June 14, 1768, to Apr. 1770. (In support of Wilkes, more than thirty petitions called for the dissolution of Parliament, signed by a quarter of the electorate, and the Society of Gentlemen Supporters of the Bill of Rights was created; see n. 110, below).

42. The anonymous political controversialist who called himself by the Latin name "Junius" published his fifty-eight or more letters (like the "Rampagers") in the *Pub. Adv.*

into his Concert some Performers on the *Corsican Shell*,[43] who were very clever in their Way, could play several smart *irregular Marches*, and good Pieces of *bold Water-Music*,[44] and would not be drowned even by *French-Horns*, unless the latter were much superior in Numbers.—While there was a terrible Confusion in the Concert-Hall, an old experienced DOCTOR of Music, remarkable for the *full Tone* of his SONOROUS BASSOON, though he had been very lazy, and played none for several Years, stepped out of JOHNSON's *Music Shop*, and gave a GRAND VOLUNTARY, which had the Effect to compose all who had a *real good* Ear.[45]

For what Reason GRAVETONE has quitted his Place I cannot tell,[46] but I see it is taken up by AUSTER, who has *Lungs of Brass*, and swears he is determined to keep it.[47] He has not yet performed enough for us to judge of his Abilities as a

---

(Jan. 1769–Mar. 1772), of which the London address was Ivy Lane, Paternoster Row. Politicians Edmund Burke ("an Irish White Boy") and William Gerard Hamilton (1729–96) ("a Man of Fashion") were, among many others, suspected of their authorship; a "White Boy" was an Irish agrarian rebel. Grafton was regarded by Junius as particularly corrupt and was the primary target of his vitriolic attacks.

43. *Corsican Shell*: from 1766, William Petty (formerly Fitzmaurice), second earl of Shelburne, a strong supporter of Pitt, was secretary of state for the southern department. In 1768, France annexed Corsica, increasing the threat France posed to Britain. Shelburne protested in warm terms to the French court but was not supported by the ministry and resigned (see Burke, *Thoughts on the Cause of the Present Discontents*, par. 70). A Corsican merchant navy was established by General Paoli in 1760, and under him the Corsican army fought a guerilla war ("smart irregular marches") against the French, until the Battle of Ponte Nuovo on May 8–9, 1769, when a French force of 34,000 defeated a very much smaller Corsican army, and the Corsican republic ended. (On May 20, 1768, JB met with the Lord Chief Justice, Lord Mansfield, and supposed himself to have "[c]onvinced him of the importance of Corsica" (*Search*, 184), although, as the journal editors note, he was mistaken.)

44. The popular *Water Music* of George Frederic Handel is a collection of three orchestral suites that were first performed in 1717, for the first Hanoverian king, George I.

45. SJ, who had been awarded an honorary doctorate of laws by Trinity College, Dublin, in July 1765, published his tract on the Wilkes case, *The False Alarm*, on Jan. 16, 1770. A music publisher and instrument seller, John Johnson (fl. 1740–62), and after his death his widow, kept a music shop in Cheapside, which offered music classes and sold tickets for concerts and advertised in the newspapers, from at least 1746. JB could have bought a ticket there for the Shakespeare Jubilee (see *St. James's Chron.*, Aug. 24, 1769). A voluntary is a piece of music, often written to be played (usually by the organ) before or after a church service; it is intended to sound as if improvised (JB is making the point that SJ's political writings were not, as was sometimes said, paid services to the ministry).

46. In the face of defections from his cabinet, the abuse of Junius, damage to his public and private reputation, and the opposition of Chatham, Grafton resigned at the end of Jan. 1770.

47. Frederick, Lord North, later second earl of Guilford (1732–92), became, at the king's request, chancellor of the exchequer and First Lord of the Treasury—i.e., prime minister—

first Musician, so we must wait a little. In the mean time I cannot help observing that there is a strange Jumble of Sounds in *Opposition* to the regular Concert.[48] You have an *Ass* with a *Bell* before it, commonly called the *Bell-Ass*, *ringing* Sedition through the Streets.[49] You have a *mad Parson* blowing a *Horn*[50]—*A Creole* squeaking on a *Sugar-Cane*[51]—*Butchers* rattling their *Marrowbones and Cleavers*[52]—*Teagues* raising the *Irish Howl*[53]—and a Set of drunken Companions at the *London Tavern*, who play on the Musical *Glasses*, and are continually roaring for a *Bill*.[54] In short, were old *Jeremy Collier* alive, he might have some Idea of the shocking *Anti-Music* as he calls it, which he schemed to form out

---

on Jan. 28, 1770. He remained in those roles until 1782. Although the opposition highlighted his supposed Toryism, he had served in governments under Newcastle, Chatham, and Grafton. *Auster* is a reference to the south wind: North's more common nickname was *Boreas* (the north wind). The basis of his long ministry was his candor and good humor in the Commons and the confidence of the king. *Lungs of Brass* is an expression meaning a strident voice.

48. At the time of writing, Lord North faced three separate groups of opponents in Parliament: the supporters of Grenville, Rockingham, and Chatham.

49. George Bellas (d. 1776), a pro-Wilkite alderman.

50. John Horne (later, Horne Tooke; 1736–1812), radical politician (and, later, philologist). Although forced into the priesthood for a living, he was more interested in the law and became a noisy partisan of John Wilkes, speaking and publishing on his behalf. (In 1768 he published a pamphlet calling for the prosecution of Edward M'Quirk; see n. 109, below.) He was one of the founders of the SSBR (see n. 41, above) and was said to have authored the two remonstrances presented to George III by the City of London (see next note).

51. *Creole* was a term used for those who had business interests in the West Indies. The "West Indians" were a sizable voting bloc in the House of Commons (see Namier, *England in the Age of American Revolution*, 234 ff.), chief among whom was William Beckford (bap. 1709–70), who, after being active in Jamaican politics, returned to England and in 1754 became an MP for London. He was Jamaica's biggest landowner (ibid., 237). He served as Lord Mayor in 1762–63 and again (unusually) in 1769–70, in which capacity he presented to the king, on Mar. 14 and May 23, two strongly worded remonstrances in support of Wilkes. The West Indians lobbied for the enforcement of the 1764 sugar tax, which delivered them market advantages but was objected to by the North Americans.

52. Marrowbones and cleavers were the principal instruments employed in "rough music" (see n. 27, above): a reference to the noisy public processions and demonstrations attendant upon the Wilkite cause.

53. *Teague* is a nickname for an Irishman (*OED*), and *Howl* suggests keening. In Feb. 1770, Lord North's government undertook to support the Lord Lieutenant of Ireland, George, first Marquess Townshend (1724–1807), in various measures to reform the governance of Ireland and wrest control from Irish politicians. Townshend prorogued the Irish Parliament, and the unpopularity of this move led to attacks in the press on him and his administration, and a pamphlet war.

54. The London Tavern in Bishopsgate Street was the meeting place of supporters of Wilkes. On Feb. 20, 1770, they subscribed £3,340 to support Wilkes and on Feb. 25 formed

of the Voices of Lions, Cats and Dogs: "An Instrument, says he, that shall sink the Spirits and shake the Nerves, and curdle the Blood, and inspire Despair and Cowardice, and Consternation at a surprising Rate."*[55] When this Noise will cease I cannot tell; but I think it is very probable that we shall soon have *Trumpets* and *Kettle-Drums*, which will effectually put an End to it.[56]

I am, Sir,

Your constant Correspondent,

RAMIGER.[57]

No. 2: The "Political Musicians," Continued

[Boswell's pseudonym was misspelled at the foot of his first contribution (above), and this incited him to consider the value of names in the peerage: with his feudal sensibilities, he is contemptuous of people taking new names for money. He continues his examination of "Political Musicians" during the tumultuous 1770 parliamentary session, which began in January with the resignation of the prime minister, the Duke of Grafton. Much to the dismay of a firmly united opposition (consisting of more than one ex–prime minister), Lord North stepped in to rob them of victory—although North himself apparently had to be convinced to take this step, in opposition to his own inclination, by George III.]

Public Advertiser, May 12, 1770, 2 (leading article)

SIR,

YOU have honoured my Essay on the POLITICAL MUSICIANS with a Place in your admirable Paper; but you have fallen into a CAPITAL Mistake in printing my Name, which you know consists of CAPITAL LETTERS. My Name, Sir, is not RAMIGER, as you have made it, but RAMPAGER. I desire that you may not be guilty of such a *Misnomer*. Suppose I should call you *Wilful* instead of *Woodfall*,

---

the SSBR (see n. 41, above). The *musical glasses* or glass harp is a musical instrument made of specially tuned wine glasses, invented in Ireland in 1741.

55. "*Collier's Essay on Music." (BOSWELL)

Jeremy Collier (1650–1726), theological writer and non-juring bishop, remembered mainly for his *Short View of the Immorality and Profaneness of the English Stage* (1698). This passage from "On Musick," in Collier's *Essays upon Several Moral Subjects* (1705–09), is quoted in *Spectator*, no. 361 (Apr. 24, 1712; 3:352); it concludes by wondering if "such anti-music as this might not be of service in a [military] camp."

56. Kettle drums (or timpani) were often paired with trumpets in military bands; JB seems to suggest that there will be royal or military intervention, or both.

57. *Ramiger*, which in Latin would mean *branch-carrier*, is a printer's error (*Cat. Yale*, P 152, 1087); see essay following.

how would you like it?[58] Sir, I glory in my Name,[59] and would not change it for that of *Holles, Dunk, Pynsent*,[60] or any other of the *golden Number*.[61] I do not mean the *Rule of Three*, though I have mentioned just three Names;[62] I mean the Names which, like Pills, have been gilt in order to induce People to *take them*.[63] *Rampager*, Sir, is a most valuable and significant Name, being derived from the Verb *to rampage*, which signifies to indulge in joyous extravagant Merriment, free of all Care and all Malice;[64] I therefore hope you will do me the Justice to insert this *Prelude* as well as what follows.

Since my last some Wags have hinted to me, that in my Account of SAWNEY I should have observed, that he played upon the *Scotch Fiddle*, and that, during his Performance, the Audience complained grievously that they were quite sick of FAVOURITE *Airs*.[65] You will best judge, you Londoners, if that was the Case;

58. Henry Sampson Woodfall (1739–1805), printer of the *Pub. Adv.* (see Chap. 3, intro).

59. An allusion to George III's famous declaration of 1760, "I glory in the name of Briton."

60. *Holles*: Pelham-Holles, Duke of Newcastle, was born Thomas Pelham. His mother's brother died in 1711, bequeathing him a vast estate, on condition that he append "Holles" to his name; he fulfilled this duty for the rest of his life. *Dunk* refers to George Montagu-Dunk, second earl of Halifax (1716–71). Born George Montagu, it was a condition of his marriage (and his receiving a dowry of £110,000) in 1741 that he took the surname of his wife, Ann Dunk. Sir William *Pynsent* (c. 1681–1765) was an eccentric baronet, who as a young man had been a whig MP and in his old age became an admirer of William Pitt. Although he was personally not even known to Pitt, at his death he gifted the bulk of his estate, Burton Pynsent, near Devizes in Somerset, to Pitt in gratitude for (it was said) his opposition to the new tax on cider. The will was challenged by Pynsent's surviving (distant) relatives but was finally decided in Pitt's favor in Apr. 1771. See *History, Military and Municipal*, 392–97.

61. Technically, the *golden number* refers to the number showing a year's place in the Metonic lunar cycle, used to fix the date of Easter for that year; the *golden ratio* (described mathematically as $a+b$ is to a as a is to b, or approximately 1.618) is a proportion represented by the Greek letter *phi*, which, in the Renaissance, was regarded as of particular importance and aesthetic pleasingness. JB's irony here is very broad.

62. In classical rhetoric, the Rule of Three is a form of comedic writing whereby the joke is set up, the setup is reinforced, and the punchline violates the pattern: here, Pitt violates the pattern by not taking the name of his benefactor.

63. The idiom *to gild* (or *sugar*) *the pill*, meaning to make something unpleasant more palatable, dates from the late 1700s.

64. *Rampage* is not in SJ's *Dictionary*, probably owing to its Scots origins. The *OED* dates the verb to 1692.

65. Although, as prime minister, Lord Bute ("Sawney") brought peace after the Seven Years' War, he was unpopular for being a Scot and because he was the "favourite" of the king and gave government appointments to favorites of his own. The Ayr Burghs ("Air") par-

but *e contra*,[66] I have found in Dr. *Armstrong's* Miscellanies a Passage excellently *adapted* for the Performers in *Opposition*. It is in his own *sharp* Stile as follows:

"What Pleasure can you feel from the Applause of those Animals? You may, indeed, make it conducive to some selfish Designs, and use it as a Tool of Ambition. I allow there is some Meaning in that. But what is quite beyond my Comprehension, supposing you still to be a Man of some Sense, this *discordant* Cry of an ignorant, worthless, stupid, dirty Rabble flatters your Vanity. Indeed it does; and it delights you to hear this Variety of a most brutish Creation bellow, bleat, bray, grunt, squeak, roar, bark, mew, cackle, prate, and chatter in your Praise. You must have a delicate *Ear*, Sir, to relish such a *Concert*. Your solid, wirey Nerves are asleep it would seem to the Lute, the Welch-Harp, and the Violoncello.—They thrill only to Marrowbones and Cleavers, or the Bob-Majors of St. Giles's."[67] Vol. I. Page 198.[68]

It is worthy of Observation that our *Political Musicians* of this Age have been not a little divided as to the *Key* on which they ought to play. One and all of them pretend a strict Adherence to what may be called the G. R. *Cliff*,[69] while at the same Time the *three* Brothers have played the highest *Treble*.[70] You may

---

liamentary constituency in Scotland was controlled by Bute (see Burn, "General Election of 1761," 104). To play on the "Scotch fiddle" is to scratch because of "the itch" (see n. 100, below). As fiddlers scratch with a bow the strings of a fiddle, so persons suffering from skin irritation keep scratching the part irritated. JB also plays on *fiddle* as meaning to swindle and cheat (*OED*).

66. *E contra*: on the other hand.

67. *Marrowbones and cleavers* (see n. 52 and text, above) were often associated with weddings: "ringing the bells" on marrowbones and cleavers. *Bob-Majors* is a pattern in English change ringing (ringing a set of tuned bells in a series of patterns called "changes"). St. Giles Cripplegate is a medieval parish church in London.

68. John Armstrong (1708/9–79), Scottish physician and poet, had a turbulent career, including very public quarrels (some through the *Pub. Adv.*) with his one-time close friend, Wilkes. Armstrong's *Miscellanies* is an almost comprehensive collection of his writing. This passage (*Miscellanies*, 1:198–99) is from *The Muncher's and Guzzler's Diary* (1749), a "mock almanac with absurd observations, prognostications, and advice on husbandry month by month" (*ODNB*). After 1735, Armstrong lived in London, where JB got to know him; in the earlier volumes of his journals, JB mentions a number of meetings and alludes to Armstrong's work.

69. G. R. is *Georgius Rex* (i.e., King George, as he is denominated in Acts of Parliament and official documents). *Cliff* is an archaic term for "clef" (*OED*). In Britain, all parliamentarians swear allegiance to the king.

70. The leading opposition figures, Chatham, George Grenville, and Richard Grenville, second Earl Temple (1711–79), were brothers-in-law and referred to as "the brotherhood." When Chatham recovered from his illness in 1769, it was thought that the trio would unite

remember what an Outcry was raised against a certain CHIEF *Musician* of *the King's Band* for having altered the *Cliff* of a noted Performance to *Tenor*, which was stigmatised as *thorough Base*.[71]

The CITY *Music* seems to grow *louder* and *louder*. What *Effect* it will have nobody as yet can tell. The *Creolian* Leader of *their* Band complains that the *Music* he heard in *answer* to it sounded very *harsh*.[72] As to the Performers at St. James's, if they do not actually *shake*, it must be confessed that they give at least a good many *Demisemiquavers*. I fairly own I wish they would play with a little more *Spirit*.[73]

I am, SIR,

Your constant Correspondent,

RAMPAGER.

No. 3: Doctrine of Fatality Avowed by Dissenting Lords in Wilkes Vote

[In response to the repeated reelection of John Wilkes as member for Middlesex, the Commons had repeatedly voted that the elections were null and void and that Wilkes was "incapable of being elected." On May 1, Lord Chatham introduced a bill in the House of Lords to rescind the resolutions of the House of Commons the previous year concerning the Middlesex election; it was unsurprisingly rejected, 89 to 43. The ostensible starting point for this essay is the phrase "an over-ruling fatality,"

---

to challenge Grafton's ministry, but, when that ministry collapsed, the king turned to Lord North to form a government.

71. *Thoroughbass* (or *figured bass*) is a kind of musical notation. "Altering the clef of the performance by moving the figured bass to the tenor line would change the nature of the leading role of the bass line (in short its authority over the other voices in the musical texture) to that of an inner voice (a voice part with traditionally little role in musical leadership)" (Paul Rice, personal communication). Wilkes was tried in Feb. 1764 for libel, for publishing the *North Briton*, no. 45, and the *Essay on Woman* (and its notes: hence, the "noted Performance"). Before the trials, the Lord Chief Justice, William Murray, first earl of Mansfield (1705–93), altered the wording of the charge against Wilkes, from "purport and effect" to "tenor and effect." This ensured that he was found guilty (Cash, *John Wilkes*, 171–72). Mansfield was regarded by many as the leading figure in the government, because of his close relationship with the king.

72. For William Beckford, Lord Mayor, 1769–70, see n. 51, above. "The king's answer to the remonstrance [of Mar. 14] was couched in words of strong reproof" (*ODNB*).

73. The Court of St. James is the British royal court. JB wants the court to be stronger, and not to shake or quaver, against the populism of the city of London and of Middlesex, which in his view threatened the balance of the constitution. The use of the terms "shake," "quaver," and "Spirit" alludes to Christian sects such as the Quakers and to religious "enthusiasm" in general, such as found among Methodists.

which Boswell finds (to his mind) ludicrously applied in the statement, which he quotes, issued after the vote by the dissenting Lords.]

Public Advertiser, June 16, 1770, 1–2; with Boswell's MS corrections

SIR,

THE great Question with Regard to Liberty and Necessity, Fate and Free-will hath perplexed and divided Philosophers both Heathen and Christian, and seems like to do so while the World lasts.[74] Various have been the Opinions upon this intricate Subject, and various the Methods in which Authors and Churches have expressed themselves concerning it. But the most extraordinary Testimony with Respect to it, which I have been able to discover, is the late *Protest* of so many *patriotic Peers* against rejecting the Earl of CHATHAM's *ingenious* Bill, to make a Great House *resolve* in direct Contradiction to what they had but a few Weeks before solemnly resolved, and, with great Propriety, uttered to the Ear of Majesty.[75] The PROTEST, instead of *declaiming* against *secret Influence*, like the Author of *Thoughts on the Cause of the present Discontents*,[76] or *raving* against *Monarchy*, and *Placemen sitting in Parliament*, like *Mrs. Catharine Macaulay*[77]—*Caput inter nubila condit*[78]—soars at once into the Clouds of metaphysical Speculation; and pronounces the dreadful Cause of all our Woes, to be AN OVER-RULING FATALITY. Thus it runs—

74. JB was long disturbed by ideas about "divine foreknowledge and the human freedom to choose—the question, as he phrased it, of liberty versus necessity," which ideas he first encountered in John Stevenson's course on logic at the University of Edinburgh (*ODNB*, s.v. "Boswell, James").

75. On May 1, 1770, Chatham presented in the House of Lords "A Bill for reversing the Adjudications of the H. of C. whereby John Wilkes, Esq; has been adjudged incapable of being elected a member in this present Parliament, and the freeholders of the county of Middlesex have been deprived of one of their legal representatives." See an account of the proceedings of the House of Lords on May 1, 1770, under the heading "A remarkable Protest in an illustrious Assembly," *London Magazine*, 39 (May 1770), 247–48.

76. Burke's *Thoughts on the Cause of the Present Discontents*, published Apr. 1770, argued that strong whig government was needed to protect the nation against the "secret influence" (of the Crown).

77. Whig historian and polemicist Catharine Macaulay (1731–91); in her reply to Burke, *Observations on a Pamphlet Entitled "Thoughts on the Cause of the Present Discontents"* (1770), she traced the causes of political corruption to the constitution itself. "Placemen" were government employees who would vote with the ministry. Her pamphlet was said to have influenced Americans to reject constitutional monarchy as the model for a free government. For more on Burke and Mrs. Macaulay, see nn. 112, 113, below.

78. *Caput inter nubila condit* (She hides her head among the clouds). In the *Aeneid* (4.177), the expression is applied to the monster *Fama*: Fame or Rumor.

"Dissentient,[79]

Because the Foundations of this Bill, being so fully laid in the Reasons contained in two Protests, entered upon the Journals of this House, on the Second Day of February last, We think it indispensibly necessary to protest against the Rejection of the same, to the Intent that it may be delivered down to Posterity, that this great constitutional and effectual Method of remedying an unexampled Grievance, hath not been left unattempted by Us; and that to Our own Times We may stand as Men determined to *persevere* in renewing, on every Occasion, our utmost *Endeavours* to obtain that Redress, for the violated Rights of the Subjects, and for the injured Electors of Great-Britain, which, in the present Moment, AN OVER-RULING FATALITY hath prevented from taking Effect, thereby refusing Reparation and Comfort to an oppressed and afflicted People."[80]

Here is certainly as formal an Avowal of the Doctrine of *Fatality* as was ever made, in direct Terms, by the *Stoicks* of old, or in the round-about Method of *Predestination*, by the *Mahometans*, or *Calvinists*, of more modern Times. This Protest will, no doubt, mightily rejoice the Calvinists, as it seems calculated to give a Sanction to one of their grand Principles. That it was certainly intended so to do, must appear from a Circumstance, for which we have the Authority of the News-papers, viz. That *Earl Stanhope* came all the Way from *Geneva, the City of John Calvin*, "to bear witness against the present Mode of Government."[81]—It is farther to be remarked, that our News-papers have designed his Lordship the *venerable* Peer, which is the very Title given to the Clergy of *Geneva*, who are designed *La venerable Compagnie*.[82] We are also told, that he *read* his Speech;

79. A term used to introduce a dissenting opinion, one that differs from that of the majority.

80. This passage was quoted in the *London Magazine* article (248), with here two very minor differences, apart from the *Pub. Adv.*'s old-fashioned capitalization, and JB's underlining and capitals for emphasis.

81. William Stanhope, second earl of Harrington (1719–79), soldier and politician. According to the *Middlesex Journal* (May 3, 1770), 3, "This worthy Nobleman, having retired from his native country to spend the remainder of his days at Geneva, on hearing of so important a business, as the right of the Electors of Middlesex brought into question, left the place of his retreat, and came with all imaginable haste to his native country. The venerable Peer was determined to bear witness against the present mode of Government. He read his speech, which breathed the spirit of Liberty, and was heard with that attention which it deserved."

82. Geneva, on Lake Leman in Switzerland, was from 1536 a Protestant republic, under the leadership of the reformer John Calvin. The Venerable Company of Pastors was the

from which we may infer, that it did not spring up in a Day, but was a *Plant* of the Growth of that same little Republican Spot: And however *mathematically* it may have been *pruned*, hath had a *watering* of the *Leman Lake* from that zealous Divine *M. Vernet*, the *Apollos* in that Quarter.[83] I would, however, humbly suggest to the *venerable Peer*, that, upon some Occasions, *Silence*, a Virtue so much approved by *Pythagoras*, is as sure a Sign of Wisdom, as to know the *Pythagorean Proposition*.[84]—The Sentiments of a pure Republican, and those of a British Constitutionalist, are like *parallel Lines*, which will never meet while the World lasts. It is in vain for a few Peers, though ever so patriotic, to oppose the whole House; for *the Whole is greater than any of its Parts*; and it is the same Thing to the People *who* are Ministers, and basking in the Sun-shine of Court Favour.

—Sit in the *Centre*, and enjoy bright Day;[85]

For *all the Radii drawn from the Centre of a Circle, to its Circumference, are equal.*

The Title of the *Bishop of Bangor* hath been an Age ago renowned in *Controversy*.[86] But I am amazed that the present Right Reverend Father of that See hath risen in Opposition.[87] I grant that a *Bishop opposing the Ministry* is next to a *Miracle*. But his Lordship might have considered, that: if they believe not the *Mayor of*

---

group of reformed ministers that Calvin organized in the 1540s to manage church affairs. JB visited Geneva Dec. 22, 1764–Jan. 1, 1765, on his Grand Tour (*Grand Tour 1*, 265–304).

83. Jacob Vernet (1698–1789) was from 1730 the leading Calvinist pastor in Geneva; he had been a friend of Rousseau but later became a bitter enemy (*Holland*, 250 n. 1; *Grand Tour 1*, 219 n. 1). See Sorkin, "Geneva's 'Enlightened Orthodoxy.'" By describing him as "Apollos," JB implies that he is a factional leader, like the early Jewish Christian mentioned in 1 Corinthians 1:10–12.

84. It was said that those who belonged to the school of the ancient Greek philosopher Pythagoras were required to maintain a strict silence, even among themselves, about Pythagoras's teachings. Pythagoras is best known for his theorem about ratios within right-angled triangles. JB goes on to allude to other mathematical commonplaces: that parallel lines never meet, that a whole is greater than its parts, that all points on the circumference of a circle are at an equal distance from the center.

85. Milton, "Comus: A Mask," line 382.

86. In 1717, the then Bishop of Bangor (in Wales), Benjamin Hoadly (1676–1761), initiated the so-called Bangorian Controversy, concerning important issues of ecclesiastical and state authority. He was an extreme whig whose views challenging the non-juring clergy were in fact opposed by most clergy but were favored by King George I.

87. John Ewer (1703–74), Bishop of Bangor from 1769. In a sermon of Feb. 1767, as Bishop of Llandaff, he sparked controversy by attacking the government's failure to supply the American colonists with their own bishops.

"*London*, and the *Sheriffs*, neither will they believe though one riseth from the *Woolpack*."[88]

The DIGNIFIED FATALISTS, with great Deference be it spoken, have not made the Use of their Doctrine which might have been expected.[89] Mr. *Pope*, the Bard of their Sect gravely asks,

> "If Plagues or Earthquakes break not Heav'n's Design,
> Why then a Borgia or a Cataline?"

And seems perfectly satisfied with the Conclusion, that WHATEVER IS IS RIGHT.[90] Why do not they, in Conformity with this Principle, quietly submit to the *Decree* of *Destiny?* The Exclusion of *Jack Wilkes* from a Seat in Parliament, is not surely more tremendous and horrible than a Plague or an Earthquake. But instead of behaving with calm Resignation, their Spirit of *Liberty* is rouzed against *Necessity*, and they stand determined to *persevere* (like *Saints*)[91] "in renewing their Endeavours" to have their *Pius Æneas*—FATO *profugus*, reinstated.[92]

It is pleasant to consider, that all your *Fatalists* are every Moment forgetting the Nature of their *Creed*, which, without *Universality*, without being literally χαθόλιχη,[93] is nothing. How can *they* "endeavour" who are included in the *fatal* System of Things? They are like ignorant Passengers aboard a Ship, who pull by one of the Cables, to stop the Progress of the Vessel, which contains them and all their Force. Could *Fatalists*, indeed, detach themselves from their supposed Torrent of *pre-determined* Causes and Effects, they might attempt to thwart or

88. An allusion to Jesus' parable of Dives and Lazarus: "And he said unto him, If they hear not Moses and the prophets, neither will they be persuaded, though one rose from the dead" (Luke 16:31). In the House of Commons, the Woolsack (not Woolpack) is the seat of the presiding officer, the Lord Chancellor.

89. Throughout the next two paragraphs, JB treats the opposition MPs behind the dissenting motion as religious dissenters and therefore adherents to the Calvinist doctrine of predestination, which would militate against dissenting against fate in any form—particularly in the form of a vote in the House of Commons.

90. Pope, *Essay on Man*, epistle 1, lines 155–56, 294. Pope's poem caused much controversy as it was taken—despite Pope's Catholicism—to deny revelation and, in SJ's later words, to represent "the whole course of things as a necessary concatenation of indissoluble fatality" (*Lives of the Most Eminent English Poets*, ed. Lonsdale, 4:40; ¶183).

91. Based on Hebrews 3:13, the "perseverance of the saints" is a Calvinist doctrine that those who are truly saved can never fall away from salvation.

92. Aeneas, the hero of Virgil's *Aeneid*, is often referred to as "Pious Aeneas." *Fato profugus*: exiled by fate (*Aeneid*, 1.2).

93. χαθόλιχη: catholic, in the sense of *universal*; hence, the irony of preaching a universal doctrine and yet belonging to a particular sect.

impede its Course, as *Archimedes* boasted, that if he had a Place whereon to rest himself and his Engine, he could raise the Globe.[94] But this they cannot do. Since, however, they *are* to "persevere," and it may be long enough before they effectuate their Purpose, I would have them *enjoy* Life, as Individuals, whatever happens, and take the Advice of old *Chiron*, when preaching to his Pupil *Achilles*, "what the *Fates did decree*."

> All the Time you lie before the Town drink,
> All the Time you lie before the Town drink,
> Drink, drink, drink and be merry;
> You'll ne'er go the sooner to the Stygian Ferry.[95]

I am, Sir,
Your constant Correspondent,
RAMPAGER.

No. 4: The "Smelling Medicine," Politically Applied

[Boswell applies to British politics the claims of a medicinal preparation he has seen advertised in Scotland, which professes to cure all skin diseases by smelling. After describing various supposed Scottish responses, elaborating in particular upon the interpretation of the advertisement as a satire upon the Scottish nation, he then suggests that it is to be understood politically, as a "*Type* of the *Times*," in which various factions and commentators are proffering a variety of drastic single remedies for the current political problems. Boswell wishes that there were a simple remedy for "the factious *Heat*"—a skin disorder particularly affecting Wilkes and his supporters, making them "peevish and froward"—but predicts that the only smell to cure faction and sedition is the smell of gunpowder.]

Public Advertiser, July 6, 1770, 1 (leading article); with Boswell's MS corrections

SIR,
A FRIEND of mine in Scotland informs me,[96] that the Inhabitants of the *good Town of Edinburgh* have been of late very much puzzled with an Advertisement,

94. In these words, ancient Greek mathematician Archimedes described the power of leverage.

95. This verse and the preceding line are from a seventeenth-century ballad, "Old Chiron thus Preach'd to His Pupil Achilles"; see "Song XVII," *Lark*, 16. In Greek mythology, Achilles was educated by the centaur Chiron. The Stygian ferry crosses the river Styx, which forms the boundary between Earth and Hades.

96. JB is apparently pretending *not* to be writing from Edinburgh; his MS note on his file copy says, "Written at Edinburgh Spring 1770."

pasted up in large capital Letters in the most conspicuous Parts of their City, and exhibited at greater Length, and with more copious Illustrations, in every one of their News-Papers. The Advertisement is in these Words: "MOLINEAX's SMELLING MEDICINE, OR NEW DISCOVERY *for the Cure of the* Scurvy, Pimpled Faces, Scall'd Heads, *and* ALL CUTANEOUS ERUPTIONS *by* SMELLING ONLY; *Price One Shilling the Box.*"[97]—Various have been the Interpretations which have been put upon this Advertisement—Some would have it to be nothing else than the usual Puff of a Mountebank, or Quack Doctor, who goes about the Country to impose upon the foolish and credulous Multitude, with some *Nostrum*, of which he boasts the wonderful Effects;[98] and did he sell his Medicine in a *Bottle*, instead of a *Box*, they would call him another *Bottle-Conjurer.*[99]—Others actually believe all that is set forth concerning this *Smelling Medicine.* They cannot, indeed, as in ordinary Cases, be said to *swallow* the Cheat, because this Medicine is not given as a Pill or a Potion, but is applied solely to the Sense of Smelling. Others, of the true Caledonian Spirit, zealous of the Honour of their Country, and quick to every national Reflection, are perfectly enraged at this Advertisement, looking upon it as a Satire on the Inhabitants of that ancient Part of the united Kingdoms, who have, for Time immemorial, been ridiculed, on Account of their being remarkably subject to a certain *cutaneous Eruption,* called the *Itch,*[100] insomuch that the Gesticulations occasioned by that Complaint, have been waggishly denominated *playing on the Scotch Fiddle;*[101] not to mention that

97. JB made a cutting of this advertisement from the *Edinburgh Evening Courant,* May 9, 1770, now in his file *Cat. Yale,* P 114(5); see Figure 9. The medicine was also advertised and sold in London. I have found nothing further about Molineux or his medicine. *Scall:* "Leprosy; Morbid baldness" (*SJ Dict.*).

98. *Nostrum:* "A medicine not yet made publick, but remaining in some single hand" (*SJ Dict.*); also a pun on *nose.* The "noses" theme of this essay is reminiscent of the frequently suggestive mention of noses in Sterne's novel *Tristram Shandy,* which JB admired.

99. In Jan. 1748, a large paying crowd was attracted by advertisements to the Haymarket Theatre in London on the promise of seeing a man climb into a quart bottle on stage. At the appointed time, the audience found themselves before a stage with nothing on it but a bottle on a table; they waited an hour then set about badly damaging the theater. An Irish adventurer, Captain Dudley Bradstreet, later claimed to have perpetrated this swindle; see *Gent. Mag.,* 101 (Dec. 1831), 494–97; also *ODNB*; other suspects were Samuel Foote, second duke of Montagu, and the Earl of Chesterfield (Benedict, *Curiosity,* 164).

100. The *itch*: "A cutaneous disease extremely contagious, which overspreads the body with small pustules filled with a thin serum, and raised as microscopes have discovered by a small animal. It is cured by sulphur" (*SJ Dict.*). Accompanied, as one would guess, by extreme irritation, it is now known to be produced by the itch mite, a small parasitic arachnid (*Sarcoptes scabiei*). "The itch" was a common Scottish skin disease; see Walker, "Development of Dermatology," 457–66.

101. *Scotch fiddle*: see n. 65, above.

the *Smell* of the *City of Edinburgh*, at Ten o'Clock at Night, is *odoriferous* to a Proverb.[102] These Interpreters, like the present English Patriots, are prodigiously violent. *Their* "Grievance and Apprehension,"[103] like those of the South, is magnified beyond Measure, and imagined to be severe beyond Tollerance, for the very same Reason, because it exists only in the Fancy, and may be either one Thing or another, as the Cloud was to *Polonius*, either an Ousel or a Whale.[104] They are for putting an immediate *Stop* to this *Molineux*—They are for *taking him by the Nose*, for his Impertinence;[105] and, in return, would have him forced to *smell* to a stout *Scotch Thistle*, and then to judge of the Poignancy of the Motto, *Nemo me impune lacesset*.[106] They very gravely declaim, that they have been duped into *a subscription for preserving the Police*;[107] and yet it is shamefully neglected. They are, indeed, amused now and then with a few Thieves being catched; but what signifies that, when such an Offender as MOLINEUX, *the public Defamer of Millions*, escapes.—They say, with *Othello*,

> Who steals my Purse, steals Trash—'tis something—nothing—
> 'Tis mine—'tis your's—and may belong to Thousands;
> But he that filches from me my good Name,
> Robs me of that which not enriches him,

102. Although the nickname for Edinburgh, *Auld Reekie*, referred originally to the chimney smoke in the city's air (*reek*: "smoke produced by burning or smouldering material"), the term had by this time also come to mean "a fume or odour" (*OED*); Edinburgh's less than sanitary living conditions led to a strong odor pervading the city. (SJ noted this when he arrived Aug. 14, 1773, joking to JB, "I smell you in the dark!" See *Life*, 5:23 and n. 1.)

103. The 1769 petition to the king from 1565 freeholders of Middlesex, concerning the actions of the ministry regarding the Wilkes case, concluded its list of grievances with the words "Such are the grievances and apprehensions which have long discontented and disturbed the greatest and best part of your Majesty's loyal subjects"; see *Gent. Mag.*, 39 (June 1769), 291. The terminology was fixed upon by many subsequent commentators; e.g., "Grievances under the present government being not easily felt, it was a lucky thought of the late petitioners to add to their grievances, apprehensions" (*General Evening Post*, Aug. 4, 1770).

104. In *Hamlet* (3.2), Polonius and Hamlet discuss whether a cloud looks more like a camel, an ousel (weasel), or a whale.

105. *To take by the nose*: an idiomatic expression meaning to fool someone: equivalent to *pull (some) one's leg*.

106. *Nemo me impune lacessit*: "No one provokes me with impunity"; this is the motto of the Order of the Thistle and of three Scottish regiments of the British Army.

107. What this refers to is unclear, but it possibly is related to threats to disband or replace the Edinburgh Town Guard, a cause about which JB was anxious (see below, Chap. 5, n. 268 and text).

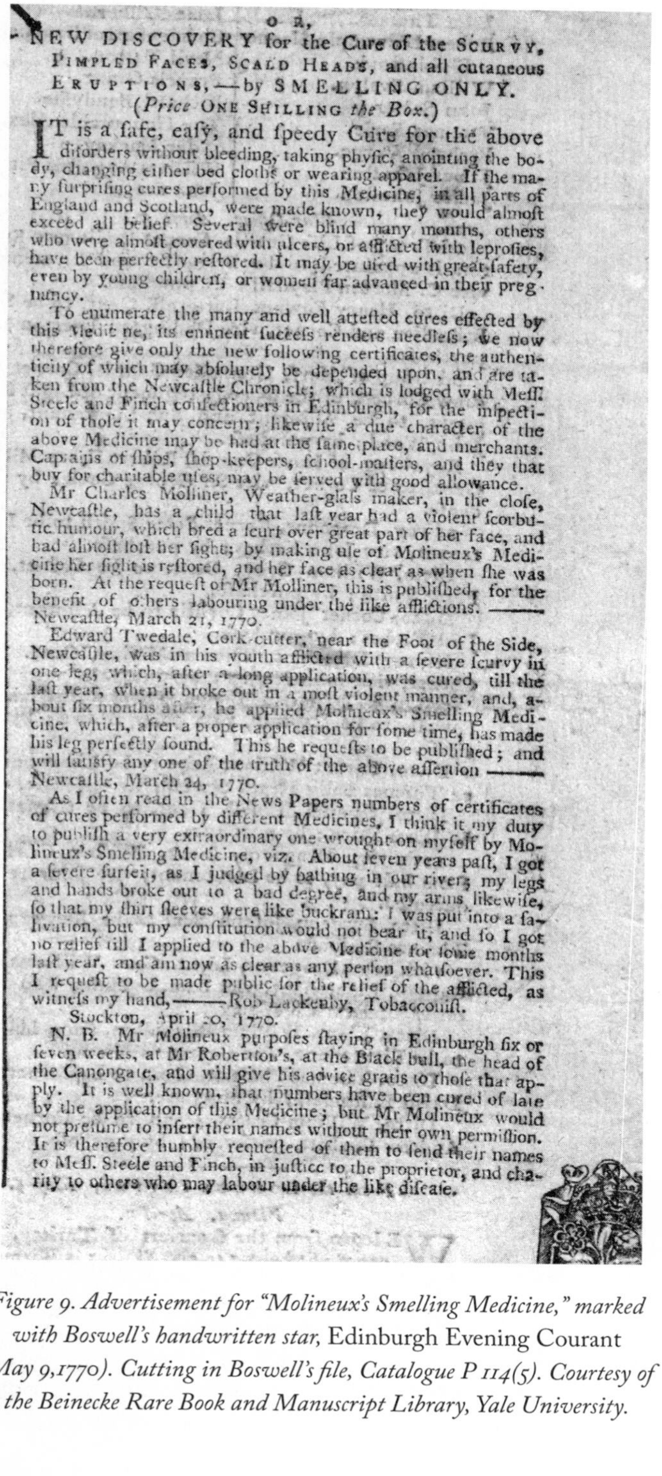

OR,

NEW DISCOVERY for the Cure of the SCURVY, PIMPLED FACES, SCALD HEADS, and all cutaneous ERUPTIONS,—by SMELLING ONLY.

(Price ONE SHILLING the Box.)

IT is a safe, easy, and speedy Cure for the above disorders without bleeding, taking physic, anointing the body, changing either bed cloths or wearing apparel. If the many surprising cures performed by this Medicine, in all parts of England and Scotland, were made known, they would almost exceed all belief. Several were blind many months, others who were almost covered with ulcers, or afflicted with leprosies, have been perfectly restored. It may be used with great safety, even by young children, or women far advanced in their pregnancy.

To enumerate the many and well attested cures effected by this Medicine, its eminent success renders needless; we now therefore give only the new following certificates, the authenticity of which may absolutely be depended upon, and are taken from the Newcastle Chronicle; which is lodged with Mess. Steele and Finch confectioners in Edinburgh, for the inspection of those it may concern; likewise a due character of the above Medicine may be had at the same place, and merchants. Captains of ships, shop-keepers, school-masters, and they that buy for charitable uses, may be served with good allowance.

Mr Charles Molliner, Weather-glass maker, in the close, Newcastle, has a child that last year had a violent scorbutic humour, which bred a scurf over great part of her face, and had almost lost her sight; by making use of Molineux's Medicine her sight is restored, and her face as clear as when she was born. At the request of Mr Molliner, this is published, for the benefit of others labouring under the like afflictions. ——— Newcastle, March 21, 1770.

Edward Twedale, Cork-cutter, near the Foot of the Side, Newcastle, was in his youth afflicted with a severe scurvy in one leg, which, after a long application, was cured, till the last year, when it broke out in a most violent manner, and, about six months after, he applied Molineux's Smelling Medicine, which, after a proper application for some time, has made his leg perfectly sound. This he requests to be published; and will satisfy any one of the truth of the above assertion ——— Newcastle, March 24, 1770.

As I often read in the News Papers numbers of certificates of cures performed by different Medicines, I think it my duty to publish a very extraordinary one wrought on myself by Molineux's Smelling Medicine, viz. About seven years past, I got a severe surfeit, as I judged by bathing in our river; my legs and hands broke out to a bad degree, and my arms likewise, so that my shirt sleeves were like buckram: I was put into a salivation, but my constitution would not bear it, and so I got no relief till I applied to the above Medicine for some months last year, and am now as clear as any person whatsoever. This I request to be made public for the relief of the afflicted, as witness my hand,——— Rob Lackenby, Tobacconist. Stockton, April 20, 1770.

N. B. Mr Molineux purposes staying in Edinburgh six or seven weeks, at Mr Robertson's, at the Black bull, the head of the Canongate, and will give his advice gratis to those that apply. It is well known, that numbers have been cured of late by the application of this Medicine; but Mr Molineux would not presume to insert their names without their own permission. It is therefore humbly requested of them to send their names to Mess. Steele and Finch, in justice to the proprietor, and charity to others who may labour under the like disease.

Figure 9. Advertisement for "Molineux's Smelling Medicine," marked with Boswell's handwritten star, Edinburgh Evening Courant *(May 9, 1770). Cutting in Boswell's file, Catalogue P 114(5). Courtesy of the Beinecke Rare Book and Manuscript Library, Yale University.*

And makes me poor, indeed.[108]

Shall any Outcry, say they, be made in England, that *Balfe* and *M'Quirk*, who are said to have murdered only one Person, have been pardoned?[109] And shall we tamely submit to the Impunity of *him* who thus murders the good Name of a whole Nation; more especially when we suspect this Murderer to be an Emissary of *Wilkes*, a *hired Ruffian*, patronized by the *Supporters of the Bill of Rights*, and receiving a Reward out of those Sums which that noble Society have set a-part [sic] for *secret Services*;[110] or, perhaps, out of that generous Tobacco, sent by some congenial Spirits in *America*, as a Present to the *Middlesex Patriot*, being very proper for regaling the *Nose* of *every true Friend of Liberty*;[111] insomuch, that it is believed a *copious* Portion of it is made into *Snuff*, for the Use of Mrs. Catharine Macaulay, *the celebrated Female Historian*.[112]

For my own Part, Mr. Printer, I think I can penetrate a little farther into the Meaning of *Mr. Molineux's* Advertisement. I think I can *smell a Rat* in this *Box* of his; for I am one of those who can *look a little beyond my Nose*. In short, Sir,

108. Shakespeare, *Othello*, 3.3; from a speech by Iago, concerning reputation.

109. In a trial at the Old Bailey, Jan. 12, 1769, Laurence Balfe and Edward Quirk (both names are spelled in various ways) were found guilty of murder, having caused a riot at the Brentford election on Dec. 8, 1768, in which a Mr. George Clarke was beaten to death. They were both sentenced to death (see Proceedings of the Old Bailey, t17690112–22). However, through the influence of Sir William Beauchamp Proctor, whose candidacy they had been hired to support, they were granted a reprieve, the evidence was reviewed, and on Mar. 10 they were pardoned by a royal warrant. See "Narrative of the Trial," 4:233–38. Proctor, a Rockingham whig, was standing against a Wilkite; on Mar. 1 a letter to Wilkes, said to be by JB, was published in the *Pub. Adv.*, appealing to Wilkes not "to insist upon the Execution of the poor Irishmen, who certainly did not intend to kill any Body" (see *Corres. 7*, 147–49).

110. The Society of Gentlemen Supporters of the Bill of Rights (SSBR, or Bill of Rights Society) was founded in Feb. 1769, on the initiative of John Horne Tooke, to aid Wilkes after his expulsion from Parliament and to press for parliamentary reform. The group successfully campaigned and provided financial support for Wilkes, helping him become elected as an alderman of London in 1769. The members were generally young lawyers and merchants and others of means. See *ODNB*, s.v. "Society of Gentlemen Supporters of the Bill of Rights." They opposed Bute and his favoritism to Scots, and JB jokes that the SSBR has (like the ministry) funds for secret intelligence gathering and subversion and that Molineux is in their pay. (However, there was a Crisp Molyneux, a planter from St. Kitts, a radical who was associated with the SSBR; see Brewer, *Party Ideology and Popular Politics*, 197.)

111. It was reported in the *St. James's Chron.*, Feb. 10, 1770, that Wilkes was sent gifts of tobacco (*forty-five* hogsheads) from Maryland and Virginia, as thanks for his support for the cause of liberty. See Thomas, *John Wilkes*, 161 and 261 n. 16.

112. Catharine Macaulay's eight-volume *History of England* was published 1763–83. She was known to be involved with John Wilkes and the Bill of Rights Society. The suggestion that she uses snuff is intended to imply her indulgence in unladylike activities.

I understand the Advertisement, not in a *physical*, but in a *political* Sense; and consider it as a shrewd *Type of the Times*, if one may say so. Does not *Mr. Molineux's* pretending to cure *all cutaneous Eruptions* by *smelling only*, aptly figure our State Quacks, who think *all* our *present* Disorders or *Discontents* may be cured by some one Remedy only?[113] I do, indeed, think that our present Discontents may well be represented under the Metaphor of *cutaneous Disorders*, because, in the *first* Place, they are occasioned by too great *Indulgence*, and a consequent *Heat* of Blood.[114]—*Secondly*, because I do not think them more than *Skin deep* on the *Body Politic.*—*Thirdly*, because many of those who *complain* are *Scurvy* Fellows,[115] who most insolently aver, that the House of Commons labour under the *King's Evil*;[116] when the Truth is, that they themselves are fretting and wasting away with the *Itch* of Power; whereas, the House of Commons are of a *sound Constitution*,[117] and would not admit amongst them a *Varlet* infected with the *Jail* Distemper.[118]

I heartily wish we had in Reality such a *Smelling Box* as *Mr. Molineux's*, to prove an effectual Cure for our *political Eruptions*. It would be the Reverse of a *Pandora's Box*, out of which we are told, by the Poets of Antiquity, there flew out [*sic*] all Manner of Plague;[119] amongst which I doubt not *Faction* was one.

---

113. Burke's *Thoughts on the Cause of the Present Discontents* argued that the causes of the present political discontents were unrestrained royal power and governmental factions. Mrs. Macaulay's *Observations*, in response to Burke, proposed different cures to the discontents involving introducing shorter parliaments, a system of rotation of office, a bill to exclude placemen from Parliament, and a more extended and equal power of election.

114. Skin diseases, such as scarlet fever, leprosy, ringworm, measles, and—as JB goes on to mention—a virulent form of typhus referred to as "jail fever" or "jail distemper," were thought to be caused by a vice of the blood. See Gowland, *Essay on Cutaneous Diseases*.

115. Scurvy, a disease resulting from a deficiency of vitamin C, was at this time common at sea and was classified as a cutaneous disorder, because dark spots on the skin were among its symptoms. *Scurvy* was also used as an insult; see *SJ Dict.*: "vile; bad; sorry; worthless; contemptible; offensive."

116. *King's Evil* was a common name for scrofula, a form of tuberculosis affecting the lymph nodes that manifests as painless, purplish growths on the neck; it was thought (in England and France, from the eleventh to eighteenth centuries) to be curable by the touch of a monarch: the Royal touch. JB alludes to the radical opinion that the House of Commons was subject to excessive influence of the Crown.

117. A pun on bodily/political constitution.

118. *Varlet*: A person of a low, mean, or knavish disposition; a knave, rogue, rascal (*OED*). This is Wilkes again, referring to his time in prison. *Jail distemper* or *jail-fever*: "A virulent type of typhus-fever, formerly endemic in crowded jails, and frequent in ships and other confined places" (*OED*).

119. In Greek mythology, as related in Hesiod's *Works and Days*, Pandora was given a large jar or box and instructed by Zeus to keep it closed. Out of curiosity, she opened it, unleashing all evils on the world.

If such blessed Effects could be obtained by a *Smelling Medicine*, it would be very sure of His Majesty's Royal Patent.[120]—And as the barbarous Tyrant, *Nero*, wished that his Subjects had all but one *Neck*, that he might behead them all at a single Blow,[121] our most gracious Sovereign, who is in every Thing the Reverse of *Nero*, would wish that all his Subjects had but one *Nose*, that they might at once be cured of that factious *Heat*, which makes them as peevish and froward as Children who have got the *Measles*.[122] I should like exceedingly to see the *Noses* of the *Heads of the Opposition* soothed and *restored* by the *Smelling Medicine*.—How pleasing would it be to behold the two *patriotic Sheriffs* of London, Messrs. *Townshend* and *Sawbridge*,[123] like the two Kings of Brentford; *smelling* to one Nosegay;[124] but most of all would it delight us to observe the salutary Effects of this Medicine on the noble Orator the Earl of Chatham.[125] Such a *Box* would be as suitable for him now, as were formerly the *Gold Boxes* with which he was presented by many of our Corporations during the last War, while he was the Great Commoner.[126] An Application to the Sense of *smelling*

120. *Patent*: "A licence conferring the sole right to manufacture, sell, or deal in a product or commodity" (*OED*).

121. In *The Twelve Caesars* (chap. 30), Roman historian Suetonius attributes these words not to Nero but to his predecessor Caligula.

122. George III was strongly opposed to the factionalism in the British Parliament: he used "party" and "faction" as pejorative terms.

123. James Townsend (bap. 1737–87) and John Sawbridge (1732–95) were MPs, supporters of Wilkes, and founding members of the SSBR. They were elected as London's two annual sheriffs in 1769. (Sawbridge was the younger brother of Catherine Macaulay.)

124. Said of two reconciled rivals. The allusion is to the Duke of Buckingham's immensely popular farce *The Rehearsal* (1672), in which, as the stage direction says, "The two kings of Brentford enter hand in hand" (2.2), and the actors, to heighten the absurdity, used to make them enter "smelling at one nosegay" (*Brewer's Dict.*; the allusion is reprised by JB in Chap. 5). Brentford was the site of the hustings for the Middlesex election. Townsend and Sawbridge, though allies in the Wilkite cause, started with different parliamentary allies (Shelburne and Grafton, respectively) and later sometimes disagreed with each other and with Wilkes.

125. For Pitt, now Earl of Chatham, see n. 10, above.

126. In Apr. 1757, Pitt was dismissed from office by the king. However, he was strongly supported by the public, in the press, and in the award of the freedom of a dozen or more boroughs and cities. The charters were sent to him handsomely packaged; Horace Walpole made the observation, "for some weeks it rained gold boxes" (Langford, "William Pitt and Public Opinion," 54–55). It was soon clear that any workable government had to include both Pitt and the king's favorite, Newcastle; in June 1757, a coalition was formed in which Pitt became de facto prime minister, nominally under Newcastle. From this time, "Pitt's rhetorical power gave him command of the Commons. It turned the sarcastic title Great Commoner (*The Test*, 1 January, 9 April 1757) into a generally recognized honorific" (*ODNB*).

is peculiarly proper for this eloquent Opposer, because his *Nose* is one of his most distinguished Features[127]—Let those who have witnessed his Harangues in the Senate, tell with what a superlative Contempt they have seen him, NASO *suspendere adunco*, his quaking Antagonists.[128] Mr. *Wilkes*, in the Character he has drawn of him (which, by the by, many good Judges allow to be the best Thing *Wilkes* ever wrote) says he has "the Eagle Face of the great *Condé*."[129] In like manner it may be said that he has the Boar-and-Sow-*Nose* of the humourous *Buckingham's*. For as

> ——Bear and Sow when any Storm is nigh,
> Snuft up, and smell it, gathering in the Sky;[130]

so does our NOBLE ORATOR—He can *smell* Armies gathering in the Sky, as he can *see* Castles building in the Air.[131] It is in this Sense that he like the famous Horse in Job "*smelleth* the Battle from afar."[132] It is in this Sense that he "pledges himself to the House that a Blow is struck in some Quarter of the Globe against the Honour and Interest of Great Britain."[133]

As however there is but little Probability that any such effectual political Medicine will speedily be invented, "the Powers that be who are ordained of God" must make use of what they have;[134] and if Faction and Sedition should

127. Pitt was described, by the Earl of Shelburne, as having a "long aquiline nose" (*ODNB*).

128. *Naso suspendere adunco*: "to turn up the nose at, ridicule, mock"; Horace, *Satires*, 1.6.5.

129. In the notes to a propagandistic collection of his own letters, Wilkes describes Pitt as a "manly figure, with the eagle-face of the famous *Condé*." See Wilkes, *Letters*, 166 n. Louis II de Bourbon, Prince de Condé (1621–86), known as the Grand Condé, is portrayed in sculptures as having an "eagle-like profile and hooked nose" (Valérie Montalbetti, "Sculptures: France, 17th and 18th Centuries," Musée du Louvre, http://www.louvre.fr/llv/oeuvres).

130. Buckingham, *The Rehearsal*, 1.1.

131. *Castles building in the air*: a proverbial expression for contemplating impossible schemes. JB alludes to the "improvements" Chatham was making to the house and estate at Burton Pynsent (see above, n. 60), supervised by "Capability" Brown.

132. Job 39:25, concerning the war horse: "He saith among the trumpets, Ha, ha; and he smelleth the battle afar off, the thunder of the captains, and the shouting" (*AV*).

133. Before the close of the previous parliamentary session in May, Chatham said, "I do now pledge myself to this honourable House for the truth of what I am going to assert: that at this very hour, that we are sitting together, a blow of hostility has been struck against us by our old inveterate enemies in some quarter of the world" (Pitt, *Speeches*, 114 n.).

134. Romans 13:1, "Let every soul be subject unto the higher powers. For there is no power but of God: the powers that be are ordained of God" (*AV*). This text is sometimes given as the biblical warrant for the doctrine of the Divine Right of Kings.

unhappily become much more violent, I am afraid there is no *Box* will do for them but a *Cartridge-Box*; nor no *Smell* but *the Smell of Gunpowder.*

I am, SIR,
Your constant Correspondent,
RAMPAGER.

1771

No. 5: The "Touching Medicine": An Old Political Cure

[Continuing to employ the allegorical procedure of his earlier letters, Boswell likens "political eruptions" to skin disorders, such as scrofula, that the king should similarly be able to cure by use of the royal "touching medicine." Much of this essay is taken up with a long quotation from the historian Thomas Carte regarding the history of the literal, medical disease, which Boswell then analyzes and uses to form his own argument regarding the metaphorical, political illness, with reference to much contemporary political history.]

Public Advertiser, May 20, 1771, 2 (leading article); with Boswell's MS correction

SIR,

IN my last I treated of that famous Remedy said to be invented by that wonderful Genius, *Mr. Molineux*; a Remedy, which, according to his Account of it, cures *all cutaneous Eruptions by Smelling only*;[135] and I fondly expressed my Wishes that we had such a *Smelling Medicine*, for the Cure of our *political Eruptions.* I at the same Time intimated my Apprehensions that it might be sometime before such a Medicine could be discovered, and I own these Apprehensions still continue with me. However, Sir, after due Reflection, though I cannot pretend to any extraordinary Degree of Sagacity and Penetration, so as to make *new Discoveries*, I find that I can illustrate *an old political Cure* well known and practised in these Kingdoms, which is not greatly removed from a Smelling Medicine, no farther indeed than one of the five Senses differs from another. The Medicine which I mean is the *Touching Medicine.*

That our Kings have possessed the Power of curing the worst of all cutaneous Eruptions *by Touching only*, is a Fact which, however mysterious, has the Sanction of History for it's Truth.[136] THOMAS CARTE, an ENGLISHMAN, in his

135. For Molineux and the *smelling medicine*, see "Rampager" 4, above.
136. For the Royal touch, see n. 116, above, and below.

History Book IV. § 42. thus gravely writeth concerning the Cure of what is called the *King's Evil*.[137]

"It was to the hereditary Right of the Royal Line, the People in *Malmsbury's* Days ascribed the supernatural Virtue of our Kings in curing the scirrhous Tumour called the King's Evil. Though this Author is willing to impute it to the singular Piety of *Edward*, there is no Proof of any of our Kings touching for that Distemper more ancient than this King, of whom *Ailred* as well as Malmsbury observe, that he cured a young married Woman, reduced by it to a deplorable Condition, by the stroking the Place affected with his Hand, upon which she grew sensibly better, the Tumour dispersed, the Scar wore off, and in a Week's Time the Cure was perfected.[138] There are no Accounts of the four Kings of *Norman* or foreign Race ever attempting to cure that Complaint, but that Henry the Second both touched those afflicted with it and cured them, is attested by *Petrus Blesensis*, who had been his Chaplain.[139] *Bradwardine*, Archbishop of *Canterbury* under Richard the Second, the Lord Chancellor *Fortescue*, and other grave Authors give the like Testimony in Behalf of the Cure, as well as Practice of that Prince's Successors;[140] besides a great Number of Evidences that may be drawn from Records, many of which are printed by *Tucker*, having been communicated to him by the late *Garter*, the learned Mr. *Anstis*.[141] There

137. Carte, *History of England*, 1:357. The writers and works mentioned by Carte are identified in a list of authorities at the front of his book.

138. Ailred (Ælred, Æthelred) (1110–67), abbot of Rievaulx and writer of historical, hagiographical, spiritual, and theological works, including two works concerned with Edward the Confessor and the royal line of kings. William of Malmesbury (fl. 1090–1142), a Benedictine monk who gathered, studied, and wrote about the history of England. Saint Edward "the Confessor" (c. 1003/5–66), king of England, is credited with being the first English monarch to cure the king's evil.

139. Henry II (1133–89), king of England from 1154. Petrus Blesensis, or Peter of Blois (1125/30–1212), a French poet and diplomat who served as secretary under three successive archbishops of Canterbury.

140. Thomas Bradwardine (c. 1300–49), theologian, Archbishop of Canterbury for thirty-eight days in 1349, and author of *De causa Dei contra Pelagium* (1618). Richard II (1367–1400), king of England 1377–99. Sir John Fortescue (c. 1397–1479), justice, political theorist, chancellor to Henry VI, and author of *De laudibus legum Angliæ* (In Praise of the Laws of England, 1468–71).

141. John Anstis (the Elder, 1669–1744), Garter King of Arms (the senior King of Arms of the Order of the Garter), could not have "communicated" his collection of evidences for the Royal touch to "Tucker," who is identified in Carte's notes as the author of *Charisma, sive, Donum Sanationis* (1597)—i.e., author and cleric William Tooker (1553/4–1621). Carte admitted that he had mistakenly given Tucker's name for that of William Beckett, a surgeon whom Anstis had mentioned in an unpublished essay (on coronations) that Carte had

is a particular religious Office used at the Time of Touching, not disagreeable
to the Simplicity of the *Saxon* Times; in the ceremonial where of the King,
at the reading of the first Gospel, gently draws both his Hands over the Sore,
much after the Manner used by *Edward*.[142] All our *English* Kings have continued to use the same Right [*sic*] to this Day: And the *French*, from the Time of
St. *Louis* if not of *Philip Auguste*, have imitated them in it with the like salutary
Effect.[143] Some of the *French* Writers ascribe this Gift of Healing to their Kings
Devotion towards the Relicks of Saint *Marculf*, in the Church of *Corbigny* in
Champagne, to which the Kings of *France* immediately, after their Coronation
at *Reims*, used to go in solemn Procession:[144] And it must be owned there was
formerly a Veneration paid to this Saint in *England*. It was in Memory of him
that a Room in the Palace of *Westminster*, frequently mentioned in the Rolls of
Parliament, at the Time of its assembling, was called the Chamber of St. *Marculf*, being probably the Place where our Kings used to touch for the Evil. It is
now called the Painted Chamber;[145] and though the Name of that Saint hath
been long forgot in this Nation, yet the sanative Virtue of our Kings still continues. Nor is it confined to them alone; for though *Fortescue* (at the Time of whose
writing there had been no Sovereign hereditary Queen crowned in this Realm)
imagined it was not communicated to Queens, because they were not anointed
in the Hands,[146] the contrary hath been since proved by abundant Experience.
Tucker relates one remarkable Instance in the Cure of a Roman Catholic, who

---

read years before, but whose pamphlet, *An Enquiry into the Antiquity and Efficacy of Touching for the King's-evil* (1722), he had not actually seen. See letter from Carte, dated Feb. 13,
1748, in *Lit. Anec.*, 2:498 n.

142. The service was called "At the healing": "This was another 'traditional' service at
which sufferers from scrofula were brought to be healed by the laying on of the monarch's
hands. The ceremony dated back to King Edward the Confessor, but these prayers were
printed in the BCP [the Anglican *Book of Common Prayer*] on only a few occasions between
1706 and 1732" (Griffiths, *Bibliography of the Book of Common Prayer*, 112).

143. Louis IX, also St. Louis (1214–70), king of France from 1226. Philip II Augustus
(1165–1223), king of France from 1180.

144. French kings were traditionally crowned at Reims in northern France, ninety miles
northwest of Paris. As Carte says, they would proceed to the nearby abbey of Corbigny in
Champagne, to venerate the relics of the sixth-century Saint Marcouf, best known for the
laying on of hands to heal scrofula and whose relics were supposed to convey this gift to the
monarch (*ODNB*). See Finley-Croswhite, "Henry IV and the Diseased Body Politic," 139.

145. A chamber in the original Palace of Westminster (destroyed by fire in 1834), where
important state ceremonies were held.

146. Sir John Fortescue's writings in defense of the Lancastrian claim to the throne were
based on showing that women could not convey a right to the crown and were excluded by
natural law from ruling.

being put into Prison, perhaps for Recusancy, and terribly afflicted with the King's Evil, was, after he had been there for a tedious Time, at a vast Expence to Physicians without the least Relief, touched by Queen *Elizabeth*, and perfectly cured. This gave him Occasion to say, he was now convinced, by undoubted Experience, that the Pope's Excommunication of that Queen signified nothing, since she still continued blessed with so miraculous a Quality."[147]

Such is the intelligent and laborious Mr. *Carte*'s Account of this Matter. I am not ignorant that it did him considerable Hurt, insomuch that although his History was undertaken under the Patronage of the *Duke of Beaufort*, the *University of Oxford*, and the *City of London*, his Credulity was so much satirized, that his Work fell into Disrepute.[148] This however will never make me alter my Opinion of its Merit, for Credulity in some Things, is very consistent with a good Historian. As witness *Livy*, who gives us strange Stories, almost as frequent as the Writer of the *Persian Tales*,[149] and some of them to Appearance as ridiculous as that of *Elizabeth Canning*,[150] or the *Cock Lane* Ghost.[151] I would

147. *Recusancy* was the crime, in England, of nonconformity to the established church; most recusants were Roman Catholics. Elizabeth I (1533–1603), queen of England from 1558, was excommunicated by Pope Pius V, on Feb. 25, 1570 (*ODNB*).

148. The first volume of Carte's *History of England* (1747) included in a note (1:291 n. 4) a detailed account of a Bristol laborer, Christopher Lovel, who in 1716 had gone to France, where he was cured of scrofula by the "Old Pretender," James Francis Edward Stuart, son of the deposed James II/VII of England/Scotland; implying as it does that James had a hereditary divine right to the British thrones, this evidence of Carte's Jacobitism caused an outcry from whig letter writers in the press and lost Carte some of his financial support, postponing the publication of the later volumes of his *History*. The book was dedicated to Charles Noel Somerset, fourth duke of Beaufort (1709–56), head of the tory party and staunch Jacobite supporter (*ODNB*), as well as the chancellor and scholars of Oxford and the mayor and aldermen of London.

149. Roman historian Titus Livius (59 B.C.–A.D. 17); his *Ab Urbe Condita* (known in English as the *History of Rome*) includes much mythical and legendary material, particularly at the beginning. *Persian Tales: Or, The Thousand and One Days*, translated from French by Ambrose Phillips (1709), was frequently reprinted.

150. Elizabeth Canning (1734–73) was a London woman who, in 1753, disappeared for twenty-eight days. She claimed to have been abducted, imprisoned in a whorehouse in Moorfields, and starved in an effort to force her into prostitution, and that she then escaped and ran home. Her story was debated in the newspapers and the courts. Suspects were identified and arrested, which led to a trial and convictions, although some of these were overturned and Canning herself was charged with perjury. The case remained unsolved, though she was sentenced to transportation and died in New England (*ODNB*).

151. The Cock-Lane Ghost was a famous London hoax. In 1759, a woman named Fanny Lynes claimed to have heard knocking and scratching on the bedroom wall in the house at which she boarded in Cock Lane, near Smithfield Market. Believing this to be a ghostly

not however take up your Paper and your Readers'Time with a full Vindication of Mr. *Carte*, for believing that our Monarchs possess the Power of curing the *King's Evil* by a *Touch*, it is sufficient for my Purpose that such a Notion has prevailed, and is well known among us; and for this I can give not only historical but poetical Authority. In a little Poem, called THE GUINEA, I find the following Lines:

"The Royal Touch, so thought our Sires of old,
Gave Sovereign Power, and mystic Worth to GOLD:
Where Physic failed, the charm'd Jacobus came,
Nature did Homage, and Disease grew tame."[152]

As the *physical Touch* of MAJESTY has been an effectual Cure for the *King's Evil*, so is the *political Touch* of MAJESTY a *sovereign* Cure for the *factious*, or *popular Evil*. Let a *Patriot* be ever so much *distempered*, let his Republican *Inflammation* be ever so violent; let him have *Paroxysms* in Parliament, and even arrive at the *Mania* of Remonstrance,[153] there is a *Royal Touch* which will recover him. This *Touch* is generally applied to the *Palm of the Hand*,[154] but it must be done with some Address, so as not to be discovered by any Body but the *Patient*, as all those unhappy People who labour under the *factious* or *popular Evil* have a strange Unwillingness to have it known that they are cured by the *Touching Medicine*, flattering themselves that People will believe they have recovered

---

warning, she and her husband moved out. Shortly afterward she died of smallpox. The noises at the house in Cock Lane started again in Jan. 1762, and the landlord, Richard Parsons, claimed the ghost was that of Fanny Lynes and that she accused her husband (who had recently sued Parsons over a debt) of having poisoned her. Parsons charged people to come and talk to the ghost, which would answer questions by knocking. In Feb. 1762, a local clergyman organized an investigation, which found that Parsons's young daughter Elizabeth had been impersonating the ghost's knocking with a hidden wooden clapper. SJ, who was one of the investigators, published an account in the *Gent. Mag.*, 32 (1762), 81. In July 1762, Parsons and others were tried, and he was convicted of conspiracy and imprisoned for two years.

152. "The Guinea," *Lond. Chron.* (no. 1569, as JB adds at this point in a handwritten note), Jan. 6, 1767, 4; the poem was reprinted from the *Gent. Mag.*, 36 (Dec. 1766), 589. *Jacobus*: King James (as in Jacobite).

153. Soon after entering Parliament in 1735, Pitt was associated with the faction called *Patriot* Whigs. A *remonstrance* is a formal protest or list of grievances, such as Lord Mayor Beckford delivered to the king (see n. 51, above); it was a far from ordinary procedure. SJ wrote, in his pamphlet *Thoughts on Falkland's Islands*, published Mar. 1771, of "the insolence of Common Councils, . . . the howl of plebeian patriotism, . . . of rabbles and riots, of petitions and remonstrances" (*Political Writings*, 385).

154. That is, as a bribe.

merely by the *Goodness of their own Constitution*. The *Touching Medicine* so far resembles Mercury or *Quicksilver*, that it must be given in very different Quantities to different *Patients*.[155] Many a one has been given over as incurable merely because he was not *touched* sufficiently, it being certain that the *Touching Medicine* will infallibly cure the most virulent *Patriot* that ever existed if it be applied to him in a proper Degree; for as a great Prime Minister in France said, "Every Man has his Price."[156] *Pulteney* was given over by many Physicians, but a wiser Man than all of them found out that they had been only *tampering* with his Disease, and by boldly *touching* him *Quantum sufficit* produced an immediate Cure.[157] Numberless Instances of such Cures may be produced, but they will readily occur to my Readers.

As the *Touching Medicine* is an infallible Cure for those who are *really infected* with the *popular Evil*, it is also a Medicine *so pleasant to take*, that many People pretend to have the Distemper in order that the Cure may be administered to them, like Children who complain of a Cold, that their Mothers may give them a little Honey. I have a Notion that most of our modern *popular Gentlemen* fall under the latter Predicament. We are told that the one amongst them, who has made the most Noise, whose Distemper *apparently* broke out to such a Degree, that it was necessary first to drive him out of the Kingdom, and afterwards to shut him up in the *King's Bench Ward*.[158] We are told, that in the Beginning of

155. Mercurial preparations were used extensively in Western medicine from the late fifteenth to the early twentieth centuries, notably for the treatment of syphilis and gonorrhea.

156. This is recorded as a proverb from the mid-eighteenth century. Robert Walpole is supposed to have said (concerning "the declarations of pretended patriots"), "All those men have their price"; see Coxe, *Memoirs*, 1:757. However, it is also attributed to an opponent of Walpole, William Wyndham, who, in 1734, said that "every man has his price" was an old maxim (Shapiro, *Yale Book of Quotations*, 611). Stephen Taylor suggests that "in France" could indicate an earlier attribution of the comment to Richelieu (personal communication).

157. William Pulteney, first earl of Bath (1684–1764), a whig politician who was first an ally and then a political foe of Robert Walpole. Pulteney was overlooked for a ministerial office in 1720 and again in 1724 when he expected to be made secretary of state, possibly because Walpole considered him to be a potential rival. In 1726 he took himself into opposition, though he remained a whig. He opposed Walpole's foreign policy and the excise necessary to fund it. When Walpole stepped aside in 1742, Pulteney was invited by George II to form a government, on the condition that there be no inquiry into Walpole's conduct of government and the war. Pulteney declined and was in July 1742 created Earl of Bath. This led to an outpouring of satire and abuse, from which his reputation as a country whig and a patriot never recovered. *Quantum sufficit*: (lit.) "as much as is sufficient"—i.e., "just enough."

158. This is Wilkes, who fled to France in Dec. 1763 to avoid imprisonment for seditious libel; he stayed there for four years and on his return was imprisoned in the King's Bench

this Reign he made Application to *John Stuart*, the *Royal Apothecary*, fairly told him that he was sound as a Roach;[159] and if he could procure him the *Touching Medicine* as a *Douceur*,[160] he would with Pleasure go and serve the King in *Canada*; but his Request not having been granted, and finding Poverty to be as bad as any Disease, he bethought himself, like many another *Sturdy Beggar* of getting a Livelihood by pretending to be very ill of the *Popular Evil*;[161] and we all know how well he has succeeded in this *Vocation*; the Fellow having a clear, shrill Voice, and his *Bless your Honours* so ready,[162] as to get a better Subsistence in this Way than he had a Chance of getting by any honest Employment; nay, I am not quite certain but by frequenting the Distempered, he may by this Time have catched the Disease in good Earnest.

My Readers will remember, that when our Monarchs have been graciously pleased to employ their mystical Power in *Touching* for the Cure of the *King's Evil*, it was customary to have a Piece of Gold which had received the *Royal Touch* hung round the Patient's Neck by a *Ribband*.[163]—Here too the *political* Cure is similar to the *physical* one; For one of it's most efficacious Methods is hanging a Piece of some Kind or other round the diseased Person's Neck by a *Ribband*, of which three Colours are in use, *Green*, *Red*, and *Blue*.[164] This Method of Cure by the *Ribband* has its Effect by *operating strongly on the Imagination*;[165] and there are *Patients* whom the King might *touch upon the Palm of the Hand* long enough without producing a Cure, who will be instantly recovered by Means of

---

Prison in Southwark, south London, which operated from medieval times until 1880 and was essentially a debtors' prison. The story that JB goes on to tell alludes to a persistent rumor—which Wilkes did not deny—that, despite his radicalism, Wilkes had in 1761 approached the prime minister, Lord Bute, to be appointed as governor of the Province of Quebec.

159. *Sound as a roach*: quite sound; it is a pun upon *roach* or *roche*, the fish, and the French *roche*, a rock (*Brewer's Dict.*).

160. *Douceur*: "'something pleasant or agreeable'; . . . A conciliatory present or gift; a gratuity or 'tip'; a bribe" (*OED*), or, as we might say, a sweetener.

161. From 1531, the English Poor Laws distinguished between the "impotent poor" (the aged, sick, and disabled) and "sturdy beggars," or able-bodied unemployed folk.

162. *Bless your honour*: a phrase used by a beggar to his benefactor.

163. SJ received this medal in 1712, when, as an infant, he was "touched" for scrofula by Queen Anne, at the last such ceremony; he wore it all his life (*Life*, 1:41–43).

164. Green, red, and blue signify the colors of the ceremonial sashes of the three most senior British orders of chivalry, the Thistle, the Bath, and the Garter. The broad ribband or sash goes over one shoulder and across the chest and back, with the badge hanging at the hip.

165. In the *Treatise of Human Nature*, book 2, sec. 5: "Of Our Esteem for the Rich and Powerful," Hume says, "Every human creature resembles ourselves, and by that means has an advantage above any other object, in operating on the imagination."

the *Ribband*. I have heard it said, that a late *spirited and intrepid Chief Magistrate* was a *Patient* of this Kind; and I am persuaded that if prudent Methods were taken to *feel the Pulse* of many others, they would be found in the same State.[166]

It may perhaps be said by some Critics, that the *Touching Medicine* is but a gross Cure; the *Touch* being a Sense much coarser than any of the others. The *Reverend Critic Warburton*, the *Bishop of Gloucester* must certainly be of this Opinion. In the second Scene of the 1st Act of *King Lear*, when *Regan* is expressing in extravagant Terms her Love for her Father, she says,

> ———— ————*I profess*
> *Myself an Enemy to all other Joys,*
> *Which the most* precious Square of Sense *possesses.*

Upon the last Line of which Doctor Warburton has this curious Annotation: "By the Square of Sense we are here to understand the four nobler Senses, viz. the *Sight, Hearing, Taste* and *Smell*. For a young Lady could not with Decency insinuate, that she knew of any Pleasures which the *Fifth* afforded."[167] This is a Degree of squeamish Decency, or rather Prudery, that, in my humble Opinion, SHAKESPEARE never intended, and which it must be acknowledged gives some Reason to suspect, that the roguish Jests of *Wilkes* and *Churchill* on the *Reverend Critic's* Deficiency in the *Operations* of the *fifth Sense* may have more Truth in them than one would willingly allow in the Case of a *married Prelate*;[168] however, if *Doctor Warburton* really thinks with so much Delicacy, it would be well if he could communicate the same Disposition to some of our factious *Clergy*,[169]

166. The first chief magistrate of London was Thomas de Veil (1684–1746); "ambitious, courageous, and active," he was knighted in 1744 (*ODNB*). Alternatively, JB may be alluding to William Murray, who, on his appointment as Lord Chief Justice, "insisted that the appointment be accompanied by a peerage, eventually overcoming the resistance of George II. On 8 November 1756 he was . . . created Lord Mansfield, baron of Mansfield" (*ODNB*).

167. In modern editions, the passage is *King Lear*, 1.1.74–76. For Warburton's note, see Pope and Warburton, *Works of Shakespeare*, 8:6. The fifth sense to which he alludes is, of course, that of touch.

168. Charles Churchill was the general editor and contributed up to ten issues of Wilkes's paper, the *North Briton*. In the obscene *Essay on Woman*, Wilkes parodied Warburton's "minute and pugnacious style of annotation" (*ODNB*, s.v. "Warburton, William"), to the extent that Warburton sought through Parliament to have it suppressed. Warburton was then further attacked in Churchill's *The Duellist* (1764) and *Sermons* (1765). His supposed "Deficiency in the *Operations* of the *fifth Sense*" stems from Churchill's accusation in *The Duellist* that Warburton's son was in fact not his own (3.38–39), and therefore his wife must be getting her touching from someone else.

169. "Factious clergy": the Feathers Tavern petitioners, who first met around this time (the summer of 1771). See "Rampagers" 9 and 10, below.

we should then be less disturbed with them, as they would not shew so eager a Desire for this same *Touching Medicine*.

It must be observed, that altho' the *touching Medicine* is an infallible Cure for the Time, it will not prevent a *Relapse*, nor will it always serve as a *Preventative*. The NOBLE ORATOR was certainly very well *touched* and yet he has of late been as bad of the *popular Evil* as ever any Man was of the *Gout*.[170] One would have thought that it was so *handsomely* administered to the *hopping Sheriff*, that he must have continued in good Health for Life, and yet we see him, I must say, *shamefully* blotched with the *factious Evil*;[171] and the *Ribband* has been no Security to *Sir Francis De-la-Fool*, as they call him, for he, poor Man, has been as bad as he could be, having placed his plump Body in the *Chair of Sedition* at the *London Tavern* with the Badge of Loyalty round his Neck,[172] like a Deserter

---

170. *Noble orator*: Chatham. After the (first) Rockingham ministry was dismissed in July 1766, Pitt was invited to form a government. He chose for himself the office of Lord Privy Seal, which required his removal from the Commons to the House of Lords, so in Aug. 1766 he became the Earl of Chatham—thus he could no longer be referred to (with respect) as the Great Commoner. He moved a motion in the Lords in defense of the populist Wilkes. He was subject all his life to attacks of gout, which in 1765 seem to have completely incapacitated him. His large gout-stricken foot swathed in bandages enhanced the drama of his appearances in Parliament.

171. Brass Crosby (1725–93), who had served as sheriff in 1764–65, was elected MP for Honiton in 1768 and Lord Mayor on Sept. 29, 1770, in the Wilkite interest. (Wilkes himself was elected sheriff in the month following this publication, in June 1771.) In Mar. 1771, Crosby opposed the efforts of the House of Commons to arrest a London printer (for printing reports of its debates), asserting his oath to protect the liberty of the city. He was summoned by the Commons and, for his continued defiance, was imprisoned in the Tower of London, to which he was escorted by huge crowds and where he received many highly placed opposition visitors for the term of his imprisonment. When the parliamentary session ended on May 8, Crosby was released and returned to the mayoral residence, again accompanied by crowds of supporters. At the time he was suffering so badly from gout that one of his appearances before the Commons was postponed; it is not unlikely that he was "hopping." On Apr. 30, 1771, he was admitted to the SSBR.

172. Sir Francis Delaval (1727–71), MP for Andover 1754–68, was known as a man of fashion, racing enthusiast, and holder of riotous parties. He was a member of the SSBR. Some years before, he had stopped voting against the government, his loyalty having apparently been bought by a pension of £300 p.a. (Namier and Brooke, *History of Parliament*, 2:310). On Mar. 19, 1771, he chaired an extraordinary meeting of the Society, at which a faction led by John Horne attempted to expand its program beyond the immediate concerns of Wilkes. Wilkes challenged this at the next regular meeting on Apr. 9, and Horne and his supporters, including Delaval, broke away to form the Constitutional Society. See "The Delavals," Seaton Sluice & Old Hartley Local History Society, http://www.seaton-sluice .co.uk/content/delavals.html. JB mentions him in his journal (*Search*, 283), and in Mar. 1795 he dined with his younger brother, John Hussey Delaval (*Great Biographer*, 312).

who appears in the Enemies Ranks in the Regimentals of his own King, or a Dog who is found worrying his Master's Sheep while he wears his Master's Collar. Mr. Donaldson, the Miniature Painter in *Prince's Street, Leicesterfields,* has given a very droll Etching of this Knight in the Chair, with *Samuel Vaughan,* and divers other *Enemies of ministerial Corruption,* croaking around him, with a most ludicrous Anxiety for the *Support of the Bill of Rights.*[173] I observe that there is now coming out in Numbers *a Biographical History of Patriots,* which is to be embellished with above eighty Heads of *illustrious Persons.*[174] I would advise the Editors to employ *Mr. Donaldson* to *execute* the *Heads* of the *living Patriots,*[175] as I am certain from the Specimen I have mentioned, that no Body can give the World a juster Idea of the true Characters of such *Worthies* as those whom our present infatuated People are pleased to admire.

I am, SIR,

Your constant Correspondent,

RAMPAGER.

No. 6: A Political Parody on Cato, Act V, Sc. 1

[Joseph Addison's play *Cato: A Tragedy* (1713) was immensely popular from the time it was first produced and was frequently performed and reprinted throughout the century. It is based on the life of Cato (the Younger), a Roman statesman in the last days of the Republic, who opposed Caesar and the empire and was regarded as a model of integrity; the play deals with important political themes, including personal liberty and the power of government, and was widely quoted in political contexts. At this time, it was particularly popular in the American colonies; "*Cato* was Washington's favorite play, and Martha Washington had arranged to have it performed by soldiers when she visited wintry Valley Forge" in 1777–78 (Weintraub, *Iron Tears,* 182).]

Public Advertiser, October 26, 1771, 4 (under "Poetry")

173. John Donaldson (c. 1737–1801), Edinburgh-born painter of miniatures; his radical social views harmed his artistic career (*ODNB*). JB knew him from at least 1759 and became reacquainted with him in London (*Lond. Journ.,* 210–11; *Search,* 296, 341); from Oct. 1775, they met socially, but only in Edinburgh (where Donaldson appears to have been living, contra *ODNB*). Samuel Vaughan (1720–1802), a wealthy merchant, was an enthusiastic supporter of Wilkes and the American rebellion; JB knew him through his fund-raising for the Corsican cause, as he recorded Sept. 13, 1769 (*Search,* 307–8; *Earlier Years,* 397). The etching JB describes is not otherwise known.

174. The announcement for this work, by Rowland Harries and Launcelot Burke, was made in a two-page sheet published in 1770 and in some newspapers, with the work scheduled to come out on July 21, 1770. The book itself appears not to have been published.

175. Execute—i.e., to draw—puns on the alternative meaning, to capitally punish.

A POLITICAL PARODY *on* CATO. ACT. V. SCENE I.

CATO, *Solus, sitting in a thoughtful Posture, in his Hand Plato's Book on the Immortality of the Soul.*[176] *A drawn Sword on the Table by him.*

IT must be so.—Plato thou reason'st well.

Else whence this pleasing Hope, this fond Desire,

This longing after Immortality?

Or whence this secret Dread, and inward Horror

Of falling into nought? Why shrinks the Soul

Back on herself, and startles at Destruction?

'Tis the Divinity that stirs within us,

'Tis Heaven itself that points out an Hereafter,

And intimates Eternity to Man.

Eternity! thou pleasing dreadful Thought!

Through what Variety of untry'd Being,

GEORGE, *Solus, sitting in a thoughtful Posture; in his Hand* JOHNSON'S *False Alarm.*[177] *A Public Advertiser, containing Junius, on the Table by him.*[178]

IT must be so.—Johnson thou reason'st well,

Else whence this pleasing Hope, this fond Desire,

This longing after great Authority?

Or whence this secret Dread and inward Horror

Of falling into nought? Why shrinks my Soul

Back on herself, and startles at *dissolving*?

'Tis the *Divinum Jus* that stirs within us;[179]

'Tis Heaven itself that points out Resolution,

And intimates Supremacy to Kings.

Supremacy! thou pleasing dangerous Thought!

Through what Variety of untry'd Ministries,

176. That is, *Phaedo*.

177. SJ's political tract *The False Alarm* (1770) was written, as JB says, "to justify the conduct of ministry and their majority in the House of Commons, for having . . . declared Colonel Lutterel to be duly elected for the county of Middlesex, notwithstanding Mr. Wilkes had a great majority of votes. This being justly considered as a gross violation of the right of election, an alarm for the constitution extended itself all over the kingdom. To prove this alarm to be false, was the purpose of Johnson's pamphlet; but even his vast powers were inadequate to cope with constitutional truth and reason, and his argument failed of effect" (*Life*, 2:111–12).

178. For Junius and the *Pub. Adv.*, see n. 42, above.

179. *Divinum Jus*: divine law.

Through what new Scenes and
   Changes must we pass.
The wide, th' unbounded Prospect lies
   before me,
But Shadows, Clouds, and Darkness
   rest upon it.
Here will I hold. If there's a Power
   above us,
(And that there is all Nature cries
   aloud
Through all her Works) he must
   delight in Virtue,
And that which he delights in must
   be happy.
But when! or where!—this World
   was made for *Cæsar*,
I'm weary of Conjectures.—This must
   end 'em.
      (Laying his Hand on his Sword.
Thus am I doubly arm'd: My Death
   and Life,
My Bane and Antidote are both
   before me:
This in a Moment brings me to an
   End;
But this informs me I shall never
   die.
The Soul secur'd in her Existence
   smiles
At the drawn Dagger, and defies it's
   Point.
The Stars shall fade away, the Sun
   himself
Grow dim with Age, and Nature sink
   in Years.

Through what News-papers and
   Pamphlets must we pass!
The wide, th' unbounded Prospect lies
   before me,
But Factions rage, and Dullness rest
   upon it.
Here will I hold. If Englishmen be
   generous,
(And that they are, all London cries
   aloud
Through all her Streets) they must
   delight in Goodness,
And he whom they delight in must
   be happy.
But how! or why!—this Noise is
   made for *Wilkes*,
I'm weary of Conjectures.—Let me
   read then,
      (Laying his Hand on Junius.
Thus am I doubly arm'd: My Death
   and Life,
My Bane and Antidote are both
   before me,
This in a Moment drives me from my
   Throne;
But this informs me I shall ever
   reign.
A King secur'd in his own Con-
   science, smiles
At the keen Junius, and defies his
   Point.
The Mob shall slink away, *Chatham*
   himself
Grow dim with Age, and *Temple* sink
   in Years;[180]

180. For William Pitt, Lord Chatham, see n. 10 ff., above; for Richard Grenville, second
Earl Temple, see above, n. 70.

But thou shalt flourish in immortal Youth,	But I shall flourish in immortal Power
Unhurt amidst the War of Elements,	Unhurt, amidst the War of Parliaments,
The Wrecks of Matter, and the Crush of Worlds.	The Wrecks of Boroughs, and the Crush of Parties.

RAMPAGER.

No. 7: "Rampageneana," and Other Fruit

[Boswell begins by admiring the letters that he receives from two friends in London, and comparing them with apples for the refreshment and nourishment they provide. As he notices at the end of the essay, he wanders from this topic, and ruminates on the names and claims of various contemporary physicians, although he does return to the theme of trees at the end.]

Public Advertiser, November 25, 1771, 1–2 (leading article); with Boswell's MS correction.

SIR,

I HAVE a Friend in London of the same *rampageneous* Disposition with myself, so that you may believe we keep up a pretty frequent Correspondence by Letters.[181]

> ——RAMPAGERS *ambo,*
> *Et cantare pares et respondere parati.*[182]

My Friend has indeed greatly the Advantage over me by residing in your Metropolis, that great Emporium of Men and Manners, News and Nonsense, Politics and Play-houses, and all other Subjects of Entertainment, while I live at a great Distance from you, and move in a narrow Sphere, little diversified with enlivening Objects. I do however as well as I can, and my Friend is pleased, aye and yourself too, Mr. Woodfall, sometimes.

181. That is, George Dempster; see n. 37, above. JB saw Dempster in London, 1762–63, and they corresponded frequently until JB's death. Dempster was co-author with JB and Andrew Erskine of the *Critical Strictures on the New Tragedy of "Elvira"* (1763). The first known written use of the term *rampageneous* is in a letter to JB from Dempster, Mar. 7, 1769 (*Corres. 7*, 152). For *rampageneousness*, see Chap. 3, intro., above.

182. "Arcades ambo, Et cantare pares et respondere parati" ("Arcadians both, well-matched in singing and ready to reply," Virgil, *Eclogues*, 7.5).

As my Friend's Letters always bring me some *Bon Mots*, or pleasant Stories of one Kind or other, a whimsical Similitude has come into my Head, that he is as it were mounted on a large Apple-tree, from whence he shakes me down excellent Fruit from Time to Time, which I gather very busily, and am much refreshed withal. Every body who has frequented Gardens when a Boy, will understand me at once. I think something may be made of this Similitude, Sir. Its Branches are spreading, and its Foliage luxuriant, and with a little Pains [*sic*] and Care, it may be made to cover a Column of the Public Advertiser, as we have seen a Bush of Jessamine or Honey-suckle extended over the Front of a little Country-house.

The *Rampageneana* communicated to me by my Friend may be well compared to Apples shaken from a Tree, because they come from a good *Stock*, they are quite *fresh*, and *leaves* come along with them; and if they are not *red and white*, which they may be if he pleases, they are *black and white*, which does just as well. I have had Apples shaken to me by many other Friends. Some have shaken me Apples, which may do very well for some People, but which are of that sour Kind that does not suit my Palate, and I shrewdly suspect that their Intention in shaking them down to me was not so much that I should be regaled, as that they should be diverted with the Wry-faces which I made when my Teeth were set on Edge. I have an ILLUSTRIOUS FRIEND, who has shaken me down *the best Fruit in England*, Apples indeed of a superior Quality; but he will sometimes take a Fancy to make some of them hit me upon the Head, and as they are of a very large Size, they give me a confounded Rap.[183] I indeed take it patiently, because his Apples are all uncommonly excellent, and of the highest Flavour; and even such of them as have hit me, will afterwards afford a most agreeable Relish.

My *rampageneous* Friend's Apples are always sweet. *Sunt nobis mitia poma*, his own Motto.[184]—Then he makes them fall gently around me with such a delicate Address, that the Fairies nor Nymphs, nor any other Genii of the Woods, could not convey them to me with more Softness. How refreshing is it to me to get a few of them while I am digging deep for Antiquities, planting out the Thorns of Law, weeding a Crop of Poetry, or making Hay of human Existence, while the Sun of Cheerfulness shines.[185] Such Fruit are to my Taste the best

183. This "illustrious friend" is surely SJ. In his most recent letter to JB prior to this publication (June 20, 1771), he exhorts him, "Mind your studies, mind your business, make your lady happy, and be a good Christian"; see *Letters SJ*, 1:362–63; also *Life*, 2:140–41.

184. *Sunt nobis mitia poma*: we have some ripened apples (Virgil, *Eclogues*, 1.80).

185. On Oct. 20, 1771, JB wrote from Auchinleck to John Johnston, "I have been serving an apprenticeship with my father in the art of pruning, and I hope in time, to be a

Desert of any, far exceeding your expensive *foreign* Productions. Your *far-fetched* Delicacies, which are either raised in fashionable Hot-beds, or so confected that there is little or nothing of the natural Relish to be perceived. And I confess I do not like your *high-seasoned* Things, in which there is a great deal either of *Salt* or *Spicerie*. *Doctor Cadogan's* System is altogether congenial with my Way of thinking; for it seems to be just Simplicity and Cheerfulness.[186] He prescribes "Activity, Temperance and Peace of Mind," the very Things in which a true *rampageneous Animal* delights. Then I observe he is a great Friend to *Fruit*. "Instead of Supper (says he) any good *ripe Fruit* of the Season would be very salutary, preventing Costiveness, and cooling, correcting and carrying off the Heats and Crudities of Indigestion." This is a Physician after my own Heart. I would give my *Golden Pippins* to him with much more Pleasure than to any of *Hogarth's* Groupe.[187]

—Et Plurima mortis Imago.[188]

His very Partiality to Fruit would win my Regard, and I care not though his snarling Enemies twit him with having tasted *forbidden Fruit* in *Portugal*.[189] I

---

skillful and diligent Guardian of the trees here. My father has been as good as his word, in giving me a college [i.e., a course of lectures] upon the Election-Law of Scotland, mixed with it's [sic] Antiquities, which illustrate it in an entertaining manner" (*Corres. 1*, 273). "Making hay while the sun shines" is a proverbial expression dating from the sixteenth century.

186. William Cadogan (1711–97), physician, author of the recently published *A Dissertation on the Gout, and All Chronic Diseases: Jointly Considered as Proceeding from the Same Causes* (1771); JB quotes from pages 80 and 92–93. Cadogan argued that gout was a result of inactivity and indulgence; in this, he "was perceived to be challenging the hereditary principle not only in medicine but also in politics, and in doing so aroused the hostility of conservatives" (*ODNB*); he was abused in a flurry of contemporary pamphlets. JB and SJ discussed his book (*Tour*, Sept. 14, 1773; *Life*, 5:210–11), and in a footnote (210 n. 2) JB said that he was acquainted with Cadogan, although I find no record of them meeting in JB's journals or published correspondence.

187. *Golden pippins* are a variety of apple. Engraver and painter William Hogarth (1697–1764) was a pictorial satirist and social critic; much of his work pointedly criticized contemporary morals, customs, and politics.

188. "And full many a shape of death" (from Virgil, *Aeneid*, 2.369; trans. Fairclough, 1:341) is used by Hogarth as the motto on an engraving called "The Company of Undertakers" (1736–37), which shows a group of well-known contemporary doctors examining the contents of a urinal. See Paulson, *Hogarth's Graphic Works*, 1:173.

189. JB seems to imply that, while in Portugal, Cadogan had a love affair and possibly illegitimate offspring. This rumor is not found elsewhere, although Cadogan was briefly in

suppose he approves of the Song of *Randal* in the *Jovial Crew*, which beautifully alludes to Fruit which the Doctor allows, "*of all Kinds and Seasons.*"[190]

> Would you try to persuade
> A pretty, pretty Maid,
> As *ripe as a Peach, or a Plumb, Plumb, Plumb,*
> You have nothing else to do
> But to swear you will be true,
> And then you may kiss—But Mum, Mum, Mum.[191]

If he keeps his own Secret, what have we to do with the Doctor's private Exercises? Besides, let us not forget that he has published an *Essay upon Nursing*, under the Designation of late *Physician to the Foundling Hospital*; so that whatever may be the Consequences, the Doctor is prepared.[192]

As I do not think myself obliged to observe any Connection or Regularity in my Essays, you will allow me to laugh at a Conceit which strikes me concerning Physicians, on reading your Paper, which is, that we seem now to go upon the Principle of "one Devil driving out another."[193] For we have Dr. *Fevre* to cure the *Gout*, and Dr. *Rush* to cure the *Asthma*; the one of *Liege*, the other of *Philadelphia*.[194] In short, one would imagine Medicine to have

---

Portugal in 1762 as a physician to the army; see Rendle-Short and Rendle-Short, *Father of Child Care*, 44.

190. For the quotation, see Cadogan, *Dissertation on the Gout*, 88.

191. *The Jovial Crew, or The Merry Beggars* (1652) a "tragi-comic opera," initially a popular stage play by Richard Brome, was adapted into a "ballad opera" in 1731. JB quotes "Air XLIV," "There was a Bonny Blade," sung by Randal. *Mum* means to keep silent or secret.

192. Cadogan's *An Essay upon Nursing, and the Management of Children, from Their Birth to Three Years of Age* (1748) was used as a guide in the London charitable institution for orphaned and abandoned children, the Foundling Hospital (established in 1741).

193. *One devil will drive out another* seems to have been a proverbial expression from the sixteenth century.

194. JB alludes to the work of Pierre François Alexandre Lefèvre (1741–1813), as described in two recently published medical works by Edmund Marshall, *A Candid and Impartial State of the Evidence of a Very Great Probability: That There is Discovered by Monsieur Le Fevre, a Regular Physician, Residing and Practising at Liege in Germany, a Specific for the Gout* (London, 1770) and *A Candid and Impartial State of the Farther Progress of the Gout-Medicine, of Doctor Le Fevre* (London, 1771). Benjamin Rush (1746–1813), who was later one of the signatories of the American Declaration of Independence, was born in Pennsylvania, studied medicine in Edinburgh, practiced briefly in London, and in 1769 moved to Phila-

become altogether metaphorical. Upon this Principle I take *Sterne's Balsamic Æther* to be nothing else than the *volatile Spirit* of *Laurence Sterne*, alias *Tristram Shandy*.[195] *Cadogan*, however, must be *Generalissimo* of Physic, as his Namesake was of our Army;[196] and since his great *Victory* in the *Kitchen*, there is a *Doctor* of whom we have often and often heard, who must be quiet, and that is Dr. *Cook*.[197]

I began this Essay, comparing my Thought to a Fruit-Tree, and was happy to imagine that I might perhaps be able to supply you with a few tolerable Apples; but behold it has turned out a Tree as curious as any of the *Ænigmas* of *Virgil* or *Pope*. The latter mentions "a wondrous Tree that sacred Monarchs bear."[198]

---

delphia. He published *A Dissertation on the Spasmodic Asthma of Children* (London, 1770). It is likely that JB is punning on *rush*, meaning diarrhea (see *OED*, s.v. "rush": "dysentery in cattle"; dating from 1799, with a Scottish citation). He is also contrasting Liege (loyalty) with Philadelphia (brotherly love).

195. *Dr. Stern's Balsamic Aether*: a medicine by Dr. Philip Stern, M.D., advertised in the papers from 1768 as "the only possible cure for consumptions and asthmas," to be inhaled in the steam of hot water (see *Gazetteer*, Jan. 5, 1768). Laurence Sterne (1713–68) was the author of the eccentric novel *The Life and Opinions of Tristram Shandy, Gentleman* (1760–67). The term *volatile spirit*, in early chemistry, applies to distilled liquids with a tendency to vaporize, of which one of the best known is alcohol, but the term is often used metaphorically to suggest changeability. Sterne was referred to as a "volatile spirit" in the *Monthly Review*, 69 (1783), 493.

196. Dr. Cadogan's namesake is William Cadogan, first Earl Cadogan (1671/72–1726), an army officer who fought in the Netherlands. He rose through the army ranks, eventually becoming a major general and, personally, a valued confidant of Marlborough (*ODNB*).

197. John Cook, M.D. (c. 1705–77), was the author of, among other works, *The Natural History of Lac, Amber and Myrrh* (published by Dilly, 1769, and Woodfall, 1770: JB knew both printers), a pamphlet that mainly served to recommend various medicinal essences and a balsamic tincture that were made and sold for the author. A long letter from him appears in the *London Evening Post*, Sept. 25–27, 1770, in which he suggested treatments for several kinds of scurvy, arguing that "An exact diet is better than medicines, and with it medicines will do much, but without it little or none at all." This may be his "victory in the kitchen," although why he "must be quiet" remains unclear.

198. This "aenigma" or riddle from Pope's "Spring," the first of his *Pastorals* (1717), line 86, is an allusion to the oak tree, later known as the Royal Oak, at Boscobel in Shropshire, in which Charles II hid from pursuit by Roundhead soldiers after the Battle of Worcester in 1651. Pope's Pastorals were imitations of Virgil. Joseph Warton, quoting this line in *An Essay on the Genius and Writings of Pope*, says, "the riddle of the *Royal Oak*, in the first Pastoral, invented in imitation of the Virgilian aenigmas in the third eclogue, savours of pun, and puerile conceit" (8).

My Tree aspires not to Monarchs, but I think it is pretty well to see it bearing Physicians; nor can I think but their Perriwigs will look as bushy and grave as that of Charles the IId. in the Royal Oak, according as he is represented by our best Sign-Post Painters.[199]

I am, SIR,

Your constant Correspondent,

RAMPAGER.

1773

No. 8: The *Public Advertiser* as a Noah's Ark

[The Rampager gives something of a self-description, appropriating to himself a description of an Archbishop of Glasgow, before giving an account of the various correspondents to the *Public Advertiser*. It was a common practice to write under a pseudonym, so it is virtually impossible to be sure of the identities of many of these writers. Even the identity of the most notorious writer, Junius, remains in doubt.]

Public Advertiser, May 15, 1773, 2

SIR,

I HOPE I may still be allowed, without Offence to any body in the present Reign, to quote Bishop *Burnet*, who, without having ever seen me, has drawn the Character of *Rampager* as well as if I had done it myself; and that is, when describing the great and worthy Archbishop *Leightoun*. The Words are: *His Thoughts were lively, oft out of the Way, and surprising, yet just and genuine.*[200] So much for myself; and now, Sir, let me say something of the *Public Advertiser*. It is a Paper, Sir, which, in the *Deluge* of Politics, Commerce and Diver-

---

199. The Royal Oak became a name and emblem for taverns, hence tavern signs would depict Charles II hiding in a tree, wearing a periwig. (The shoulder-length peruke or periwig was introduced from France as an aristocratic male fashion item after the Restoration in 1660.)

200. Gilbert Burnet (1643–1715), Bishop of Salisbury from 1689. He describes Robert Leighton (1611–84), Archbishop of Glasgow 1670–74, in book 2, chap. 3, of his much-reprinted *History of His Own Time*, published after his death (1724–34); see Airy, *Burnet's History*, 1:240. Burnet was seen as William III's right-hand man and court historian (see *ODNB*), and therefore a staunch ally of the revolution principles, which appeared to be under some attack during the reign of George III.

sions, resembles *Noah's Ark*, being filled with all Kinds of Animals, clean and unclean.[201] Here growls the Bear *Cinna*;[202] there snarls the Cur *Antignatho*;[203] there roars the Lion JUNIUS;[204] there crows the little cock *Modestus* to frighten the Lion forsooth;—but he is soon discovered to be a Dunghill Cock, a ministerial fed Fowl;[205] here hop the two theatrical *Magpies*;[206] there buzz the *Spanish Flies* of Quackery;[207] here trudges the mule *Canana*;[208] there frisk [*sic*] the

201. In Genesis 7:2, Noah is instructed to take on the ark every kind of animal, (ritually) clean and unclean, to save them from the Deluge. The names given in what follows are pseudonyms of letter writers to the *Pub. Adv.*

202. Cinna was the pen name on a number of contributions to the *Pub. Adv.* in 1770–71 in support of Lord Sandwich. In an undated letter of this period, SJ reports George Steevens saying that Cinna was tory satirist John Shebbeare (1709–88), SJ's fellow pensioner (*Letters SJ*, 5:27). In the *Life*, Boswell reports, "I recall a ludicrous paragraph in the newspapers, that the King had pensioned both a *He*-bear [i.e., SJ] and a *She*-bear" (*Life*, 4:113 n. 2). (Cinna's letters are now thought to have been written by James Scott (1733–1814), a clergyman and writer under Sandwich's patronage.)

203. *Antignatho* was probably, according to Pottle (*Lit. Car.*, 257), William Kenrick (1729/30–79), translator, playwright, and miscellaneous writer, much of whose career was spent picking fights with other writers. He had ridiculed Garrick's *Jubilee Ode* in the *Pub. Adv.* in 1769 and subsequently JB, who had joined in the correspondence with a signed letter (Oct. 13, 1769). Kenrick's other enemies included Fielding, Goldsmith, and SJ; JB met him on Apr. 3, 1772, and found him, unexpectedly, to be "a bluff, hearty little man, full of spirits and cheerfulness" (*Defence*, 95–96; see also *Corres. 6*, 260–61 n. 6).

204. For Junius, see n. 42, above.

205. John Cleland (1710–89), author of *Fanny Hill*, writing as "Modestus," was one of the correspondents employed by the administration to respond to Junius's attacks. At least five times between Nov. 1769 and June 1770, "Modestus" provided the *Pub. Adv.* with partisan answers to the revelations of Junius; Cleland was identified as "Modestus" by John Nichols (Epstein, *John Cleland*, 151; see also 145 and n.). At the time, "Modestus" was thought to be Sir William Draper (see Chap. 1, n. 98). JB met Cleland at Garrick's, Mar. 31, 1772 (*Defence*, 84–85). A *dunghill cock*—from the saying "Every cock will crow upon his own dunghill"— suggests petty or ridiculous pride; also a dunghill cock, only crowing when it is safe on its own territory and as distinct from a fighting cock, is a proverbial indication of cowardice (JB uses the image again in "Rampagers" 10 and 13, below).

206. "Formerly bishops were humorously or derisively called magpies because of their black and white vestments" (*Brewer's Dict.*); by *theatrical magpies* JB may mean clerical rather than specifically episcopal playwrights.

207. A *Spanish fly* or cantharides is a medicinal powder, made from crushing a species of beetle, used as an aphrodisiac. As Bob Clarke observes, eighteenth-century newspapers "were full of advertisements for quack medicines" (*From Grub Street*, 142). It is unclear if JB has a specific reference in mind.

208. *Canana*, a frequent correspondent to the *Pub. Adv.* and other papers (particularly from Nov. 1769 to Sept. 1770), wrote mainly to oppose Junius, the petitioners, and the remonstrances. A collection, *The Twelve Letters of Canana, on the Impropriety of Petition-*

squirrel *Quidnunc*;[209] there mew the *Cats* of the London Tavern to let us know that they can *look at a King*, tho' take my Lord *Pomfret's* Word for it, they blink like *Owls* in the Sun;[210] and indeed when they march up to the Palace, *Welch Poney* and all, they should, instead of Cake and Caudle, get nothing but a *Pomfret Cake* to teach them to be so very *liquorish* in their taste of Government;[211] here bray the *Asses* who must needs be biting at the *Scotch* by way of chewing *Thistles*; but they find the *nemo me impune lacesset* among their Provender, and are like the *Viper* gnawing the File;[212] here bellows the formidable Bull *Regulus*, and, like the *brazen* Bull of *Phalaris*, destroys all whom he encloses within his glowing Frame.[213] I speak not of the *Bulls* and *Bears* at *Jonathan's*,[214] the lame

---

ing the King to Dissolve the Parliament, was published in Jan. 1770. The writer's identity is unknown.

209. *Quidnunc*: a person who constantly asks, "What now?"; an inquisitive or nosy person; a gossip (*OED*). This name—possibly taken from the much-performed two-act farce *The Upholsterer*, by Arthur Murphy (1758)—was the pseudonym of a number of correspondents to the *Pub. Adv.* (see letter of May 20, 1768). Grose's *Dictionary of the Vulgar Tongue* (1811) records the name as having become a byword for a politician.

210. For the London Tavern, see n. 54, above. Regarding the remonstrances, George, second earl of Pomfret (1722–85), privy councilor, and the Ranger of St. James's Park, was said to have declared in the House of Lords that "however swaggering and impudent the behaviour of the low Citizens might be on their own dunghill, when they came into the Royal Presence, . . . they blinked with their eyes like owls in the sunshine of the sun" (*North Briton*, May 26, 1770). "A cat may look at a king": even a subordinate has certain inalienable privileges (a sixteenth-century proverb).

211. The *Welsh pony* is a small, hardy breed of pony; a *pony* is also a measure of alcohol. But here, the "Welch Poney" alludes to a particular beast that Horne Tooke accused Wilkes of buying with money appropriated from him (Horne); see Wilkes, *Controversial Letters*, 41, 73. Also Robert Lloyd, Churchill's friend and colleague, was described as his "Welsh pony" by Wilkes (Cash, *John Wilkes*, 66). *Caudle* is a warm spiced wine. *Pomfret* is a variation of the name *pontefract*, for a licorice confection (typically a flat black circular sweet) of a type originally made in Pontefract (*OED*). Since these gentlemen meet in a tavern and are "liquorish," there is a labored suggestion that they are drunk.

212. The critics of the Scots, because they chew at (Scotch) thistles, are compared to donkeys. *Nemo me . . .*, see n. 106, above. The viper gnawing the file refers to Aesop's Fable no. 70, of which the moral is "Do not attempt impossibilities."

213. *Regulus* (the name means "little king"), who was from 1771 a very frequent correspondent to the *Pub. Adv.*, was a critic of the government and supporter of Wilkes. His name, like that of Junius, alludes to a Roman patriot who opposed the tyrant Nero. The *brazen bull* was an instrument of torture and execution by roasting, reportedly built for the Sicilian tyrant Phalaris in the sixth century B.C.

214. Jonathan's Coffee House in Exchange Alley, opened in 1680 by Jonathan Miles, became the site of the London Stock Exchange, hence the reference to bulls and bears, terms still used for speculators.

Ducks in the *Alley*,[215] the queer *Fishes*, the jovial *Bucks*, the hearty *Cocks*, and the jolly *Dogs* with which this metropolis abounds, and who in their Turns are *exhibited* in your Paper.[216] In my next I shall offer a few Thoughts on the petitioning Clergy,[217] and in the mean time am most faithfully

Your's

RAMPAGER.

1774

No. 9: On the Feathers Tavern Petitioners

[In the summer of 1771, a group of clergy, opposed to the requirement that those ordained to the Anglican priesthood subscribe to the Thirty-nine Articles, met in the Feathers Tavern in the Strand.[218] Under the leadership of Theophilus Lindsey (1763–1808), John Jebb (1736–86), and others, the movement took in a variety of protestant viewpoints, some rather extreme: some who simply opposed vows as offending against the Christian freedom of conscience, some who believed that the Articles required more than was warranted by scripture, and others who rejected the doctrine of the Trinity. A petition to Parliament was prepared and, on February 6, 1772, presented to the House of Commons. The House voted 217 votes to 71 not to receive it. The petitioners "were a tiny, albeit articulate, minority within the Church of England. Their campaign seemed to challenge the authority of the church at the very time when threats to authority at home (with the agitation surrounding John Wilkes) and in the colonies (with American protests against the duties introduced by the chancellor of the exchequer, Charles Townshend) raised anxieties about threats to order" (*ODNB*, s.v. "Feathers Tavern Petitioners"). Boswell attends to the subject now because the petition was due shortly to be reintroduced to the Parliament.

215. The *Alley*: Exchange Alley (see previous note); *Lame Ducks* are brokers who default on their debts.

216. The queer Fishes, Bucks, Cocks, and Dogs: these are presumably colloquial terms for various contemporary social types, rather than for particular correspondents. They are "exhibited" in the way animals (especially unusual ones) were shown at fairs or in collections at taverns, etc.

217. For the petitioning clergy, see "Rampager" 9, following.

218. The Thirty-nine "Articles of Religion," which establish the Protestant character of the Church of England, were formulated 1563–71 under Elizabeth I. Although intended not as a comprehensive statement of Anglican doctrine but to define it against the extremes of Anabaptists and the Roman Church, the articles are included in the *Book of Common Prayer*, and assent to them was required for holding civil office, ordination to the Anglican priesthood, and graduation from the universities.

For a consideration of Boswell's own religious position, see Tankard, "'A Most Agreable Way of Thinking.'"]

Public Advertiser, February 23, 1774, 2 (leading article)

SIR,

ACCORDING to my Appointment I am now to give you a few Remarks, Animadversions, or whatever else you may please to call them upon the Petitioning Clergy, whether Dissenters or Churchmen.[219] The Subject has been nobly treated both in Writing and in Speaking with that Seriousness which becomes its Importance; and, indeed, I have had a most sincere Satisfaction in observing, that in an Age peculiarly disgraced by Infidelity, not only many of our Clergy, and others devoted to Study, have repelled what I cannot help considering licentious Attacks, but several of our Noblemen and Members of the House of Commons have displayed Abilities and Spirit in Defence of a public, religious Establishment:[220] Be it my humble Province to flank the Male-contents [*sic*] with a little well-meant *rampageneous* Ridicule.

And first: As to the *Dissenters*, how can they possibly imagine that the Church will set them quite free at the very Time when they are attacking her with unprecedented Impudence, and calling her *Idolatrous*, as has been flatly done by Dr. *Priestly*, whose Name is like a Contrast to his Principles,[221] as *lucus* has been derived *a non lucendo*.[222]—It is just like supposing, that if I have a troublesome Enemy hand-cuff'd, and he calls to me, "You *Scoundrel* set

219. The petition was signed by about 250 people, of whom over 200 were clergy. "Dissenters" refers specifically to those who belong to religious organizations other than the state-established (Anglican) church.

220. Although much of the parliamentary support for the petition was from the opposition, it was not a party issue, and members were able to vote according to their consciences.

221. Joseph Priestley (1733–1804), dissenting minister and radical theologian, grammarian, educationalist, and scientist. He had been raised in a dissenting evangelical household but later rejected Calvinism and tried to combine materialism and Unitarianism with theism. He was a friend of Benjamin Franklin and of Theophilus Lindsey. He was a prolific writer, and his theological works excited a great deal of controversy. In his *Institutes of Natural and Revealed Religion* (1772–74), he writes: "this great article, the worship of one God only, is guarded in all the books of scripture, . . . and yet . . . this very article was the subject of one of the first and the most radical of all the corruptions of christianity. For . . . there was introduced into the christian church, in the first place, the idolatrous worship of Jesus Christ, then that of the Virgin Mary . . . and this *modern christian idolatry* has been attended with all the absurdities . . . of the antient heathen idolatry" (2:215–16; Priestley's italics). JB met Priestley on Mar. 26, 1772, noting that although his "works of religious controversy . . . are in my opinion insolent . . . *he* appeared to be very civil" (*Defence*, 68).

222. *Lucus a non lucendo*: "The word for grove is *lucus* because it is not light [*non lucet*] in a grove." "This etymology by opposites is a byword for a notoriously far-fetched explanation

me loose," I should be simple enough to do it; when it is plain that if he rails at me when manacled—were he loose—he would endeavour to knock out my Brains.

As to the Association at the *Feathers Tavern*, they, indeed, do well to meet at a *Tavern* for their *free* Schemes, as I suppose were they to obtain a *Victory*, they would in place of *Te Deum*, that *Form* of the *Church*, to which they are so averse,[223] have a jolly Chorus, singing

> *Nunc est bibendum nunc pede libero*
> *Pulsanda tellus,*[224]

and dance to the Tune of Nancy *Dawson*'s Hornpipe, while the *Arch-Deacon* beats Time to them.[225]

The *Feathers* too may serve as a good Emblem of their *flighty* Genius, which leaves the Establishment behind *fugiente penna* that could be found;[226] neither do I think that this *Feathers* Association has produced many good *Pens*. We have, indeed, had *Goose-Quills* enough; but I do not imagine that it can be justly said of any of *their* grey Goose-Quills as of the one in Chevy Chace, that it was "wet in the Heart's Blood."[227]

---

of the derivation of a word" (Webster's Online Dictionary). Addison uses the expression in *Spectator*, no. 59 (May 8, 1711; 1:249).

223. *Te Deum Laudamus* ("We praise Thee, O God") is the ancient Christian hymn of praise regularly used in the Anglican service of Morning Prayer, as found in the *Book of Common Prayer*. Musical settings, such as Handel's *Dettingen Te Deum* (1743), were sometimes composed for victory celebrations. Dissenters objected to liturgical worship as consisting of "empty forms."

224. Horace, *Odes*, 1.37.1–2. This frequently quoted text is translated, "Now is the time to drink, now is the time to dance footloose upon the earth."

225. At Covent Garden in 1759, Nancy Dawson (1728–67) first danced the hornpipe in *The Beggar's Opera*, to a tune that soon became known by her name. JB knew the tune from his first period in London; see *Corres.* 9, 198 and n. 3. Benjamin Dawson (1729–1814) was a clergyman who defended the petition in a series of pamphlets. Francis Blackburne (1705–87) wrote *The Confessional* (1766), a strong attack on compulsory subscription to the Articles of Religion; he was made an archdeacon in 1750 but decided not to subscribe to the Articles of Religion and advanced no further in the church.

226. *Fugiente penna*: "winged flight," from Horace, *Odes*, 3.2.24: *spernit humum fugiente penna* ("spurns the dank soil in wingéd flight").

227. The later and more popular of the two English ballads known as "Chevy Chase," from which this line is taken, is thought to have been written in about 1620. It tells of a hunting party (or *chase*) in the Cheviot Hills in Northumberland in the late fourteenth century. It became well known through Thomas Percy's influential *Reliques of Ancient English Poetry* (1765); the passage reads, "The swane-fethars that his arrowe bar / with his hart-blood

Feathers have a Connection with this Society in many more Ways than one would imagine. I take it several of its Members are what the celebrated Mr. *Whitfield* used to call *Downy* Doctors.[228]—A few *Feathers* stuck into *Cork* make a *Shuttlecock*; and who doubts that the *Cork Heads* of the *Feathers Tavern* may be beat about by the Battledores of Novelty and Whim;[229] yet, though Mr. *Pope* calls "a *Wit* a *Feather*,"[230] it must be thought that there is not *Dulness* enough in this Association; for I believe the arithmetical Rhyme will apply here with great Justice;

A Pound of *Feathers* and a Pound of *Lead* are *equal*————[231]

John Milton, who was a wonderous Reformer and for whom we must make Allowance, seems to have had a prophetic Eye to this *Feathers* Association in the following Passage in *Comus*:

————————"Wisdom's Self
Oft seeks a sweet retired Solitude,

---

the wear wete." Addison devoted two essays of the *Spectator*, nos. 70 (May 21, 1711; 1:297–303) and 74 (May 25, 1711; 1:315–22), to a critique of the ballad.

228. Methodist preacher George Whitefield (1714–70) uses this expression in a sermon, "The Burning Bush," in which he argues that scripture and history show that neither the church nor individual believers should expect to be at peace with the times: "I know very well that 'tis said, that now the case is altered: modern commentators therefore, and our great Dr. Young, calls them downy Doctors; they tell us, now we have got a Christian king and governor, and are under the toleration act, we shall have no persecution; and, blessed be God, we have had none since this family has been on the throne: may God continue it till time shall be no more" (Sermon XI, *Eighteen Sermons*, 259). JB seems to have met Whitefield and probably heard him preach on a number of occasions (see *Earlier Years*, 32–33 and n.). The expression "downy doctors" is from Edward Young's *Night Thoughts* (1742–46):

> Shall Heaven, which gave us ardour, and has shown
> Her own for man so strongly, not disdain
> What smooth emollients in theology,
> Recumbent Virtue's downy doctors, preach;
> That prose of piety, a lukewarm praise?"

(Night IV "The Christian Triumph," lines 641–45).

229. A *battledore* is an old name for a shuttlecock (made, of course, of a cork and feathers).

230. "A Wit's a feather, and a Chief a rod; / An honest Man's the noblest work of God" (Pope, *Essay on Man*, epistle 4, lines 247–48).

231. This is the answer to a very old trick question, which makes a point about the difference between weight and volume.

> Where, with her best Nurse Contemplation,
> She plumes her *Feathers*."[232]

We are not publicly told who is the Leader, the Commanding Officer, the Captain *Plume* of this *Feathers Association*.[233] Perhaps indeed they have many "*Feather-cinctured Chiefs*," as Mr. *Gray* says; but as yet they cannot *plume* themselves on their Success, although their Boast is,

> "Yet we shall *wing* our distant Way
> Above the Tenor of a vulgar *Creed*."[234]

Mr. *Addison* tells us in the *Spectator* that some Geniuses, remarkable for laborious Conceit, piqued themselves on making Poems in various Shapes, as in that of a Wing, an Ax, or an Egg.[235] I would suggest to the *Feathers Clergy* to imitate such bright Examples, and draw up their Petition in such Forms. The *Wing* is most happily suited to what is composed at the *Feathers*; the *Ax* is well fitted to typify their hacking and hewing the Thirty-nine Articles,[236] the *Egg* will appear with double Propriety, both as being the Production of a *Bird*, and as containing one of the most *insipid* Substances that we know. But indeed as they seem determined to *persevere* in their Applications, and I trust Parliament will be equally firm in rejecting them, they may have an Opportunity of putting their Petition into Abundance of fantastical Shapes, into that of a *Serpent*, an *Ass*, a *Mole*, or any Thing else they please; they will however carefully avoid a *Perriwig*, because the *Lord's Prayer* was written by some odd Fellow in the Curls of *Charles the First*'s Wig in a Drawing of that Monarch.[237]

232. Milton, "Comus: A Mask," lines 375–78; these lines are spoken by the Elder Brother.

233. Captain Plume is the hero of George Farquhar's popular comedy *The Recruiting Officer* (1706).

234. "Their feather-cinctured Chiefs, and dusky Loves," from Thomas Gray (1716–77), *Progress of Poesy* (1757), line 62. The poem's concluding lines read, "Yet shall he mount, and keep his distant way / Beyond the limits of a vulgar fate, / Beneath the Good how far—but far above the Great" (121–23).

235. *Spectator*, no. 58 (May 7, 1711; 1:244–48). The poem "Easter Wings" by George Herbert (1593–1632) is probably the best-known poem of this kind.

236. See headnote and n. 218, above.

237. Addison, in *Spectator*, no. 58 (May 7, 1711; 1:248), refers to a famous picture of King Charles I that has the whole of the biblical book of Psalms written in the lines of the face and the hair of the head: "When I was last at Oxford, I perused one of the whiskers; and was reading the other, but could not go so far in it as I would have done, by reason of the impatience of my friends and fellow-travellers, who all of them pressed to see such a piece of curiosity. I have since heard that there is now an eminent writing-master in town who has transcribed all the Old Testament in a full-bottomed periwig; and if the fashion should

The Definition which one of the ancient Philosophers gave of Man was, "a two-legged Animal without Feathers;" upon which a Rival Philosopher pulled the Feathers off a Cock, and turned him thus stripped into the other's School, by which he at once refuted the Definition, and exposed him to the Laughter of his Scholars.[238] But in this Age, when Metaphor is well understood, the Definition of a good Churchman might very well include in it that he is *"without Feathers."*[239]

I have only to add, that my Intention in this waggish Skirmish is, that the *Feathers Men* may not, like the Dunghill Cock, crow in Sign of Victory because they see none to oppose them.[240] I hope I have *ruffled* their *Feathers* a little for them, and that they will be glad to *petition* for Quarter.[241]

RAMPAGER.

No. 10: Reply, Serious and Otherwise, to "A Feather's Man"

[On April 23, 1774, the *Public Advertiser* printed (p. 2) the following letter from "A Feather's Man," in response to the "Rampager" (no. 9), above, published the previous week. Boswell made a cutting of this letter, now in his files at Yale (*Cat. Yale,* P 152(7)).

SIR,

WE are to suppose that Rampager stands up for a Wit, and such I will readily allow him to be, though of an inferior Kind. His Wit seems to consist chiefly in darting suddenly from one Idea to another, in unexpected Allusions, and in quaint Applications of little proverbial Phrases. But I would beg Leave to remind him of the Distinction the great Mr. Locke has made between Wit and Judgment;[242] or, if Mr. Locke is an Author too much out of

---

introduce the thick kind of wigs which were in vogue some few years ago, he promises to add two or three supernumerary locks that shall contain all the Apocrypha. He designed this wig originally for King William, having disposed of the two books of Kings in the two forks of the foretop; but that glorious monarch dying before the wig was finished, there is a space left in it for the face of any one that has a mind to purchase it."

238. In the Life of Diogenes the Cynic, Diogenes Laertius tells this story about Plato; it concludes, "Diogenes plucked a cock and brought it to his school, and said, 'This is Plato's man.'" See Diogenes Laertius, *Lives and Opinions of Eminent Philosophers* (book 6), 231.

239. That is, that a good churchman will not be *within* the *Feathers* (Tavern).

240. *Dunghill cock*, see n. 205, above.

241. To *petition for quarter*: for those defeated in battle to ask for mercy from their conqueror.

242. John Locke (1632–1704), English philosopher. In *An Essay Concerning Human Understanding* (1690), he says, "wit lying most in the assemblage of ideas, and putting those

his Way, I will refer him to the Spectator, an Author which he mentions, and
who has quoted that Passage of Locke, and has descanted upon it in a very
sensible Manner.

> "Wit has been called a two-edged Sword. It may be, and it is, equally
> employed on the Side of Truth, and on that of Falshood. Wit proves
> nothing of itself, and is of no Service, or of any real Worth, unless
> preceded by Truth and Justice; at best, it only proves, it only displays,
> the Talent of him who employs it, and his Character, as he employs it
> a-propos or otherwise."[243]

I would beg Leave to remind Rampager of another Thing, which is, that
grave, serious Subjects ought to be treated in a grave, serious Manner. Now
surely there is nothing in the World more grave, more serious than Religion,
and religious Professions.

Since Rampager has mentioned the *Spectator*, I will inform him, if he does
not know it, that Mr. Addison, who was one of the principal Writers in it, was
no Friend to the Thirty-nine Articles, and that he was particularly averse to
those of them which are distinguished by the Name of CALVINISTICAL. This
I have read in some Account of his Life;[244] and besides, nothing can be more
diametrically opposite to what he says in some of his Papers, wherein he has
Occasion to speak of the Divine Attributes.

Whenever Rampager is disposed to make use of his Judgment instead of
his Wit, or even jointly with it, I will readily submit it to him, whether they
deserve to be censured who take Revelation, Revelation itself, for their sole
Guide and Rule in Matters of Religion, who think they are bound to make

---

together with quickness and variety wherein can be found any resemblance or congruity,
thereby to make up pleasant pictures and agreeable visions in the fancy" (book 2, chap. 11:
"Of Discerning," § 3). JB quotes the rest of the passage, concerning judgment, in the "Rampager" following.

243. The passage from Locke concerning the distinction between wit and judgment
is quoted in *Spectator*, no. 62 (May 11, 1711; 1:263–64); however, the passage quoted as the
Spectator "descanting" upon Locke is not to be found there or elsewhere. (Cf. *Un bon mot ne
prouve rien*: a witty saying proves nothing, from Voltaire, *Le dîner du* comte *de Boulainvilliers* (1767): Deuxième Entretien.)

244. The supposed Calvinist elements in the Thirty-nine Articles include the articles
on baptism (no. 27) and the Lord's supper (no. 28), although article 17 on the important
Calvinist issue of predestination and election explicitly rejects the idea of predestination to
damnation (Mark A. Noll, "Thirty-nine Articles (1563)," http://mb-soft.com/believe/txc/
thirtyni.htm). I have not identified the passage suggested here; Addison's religious opinions
are usually understood to be "broad Church Anglican, and while he no doubt harboured
some of the old prejudices against 'extreme' protestants, . . . he's much more virulent against
the high church" (Pat Rogers, personal communication). Addison's vision of religious moderation, of the desirability of a balance between unity and freedom, is presented in *Spectator*,
no. 3 (March 3, 1711; 1:14–17).

use of their own Reason and Understanding in order to understand it, and who abide by what appears to them true and right.

I am, SIR,

Your humble Servant,

Feb. 24.   A FEATHER'S MAN.

On May 5, 1774, the issue of clerical subscription was reintroduced to the Parliament, in a motion that a committee be established to consider the plight of clergy who had conscientious objections to the Articles. This motion was rejected, so Boswell was on firm ground when he replied to "A Feather's Man" in his next "Rampager," many months later.]

Public Advertiser, August 16, 1774, 1 (leading article); with Boswell's MS corrections (see Figure 10).

SIR,

A *Feathers-Man* has been pleased to animadvert upon *Rampager*; he characterizes my Wit, by saying, that "it seems to consist chiefly in darting suddenly from one Idea to another, in unexpected Allusions, and in quaint Applications of little proverbial Phrases." This is well enough; but I would rather chuse to adopt what Bishop *Burnet* says, in his History of his own Times, of Bishop *Leightoun*: "His Thoughts were lively, oft out of the Way and surprizing, yet just and genuine."[245] And since I have quoted *Burnet*, I would beg Leave to refer this *Feathers-Man* to that Prelate's Commentary on the *Thirty-nine Articles*,[246] which I am persuaded he and his Brethren have not read, otherwise they must have been satisfied that they are contending against Propositions which the Church does not hold, and frightened with Scruples for which there is no Cause but their own mistaken Apprehensions. I must also send *him* to Mr. *Locke*, to whom he sends *me*, and must beg his Attention to what that Philosopher says of Judgment, which he tells us "separates carefully one from another, Ideas wherein can be found the least Difference thereby to avoid being misled by Similitude, and by Affinity to take one Thing for another."[247] I wish the *Feathers-Men* to be upon their Guard, lest they mistake a Fondness for Novelty and Singularity for Tenderness of Conscience, and a Spirit of Forwardness and Presumption for Zeal for Truth. Far be it from me to censure any Man who takes Revelation itself for his sole Rule in Matters of Religion. The modest and humble Christian, be

245. JB has already used this quotation from Burnet in "Rampager" 8, see above.

246. Gilbert Burnet, *An Exposition of the Thirty-nine Articles of the Church of England* (1699).

247. This passage from Locke immediately follows that to which a Feather's Man referred JB, above; see n. 242.

Figure 10. Letter signed "Rampager" [no. 10], with Boswell's handwritten star, corrections, and annotation, Public Advertiser, *August 16, 1774. Cutting in Boswell's file, Catalogue P 152(8). Courtesy of the Beinecke Rare Book and Manuscript Library, Yale University.*

his Opinions ever so different from the Standard of the Church of England, shall have my best Wishes; but I cannot help feeling an Indignation to see Men forming themselves into a regular Body to attack a respectable Establishment, by which our holy Religion hath been carried on with Dignity and Beneficence for Ages. I am for an Indulgence sufficiently liberal: but every regular Society has surely a Right to prescribe its own Terms: And are these to be abolished because certain Individuals do not like them, when those Individuals need not be of the Society unless they chuse it?

But it is not my Intention to enter upon a serious Argument with the *Feathers-Men*; for that has been done already by Writers of distinguished Ability. In my last I played a little with the Name of Dr. *Priestly*, as being by no Means consonant to the Task which he has assumed of *arraigning* our *Priest-hood*. Since that Time a Writer has appeared, whose Name is much better suited to his Principles, the Reverend Mr. TEMPLE, Rector of *Mamhead*, in *Devonshire*, who has given us an *"Essay on the Clergy,"* in which, amongst other Topics, he, with equal Perspicuity and Elegance, shews the Reasonableness and Propriety of having Articles of Faith, and the Danger of throwing them loose.[248] Whatever *Feathers-Man* perseveres in his *Flights*, without reading this excellent Essay, I pronounce to be an Apostate from his own Professions of free Enquiry and diligent Information; one who shuts his Eyes against the Light, or who at least will not turn them towards the Quarter where he is told that it shines;— though perhaps some Members of that Association may have the Boldness and vigorous Eyes of the Eagle that can fly directly in the Face of the Sun.[249] I must observe, too, that Mr. *Temple*'s Essay claims the peculiar Attention of the *Feathers-Men* from this Circumstance, that it is printed for Mess. *Dilly* in the POULTRY.[250]

248. JB's intimate and lifelong friend and correspondent, clergyman William Johnson Temple (1739–96): his *An Essay on the Clergy: Their Studies, Recreations, Decline of Influence, &c.* was published in May 1774; Temple first mentions it in a letter to JB, Jan. 5, 1773 (see *Corres.* 6, 322 and n. 5).

249. In his *Natural History* (book 10, chap. 3), Pliny writes that the eagle will compel her chicks "to looke full against the Sunne beames. Now if shee see any one of them to winke, or their eies to water at the raies of the Sunne, shee turnes it with the head forward out of the nest, as a bastard, and not right; nor none of hers: but bringeth up and cherisheth that whose eie will abide the light of the Sunne as she looketh directly upon him." Lucan repeats this (*Civil War*, 9.1057–61), and it became a commonplace piece of lore in, for instance, seventeenth-century emblem books.

250. JB's friends and publishers Charles Dilly (1739–1807) and, from 1764, his brother Edward (1732–79) ran a successful bookselling business at 22 Poultry, London, near the Mansion House, an address given in their colophon as "In the Poultry." The Dillys were

The *Feathers-Man* begs Leave to remind me, that "grave, serious Subjects ought to be treated in a grave, serious Manner, and that there is nothing in the World more grave, more serious than Religion and religious Professions." As to this I in general agree with him; for I am perfectly convinced that nothing can be more false than Lord *Shaftesbury's* Maxim, that Ridicule is the Test of Truth.[251] At the same Time Instances do occur where People, who are very grave and serious, are also not a little foolish, to say no worse: and the Consequences of their Conduct, if successful, may be exceedingly destructive of what is indeed grave and serious, nay sacred and venerable. Upon such Occasions Ridicule may be well applied, and have good Success, according to the Maxim of the Roman Poet.

————————————*Ridiculum* acri

Fortius ac melius magnas plerumque secat res.[252]

We have an Example in the HOLY SCRIPTURES of Ridicule being admirably used against pretended Religionists; and sure the *Feathers-Men* will not object to the Authority of *the Scriptures themselves.*

"ELIJAH (the Prophet of the LORD said unto the Prophets of *Baal*, choose you one Bullock for yourselves, and dress it first; for ye are many; and call on the Name of your Gods, but put no Fire under.

And they took the Bullock which was given them, and they dressed it, and called on the Name of Baal from Morning even unto Noon, saying, O, Baal, hear us! But there was no Voice, nor any that answered. And they leapt upon the Altar which was made.

---

generous literary patrons and very supportive of their authors, who included JB, SJ, Benjamin Franklin, Elizabeth Montagu, and many others. Charles became sole proprietor of the firm after Edward's death. The Dillys were known to be religious dissenters, like the Feathers Men, making it the more striking that they should publish Temple's *Essay.*

251. Anthony Ashley Cooper, third earl of Shaftesbury (1671–1713), English philosopher; his famous test seems to be expressed by him not in this particular "maxim," but in a number of places throughout his writings: "How comes it to pass, then, that we appear such cowards in reasoning and are so afraid to stand the test of ridicule?" ("A Letter Concerning Enthusiasm," sec. 2); "Truth, it is supposed, may bear *all* lights, and one of those principal lights, or natural mediums, by which things are to be viewed, in order to a thorough recognition, is ridicule itself" ("Sensus Communis, An Essay on the Freedom of Wit and Humour," sec. 1). See Shaftesbury, *Characteristics of Men, Manners, Opinions, Times,* 8, 30.

252. Horace, *Satires,* 1.10.14–15: "Jesting oft cuts hard knots more forcefully and effectively than gravity" (117); i.e., ridicule often settles difficult questions better than a serious response.

And it came to pass at Noon that Elijah *mocked* them, and said, Cry aloud; for he is a God; either he is talking, or he is pursuing, or he is in a Journey, or peradventure he sleepeth, and must be awakened.

And they cried aloud, and cut themselves, after their Manner, with Knives and Lancets 'till the Blood gushed out upon them."[253]

I take it, Mr. Woodfall, the Prophets of Baal were at least as grave and serious as the *Feathers-Men*; nay, more so; for I have not heard of any of the latter cutting themselves with Knives. No; no; these they employ in cutting the fat Tythe Pigs at their Livings,[254] which they enjoy, upon that very Establishment against which their Quivers are discharged.

Having thus I hope cleared myself from all Suspicions of Prophaneness while I *rampage* against the *Feathers-Men*, I take the Field again with that hearty Good-humour and sportive Spirit which has ever distinguished my Essays in the *Public Advertiser*. With Joy did I read the ludicrous Fate of their renewed Application to Parliament which had indeed a *Merry death (Meredith)* and had its Grave richly strewed with Flowers by *Edmund Burke*, so that I really think the next Meeting of the Petitioners should have been at *Edmunsbury*.[255] Sir Roger *New*digate was by much too *Old* for them; and Lord NORTH effectually *blasted* their Hopes;[256] teaching them, that like *Dedalus*, they had *waxed* wanton in Project, and were endeavouring to fly loose *pennis non homini datis*.[257]

---

253. 1 Kings 18:25–28 (*AV*).

254. *Living*: the benefice of a clergyman (*SJ Dict.*).

255. The new motion concerning clerical subscription was introduced to the House of Commons on May 5, 1774, by opposition MP Sir William Meredith (bap. 1724–90). But it was not a party-political matter, and Edmund Burke sided with Lord North in defending the status quo. Burke's speech on this occasion was mainly devoted to mocking Meredith, who had just accepted a government appointment to the Privy Council. See Burke, *Writings and Speeches*, 2:465–67. St. Edmundsbury, also known as Bury St. Edmunds, is a town in Suffolk associated with the Magna Carta. JB is punning on the petition having been *buried* by *Edmund* (Burke).

256. Sir Roger Newdigate (1719–1806), tory MP for Oxford University, argued that such a bill could not be assented to by the king without breaking his Coronation oath; by *old* here, JB suggests the connotation of wise, mature, canny. Lord North said that the Church already allowed sufficient moderation and that, in any case, motions on Church matters should originate in the House of Lords. The motion was rejected, without a division being required. See *St. James's Chron.*, May 5, 1774. JB puns on the cold *blasts* of the *North* wind.

257. JB alludes to the Greek story of Daedalus the craftsman who, with his son Icarus, attempted to escape exile in Crete by making wings out of wax and feathers. Icarus flew too close to the sun, his wings melted, and he plunged into the sea. In the ode quoted, Horace describes Daedalus flying "on wings unnatural to man" (*Odes*, 1.3.35).

We are told in the Heathen Mythology, that *Juno* turned *Argus* into a Peacock, and scattered his 100 Eyes about the Tail of that Bird:

> Excipit hos, volucrisque suæ Saturnia Pennis
> Collocat, & gemmis caudam stellantibus implet.[258]

These Feathersmen had need of some extraordinary Priviledge of more Eyes than their Neighbours, as a Justification of their pretending to see with much more Clearness than the greatest Luminaries of the Church. Nor am I much moved by an Assertion, that Mr. *Addison* was no Friend to the Thirty-nine Articles, which the Feathersman says, "he has read in *some* Account of his Life." I fancy it will not be easy to point out any explicit Evidence of the Charge; and supposing it were true, it would avail the *Feathersmen* no more than Mr. *Addison*'s drinking rather too much Strong Beer, would avail a Club of Soakers;[259] or his Usage of *Pope* justify the like Conduct in other Men of Genius. *Addison*, however illustrious for Talents, for Virtue, and for Piety, was not perfect:

> "Who would not weep if *Atticus* were he."[260]

What Title have the *Feathersmen* to complain of the Regulations of an established Church, of which No-body desires them to be Ministers? In all other Societies, those who cannot conform to their Rules, or in any Way differ from the Establishment, never dream of making the Society subservient to them; but endeavour to do for themselves in the Manner that is most agreeable to them. Thus *Kenrick*, the learned *Aberdeen Doctor of Laws*, being a Non-Conformist to *our Theatrical Establishments*, has very properly betaken himself to the *Devil Tavern*, and there delivered Lectures upon *Shakespeare*.[261] Why do not the *Feathersmen* also *Lecture* at *their* Tavern.

---

258. "Saturnia took these eyes [of Argus] and set them on the feathers of her bird, filling his tail with star-like jewels" (Ovid, *Metamorphoses*, 1.722–23).

259. *Soaker*: "A great drinker. In low language" (*SJ Dict.*).

260. Pope, *Epistle to Dr. Arbuthnot*, line 214. This is the final line of a verse paragraph on Addison, whom Pope names Atticus, after the friend of Cicero, for his generous patronage and good taste. But the point of Pope's portrait is to regret a great talent flawed by petty tyranny.

261. The satirical writer and controversialist William Kenrick had in Feb. 1772 received the degree of LL.D. from Marischal College of the University of Aberdeen. JB also alludes to his being a (religious) nonconformist and to his being cut off from the theatrical establishment: in 1766 he lost the contract for an edition of Shakespeare, and production of his plays was hampered by his attacks on actor-managers Garrick and George Colman. Kenrick used the notes for his aborted edition of Shakespeare as the basis for a successful series

"And all the aerial Audience clap their Wings."[262]

Let us give due Praise to one Example: Let us commend in suitable Terms, that *honest Yorkshire Man,* The: *Lindesay,* who has resigned his Living at *Catterick,* and come up to the Metropolis;[263] and to whom we may sing

"You ne'er like a Clown, shall leave London dear Town,
To dwell in your own Country."[264]

Doubtless, he has done well in exchanging his *Northern Sheep,* for a Flock of *Essex Calves,* and his *humbler Fold,* for *Essex House* in the *Strand.*[265] I would therefore say to each *Feathersman,* that if he can continue calmly and steadily at his Living, *laudi manentem:*—If he cannot do so, and is able to *Feather his Nest* as well as good Mr. *Lindesay,* I shall say nothing against him, though *Celeres quatit pennas,*[266] and comes off. All I insist is, that he may have to say with *Hecate* in the Tragedy of *Macbeth,* "Now I am *furnished* for my *Flight.*"[267]

It is a Wonder to me, that the Zeal of the *petitioning Clergy* does not rise to such a *Pitch,* as to make them like the Liberty Boys in *America,* not only *Featherers* but *Tarrers.*[268] They may indeed be thankful, that they live in a mild and indulgent Reign; for they very well know, that the Time has been, when such

---

of lectures at the Devil Tavern at Temple Bar, London, which were afterward published as *Introduction to the School of Shakespeare* (1774).

262. Pope, "Spring," line 16.

263. See "Rampager" 9, headnote. After the rejection of the petition by the Commons, Theophilus Lindsey resigned his living at Catterick in Yorkshire. He came to London and in Apr. 1774 was assisted by friends, including Joseph Priestley, to set up a Unitarian chapel in Essex Street (*ODNB*).

264. Carey, *Honest Yorkshireman,* 11. "Air VII": "Thou ne'er, like a Clown,/Shalt quit London's sweet Town,/To live in thine own Country." *Clown:* "a rustick; a country fellow" (*SJ Dict.*).

265. The temporary chapel in Essex House was opened for public worship on Apr. 17, 1774. "Essex calves" is a nickname for people from Essex.

266. *Laudi manentem:* I praise her while she stays. *Celeres quatit pennas:* she shakes her wings for flight. Both phrases are from the same passage: "I praise her [Fortune] while she stays; but if she shakes her wings for flight, I renounce her gifts," Horace, *Odes,* 3.29.53–54).

267. Shakespeare, *Macbeth,* 3.5.55. (This line, spoken by the witch Hecate, is from a song by Thomas Middleton, of which the title but not the text was included in the First Folio; it is therefore omitted in some modern editions.)

268. For Liberty Boys, also known as the Sons of Liberty, see Chap. 1, n. 1. The old British punishment of tarring and feathering was reported, from 1769, to have been much in use among the Liberty Boys. See Evelyn, *Memoir,* 27–28.

Heretics as they would have had a *Tar-Barrel* in *Smithfield*.[269] But I really think, a little *Tarring* would not be amiss for the *Feathersmen*, to shew a congenial Spirit in Ecclesiastical Matters, with the Bostonians in Civil. Besides, it must be remembered, what an Enthusiast the ingenious *Berkeley* Bishop of *Cloyne* was for *Tar-Water*, which is humourously illustrated in Verse by Sir *Charles Hanbury Williams*.[270] Now, *Berkeley* was a glorious Demolisher of Establishments, for he disproved the Existence of Matter itself, which was far beyond the little Strokes of any of the Petitioners.[271]

I have but one more Word to say at present to the *Feathersmen*: Let them consider the Inconvenience of being "tossed about by every Wind of Doctrine,"[272] and recollect that *Feathers* and *Cork* compose that Emblem of Levity a *Shuttle-Cock*.

RAMPAGER.

1775

No. 11: On the American Tea War:
Rhubarb Recommended[273]

[In April 1770, the British Parliament repealed various of the taxes on products imported into America but refused to repeal the tax on tea, for the sound reason that

269. Smithfield, just outside the old city walls of London, was a site for markets and fairs and was also for many years the main site for executions of religious dissidents. During the persecution of Protestants under Queen Mary, in 1555–57, fifty or more people were martyred by burning at Smithfield; the condemned person would be stood in an empty tar barrel and tied to the stake, before dry brush and branches were heaped around them. (See *ODNB*, s.v. "Marian Martyrs.")

270. Bishop and idealist philosopher George Berkeley (1685–1753) was an advocate for the virtues of tar-water—which he prepared from pine resin and water—as a specific for a great variety of distempers, and his last two lifetime publications were devoted to this cause: *Siris: Philosophical Reflexions and Inquiries Concerning the Virtues of Tar-Water* (1744) and *Further Thoughts on Tar-Water* (1752). This eccentric enthusiasm was satirized by politician, diplomat, and poet Charles Hanbury Williams in *Tar-Water: A Ballad*, first published in 1743.

271. Berkeley is better known for his proto-empiricist philosophy, which argued that the only secure knowledge we have is of sense-data and that the material world is an abstraction that exists only insofar as it is an idea in the mind of God.

272. Ephesians 4:14 (*AV*).

273. This title adapts JB's MS note on his file copy (see textual notes).

this was the only tax that actually produced any meaningful income. The colonists
boycotted the British East India Company's tea, and on May 10, 1773, in order to
assist the company, Parliament passed the Tea Act, which allowed tea to be exported
directly to the colonies without being taxed in Britain. Tea thus became cheaper
in the colonies, but acceptance of the new measures was seen by some to imply an
acknowledgment of Parliament's right to have retained the tea duty since 1770. Furthermore, the cheaper price of tea undercut the local merchants. When in December
1773 the first tea-bearing ships arrived in Boston, some citizens (and tea merchants),
disguised as Native Americans, seized them and emptied the chests of tea into
Boston Harbor; the episode is known as the Boston Tea Party. This attack on British
property provoked the North government into passing the Coercive or Intolerable
Acts of 1774 to punish the colonists of Massachusetts, which further angered the
colonists.

In response, the First Continental Congress was held in October 1774, in Philadelphia, with delegates from twelve of the thirteen American colonies, at which it
was agreed to urge all colonists to avoid using British goods and to form committees to enforce this ban. In January 1775, the prime minister, Lord North, desperately
tried to forestall Britain's inevitable civil war with the American colonies, now almost
wholly united in their resistance to Parliament's authority over their internal affairs
and their rights and liberties. North attempted some measure of compromise with
the Continental Congress and persuaded his cabinet to allow individual colonies to
tax themselves, to cover the cost of their own defense and administration; however,
events had overtaken the initial taxation difficulty, and taxation compromise would
not solve the impending crisis. The war had already broken out before the news
reached the colonies.]

Public Advertiser, March 11, 1775, 2; with Boswell's MS correction

SIR,

LORD *North*'s late Motion with regard to the Americans[274] has deprived me
of some little Amusement which I proposed to have had upon the Embarkation of the 17th Regiment of Horse from Ireland for America.[275] We have all

---

274. On Feb. 15, 1775, Lord North put to Parliament a motion setting out his proposals for conciliation with the American colonies; this motion followed the more generous
proposals of Lord Chatham, which had been rejected by Parliament. See Cobbett, *Parliamentary History of England*, cols. 319–58.

275. The 17th Regiment of (Light) Dragoons (later to become the 17th Lancers)—a kind
of mounted infantry—was established (as, briefly, the 18th Regiment) in 1759, under Col.
John Hale. The regiment was stationed in Scotland, 1760–64, and was moved to Ireland in
1765. In 1770, George Preston became colonel of the regiment. In Feb. 1775, the 17th was the
first cavalry regiment selected for service in the American war, with orders "to reinforce the
Troops under General Gage at Boston" (*Pub. Adv.*, Feb. 11, 1775), which was then besieged

heard of the ludicrous Expression, "a Captain of *Horse* by *Sea*," said to be of Hibernian Extraction;[276] and we were very near having it realized by the Hibernian Embarkation which I have mentioned. It would have been a pretty Piece of Work to have transported such a Number of Horses across the Atlantic.[277] What a Quantity of Hay and Corn must have been put on board; and the Water for their Drink would have been sufficient to make a Ship swim. I could not help being diverted with the Names of two of the Officers of this Regiment of Horse, Lieutenant Colonel *Birch* and Captain *Nettles*; for, indeed, *Birch* and *Nettles* might be very properly applied to some of our American Children.[278] It is, however, more agreeable, if we can bring them to a proper Submission without making them smart.

I remember to have seen, in the Public Advertiser, a Poem upon Tea by the Emperor of China.[279] Had that Monarch known that this trifling Herb had nearly embroiled the Western World, it would have afforded a good Addition to his Verses, and given a kind of horrid Grandeur to the Subject. We have read of a *Teterrima* Belli Causa; but a *sillier* one than Tea cannot be imagined.[280] That Scandal and little female Altercations have been promoted by it, is almost proverbial;[281] but it is truly wonderful to find it the Cause of national

---

by American rebels; they embarked from Cork toward the end of March. (On June 17, the 17th fought at the Battle of Bunker Hill.) See Fortescue, *History of the 17th Lancers*, chaps. 1–3.

276. Not found in this form as a "common expression," but the "horse marines" is a jocular reference to an unknown or imaginary force (the Royal Marines being either artillery or infantry, rather than cavalry), which is preserved in the expression "tell it to the [horse] marines": i.e., tell something unbelievable to an imaginary audience (*Brewer's Dict.*).

277. Horses for the regiment were actually bought in America (Fortescue, *History of the 17th Lancers*, 32).

278. Lt. Col. Samuel Birch was an officer of the regiment from its formation; both he and Lt. Henry Nettles are listed in the final muster of the regiment before its embarkation (Fortescue, *History of the 17th Lancers*, 8, 33). JB could have read the names in a number of contemporary publications.

279. "*A Prose Translation of an Ode on Tea, composed by* Kien-long, *the Present* Emperor *of* China *and* Tartary," introduced by a letter signed "Publicola" (*Pub. Adv.*, Mar. 9, 1772, 2). In a later issue (Mar. 23, 1772), there is a long letter from the same correspondent, purporting to explain and authenticate the poem (2); nevertheless, it is also printed in *School for Satire*, 45–92. Qianlong (1711–99) was emperor of China from 1735.

280. Horace, *Satires*, 1.3.107–8: "the *most dreadful* cause of war"—which was a woman (literally, *cunnus*), according to Horace.

281. An allusion to the idiom *a storm in a teacup*: a small disturbance of which the seriousness has been exaggerated.

Animosities, and almost of the Horrors of Slaughter and Devastation; though a *Leaf*, it is in its Effects like "the insane *Root* that takes the Reason Prisoner."[282]

Sir *Alexander Dick*, who practised for some Time as a Physician in Wales, suggested lately a very good Prescription for the Americans: He would have them to drink *Rue* Tea,[283] which, as it grows in the Country, will correspond with their Non-importation Scheme;[284] and will also clear up their Eyes, if we can believe the Precept of the *Schola Salernitona, bona est ruta quia lumina reddit accuta*.[285]

It would not be amiss too that Sir *Alexander* should send them a Quantity of the *Rhubarb* which he raises in his Garden, and for which he lately had the Honour to obtain a Gold Medal from the Society of Arts and Sciences; for since the Americans are not to be *blooded*, it is fit that they should be *purged*.[286]

---

282. Shakespeare, *Macbeth*, 1.3.84–85. After their encounter with the witches, Banquo asks if he and Macbeth have "eaten on the insane root"—i.e., some root believed to cause hallucinations or madness, usually thought to be henbane or hemlock.

283. In 1768, Sir Alexander Dick told JB that he was writing without spectacles, "by the help of Rue tea" (Oct. 1; *Corres. 7*, 113). In an as-yet unpublished letter to JB of Sept. 12, 1782, Dick describes his daily regimen, which included the taking of rue tea (James Caudle, personal communication). It is not known when he made the suggestion recorded here. The Common Rue (*Ruta graveolens*) is a bitter herb used around the Mediterranean medicinally (traditionally, as a tea) and as a condiment. The plant that grows in North America is not this but an unrelated plant called harmal (*Peganum harmala*), commonly called "Syrian rue."

284. That is, the extended boycott of British products, such as tea and sugar, agreed at the First Continental Congress. The boycott gained the attention of British policy makers, but its success was cut short by the outbreak of war.

285. In the letter mentioned in n. 283, above, Dick quotes this passage—*Nobila est ruta, quia lumina reddit acuta*: "rue is noble; it makes the eyes sharp" (noted as untraced in *Corres. 7*, 113)—from the *Regimen Sanitatis Salernitatum* (the Salernitan Rule of Health) attributed to Joannes de Mediolano (c. 1050), 60; the *Regimen* is a medieval rhyming poem concerning medical practice. There were English versions by Thomas Paynell (1528), Philemon Holland (1649), and *The Englishmans Doctor*, trans. Sir John Harrington (1607). Ancient Egyptians and early Greeks believed that rue taken orally could improve eyesight; it was taken commonly by medieval artists, craftsmen, and writers who needed good vision to perform close work (www.DrugDigest.org).

286. Rhubarb, which was long cultivated as a purgative, was first introduced into Britain from Russia in 1761 by James Mounsey of St. Petersburg. Dick obtained seeds, cultivated it, and prepared medicines, and in Dec. 1774 the Royal Society of Arts, founded in London in 1754, awarded him the first of its "annual" gold medals. See Foust, "Society of the Arts and Rhubarb." Being "blooded" or bled was at the time, like purgation, a routine medical procedure for the alleged release of pent-up humors.

I cannot help feeling some Indignation at the Perverseness of the Gentlemen in Opposition for abusing the Minister with Keenness and Acrimony now,
when he is in Effect doing what they a little Time ago warmly insisted should
be done.[287] It is even *impolitic* to let the People see clearly that they have no
other Principle of Action than the *Reverse* of what the Minister chooses. They
put one in Mind of a Set of Jolly Fellows, who parading through the Streets of
a Burgh at an Election,[288] and hearing the Party who were of *the other Interest*,
crying Liberty and Property, and no Excise, they, with the true Spirit of Opposition, called out, *no* Liberty, *no* Property, and *Excise for ever.*

For my own Part, it is very seldom that I think Administration in the wrong;
for I own that I wish to reverence and support "the Powers that be," both in
Church and State.[289] But I have had my Doubts concerning American Measures, and it gives me sincere Satisfaction that our Rulers are now disposed to
be more calm and gentle.

The Literary World is obliged to Mr. *Thomas Davies* for having lately published a neat Edition of *George Lillo*, by which many have been induced to
read that worthy Poet's Works, who might not have sought after them when
scattered.[290] In the Epilogue to *Marina*, a Tragedy by *Lillo*, I found some Lines
which struck me, as what might be spoken with admirable Effect by an American Ambassador to the Mother Country.

> When to a future Race the present Days
> Shall be the Theme of Censure or of Praise;
> When they shall blame what's wrong, what's right allow,
> Just as you treat your own Forefathers now;
> I'm thinking what a Figure you will make:
> No light Concern, Sirs, where your Fame's at Stake.
> I hope we need not urge your Country's Cause;
> You'll guard her Glory, and assert her Laws;

287. Lord North's conciliatory proposals were criticized by many opposition politicians,
including Fox, Isaac Barré, and Burke, for being insincere and too little and too late.

288. In Scottish usage, *burgh* is a self-governing administrative division, usually a town,
having (before the Union of 1707) the right to representation in the Scottish Parliament; by
this time, it was an archaism.

289. This passage was echoed by JB in a letter to Temple a few weeks after this publication; see section intro, above. For "the powers that be," see n. 134, above.

290. Thomas Davies (1712–85), London actor and bookseller; he first introduced JB to
SJ on May 16, 1763. His edition of the *Works* of George Lillo (1693–1739) was published in
1775. Lillo's play *Marina* (1738) was an adaptation of acts 4 and 5 of Shakespeare's *Pericles*.
For this passage, see Lillo, *Works*, 59.

Nor force your ruin'd Race, mad with their Pains,
To curse you as the Authors of their Chains.
We dare not think, we wou'd not fear, you will;
For Britons, though provok'd, are Britons still.

RAMPAGER.

No. 12: End the American War by Arming the Jews

[With the failure of Lord North's conciliatory proposals, in April 1775 the first shots were fired in what was to become the War of Independence, in the Battles of Lexington and Concord. On May 10, 1775, a Second Continental Congress was held, at which the decision to move toward independence was made, and on June 14, 1775, Congress voted to form the Continental Army. Within a few days, the British suffered massive losses (1,500 out of 2,000) in winning the Battle of Bunker Hill. News of this engagement reached Boswell, as he proposes a plan to put an end to the war.

There was at the time only a very small Jewish population in England. Jews had been expelled from England in 1290 under Edward I, and, although from the mid-seventeenth century the ban was not enforced, Jews still could not become naturalized British subjects. Legislation passed in 1753 allowed naturalization, but it was quickly repealed after a public outcry, making life very difficult for the disenfranchised Jewish community. Indeed, many opted to abandon their faith. So, why not send them to America to take on the colonists?]

Public Advertiser, August 14, 1775, 1–2; with Boswell's MS corrections

SIR,

WHILE our great Men seem to be very much at a Loss in what Manner to conduct themselves towards the *Americans*, I take it for granted that no Man whatever need be ashamed to suggest any Plan that occurs to him, even although it should appear whimsical and ridiculous. I do declare that I cannot as yet bring myself to any settled Opinion with regard to the Affairs of America, and I can with great Justice adopt the Saying of an eminent Wit, that one should have an *American Master*.[291]

In my last Letter to you, Mr. Woodfall, I was rather inclined to lenient Measures,[292] but now I would offer my Plan for violent Measures. It is, indeed, strange, that although we are told by Mr. Pope, that *Coffee* makes the Politician *wise*—*Tea* should produce so very different an Effect, so as to make so many

291. I have not identified this saying or its source.
292. See previous "Rampager," above, in which JB suggested the application of rue tea and rhubarb.

Politicians both in Great Britain and America *mad*.[293] We may, indeed, very well dispense with both of them, and at no Time sing with greater Glee that Passage in the Roast Beef of Old England:

> "When good Queen Elizabeth sat on the Throne,
> Ere Coffee and *Tea*, and such Slip-slops were known."[294]

And when in my last Letter I mentioned Sir *Alexander Dick*'s Prescription, that instead of Tea, the Americans should be obliged to drink *Rue*,[295] I might have added, that it should be infused in the Waters of *Lethe*, that the Americans might "*drink an Oblivion*" to all Differences with their Mother Country.[296]

But I am rambling from my Purpose, and forgetting my Plan for violent Measures, in which I have at the same Time an Eye to what seems to be thought generally expedient, viz. to take off a distinguished Hero of Opposition by giving him an Office.

My Plan then, Sir, is to *embody the Jews*,[297] and appoint a young Orator of very forcible Powers their Colonel Commandant. It is unnecessary to name him, as all who have read the *Heroic Epistle to Sir William Chalmers* will recollect the humourous Description of his being *qualified* for being put at the Head of this Army of *Hebrews*.[298]

---

293. See Pope, *Rape of the Lock*, canto 3, lines 117–18: "Coffee, (which makes the politician wise,/ And see thro' all things with his half-shut eyes)."

294. "The Roast Beef of Old England" was a popular patriotic song, from Henry Fielding's *Grub Street Opera* (1731). *Slipslop*: "Bad liquor. A low word formed by reduplication of *slop*" (*SJ Dict.*).

295. For rue tea, see previous "Rampager." *Rue* may obliquely call to mind Ophelia's mad speeches in *Hamlet*, 4.5.

296. The *Lethe*: in Greek mythology, a river in Hades; those who drank from it would lose all remembrance of the past. Hence it signifies the "waters of oblivion," or forgetfulness.

297. That is, form a (military) corps of Jews. It should be remarked that although, on his Continental tour, Aug. 5, 1764, Boswell mentions finding himself in the company of "a Jew and many other blackguards" and seems thus to accept the negative stereotype common at the time (Aug. 5, 1764; *Grand Tour 1*, 49); on Apr. 3–4, 1772, when he visited two London synagogues, he admired the plainness and lack of solemnity in Jewish worship and wrote, "I could not help feeling a kind of regret to see the certain descendants of venerable Abraham in an outcast state and sneered at and abused by every fool" (*Defence*, 96).

298. A pamphlet by William Mason, published anonymously in 1773. It is actually addressed to Sir William Chambers (not "Chalmers"), a garden designer and architect and author of the *Dissertation on Oriental Gardening*, and is a political satire employing gardening imagery. The "young orator" is "C*s F*"—i.e., whig politician Charles James Fox (1749–1806), then aged twenty-six, who entered the House of Commons in 1768 and, in the

I do not believe that the Ministry will allow the *Golden Calf* to be carried over to Boston, as they have, we are told, constant Occasion for that at home;[299] but the Jews may be certainly spared from this Country, and a most terrific Appearance they would make among the Oliverian Puritans on the other Side of the Atlantic.[300] I would have them armed with monstrous Knives, like that which *Macklin* draws forth when he plays *Shylock*;[301] and, as a Friend of mine very well observed, the Terror of *Circumcision* would affect the Colonists still more than that of *Scalping*.[302]

In this Reign it is not a little remarkable that there is at least an Appearance of *Jewish Influence*, though there has been such a prodigious Noise about *Scottish Influence*, that I do not remember that any of our most anxious Patriots have ever taken Notice of it. We find even *a County* in England represented by a Sir *Sampson*; and when we look at the List of those who have been honoured by his Majesty, do we not find a Sir *Joshua* Reynolds, a Sir *Elijah* Impey, a Sir *Noah* Thomas? Nay, who is it that prints the Public Advertiser itself? Henry SAMPSON Woodfall.[303]

Let us then make a fair Trial of what the *Israelites* can do. Methinks I see their Colonel Commandant kissing Hands upon his Promotion, and the First Lord of the Treasury receiving him with open Arms,[304] chucking him under

---

next six years, spoke there hundreds of times, gaining a reputation as a powerful speaker. In the *Heroic Epistle*, 15 (lines 129–34), Fox is "qualified" by being forcibly circumcised.

299. See Exodus 32, a warning against idolatry. When the Jewish people tired of waiting for Moses while he was receiving the Ten Commandments, Aaron had them cast a golden calf, which they idolized. JB may not be referring to anything more specific than the ministry's need for cash to prosecute the American war.

300. Oliver Cromwell (1599–1658), Britain's Lord Protector, 1653–58, after the execution of Charles I; he was connected to prominent Puritans who went to New England.

301. From 1741, actor Charles Macklin (c. 1699–1797) became famous for his portrayal of the Jew, Shylock, in *The Merchant of Venice*, and played the role for fifty years. JB "seems not to have seen Macklin's performance and would not meet him until 1769" (Boswell, *Journal of His German and Swiss Travels*, 60 n. 1).

302. No such observation from a friend of JB's has been found in his journals or letters; the reference is possibly just rhetorical.

303. JB plays on the Old Testament origins of the Christian names of various public figures: Sir Sampson Gideon (1744–1824) represented Cambridgeshire, 1770–80; Sir Joshua Reynolds, see Chap. 1, n. 74; Sir Elijah Impey (1732–1809), a lawyer and chief justice in Bengal; Sir Noah Thomas (1720–92), physician to George III; for H. S. Woodfall, see intro. to this Chap., and n. 58, above.

304. *First Lord of the Treasury*: this was the post held by Lord North, and almost all prime ministers to the present day. "Kissing hands" is the formal ceremony of receiving a commission from the Crown.

the swarthy Chin, and addressing him with a Leer of Satisfaction in the Words of Sir Archy Macsarcasm, "*My bony Girgashite.*"[305] Methinks I hear the horrid Sound of their Shoutings upon the American Shores, and see rifle-barrelled Rioters running before them; and if the Theory of Mr. *Adair* in his late History be true, that the *North American Indians* are *Jews*, with what Alacrity will they come to the Aid of their own Kindred?[306] so that we shall have our unruly Descendents between two Fires,[307] and Dr. *Franklin's* Electricity, with which he with *Wires* directs his *Puppets* of Countrymen, shall be no better than a *Will o' the Wisp.*[308]

RAMPAGER.

1776

No. 13: Metaphorical Groupe of Birds[309]

[The avian similes in this article, drawn from a premise of commenting on a recent article denying the migration of birds in favor of hibernation, engage the audience in a series of light-hearted jibes at the expense of other contributors to the *Public Advertiser*. Boswell then moves on to imagining politicians in the characters of birds, ending with a commentary on the situation in America.]

Public Advertiser, March 9, 1776, 2 (leading article)

305. Sir Archy Macsarcasm is a character in Charles Macklin's comedy *Love à-la-Mode* (1759); "What, my child of circumcision, how do you do, my bonny Girgashite?" (act 1). Girgashites or Girgasites were one of the original tribes inhabiting the land of Canaan before the time of the Israelites (Genesis 10:16 and 15:21; Deuteronomy 7:1).

306. James Adair (1709–83) lived among the Chickasaw in South Carolina; he wrote *The History of the American-Indians, Particularly Those Nations Adjoining the Mississippi, East and West Florida, South Carolina, &c.* (London, 1775), which argues that American Indians were descended from the Jews.

307. *Between two fires*: to be in two or more directions within the range of an enemy's gunfire.

308. In 1749, American printer, politician, and inventor Benjamin Franklin (1706–90) described an experiment—soon conducted by others and in June 1752 himself, using a kite—to attract electric sparks from thunderclouds. Franklin's experiment was drawn to general attention by Joseph Priestley in *The History and Present State of Electricity* (1767). "Will o' the wisp" is the name in folklore for phantom lights seen over bogs, in graveyards, etc. JB knew Franklin from at least May 14, 1768 (*Search*, 178), and possibly earlier, and met socially with him on a number of occasions.

309. This title is from JB's MS note on his file copy.

SIR,

THE Honourable *Daines Barrington*, of whose Writings I am an Admirer in my serious Moments, has entertained the Philosophical World with a very ingenious Discourse against the long-received popular Opinion of the *Migration* of certain Birds, and has brought Arguments and Evidence to convince us, that they *sleep* in our own Country.[310] For my Part, I am convinced of the Truth of his System, from what I have experienced in my own Life; for I perceive that I have been asleep for a long Time, and indeed had not this been the Case, I should have been taking my *Flights* in the Hemisphere of the *Public Advertiser*.[311] In that Hemisphere we have all Manner of *Birds*, who play their Part in successive Rotation; sometimes we have a *Nightingale* in the *poetical Corner*, sometimes a chirping *Linnet*.[312] Any *Magpy* can chatter in a single Paragraph, and you certainly have a tame *Parrot* who sits on your Shoulder, and furnishes many Articles of *private Intelligence*.[313] Many of your *City Disputants* fight as bitterly as *Game Cocks*, tho' they are but of the *Dunghill* Breed;[314] and Correspondents at the West-End of the Town seem so totally to have forgotten their natural Notes, that like Blackbirds or Thrushes who have been brought up in Tradesmens Shops, they whistle only the Tunes which they have been taught.[315] Mr. *Burke*, in one of his Speeches in the House of Commons, compared JUNIUS

310. Daines Barrington (1727/28–1800), English judge, legal scholar, antiquarian, and natural historian. The piece in which he contested the migration theory in favor of a type of hibernation was printed in the Royal Society's *Philosophical Transactions*, 62 (1772), 265–326, as "An Essay on the Periodical Appearing and Disappearing of Certain Birds, at Different Times of the Year"; it was reprinted "with considerable additions" as Essay IV in Barrington's *Miscellanies* (225–44). SJ discussed this theory, Spring 1768 (see *Life*, 2:55, 248); he had met Barrington in 1766 (*Life*, 3:314). Barrington was a founding member of Johnson's Essex Head club and proposed JB for membership (*Life*, 4:254 n. 2).

311. The previous "Rampager" essay was published on Aug. 14, 1775, almost seven months earlier.

312. JB characterizes the contributors of poetry to the *Pub. Adv.*: the nightingale is associated with melancholy and elegant expression (see Ovid, *Metamorphoses*, 6.424–674). By contrast, the linnet is known for its cheerful song. If JB is referring to particular individuals, they have not been identified.

313. Magpies are proverbial for their indiscriminate gathering of objects; parrots are associated with ostentation and mindless repetition: the former may represent those who furnish paragraphs for the papers, and the latter may refer to the many items that each paper copied from its competitors.

314. For dunghill cocks, see n. 205, above. "City disputants" are presumably those who dispute about the politics of the City of London.

315. The West End is the wealthy and fashionable area of central London, west of Charing Cross.

to the *Eagle*, and with Richness of Imagery, for which that eloquent Gentleman is distinguished, gave a most picturesque Description of him as pouncing even upon *Sir Fletcher* himself.[316]

The Speeches in Parliament which you give us, are as different as the various Voices of Birds;[317] some Speakers have what is called a *fat* Tone, the Birds being well fed in the Treasury Coop;[318] some have that keen Pipe, which Want occasions, for the feathered Race, express Want by Sound, as well as other Animals. Dr. *Johnson* says of a mighty patriotic Orator, "the Howling of the Savage only marks his Hunger;"[319] and perhaps we may with Justice observe, that many a Parliamentary Bird sings most loud and shrill while urged by Necessity. I have sometimes thought that the Prime Minister resembles *Prometheus*, with a *Vulture*-like *Barré*, or some other fierce Bird of Opposition gnawing his Liver.[320] This Simile,

316. On Nov. 27, 1770, in a debate in the House of Commons on the powers of the attorney general, Edmund Burke delivered a powerful speech in which he railed against the power of Junius, especially his famous letter of Dec. 19, 1769, addressed to the king: "How comes this *Junius* to have broke through the cobwebs of the law, and to range uncontrolled, unpunished, through the land?" In this speech, addressed formally to the Speaker of the House (Sir Fletcher Norton, 1716–89), Burke asserted that having already attacked "our Royal eagle, . . . he [Junius] has laid you prostrate, and Kings, Lords, and Commons, thus become but the sport of his fury." The whole debate was widely reported at the time, and the version printed in the *Morning Chronicle* was reprinted as *Vox Senatus: The Speeches at Large which were Made in a Great Assembly, on Wednesday the 27th of November Last* (1771); see 21–24. In thinking Burke described Junius as an eagle, JB has either misread the report or has read an account in which the speech was given differently. A *fletcher* is a maker—specifically a featherer—of arrows.

317. The British Parliament had long considered the reporting of its debates to be a breach of privilege. The *Pub. Adv.* had printed parliamentary reports in 1760 and 1765 and been prosecuted and fined in both instances. In 1771, Wilkes and his supporters in their roles as city magistrates defended the rights of the printers, and, in the face of mob violence in support of Wilkes, the government backed down and never again attempted to prevent the reporting of its proceedings (see Clarke, *From Grub Street*, 91–93).

318. *Fat*: "Of the voice: Full" (*OED*). The term *fat tone* is still used to describe the tone of certain instruments, such as guitars or horns. The *well fed* birds are placemen (see n. 77, above).

319. "The noise of a savage proves nothing but his hunger" (Johnson, "Thoughts on Falkland's Islands," *Political Writings*, 386). JB implies that this is a reference to Pitt.

320. Lord North is depicted as Prometheus, the mythical hero who, for stealing fire from the gods, was chained to a rock for eternity; every day he was savaged by an eagle, which would tear out his liver, which each night would regrow only to be torn out and eaten again the next day (Hesiod, *Theogony*, lines 507–43). Col. Isaac Barré (1726–1802), a former army officer and leading opposition politician, was a particularly effective speaker and took delight in taunting the mild-mannered North.

however, like all other Similes, is, when Circumstances are more considered, not completely exact; for I do not think the Situation of a Prime Minister of this Country can be likened to a *Rock*; nor do I suppose that the Prime Minister is *chained* to his Seat; but let me do Justice to Lord NORTH, and acknowledge that he at Times displays the Resolution of the young Spartan, who never uttered the least Complaint, or even changed Countenance, while a *Fox*, with sharp and ravenous Teeth, worried his Side.[321] I must, however, take care not to quit my *winged* metaphorical Stile, but to continue as long as I can hovering amongst Birds. Many a *Raven* is now croaking Destruction to Great Britain, unless she will fly from her own Grove, invite the Assistance of foreign Birds, and crush her vigorous Offspring on the other Side of the Atlantic:[322] But I much fear that we are egregiously mistaken, that our Offspring are too numerous and too well fledged to be reduced to an *infantine Dependence* on their Mother, which Nature never intended, and which is really not desirable for the Mother; and although there are, no Doubt, some harmonious Voices in the Choir of Compulsion I must modestly observe, that if our State is to be saved by Ministerial Harrangues at present, it will be saved, like the Capital at Rome, by the Cackling of Geese.[323] Sincerely do I wish to see the *Dove*, with the Olive Branch;[324]

321. In the "Life of Lycurgus," Plutarch tells of a Spartan youth who hid a stolen fox under his jacket, and although the animal ate into his side, finally disemboweling and killing him, he did not cry out or give it up. Charles James Fox (see n. 298) had supported the Grafton ministry and held offices under North, but came to resent North and moved toward the Rockingham whigs, becoming North's most prominent critic. In the Commons on Oct. 26, 1775, he denounced him as "the blundering pilot who had brought the nation into its present difficulties. . . . Lord Chatham, the King of Prussia, nay, Alexander the Great, never gained more in one campaign than the noble lord has lost—he has lost a whole continent"; see *Parliamentary Register*, 2:226.

322. The raven was thought to be a bird of ill omen (see *Macbeth*, 1.5.36: "the raven himself is hoarse"). JB alludes, perhaps, to the British alliances with various German states in the Seven Years' War (see above, n. 9 ff.). But there was at this time a widespread belief that the American war could be successfully and promptly concluded only if Britain would boost its forces by hiring foreign troops. As a result, in Aug. 1776, the first 18,000 of an eventual 30,000 German soldiers were dispatched to fight in America. Known as Hessian mercenaries, because most were from the state of Hesse, they eventually composed upward of a quarter of the total forces in America under British command.

323. According to Livy, *History of Rome*, book 5, the geese in Juno's temple on the Capitoline hill in Rome prevented an invasion one night when their startled cries woke the city.

324. In the story of Noah's Ark, a dove bearing an olive branch is a symbol of peace and safety; see Genesis 8:11. In July 1775, the Second American Continental Congress adopted

and when Ambassadors of Conciliation are sent out I shall sing with the young
'Squire in Dr. Goldsmith's Comedy,[325]

> But of all the Birds in the Air,
> There is none like the three jolly Pidgeons.[326]

RAMPAGER.

1777

No. 14: John the Painter and John the Peer[327]

["John the Painter" was the name adopted by arsonist James Aitken (alias Hill and
Hind, 1752–77), who, from a desire to aid the American Revolution, on the night of
December 7, 1776, lit a fire that burned down the ropehouse in the royal dockyards
at Portsmouth. The ropehouse was a huge building, over a thousand feet long, and
up to one hundred ropemakers were employed there at a time. Two days after the
fire, the First Lord of the Admiralty, Lord Sandwich, under pressure from the king
to discover that it was not an accident but a political crime, ordered an investigation.
Aitken lit similar fires at the docks in Plymouth and Bristol the following January. Through a combination of indiscretion and bad luck, he was apprehended in
Hampshire on January 27. He was tried at Winchester and hanged at Portsmouth on
March 10, 1777.]

Public Advertiser, August 21, 1777, 1 (leading article)

---

the so-called olive branch petition, which proposed measures aimed to prevent further
warfare and a complete break with Britain. It was drafted by Thomas Jefferson and rewrit-
ten by John Dickinson.

325. *Ambassadors of Conciliation*: in 1774, Lord North had proposed a peace commission;
the king at first rejected the idea but then agreed that the brothers Admiral Richard, first
Earl Howe, and General Sir William Howe (see n. 348, below), commanders respectively of
the naval and military forces, should be empowered to negotiate for peace, if possible. The
actual instructions, formulated by Lord George Germain, who opposed the commission,
were impossibly harsh; in the event, war had already broken out, and the Americans had
declared themselves independent before North's plan could be presented. (See Cook, *Long
Fuse*, 248.)

326. In Oliver Goldsmith's *She Stoops to Conquer* (1773), 1.2, this song is sung by the
bibulous country booby Tony Lumpkin; the "three jolly Pidgeons" is the local ale-house.
The third and final verse from which JB quotes mentions, like this essay, the names of a
number of birds.

327. This title is from JB's MS note on his file copy.

SIR,

JOHN the Painter's having assumed the Name of *James Boswell*, when he inlisted in the Army,[328] is a Circumstance that has occasioned a few desultory Reflections in my Mind, which I hope you will allow to frisk about upon a Page of your Paper, with that Ease and Freedom which my Fancies have ever done since first you saw "me *sportive* move."[329] With the Surname of *Boswell* I have nothing to do in my present Disquisition, though I am as zealous for *Corsica* and *General Paoli* as *the original James Boswell* himself, and admire the beautiful Miss *Bosville* or *Boswell*, of Yorkshire, as warmly as any Peer or fine Gentleman in England.[330] It is the *James* only for which poor *John* thought fit to change his own Name for a Season, that is to be the Subject of this my Meditation; and truly I am at a Loss to divine what could be the Fellow's Meaning; he surely could not be foolish enough to imagine, that he would have a Chance of making a Party amongst the *Jacobites*[331] in case of his engaging in any desperate Enterprize; and yet as wild a Head as his was capable of conceiving any Extravagance; nay, I am not perfectly sure, whether in the strange Revolutions of Politicks it might not be possible to have made *Jacobites* and *Americans* coalesce; for I see as strange Coalitions in both Houses of Parliament, though not upon so wide a Scale.

I cannot however help attempting a short Parallel, *in the Manner of Plutarch* (as the Phrase is) between *John the Painter* and his illustrious Prosecutor *John Earl of Sandwich*[332]—As to one Particular only though, for I have not sufficient

328. Aitken used a variety of aliases. According to reports of his confession in Winchester, dated Mar. 7, 1777, "In October, 1775, by the name of James Boswell, [he] enlisted as a private soldier in 32d reg. at Gravesend, marched to Chatham next day from whence he soon deserted" (*Hampshire Chronicle*, Mar. 24). Boswell was Aitken's mother's maiden name (Warner, *John the Painter*, 89).

329. Thomas Parnell, *An Essay on the Different Stiles of Poetry* (1713), lines 105–7: "No nervous strength of Sense maturely wrought,/ Possess this Realm; but common Turns are there,/ Which idely sportive move with childish Air" (*Collected Poems*, 52).

330. Elizabeth Diana Bosville (1748–89), daughter of the wealthy Godfrey Bosville of Yorkshire, whom JB regarded as his clan chieftain, had, for a short time after he met her in Feb. 1766, been one of JB's marital prospects (*Earlier Years*, 284). Here, JB deliberately glosses over the fact that "Miss Bosville" had been since 1768 the wife of Sir Alexander Macdonald (c. 1745–95), who had a year earlier become first Baron Macdonald of Slate (hence, "as any Peer"). (JB attended a masquerade with the Macdonalds in Jan. 1773, see Chap. 5; in Sept. 1774, JB and SJ stayed with the Macdonalds on their Scottish tour, and JB gave an unflattering account of the visit in the *Tour*, see Chap. 4, n. 330.)

331. For *Jacobites*, see Chap. 1, n. 17.

332. The political implications of John the Painter's crimes were emphasized for the public by the attendance of Lord Sandwich and other lords of the Admiralty at some of Aitken's interrogation and the first days of his trial in Winchester. The *Vitae Parallelae*

Knowledge to be extensive in my Lucubrations. The Particular on which I touch is merely to ring the Change upon *John* and *James*. *John the Painter* voluntarily assumed the Name of *James*. *John the Peer* has had its Contraction *Jemmy* involuntarily bestowed upon him.[333] *John the Painter* had nothing *emphatic* in his *alias*, whereas in that of *John the Peer* there is *Emphasis enough*, if we allow *John Wilkes* to lay it on: Fifty ridiculous Conceits I know might be uttered as to the *Peer* and the *Painter*. The Alliance between the Sister Arts of Musick and Painting is obvious, and *the one John* did not handle the *Brush* with more Eagerness than *the other John* vociferates a jovial *Catch*.[334] *John the Painter* was *impeached by a Companion*, but *there* is a *wide Difference* indeed between the *two Johns*.[335] I find myself exhausted in Prose; and as a lame Man, who cannot walk, may yet hobble a little so as to make it appear as if he danced, I shall now try to jump a few Steps in Verse.

> WHEN *John the Painter* over Beer,
>   By a sly Serjeant was made mellow,
> He listed with a thoughtless Cheer,
>   And bragg'd he was a pretty Fellow.[336]
>
> His old Name *John* he threw away,
>   Thinking that *James* would have more Lustre;
> And being thus all new and gay,
>   He stood *James Boswell* in the Muster.
>
> But the more potent *John the Peer*,
>   For *something better than a Shilling*,[337]
> Chose to *Decorum's Point* to veer,
>   And was call'd *Jemmy*, tho' unwilling.

(Parallel Lives) of Plutarch (c. 50–120 A.D.) survives as fifty Greek and Roman lives, mostly arranged in pairs, followed by an ethical comparison.

333. For Sandwich's nickname *Jemmy Twitcher*, see n. 28, above.

334. *Brush* suggests tinder, as well as the paintbrush. A *catch*: "A song sung in succession, where one *catches* it from another" (*SJ Dict.*); Sandwich had an enthusiasm for music and held private concerts and musical parties.

335. Evidence against Aitken was obtained by a man named John Baldwin, sent by the prosecutors to visit and befriend him in prison. Wilkes and Sandwich were fellow members of the infamous Hell-fire Club, and Wilkes encouraged the public impression that Sandwich's speech against him was the betrayal of a friend.

336. Accounts of Aitken's apprehension and arrest differ; see Warner, *John the Painter*, 185–88, 209–10.

337. That is, the so-called King's Shilling, which a soldier would receive upon enlisting.

> These two *John Jameses* wild *Rousseau*
> Let thy capricious Fancy picture
> At flowing Length—while I but show
> What good plain English calls a *Stricture*.[338]

RAMPAGER.

No. 15: American Allusions from a Bookseller's Catalog

[Only a week after the previous "Rampager," Boswell in this letter uses the names of books and authors from a catalog as the basis for satirical mention of and comment upon many of the characters and events of the American Revolutionary War. The original titles have little to do with Boswell's leaps of imagination: they simply include coincidental names and subjects that inspired his political puns. Boswell here calls the American war a "Civil War," but that does not betoken a lack of sympathy for the American cause: after Washington's retreat from Long Island the previous year, Boswell wrote in his journal, on October 16, 1776, "General Howe's having defeated the Americans . . . I was sorry that the *Ministerial* Army had prevailed" (*Extremes*, 43, also 53). In his journal entry for August 11, 1777, he notes, "finished [essay about] books for *Public Advertiser* as to America" (ibid., 138).

The books he alludes to are the following:

1. Joseph Washington (d. 1694), *An Exact Abridgement of All the Statutes of King William and Queen Mary, now in Force and Use* (London, 1694); was revised and continued in new editions, at least until 1704.
2. Patrick Abercromby (1656–1716?), *The Martial Atchievements of the Scots Nation*, 2 vols. (Edinburgh, 1711–16); an important historical work, with a strong Jacobite bias.
3. John Graunt (1620–74), *Natural and Political Observations . . . Made upon the Bills of Mortality* (London, 1662); a pioneering demographical work, frequently reprinted, with updated tables, etc.
4. Thomas Daniel (n.d.), *The Present State of the British Customs: . . . Being the only Complete System of Duties Extant* (London, 1752); consists of tables of duties payable on various products and of exchange rates of different currencies, etc.
5. Henry Crouch (d. 1732), *A Complete View of the British Customs: Containing the Rates of Merchandize* (London, 1724).

338. That is, Jean-Jacques Rousseau (1712–78), the infidel philosopher, whom JB visited at his home in Switzerland in 1764, could describe these two characters in a novelistic manner. JB will attempt only a *stricture*—i.e., "a slight touch upon a subject; not a set discourse" (*SJ Dict.*). (The English equivalent of the French name Jean-Jacques is John James.)

6. John Howe (1630–1705), *The Blessednesse of the Righteous: Opened, and Further Recommended, . . . in Two Treatises* (London, 1668). Howe was a prolific Puritan writer.

7. Charles Leslie (1650–1722), *The Rehearsal*, 1705–09; a semi-weekly periodical paper, of tory and Jacobite stamp, of which Leslie, a nonjuring Anglican clergyman, was the editor and main author. Many issues are wholly devoted to attacks on Daniel Defoe.

8. Alexander Cruden (1701–70), *A Complete Concordance to the Holy Scriptures of the Old and New Testament* (London, 1737). This remains to the present day a standard work of its kind.

9. Sir James Steuart (1635–1713), *Dirleton's Doubts and Questions in the Law of Scotland, Resolved and Answered* (Edinburgh, 1715). This work is a commentary upon Sir John Nisbet (of Dirleton) (1609?–87), *Some Doubts & Questions, in the Law; especially of Scotland* (Edinburgh, 1698). See *Brewer's Dict.*, s.v. "Dirleton": "*Doubting with Dirleton, and resolving those doubts with Stewart.* Doubting and answering those doubts, but doubting still. It applies to law, science, religion, morals, etc." The two books are, Brewer says, "works of established reputation in Scotland, but the *Doubts* hold a higher place than the *Solutions.*" In the *Life*, Boswell mentions *Dirleton's Doubts* and quotes praise of the work (Sept. 23, 1777; *Life*, 3:205).

10. John Webster (1610–82), *The Displaying of Supposed Witchcraft* (London, 1677). While skeptical of many claims, Webster nevertheless asserts, "there is a Corporeal League made betwixt the Devil and the Witch."

11. James Lee (1715–95), *An Introduction to Botany* (London, 1760). Based on the work of Linnaeus, this work, by a nurseryman, went through a number of editions, being revised and expanded.

12. Boethius (d. 524), *Anicius Manlius Severinus Boetius, Of the Consolation of Philosophy*, trans. Richard, Lord Viscount Preston (London, 1695). Preston (1648–95), a politician and diplomat, was a leading Jacobite conspirator, who translated this classic early Christian work after he was pardoned, having given evidence against his co-conspirators.

13. Ralph Erskine (1685–1752), *Gospel-Canticles: Or, Spiritual Songs* (Edinburgh, 1720); all later editions (sixteen by 1775) called *Gospel-Sonnets*. One section, called "The Believer's Riddle," was much quoted.

14. Samuel von Pufendorf (1632–94), *An Introduction to the History of the Principal Kingdoms and States of Europe*, trans. Joducus Crull (London, 1695). Published throughout the eighteenth century in revised and expanded editions and other translations, it was a translation of *Einleitung zur Geschichte der vornehmsten Staaten Europas* (1682). ("Puffendorf" is often referred to in Sterne's *Tristram Shandy*.)]

Public Advertiser, August 27, 1777, 1 (leading article)

SIR,

AS I confess that I have wavered a good deal upon the American Controversy since the present unhappy Civil War began, I now endeavour, instead of heating my Blood by keen Disputation, to temper and sweeten it by every Species of Pleasantry.

While perusing a Catalogue of Books for Sale,[339] I found myself unexpectedly amused with Conceits which the Names of Authors suggested concerning the Contest with our Colonies; Conceits which seem to me to fall under Mr. Locke's Definition of Wit, by bringing together Ideas very distant from each other;[340] and as I never feel myself any how diverted, but I wish to communicate the Amusement to my Friend Woodfall, who has many Friends to entertain, and very liberally pushes about the Jorum of Amusement in public, as of generous Liquor in private.[341]

Be pleased then, Sir, to accept of some Specimens of my *Catalogue raisonnée*, or rather *Catalogue risible*.[342]

1. *Washington's Abridgement of the Statutes*—The severe *Statutes* against our Fellow Subjects in *America* have been controverted in great Length of Argument, both in America and Britain, but in vain; *General Washington* therefore has taken the Field to make *short Work* with them, and, like the Hero of Old, *cut the Gordian Knot* with his *Sword*.[343]

2. *Abercrombie's Martial Atchievements*—The gallant *Lieutenant Colonel James Abercrombie*, who fell at *Bunker's-Hill*,[344] candidly acknowledged that he had

339. An actual catalog has not been identified; it may well be a fiction.

340. "A Feather's Man" referred to this passage from Locke in his letter to JB; see above, n. 242.

341. A *jorum* is a large drinking-bowl or vessel, or its contents, esp. a bowl of punch (*OED*). In his journal entry for Mar. 26, 1783, JB describes Woodfall, editor of the *Pub. Adv.* (see n. 58, above), as "a fine hearty fellow, and one who loves a bottle" (*Applause*, 86).

342. A *catalogue raisonnée* is a descriptive catalog arranged according to subjects or branches of subjects; hence, generally or loosely, a classified or methodical list; *risible*: capable of exciting laughter; laughable, ludicrous, comical (*OED*).

343. George Washington (1732–99), commander of the Continental Army in the American Revolutionary War and (later) first president of the United States. To *cut the Gordian knot* is to solve a difficult intellectual problem by forceful action, after Alexander the Great, who was reportedly challenged at Gordium, Phrygia, to undo a near-impossible knot and, having pondered the difficulty, eventually slashed through the knot with his sword.

344. James Abercrombie (1732–75), British army officer. He arrived in Boston in late Apr. 1775. His private correspondence reveals that he was critical of the leadership of the commander in chief, General Gage. He received a gunshot wound in the Battle of Bunker Hill at Charleston during the siege of Boston, on June 17, 1775, and died a week later—i.e.,

lived to have a different Opinion of the Courage of the Americans from what he had once entertained.

3. *Grant on the Bills of Mortality—General Grant*, we have been told, boasted that he could go through America with a Couple of Thousand Men;[345] but it is believed that if the *Bill of Mortality of the British Army* was laid before the Public, it would appear that by Battle, Famine, and Disease, six Times the Number have perished; and, it may be asked, *how far* has the British [*sic*] yet advanced?

4. *Daniel's British Customs*—Alas! we have no *second Daniel* to direct the levying the *Customs of this great Empire*.[346]

5. *Crouch on the Customs*—Our Brethren in *America*, who have *British Blood* in their Veins, will not *crouch* to *Custom-house Officers*,[347] when they think the Exactions *unconstitutional*.

6. *Howe's Blessedness of the Righteous*—Gen. *Howe* has as yet been no very successful *Apostle* to the *Saints at Boston*.[348]

---

only weeks before this essay (see Dictionary of Canadian Biography, s.v. "Abercrombie, James"). It was reported in the *Morning Chronicle*, July 31, 1775, "Lieutenant-Colonel Abercrombie wrote a letter to General Hervey a very little time before he expired, wherein, it is said, he gives the Provincials a much better character than he had conceived of them before the action."

345. James Grant of Ballindalloch (1720–1806) climbed the military ranks while fighting in America in the 1760s and became governor of East Florida. Returning to Scotland, in Apr. 1773 he became an MP for Tain Burghs (*ODNB*). Grant is said to have told the Commons, on Feb. 2, 1775, that the Americans "could not fight" and that he would "undertake to march from one end of the continent to the other with five thousand men." "The source of this information was William Alexander, known as Lord Stirling, who was sitting in the gallery of the House of Commons when Grant supposedly made his claim. This entire incident has been called into question since there is no record of Alexander's being in London at the time cited, according to his current biographer, Alan Valentine" (Sanborn, "James Grant," 665). (Contemporary newspaper accounts record Grant speaking that day but not these actual words [see *London Evening Post*, Feb. 11, 1775]; within a few years, they were attributed to him—though also to others, such as John Burgoyne, Lord Townshend, and particularly Lord Jeffrey Amherst—in the press.) By this stage, total British casualties, including the sick, could have numbered 12,000.

346. In Shakespeare's *Merchant of Venice* (4.1.333, 340), Gratiano twice calls the disguised Portia "a second Daniel" (alluding to the apocryphal addition to the Old Testament book of Daniel, called "Susanna and the Elders"); JB implies that the war would have been avoided with better political judgment about taxing the American colonies.

347. *Crouch*: "To fawn; to bend servilely; to stoop meanly" (*SJ Dict.*).

348. Sir William Howe, later fifth Viscount Howe (1729–1814), British army officer. He went to Boston in 1775 as second in command of British forces hoping to negotiate peace but was, with his troops, immediately engaged in the Battle of Bunker Hill and suffered a costly victory. When General Gage was recalled, Howe became commander in chief of the

7. Leslie's Rehearsals—The Marches and Counter-marches which *Brigadier Leslie*, and our other General Officers, have been obliged to make, may be considered as *Rehearsals* of something *very important*—when it is Time for the Play to begin.[349]

8. *Cruden's Concordance*—It is to be feared that any Schemes which are as yet formed of *Concord* between Britain and America are *crude* indeed.[350]

9. *Stuart's Decisions on Dirleton's Doubts*—Who was the *doubting Dirleton* at *Danbury*, I shall not say;[351] but surely all Parties must admire the *decisive* Bravery of Major *Charles Stuart*, who, at the Head of a few fine young Fellows, rushed upon the Provincials with Bayonets, and prevented the British Troops from being routed and disgraced. That this distinguished Officer is a Son of the *Earl of Bute* cannot be denied, and it is curious to think that when he returns with the Laurel in his Hat we shall have in the *Palace of St. James's* what few even of the most *zealous* Friends of *the good old Cause* ever expected to hear *in that Place*—"You're welcome, Charles Stuart."[352]

British army. With his brother, Admiral Richard, fourth Viscount (and first Earl) Howe (1726–99), in charge of the navy, General Howe spent late 1776 trying to negotiate peace and avoided opportunities for a decisive victory. During 1777, he failed to link up his forces with Burgoyne's advancing south from Canada, preferring instead to take his troops from New York to attack Philadelphia. He captured what he regarded as the American capital but left Burgoyne to surrender at Saratoga, because he had not been reinforced and resupplied. JB later met Howe socially from time to time; see journal for 1781; *Laird*, 335, 360–61. The term *Saints* was "used by some religious bodies as their own designation, e.g. by some puritanical sects in the 16–17th c." (*OED*, 3).

349. British Brig. Gen. Alexander Leslie (1740–94) was in charge of a brigade near Princeton that was obliged to make marches and countermarches in an attempt to prevent the American forces from advancing from Trenton to Princeton. Washington's army, marching at night in great secrecy, took the town on Jan. 3, 1777. It was a very important American victory (Fischer, *Washington's Crossing*, 197).

350. The towns of Concord and Lexington, Massachusetts, were the sites of the first battles in the American war, on Apr. 19, 1775.

351. Danbury, Connecticut, an important military supply depot for the Continental Army, was burned and looted by British forces under Maj. Gen. William Tyron, sent from New York by General Howe, on Apr. 26–27, 1777.

352. Maj. Charles Stuart (1753–1801) "served with distinction in the war in America . . . was promoted lieutenant-colonel of the 26th foot (Cameronians) in 1777" (*ODNB*). "Major Stuart, who rallied the troops at the affair of Danbury, and charged the Provincial lines, is fourth son of the Earl of Bute" (*Lond. Chron.*, June 7, 1777). JB plays on the coincidence of his name with that of Prince Charles Edward Stuart (1720–88), "Bonnie Prince Charlie," the Jacobite claimant to the English, Scottish, and Irish thrones, as well as that of the executed monarch to whom he traced his claim to the throne, Charles I. After the restoration of the monarchy, supporters of Cromwell's commonwealth referred to it as "the good old cause," and the term was also used later by the Jacobites, as a code for their own

10. *Webster's Witchcraft—New England* is very famous for *Witches*,[353] and most certainly some of these old Hags have been too busy with Lord *Cornwallis* and his Lieutenant Colonel *Webster*, else they never would have solicited for Leave to go themselves, and carry the *22d Regiment*, trained to the highest Pitch of Perfection, into disagreeable Service, as to the Justice of which *Old England* is so much divided.[354]

11. *Lee's Botany—Mr. Lee* has rather shewn himself to be a *Simple* in the *Plantations* for taking up such *Ground* as to be pickt up as easily by *Herbalist Harcourt*. Why did he not take care to have himself *better placed* as an *Exotic*; for Plants which are not of the native Growth of a Country require the most *Shelter*.[355]

12. *Preston's Boethius the Consolation of Philosophy—General Preston's* Regiment of Horse has much Need of *Consolation*.[356] Taking a Hint from what is of-

----

partly nostalgic ambitions. St. James's Palace was George III's principal London residence; foreign ambassadors are still accredited to the Court of St. James, and today it is used as a venue for official receptions.

353. New England's reputation for witchcraft dates from events in Salem, Massachusetts, in 1692 that led to trials in which nineteen people, mostly women, were executed for occult practices.

354. Charles Cornwallis, first marquess Cornwallis (1738–1805). Despite having, during his short political career, opposed the policies that led to war, Cornwallis volunteered for service and sailed for America in Feb. 1776 as a major general in charge of seven regiments, including the 33rd Regiment of Foot, of which he had been colonel since 1766 and of which the commanding officer was Lt. Col. James Webster (1740–81), JB's first cousin; see *Laird*, 262–63 (Oct. 16, 1780). JB or the printer has mistakenly given 22 for 33. The 33rd saw a great deal of action in the war, and were in August 1776 involved in the British victory at the Battle of Long Island. Moreover, it had a reputation as a crack regiment, known for its professionalism, and was nicknamed "the pattern" as it was a model for other units—hence JB saying they were "trained to the highest Pitch of Perfection." (Webster was an outstanding officer, and was mortally wounded in battle in March 1781; see *Laird*, 378 and n. 2.)

355. On Dec. 13, 1776, (British-born) American Maj. Gen. Charles Lee (1732–82) was captured by troops of William, third Earl Harcourt (1743–1830), lieutenant colonel in the 16th Light Dragoons. Lee was a cantankerous and controversial figure who had joined the American forces in 1773 after a restless career including travels, political activity in Britain, and having children with a Native American woman during service with the British army in 1755. His capture, after a daring seventy-mile raid, was much celebrated. A *simple* is "A single ingredient in a medicine . . . ; it is popularly used for an herb"; *plantation*: "A colony"; *exotick*: "A foreign plant" (*SJ Dict.*).

356. Maj. Charles Preston (later Sir Charles, fifth baronet, c. 1735–1800) was a cousin of JB's mother. He was in charge of the 26th (Cameronian) Regiment at Fort St. John, Quebec, which he was forced to surrender after a fifty-five-day siege on Nov. 3, 1775. On Dec. 24, 1775, JB notes reading of this with alarm and the "high esteem" of Thayendanegea for Preston (*Ominous Years*, 204, 342). On Preston's return to England, JB met him (Mar. 26, 1777; *Extremes*, 102), and continued to see him socially in London and Scotland for the rest of his life.

ten inscribed on the Front of an Inn I would let them have *Consolation for Man and Horse*; and for this Purpose let some ingenious Translator, who *knows Fingal in the Original*,[357] be employed to give a Version of Boethius in the *Howhynm* Language.[358]

13. *Erskine's Riddles*—We were told in the *Gazette* that a Detachment, commanded by *Sir William Erskine*, had killed 400 Provincials, yet it did not appear that a single British Soldier was touched.[359] This surely is a *Riddle*, and nobody will deny Sir William Erskine's *secret Expedition* to be a *Riddle*.

14. *Puffendorf's Introduction to the History of Europe*—There has been a great deal *too* much *puffing* in the Introduction to the War with America.[360]

RAMPAGER.

1778

No. 16: On the Manchester Regiment[361]

[In a major turning point of the American war, a British army of 6,000 men was defeated and surrendered at Saratoga, New York, on October 17, 1777. When news of this reached England on December 2, there was across the country a groundswell of

357. *Fingal* (1762) is an epic poem supposedly composed anciently and in Gaelic by Ossian, the son of Fingal, but is actually the work of the alleged translator, James McPherson (1736–96), although drawing on traditional oral materials. (SJ was well known to be skeptical about its authenticity.)

358. A misspelling of "Houyhnhnm," the race of talking horses in Jonathan Swift's satire *Gulliver's Travels* (1726). JB wants a translation of Boethius for Scottish horses, to console them after their surrender.

359. Sir William Erskine (1728–95) of Torrie, first baronet, was second in command of the detachment of troops that attacked the supply depot at Danbury. JB's source in the *Gazette* has not been found, but the *Derby Mercury* (Mar. 21, 1777), quoting the *Gazette*, gives "an Account of several Advantages gained by Parties composed of British and Hessian Troops, employed in escorting Convoys in the Jerseys, over large Bodies of the Rebels, by which they had been attacked: Particularly, that a Party of the 42d., which was escorting some Forage Waggons from Brunswick, having been attacked by a great Number of the Rebels, Sir William Erskine marched out with a Detachment to their Relief, and taking a Position which placed the Rebels between two Fires, obliged them to retreat in great Confusion, leaving between 3 and 400 dead upon the Spot." Several other "advantages" are then described, and no British casualties are mentioned. Erskine moved up through the ranks to become major general in 1779, before his return to Britain. JB met him on Dec. 14, 1774 (*Ominous Years*, 45).

360. *To puff:* "to make the subject of a laudatory advertisement, review, etc.; to make favourable mention of, promote, publicize" (*OED*).

361. This title is from JB's MS note on his file copy.

patriotic support for the ministry's policies in America. Within a week of the news, George III received a letter from a committee of eminent citizens of Manchester, offering to raise a corps of a thousand men. Manchester, a fast-growing industrial town, was regarded as a bastion of Toryism and lingering Jacobitism. The offer being gratefully accepted, a campaign of fund-raising and recruitment began, and by the end of March 1778 the Royal Manchester Volunteers (to become officially the 72nd Regiment of Foot) had reached its full strength of over a thousand men. On April 20, the regiment was reviewed by the king, prior to embarkation for Gibraltar. Other cities soon followed Manchester's example. Boswell visited Manchester on September 13, 1777, en route to meeting Johnson at Ashbourne (*Extremes*, 146–48).]

Public Advertiser, March 21, 1778, 2 (leading article); with Boswell's MS correction

SIR,

I SUPPOSE the Ministry think they shall "play upon *Velvet*,"[362] now that they are getting a *Manchester* Regiment.[363] When the gallant little *Highland Army* struck Dismay through the rest of the Nation in 1745, diverse strange, alarming Notions were propagated; in particular it was said that there was amongst them a *Clan* or *Tribe* called the *Mac Craws*, who were most dreadfully ferocious, and who like some distant Savage Nations were *Man-eaters*.[364] Such Notions as these had a wonderful Effect upon the good and *fat* People of England, and therefore it might be well of the *Manchester Volunteers* if they should really go to America, could take a *Pattern* from their old *Acquaintances*,[365] I shall not say *Friends*, though Lord *Camden* t'other Day alleged in the House of Lords, that

362. *On velvet*: in a position of ease or advantage; in an advantageous or prosperous condition (*OED*); cites John Cleland's *Memoirs of a Woman of Pleasure* (1749): "The deceiving him became so easy, that it was perfect playing upon velvet" (2:114). To "play on velvet" was, in gambling slang (dated as from c. 1880), "to gamble with winnings"; see Partridge, *Dictionary of Slang and Unconventional English*, 1297.

363. From the sixteenth century, Manchester was a center for weaving and textile manufacture, subjects that give rise to much of the wordplay and imagery in what follows. Manchester velvet was a cotton corduroy that during the eighteenth century became popular as the material for men's breeches and trousers (Glynis Greenman, "Men's Wear," Spinning the Web, http://www.spinningtheweb.org.uk).

364. The *Mac Craws*: the Macrae clan from the Scottish Highlands, who fought in the Jacobite rebellions of 1715 and 1745, were often referred to as "the wild Macraes" because of their reputation as ferocious warriors, and so was the regiment of Highlanders, raised in early 1778 by Lord Seaforth (see Chap. 1, n. 188). *Craw* also suggests the crop or throat of a bird.

365. Regiments from Manchester were sent in support of the Jacobite risings of 1715 and 1745, and the town long retained a reputation for Jacobite sympathies. An American visitor in 1777 remarked that Jacobitism was "openly professed" and saw houses with public displays of allegiance to celebrate the Stuart restoration on May 29 (Marshall, "Manchester

the Highland Army was *embraced* by Manchester.[366] Suppose they could circulate through the Western World, a Report that a Battalion of Lancashire *Giants* is coming over, Imagination would magnify them prodigiously, even against the Evidence of Eye-sight. What gave Rise to the Thought of figuring those Volunteers to be Giants, was the Recollection of having read of *Goliath* of *Gath*, the warlike Giant of old, that the Staff of his Spear was like a *Weaver's Beam*.[367] And methinks whatever Arms shall be put into the Hands of the *Manchester Weavers*, will still have something of the Appearance of the old Trade; brandish them as they will, Men accustomed to *mount a Loom*, I should think will be but aukward in *mounting a Breach*;[368] and I am afraid these Men of Manchester have been too much accustomed to the Use of their *Heels*, to be fit for making *forward Movements*.[369]

Perhaps indeed these warlike Weavers may be sent forth as a Body of allegorical Personages in the Words of *Gray's* Ode on the Destruction of the Welsh Bards:

> "Weave the Warp and weave the Woof,
> The Winding-sheet of Edward's Race,
> Give ample Verge and Room enough,
> The Characters of Hell to trace."[370]

Dismissed with so solemn a Commission, let them weave as their Colours[371] General *Burgoyne's Proclamation*, *embellished* with Tomahawks and Scalps, as a

---

and the American Revolution," 175–76). JB puns on *pattern*: "Any thing cut out in paper to direct the cutting of cloth" (*SJ Dict.*).

366. Charles Pratt (1714–94), first Earl Camden, lawyer and whig politician, Lord Chancellor (1766–70) under Pitt and Grafton. He was known as a champion of liberty (he defended Wilkes) and for speaking out about the American War of Independence. On Feb. 4, 1778, there was a motion in the Lords, "That this House taking into consideration the legality . . . of raising forces by subscription, do look upon this practice as contrary to law" (*Morning Post*, Feb. 5, 1778). Camden spoke in the debate and was "critical of expressions of loyalism emanating from places that had supported the Jacobite rebels in 1745—citing Manchester, but not using the words JB used" (Harry Dickinson, to author, Apr. 29, 2010). A version of his speech can be found in Cobbett, *Parliamentary History of England*, 19 (1814), col. 643.

367. The biblical Goliath was a giant Philistine warrior defeated in battle by the young David (1 Samuel 17); "the shaft of his spear was like a weaver's beam" (v. 7; *AV*).

368. The fancy that the Manchester Regiment is composed of weavers leads to the comparison of *mounting a loom*—i.e., to prepare a loom for weaving (also to *dress* the loom)— with *mounting a breach*—which is to ascend a gap in a fortification, made by a battery, for the purpose of assault or attack.

369. Weavers on a hand loom use a heel-toe action to work the treadle.

370. Thomas Gray, *The Bard: A Pindaric Ode* (1757), 2.2, lines 1–4. The poem is based on a tradition that in 1277 King Edward I of England had all the bards of Wales put to death.

371. The "colours" of a regiment is the regimental flag, showing the badge of the regiment.

Funeral Sermon is with Cross-bones and Death-heads;[372] and while "in Consciousness of Christianity," it "flouts the Sky," can we doubt of its "fanning the People of America cold."[373]

I am aware that *Elliot's* Light-horse, who behaved so remarkably well during [the] last War in Germany, were mostly *Taylors*, at least we are told so; and why should not *Weavers* make as good Soldiers as *Taylors*?[374] I shall not enter into a *Dispute* on that Question, for my Readers will do me the Justice to say that I have never been *argumentative*; and as I am a very impartial Writer, I appeal to the whole *Bedford* Faction,[375] "if the Time has not been when *Weavers* appeared formidable enough, when a great Dinner in *Bloomsbury-square* was served up cold at Supper-time, the Afternoon having been passed rather unpleasantly, while *Rigby*, stout as he is, had neither his Wit nor his Wine."[376]

372. General John Burgoyne (1722–92) was a British army officer, politician, and dramatist. Appointed by Lord North as head of the British forces in Canada, he led almost 10,000 troops down the Hudson to invade New York, but his forces were overwhelmed at the Battle of Bemis Heights (the second of the Battles of Saratoga) on Oct. 7, 1777, and Burgoyne surrendered his entire army ten days later. He returned to England in 1778 to answer charges in Parliament. The British defeat at Saratoga is generally seen as the turning point of the American war. En route to his defeat, Burgoyne had, on June 29 at Putnam's Creek, issued a grandiose "proclamation," intended to threaten and demoralize his enemy, which JB suggests should be printed like an old-fashioned funeral sermon with, in place of the customary woodcuts of skulls and crossbones, emblems alluding to the Native Americans whom Burgoyne had induced to join his army (and to whom he referred in his proclamation as "the Indian forces under my direction").

373. The phrase "in consciousness of Christianity" is from Burgoyne's proclamation. See "General Burgoyne's Proclamation" (Teaching American History, http://teachingamerican history.org/library/index.asp?document=871). In *Macbeth*, 1.2.48–50, Ross tells King Duncan that he is "From Fife, great King;/Where the Norweyan banners flout the sky/And fan our people cold."

374. The 15th King's Hussars was a cavalry regiment raised in 1759 by George Augustus Elliot, first Baron Heathfield (1717–90), as the first of the new regiments of light dragoons and was named at first Elliot's Light Horse. "Many of the recruits were tailors who happened to be on strike at the time" (Charles Griffin, "15th, the King's Light Dragoons: The King's Hussars," The British Empire, http://www.britishempire.co.uk). In 1760, the regiment became the first British Army unit to be awarded a battle honor, as a result of its actions in the Battle of Emsdorf in the Seven Years' War.

375. From the early 1750s, John Russell, fourth duke of Bedford (1710–71), led a faction in the governments of Pelham, Newcastle, and Pitt. In May 1765, Bedford opposed the imposition of a harsh duty on foreign silks, and on May 17 his house in Bloomsbury Square, London, was stoned and besieged by rioting weavers. The Bedfordites took a strong line against the Americans.

376. Richard Rigby, MP (1722–88), was the most effective speaker of the Bedford faction, in the House of Commons. He is described as well built, high spirited, and brash;

I would however observe, that it does not seem to be altogether the wisest Measure of a wise Administration to encourage their most valuable Manufacturers to emigrate. But if that is to be the Case, I would suggest that the Thing may be completely done; and that if a whole Regiment of *Weavers* is to be landed upon the American Continent, we should at least take Care that there be two *Taylors* to each Company, and then we may expect that *Clothing* will go on admirably.

Whitaker, the Historian of Manchester, ought certainly to be appointed Chaplain to the Regiment, that we may have the Military Exploits of his much-valued Town recorded in full Detail;[377] and let Doctors *Brown* and *Percival* draw *Cuts* which of them shall go *Physician* to the Corps;[378] for one who is to have the Care of the Health of so many *extraordinary Troops*, should be a *Degree* higher than a *Surgeon*.[379]

After all, I could not help making a serious Reflection, in my serious Way, upon a Circumstance of Sir *Thomas Egerton's* Theatrical Exhibition, as an Encouragement to the Manchester Recruiting; which was, that *Rule Britannia* was sung from the Stage, and re-echoed in Chorus from every Part of the House.[380] This, in my Opinion, is by no Means an Omen, that those who conduct the Affairs of this Nation at present, shall conquer our Fellow-Subjects in America. On the contrary, it seemeth to me to portend that the Remains of the British Army, unable to support themselves at *Land*, must even take to their *Ships*; and

---

he was well known for his convivial habits and was mocked in the letters of Junius for his purple face (*ODNB*). He was Bedford's intimate friend, had been his secretary, and may well have been present when his house was attacked.

377. John Whitaker (1735–1808), historian and clergyman. In 1771 and 1775, he published the first and second volumes of his (unfinished) *History of Manchester*, of which SJ did not think highly (Apr. 29, 1778; *Life*, 3:333). JB met him in London, Mar. 26, 1772 (*Defence*, 67), and later Sept. 10, 1792 on his trip to Cornwall (*Great Biographer*, 180 and n. 5).

378. Philip Brown (d. 1779) was a Manchester doctor of medicine, on whom JB called on Sept. 13, 1777, passing an agreeable evening. JB's other Manchester friend, Mr. Naylor, told him that Brown "was one of two physicians who had the most practice here" (*Extremes*, 148). The other doctor was presumably Thomas Percival (1740–1804), who lived in Manchester from 1767 and who is remembered for his early work in occupational health. *Drawing cuts*: to draw lots or straws (*OED*), but also a punning allusion to bloodletting.

379. The Company of Surgeons split from the Company of Barber-Surgeons in 1745. Surgeons did not require a degree in medicine so were not regarded as "doctors."

380. Sir Thomas Egerton (1749–1814), later first earl of Wilton. He was MP for Lancashire, 1772–84, and is remembered for his support for the interests of Manchester in the House of Commons. He chaired the committee to raise the regiment (Stead, "'Poor distress'd weavers,'" 204), and the minutes show that he authorized a free performance of Farquhar's *Recruiting Officer* for the recruits at Manchester's Theatre Royal on Jan. 2, 1778. This was reported in many of the London papers, including the *Pub. Adv.* (Jan. 8), in an "Extract of a Letter from Manchester, 3 Jan.," which confirms the details given here by JB.

making as good a Mock-Triumph as they can, while they *"retire as conquering Troops,"*[381] must be contented to sing,

Rule Britannia, Britannia rule—*the Waves.*[382]

RAMPAGER.

No. 17: The Lads at Water Still

[The recent disastrous surrender at Saratoga had seriously damaged the morale of the British forces. Moreover, by the spring of 1778, the Americans were breaking the British naval blockade of their coast, had blocked any British advance up the Hudson River by placing heavy chains, reinforced with logs, across it, and, most serious of all, had signed a military alliance with France. Boswell praises the behavior of the American troops and castigates the British commanders, while celebrating his own Scottish heritage.]

Public Advertiser, April 18, 1778, 2

SIR,

POETS of every Rank, from sublime Epic and Tragic Bards, to lively Lyric or Song Writers, are allowed to make the greatest Men of former Ages say or sing what they please: But I believe even poetical Licence seldom ventures to put Words into the Mouths of great Men while living; Instances however there have been of this, and I lately met with a pretty good one in your Paper, viz. a Parody upon Lord *Dorset*'s famous Song, *To all ye Ladies now at Land*, in the Person of the Whig Earl of *Abingdon*.[383] Having thus a recent Precedent,

---

381. In an official letter from Saratoga to Whitehall, dated Aug. 20, 1777, Burgoyne reported that "The failure of ammunition unfortunately obliged Lieutenant Colonel Breyman to retire conquering troops, and to leave behind two pieces of cannon" (*London Evening Post*, Nov. 1, 1777). Although the expression "to retire conquering troops" was assumed to be a euphemism for "to retreat," Burgoyne was emphasizing that his troops had not been defeated in the field but had had to withdraw from battle simply because they were running out of ammunition.

382. The British patriotic song "Rule, Britannia!" appeared first in the final scene of *Alfred: A Masque* (1740), 2.5, by James Thomson (1700–48), with music by Thomas Arne.

383. Willoughby Bertie, fourth earl of Abingdon (1740–99), was a political opponent of Lord North and a friend of Wilkes. The original song is a 1644 ballad by Charles Sackville (1643–1706), sixth earl of Dorset; it was often used as a basis for parody. Two parodies on this subject that had recently appeared in the *Pub. Adv.* are "Who's Been to Abington, etc., etc." (Oct. 11, 1777), and a song purporting to "correct" it, "The Abington Garland" (Oct. 14, 1777), though neither of these conforms closely to the style of Dorset's song.

I presume to offer a few Lines, which might be very well sung by a celebrated British General, of whom we may say, without Offence, that the Americans have been *too many* for him.[384] I think my Lines will have additional *Zest*, by being a Parody upon a *Scotch Song*.

<table>
<tr><td align="center">ORIGINAL.</td><td align="center">PARODY.</td></tr>
<tr><td align="center">*The Lass of Peaties Mill.*[385]</td><td align="center">*The Lads at Water Still.*[389]</td></tr>
</table>

The Lass of Peaties Mill,	The Lads at Water Still,
So bonny, blyth, and gay,	So fierce in their Array,
In spite of all my Skill,	In spite of all my Skill,
Hath stole my Heart away.	They've borne our Arms away.[390]
When Tedding[386] of the Hay,	For while encamp'd we lay,
Bare-headed on the Green,	With Hunger, Cold and Care,
Love 'midst her Locks did play,	Lead midst our Ranks did play,
And wanton'd in her Een.[387]	And rattled in the Air.
Her Arms, white, round, and smooth,	Brave Lincoln, Arnold, Gates,[391]
Breasts rising in their Dawn,	Troops rising into Fame,
To Age it would give Youth,	Resistless as the Fates
To press 'em with his Hand.	Against our Veterans came.
Through all my Spirits ran,	Through all our Soldiers ran
An Ecstasy of Bliss,	Amazement, but not Fear,
When I such Sweetness fand,[388]	When the Attack began
Wrapt in a balmy Kiss.	With a loud Yankie Cheer.

384. Burgoyne's defeat at Saratoga was particularly alarming because the force sent to America was the largest up to that time ever to cross the Atlantic, and the ministry had often claimed that only a minority of Americans supported the rebels. There is some (unidentified) specific reference in the phrase "too many": it is frequently used allusively in the newspapers around this time. After hearing of Burgoyne's surrender, General Howe asked to be relieved of his position as North American commander in chief of the British army. (As the Americans had by this time broken the British naval blockade, Howe's brother, Admiral Howe, also asked to resign, and both men returned to London later in 1778 to face their parliamentary critics. This was the beginning of the end of the war.)

385. This is another song from Ramsay's *Tea-Table Miscellany*; it was in the first volume (1724), 24–27. JB sang this with other "beautiful old Scots tunes" in Corsica in Oct. 1765 (Boswell, *Account of Corsica*, 188; *Grand Tour 2*, 185).

386. *To ted*: "To lay grass newly mown in rows" (*SJ Dict.*).

387. *Een*: (Scots dialect) eyes.

388. *Fand*: (Scots dialect) found.

Without the Help of Art,
   Like Flow'rs which grace the Wild,
She did her Sweets impart,
   Whene'er she spoke or smil'd.
Her Looks they were so mild,
   Free from affected Pride,
She me to Love beguild'd,
   I wish'd her for my Bride.

Without one *Martinet*,[393]
   These Heroes of the wild
Shew'd *Roman Etiquette*
   To conquer, yet be mild.[394]
Such Nobleness of Mind
   Above all sordid Ends
My Breast to Warmth inclin'd
   I wish'd they were my Friends.

O had I all that Wealth,
   Hopetoun's high Mountains fill,[392]
Ensur'd long Life and Health,
   And Pleasures at my Will;
I'd promise and fulfil,
   That none but Bonny she,
The Lass of Peaties Mill,
   Shou'd share the same with me.

O had I all the Troops
   Howe's tardy Trenches fill,[395]
Supplied with Wines and Soups,
   And Mutton at my Will;
I'd promise and fulfil,
   That this same Enemy,
The Lads at Water Still,
   Shou'd share the same with me.

RAMPAGER.

389. Stillwater, New York, was the site of part of the Battle of Saratoga in 1777 (see "Rampager" 16, headnote and n. 372, above).

390. When Burgoyne's army surrendered, one of the agreed conditions was that his army should be allowed to "march out of the camp with all the honours of war . . . to a fixed place where they were to deposit their arms." This (from *Ann. Reg.*) JB quoted in *Life*, 3:355 n. 3, in the context of an account of a dinner party on May 16, 1778, a month after the publication of this essay, at which the surrender was discussed; as he says, "the disaster of General Burgoyne's army was then the common topick of conversation." Later that day JB wrote to Burgoyne, introducing himself and asking if he might call on him. Burgoyne replied positively, and JB called on him the next day. He wrote up the interview but unfortunately enclosed the document in a letter to W. J. Temple, and it was not returned (*Extremes*, xxii, 345 n. 7, 346).

391. These three were generals in charge of forces of the revolutionary army at the Battle of Saratoga: Benjamin Lincoln (1733–1810), major general and later a politician; Benedict Arnold (1741–1801), a fiery and talented officer who later defected to the British forces; and Horatio Gates (c. 1727–1806), second in command of the campaign.

392. The earls of Hopetoun owned large estates in East and West Lothian, Fife, and Lanarkshire.

393. *Martinet*: a strict disciplinarian (*OED*).

394. "Roman . . . you have to guide the nations by your authority, for this is to be your skill, to graft tradition onto peace, to shew mercy to the conquered, and to wage war until the haughty are brought low" (Virgil, *Aeneid*, trans. Jackson Knight, p. 173 [6.848]).

395. Howe's strategy in the war shifted back and forth between an early desire to make peace and the recognition that only a decisive victory would end the rebellion. His caution made it seem to those in London that he was constantly waiting upon events.

1779

No. 18: On the Parliamentary Inquiry into the War

[During the American campaigns of 1777–79, the British had suffered consistently humiliating losses, such as at Saratoga—or, at best, far too costly victories (Philadelphia). The failure of the British forces became a major political issue and was seen in Parliament to be the fault of the military commanders in America, such as Howe and Burgoyne. The generals at the front, however, blamed the disastrous war on the secretary of state for the American colonies, Lord George Germain, and mismanagement of the campaign at home. Many of the generals, defeated and disillusioned, resigned their posts and returned to England. General William Howe and his brother, Admiral Lord Richard Howe, were, like a number of other commanders, also members of Parliament. Finding themselves implicitly or explicitly blamed, they joined the opposition and asked for a House of Commons committee of inquiry to be set up into the conduct of the war. The inquiries ran for two months (April 22–June 30, 1779), assuming something of the character of a court case, with the ministry and the generals calling witnesses; they were extensively reported in the newspapers. Boswell writes here about the inquiries, undercutting his ruminations by making puns on the names of the recently newsworthy military men—and ends somewhat abortively, apparently like the inquiries themselves.]

Public Advertiser, August 14, 1779, 1–2 (leading article); with Boswell's MS corrections

SIR,

I Wonder that the late Enquiries in the House of Commons into the Conduct of our Generals in America, have not produced more lively Essays in your entertaining Paper.[396] As Love begets Love,[397] so Laughter begets Laughter. But your Authors have of late been mostly so grave and serious, that upon my Word I begin to sit down to the Public Advertiser as a downright Paper of *Instruction*, instead of the Morning *Amusement* which I used to find it, cheering my Animal Spirits, and quickening the Circulation of my Blood.[398] It is a *Breakfast*

396. General Howe returned to London in July 1778, and his brother, Admiral Howe, in October.

397. A proverbial expression, dating from the early sixteenth century; found in English as "Love love begets, then never be/Unsoft to him who's smooth to thee"; see Herrick, *Hesperides*, 297.

398. In ancient medical theory, the term "animal spirits" (from the Latin *spiritus animales*) referred to fine substances that were believed to be transmitted through the body by various systems, such as the blood and nerves. Although discussed by Descartes and Locke, the theory was regarded as old-fashioned but picturesque when notably mentioned by Sterne in chap. 1 of *Tristram Shandy*, vol. 1 (1759), in connection with his hero's conception.

Paper, Mr. Woodfall, and therefore should be *light reading*, whether in Summer or in Winter, especially so very warm a Summer as this, in which if *Wits* really be *Feathers*, as Mr. *Pope* calls them, you should have an extraordinary Number of them flapping and fanning your languid Readers;[399] whereas you serve us up such heavy Food, that I am apt to think the Days of Queen Elizabeth are returned again, when People breakfasted on Beef Steakes.[400] I beseech you therefore, my good Friend, either give us a more slender Repast, or don't publish till Dinner Time.[401] I own I love to write in my own Way; but having had so little in a congenial Stile of late, I begin to lose the Habit of *Rampageneousness*.

Give me Leave to try if I can revive myself a little upon this same Committee. It is not quite similar to that before which *the First Lord of the Admiralty* was tried in the House of Lords;[402] for upon that there was one of the best News-paper Jokes I have read of a long Time, viz. That his Lordship would send about Cards to the Minority Lords, returning them many Thanks for their *obliging Enquiries*.[403] Were all Enquiries to end as that has done, our Generals and Admirals would call for them as readily as we call for *Sandwiches* when we want a tasty Bit at Night.[404]

My Province in these Essays is not Business and Order. My Readers, therefore, must not expect any Thing like Accuracy. I aim only at a little Diversion,

399. See n. 230, above. There was a heat wave across much of Europe in the summer of 1779.

400. The reputation of the English as dedicated beef-eaters certainly dates back to Elizabethan times. In 1562, a visiting Italian merchant, seeing the London cattle market, commented, "it is almost impossible to believe that they could eat so much meat in one city alone. The beef is not expensive, and they roast it whole, in large pieces" (quoted in Rogers, *Beef and Liberty*, 11). JB paid homage to this enduring image by dining on "a large fat beefsteak" at Dolly's Steak-house on his second visit to London (Dec. 15, 1762; *Lond. Journ.*, 86).

401. The time of dinner, the main meal of the day, changed during the eighteenth century, from midday to late afternoon, to early evening. See Lehmann, *British Housewife*, 385–86.

402. Lord Sandwich was at this time in his third and longest stint in the office of First Lord of the Admiralty. Trial in the House of Lords could only take place by impeachment, and Sandwich was never impeached. He was called into question by the Lords in 1778 and, during the American war, was subject to a number of hostile motions in the House of Commons, including one on Apr. 19, 1779, moved by Fox, all of which he easily survived.

403. I have not found this "News-paper Joke." The sending and leaving of engraved calling and greeting cards was an aristocratic practice adopted from Europe (in the nineteenth century, it evolved into a highly elaborate social ritual).

404. This name for the portable light meal that Lord Sandwich was said to have invented dates from the early 1760s.

and while pursuing my Sport, I may run from the Southern Provinces to the
Northern, and from the Northern to the Southern: In short, I may move about
as unexpectedly as Sir William Howe himself did;[405] and without regard to
the Distinction between the two Enquiries, I may, just as the humorous Play
of Words shall answer, groupe together detached Ideas concerning Sir William Howe and concerning General Burgoyne indiscriminately;[406] and thus in
one Way at least exhibit something like a realizing of the *peremptory* Orders of
Administration—to effectuate a Junction *between these two Generals.*[407]

If by the mere Magic of Words, *Realities* at three thousand Miles Distance
could be changed, as we are told that Witches by their mumbling and mutter-
ing can produce very strange Alterations very far off, I should not wonder at
the extraordinary Pains which were taken upon one Side of the House to have
it *said,* that the Americans were not firmly united against the unconstitutional
Attempts of the present Ministry, and that upon several Occasions they might
have been conquered.[408]

Montresor, that skilful and experienced Engineer, gave me full Satisfaction;
but I believe the Ministry would have been glad he had continued a *hidden
Treasure,* instead of being dug up by a *How.*[409]

In Point of *Dignity* between the two Parties, there is certainly no Comparison, one being mounted upon a generous *Grey,* (though indeed not a *Scots*

405. In 1777, Gen. Sir William Howe, who had an affection for the American people
and stubbornly believed that peace was still negotiable, took advantage of delays and ambiguities in his orders and constantly moved his troops around in a deliberate effort to avoid
decisive military action.

406. The "two enquiries" are the examination of Sandwich by the House of Lords and
of General Burgoyne by the Commons. Burgoyne returned to England in May 1778 and
was examined by the House of Commons in May 1779. He attempted to show "that his
instructions were *peremptory,*" to force his way to Albany, and that the secretary of state for
the American colonies, Germain, had given him no discretion and then had attempted to
cover up the fact (*Gazetteer and New Daily Advertiser,* May 1, 1779).

407. In 1777, the government's orders were for Howe to join his army, coming from New
York, with Burgoyne's forces coming south from Canada. Howe delayed, Burgoyne met
little resistance and did not wait, and the longed-for junction was not effected.

408. The ministry claimed, with some truth, that the Americans were not united—i.e.,
that a sizable proportion supported British rule.

409. John Montresor (1736–99) was engineer in chief with the British army in Boston
at the start of the American war. His home was in New York, where he was based during
the British occupation; in 1777, he was with Howe's expedition against Philadelphia. He
returned to England in 1778, resigned his commission, and testified for Howe ("a how")—
and thus against the ministry—at the inquiry (*ODNB*). By "dug up" and "a how" (i.e., *hoe*),
JB alludes to Montresor's work on military earthworks and fortifications.

Grey)[410] the other upon a *black* little *Galloway*.[411] It is surprizing to me how so much notice has been taken of this last. I only ask if any Body doubts that he has a *golden Curb?*[412]

Administration seemed to be chiefly delighted with *"Robertson's* History of America,"[413] but I received the greatest Pleasure from *"Balcaras's* Memoirs;"[414]

410. The two parties to the inquiries are the generals and the ministry. The generals were supported by (among many other witnesses) Charles Grey, later the first Earl Grey (1729–1807), who had served as a major general in America under Gen. Howe. Grey was a ruthless warrior who was detested by Americans for twice leading his forces in bayonet "massacres" of sleeping American troops. At the inquiry, he loyally "defended his chief by claiming that 'there could be no expectation of ending the war by force of arms' with the inadequate numbers of troops 'assigned to its prosecution'" (Weintraub, *Iron Tears*, 192; see *General Evening Post*, May 6, 1779). "Scots Greys" is the nickname of the Royal Scots Dragoons, a regiment of the British army who always used gray horses; they were on home service 1764–1815 and did not see any action during the American war.

411. Joseph Galloway (c. 1731–1803), an American loyalist politician and author who believed that strong measures were necessary to preserve British sovereignty. He joined the British army in 1776 and served in various posts under Howe's command. He lost his considerable properties in Philadelphia and moved to London, where he campaigned for the loyalist cause. "Galloway turned furiously against William Howe in particular and attacked him repeatedly as responsible for the loss of the American colonies" (Fischer, *Washington's Crossing*, 426); in June, he spent a number of days addressing the committee of inquiry in these terms. JB puns on Galloway and Grey as types of horses. The Galloway pony was a breed of small horse, once native to Scotland.

412. A curb is a bit in the mouth of a horse. JB is suggesting that Galloway is in the pay of the ministry; in Mar. 1779, Galloway sent to Germain two plans for Anglo-American union (Schuyler, "Galloway's Plans," 281–85).

413. *The History of America* (1777) by William Robertson (see Chap. 1, n. 212), historian and Church of Scotland minister, was very popular, especially on the Continent. However, JB alludes to Maj. Gen. James Robertson (1717–88), who was the military commandant of New York in the first years of the British occupation and was appointed as civil governor on May 12, 1779 (see *London Evening Post*, May 15, 1779). When Germain opened his defense before the inquiry, in particular "to repel that part of the evidence, which described the majority of the people of that country as hostile to a British government, he had [first] summoned General Robertson to the bar" (*Gazetteer and New Daily Advertiser*, June 11, 1779). Robertson was examined for almost thirty hours, on June 8–10 and 14. His testimony was, however, regarded as based on hearsay and on experience that, though long, had since been overtaken by events, as he had for some years been confined to New York City. One paper commented, "The General, instead of giving that warm evidence for the Ministry, which they pretended he would, supported in fact every part of the conduct of the noble brothers" (*General Advertiser*, June 10, 1779).

414. "Balcaras's Memoirs" is *An Account of the Affairs of Scotland, Relating to the Revolution in 1688* (1714), by Colin Lindsay (1652–1722), third earl of Balcarres. JB alludes to

and I believe the most *striking Likeness* was given by *Harrington*,[415] tho' out a *Shade*.[416]

As I am only beginning again to write, I find myself very aukward at it, and shall therefore, in Imitation of the Enquiries, stop short.[417]

RAMPAGER.

1780

No. 19: On the Duel between Lord Shelburne and Col. Fullarton[418]

[On Monday, March 7, in the House of Lords, a leading member of the opposition, William Petty, second earl of Shelburne, complained that various government appointees were being given high rank in the army without regard to previous military rank or service. He commented furthermore that "there appeared an actual intention to drive the English [i.e., not Scottish] noblemen and gentlemen from the service." According to the *London Evening Post*, March 4, 1780, "He instanced the gross abuse of the service in the unaccountable and novel institution of temporary rank in the preferment of Mr. Fullerton [*sic*], Lord Stormont's clerk, to the command of a corps. This gentleman was raising a regiment for the professed purpose of *buccaneering*."

Alexander Lindsay, sixth earl of Balcarres (1752–1825), army officer and, later, colonial governor. He commanded an elite battalion of light infantry at the Battle of Ticonderoga in July 1777, which he led bravely and skillfully. He surrendered at Saratoga with General Burgoyne and remained a prisoner until 1779, when he returned to England. JB dined with him in London on Apr. 21, 1779 (*Laird*, 95), and may have heard an account of his experiences.

415. Charles Stanhope (1753–1829), third earl of Harrington. As Viscount Petersham, he served in America as aide-de-camp to General Burgoyne. He fought in the disastrous Hudson Valley campaign of 1777. Burgoyne sent him to England with dispatches announcing the surrender at Saratoga. On his father's death in Apr. 1779, he succeeded to the title. On June 1, he defended Burgoyne at the inquiry, when, according to Horace Walpole, he "did himself and Burgoyne honour" (*ODNB*).

416. From 1778 to 1784, but particularly in the early part of 1779, Mrs. Sarah Harrington advertised in the newspapers that she would take from life a "striking likeness" of "the first personages and most distinguished Nobility," which she also sold "in Shade 2s. 6d. Etching 1s. 6d." from her shop in Oxford Street. Her portraits were silhouettes ("shades"), cut using a patent device of her own design.

417. "[O]nly beginning again to write," in the sense that it was sixteen months since the last "Rampager." The Inquiry ended on June 30 and was generally regarded as inconclusive; in the words of one MP, the "Enquiry was concluded without any propositions being drawn from it" (*General Advertiser*, July 1, 1779).

418. This title is from JB's MS note on his file copy.

Although it was accepted practice for individuals to raise private regiments that would serve the state without public cost, and to receive a rank, the implication was that such appointments were political in nature and intended to enrich the appointees. After some delay, on March 20, Scottish MP William Fullarton made an impassioned response in the House of Commons, naming Lord Shelburne and mentioning *"that aristocratic insolence that so peculiarly marks his character"* (*General Evening Post*, Mar. 18). Receiving no satisfaction to a private demand to Shelburne, Fullarton challenged him to a duel. The whole matter at every stage received a great deal of attention in the press.]

Public Advertiser, August 23, 1780, 1 (leading article); with Boswell's MS corrections

SIR,

FOR sometime past our News-papers have been much taken up with the Operations of Sir *Hyde Parker*;[419] but from the Number of political Duels which have been of late, it would seem that we are getting too many HYDE-PARKERS; for the celebrated Royal Park, which has so often been the Scene of single Combat, has been for sometime past plentifully stocked, not with timorous Deer, but with Animals of a bold fighting Disposition.[420]

The Duel which chiefly attracted my Notice, is that between the Right Honourable the *Earl of Shelburne* and *Colonel Fullarton*, where, instead of "Lead being turned to Gold," Words were turned to Bullets.[421]

419. Sir Hyde Parker, later the fifth baronet (1714–82/83), was a naval officer whose exploits were much in the news around this time. In 1779–80, he commanded British fleets in various actions in the West Indies. In July 1780, he returned to England (until Mar. 1781). His son, another Sir Hyde Parker (1739–1807), was also a naval officer (he was knighted in Apr. 1779); his ship, the *Phoenix*, was deployed in American waters and the West Indies, 1776–80. Newspaper accounts occasionally confuse the two men, hence JB's reference to "too many HYDE-PARKERS." JB knew both of them and records social occasions with them (June 15–27, 1781; see *Laird*, 379–81).

420. In 1536, London's Hyde Park was acquired and stocked with deer for Henry VIII's private use, while James I allowed limited access, and Charles I opened it to the general public in 1637. It was a favorite place for settling affairs of honor by dueling.

421. William Petty (Fitzmaurice), second earl of Shelburne (1737–1805), would become prime minister two years later. Scottish MP William Fullarton (1754–1808) only two months later was appointed lieutenant colonel of the 98th. The duel was fought on Mar. 22; Shelburne was wounded slightly in the groin, but the incident temporarily amended his popularity, as the Scots were hated more than he was (*ODNB*). Turning lead to gold was supposed to have been the main endeavor of medieval alchemists.

Honest *Sir William Petty*, the plain sensi-Citizen of London, from whom *Lord Shelburne* is descended, little Thought when composing his *Political Arithmetic*, that a *Calculation* of the *Chances* of being run through, or shot through, must be taken in to the Account in computing the *Value* of a *Parliamentary Life*:[422] But a few such Instances as we had last Winter make that Consideration of some Influence;[423] and as Gallantry is said to be very prevalent in this Age, we should find Men of great Influence who are *attached*, as it is called, to married Women, take a different Method from what David did with *Uriah*, the Hittite, which has been followed by some distinguished Personages in modern Times;[424] and instead of contriving that the Husbands should go abroad, and be exposed to the Dangers of War, put them into Parliament.

Lucy in the *Beggar's Opera* sings

> *What are Cannon, or Bombs, or the clashing of Swords,*
> *For Death is more certain by Witnesses Words.*[425]

But if Words spoken in Parliament are extorted by lethal Weapons, St. *Stephen's* Chapel, though no body be *stoned to Death* within its Walls, may be considered as the Porch of extreme Danger,[426] and the greatest Orators should ever be mindful of that Line in Mr. *Gray's* Elegy in a Country Church-yard,

> *The Paths of Glory lead but to the Grave.*[427]

422. Sir William Petty (1623–87), natural philosopher and public administrator, author of the posthumously published *The Political Arithmetic* (1690), a statistical approach to the understanding and government of Ireland. He was known for his rigorously utilitarian and arithmetical approach to social policy, including proposals to reorganize the London parishes by population. His daughter was the Earl of Shelburne's paternal grandmother (*ODNB*). I have been unable to penetrate the description of him as the "plain sensi-Citizen of London."

423. Many of the British commanders in the American war were also members of Parliament, such as the Howes, Burgoyne, Amherst, and Harrington.

424. When King David's adultery with Bathsheba resulted in her pregnancy, David ordered her husband Uriah the Hittite to leave his military post in order to visit her, in the hope this would conceal the adultery; when Uriah refused, David had Uriah killed by sending him to the front line of battle (2 Samuel 11:1–16). It is not clear who JB thinks "in modern times" has followed David's method, by putting his rival into parliament.

425. Gay, *The Beggar's Opera* (see Chap. 2, n. 71), 1.11.

426. The former St. Stephen's Chapel at Westminster was used as the House of Commons; it was named for the proto-martyr Stephen, who was stoned to death.

427. Thomas Gray's famous *Elegy Written in a Country Church-Yard* (1751), line 36.

We are informed in the News-papers, that the Force of the Bullet which wounded Lord Shelburne, was broke by some *Papers* which his Lordship happened to have in his Waistcoat Pocket.[428] These were indeed *valuable Papers*, and one cannot help conjecturing what they were. If they were Letters or Memorandums from the Veteran *Colonel Barré*, we may suppose them to be strongly impregnated with *Martial Spirit*, as we are told that the Effluvia by which the Pestilence is communicated, may be carried Thousands of Miles over Land and Sea in a Letter:[429] Or if they were Hints from *Mr. Dunning*, they were fit for being opposed to *Arguments of hard Contents*, such as Milton *punningly* describes in Paradise Lost.[430] Perhaps they were some of the Lucubrations of the ingenious and worthy *Dr. Price*, whose Character being that of *integer vitæ scelerisque purus*, so beautifully illustrated in one of *Horace's* Odes, we may imagine his Writings to be like *Talismans* to ward off Evil, and that the Bullet was softened by their benignant Influence, as the fierce Wolf fled from the Poet while innocently musing in the Sabine Wood.[431] Finally, if we may argue from *natural Philosophy* and *material* Causes only, is it not very probable that the Papers in Lord Shelburne's Waistcoat Pocket, may have been the Compositions of *Dr. Priestly*?[432] If that was the Case, the Earl—stood like the *Turk*—not indeed

428. Various newspaper accounts of the duel appeared; the *Pub. Adv.* published two in the one issue (Mar. 23, 1780), of which the second and more detailed reports that "Mr. Fullarton's second Fire lodged a Ball, which passed through Lord Shelburne's Waistcoat Pocket, and being full of Papers the Force of it was impeded, and it only slightly wounded his Lordship in the upper Part of the Thigh."

429. Isaac Barré was a protégé of Shelburne and his "chief voice in the Commons and his close personal friend. . . . [T]hroughout his parliamentary career he was noted for virulence and abuse, a terror to ministers" (*ODNB*).

430. John Dunning, later the first Baron Ashburton (1731–83), barrister and politician, ally and good friend of Shelburne's, who at this time was campaigning for economical reform. In *Paradise Lost*, Belial describes a barrage of thunderbolts and cannonballs as "terms of weight,/ Of hard contents" (6.622).

431. Richard Price (1723–91) was a dissenting minister and political radical who published many works, including *Four Dissertations* (1767), which comforted the Earl of Shelburne after his first wife's death, leading to a friendship between the two (*ODNB*). JB records meeting him on July 6, 1785 (*Applause*, 320). The phrase from Horace, *Ode*, 1.22.1, means "upright of life, and free from wickedness"; the ode celebrates the fact that a good man will be preserved, as the poet asserts he was once, from a wolf, as JB describes. Horace's farm was in the *Sabine Wood*, in the hills outside Rome.

432. Joseph Priestley obtained a post as librarian and companion to the Earl of Shelburne in 1773, thanks to the influence of his friend Benjamin Franklin (*ODNB*). The italicized terms—fate and necessity, cause and effect—allude to Priestley's writings (which publicized the work of Franklin, hence the allusions to force, velocity, electricity).

with his Doxies[433] around—but fortified by *Fate* and *Necessity*—or as the *Impetus* of the Bullet was occasioned merely by an *Explosion of Air*, he might have as much *fixed Air* about him as would match it with *equal Force*,[434] or he might be possessed of such *Power of Electricity* as to deaden its Velocity by one *Shock*.

Such are the Conjectures which one may form as to the *Cause* of Lord Shelburne's Preservation, while the City of London and other patriotic Bodies concern themselves only with the *Effect*.[435] I cannot however conclude without observing that it is very lucky for Mr. Fullarton that Death did not ensue; for if he had been brought to his Trial,[436] he was barred from pleading one great Indulgence granted by the Law of England.—He took it as an Injurious Affront to be called [a *Commis* or] a *Clerk*,[437] and therefore he could not have been entitled to *the Benefit of Clergy*.[438]

RAMPAGER.

433. Turks were proverbial for their bravery in battle and for keeping multiple wives or concubines in harems. JB implies that Priestley is a kind of infidel; *doxy* is slang for a mistress or prostitute (*OED*), and a pun on Priestley's heterodox views.

434. *Fixed air* was the name given in 1754 to carbon dioxide. Priestley isolated oxygen from fixed air in 1774.

435. Shelburne was one of a number of parliamentarians who, in reports published in the newspapers from various "patriotic" committees, were praised for their "patriotism": see, for example, the "Thanks" of the Middlesex committee, "to the earl of Shelburne . . . [and others] for the active and honourable Part they have taken in Parliament, tending to promote the Objects of the Petition of this County" (*Pub. Adv.*, Mar. 1, 1780). After the duel, a number of the committees issued statements, professing to be "anxious for the Preservation of the valuable Life of so true a Friend of the People, and defender of the Liberties of Englishmen, as the Earl of Shelburne, [and to] respectfully enquire after his Lordship's Safety, highly endangered in consequence of his upright and spirited Conduct in Parliament" (*Pub. Adv.*, Mar. 24, 1780).

436. Had Fullarton killed Shelburne, he would have been brought to trial, as dueling was illegal.

437. Both these terms mean *subordinate* (*OED*). In responding to Shelburne, Fullarton had said that "The contemptuous name of *clerk* and *commis* had been bestowed upon him: he was neither the one or the other; his Majesty had honoured him with the office of secretary to his embassy at Paris. The appointment he held to be highly honourable" (*General Evening Post*, Mar. 18). JB's puns on *clerk*, as meaning both "a clergyman" and "a man employed under another as a writer" (*SJ Dict.*).

438. The "benefit of clergy" was a legal provision allowing first-time offenders who could claim to be clergymen to have their cases tried in an ecclesiastical court, where punishments were not capital. As there was no clear register of clergy, laymen (even illiterates) could pass themselves off as clergymen by reciting Psalm 51. To avoid such abuses, the provision had actually been abolished the previous year.

1782

No. 20: On the Change of Ministry[439]

[After the war turned against the British in October 1777, with Saratoga, the French entered the war against them by way of the Treaty of Alliance in February 1778; this pitted the British against the French in Europe and other colonies. Then the Spanish and the Dutch came in on the side of the French. In 1780, George III recognized his inability to win but refused to ever "acknowledge the independence of the Americans" and determined to keep the war going indefinitely to "punish their contumacy" (Trevelyan, *George the Third and Charles Fox*, 1:4). On October 19, 1781, however, General Earl Cornwallis was forced to surrender at Yorktown. That brought about a change of government in the British Parliament—Lord North resigned March 20, 1782—and the effective end of the war in America but not elsewhere, and the war dragged on until it was ended by the Treaty of Paris, September 3, 1783.

Twenty months after his previous "Rampager," the change of government provoked this piece from Boswell, who perhaps detected satirical possibilities in the juxtaposition of *Min-orca*, *Min-den*, and *Min-istry*. He ironically contrasts the end of the campaign in America with another British international defeat: the rather more noble withdrawal by General Murray from Fort St. Philip in Minorca. Twelve years after writing the first "Rampager," he finishes with a reference to political discord, just as he started.]

Public Advertiser, April 23, 1782, 2 (leading article); with Boswell's MS correction

SIR,

THE American War has more than once been the Subject of my desultory Lucubrations,[440] but at last it became such a wild-Goose Business, that it was too extravagant even for my Fancy. The present Session of Parliament has, indeed, produced an amazing Change,[441] to which the previous Proceedings

439. This title is a phrase from JB's MS note on his file copy.

440. Most notably in the pieces written Mar. 11, 1775 (no. 11); Aug. 14, 1775 (no. 12); Aug. 27, 1777 (no. 15); and Mar. 21, 1778 (no. 16).

441. The government and the direction of American policy changed dramatically in the early part of 1782. In February, the vote went against a continuation of the war in America, then on Mar. 5, Parliament gave George III power to negotiate a peace. Lord North resigned on Mar. 20, 1782, following a vote of no confidence, and was on Mar. 22 replaced by Lord Rockingham, whose first task was to seek peace. (Rockingham, however, died in July 1782, at which point Shelburne became prime minister.)

appeared whimsical enough. For Instance: The sanguine Encourager of the Subjugation of our Brethren obtained a Call to the House of Lords, as one who was in Danger of being devoured by wild Beasts scrambles up into a Tree;[442] I hope the Word *Tree* will not alarm him as a *fatal* Sound; the *Royal Oak* may secure him.[443]—Upon a Division in the House of Commons the Minister found himself left with *one* Vote,[444] and *one* Arnold.[445] The American War had long been a *Bore*, so they set to it a WELL *-bore*, and it was foolishly imagined that old Mr. Ellis could turn hostile Plains into ELLIS*ian* Fields.[446]

442. Lord George Germain was, from Nov. 1775, secretary of state for North America in Lord North's ministry and had direct control of the war effort (on land), until late Jan. 1782, when the Lord Advocate, Henry Dundas, made it clear to North that Germain's resignation would be the price of his continued support of the ministry. Germain was given a seat in the House of Lords as Viscount Sackville. JB alludes to the Minden scandal of Aug. 1759, when Germain—then named Sackville—was commanding British troops against the French. As a result of some misunderstanding as to his orders, instead of going to aid his German superior, Prince Ferdinand, he apparently retreated into some woods and was later branded a coward and faced trial, public disgrace, and the furious enmity of George II (*ODNB*). He was rehabilitated by later developments, but his enemies would persist in reminding the public of the scandal.

443. Alluding to the "fatal tree" (the gallows at Tyburn), JB suggests that the king will give Germain better protection from his enemies than the tree in which he hid at Minden. For *Royal Oak*, see nn. 198–99, above.

444. The (prime) minister, Lord North. On Mar. 22, a motion in the Commons to cede the American colonies their independence (moved by Henry Conway; see n. 447, below) was defeated by only one vote (the division was 194 votes to 193).

445. After Benedict Arnold went over to the British side in 1780, he was awarded a pension and made a brigadier general in the British army. He led British forces in a number of raids in 1780–81 and left America for England at the end of 1781. At around this time, it was rumored that he was ordered to command another military assault; see Christie, *End of North's Ministry*, 297. Arnold had led the American forces at the siege of Quebec in Sept. 1775, and on Dec. 19 the *Gazette* reported a letter from Lieutenant Governor Cramahé of Quebec referring to Arnold with feigned ignorance and condescension as "one Arnold." After this, Arnold was often referred to that way in the press, as an ironical reminder of British stubbornness (although the expression was often attributed to the governor, Sir Guy Carleton). See the letter signed "American" (*Pub. Adv.*, Dec. 29, 1775): "this ONE *Arnold* is at least worth Ten *Carletons*."

446. After Germain's forced resignation, Welbore Ellis, later the first Baron Mendip (1713–1802), became in Feb. 1782 the secretary of state for the colonies, for the last month of Lord North's ministry. The *Plains* (plural) was a common term for the flat treeless farmland of colonial America; the *Elysian fields* are, in Greek mythology, the home of the blessed after death—i.e., paradise.

All these Circumstances, however, are forgotten—are overwhelmed in "CONWAY's foaming Flood,"[447] and the *Change of Ministry*, or rather, indeed, the *Revolution of Government*, hath stunned us like the Noise of many Waters.[448]

To me, whose Fancy is apt to perceive remote Resemblances, the Resignation of the late Ministry appears like the Surrender of Minorca.[449] The doleful History of it is thus given in the News-Papers of the Day.[450]—"Yesterday at One o'Clock his Majesty went to St. James's, when the old Ministry went into the Closet to resign in the following Order:[451] Lords North, Stormont, Hillsborough, Bathurst, Sandwich, Dartmouth, Mr. Ellis, Lords Amherst and Townshend;[452]

447. Henry Seymour Conway (1719–95), army officer and whig politician, had opposed the American war from the beginning; his successful motion of Feb. 27, 1782, against the further prosecution of the American war, was partly responsible for the fall of Lord North's government. In the new Rockingham ministry, he became commander in chief of the armed forces and a cabinet minister, with the task of negotiating a peace and independence. (On Apr. 18, 1782—a few days before the publication of this column—JB wrote to Burke, appointed by the new ministry as paymaster general of the forces, soliciting him to approach Conway with a view to gaining him the office of judge advocate of Scotland. Burke made application to Conway, who replied cordially enough, but JB was not appointed; see *Corres. 4*, 120–23). For "CONWAY's foaming Flood," see Thomas Gray, *The Bard: A Pindaric Ode* (1757), line 16 (the Conway is a river in North Wales).

448. *Noise of many waters*: Psalm 93:4 (*AV*).

449. The island of Minorca, in the Mediterranean off Spain, was an important strategic naval base held by Britain for most of the eighteenth century. In 1756, it was lost to France (and Admiral Byng was famously executed for supposed neglect of his duties) but was returned to Britain at the conclusion of the Seven Years' War, and in 1774 Gen. James Murray (1721–94) was appointed governor. When the American war broke out, Spain made an alliance with France, in hopes of recapturing Minorca. Fort St. Philip came under attack from French and Spanish forces on Aug. 19, 1781: something under 3,000 fighting men were besieged by 10,000 or more Spanish troops. After a five-month siege, starvation and scurvy compelled Murray's forces to surrender on Feb. 6, 1782.

450. North and his ministers presented their resignations to the king on Mar. 27, 1782, as reported in the passage JB goes on to quote, from the *St. James's Chron.*, Mar. 26–28, 1782, 3. Members of the new ministry, about which there had been much speculation in the papers, received their appointments from the king immediately afterward.

451. The Royal Closet, St. James's Palace, is a room in which the king or queen traditionally receives ambassadors.

452. Lord North's ministers: David Murray (1727–96), seventh Viscount Stormont, was secretary of state for the northern department; Wills Hill (1718–93), Earl of Hillsborough (later the first marquess of Downshire), was secretary of state for the southern department; Henry Bathurst (1714–94), second Earl Bathurst, was Lord President of the council (the fourth-ranked minister); the Earl of Sandwich (see Chap. 2, n. 66; and n. 402, above) was

each of whom, after their Return from the Closet, left St. James's, not waiting till the Levee began."[453]

And there are Passages in General Murray's Letter which apply so exactly to this Resignation or Expulsion, or whatever else it shall be called, that there is very little Variation to be made in the Way of Parody to make them at once almost exact, and yet ludicrous.

I shall transcribe them for the Amusement of your Readers, marking at the Bottom of the Page the Words in the Original, which are varied.[454]

"I have the *Honour* to acquaint your Lordship, that (*a*) the Administration of Great Britain was surrendered to the Opposition. I flatter myself all Europe will agree the (*b*) late Ministry shewed uncommon (*c*) Fool-Hardiness, and that Thirst for (*d*) Lucre, which has (*e*) generally distinguished the (*f*) Servants of my Royal Master. Our necessary (*g*) Support required (*h*) 329 Members, the Night before the Capitulation the whole Number amounted to (*i*) 229 only.[455]

a. Fort St. Philip.	f. Troops.
b. Brave Garrison.	g. Guards.
c. Heroism.	h. 415 Men.
d. Glory.	i. 660 Men.
e. Ever.	

First Lord of the Admiralty; William Legge (1731–1801), second earl of Dartmouth, was Lord Privy Seal (the fifth-ranked Minister); Welbore Ellis (see above, n. 446); General Jeffrey Amherst (1717–97), first Baron Amherst, a career soldier, was commander in chief of British armed forces; George Townshend, now Viscount Townshend, was master general of the ordnance, a post equivalent to commander in chief.

453. A *levee*: in Great Britain and Ireland, an assembly held (in the early afternoon) by the sovereign or his representative, at which men only are received (*OED*).

454. After the surrender of Minorca (see n. 449, above), Murray wrote on Feb. 16 to the Earl of Hillsborough. His letter was published in the *Gazette* and reprinted in the newspapers—e.g., *St. James's Chron.*, Mar. 26–28, 1782, 1, and the *Morning Herald*, Mar. 27, 1782, 1. Murray wrote of the "noble" and "tragical scene" of his much depleted troops leaving the garrison, with the massed ranks of the Spanish and French armies forming a way for them to pass through. He reported that his men were in such a pitiful condition "that many of the Spanish and French troops are said to have shed tears as they passed them." For his parody, JB extracts sentences amounting to about a third of Murray's letter. (Murray was court-martialed in Nov. 1782, but George III effectively overruled the minor charges on which he was convicted.)

455. The *Morning Post* (Mar. 16) reports the debate of Mar. 15 in the House of Commons on the removal of the ministry; the vote was 229 for the motion, 238 against. The size of the Commons at this time was 558, half of which would be 279, not 329. I have not identified JB's source for his figures, and it is uncharacteristic of him to be mistaken in reporting such matters.

"The most inveterate (*k*) Blundering which I believe has ever infected Mortals, reduced us to this Situation. The (*l*) Votes of the House fully explain the dreadful Havock it made, and that three Days further *Obstinacy* must have inevitably destroyed (*m*) this Government.

"Such was the uncommon Spirit of the King's (*n*) Ministers, that they concealed their Disorders and *Inability* rather than go (*o*) out of their Offices.

"Perhaps a more noble nor a more tragical Scene was never exhibited than that of the March of the (*p*) late Ministry through the (*q*) Rockingham and Shelburne Parties.[456] It consisted (*r*) of a Number of old decrepid Courtiers, two hundred Scotsmen, a hundred and twenty American Refugees, who call themselves *Royalists*, and a hundred and fifty Placemen, Pensioners, Contractors, Jews, &c.

"Such was the distressing Figures of our Men, that many of the (*s*) Rockingham and Shelburne Parties are said to have (*t*) laughed as they passed them. The (*u*) Duke of Richmond and the Baron of Ashburton declare it is true.[457] I cannot aver this, but think it was very natural.

"I shall wait here until I see the last Man of my (*v*) Party safely and commodiously (*w*) removed. If my accompanying them would be of the smallest Service to any of them, I would cheerfully go with them; but as I can be of no further Use to them, I trust his Majesty will approve of my (*x*) taking Care of my Wife and Children."

k. Scurvy.
l. Reports of the Faculty.[458]
m. The brave Remains of this Garrison.
n. Soldiers.
o. Into the Hospitals.
p. Garrison of St. Philips.
q. Spanish and French Armies.
r. Of no more than 600 old de-
    crepid Soldiers, 200 Seamen, 120
    of the Royal Artillery, 20 Corsicans,

and 25 Greeks, Turks, Moors, Jews,
    &c.
s. The Spanish and French Troops.
t. Shed Tears.
u. Duke de Crillon and the Baron de
    Talkanhayn [*sic*].[459]
v. Noble Garrison.
w. Embarked.
x. Going to Leghorn[460] to bring home
    with me.

456. The parliamentary opposition to Lord North's administration was divided, over parliamentary reform, the Gordon Riots, and other issues, between supporters of Rockingham and Shelburne, so that, by the time Lord's North's ministry resigned, there was hardly a policy uniting the opposition. The king, however, insisted that the Shelburne party should be included in the new ministry, and Shelburne became home secretary.

457. Charles Lennox, third duke of Richmond (1735–1806), became master general of the ordnance in the new ministry, and John Dunning was raised to the peerage as Baron Ashburton. They were supporters of Rockingham and Shelburne, respectively.

458. That is, medical men.

459. Don Luis Berton de los Blats, duc de Crillon (1717–96), a distinguished French

How the Lord CHANCELLOR remains alone amidst the Victors of the old Ministry, I cannot explain;[461] I hope they do not keep him in Chains, in Imitation of the famous Story of *Tamerlane* and *Bajazet*.[462]—What will be the Result of this Assemblage of *non bene junctarum discordia semina rerum*, Time must shew.[463]

RAMPAGER.

---

soldier who joined the Spanish Army and became its supreme commander, was honored for his victory over the British at Minorca. The French commander Major General Count de Falkanhayn was in charge of six French regiments sent by Louis XVI to support the Spanish.

460. *Leghorn* is the traditional English name for Livorno, a port city in Tuscany, Italy.

461. The Lord Chancellor in the North ministry was Edward Thurlow, first Baron Thurlow (1731–1808). Despite the change of ministry, he retained the Lord Chancellorship, which is primarily a judicial role rather than a political office. Thurlow's appointment avoided a conflict between the two factions of the new administration: Shelburne wanted to appoint Dunning, and Rockingham, Sir Fletcher Norton (*ODNB*, s.v. "Dunning, John"). (Because of his closeness to the king, Thurlow was able to continue as Lord Chancellor after Rockingham's death, under Shelburne and then—after a brief period out of office—under Pitt.) An allusion follows to his ceremonial chains of office.

462. The Islamic warlord Timur Lenk (also called "Tamerlane," 1336–1405), whose empire spread from southeastern Turkey to India, captured Bayezid I (also called Bajazet, 1354–1403), sultan of the Ottoman Empire, in the Battle of Ankara on July 20, 1402. Bayezid died in captivity, and it was reported that Timur kept him chained in a cage as a trophy. The story was well known through retellings such as Marlowe's *Tamburlane the Great*, Handel's opera *Tamerlano*, and Vivaldi's opera *Bayezid*.

463. *Non bene iunctarum discordia semina rerum* ("warring seeds of ill-matched elements"; Ovid, *Metamorphoses*, 1.9). In the opening lines of the poem, the elements that constitute the earth, sea, and heaven are depicted as being in a state of primordial chaos. JB is (accurately) anticipating discord in the new government, between the former opposition leaders and Thurlow, but also between the Rockingham and Shelburne groups, which had often been at loggerheads in opposition.

4

The Lives of Johnson

In the days before Samuel Johnson died, on the evening of Monday, December 13, 1784, he was visited on his deathbed by many of his friends, including Sir Joshua Reynolds, Sir John Hawkins, Edmund Burke, Bennet Langton, William Windham, and various doctors, booksellers, and clergymen who were also friends. Two of the people whom we perhaps think of as his more intimate friends and who did not visit him were Hester Piozzi and Boswell. The former Hester Thrale was on an extended honeymoon in Italy with her new husband, Gabriel Piozzi, her twenty-year intimacy with Johnson having effectively ended with Henry Thrale's death in 1781. The then-cooling friendship was shattered when, in July 1784, she married her daughters' Italian music-master.

Boswell was in Edinburgh. He had last seen Johnson on June 30 (*Life*, 4:339), and first heard of Johnson's death on Friday, December 17, when he received a letter from Johnson's physician, Richard Brocklesby (*Corres. 2*, 21–22). The following day, he had a letter from bookseller Charles Dilly, to inquire (as Boswell says, "in the true spirit of *the trade*") whether he could have a 400-page octavo volume of Johnson's conversations ready for the press by February (*Applause*, 272). Boswell had long intended to write Johnson's life: in his journal for March 31, 1772, he wrote, "I have a constant plan to write the life of Mr. Johnson. I have not told him of it yet, nor do I know if I should tell him" (*Defence*, 86). Johnson was aware of Boswell's intentions, telling him on April 11, 1773, "I hope you shall know a great deal more of me before you write my Life" (ibid., 183). However, Boswell had as early as September 1764 composed a letter to the great man (unsent, however, until 1777), written melodramatically while he was lying on the tomb of the reformer Philip Melanchthon in Wittenberg, vowing that "if you die before me, I shall endeavour to do honour to your memory" (*Grand Tour 1*, 115–16). Over the next decades, as his friendship with Johnson developed, he made sure that he was widely known to be both collecting materials and recording conversations. Shortly before Johnson's death, Dilly inquired if Boswell would "be the editor of all his works and write his *Life*," and Boswell recorded that "I answered him that I had a large collection of materials for his life, but would write it deliberately. I was now uneasy to think that there would be considerable expectations from me of memoirs of my illustrious friend, but that habits of indolence and dejection of spirit would probably hinder me from laudable exertion" (*Applause*, 272). However, to the now-posthumously repeated request, Boswell replied firmly, on December 23, that he would first "publish in the Spring my tour [to the Hebrides] with Dr. Johnson, a good Prelude to my large Work his *Life*" (*Corres. 2*, li). That same day he wrote to Reynolds, among others, soliciting material for the great biography (ibid., 26).

In the meantime, a consortium of London booksellers, represented by Thomas Cadell and William Strahan, approached Sir John Hawkins, a lawyer and sometime writer—and, more importantly, one of Johnson's oldest friends—and was able to announce on the day after Johnson's funeral that "an authentic Life of him by one of his Executors, and also a complete Edition of his Writings . . . are preparing, and will be published with all convenient speed" (*St. James's Chron.*, Dec. 21, 1784). The magazines and newspapers could call on innumerable writers with some acquaintance with Johnson for reminiscences and anecdotes, and these were rushed into print. The lively and versatile minor writer Thomas Tyers contributed an account to the *Gentleman's Magazine* for December.[1] Inevitably, these essays and announcements responded to and fed off the interest generated by one another. In January 1785, over five successive issues of the *St. James's Chronicle*, a series of anonymous articles attacked the pretensions of Hawkins, made sarcastic mention of Hester Thrale Piozzi and her husbands, and flattered Boswell—drawing forth from the latter the grateful acknowledgment that is the first item in this chapter.

Unsurprisingly, Hester Piozzi suspected—notwithstanding Boswell's disclaimer—that Boswell was himself the author of this sequence of articles in the *St. James's Chronicle*. She determined to publish on Johnson herself (Hyde, *Impossible Friendship*, 96). However, she was not in a convenient location to gather material. Her own papers, including her great collection of letters from Johnson, were in storage in London, and various friends from whom she had hoped to receive material had in the first months of 1785 already supplied Boswell or Hawkins (ibid., 98). She decided to prepare a book of anecdotes that she could extract from the volumes of her notebooks, the *Thraliana*, which she had with her in Italy. In June 1785, she offered her book to Thomas Cadell, who accepted immediately and had the book announced in the papers (ibid., 99).

Boswell's *Tour to the Hebrides* was virtually ready for the press, as he had taken particular care when keeping the journal in 1773, with half an eye to its publication during Johnson's lifetime. When he arrived in London at the end of March, it was a month before he began to revise in earnest, but, with the almost constant encouragement, advice, and assistance—amounting almost to collaboration—of Shakespearean scholar

---

1. Various of these sub-Boswellian biographical materials have been gathered up in a number of editions: *Johnsoniana* (1884), *Johnsonian Miscellanies* (1897), and Brack and Kelley, *Early Biographies of Samuel Johnson* (1974).

Edmond Malone, the 500-page volume was published on Saturday, October 1, 1785 (*Applause*, 342 n. 7). The whole edition sold out in under three weeks. The book concluded with an announcement that the *Life of Johnson* was "preparing for the Press." In the second edition of the *Tour*, published in December, and the third, on September 23, 1786, the announcement was extended by two paragraphs; the same advertisement appeared in Dilly's catalog for May 1787.

But the first book-length biography was Hester Piozzi's *Anecdotes of Samuel Johnson*, which was published on March 25, 1786, and sold out that day. The author was still abroad, but Cadell was able to arrange for her book—unlike Boswell's *Tour*—to be accompanied on publication by excerpts in most of the newspapers. With Mrs. Piozzi's book published and Hawkins's and Boswell's in anticipation, a competitive atmosphere was fostered in the press. This activity was not gratuitous. All three writers were concerned to elevate publicly (at the expense of the others) their authority as Johnson's biographer. Boswell was annoyed at his portrayal—or, more, his non-portrayal—in the *Anecdotes*; while Mrs. Piozzi was the subject of an unflattering remark (of Johnson's) in the *Tour*, to which her agents had—in her absence—chosen to respond in a postscript to the *Anecdotes* (using her own words from letters). This was ill advised, as Boswell's weapons were more finely honed than hers, and he was always ready to rush instantly into print.

Encouraged by the spectacle of Boswell and Mrs. Piozzi sniping at each other, John Wolcot, as "Peter Pindar," published in 1786 two verse satires, *Epistle to James Boswell* and *Bozzy and Piozzi: Or, the British Biographers*, both of which were much reprinted. The two series of satirical prints, *Picturesque Beauties of Boswell*, by Thomas Rowlandson (after designs by Samuel Collings), illustrating the *Tour*, were published in the middle of the year, and the *Morning Post*, as Lucyle Werkmeister has shown (*Jemmie Boswell*, 13–15), took to mocking Boswell and the biographers generally in a series of paragraphs in the second half of the year. (See Figure 11 for another characteristic print of the time.)

Sir John Hawkins remained aloof from all this skirmishing, and in March 1787— just as the Piozzis returned to London—his *Life of Samuel Johnson* was published, as the first volume of a collected edition of Johnson's *Works*. A second, separate edition of Hawkins's book appeared three months later; but this edition was—until O M Brack's edition of 2009—the last of the whole book. Although the *St. James's Chronicle* and the *London Chronicle* published a series of excerpts in March–April, and some of the monthlies also reprinted parts, by May reviewers in the *Monthly Review*, *European Magazine*, *Critical Review*, and others were taking Hawkins to task for his dull style, uncharitable attitude, and tedious digressions. Boswell, heartened, put a notice in the newspapers in May 1787 and on the front wrapper of the *Gentleman's Magazine* for June, in which he promised that his *Life* will correct any "unfavourable impressions" of Johnson's character that may have been made upon readers' minds by "the light Effusions of Carelessness and Pique, or the ponderous Labours of solemn Inaccuracy and dark uncharitable Conjecture."

Figure 11. "The Biographers," cartoon by James Sayers (1786), depicting Hester Piozzi, John Courtney, and Boswell. © Trustees of the British Museum. Courtney's Poetical Review of the Literary and Moral Character of the Late Samuel Johnson, L.L.D. *(1786) went through three editions.*

He was by now working hard at the *Life*, and in July 1787 he advised a correspondent, "It will be in January or February next at soonest that my volume will be
ready for publick inspection" (*Corres. 2*, 175). He badly underestimated both the time
needed and the size of the work. The next major Johnsonian publication was not Boswell's but Hester Piozzi's edition of *Letters to and from the Late Samuel Johnson, LL.D.*,
which Cadell had commissioned on her return to London, after the *Anecdotes* had
gone through four editions in a year. The *Letters* was published on March 8, 1788,
in two volumes. Boswell's jealousy was piqued by the unexpected size of the collection—347 letters of Johnson's and 27 of Mrs. Thrale's—as well as by the affection and
familiarity apparent in their correspondence. He consoled himself with the thought
that the letters were, in comparison with his own correspondence with Johnson, disappointingly trivial; and extracted some righteous indignation from the realization that
she had suppressed the letters that she and Johnson had exchanged after her marriage
to Piozzi; but he confessed to his journal that, from the tone of the few references to
himself, "I felt myself degraded from the consequence of an ancient Baron to the state
of an humble attendant upon an author" (*Experiment*, 194). In this mood, he dredged
out his obscene *Ode by Dr. Samuel Johnson to Mrs. Thrale, upon Their Supposed Approaching Nuptials*, written years earlier, and published it as a pamphlet, with the addition of
a long preface in which he attacked the *Letters*.

For the next three years, Boswell worked at the *Life*, with the vital encouragement
and practical assistance of Malone. But he did so intermittently; he had a law practice
to attend to, political ambitions to pursue, and a family and an estate in Scotland to
return to. After some years of cultivating the wealthy and imperious political manipulator Sir James Lowther, now Lord Lonsdale, Boswell had been rewarded in January
1788 with the recordership of Carlisle. From May to September 1788 and from April to
October 1789, he was in Scotland, on the Northern Circuit, or in Carlisle or London
dancing attendance on his tyrannical patron; during both of these periods, he did
nothing toward the work he was now referring to in correspondence as his magnum
opus. His wife was ill, and on June 4, 1789, while he was in London, having been summoned thither by Lonsdale, she died. He returned to Scotland, but after two months
he was again in Lonsdale's clutches, returning to London only in October. He was
cheered to find that Malone had prepared the first thirty pages of the *Life* for the
press. An introduction for the book was with the printer by January 1, 1790, and—now
that the book appeared to be a real prospect rather than a thing of the imagination—
Boswell was moved to stir up interest via the periodical press.

In 1790, while the processes of finishing the manuscript and revising for the press
were going on simultaneously, Boswell generated for the newspapers a succession of
anonymous paragraphs about Johnson and by implication his own forthcoming book.
His main topics were Mrs. Piozzi—her supposed terror in anticipating the book and her
general lowness and ludicrousness—and the proposed public monument to Johnson,
which was an ongoing subject of discussion and indecision and hence perfect as a hook
for Boswell's periodical mockery. By June 13, when he was summoned to Carlisle for

recordership duties, one-third of the book had been printed. After resigning his demeaning post, he was able to return to London in August. He was finding the revision process onerous, and it is easy to suspect that part of him was reluctant to finish what was in many ways his only reason for living. He was still collecting new material, even though it was apparent now that the book would have to be two volumes. In October, he appeared at Windsor, to try (unsuccessfully) to solicit more of Johnson's letters from Frances Burney (and earned himself a memorable appearance in her diary; see Larsen, *James Boswell*, 151–52). Malone departed for Ireland in December, but Boswell was still acquiring new material: a twenty-seven-page manuscript of anecdotes from Bennet Langton and, on February 4, 1791, a story from actor John Philip Kemble (*Great Biographer*, 119–20)—both of which were duly inserted into the last pages of the *Life*. By February 10, he was writing to Malone, asking, "Pray how shall I wind up [?]" (*Corres. 2*, 296).

After the *Life of Johnson* was finally published on May 16, 1791, Boswell fanned the flames of its fame with literally dozens of items sent to the papers. Many such items (some omitted here) were extracts or quotations from the book, relevant to topical issues, kindly brought—so it seemed—to the public's attention by enthusiastic anonymous readers of the great book. Johnson's monument and Mrs. Piozzi continued as productive themes, and five of his items played on a contrast and competition between Boswell's book, and its subject, and Edmund Burke's recent and best-selling book, *Reflections on the Revolution in France*.

Although the *Life of Johnson* was as successful as he could have hoped, Boswell struggled to find another project to engage his attentions. He prepared a second edition of the *Life* (1793) and a set of *Principal Corrections and Additions to the First Edition* (1793). The other matters he toyed with—a life of Sir Joshua Reynolds, a play ("Favras") on the French Revolution, the possibility of remarriage, a parliamentary career—went nowhere. He continued taking in material for a third edition, which, after he died on May 19, 1795, was published on May 18, 1799, having been seen through the press by Edmond Malone.

1785

Boswell Honored to Be Recommended as Johnson's Biographer

[During January 1785, a series of articles in the *St James's Chronicle* cast aspersions upon Sir John Hawkins's pretensions as Johnson's official biographer and specified Boswell's superior qualifications. In Edinburgh, Boswell recorded in his journal his pleasure in reading these items ("Such attention to me was truly flattering"), sending this letter, and receiving the printer's reply (*Applause*, 279 and n. 3).]

St. James's Chronicle, January 25, 1785, 4; with Boswell's MS correction

To the Printer of the St. J. CHRONICLE.

SIR,

I Read in your Paper with the highest Satisfaction a Character of my illustrious Friend Dr. Samuel Johnson, by a Writer who does me the Honour to pay me distinguished Compliments, as the intended Biographer of that great and good Man.[2] I am only afraid, that while he animates my Mind to its best Exertions, he may teach the Publick to expect too much from me. Upon my Honour I have not the least Notion who this Writer is. But his Knowledge of the Intimacy between Dr. Johnson and me, and of my Means of obtaining Information for writing his Life, is so particular, that were it not expressed with more Elegance than I am Master of, I should almost believe that his Essay was written by myself. If the Writer will have the Generosity to avow himself in your Paper, I shall be very much obliged to him. But if he has any Objection to a publick Discovery, I entreat he may be kind enough to let me know by a private Note to whom I am indebted for such encouraging Notice, that I may testify my Gratitude, and may be further indebted to him for his Advice in the Progress of my Labours.[3]

And as my Name has, upon the late much lamented Occasion been often mentioned in the News-Papers, I think it proper solemnly to declare, that I have not sent a single Article, nor shall I send one, without being signed with my Name.[4]

JAMES BOSWELL.

Edinburgh, Jan. 18, 1785.

2. JB is here responding in particular to an item in the issue of Jan. 8–11 (4), the second of two sets of strictures on Thomas Tyers's "Biographical Sketch" of SJ (which was published in the December *Gent. Mag.*). The article was reprinted in part in the *Edinburgh Advertiser*, to which it seems to have been submitted by JB, as suggested by a corrected copy of the proofs in his files (*Cat. Yale*, P 50).

3. The items, including three pieces about Tyers's work (one of these has been quoted in the Introduction, above), three installments of *ana* or tabletalk, an account of Robert Levet, three poems attributed to SJ, and six "Postscript" paragraphs, continued throughout January. The printer of the *St. James's Chron.*, Henry Baldwin, replied to JB privately that "the whole (almost) have been the Communications of Mr. Steevens of Hampstead, (Dr. Johnson's colleague)" (*Corres. 2*, 40). A selection of nine of these items was reprinted, with this letter of JB's, as "Letters and Detached Pieces Relative to Dr. Samuel Johnson," *London Magazine*, 4 (Apr. 1785), 246–60. See Tankard, "Boswell, George Steevens." George Steevens (1736–1800), friend of SJ (but few besides) and editor of Shakespeare, was famously malicious and had, in particular, "an antipathy for Hawkins which must have been festering for years" (Davis, *Johnson Before Boswell*, 4).

4. As will be seen below, JB did not strictly adhere to this declaration.

Boswell Disclaims Authorship of Certain Newspaper Paragraphs

Public Advertiser, March 17, 1785, 2

To the Printer of the Public Advertiser.

SIR,

AS there have been innumerable paragraphs in the newspapers concerning my illustrious departed friend, Dr. Johnson, since his much lamented death, and in many of them my name has been mentioned, I think it proper to declare upon my honour, that not one of them was of my writing, nor do I know who wrote any one of them,[5] nor shall I send a single sentence upon the subject that is not signed with my name.

The compliments which some of your benevolent correspondents have been pleased to pay me as his biographer, I do own have flattered me, and will encourage me to persist in my ambitious designs of erecting a literary monument worthy of that great and good man. The materials at least will be valuable, being chiefly furnished by himself.

I am, SIR,

Your most humble servant,

JAMES BOSWELL.

Edinburgh, March 10, 1785.

Advertisement for the *Tour*

London Chronicle, September 10–13, 1785, 255

In a few Days will be published,[6]
In One Volume, Octavo, Price 6s. in boards,
THE JOURNAL of a TOUR to the HEBRIDES,
with SAMUEL JOHNSON, LL.D.
By JAMES BOSWELL, Esq.

Containing some Latin Poems, by Dr. Johnson, relative to the Tour, and never before published; a Series of his Conversation, literary Anecdotes, and Opinions of Men and Books. Together with an authentic account of the Distresses and Escape of the Grandson of King James II in the year 1746.[7]

---

5. Not true: he knew Steevens's identity by Jan. 29 (*Applause*, 279).

6. The *Tour* was published on Saturday, Oct. 1, 1785 (*Applause*, 342 n. 7).

7. The "Grandson of King James II" is Prince Charles Edward Stuart (see Chap. 3, n. 352). On June 15, 1785, JB consulted the king as to his preferred means of referring to

Printed for C. Dilly, in the Poultry, London;[8] sold also by W. Creech, Edinburgh.[9]

Advertisement for the *Life of Johnson*

A Journal of a Tour to the Hebrides, 2nd edition (December 1785), 531

Preparing for the Press, in one Volume Quarto,
THE LIFE OF SAMUEL JOHNSON, LL.D.
By *JAMES BOSWELL*, Esq.

MR. Boswell has been collecting materials for this work for more than twenty years, during which he was honoured with the intimate friendship of Dr. Johnson; to whose memory he is ambitious to erect a literary monument, worthy of so great an authour, and so excellent a man. Dr. Johnson was well informed of his design, and obligingly communicated to him several curious particulars. With these will be interwoven the most authentick accounts that can be obtained from those who knew him best; many sketches of his conversation on a multiplicity of subjects, with various persons, some of them the most eminent of the age; a great number of letters from him at different periods, and several original pieces dictated by him to Mr. Boswell, distinguished by that peculiar energy, which marked every emanation of his mind.

Mr. Boswell takes this opportunity of gratefully acknowledging the many valuable communications which he has received to enable him to render his Life of Dr. Johnson more complete. His thanks are particularly due to the Rev. Dr. Adams, the Rev. Dr. Taylor, Sir Joshua Reynolds, Mr. Langton, Dr. Brocklesby, the Rev. Thomas Warton, Mr. Hector of Birmingham, Mrs. Porter, and Miss Seward.[10]

---

the prince and gained royal approval for this formula (*Applause*, 310–11). On Sept. 13, 1773, during their Scottish tour, JB and SJ lodged at Kingsburgh in Skye, the home of Flora Macdonald (1722–90), who was celebrated for having in June 1745 helped the prince to escape, disguised as her Irish maid, after his defeat at the Battle of Culloden. Largely from the account that she gave them, JB fashioned a lengthy self-contained passage in the *Tour* (*Life*, 5:187–205), which he expected would be a selling point of the book.

8. For Charles Dilly, see Chap. 3, n. 250.

9. William Creech (1745–1815), Edinburgh bookseller; well traveled and well connected, professionally and socially, he particularly aimed to publish works of literary and patriotic value; he was the first Edinburgh publisher of Robert Burns. His bookshop was a literary meeting place; JB called by there on Jan. 12, 1786 (*Experiment*, 27).

10. William Adams (1706–89), tutor at Pembroke College, Oxford, in SJ's time there, and later Master of Pembroke and host to SJ on his Oxford visits; John Taylor (1711–88), farmer and clergyman, lifelong friend of SJ, of Ashbourne, where SJ often visited him; Sir Joshua Reynolds, renowned portrait painter, first president of the Royal Academy, and SJ's

He has already obtained a large collection of Dr. Johnson's letters to his friends, and shall be much obliged for such others as yet remain in private hands; which he is the more desirous of collecting, as all the letters of that great man, which he has yet seen, are written with peculiar precision and elegance; and he is confident that the publication of the whole of Dr. Johnson's epistolary correspondence will do him the highest honour.

1786

Boswell Denies Suppressing Passage in Second Edition of the *Tour*

[On their tour to the Hebrides in 1773, Johnson and Boswell stayed September 2–6 at Armadale in Skye at the home of Sir Alexander Macdonald (see Chap. 3, n. 330). In the published *Tour*, the account of this visit was critical of their reception and depicted Sir Alexander as parsimonious and neglectful of his feudal responsibilities. Boswell grew uneasy about the passage and made substantial cuts when revising the book for its second edition. However, Sir Alexander (by then, Lord) Macdonald sent Boswell an angry and threatening letter and somehow broadcast the fact so that, despite Boswell's managing to reach an accommodation with him, when the second edition appeared in December 1785, it was assumed by all that the muted account of the visit to Armadale was a result of Boswell's caving in to his threats. This episode is illustrated in the Collings-Rowlandson series of caricatures *Picturesque Beauties of Boswell*, published in June 1786, the first of which, entitled "Revising for the Second Edition," shows Boswell cowering and being held by the throat by an angry Lord Macdonald, who is pointing his stick at an open copy of the *Tour of the Hebrides*. Another prominent retailer of this version was the satirical poet "Peter Pindar." (For a more detailed account, see *Later Years*, 306–11.)]

St. James's Chronicle, March 9–11, 1786, 2

To the PRINTER.

SIR,

IT having been asserted in a late scurrilous Publication, that some Passages relative to a noble Lord, which appeared in the first Edition of my Journal of

---

great London friend; Bennet Langton (1737–1801), aristocrat and scholar, younger friend of SJ, frequently mentioned in the *Life*; Richard Brocklesby (1722–97), SJ's physician; Thomas Warton (1728–90), poet and literary scholar, fellow of Trinity College and professor of poetry at Oxford; Edmund Hector (1708–94), surgeon, lifelong friend of SJ; Lucy Porter (1715–86) of Lichfield, SJ's unmarried stepdaughter; Anna Seward (1742–1809), poet, of Lichfield, whose vexed relationship with SJ later drew her into public controversy with JB (see the final two items in this chapter).

a Tour to the Hebrides, were omitted in the second Edition of that Work, in Consequence of a Letter from his Lordship,[11]—I think myself called upon to declare, that, that Assertion is false.

In a Note, P. 527, of my second Edition, I mentioned that "having found, on a Revision of this Work, that, notwithstanding my best Care, a few Observations had escaped me, which arose from the instant Impression, the Publication of which might perhaps be considered as passing the Bounds of a strict Decorum, I immediately ordered that they should be omitted in the present Edition."[12]

I did not then think it necessary to be more explicit. But as I now find that I have been misunderstood by some, and grossly misrepresented by others, I think it proper to add, that soon after the Publication of the first Edition of my Work, from the Motive above mentioned alone, without any Application from any Person whatever, I ordered twenty-six Lines, relative to the Noble Lord, to be omitted in the second Edition (for the Loss of which, I trust, twenty-two additional Pages are a sufficient Compensation); and this was the sole Alteration that was made in my Book relative to that Nobleman.[13]

To any serious Criticism, or ludicrous Banter, to which my Journal may be liable, I shall never object; but receive both the one and the other with perfect good Humour; but I cannot suffer a malignant and injurious Falsehood to pass uncontradicted.

> I am, Sir, your most humble Servant,
>
> JAMES BOSWELL.

March 9, 1786.

11. See *A Poetical and Congratulatory Epistle to James Boswell, Esq., on his Journal of a Tour to the Hebrides, with the Celebrated Dr. Johnson* by "Peter Pindar" (i.e., John Wolcot [1738–1819]) (1786), 16: "Let LORD M'DONALD threat thy breech to kick,*/And o'er thy shrinking shoulders, shake his stick"; the footnote says, "A letter of *severe* remonstrance was sent to Mr. B. who, in consequence, omitted, in the second edition of his Journal, what is so generally pleasing to the public, viz. the *scandalous passages* relative to this nobleman."

12. This note is attached to the penultimate paragraph of the *Tour*; see *Life*, 5:415 n. 4. In the third edition (1786), JB added a further paragraph to the note, denying that the omitted passage was defamatory and labeling Wolcot a "contemptible scribbler, . . . [who,] having disgraced and deserted the clerical character, . . . picks up in London a scanty livelihood by scurrilous lampoons under a feigned name."

13. In the first edition of the *Tour to the Hebrides*, the passage subsequently omitted describes a small company and poor entertainment at Armadale and relates complaints of high rents on the estate driving tenants to emigrate (165–66); see *Life*, 5:148–49 n. 1 (Sept. 2, 1773).

Boswell's Reply to the Postscript of Mrs. Piozzi's *Anecdotes*

[Hester Piozzi's *Anecdotes of Samuel Johnson* appeared on March 25, 1786, and Boswell, who was engaged in legal work on the Northern Circuit at the time, received a copy by post (from Malone) on March 30 and "devoured her" immediately (*Corres. 2*, 114). As this reply relates, the postscript to the *Anecdotes* was occasioned by Boswell's having printed in his *Tour* a passage of Johnson's conversation that offended Elizabeth Montagu and embarrassed Hester Piozzi. As Mary Hyde writes, Boswell "had vacillated, whether or not to include Mrs. Thrale's name. He cancelled it in the manuscript, restored it in proof, then took it out again" (*Impossible Friendship*, 101–2); her name was finally reinstated on the advice of Malone and their friend John Courtenay. Boswell sent a first draft of his reply in a letter to Malone (Apr. 3; *Corres. 4*, 319–21); the published version was concocted by Boswell, Malone, and Courtenay (see n. 21, below) (Apr. 15; *Experiment*, 59). A version omitting the two paragraphs following Mrs. Piozzi's postscript was published as a footnote to the offending passage in the third edition of the *Tour* (Sept. 23, 1786; *Life*, 5:245 n. 2).]

Public Advertiser, April 18, 1786, 2 (leading article)

To the Printer of the Public Advertiser.

SIR,

NO man has less inclination to controversy than I have, particularly with a lady. But as in my *Journal of a Tour to the Hebrides* I have claimed, and am conscious of being entitled to, credit, for the strictest fidelity,[14] my respect for the public obliges me to take notice of an insinuation which tends to impeach it.

Mrs. Piozzi, (late Mrs. Thrale) to her *Anecdotes of Dr. Johnson*,[15] has added the following Postscript:

Naples, Feb. 10, 1786.

"Since the foregoing went to the press, having seen a passage from Mr. Boswell's Tour to the Hebrides, in which it is said that *I could not get through Mrs. Montagu's Essay on Shakespeare*,[16] I do not delay a moment

---

14. In the dedication of the *Tour*, to Edmond Malone, JB promises the "authenticity ... , accuracy ... [and] strict fidelity" of the work (*Life*, 5:1).

15. Hester Lynch Piozzi (1741–1821), writer, diarist, and literary hostess; with her first husband Henry Thrale (1728–81), MP and brewer, she befriended and provided hospitality to SJ from 1764 until her remarriage in 1784 to Gabriel Piozzi.

16. Elizabeth Montagu (1720–1800), author and literary hostess, "the queen of the blue-stockings"; *An Essay on the Writings and Genius of Shakespear* (1769). Mrs. Montagu dined at Streatham in 1777, and she and HLP became more friendly during a visit to Bath in 1780.

to declare, that, on the contrary, I have always commended it myself, and heard it commended by every one else; and few things would give me more concern than to be thought incapable of tasting, or unwilling to testify my opinion of its excellence."

I might perhaps with propriety have waited till I should have an opportunity of answering this Postscript in a future publication; but, being sensible that impressions once made are not easily effaced, I think it better thus early to ascertain a fact which seems to be denied.

The fact reported in my Journal, to which Mrs. Piozzi alludes, is stated in these words, p. 299: "I spoke of Mrs. Montagu's very high praises of Garrick. *Johnson*. Sir, it is fit she should say so much, and I should say nothing. Reynolds is fond of her book, and I wonder at it; for neither I, nor Beauclerk, nor *Mrs. Thrale*, could get through it."[17]

It is remarkable that this Postscript is so expressed, as not to point out the person who said that Mrs. Thrale could not get through Mrs. Montagu's book; and therefore I think it necessary to remind Mrs. Piozzi, that the assertion concerning her was Dr. Johnson's, and not mine. The second observation that I shall make on this Postscript is, that it does not deny the fact asserted, though I must acknowledge, from the praise it bestows on Mrs. Montagu's book, it may have been designed to convey that meaning.

What Mrs. Thrale's opinion is or was, or what she may or may not have said to Dr. Johnson concerning Mrs. Montagu's book, it is not necessary for me to enquire. It is only incumbent on me to ascertain what Dr. Johnson said to me. I shall therefore confine myself to a very short state of the fact.

The unfavourable opinion of Mrs. Montagu's book, which Dr. Johnson is here reported to have given, is known to have been that which he uniformly expressed, as many of his friends well remember. So much for the authenticity of the paragraph, as far as it relates to his own sentiments. The words containing the assertion, to which Mrs. Piozzi objects, are printed from my manuscript journal, and were taken down at the time. The journal was read by Dr. Johnson, who pointed out some inaccuracies, which I corrected, but did not mention any inaccuracy in the paragraph in question:[18] and what is still more material, and very flattering to me, a considerable part of my journal, containing this

17. See *Tour* (*Life*, 5:245; Sept. 23). SJ's cultivated and frivolous young friend Topham Beauclerk (1739–80), aristocrat and book collector, was a foundation member of the Literary Club and is frequently mentioned in the *Life*.

18. JB reports SJ reading and commenting favorably on his journal of the Tour (*Tour*, Sept. 19; *Life*, 5:226–27).

paragraph, *was read several years ago, by Mrs. Thrale herself,* who had it for some time in her possession, and returned it to me, without intimating that Dr. Johnson had mistaken her sentiments.[19]

When my journal was passing through the press, it occurred to me, that a peculiar delicacy was necessary to be observed in reporting the opinion of one literary lady concerning the performance of another; and I had such scruples on that head, that in the proof sheet I struck out the name of Mrs. Thrale from the paragraph in question, and two or three hundred copies of my book were actually printed and published without it; of these Sir Joshua Reynolds's copy happened to be one.[20] But while the sheet was working off, a friend for whose opinion I have great respect,[21] suggested that I had no right to deprive Mrs. Thrale of the high honour which Dr. Johnson had done her, by stating her opinion along with that of Mr. Beauclerk, as coinciding with, and, as it were, sanctioning his own. The observation appeared to me so weighty and conclusive, that I hastened to the printing-house, and, as a piece of justice, restored Mrs. Thrale to that place from which a too scrupulous delicacy had excluded her.

On this simple state of facts I shall make no observation whatever.

JAMES BOSWELL.

London, April 17, 1786.

Piozzian Rhimes

[As Mary Hyde comments, Boswell sought the counsel of sensible friends concerning his signed "official" riposte to Mrs. Piozzi's *Anecdotes* (above), but, "characteristically, he could not let the incident rest without some independent show of spirit" (*Impossible Friendship*, 112). The following verses were published the same day and alongside the letter above. In his journal, Boswell mentions that Courtenay and Ma-

19. Hester Thrale borrowed and read JB's journal; see SJ to Thrale, May 22, 1775 (*Letters SJ*, 2:209; also *Ominous Years*, 157).

20. A copy of the first edition of the *Tour to the Hebrides* signed by Sir Joshua Reynolds and inscribed by him, "From the Author," is now owned by Paul Ruxin, who reports that Mrs. Thrale's name is *not* omitted from the relevant passage in this copy; furthermore, no copies of the first edition have ever been seen without her name, suggesting that if JB did temporarily make this "too scrupulous" correction, he did so before the sheet could be printed. See Ruxin, "Other People's Books," 7.

21. John Courtenay (1738–1816), Irish-born, MP from 1780, became from the summer of 1785 a good friend and regular companion of JB; he was elected to the Literary Club in Dec. 1788. See also Figure 11.

lone enjoyed the poem and did not suspect his authorship (*Experiment*, 60). A note in the manuscript of the *Life of Johnson* indicates that he planned to include these verses in the *Life*; see Lustig, "Boswell at Work," 18.]

London Chronicle, April 18–20, 1786, 373

PIOZZIAN RHIMES.

THINKING, no doubt, to rival *Bozzy*,
From Naples comes Signora *Piozzi*,[22]
Bringing (like former wits to *Tonson*)[23]
Her curious scraps of SAMUEL JOHNSON;
Old tales and private anecdotes,
Growling replies, uncouth *bon-mots*;
Latin and also English verses,
And counsel sage for babes and nurses,
Drest with Italian *goût* so nice,[24]
With sugar now, and now with spice;[25]
And that her bantling might not fail[26]
To please Monboddo with a *tail*,[27]

22. In July 1784, three years after the death of her first husband, HLP married Italian musician Gabriel Piozzi (1740–1809); the couple left London soon after to travel to Italy, where she wrote her *Anecdotes* and (with some inconvenience) arranged for the book's publication in London. The postscript to the book, given by JB in the item above, is dated as from Naples.

23. Jacob Tonson (1655/56–1736), bookseller-publisher, whose energy, learning, and business sense enabled him to dominate the nascent industry. He published Dryden, Milton, and Pope, popularized translations from the classics, and was the linchpin of the Kit-Kat Club.

24. *Goût*: flavor, taste, style. However, *gout* is also recorded as slang for venereal disease (*OED*). In the *St. James's Chron.* text, this line reads, "Drest with Italian *gusto* nice," as E. K. Denton-Willing pointed out in a letter to the *TLS* (Apr. 20, 1933, 276).

25. According to the old nursery rhyme, "sugar and spice / And all things nice" are what little girls are made of.

26. *Bantling*: brat, bastard; also young child (*OED*).

27. James Burnett, Lord Monboddo (c. 1714–99), eccentric Scottish judge and an important figure in the Scottish Enlightenment. He admired the primitive life, held proto-Darwinian views, and was mocked for his credulity concerning the discovery of a race of men with tails. JB knew him through his involvement with the Douglas Cause and sought his advice on family matters. JB took SJ to visit Monboddo on their tour to the Highlands and Hebrides (*Tour*, Aug. 21; *Life*, 5:76–83). The pun following, on *cue* (hint) and *queue* (pigtail), links another reference to Mrs. Thrale's footnote (or tail) to the vestigial tail joke.

Behold a postscript!—Mark the *cue*,
To flatter Mrs. Montagu.

    How strange seems this to me, who knew her,
The wife of honest Thrale the brewer,
Whose kind indulgence gave her leave
The *Literati* to receive,[28]
Who at his hearty plenteous table
Might eat and drink while they were able;
While she, elated, took great pride
O'er feasting, genius to preside;
But seem'd most willing to stoop low,
On JOHNSON honours to bestow.

    Ah, luckless JOHNSON, hadst thou thought
Thou shouldst be thus to market brought;
That thy lax sayings, good or bad,
Nay, thy dire fears of going mad,
Should all be *case'd*,[29] and keept in store,
For *sale*, when thou should'st be no more,
Not the luxurious board of Thrale,
Not oceans of his wine and ale,
Not honey'd words from coaxing tongue,[30]
In thy dull ears for ever rung,
Would have seduc'd thee to forsake
Thy own Bolt-court and plain beef-steak.[31]

                        OLD SALUSBURY BRIAR.[32]

---

28. From 1765, when he entered Parliament, Henry Thrale enabled his wife to host a virtual salon at Streatham, where the presence of SJ also attracted Goldsmith, Garrick, Burke, James Beattie, Charles Burney and his daughter Frances, Reynolds, and others.

29. JB is punning on different senses of *to case*, as "to put up in a case or box" (as goods for the market) and "to glue a book after sewing into its 'case' or covers" (*OED*).

30. JB notes that SJ "despised the honeyed words" of Lord Chesterfield (1754; *Life*, 1:259)—i.e., the essays Chesterfield published in *The World* as SJ was about to complete his *Dictionary*.

31. Bolt Court, No. 8 Fleet Street: where SJ lived from Mar. 1776 until his death in 1784 (Mar. 15, 1776; *Life*, 2:427; also App. F, 3:535).

32. "Salusbury" was HLP's maiden name. *Salisbury briar* may refer to a type of tobacco pipe or simply to the prickly bush or shrub, the white heath, of which the hard gnarled burl between the stem and the roots was used for carving tobacco pipes (as well as for making cudgels). Pottle suggests that the initial letters of the pseudonym "OSB" may signify "BOS" (*Lit. Car.*, 266).

Boswell's Retort to Mrs. Piozzi Has Upset the Bluestockings

Public Advertiser, April 21, 1786, 3

Mr. Boswell's retort courteous to the *stiletto* postscript,[33] has played the very devil in the assembly of *stockings*, whose *colour* shall be nameless. It has run amongst the learned *legs*, flaming and *hissing* like a well-charged *cracker*. But, as is foretold in the celebrated motto ALTIUS *ibunt*,[34] the *sparks* have flown *up* and singed *hairs less in sight* of several *grey cats*.[35] *Goody Galimatias* herself may well say, "I wish that designing woman had let me alone."[36]

Mrs. Piozzi, with Her Husband, Will Soon Return to England

[Hester Piozzi and her husband had been based in Milan from November 1784, although they frequently went on extended visits to other parts of Italy, from whence reports of them reached the London papers.]

General Evening Post, May 2–4, 1786, 4

We hear that Madam Piozzi, with her *cara Sposa*, will soon return to England[37]—when she intends to have him naturalized, and take the name of her Ancestors; how far the name and family of *Salisbury* may be enriched or en-

33. In the first draft of his "retort courteous" ("Reply to the Postscript"; see above), JB had written, "there seems to be an oblique *stiletto* in the paragraph" (Apr. 3, 1786; *Corres. 4*, 320); John Wilkes had earlier described the then-anticipated *Anecdotes* in a letter to JB as "the stilletto [*sic*] of Piozzi" (Oct. 1, 1785; *Corres. 4*, 217 n. 69). The stiletto is a specifically Italian dagger.

34. *Altius ibunt*: they will rise highest; from the motto *Altius ibunt qui ad summa nitun-tur*: "They will rise highest who strive for the highest place," which was the motto of the family of Sir William Forbes of Pitsligo, JB's banker and later one of his executors.

35. For "hairs less in sight," see Pope, *The Rape of the Lock*, 4.176; "several *grey* cats" suggests old witches and/or prostitutes.

36. *Goody Galimatias*: Elizabeth Montagu; JB refers to her as "old Goody of a dusky hue" in an unpublished and unfinished poem (Yale MS 310, quoted in Hyde, *Impos-sible Friendship*, 113; see also *Experiment*, 62 n. 4). *Goody*: (term of address for) an elderly woman of humble status. *Galimatias*, meaning "confused language, nonsense," was a word used by Mrs. Montagu in the chapter "On the Cinna of Corneille," in her *Essay on Shakespear* (214).

37. In Sept. 1786, the Piozzis left Milan to travel to England (Clifford, *Hester Lynch Piozzi*, 285). *Cara Sposa*: dear wife or bride; the male form would be "Sposo." JB may be us-ing the female form deliberately, especially given the suggestion here that Piozzi will take his wife's name.

nobled by such an alliance and union,[38] she certainly can best explain to the publick, who has it under Johnson's own hand for the purpose.[39]

1787

Johnson's Biographers

[Sir John Hawkins's eleven-volume edition of the *Works of Samuel Johnson, LL.D.* was published on March 20, 1787, with Hawkins's *Life of Johnson* as volume one. Hawkins's *Life* was available for separate purchase two days later (see Brack, Introduction, xxviii). The work was advertised prominently in the press, with a front-page announcement in the *Public Advertiser* on February 2 (repeated February 7 and also published in the *London Chronicle*, February 3–7). In response, Boswell sent the following, asserting that what matters is no longer which biography is first, but which outlasts the others. Some weeks later, he had the satisfaction of reading the mainly hostile reviews of Hawkins's work (*Experiment*, 132).]

Public Advertiser, February 9, 1787, 1 (first item)

JOHNSON's BIOGRAPHERS.

THE *etiquette* of *precedency* between *Hawkins* and *Boswell*, for both of whom the public has been so long waiting, is not a little curious.[40] The truth is, that the competition between them is not who shall be *first*, but who shall be *last*;[41] in short which shall *see the other's back*, so as to hold the lash of animadversion. Pray walk, Sir, says Sir John, you are a *Laird*.——Excuse me, Sir, answers Boswell, you are a Knight, and you *was* chairman of the Middlesex Justices. Thus they bow, and thus they compliment, while our curiosity is all impatience.[42]

38. See n. 32, above; JB also misspelled HLP's maiden name in the *Tour* (Oct. 2; *Life*, 5:276).

39. An allusion to SJ's letter to HLP on her marriage, in which he charged her, "[you have] abandoned your children and . . . forfeited your Fame, and your country" (July 2, 1784; *Letters SJ*, 4:338). The actual text was first published in Hayward, *Autobiography, Letters, and Literary Remains*, 1:239; however, the existence of such a letter was well known, and a version of its contents had been published in the *Gent. Mag.*, 54 (Dec. 1784), 893; see Hawkins, *Life*, 343–45.

40. Sir John Hawkins (1719–89), lawyer and writer, was a good friend of SJ's from his earliest days in London and an executor of his will; see Figure 12. *Etiquette of precedency* describes the prescribed forms of behavior at court, specifically, of who by rank should rightfully precede another in matters of entrance, seating, etc.

41. Cf. Mark 9:35: "If any man desire to be first, the same shall be last of all, and servant of all."

42. This short fantasy is oddly prescient of JB's actual meeting with Hawkins a year later, recorded in his journal (Apr. 19, 1788; *Experiment*, 212–13): "He complimented me on my

*Figure 12. "Sir John Hawkins" (1794), engraving by S. Harding, from
a portrait by James Roberts. © Trustees of the British Museum.*

If Dr. Johnson's various Biographers do not come forward with more expedition, they will not all see each other's works.—Poor Tyers is already gone.[43]

Life of Johnson Delayed, Now in Forwardness

[Although Boswell was working on the *Life*, the work was far more complex and
laborious than he expected, and he consistently underestimated the time it required.
On March 29, 1787, he, "Laboured at *Life* all day, yet did no more than seven pages"

---

coming exactly to time. . . . Sir John said to me, 'You are Recorder of Carlisle, Sir.' 'I have
that honour, Sir'; upon which he presented me with his *Charge to the Grand Jury of Middlesex*, for which I returned him thanks. . . . We parted quite placidly."

43. Thomas Tyers (1724/25–87), a minor writer, on friendly terms with SJ and JB, whose
"Biographical Sketch of Dr. Samuel Johnson" was first published in the *Gent. Mag.* (Dec.
1784) and revised and issued as a pamphlet in 1785, had died just the week before this, on
Feb. 1, 1787.

(*Experiment*, 125). In letters to friends, as the months progressed, the anticipated publication date was pushed back further and further: "I shall not be able to have it to the press till July or August" (letter of May 8); "My book will not be ready for the press before August" (c. June 10); "January or February next at soonest" (July 4) (*Corres. 2*, liv–lv). At the royal Levee on May 11, the king asked him, "How does writing go on?" and "When will you be done?" (*Experiment*, 134). The following week Boswell sent the following explanation to the waiting public.]

London Chronicle, May 19–22, 1787, 487

Mr. BOSWELL'S LIFE of Dr. JOHNSON.

THE Public are respectfully informed, that Mr. BOSWELL's LIFE of Dr. JOHNSON is in great forwardness. The reason of its having been delayed is, that some other publications on that subject were promised, from which he expected to obtain much information, in addition to the large store of materials which he had already accumulated. These Works have now made their appearance; and, though disappointed in that expectation, he does not regret the deliberation with which he has proceeded, as very few circumstances relative to the History of Dr. Johnson's private Life, Writings, or Conversation, have been told with that authentic precision which alone can render biography valuable. To correct these erroneous accounts will be one of his principal objects; and, on reviewing his materials, he is happy to find that he has documents in his possession which will enable him to do justice to the character of his illustrious friend. He trusts that, in the mean time, the Public will not permit unfavourable impressions to be made on their minds, whether by the light effusions of carelessness and pique, or the ponderous labours of solemn inaccuracy and dark uncharitable conjecture.[44]

London, May 1787.

1788

Ode by Dr. Samuel Johnson to Mrs. Thrale, upon Their Supposed Approaching Nuptials

[Hester Piozzi, with her husband, returned to London from Italy in March 1787, with the aim of preparing an edition of Johnson's letters. With access to her papers, she set to work promptly, and the collection was published in two volumes on March 8, 1788.

---

44. The "light effusions" are Mrs. Piozzi's *Anecdotes*; the "ponderous labours," Hawkins's *Life*.

She had again beaten Boswell into print, and the size of the work (338 of Johnson's letters), its popularity (the edition of 2000 copies sold out within days), its success with the critics, and in the book itself the "clear evidence of Johnson's deep affection for Hester—and his own near-invisibility" (McIntyre, *Hester*, 257), all predictably roused Boswell to a pitch of jealousy, embarrassment and vexation. In retaliation, Boswell was moved to publish this scurrilous item, which he had composed seven years earlier on April 12, 1781 (eight days after the death of Henry Thrale); for the earliest text from manuscript, an account of its composition, and as good an apologia as could be made for it, see *Laird*, 316–21. The first three verses of the *Ode* were later excerpted in a footnote to the *Life*, as an (anonymous) example of imitations of Johnson's style (4:387 n. 1). Hester Piozzi had not seen the verses before then, and her marginalia suggest that she did not suspect Boswell's authorship (Fletcher, *Life*, 3:439). The mock-scholarly preface, Pottle says, "does not in any part of it sound like Boswell"; he suggests that "Wilkes perhaps lent his aid in composing the prose part of the pamphlet" (*Lit. Car.*, 132, 134). The *Ode* was not the hit Boswell had hoped it would be; in response to his repeated inquiries about its sales, Malone advised him, "The poem, I fear, has done nothing" (Aug. 12; *Corres. 4*, 351), and Mary Hyde suggests that the printer Faulder later returned a quantity of folded, unstitched sheets of the work to Boswell (*Impossible Friendship*, 136).]

A pamphlet of 16 pp. in quarto (London, for R. Faulder, New-Bond-Street), priced at 1 shilling, printed May 9, 1788 (dated 1784); see *Experiment*, 223.

ODE
BY
DR. SAMUEL JOHNSON
TO
MRS. THRALE,
UPON THEIR SUPPOSED APPROACHING NUPTIALS
————*Tauri ruentis*
In venerem tolerare pondus.—HOR.[45]
PREFACE BY THE EDITOR.

MR. HENRY THRALE, brewer, in the borough of Southwark (I say it without flattery, or interested hopes of reward from his surviving relict and daughters), was one of the most eminent and opulent traders that England ever had. He was, moreover, a well-built, stout man, in his person. His wife, Mrs. Hester

---

45. Horace, *Odes*, 2.5.3–4: "[No, she is not yet able to stand the yoke/on her yielding neck, not able to do her/share of the job, or] to take the shock/of the bull's rush in the act of coupling" (trans. Clancy, 79).

Lynch, whose maiden name was Salusbury, was of creditable Welch extraction. She was rather a little woman, but smart, of pregnant parts,[46] and some share of book-learning. They kept a very plentiful table, both of meat and drink, to which those who are called *Wits*, and also many ingenious artists, gladly repaired as to a convenient house of call, where they had nothing to pay, except their court to Mrs. Thrale, who doubtless deserved, while she was flattered by their compliments. The most distinguished of them, and, as one may say, the foreman of the whole, was Dr. SAMUEL JOHNSON, the celebrated Lichfield authour, who wrote an English Dictionary, and several works of a good moral tendency, and was famous, besides, for shrewd sayings and lively jokes. He was a very large man, and by no means well-looking, but rather the contrary; neither was he neat and cleanly in his person and dress. He was, notwithstanding, a no small favourite with Mrs. Thrale, both in her husband's life-time, and for some short while after; and from a collection of their letters, which is extant, and has been put forth in print by herself,[47] it appears that there was no over-delicate niceness, but truly the plainest familiarity between them; as witness these, and the like passages:[48] —"I hope, in time, to be like the great bull." lett. 34.—"Dr. Taylor desires always to have his compliments sent. He is, in his usual way, very busy getting a bull to his cows, and a dog to his bitches. Old Shakespeare is dead, and he wants to buy another horse to his mares." lett. 180.—"You must take the chance of finding me, *better or worse.*[49] This you may know at present, that my *affection* for you is not diminished, and my *expectation* from you is increased." lett. 277.—"I am harrassed by a very disagreeable operation of the *cantharides*,

46. "Of pregnant parts": a contemporary idiom, meaning having faculties of wit, invention, resourcefulness, etc.

47. This comment undermines the claim of the pamphlet to have been published in 1784. HLP's *Letters to and from the Late Samuel Johnson, LL.D.: To which are Added Some Poems Never before Printed*, 2 vols. (London, 1788), was published Saturday, Mar. 8. JB had a copy the day before publication; he was disturbed at its image of SJ, was annoyed at the appearance he himself made (*Experiment*, 194 ff.), and suspected that HLP had suppressed passages that flattered him. She had in fact suppressed "only two significant references" to JB in SJ's letters (*Later Years*, 367), although, as Hyde observes, "for several omissions Boswell should have been grateful" (*Impossible Friendship*, 127).

48. The letters are numbered as in HLP's edition; these are the dates and references to Redford's edition: 34 (July 3, 1771; 1:366–67), 180 (Michaelmas Day, 1777; 3:77–80), 277 (Dec. 8, 1781; 3:379), 303 (June 21, 1783; 4:155–56), 342 (Mar. 2, 1784; 4:292–93), and, in the next paragraph, 275 (Nov. 24, 1781; 3:374–75). As well as illustrating the "plainest familiarity," the extracts emphasize animal husbandry and thus echo the Horatian epigraph.

49. "Better or [for] worse" is well known as a phrase from the marriage vows in the Anglican rite.

which I am endeavouring to *control* by copious dilution." lett. 303.[50]—"On the 19th of last month I evacuated twenty pints of water." lett. 342.

Mr. Thrale and his wife had a family of five daughters, to whom they did not grudge to give every piece of genteel education. Signor Baretti was entertained in the house, at bed and board, to teach them the Italian tongue;[51] and Signor Piozzi, it is believed, was liberally rewarded for teaching them to sing, and play on the harpsichord. Mrs. Thrale had not an *ear*, as the saying is, but she had an *eye* to this her daughter's music-master, who, it appears, by her said publication, was permitted to *love* her. "Piozzi, I find, is coming, and when *he* comes, and *I* come, you will have two about you that *love* you." lett. 275. This was in her widowhood; and indeed it is plain that Dr. Samuel Johnson himself had then also pretensions to her; the disappointment of which, by her preference of Signor Piozzi, whom she afterwards married, no doubt contributed, with other considerations, to his writing that severe answer on her informing him of her resolution, which answer she has very prudently suppressed.[52]

Indeed, recently after the death of Mr. Henry Thrale, there were not wanting many who conjectured that a matrimonial union would take place between the widow and Dr. Samuel Johnson; and some went so far as to assert, that it was his determined purpose, not only to carry on the business under the *firm* of the brewery, but even to assume the name and arms of Thrale.[53] Upon this foundation, and no better, the bell-man,[54] or some other such rhymster of the Borough, bantered the business in the following homely lines:

50. For *Cantharides* or "Spanish fly," see Chap. 3, n. 207. In a later letter, SJ wrote to his physician Brocklesby that he was using tincture of cantharides as a diuretic (Aug. 12, 1784; *Letters SJ*, 4:364–66). For its supposed aphrodisiac effect it was also used in animal husbandry.

51. Guiseppi (Joseph) Baretti (1719–89), an Italian writer who lived mostly in London, was a friend of SJ's and one of the Streatham circle; he had lived in the Thrale household as a tutor to the eldest daughter, Hester Maria ("Queeney").

52. SJ's letter of July 2, 1784 ("you are ignominiously married") is indeed omitted from HLP's edition (see 2:375), in which she proceeds to his more conciliatory letter of July 8. See n. 39, above.

53. In Scottish law, the heraldic title of "Chief of the Name and Arms" confers social dignity and precedence on the head of a Scottish family. JB's joke is at the expense of Thrale's not having a coat of arms.

54. *Bellman*: a man who rings a bell; esp. a man employed to walk through the streets of a town and make public announcements, to which he attracts attention by ringing a bell; a town crier (*OED*).

Hail, Johnson!
Thrale Johnson,
Brewer of good ale, Johnson;
While thus you drive so bold a trade,
Your cash will never fail, Johnson.
Though Madam's somewhat stale, Johnson,
You'll find she'll yet be frail, Johnson;
For many years she tried your head,
And now she'll try— —, Johnson.[55]

Whether it was that a copy of this balderdash reached Dr. Samuel Johnson, and made him anxious lest posterity should look upon his tender passion as of a very coarse and vulgar nature, or whether he was merely incited by her blandishments to give a specimen of his juvenile vivacity, or from whatever other cause, it would seem, that in the confidence of their being speedily joined in marriage, he sent her the following wedding verses; of which, it is probable, she gave a copy to Signor Baretti, or to some other person with whom she at that time was intimate.

The same having, by some strange chance, fallen into my hands, I thought I could not do better than lay them before the publick.

With respect to their being certainly written by Dr. Samuel Johnson, I honestly confess I am no judge of such matters, and therefore will not pretend to say any thing of my own knowledge upon that head. But I am well assured by a person of skill, that they have the undoubted sterling mark,[56] and that no other man in the kingdom could make them but himself.

ARGUMENT.

THE Poet, pleased with the reminiscence of his poetical powers, prepares to concentrate them in his Mistress—He prostrates his dignity to her in versatility of character—Plumes himself on his fancied felicity, and, by a bold image, equal to any in Anacreon,[57] at once personifies, and personates that Beer which was the glory of her house—Touches on his jealousy of Signor Piozzi—Exults in his supposed victory over his rival—Describes the congratulations on the nuptials between him and his dearest

---

55. The words represented as deleted are, doubtless, "your tail"; *tail*: penis (*OED*).

56. Objects of sterling silver are given a mark (a *hallmark*) or marks to indicate the purity of the silver and its origin.

57. *Anacreon*: Greek lyric poet of the sixth century B.C., whose poems are supposed mainly to have concerned love and wine, but little of whose work survives. JB's father, Lord Auchinleck, had a special interest in Anacreon (see *Tour*, Nov. 2, 1773; *Life*, 5:376); JB consulted SJ about doing an edition (Sept. 30, 1783; *Life*, 4:241).

dear lady; but characteristically hints at the malignity of human nature—Represents
the envy with which their happiness is beheld—Weary of continence, solaces himself
with the prospect of future enjoyment—Paints it with vigorous strokes and glowing
colours—Takes care to give it the delicate sanction of sentiment—Assumes a reflex
honour, by projecting illustrious matches for his lady's daughters by her first husband;
but maintains his own superiority, by figuring himself the father of an heir male—
Concludes, in mythological enthusiasm, that he is greater than Atlas.

ODE.

IF e'er my fingers touch'd the lyre,
    In satire fierce, in pleasure gay,
Shall not my THRALIA's smiles inspire?
    Shall SAM refuse the sportive lay?

My dearest lady! view your slave,
    Behold him as your very SCRUB,[58]
Eager to write as authour grave,
    Or govern well the brewing tub.

To rich felicity thus rais'd,
    My bosom glows with amorous fire;
Porter no longer shall be prais'd;[59]
    'Tis I MYSELF am *Thrale's Entire!*[60]

PIOZZI once alarm'd my fears,
    Till beauteous MARY's tragick fate
And RIZZIO's tale dissolv'd in tears[61]
    My mistress, ere it was too late.

58. *Scrub* denotes a loyal servant, named for the character in Farquhar's comedy *The Beaux' Stratagem* (1707) who serves Squire Sullen in half a dozen different capacities.

59. SJ's wife Elizabeth, née Jervis (1689–1752), was Mrs. Porter before their marriage in 1735. *Porter* is also a dark bitter beer.

60. Another pun: *entire* is another kind of beer; "Thrale's Entire" was a popular product of his brewery. In husbandry, *entire* is used for a male animal that has not been gelded.

61. Mary I, Queen of Scots (1542–87). On Mar. 9, 1566, her secretary and favorite courtier, Italian musician David Riccio or Rizzio (c. 1533–66), was murdered by jealous nobles and with the connivance of her estranged husband in her presence. Mary herself, as a threat to Protestant succession in England, was under house arrest in England for the last twenty years of her life and was eventually executed. In his last letter to HLP, of July 8, 1784, SJ drew a parallel between her situation and that of Mary departing for England, with himself as the Archbishop of St. Andrews attempting to dissuade her (*Letters SJ*, 4:343–44 and n. 5).

Indignant thought to English pride!
    That any eye should ever see
JOHNSON one moment set aside
    For *Tweedledum* or *Tweedledee*.[62]

Congratulating crowds shall come,
    Our new-born happiness to hail,
Whether at ball, at rout, at drum;[63]
    —But human spite will still prevail.

For though they come in pleasing guise,
    And cry, "The wise deserve the fair!"[64]
They look askance with envious eyes,
    As Satan look'd at the first pair.[65]

Ascetick now thy lover lives,
    Nor dares to touch, nor dares to kiss;
Yet prurient fancy sometimes gives
    A prelibation of our bliss.

Convuls'd in love's tumultuous throws,
    We feel the aphrodisian spasm;
Tir'd nature must, at last, repose,
    Then Wit and Wisdom fill the chasm.

Nor only are our limbs entwin'd,
    And lip in rapture glued to lip;
Lock'd in embraces of the mind;
    Imagination's sweets we sip.

---

62. An epigram of 1725 by poet John Byrom, about the rivalry between the composers Handel and Bononcini, concludes, "Strange all this difference should be/Twixt tweedle-dum and tweedle-dee." The terms therefore denote two insignificant and indistinguishable alternatives, both foreigners, and have musical resonances.

63. A *rout*: "A group of people gathered or assembled together; a company, a troop; a gathering, a crowd" (*OED*). A *drum*: "An assembly of fashionable people at a private house, held in the evening: much in vogue during the latter half of the 18th and beginning of the 19th century; a rout" (ibid.).

64. Dryden, *Alexander's Feast, or, The Power of Music* (1697), lines 13–15; though Dryden has "brave" rather than "wise."

65. Satan looking upon Adam and Eve, as depicted by Milton in *Paradise Lost*, 4.504: "aside the Devil turnd/For envie, yet with jealous leer maligne/Ey'd them askance."

> Five daughters by a former spouse
>> Shall match with nobles of the land;
> The fruit of our more fervent vows
>> A pillar of the state shall stand!

> Greater than Atlas was of yore,[66]
>> A nobler charge to me is given;
> The sphere he on his shoulders bore,
>> I, with my arms, encircle Heaven!

THE END.

Did Johnson Court Mrs. Thrale? Do His Biographers Know?

[After the *Ode* was published, Boswell put two pieces in the press, in an attempt to fan public suspicion about or prurient interest in Hester Piozzi's love life. The first draws attention to another published response to her edition of Johnson's letters, a series of three articles by Guiseppi Baretti. Baretti was known to have had an acrimonious parting from the Thrale household and to have been generally ill tempered, and it was thought that perhaps he would have some revelations to offer.]

Public Advertiser, May 12, 1788, 4[67]

Dr. Johnson's courtship of Mrs. Thrale, and his rage in being rejected for Signor Piozzi, which is said now to be *promulgated* by Baretti, is one of the most extraordinary things that we have yet had concerning our great Lexicographer.[68] Query, Did Hawkins know this? Does Boswell know it? What are we to believe? Why have we not a detail? Why not some documents? Let us have all out.

66. Atlas was a titan in Greek mythology who was condemned to support the heavens above his head, by his hands.

67. In the *Pub. Adv.*, the item below is followed immediately by a paragraph concerning JB's appointment as the recorder of Carlisle; JB's marked file copy, *Cat. Yale*, P 116(28).

68. Offended by passages in HLP's collection of SJ's *Letters*, Baretti published his "Strictures" on the book in three issues of the *European Magazine*, 13 (May), 313–17, and (June), 393–99; 14 (Aug.), 89–99. He responded at great length to parts of both HLP's and SJ's letters that cast him in a poor light, and reflected disparagingly on HLP's honesty, learning, childrearing practices, and second marriage. Although Baretti testifies to SJ's immense fondness for and high opinion of HLP, he says nothing about SJ having courted her.

A Thralian Epigram

Public Advertiser, May 13, 1788, 2

A THRALIAN EPIGRAM.

IF *Hesther* had chosen to wed mighty SAM,
Who it seems, drove full at her his BATTERING RAM:*[69]
A wonder indeed, then, the world would have found,
A woman who truly prefer'd SENSE to *sound*.[70]

1789

Life of Johnson in the Press

"*Morning Post* [late] 1789"[71]

Boswell's life of Johnson is at last in the press, and will shew its biographical front in May; it will not only consist of the life of this extraordinary man, but of his bon mots, letters, &c. making a large quarto volume.[72] Amongst the letters will be found that celebrated one to the late Earl of Chesterfield, requesting to be dismissed from his patronage.[73]

69. "* See Epilogue to the REGENT, a Tragedy." (BOSWELL) HLP contributed an epilogue to a play by her friend and collaborator in the Della Cruscan project (see n. 86, below) Bertie Greatheed (1759–1826), *The Regent: A Tragedy* (1788), which opened at the Theatre Royal on Mar. 29, 1788, with John Kemble and his sister Sarah Siddons taking the lead roles. The epilogue, spoken by Mrs. Siddons, included the lines:

> Unskill'd in modern tactics, rule and line,
> The floating engine, and th'insidious mine,
> Our bard disdains; with antiquated art
> He drives his battering-ram full at your heart.

JB found the expression ludicrous and used it again in the "Brewhouse Entertainment," below.

70. That is, SJ's literary accomplishments (*sense*) rather than Piozzi's musical ones (*sound*). That in poetry the sound should be accommodated to the sense was a critical commonplace; see Pope, *Essay on Criticism*, line 365, and SJ, *Idler*, no. 60 (June 9, 1759).

71. This source note (and others like it, following) is quoted from JB's MS note on a copy of the item in his files and is used in the absence of any known copy of the issue of the paper.

72. In the end, the book made two large octavo volumes.

73. On the eve of the publication of SJ's *Dictionary of the English Language* (1755), Philip Dormer Stanhope, fourth earl of Chesterfield (1694–1773), wrote in praise of the work in

1790

Mr. Boswell at the Abbey

Public Advertiser, February 8, 1790, 3

At the celebration of the anniversary of the 30th of January in Westminster Abbey,[74] when the Bishop of Carlisle (Dr. Douglas) preached,[75] Mr. Boswell, the Recorder of that city,[76] was observed attending with a most High-church Tory gravity, in a scratch wig and watch-man's great coat,[77] as like as he could be to old SAM JOHNSON.

Mrs. Piozzi's Terror of Boswell's *Life of Johnson*

"*Morning Post* 22 Febry 1790"

Mrs. PIOZZI has been taught to look with terror on the approaching biography of JOHNSON, by Mr. JAMES BOSWELL. If Mrs. PIOZZI has, indeed, any thing to apprehend respecting that work, it must be formidable indeed; for it will consist of facts only, Mr. BOSWELL being too honest and too benevolent a man to bring any charge but upon the most solid foundation and rational necessity. Mrs. PIOZZI has, however, nothing to dread, for BOSWELL will be employed in pursuing AN EAGLE, and it is not likely that he will turn from so noble a flight to pluck a feather from a *tom tit*.

---

the periodical *The World*; on Feb. 7, 1755, SJ wrote rebuffing this belated attention (*Letters SJ*, 1:94–97). Soon after, according to William Adams, this letter became "the Talk of the Town" (*Corres. 2*, 50). JB possessed two copies of "that celebrated letter of which so much has been said," dictated by SJ on separate occasions (*Life*, 1:260; 1754), and was counting on this to attract interest in his book. Here he is baiting a hook to catch potential reviewers who might like to excerpt it; see "Advertisement for Valuable Extracts" and "Apology of *London Packet*," below.

74. In high-church Anglican circles, Jan. 30 is kept as the Feast of Charles, King and Martyr, being the anniversary of the execution of King Charles I (1600–1649).

75. Rev. John Douglas (1721–1807) became Bishop of Carlisle in 1787 and Bishop of Salisbury in 1791; he wrote on political and literary topics, contributed some anecdotes to the *Life*, and was elected to the Literary Club on JB's proposal in 1792.

76. JB was elected to this post on Jan. 11, 1788.

77. A *scratch wig* or scratch periwig, sometimes shortened to *scratch*, was "a small, short wig," possibly named for the opportunity it provided the wearer for scratching the head (*OED*). A *watchman*: "a constable of the watch who, before the Police Act of 1839, patrolled the streets by night to safeguard life and property" (*OED*). A greatcoat was a traditional part of their uniform.

Johnson's Monument

[In May 1785, the Literary Club, with the permission of the dean and chapter of Westminster Abbey, started collecting money for a monument to SJ. However, little progress was made until the meeting, which Boswell attended and is here reporting, on January 5, 1790, when a committee was formed, under the chairmanship of Sir Joseph Banks, to collect subscriptions (see *Great Biographer*, 28).[78]]

Public Advertiser, February 22, 1790, 3

JOHNSON'S MONUMENT — The BOOKSELLERS OF LONDON have been most unjustly attacked.[79] Their contributions to this great and good work will be very liberal; but they are not to stand forth *individually*, but to make a *purse* in *a body*. Let it be mentioned, however, that *one* of them, Mr. George Niccol, a *Scotchman*, (who married the niece of Alderman Boydell)[80] has actually subscribed five guineas as his share, and it is not doubted that the rest of *the trade* will equal, if not exceed him.[81]

Mrs. Piozzi's Subscription to Johnson's Monument Defended

"*Morning Post* 23 Febry 1790"

MRS. PIOZZI.

This Lady, like the Minister's EXCISE,[82] has been sadly *traduced*. In particular, she has been vilified beyond measure, for giving only five guineas to *Johnson's*

---

78. Reynolds persuaded the committee that St. Paul's Cathedral was a better site than the Abbey, and the statue by John Bacon was eventually placed there in 1796 (see Figure 13). For a full account, see *Life*, 4:423 (1784) and n. 2, and App. I, 464–72; also *Corres. 4*, 419 n. 7.

79. It is not clear if JB refers to a specific "attack" on the booksellers.

80. George Nicol (c. 1741–1828) was bookseller to the king and a friend of SJ; in the *Life*, he is mentioned at 4:251 (Dec. 1783), and JB includes a letter of SJ's to him at 4:365 (Aug. 19, 1784). His second wife, Mary Nicol (1747–1820), writer and collector of prints, was the niece of John Boydell (see Chap. 2, n. 87). At *Life*, 2:293 n. 2 (Jan. 21, 1775), JB refers to Boydell as "that eminent Patron of the Arts." When Boydell became Lord Mayor of London in 1790, his niece acted as lady mayoress.

81. As is often the case with these paragraphs, this item in the *Pub. Adv.* is in suggestive proximity to other items that it is possible to imagine JB's involvement in: an evocation of SJ in defense of Warren Hastings and a couple of paragraphs in praise of Sir Joshua Reynolds.

82. The prime minister and chancellor of the exchequer from 1783 to 1801 was William Pitt, the Younger (1759–1806). The cost of the American war had dramatically increased the national debt, and Pitt set about reforming the nation's finances by simplifying customs and excises and introducing a great many new taxes. In July 1789, he replaced the customs duty

*Figure 13. Samuel Johnson, sculpture by John Bacon (1796). St. Paul's
Cathedral, London. © The Dean and Chapter of St. Paul's Cathedral.*

monument,[83] out of 737£. 14s. 6d. which she pocketed by selling his Anecdotes and
Letters.[84] But let malevolent envy be suspended only till *Wednesday next*, when
she is to exhibit an ample proof, that though she did not chuse to be *ostentatious*,

on tobacco with an excise, which was more intrusive and harder to evade. There were many
protests about this, including public petitions; on Apr. 16, 1790, Richard Brinsley Sheridan
(1751–1816), playwright and politician, led a parliamentary debate for its repeal.

83. A paragraph in *The World*, Feb. 27, 1790, noting that the subscription to the monument is nearly filled, says that Reynolds and Steevens subscribed ten guineas and that
Malone, Mrs. Piozzi, and Kemble subscribed five guineas each. However, Malone, who was
a prime mover in the monument project, recorded in his copy of the *Anecdotes*, "Mrs. Piozzi,
who had gained 500*l* [i.e., £500] by this book, and 600*l* by publishing his Letters . . . sent to
me . . . the mighty sum of *three* Guineas" (see *Life*, App. I, 4:467–68).

84. This suspiciously precise figure may be invented. It is unclear what HLP was paid
for the *Anecdotes*; it seems to have been £130 or £150 (Clifford, *Hester Lynch Piozzi*, 263 n. 3).

and deprive many eminent persons of the honour of contributing to that noble design, she is truly *liberal*. On *Wednesday next* she is to give a grand entertainment at Mr. Thrale's brew-house in Southwark, to the friends and connections of her late husband, by whose bounty she is now in affluence, suitable largesses are to be distributed to the poor, and quantities of beer to the populace.[85]

The Brewhouse Entertainment

[On returning to London, Mrs. Piozzi and her husband became involved in the theater and in the world of high-society amateur theatricals. They hosted private concerts and entertainments at their house in Hanover Square, which were reported in the papers, with lists of the guests, including "visiting foreigners, popular writers of the day, a sprinkling of the nobility, scholars and prelates, a few actors and musicians" (Clifford, *Hester Lynch Piozzi*, 334). These occasions were quite unlike the Johnsonian salons at Streatham, being focused on music rather than conversation, and involved no members of the old circle.]

"*Morning Post* [, c. March 1], 1790"

MRS. PIOZZI.

The entertainment which is to be given by Mrs. PIOZZI on occasion of her revisiting the Brewhouse of her first husband, Mr. THRALE, will undoubtedly exceed any *féte* that this country has ever seen.

It is to be truly a *Mischianza*,[86] a medley of tragedy, comedy, music, oratory; in short, of every thing. Mr. HORNE TOOKE is to assist at these "Diversions of PURL."[87]

On her return to London, HLP accepted an offer from Cadell of £500 for her book of SJ's letters, though she also claimed that the sum was 500 guineas—i.e., £525 (ibid., 295).

85. See next item.

86. *Mischianza*: a jumble. The structure of this piece and its Italian elements are parodic references to *The Florence Miscellany* (Florence, 1785), the founding text of the Della Cruscan school of poetry, which was the work of a number of English writers living in Italy: HLP, who wrote the preface and some of the poems, Bertie Greatheed, William Parsons, and Robert Merry. The poems were in a variety of styles and in English, Italian, and French. As Mary Hyde observes, this burlesque includes elements salvaged from an obscene rhyme on HLP's marriage, written some years before, which JB had not published (*Impossible Friendship*, 143).

87. The first part of John Horne Tooke's famous philological treatise, *The Diversions of Purley*, was published in 1786. JB met him for the first time only weeks before this publication, at a dinner at Dilly's, and found him ironical, irreligious, and overbearing; he wrote in his journal, "I had not met with a man so very disagreeable for a long time" (*Great Biographer*, 29). JB abbreviates *Purley* (the name of the house in Huntingdonshire where the book was

A grand procession is to take place, in which Mr. JOHN KEMBLE [88] is to walk in the character of *Hamlet*, holding two miniature pictures, and repeating the well-known comparative passage,—

"This WAS your husband," &c.[89]

And Signor SASTRES,[90] the Italian master (to whom Dr. JOHNSON left 5*£*.) is to exhibit himself in the fantastical dress of *Il Mercurio Italico*,[91] for which Sir JOHN GALLINI has obligingly lent him his best pair of wings.[92]

By way of *ground*-work there is to be a solemn dirge:

"Down among the dead men let him lie."[93]

After which, all on a sudden, a brisk *fugue* is to be played, and

"Viva, viva, la Padrona,"[94]

---

written), to allude to either or both senses of *purl*: "Originally: an alcoholic drink made by infusing wormwood or other bitter herbs in ale or beer. Later also: hot beer mixed with gin, and sometimes also with ginger and sugar, often drunk early in the day"; or (a Scots and English northern regional expression), "A hard nodule of the dung of an animal, esp. a sheep" (*OED*).

88. John Kemble (1757–1823), great tragic actor, who debuted as a "gentlemanly" Hamlet, as Hazlitt described him, in 1783. The Piozzis knew him through his playing the male lead in Greatheed's play. He and JB became good friends.

89. From Hamlet's speech to Gertrude in her chamber, comparing his father to her new husband, Claudius (*Hamlet*, 3.4.64).

90. Francesco Sastres (fl. 1776–1822), Italian tutor and translator, friend of SJ; in his will (Dec. 9, 1784), SJ bequeathed to him "the sum of five pounds, to be laid out in books of piety for his own use" (*Life*, 4:402 n. 2). He gave JB some Johnsonian anecdotes and promised copies of eleven letters from SJ (*Corres. 2*, 107), which, on thinking JB not very interested, he instead delivered to HLP (ibid., 210). The only mention of him in the *Life* is rather dismissive (Apr. 5, 1776; *Life*, 3:22). He was another of the Piozzis' guests.

91. *Il Mercurio Italico: The Italian Mercury*: a monthly periodical concerning Italian arts and culture, of which thirteen numbers only were published in London, 1789–90, edited by Sastres. A costume for Mercury, the messenger of the gods, would usually involve a winged helmet or sandals.

92. Sir John Gallini (1728–1805), opera impresario; born in Florence, he was dancing at Covent Garden by 1757. In 1763, as a young dancing master, he married Lady Elizabeth Peregrine Bertie, daughter of the third earl of Abingdon.

93. A popular song by John Dyer, published c. 1726, set to a traditional English tune. Not a "solemn dirge," it toasts the Queen (Anne), peace, wealth, female beauty, love, and wine, and curses only him that "Won't with us comply / Down among the dead men let him lie."

94. Verses by Baretti, of which SJ's translation, beginning "Long may live my lovely Hetty" (referring to the Thrale's eldest daughter, Hester or "Queeney"), was first printed in the *Anecdotes*. See SJ, *Poems*, 174–75.

To be sung by a troop of jolly *brewers*, carefully instructed by Signor SASTRES, who declares that the performance, with their English lungs, will be *Lingua Toscana in bocca Romana.*[95]

BARETTI's ghost[96] next rises, and frowns upon the Signora; she, however, not abashed, vaults upon a *black ram*, reciting—

"And for my Crinkum Crankum," &c.[97]

Parson ESTE has,[98] in the politest manner, engaged to represent the *black ram.*

The principal air is to be—

95. *Lingua Toscana in bocca Romana*: lit. "The Tuscan language in a Roman mouth," an expression meaning, in effect, *the purest Italian with the finest accent.*

96. Baretti had died the previous year.

97. By the ancient custom of *free-bench*, on certain manorial estates, a widow had the right to the tenure of her late husband's lands, until she remarried. In *Spectator*, no. 614 (Nov. 1, 1714), it is related that in Berkshire, if a widow had forfeited her estate through "incontinency," she would be readmitted to her *free-bench* if she "will come into the court riding backward on a black ram, with his tail in her hand, and say the words following":

> Here I am,
> Riding upon a Black Ram,
> Like a Whore as I am.
> And for my *Crincum Crancum*
> Have lost my *Binkum Bankum.*
> And for my Tails Game,
> Have done this Worldly shame.
> Therefore I pray you Mr. Steward let me have my Land again.

The account is presumably taken from the article "free-bench," in Thomas Blount's *Nomo-Lexicon: A Law Dictionary* (1670), where it is described in almost exactly the same terms. Voltaire, who probably read this in the *Spectator*, quoted the verse to JB at their interview on Dec. 27, 1764 (*Grand Tour I*, 291). JB was apparently amused by this ceremony and prescribed a similar one to a legal colleague who had left the Northern Circuit in Mar. 1786. On July 10, 1788, he performed the ceremony himself in York, with Mr. S. Heywood standing in for the black ram (see *Experiment*, 232–33 and n. 4). In the seventeenth century, to have the *crinkums* was to have a venereal disease (*OED*). In his burlesque "A Letter from Lexiphanes" (1767), George Colman (1732–94) gives samples from a proposed supplement to SJ's *Dictionary*, including "*Crincum-crancum*,—Lines of Irregularity and Involution"; JB quotes this entry in the *Life* (4:388 n. 1; Nov.–Dec. 1784). See Colman's *Prose on Several Occasions* (1787), 2:93.

98. Charles Este (1753–1829), clergyman and writer, a friend and literary defender of HLP and editor of *The World*, in which the Piozzis' social gatherings were frequently reported.

"By the hollow *cask* we are told,
How nobly *Thrale's entire* has sold;"[99]

accompanied by a band of *barrel*-organs: after which will be sung the good old glee,

"He that has the best wife,
She's the plague of his life," &c.

With the Chorus of—

"And ten times a day hoop her *barrel.*"[100]

The butchers of the Borough have orders to attend with their marrow-bones and cleavers.[101]

But what has excited the most eager impatience in the ladies of Southwark is, a report that the Signora is to give after dinner, an *improvisation*, founded on the much famed line in her Prologue to the tragedy of *the Regent*,

"And drives his *battering ram* FULL at your heart."[102]

---

99. A parody of the song "By the Gaily Circling Glass," from John Dalton's adaptation of Milton's *Comus*, set to music by Arne, first performed in 1738 and notably in 1750, for which performance SJ wrote the prologue spoken by Garrick.

> By the gaily circling Glass
> We can see how Minutes pass;
> By the hollow cask are told
> How the waning Night grows old.

The song became very popular and was often regarded as an anonymous madrigal. For "Thrale's entire," see n. 60, above.

100. A song from Thomas Jevons's *The Devil of a Wife: or, A Comical Transformation* (1686), which is reprised a number of times.

> He that has the best Wife,
> She's the Burthen of his Life,
> But for her that will Scold and will Quarrel;
> Let him cut her short
> Of her Meat and her Sport,
> And ten times a day hoop her Barrel.

"Hoop her barrel," here and in other texts, refers to wife-beating, although *hoop* is also "allusive of copulation" (Williams, *Dictionary of Sexual Language and Imagery*, 1:677–78).

101. For "marrow-bones and cleavers," see Chap. 3, n. 52.

102. For the *Regent* and *battering ram*, see n. 69, above. (As noted, the line is in the epilogue, not the prologue.)

Mrs. Piozzi's Nerves Shaken by Prospect of Boswell's Book

"Star, 3 March 1790"

The *frayeur* of Madam PIOZZI for the appearance of Mr. BOSWELL's book, still continues, with unabated force.[103] She takes *sedative* and *anodyne* medicines, but with little effect.[104] Her nerves, shaken by a perturbed spirit, cannot be composed.

BOSWELL has even been tampered with to expunge every passage concerning her. His good nature we know is great, but we hope his integrity, his inflexible love of truth, and his veneration for the memory of a friend, by her made to stink in the public nose, will render him callous to every such application.

Boswell to Spare Mrs. Piozzi

The Diary; or, Woodfall's Register, September 21, 1790, 2

Mr. BOSWELL has erased from his intended biography of JOHNSON, whatever was calculated to wound the feelings of Mrs. PIOZZI, of whose character he had been induced to form such unfavourable ideas, as a short intercourse with that lady cannot fail to obliterate. There are indeed, few persons more aspersed with less reason than Mrs. Piozzi, whose talents, and moral qualities are conspicuous within her sphere of action.

Boswell Will Not Spare Mrs. Piozzi

"Morning Post, 1790"

BOSWELL has been assailed by much importunity, to expunge from his intended Life of JOHNSON, all that may be unfavourable to Mrs. PIOZZI; but BOSWELL's zeal for the honour of his departed friend, renders him on that point inflexible.

Boswell to Send News of Johnson's *Life* to the Press

St. James's Chronicle, October 16–19, 1790, 4

103. *Frayeur*: fear, dread. HLP noted in her journal (Apr. 20, 1791): "Mr. Boswell's Book is coming out, & the Wits expect me to tremble: what will the fellow say?—that has not already been said" (*Thraliana*, 2:807).

104. These two terms are almost synonymous, but *anodyne* suggests reducing or alleviating pain, and *sedative* making quiet or sleepy.

To the PRINTER *of the* St. J. CHRONICLE.

SIR,

A Considerable time ago I wrote you a letter, which appeared in your Paper, declaring that I would publish no paragraph whatever concerning my *Life of Dr. Johnson*, without putting my name to it.[105]

Since that time there have been such a number written by friends, foes, and correspondents of all descriptions (of none of which I know or even suspect who the authours are) that I find it hard to be precluded from availing myself of any fair opportunity to meet them in their own way. I therefore intimate that this restraint is to last no longer, and that I hold myself at full liberty to throw into the prints whatever fancy may prompt.

I am, Sir, your most humble servant,

London, Oct. 18.   JAMES BOSWELL.

1791

Advertisement for the *Life of Johnson*

London Chronicle, March 17–19, 1791, 268

Next Month will be published,
In Two Volumes large Quarto,
Price Two Guineas in boards,
(Dedicated to Sir JOSHUA REYNOLDS,)
THE LIFE of SAMUEL JOHNSON, LL.D.

Comprehending an Account of his Studies and numerous Works in Chronological Order; a Series of his Conversations and epistolary Correspondence with many eminent Persons; including his celebrated Letter to the Earl of CHESTERFIELD. Also various Pieces of his Composition, never before published. The Whole exhibiting a VIEW of LITERATURE and LITERARY MEN in Great Britain, for near half a Century, during which he flourished.

By JAMES BOSWELL, Esq.
London: Printed for Charles Dilly, in the Poultry.

105. See the first item in this chapter. As Werkmeister notes, the earlier letter seems not to have been published in the *Gazetteer* (*Jemmie Boswell*, 19 n. 40).

¶ The extraordinary Zeal which has been shown by distinguished Persons in all Parts of the Kingdom, in supplying additional Information, authentic Manuscripts, and singular Anecdotes of Dr. Johnson, has occasioned such an Enlargement of this Work, that it has been unavoidably delayed much longer than was intended.

Dr. Johnson's Monument

Public Advertiser, April 16, 1791, 1

To the Printer *of the* Public Advertiser.

SIR,

THE discussion which is to take place this day, Whether Dr. JOHNSON's Monument shall be in Westminster Abbey or St. Paul's, is expected to last long, and to produce a great deal of singular eloquence, many of the Subscribers having studied the question with much care, and prepared speeches for the occasion.

Let those speak now who never spoke before.[106]

When it is considered that among the subscribers there are such Parliamentary orators as Messrs. Fox, Sheridan, Windham, Courtenay, Sir William, and Sir John Scott,[107] that there are Barristers and Clergymen of eminence, not to mention members of various other societies where public speaking is required, there can be no doubt of an extraordinary display. But, Mr. Woodfall, I am a plain man, and love plain dealing. I am myself a subscriber, and I did expect that I should long ere now have seen the Monument to THE FIRST LITERARY CHARACTER OF HIS AGE erected in that Temple of Fame which has long been appropriated to the illustrious dead. But, Sir, (without meaning to charge it home *directly*) if the Committee *who have my money, and that of many others for*

---

106. The fourth-century Latin poem *Pervigilium Veneris* ("The Vigil of Venus") includes the repeated line "*Cras amet qui nunquam amavit; quique amavit cras amet*" ("Let him love tomorrow who has never loved, and let him who has loved love tomorrow"). This line is quoted for rhetorical effect and allusively translated, "Let those speak now, who never spoke before; / Let those who spoke before, now speak the more," by John Dalrymple, fifth earl of Stair, *Argument to Prove*, 36.

107. Charles James Fox, see Chap. 3, n. 298; Richard Brinsley Sheridan, see n. 82, above; William Windham (1750–1810), whig politician; John Courtenay, see n. 21, above; Sir William Scott (1745–1836), judge and politician, later first Baron Stowell; and (his brother) Sir John Scott (1751–1838), lawyer and politician, later (as Lord Eldon) Lord Chancellor. All these, except Sir John Scott, were members of the Literary Club.

an express purpose, are to jump from church to church, we ourselves may want the generous tear before any thing is done, and the *money* may be—we know not where.

Yours,

A CAUTIOUS MAN.

Johnson's Monument Like Mahomet's Coffin

Public Advertiser, April 16, 1791, 3[108]

It was well observed that JOHNSON'S MONUMENT being kept in a wavering state between Westminster Abbey and St. Paul's, resembles Mahomet's coffin suspended between two loadstones.[109]

Advertisement for Valuable Extracts from the *Life of Johnson*: The *Conversation* and *Letter*

[Boswell correctly anticipated that two passages from the *Life* on subjects of public curiosity would be of particular interest to reviewers, and in order to protect his copyright he had them published separately as quarto pamphlets. They were printed in April 1790, when the relevant sheets of the *Life* were passing through the press, and were dated 1790, but they were not entered at Stationers' Hall until April 27, 1791. However, as Pottle says, Boswell's "intention was clearly to have the extracts technically on sale, but not to sell any copies" (*Lit. Car.*, 138). There is no evidence that copies were ever in circulation. In accordance with this aim, the following advertisement, for which Pottle had (in 1929) "sought in vain," seems only to have been published this once.]

Public Advertiser, April 30, 1791, 1

108. This paragraph in the *Pub. Adv.* is preceded directly by another paragraph by JB (*NCBEL*, 1227) speculating on the authorship of his anonymous poem *No Abolition of Slavery* (1791), and is followed directly by other paragraphs of plausibly Boswellian authorship, on monuments in St. Paul's and a Temple of Fame for British worthies and asking if there should not be officially appointed reporters of law cases and of speeches in the House of Commons.

109. A medieval legend in Europe said that the body of Muhammad, the prophet of Islam, was put in an iron coffin, which, in his tomb in Medina, hung suspended in the air between two magnets or lodestones. See the correspondence on this topic in *Notes and Queries* (1889), 274–75.

On Thursday the 12th of May will be published,
(Price Half-a Guinea each)[110]
Illustrated with Observations and Notes, by JAMES BOSWELL, Esq.

A CONVERSATION between His Most Sacred Majesty GEORGE the THIRD, and SAMUEL JOHNSON, L. L. D.; and, the celebrated LETTER from SAMUEL JOHNSON, L. L. D. to PHILIP DORMER STANHOPE, Earl of Chesterfield.[111] Printed for Charles Dilly in the Poultry.

✻ The above two valuable Articles are separately entered in Stationer's Hall,[112] but they will also be completely included in Mr. BOSWELL's LIFE of Dr. JOHNSON; which is to be published by Mr. Dilly on Monday the Sixteenth of May.

Johnson and Burke

[We have already noted the complexity of Boswell's feelings for and relationship with Edmund Burke. Although Boswell was too conscientious a reporter to gloss over Johnson's admiration for Burke—in the *Tour* and the *Life* Johnson is three times quoted as insisting that Burke is "an extraordinary man" (on Aug. 15, 1773; Mar. 20, 1776; and May 15, 1784; see *Life*, 5:34, 2:450, and 4:275–76)—it is interesting to notice Boswell's unwillingness to allow him a reputation as "a wit and an author"; this reluctance seems to have been exacerbated by the success of Burke's *Reflections on the Revolution in France*, published late the previous year. For further indications of Boswell's ambivalence toward Burke, see "Dilly and Dodsley" and "Sales of the *Life*," below.]

Public Advertiser, May 14, 1791, 3

JOHNSON and BURKE[113]

110. That is, 10s. 6d.; this price—25 percent of the cost of the entire book—was clearly calculated to discourage sales.

111. For the letter to Chesterfield, see n. 73, above. The account of SJ's conversation with King George III in Feb. 1767 was another passage in the *Life* over which JB had taken considerable trouble (see his note to the passage, *Life*, 2:34 n. 1).

112. The Stationers' Company was the guild of printers and booksellers; at Stationers' Hall in Ave Maria Lane, near Ludgate Hill, the company maintained a register by which members could assert their ownership of a text and prevent its publication by other company members. This protection applied only to complete texts, not extracts, so to claim ownership of these passages from the *Life*, JB had to have them separately printed and registered.

113. JB included this piece in the *Life*, in a footnote to SJ's reported remark about Burke (Apr. 17, 1778), and prefaced it as follows: "I attempted in a newspaper to comment on the above passage, in the manner of Warburton, who must be allowed to have shewn uncom-

No saying of Dr. JOHNSON's has been more misunderstood than, his applying to Mr. BURKE, when he first saw him at his fine place at Beaconsfield—
Non equidem invideo; miror magis.[114] These two celebrated men had been friends
for many years before Mr. Burke entered on his parliamentary career.—They
were both writers; both Members of THE LITERARY CLUB.[115]—When, therefore,
Dr. Johnson, saw Mr. Burke in a situation so much more splendid than that to
which he himself had attained, he did not mean to express that he thought it a
disproportionate prosperity; but, while he, as a philosopher, asserted an exemp-
tion from envy, *Non equidem invideo,* he went on in the words of the Poet, *miror
magis*; thereby signifying, either that he was occupied in admiring what he was
glad to see; or, perhaps, that considering the general lot of men of superior
abilities, he wondered that Fortune, who is represented as blind, should, in this
instance, have been so just.

Warren Hastings

[Boswell's *Life of Samuel Johnson, LL.D.* was published this day, in two volumes
quarto, in an edition of 1,750 copies. The following is the first of many extracts from
the book that appeared in the press, not all of them sent by Boswell.]

Public Advertiser, May 16, 1791, 3

WARREN HASTINGS

It is remarkable that the grand and ultimate consideration of the conduct of the
GOVERNOR GENERAL of INDIA,[116] comes before the Lords, on the very day on
which Mr. BOSWELL's Life of Dr. JOHNSON appears, in which is the following
passage—

---

mon ingenuity, in giving to any authour's text whatever meaning he chose it should carry.
As this imitation may amuse my readers, I shall here introduce it" (*Life,* 3:310 n. 4).

114. "In truth, I feel no envy; I am greatly surprised" (Virgil, *Eclogues,* 1.2).

115. The Club, or Literary Club, was a society of SJ and friends, founded by Reynolds in
Feb. 1764 for supper and conversation. Burke was a founding member.

116. Warren Hastings (1732–1818), governor-general of Bengal, 1773–85, whose trial before Parliament on charges of corruption commenced in 1788 and ended with his acquittal
in 1795. The passage that follows is an extract from the *Life,* 4:66 (1781). SJ was acquainted
with Hastings from, perhaps, 1766, and the two corresponded. JB met Hastings at a dinner at Reynolds's, on Mar. 19, 1787, and, with his customary desire for close acquaintance
with remarkable men, called on him the following day (*Experiment,* 122–23), and the two
remained on social terms. JB's sympathy for Hastings contributed to his estrangement from
Burke, who was one of the leaders of the case against Hastings.

"While my friend is thus contemplated in the splendour derived from his last, and, perhaps, most admirable work,[117] I introduce him with peculiar propriety as the correspondent of Warren Hastings, a man whose regard reflects dignity even upon Johnson; a man, the extent of whose abilities, was equal to that of his power; and who, by those who are fortunate enough to know him in private life, is admired for his literature and taste, and beloved for that candour, moderation, and mildness of his character. Were I capable of paying a suitable tribute of admiration to him, I should certainly not withhold it at a moment, when it is not possible that I should be suspected of being an interested flatterer. But how weak would be my voice, after that of the millions whom he governed."

The *Life of Johnson* a Union of Matter and Spirit

Public Advertiser, May 16, 1791, 3

Notwithstanding the numberless retailers of Johnsonianæ, we still find that Mr. Boswell has *amassed* sufficient for two quartos; in which, from what little we have yet seen of them, he seems to have baffled the arch-heretic and his late friend completely,[118] by an unexpected *union* of *matter* and *spirit*.[119]

The Engraved Portrait of Dr. Johnson

Public Advertiser, May 17, 1791, 4

THE ARTS.

THE engraved portrait of DR. JOHNSON, prefixed to Mr. BOSWELL's life of that celebrated man, we must say, in justice to Mr. HEATH, is one of the most capital

117. In the *Life*, this passage follows JB's account of SJ's *Lives of the Poets*.

118. *Arch-heretic* refers to Joseph Priestley, who was prominent at this time for his support of the revolution in France and was singled out for criticism by Burke in his recently published *Reflections on the Revolution in France* (1791); "his [JB's] late friend," to philosopher David Hume (1711–76), a noted skeptic and materialist. JB met Hume in Edinburgh in 1758 and interviewed him on his deathbed (*Extremes*, 11–15).

119. In his *Disquisitions Relating to Matter and Spirit* (1777), Priestley attempted to combine materialism with metaphysics. He argued that the soul had no material existence and that, being made of "divine substance," it was inaccessible to human knowledge.

Figure 14. "Samuel Johnson: From the original portrait in the possession of James Boswell Esq.," frontispiece to the first edition of the Life *of Johnson (1791), engraved by James Heath, from a portrait by Sir Joshua Reynolds. Courtesy of the Heritage Collections, Dunedin Public Libraries, New Zealand.*

performances that has appeared for some time.[120] The picture from which it was taken, was painted by Sir JOSHUA REYNOLDS, in 1756, when Dr. Johnson was in his 45th year; and is, therefore, of a younger cast than any of those which the public has heretofore seen. It is a large half length.—The Sage is sitting in his study, the furniture of which, is depicted with all the niceness of *costumé*, for a

120. Reynolds's first portrait of SJ (c. 1756) was specially engraved by James Heath (1757–1834), under Reynolds's and JB's close supervision, to be the frontispiece of the *Life* (see *Life*, 1:392 and 4: App. H, "The Portraits of Johnson," 463; also Kai Kin Yung, *Samuel Johnson*, 79–83). See Figure 14.

retired author:[121]—His chair, is the old-fashioned broad shape, covered with blue and white check; his table is a small one, of plain deal board.—His DICTIONARY of the ENGLISH LANGUAGE, which he had then not finished, and by which, himself, and his native tongue, will both be rendered immortal, stands upon a shelf by him. He is in profound meditation,[122] holds a pen in his hand, as if about to dip it in his inkhorn, and resume his admirable labours.

Literary Property

Public Advertiser, May 17, 1791, 4

LITERARY PROPERTY.[123]

Mr. Boswell has attempted a new and ingenious limitation of literary property,[124] by entering *separately* in Stationers Hall, two valuable articles in his life of Dr. Johnson, viz. the Conversation with the King, and the Letter to Lord Chesterfield; both of which were advertised some time ago, price half a guinea each.—And then having thus *secured* them, as he would maintain, has introduced them into his great work. How far this will be *effectual*, must be left to the *glorious uncertainty of the Law*.[125]

---

121. *Costumé*: (in historical art) the custom and fashion of the time to which a scene or representation belongs; the manner, dress, arms, furniture, and other features proper to the time and locality in which the scene is laid (*OED*).

122. In the *Life*, 1:392, in the passage describing his first meeting with SJ on May 16, 1763, JB says, "I found that I had a very perfect idea of Johnson's figure, from the portrait of him painted by Sir Joshua Reynolds soon after he had published his Dictionary, in the attitude of sitting in his easy chair in deep meditation."

123. This item is attributed to JB by Colin Horne and accepted by Pottle. Horne argues that it shows JB to have been genuine in his desire "to protect his literary property in the *Letter* and the *Conversation*," rather than to be pursuing "a cunning scheme to score off the newspapers" ("Boswell, Burke, and the 'Life of Johnson,'" 297). I do not see that the aims are mutually exclusive.

124. Early in his legal career, JB was involved in the trials of publisher Alexander Donaldson over literary property. He acted as counsel for Donaldson in *Hinton v. Donaldson* in July 1773 and in Feb. 1774, when Donaldson took the case *Donaldson v. Becket* to the House of Lords. He also published about the case; see *Later Years*, 87–88. Donaldson won both cases, which still form the basis of the law of copyright.

125. "Soon after the first Lord Mansfield was appointed Chief Justice, which was in 1756, he overruled some long established legal decisions, and introduced several innovations in the practice of his court. At that period 'the glorious memory of King William' was a standing toast; and at a dinner of the Judges and Counsel at Serjeants' Inn Hall, after the

Boswell Has Rescued Johnson from Hawkins and Thrale

St. James's Chronicle, May 14–17, 1791, 4

BOSWELL has rescued Dr. JOHNSON's memory from many imputations thrown upon it by the inaccuracy and inattention of Sir JOHN HAWKINS and Mrs. THRALE. A more minute *painting* of a great character we have seldom seen.[126] The illiberal part of the Scotch, however, have still enough to growl at.[127]

Insolvent Debtors

Public Advertiser, May 19, 1791, 3

INSOLVENT DEBTORS.

Mr. Grey's laudable motion upon this subject[128] must be greatly strengthened by the authority of Dr. JOHNSON, who has not only written an *Idler* in their favour;[129] but in a letter, for which we are obliged to Mr. BOSWELL, in his LIFE, thus expresses himself to a friend who was in straightened circumstances: "Neither the great nor little debts disgrace you. I am sure you have my esteem for the courage with which you contracted them, and the spirit with which you endure them!"[130]

---

toast of the 'glorious memory,' Mr. Wilbraham, a very eminent counsel of that day, gave 'the glorious uncertainty of the law,' which was levelled at Lord Mansfield's judgments, and created much merriment"; *Gent. Mag.*, 100 (Aug. 1830), 98.

126. In his journal for Mar. 27, 1775, JB says of his methods, "I draw him in the style of a Flemish painter. I am not satisfied with hitting the large features. I must be exact as to every hair, or even every spot on his countenance" (*Ominous Years*, 103). In the *Life*, he writes of "the Flemish picture which I give of my friend, and in which, therefore, I mark the most minute particulars" (Sept. 22, 1777; *Life*, 3:191).

127. On Dec. 18, 1785, JB described himself in a letter as "having had candour enough to speak without prejudice of Scotland in his *Tour* with Dr. Johnson has given very general offence to an irritable people" (*Experiment*, 290). In fact, the Scots who reviewed or spoke to JB about the book were in general (excluding Lord Macdonald; see nn. 11–13 and text, above) no more unfavorable to it than the English. He presumably thought it worthwhile to cultivate among the English an image of himself as a Scot who could critique his own national character.

128. In May 1791, Charles Grey (1764–1845), opposition MP, later the second Earl Grey and prime minister 1830–34, instigated the establishment of a parliamentary committee to inquire into the practice of imprisonment for debt.

129. In fact, SJ wrote two *Idler* essays, nos. 22 (Sept. 16, 1758) and 38 (Jan. 6, 1759), against the practice of imprisoning debtors; see *Idler and Adventurer*, 2:69–71, 117–21).

130. See SJ's letter of c. 1759 to his friend, barrister Joseph Simpson (1721–68), given by JB (*Life*, 1:346–47).

Living Twice, through Boswell's Pages

Public Advertiser, May 20, 1791, 3

EARL *of* ABERCORN

The late Earl of Abercorn was remarkable for strong laconick sayings.[131] Talking of the advantage of *experience*, his Lordship observed, *"We should live twice—but we don't."* Mr. BOSWELL, however, would persuade us that he is able to make Dr. JOHNSON live over again, and gravely tells his readers, that by perusing his quarto volumes, they may *"live with him."*[132]

Portable Soup

Public Advertiser, May 21, 1791, 3

PORTABLE SOUP[133]

There are many competitors for this valuable article. ARCHIBALD DUKE OF ARGYLL, a wise and sagacious Statesman, who governed SCOTLAND,[134] all his life, never travelled without it; for, upon coming into the worst inn upon earth, if there were but *fire* and *water* he had immediately a good and comfortable dish. *Doctors differ* which sort is best; whether of *beef, mutton, veal,* or *chicken.* But what shall we say to *Portable Soup* of the LION?

131. James Hamilton, eighth earl of Abercorn (see Chap. 1, n. 104), was referred to by Horace Walpole as "his taciturnity, the Earl" (*ODNB*).

132. In the *Life*, JB says that by means of his biographical method, "mankind are enabled as it were to see him live, and to 'live o'er each scene' with him" (1:30, quoting Pope's prologue to Addison's *Cato*).

133. Dating from 1758, the term "portable soup" was applied to "liquid substances congealed ... so as to be more conveniently carried or transported" (*OED*); what would now be called stock cubes or stock powder. In "Hypochondriack," no. 66 (Mar. 1783), JB wrote of keeping a daily journal, "I have thought my notes like *portable soup*, of which a little bit by being dissolved in water will make a good large dish; for their substance by being expanded in words would fill a volume" (Bailey, 2:259). JB used the same image in the ms. of the *Tour*; see *Hebrides*, 165.

134. Archibald Campbell, third duke of Argyll (1682–1761), was Lord Chief Justice and Lord Keeper of the Privy Seal of Scotland. After a short military career, he embarked on a life of politics. In 1760, when JB was taken by his father to visit him, Argyll was "unofficial governor of Scotland" and "the most impressive Scotsman then living" (*Earlier Years*, 51). In a *Letter to the People of Scotland* (1785), JB recalled the deference with which Argyll was treated, writing, "I remember *Archibald* duke of *Argyll . . . bowed to*" (9). On their Scottish tour, JB and SJ visited his castle at Inveraray and were entertained by the fifth duke of Argyll (Oct. 25, 1773; *Life*, 5:355–59).

The Poet farcically says of Achilles going to war,[135]

> "He din'd on Lion's marrow spread
> On toasts of ammunition bread."[136]

How must the BRITISH NATION now be *invigorated*, when BOSWELL feeds them with the *portable soup?*—The LION's *marrow* of a JOHNSON!

Apology of *London Packet* for Infringing Boswell's Copyright

[Boswell's intention in separately publishing the *Conversation* and the *Letter*, and in doing so unobtrusively, seems to have been to establish copyright over the passages (*Lit. Car.*, 141; *Corres.* 2, 311 n. 4), so that if and when any newspapers were lured into printing them as choice extracts from the *Life*, when published, he would be in a position to force them to print this public apology. It seems likely that Boswell wrote both the apology and the framing remarks with which it was reprinted in the *St. James's Chronicle*.]

St. James's Chronicle, May 19–21, 1791, 4

LITERARY PROPERTY.

PRIOR well observes that there should be in *the better sort* something

> "Beyond the fix'd and settled rules
> Of vice and virtue in the schools."[137]

There is no doubt much equity in maintaining *Literary Property*. But it should not be too *strictly* enforced, especially so as to *catch* any man, and *hold* him *hard*.

The Rev. Mr. William Mason prosecuted Mr. Murray, the Bookseller, for having inserted a single poem of Gray's, in his collection of that authour's works, beyond what he had a *right* to take; and refused offers of accommodation.[138]

---

135. Matthew Prior (1664–1721), "Alma; or, The Progress of the Mind" (1718), canto 3, lines 214–15.

136. *Ammunition bread*: bread supplied as rations to soldiers.

137. The opening lines of Matthew Prior's poem "Paulo Purganti and His Wife: An Honest, but a Simple Pair," which continues, "Beyond the letter of the law / Which keeps our men and maids in awe, / The better sort should keep before 'em / A grace, a manner, a decorum." These lines were well known in the eighteenth century; they were quoted by Henry Fielding in *The History of Tom Jones: A Foundling* (1749), book 15, chap. 10.

138. In 1775, poet William Mason (1725–97) published *The Poems of Mr. Gray, to which are Prefixed Memoirs of his Life and Writings*. This important work consolidated Thomas Gray's reputation, and the *Memoirs* provided something of a model of the "life and letters" style

Mr. Boswell's conduct is very different, as appears from the following article in *The London Packet*:

"Mr. BOSWELL.

From our desire to furnish interesting entertainment to our readers, we inserted Dr. Johnson's Conversation with his Majesty, and his celebrated Letter to the Earl of Chesterfield,[139] which we extracted from Mr. Boswell's Life of Dr. Johnson. We had not the smallest apprehension that we were invading Literary Property, which we hold sacred. But it seems those two articles were entered in Stationer's-Hall, as *separate publications*, which were advertised in some of the news-papers, but the advertisements escaped us.[140]—We cannot but be sorry for the mistake; but Mr. Boswell is too candid to take any advantage, and upon our assuring him of the fact, he declared he will not prosecute."

This is a fair specimen of confidence, and that liberality which shou'd subsist between the different votaries of Literature.

Dilly and Dodsley

Public Advertiser, May 26, 1791, 2

DILLY AND DODSLEY[141]

---

of biography, which JB adopted for the *Life of Johnson* (see *Life*, 1:29). In 1777, Mason prosecuted Edinburgh publisher John Murray for reprinting a passage of Gray's verse from the *Memoirs* without permission, and refused Murray's offer to settle out of court. The success of Mason's case was important in developing the law of copyright.

139. These extracts were the passages separately published as *The Celebrated Letter from Samuel Johnson, LL.D. to Philip Dormer Stanhope, Earl of Chesterfield* and *A Conversation between His Most Sacred Majesty George III and Samuel Johnson, LL.D.*; see n. 73, above.

140. On Apr. 14, 1791, Malone wrote to JB, "I have not seen the Letter to Lord Chesterfield advertised. I suppose you will publish it a day or two only before the *opus magnum*" (*Corres.* 2, 310). When Malone wrote this, JB was yet to publish the advertisement (above), which indeed announced that the extracts would be published only four days before the *Life of Johnson* itself, on May 16, 1791.

141. JB's publisher, Charles Dilly, and rival bookseller James Dodsley (1724–97). Dodsley was the younger brother of Robert Dodsley (1704–64), London's preeminent publishing bookseller, and inherited his valuable copyrights on many important works, such as early works of SJ and the last works of Swift, Gray's *Elegy*, the essay periodical *The World*, SJ's *Dictionary* and *Rasselas*, and the newspaper the *Lond. Chron.*, to which JB was a frequent contributor. The Dodsleys published Burke's *Annual Register* (from 1759) and his *Philosophical Enquiry into the Origin of our Ideas of the Sublime and Beautiful* (1757).

DILLY.

TELL me no more, Pall-mall old boy,[142]
Of BURKE, your florid writer—[143]
Than this declaming [*sic*] *Irish* shoy,[144]
BOSWELL, my *Scot*, moves lighter.

DODSLEY.

You paltry wag[145]—who minds a work,
Fill'd with JOHNSONIAN jargon?
Keep you your BOSWELL —I'll have BURKE;
Which has the better bargain?

Boswell Dining (Out) on Johnson

Public Advertiser, May 27, 1791, 2[146]

BOSWELL has so many invitations in consequence of his LIFE of JOHNSON,[147] that he may be *literally* said to *live* upon his deceased friend.

142. Dodsley's premises were in Pall Mall, London.

143. Burke's *Reflections on the Revolution in France*, the literary and political sensation of the moment, had been published by Dodsley on Nov. 1, 1790. It was "by far his [Dodsley's] most profitable publication," passing through "seven editions and 18,000 copies in 1790 alone" (*ODNB*, s.v. "Dodsley, James"). *Florid*: addicted to the use of flowery language or rhetorical ornament (*OED*).

144. In a jocular letter to JB, of Feb. 21, 1763 (*Lond. Journ.*, 198), William Cochrane uses "Shoy" as the spelling for a term JB had used in his journal some weeks earlier ("an Irish old maid ... was indeed a terrible Joy"), which Pottle (quoting Joseph Wright's *English Dialect Dictionary*) says was so commonly used as a term of friendly address among the Irish lower classes that "the words 'dear joy' are often used by way of derision to signify an Irishman" (*Lond. Journ.*, 137 and n. 8).

145. The following day in the *Pub. Adv.*, an anonymous letter was signed as by the author of these verses; a starred copy is in JB's files, *Cat. Yale*, P 100(23). JB informs readers that the poem was intended as "an imitation of Congreve's 'Tell me no more I am deceiv'd,'" a satirical song that Congreve supplied for a play in 1693 and is believed to have been his first publication. He claimed that "paltry" should read *Poultry*, alluding to Dilly's address "in the Poultry." The purported misprint may have been deliberate, in order to prolong the coverage. See Horne, "Boswell, Burke, and the 'Life of Johnson,'" 498–99.

146. In the *Pub. Adv.*, this paragraph is immediately preceded by a paragraph comparing the *Life of Johnson* to the stone monument to SJ and which quotes the epigraph to the *Life* from Horace, and it is followed by a compliment to the Pretender from the late king of Prussia.

147. JB's surviving journals do not cover the period from Apr. 11, 1791, to Aug. 16, 1792. However, as the journal editors note, "the publication of his *magnum opus* gratifyingly increased Boswell's social prominence" (*Great Biographer*, 148).

Sales of the *Life*

St. James's Chronicle, May 26–28, 1791, 4[148]

BURKE *and* BOSWELL.

A prodigious rout was made about the sale of BURKE's "Reflections on the *French Revolution.*" So much for *Politicks* and *France.* But for the honour of *Literature* and *our own nation*, it may gratify our Readers to mention that in the very first week of the publication of BOSWELL's *LIFE of JOHNSON*, no less than *Six Hundred* Copies of that work were sold. Now, as Dr. PRICE might have said, when we consider that *one hundred* of BOSWELL's book, at *Two Guineas*, amounts to *eight hundred and forty* of BURKE's book, at a *Crown*, we shall find that the sale of the former in that space, has been equal to the number of *five thousand and forty* of the latter; and it is also fair to take into the calculation that in the proportion of purchasers, there is a greater probability of eight buying a Crown book, than one buying a Two Guinea book.[149]

"Friendly Patronage," and Two Other Paragraphs

Public Advertiser, June 18, 1791, 3

FRIENDLY PATRONAGE.

Sir JOSHUA REYNOLDS, with a munificence truly princely, has not only presented Mr. BOSWELL with the large portrait of Dr. JOHNSON, from which the capital engraving by HEATH, prefixed to THE LIFE, is taken,[150] but also with his friend's own portrait, which appeared in the exhibition of the Royal Academy in 1786:[151] it is allowed to be one of Sir Joshua's very best pictures, both for like-

---

148. In the *St. James's Chron.*, this item was printed immediately following another contribution from JB, headed "Dr. Johnson and Mr. Burke" (*NCBEL*, *1232; *Cat. Yale*, P 100(26)), mainly an extract from the *Life* concerning Burke's wit.

149. Two guineas is 42 shillings; a crown, 5 shillings. In addition to his philosophical works, Dr. Richard Price (see Chap. 3, n. 431) wrote influential studies in probability, statistics, finance, and population.

150. Reynolds gave the portrait of SJ to JB (*Life*, 1:392) "sometime during the year 1789" (according to Yung, *Samuel Johnson*, 80). For the engraving of Reynolds's portrait of SJ, see n. 120, above.

151. Reynolds's portrait of JB was painted July 5–Sept. 10, 1785 (*Applause*, 317, 340). Reynolds's usual fee of 100 guineas was reduced for JB to £50 (ibid., 308 n. 5), and the debt forgiven completely when the *Life of Johnson*—dedicated to Reynolds and with his portrait of SJ as its frontispiece—was published, as described here. The portrait of JB now hangs in the National Portrait Gallery, London (ibid.).

ness, character, and colouring. The Mezzotinto from it, by Jones, is admirably executed.[152] We have only to regret that it is of too extensive a size to be bound up with Boswell's Life of Johnson, as it would be agreeable to have the images not only of the illustrious Sage, but of his Biographer, before us, while we read a work in which *both* their minds are depicted in a vivid style. If Mr. Jones would contract his plate, or would let us have another of less dimensions, he would gratify us much.

*   *   *

Boswell, when he speaks of his Life of Johnson, calls it my *Magnum Opus*;[153] but it may more properly be called his *Opera*, for it is truly a composition founded on a true story, in which there is a *Hero* with a number of *subordinate characters*, and an alternate succession of *recitative* and *airs* of various tone and effect, all however in delightful animation.

The European Magazine has given *Memoirs of Boswell*.[154] When one of the Proprietors asked him, Pray, Sir, will you give us leave to put your *Life* into our Magazine? he pleasantly answered, Why, Sir, you may put in a *part* of my Life, but I trust the *whole* of it shall be in no Magazine for these many many years.

Mrs. Piozzi to Reply to Charge of Carelessness

Public Advertiser, June 27, 1791, 3

Mrs. Piozzi is said to be preparing a reply to Mr. Boswell's charge of *carelessness in relating matters of fact*[155]—Mr. Boswell affirms, that he once *caught her*

---

152. The engraving by John Jones (1745–97) of the JB portrait was published Jan. 17, 1786 (*Experiment*, 97 n. 7). A mezzotint is a print made from a plate engraved by scraping, to achieve an effect of light and shade.

153. True; JB had been calling the *Life of Johnson* his magnum opus at least since Nov. 17, 1788; thirteen uses of the expression, quoted from his letters, appear in the "Chronology" in *Corres. 2*, lix ff.

154. The *European Magazine* was founded in 1782 by a consortium of London booksellers. Its proprietor and de facto editor was Isaac Reed (1742–1807; *ODNB*). The two-part "Memoirs of James Boswell, Esq.," published anonymously in the issues of May and June 1791, was by JB himself. The text is reprinted by Pottle in *Lit. Car.*

155. Throughout the *Life*, JB remarks on "the extreme inaccuracy with which all her anecdotes of Dr. Johnson are related" (1:416 n. 2; 1763). He records SJ rebuking HLP for "little variations in narrative" (her expression) and saying, "It is more from carelessness about truth than from intentional lying, that there is so much falsehood in the world" (*Life*, 3:228–29; Mar. 31, 1778).

with the manner[156]—in calling an *old man an old woman.*[157] A smart publication from the Lady will be an excellent advertisement for the *Life of Johnson.*

1792

Shakespeare's Mulberry Tree: Johnson's Animadversions on Rev. and Mrs. Gastrell Defended

Gentleman's Magazine, 62 (January 1792), 18

Jan. 16.

Mr. URBAN,[158]

In your Obituary for December, when you mention the death of Mrs. Gastrell,[159] you quote from my Life of Dr. Johnson an animadversion upon her husband, the Rev. Mr. Gastrell, for having cut down Shakspeare's mulberry-tree, and upon her for having participated in that offence against the reverence due to Genius;[160] and you add, "neither Mrs. G. nor her husband, we are well assured, deserved this severity of Mr. Boswell, though we are not in possession of the controverting proofs."

I think it necessary, for the sake of truth, and the authenticity of my book, to observe, in answer to your remark (and, at the same time, to a letter signed TREVOR JONES, with which I have been favoured on the subject),[161] that I have

---

156. To be *caught with the manner* (properly, *mainour*) is to be caught in the act of doing something unlawful, "in flagrante delicto" (*OED*).

157. For this story, see *Life*, 3:226 (Mar. 30, 1778).

158. The *Gent. Mag.* was edited or conducted by Edward Cave (1691–1754) and subsequent editors under the name "Sylvanus Urban," meaning "country and city." At this time, the editor was printer and antiquary John Nichols (1745–1826).

159. The death of Jane (Aston) Gastrell (1710–91) on Oct. 30 was reported in *Gent. Mag.*, 70 (Dec. 1791), 1159.

160. The *Gent. Mag.* report was accompanied by three sentences from the *Life* (2:469–70; Mar. 25, 1776) in which Rev. Francis Gastrell (c. 1707–72) is described by SJ as having cut down Shakespeare's mulberry tree to "vex his neighbours" (in JB's journal he records SJ saying, "to vex his parishioners, who had differed with him," *Ominous Years*, 297).

161. In a letter to JB of Aug. 29, 1791, Trevor Jones (1753–1832), M.D., of Lichfield tells of having been informed by a respectable gentleman and friend of Mr. Gastrell that the tree "was in a decaying state and that he was apprehensive that it would damage an adjoining wall." He describes SJ's reported remark as an "illhumoured sally" and suggests that SJ may have said this "without meaning any thing as he often did give short answers to get rid of a subject" (*Corres.* 2, 343).

quoted Dr. Johnson as my informer concerning Mr. Gastrell; and that whoever wishes to see a full account of his Gothic barbarity will find it in the first volume of Mr. Malone's admirable edition of Shakspeare, p. 118, related from the very best authority.[162] Mrs. Gastrell's accession was also told me by Dr. Johnson, though I did not mention his name while she was alive, as it might have given uneasiness to the old lady, to know that one whom she so highly respected had in any degree censured her.[163]

Yours, &c.   JAMES BOSWELL.

1793

Boswell Recovers from Street Assault

[On the evening of Wednesday, June 5, Boswell was coming home—the worse for drink—when he was knocked down, robbed, and left lying stunned in the street. Although the robbery was trifling, he was cut and bruised and two weeks later was still unable to write (*Great Biographer*, 221).]

St. James's Chronicle, July 4–6, 1793, 4

LITERARY INTELLIGENCE.

The wounds which *Mr. Boswell* received from a ruffian in the street, in consequence of which he was in a state of considerable pain and fever for some time, have doubtless been the occasion of retarding his octavo edition of Dr. JOHN-son's LIFE.[164] But, as we understand he is now quite recovered, we may hope to have our expectations gratified very soon.[165]

---

162. Edmond Malone, ed., *The Plays and Poems of William Shakspeare* (London, 1790), 1:118. Malone describes Gastrell as having cut down the tree to save himself the nuisance of showing it to tourists. Edmond Malone (1741–1812), literary scholar and Shakespearean editor, friend of SJ and JB, has already been mentioned for his collaboration on the *Tour*, which JB dedicated to him. He was one of the executors of JB's will.

163. Jane Gastrell was one of the eight daughters of Sir Thomas Aston, a number of whom SJ was, from his youth in Lichfield, on terms of warm friendship with (*Life*, 1:82; 1732); SJ would call on her when visiting Lichfield. JB also visited Mrs. Gastrell in 1776 and 1779; see *Ominous Years*, 297, and *Life*, 3:412 (Oct. 22, 1779).

164. JB's misfortune was reported in the papers; see *Lond. Chron.*, June 8–11, 1793.

165. The second edition of the *Life of Johnson* was published July 17.

PAPER-WAR WITH MISS ANNA SEWARD

[The following two substantial texts, an epilogue to our gathering of Boswell's journalistic publications concerning his books about Johnson, need to be understood in the context of the "paper war" about Johnson and Boswell's two Johnsonian books between Boswell and Lichfield poet Anna Seward (1747–1809), conducted over a number of years in the pages of the *Gentleman's Magazine*. Readers may find the controversy more usefully framed by some appreciation of the relationship between the two protagonists, as represented in letters and such accounts as there are of their previous meetings and dealings. In the first "Advertisement for the *Life*" (Dec. 1785; see above), Boswell publically thanked Anna Seward for her contributions to his book. By the time of the article to which he is responding below, he had quite fallen out with her, and, while her severe opinion of Johnson is their ostensible subject of difference, their relationship must inevitably have been complicated by Boswell's concerted attempts of a decade earlier to seduce her.

Boswell first met Anna Seward in Johnson's company, at her father's home in Lichfield in March 1776; in his journal, he notes thinking her pretty (*Ominous Years*, 294). Two years later, on April 15, 1778, they were together at a dinner in London, at which Johnson delivered what Boswell called (in a letter to Seward, before their falling out) "his tremendous Commination" concerning Jenny Harry, who had become a Quaker (*Corres. 2*, 47), an outburst that became a central topic in the later dispute over the representation of Johnson's character. Six years later, Boswell called on Seward in Lichfield, embarking at that time on a serious flirtation, by which she was moved and flattered, but resisted; when he returned to London, he wrote requesting a lock of her hair. She wrote an elegant refusal, although after he published, in the *Public Advertiser*, a flattering review of her recently published verse novel, *Louisa* (1784), the lock duly arrived in London. In early 1785, Anna Seward conveyed to Boswell two collections of anecdotes about Johnson, contributions to his stores for the *Life*. This seems to be the point at which his feelings began to cool: her writings made it clear to Boswell, and his *Tour to the Hebrides* (published October 1785) made it clear to her, that they disagreed fundamentally in their reading of Johnson's character. In a series of articles published under the name "Benvolio" in the *Gentleman's Magazine*, 1786–87, she defended Boswell for the accuracy and detail of his account, while insisting that Johnson was often prejudiced in his critical opinions and brutal in his conversational dealings. Privately, Seward and Boswell continued on cordial terms; the editors of Boswell's journals write that, as late as October 1788, when he saw her in Lichfield, "he continued an unsuccessful attempt to involve Anna Seward in an affair" (*Experiment*, 252). However, when the *Life* was published, she saw that her contributions had been almost wholly rejected, and, when in August 1793 she saw her name in a prominent place in *The Principal Additions and Corrections to the First Edition*, she wrote in her own name to the *Gentleman's Magazine*. Boswell replied promptly in the first letter following, and, when she responded, he replied again.]

Gentleman's Magazine, 63 (November 1793), 1009–11

Great Portland-street,[166]

Nov. 16, 1793.

Mr. URBAN,

MISS ANNA SEWARD, in a letter in your last Magazine, p. 875,[167] seems to apprehend that I have not treated her well in the first page of what she denominates a *pamphlet*, intituled, "The principal Corrections and Additions to the first Edition of Mr. Boswell's Life of Dr. Johnson."[168] As I should be sorry to be thought deficient in *politeness*, much more in *justice*, to any person, but particularly to a fair lady, I think it necessary to answer a charge too hastily brought against me.

This lady, as she herself has stated, did indeed *cover several sheets of paper* with the *few* anecdotes, concerning Dr. Johnson, which she did me the honour to communicate to me.[169] They were, however, not only poetically luxuriant, but, I could easily perceive, were tinctured with a strong prejudice against the person to whom they related. It therefore became me to examine them with much caution. One of them, the idle and utterly improbable story of his making verses on a duck when he was but three years old, which good Mrs. Lucy Porter had, among others, credulously related, he himself had enabled me unquestionably to refute;[170] notwithstanding which, Miss Seward adheres to her original tale,

---

166. JB and his family moved into new apartments at 47 Great Portland Street, London, in Jan. 1791 (*Great Biographer*, 117). This was his last London home. The building now on the site, at 118–122 Great Portland Street, is called James Boswell House.

167. Anna Seward's letter, dated Oct. 13, was the leading article in *Gent. Mag.*, 63 (Oct. 1793), 875.

168. *The Principal Corrections and Additions to the First Edition of Mr. Boswell's "Life of Dr. Johnson"* (1793) was published in early August (*Corres. 2*, lxix); it had its own pagination (ii+42) and was issued in its own blue paper wrappers (*Lit. Car.*, 212). (JB later explains his objection to Seward calling it a "pamphlet.")

169. JB wrote to Anna Seward on Jan. 21, 1785, soliciting "your liberal and freindly [*sic*] Assistance in procuring additional materials for the *Life of Dr. Samuel Johnson*" (*Corres. 2*, 39). She sent a package that he acknowledged on Feb. 15, asking at the same time for further information (*Corres. 2*, 47), which she delivered to him personally when he was passing through Lichfield, Mar. 26–27 (*Applause*, 285).

170. The story of the three-year-old SJ having composed four lines of verse in commemoration of a duckling, that he had accidentally stood on and killed, was related both by HLP and Hawkins; Hawkins's source seems to have been Anna Seward (Hawkins, *Life*,

and, in the letter now under consideration, still refers to them as his composition. Another story, which she sent me, was a very extraordinary fact, said to have been mentioned in a conversation between his mother and him, on the subject of his marrying Mrs. Porter, which appeared to me so strange as to require confirmation.[171] Miss Seward having quoted, as her authority for it, a respectable lady of Lichfield, I wrote to that lady, without mentioning the name of the person from whom the report was derived, inquiring only as to the authenticity of it. The lady informed me that she had never heard of the fact alluded to.—As my book was to be a *real history*, and not a *novel*, it was necessary to suppress all erroneous particulars, however entertaining. I was therefore obliged to reduce, into a very narrow compass indeed, what Miss Seward's fluent pen had expanded over many sheets. The account, however, which she gave, in contradiction to that of Mrs. Piozzi, of the circumstances attending Johnson's writing his beautiful "Verses to a Lady, on receiving from her a Sprig of Myrtle," seemed so plausible, that I with confidence inserted it in the first edition of my book;[172] nor had I any doubt of it, till Mr. Hector spontaneously assured me, by letter, that the fact was as Mrs. Piozzi has represented it.*[173] Having

---

369 n. 15). Seward sent her account to JB in her letter of Mar. 25, 1785 (*Corres. 2*, 65–66). In Lichfield, on Mar. 26, 1776, in SJ's company, JB asked SJ's stepdaughter, Lucy Porter, about the verses; despite her professed recollection of his mother's testimony, in the *Life*, JB rejected the attribution, on SJ's authority (1:40). He quotes Anna Seward's account in a footnote, as "ingenious and fanciful" (ibid., 1:40 and n. 3). Nevertheless, she maintained her account by a brief reference in her *Gent. Mag.* letter. See also Boswell, *"Life of Johnson" Manuscript*, 351–54.

171. Regarding SJ's marriage, Anna Seward passed on to JB a story that SJ had first attempted to court Elizabeth Porter's daughter Lucy but, being disregarded by her, later proposed to the recently widowed Elizabeth; the story continues with an account of SJ's conversation with his own mother, who reportedly told him, "my willing consent you will never have to so preposterous a union" (*Corres. 2*, 66). At Seward's suggestion, JB wrote to Mary Adey and Mary Cobb in Lichfield (ibid., 47); he quotes from their reply in his next letter to the *Gent. Mag.*, below.

172. Anna Seward's story of the "Sprig of Myrtle," used by JB in the first edition of the *Life of Johnson*, was that SJ, as a young man, wrote these verses for Lucy Porter (*Life*, 1:92 n. 2; Nov. 25, 1734).

173. "*The verses which occasioned this discussion having been printed in our vol. XLIX, p. 205 (where for *fears* read *hopes*), as Mr. Hammond's, and having not unfrequently been ascribed to Mr. Derrick; Dr. Johnson was asked, by the writer of this note, whilst Hammond's poems were in the press, if he knew the real author. His reply, which has already appeared in vol. LXI [i.e., *Gent. Mag.*, May 1791], p. 396, being short, is here repeated:

'I wrote them, sir, more than forty years ago, when I was at Birmingham, at the request of a friend; who, having frequently teazed me for the verses, I went one day up stairs, as if

received this decisive evidence, it became my duty to correct, in my second edition, the erroneous account which I had been induced to give in my first;[174] and, of course, to introduce that correction into the supplemental pages to my quarto edition, which I thought it incumbent upon me to publish separately, and in the same form, for the accommodation of those who were possessed of that edition.

Miss Seward says, that "I ought in justice, as well as common politeness, since I mentioned her testimony, to have stated the reasons she gave for that different evidence." Now, sir, *this I have done*. In the first edition those reasons are fully stated. It was not necessary that the Corrections and Additions, which are not, as she imagines, a *distinct pamphlet*, but *supplemental* to that edition, and to be *taken along with it*, should contain a repetition of the grounds of her testimony. It was enough that the refutation of them was there exhibited. But, in the second edition itself, after re-stating those grounds in her own words, *I let my fair antagonist down as softly as might be*, thus:

"Such was this lady's statement, which I make no doubt she supposed to be correct; but it shews how dangerous it is to trust too implicitly to traditional testimony and ingenious inference; for Mr. Hector has lately assured me, that Mrs. Piozzi's account is, in this instance, accurate."[175]

The merit of the verses in question will not be lessened by Miss Seward's attempt to depreciate them, as if good enough only for a school-boy. They have been long and universally admired. They speak for themselves, and require no defence. But I cannot help observing, that it is an aukward tale, that they were written by Dr. Johnson, in his own person, to Lucy Porter, whose *mother* he afterwards married. *Conjecture* must at once yield where *fact* appears, and *that* we have from Mr. Hector. He also, in referring to the time when they were written

---

to fetch them, and wrote them in the short space of time it required to have actually done so.' J. N." (i.e., John Nichols, editor of the *Gent. Mag.*). See also Boswell, *"Life of Johnson" Manuscript*, 354–56.

174. JB was reluctant to correct himself, much less to credit HLP, but did so in the second edition, having received a letter dated Aug. 9, 1791, from SJ's old Lichfield friend, Edmund Hector (1708–94), who says that he is writing "to set you right in regard of a Fabulous anecdote communicated to You by the fascinating Eyes and Tongue of the Lichd. Poetess. The *Sprig of Myrtle* was wrote as Mrs. Piosie [Piozzi] has related it" (*Corres. 2*, 339). HLP gives the story in her *Anecdotes* (*Johnsonian Miscellanies*, 1:167).

175. James Boswell, *The Life of Samuel Johnson*, 2nd ed., 3 vols. (1793), 1:69 n.; see *Life*, 1:92 n. 2. As Claudia Thomas Kairoff observes, "Boswell sneers at Mrs. Seward and Lucy Porter as credulous old women retailing old traditions; his witnesses, the sophisticated Thrale-Piozzi and learned Hector, are, he implies, necessarily preferable" (*Anna Seward*, 250).

and given to him, says, "Lucy Porter was then only a girl." Miss Seward would fain have us suppose, that Dr. Johnson had *first* written them to Lucy Porter; and *afterwards*, on being applied to by Mr. Hector for verses on receiving myrtle from a lady, might give them to Mr. Hector, without thinking it necessary to declare their *previous* existence. But, if Mrs. Lucy Porter was accurate in her recollection of their being presented to her by Dr. Johnson, Miss Seward's chronology, *reversed*, is much more natural and probable. Dr. Johnson might have written them for Mr. Hector when Lucy Porter was only a girl; and, when she was grown up, might have, with a pleasant economy, made them serve a second time for a compliment to her. That they were written for Mr. Hector, however, is all that is necessary to be proved; and it has been proved.

Miss Seward surely had no occasion to say one word to guard against her being suspected of "averring a conscious falsehood." No such suspicion was ever insinuated. Undoubtedly it *was* indifferent to her whether Dr. Johnson's verses were addressed to Lucy Porter or written for Mr. Hector; therefore, when she made her statement of the case, she had no motive of vanity or interest. *Now* it may, perhaps, not be indifferent, because she seems exceedingly zealous that her statement should be thought right. But there is no question, either as to conscious falsehood or conscious truth. It is merely a matter of argument upon evidence; and, I think, a very plain one.

I hope then, Mr. Urban, the fair Lady will be convinced that I have neither been impolite nor unjust to her. But, from the veneration and affection which I entertain for the character of my illustrious friend, *I* cannot be satisfied without expressing my indignation at the malevolence with which she has presumed to attack that great and good man. In the present letter she seriously accuses HIM of "*conscious falsehood,*" in an "*assertion*" that "Buchanan was the only man of genius which his country had ever produced."[176] From the frequency of what she calls "*similar false assertions*" she concludes that "his veracity was of that species which, straining at *gnats*, swallows CAMELS."[177] Miss Seward does not perceive that such sallies as those which are recorded to shew Dr. Johnson's wonderful dexterity in retort, are not assertions in the sense which concerns truth or falsehood; they are evidently *ardentia verba* (*glowing words*—I ask her pardon for quoting a Latin phrase) uttered in witty contest. They are not even expressive of his *opinion*; but, if they could be supposed to convey his real

176. JB says that SJ "uniformly gave liberal praise" to the Scottish poet and scholar George Buchanan (1506–82) and records this remark (*Life*, 4:185–86; 1783).
177. Matthew 23:24: "Ye blind guides, which strain at a gnat, and swallow a camel" (*AV*).

opinion, still they would have no concern with his *veracity*. When he did give his honest judgement on the merits of certain poets, where he differed from a shoal of small criticks, and, in a few instances, was thought, by men of a superior rank in taste, to be in the wrong, he might be charged with *error*; but it is from a defect in the *reasoning faculty* when, in such instances, he is charged with *falsehood* or *envy*. Dr. Johnson's strict, nice, and scrupulous regard to *truth* was one of the most remarkable circumstances in his character, and was often mentioned as such by his friends, particularly Sir Joshua Reynolds.[178] *Falsehood*, therefore, was at the utmost distance from him; and his transcendant abilities and acquirements, his extensive and increasing fame, set him far above *envy*. Miss Seward does not know that her injurious reflection refutes itself; but her eagerly making it, however weak and ineffectual it may be, fully discovers her *intention*.

So far from having any hostile disposition towards this Lady, I have, in my Life of Dr. Johnson, spoken of her in as handsome terms as I could; I have quoted a compliment paid by him to one of her poetical pieces; and I have withheld his opinion of herself, thinking that she might not like it.[179] I am afraid it has reached her by some other means; and thus we may account for various attacks, by her, on her venerable townsman since his decease, even in your Magazine, where I have been sorry to see them, some avowed and with her own name, and others, as I believe, in various forms, and under several signatures.*[180] What are we to think of the scraps of letters between her and Mr. Hayley,†[181] impotently attempting to undermine the noble pedestal on which the public opinion

---

178. Reynolds wrote of SJ that "Truth, whether in great or little matters, he held sacred" (*Life*, 2:433 n. 2; Mar. 16, 1776), and testified to SJ's "scrupulous adherence to truth" (ibid., 4:221 n. 2; May 15, 1783).

179. On June 25, 1784, JB received from Anna Seward some verses about Lichfield, which SJ praised; JB then confirmed with SJ his good opinion of her *Elegy on Captain Cook* (1780); see *Life*, 4:331. The opinion of her that JB claims to withhold has not been identified.

180. "* Mr. Boswell having here particularly referred to letters under the signature of *Benvolio*, vol. LVI, pp. 125, 302; and vol. LVII, p. 684; it becomes our duty to declare, that his conjecture is totally groundless; and we hope that, on this occasion, *Benvolio* will condescend to unmask. EDIT[OR, i.e., of the *Gent. Mag.*]." The three letters signed "Benvolio," which reflect critically on SJ's character as revealed in various episodes of JB's *Tour*, were published in the *Gent. Mag.*, Feb. 1786, Apr. 1786, and Aug. 1787. In her letter in reply to this, Anna Seward says that she had told the editor of the *Gent. Mag.* that she had written them.

181. "† Whatever Mr. B. may think of these scraps (and his mode of expression conveys a certain degree of insinuation), it would be injustice to the writer of them if we did not request the correspondent who communicated them (whom we really do not know) to disclose himself. EDIT[OR, i.e., of the *Gent. Mag.*]."

has placed Dr. Johnson?[182] But it is unnecessary to take up any part of your valuable miscellany in exposing the little arts which have been employed by a cabal of minor poets and poetesses, who are sadly mortified that Dr. Johnson, by his powerful sentence, assigned their proper station to writers of this description.

JAMES BOSWELL.

1794

Gentleman's Magazine, 64 (January 1794), 32–35

Great Portland-street,
Jan. 20.

Mr. URBAN,

HAVING been too hastily charged, in your Magazine, by Miss Anna Seward, with want of *politeness*, and even *common justice*, towards her, I was naturally anxious to vindicate myself, which I accordingly did in November last, by shewing, in the most satisfactory manner, that I had been careful to express myself with due delicacy, when obliged to correct an error into which she had been led, as to the true history of Dr. Johnson's writing the verses on a Sprig of Myrtle.[183] I refer to my statement, and trust it, with confidence, to the candour of all who are capable of reasoning and judging of evidence. I, at the same time, could not but discover some indignation at the malevolence with which that fair lady had presumed to attack the great and good Dr. JOHNSON, whose character was altogether unconnected with the inconsiderable matter in question. Whether he wrote those beautiful verses for himself, or for a friend, his merit as a poet must be the same. The investigation of their history was important only for the sake of truth, and in fairness to another lady, whom Miss Seward had induced me to contradict, on grounds sufficiently probable, as I admitted in my additional note.

I should have thought that there was no occasion for any more writing upon the subject; but I am sorry to find that our poetess has made a second attack, at great length, and in such temper as must be very uneasy to a gentle bosom.[184]

---

182. Extracts concerning SJ, from some letters exchanged in 1782 between Seward and minor poet William Hayley (1745–1820), were published in *Gent. Mag.*, 63 (Mar. 1793), 197–99. They mainly concern the *Lives of the Poets*.

183. See JB's letter, immediately above.

184. Seward responded to JB's previous letter with a letter dated Dec. 14, published in *Gent. Mag.*, 63 (Dec. 1793), 1098–101; page references for quotations from this letter will be provided in parentheses, below.

She, indeed, has candour enough not to resume the charge from which I vindicated myself, and which was the cause of my animadverting upon her at all. But she throws forth some censure upon me, and a great deal upon Dr. Johnson, of which, Sir, I leave you and your readers to discern the motives.

Miss Seward may be assured that *she* is as much mistaken as to me, as she certainly is as to Dr. Johnson. I am not her *foe*, though I committed to the flames those sheets of *"Johnsonian Narratives,"* with which I was favoured by her, among the almost innumerable communications which I obtained concerning the illustrious subject of my great biographical work.[185] I however first extracted from those sheets all that I could possibly consider to be authentic. Nay, so desirous was I to give Miss Seward every advantage, that after refuting the *impossible* legend of Johnson's verses on a Duck, when he was but three years old, to which, *for a woman's reason*, she still pertinaciously adheres,[186] I preserved the ingenious reflections which she supposing it to be true, had made on that idle tale. I am not her *foe*, though I cannot allow that the censure of BACON, by POPE, that prince of poets,[187] who could

"Expatiate free o'er all this scene of man,"

is any reason why it is not presumptuous in Miss *Nancy Seward* to judge and condemn Dr. JOHNSON, "the brightest ornament of the eighteenth century;" as Mr. Malone has truly and elegantly described him.[188] I am not her *foe*; though,

185. Seward described JB as "a man, who, after professing himself my friend, becomes causelessly my foe" (1101). She began her letter by asking, "If Mr. Boswell has preserved my letters to him on the subject, I desire he will send them to *you*, and that you will allow them a place in this Repository; so shall the publick judge whether they *deserve* the contempt with which he mentions them in your last Number" (1098). The "Johnsonian narratives" (Seward's expression, 1098) that JB "committed to the flames" was the first letter she sent him, concerning the conversation at Dilly's about Miss Harry, although James D. Woolley gives a text from other sources ("Johnson as Despot," 140–45). Waingrow overlooks this (*Corres. 2*, 41), but gives the text of the latter package (ibid., 64–67).

186. A *"woman's reason"* seems to imply gossip or hearsay among women: Seward reiterated her belief in the story, "because Mrs. Lucy Porter said Dr. Johnson's mother told her the circumstance" (1099).

187. In response to JB's having said "she has presumed to attack that great and good man," Seward had quoted Pope's description of "the Illustrious Lord Bacon" as "The wisest, greatest, *meanest*, of mankind" and made the point that even great men may have faults and that it is not presumptuous to point them out (1099). JB responds that it is presumptuous if one is not great oneself, like Pope, whose *Essay on Man*, epistle 1, line 5, he quotes.

188. See Malone, *Plays and Poems*, 1:lxviii. JB quotes this expression in his "Advertisement to the First Edition" (*Life*, 1:9). The name *Nancy* was originally a pet form of *Anna*.

instead of joining in the republican cry, as she does, that Johnson has been unjust to Milton,[189] I declare my admiration of his very liberal and just praise of
that great poet, who was the most odious character, both in public and private,
of any man of genius that ever lived; in public, the defender of the murderers
of his sovereign, the blessed martyr; in private, the sulky tyrant over his own
wretched, uneducated, and helpless daughters.

Why should I be my fair antagonist's *foe*? She never did me any harm, nor
do I apprehend that she ever can. She protests against entering farther into a
paper war with me.[190] If there be such *war*, it is all on one side; for it is not in my
thoughts. That kind of conflict is not what I wish to have with ladies; and I really must complain that my *old friend* (if she will forgive the expression) should
represent me so unlike myself.

It is very hard, that Miss Seward's misconceiving a *witty retort* for a *false assertion* should subject her to so woeful a deception as to imagine Dr. Johnson in
any degree deficient in a sacred regard for *truth*. It is not in my power to make
the distinction plainer than I have made it in my former letter.

The lady quotes as genuine, a sarcasm of Dr. Johnson on lord Chesterfield, in
these words: "He is a wit among lords, and a lord among wits," which, it seems,
she has heard repeated by *numbers*.[191] Here is a proof of the justice of the late
Mr. Fitzherbert's observation, that it is not every one who can *carry a bon mot*.[192]
This representation of Johnson's pointed saying is flat and unmeaning indeed.
What he *did* say is recorded p. 238, vol. I of my book, which Miss Seward handsomely, and I believe sincerely, styles "interesting memoirs:"

> "This man I thought had been a lord among wits; but I find he is only a
> wit among lords."[193]

189. The tory and Anglican SJ had a strong antipathy to Milton's political views, which
he said "were those of an acrimonious and surly Republican" (*Lives of the Poets*, 1:156). JB
writes that, "[a]gainst his Life of MILTON, the hounds of Whiggism have opened in full
cry" (*Life*, 4:40; 1781).

190. In her final paragraph, Seward wrote, "Into paper-war . . . I will no farther enter" (1101).

191. Seward introduces this saying about Chesterfield (which, as JB notes, she garbles: see
sentences following) in order to observe that, if asked to recall from whom one first heard
such a frequently repeated saying, she would "find it difficult to specify an individual": this to
justify her saying that she thought she first heard the story of SJ discussing his marriage plans
with his mother from Mrs. Cobb, whom she correctly assumes is the person JB wrote to.

192. William Fitzherbert (1712–72), MP, is quoted as having said this to JB on Apr. 10,
1775 (*Life*, 2:350).

193. See *Life*, 1:266 (1754).

It would therefore be better if Miss Seward would not boast of *all* her communications concerning Johnson, as "conveying strong internal evidence of their verity from characteristic turn of expression;" nor would it be any disadvantage to her if she should sometimes distrust the accuracy of her *memory* (I seriously protest I mean no more); for, since she has mentioned the late Mrs. Cobb as the person from whom, "to the best of her remembrance," she heard the strange conversation between Johnson and his mother, concerning his marriage with Mrs. Porter, which she communicated to me and I suppressed, I will tell her that Mrs. Cobb *was* the person whom she gave me as her authority; and Mrs. Cobb's letter now lies before me, in which she says,

> "I cannot recollect any conversation which passed between Dr. Johnson and his mother, concerning his marriage with Mrs. Porter. If I ever heard any, it has totally escaped my memory. Many things are repeated in Lichfield, as being told or said by Mrs. Cobb, and not a syllable of truth in any one."[194]

I again say, that I did not mention to Mrs. Cobb from whom I had the story; nor did she ever know that it was Miss Seward. It is, however, remarkable, that in the same letter is the following passage: "If you praise our good Johnson, Miss Seward will not love you;" a prediction, which, alas! I now begin to fear is but too true, if I may venture to judge from the strain and tenor of her last epistle.

The detection of so considerable a mistake should make Miss Seward not so *sure* of having read either in Dr. Johnson's Works, or in the records of his biographers, "an assertion concerning Dr. Watts, which she calls a *base stigma*, and *slander*, and *unchristian like*; and pours forth, in her customary manner, a *profusion of words* to abuse. *It is not* in his Life of that excellent man; and, if Miss Seward has read it any where, she has read what *was not true*.[195] That

194. For Mary Cobb's letter of Mar. 29, 1789, to JB, including the sentence JB quotes in the following paragraph, see *Corres. 2*, 225.

195. Seward wrote, "I am *sure* I have read, in either Dr. Johnson's Works, or in the records of his biographers, the assertion, that [hymn writer Dr. Isaac] Watts was one of the few poets who could look forward with rational hope to the mercy of their God" (1100). She had referred to this expression in her earlier correspondence with the *Gent. Mag.*; see the third "Benvolio" letter (Aug. 1787, 685). What in all likelihood Seward read was Johnson on the poet Gilbert West: "a stroke of the palsy brought to the grave one of the few poets to whom the grave might be without its terrors" (see *Lives*, 3:331 and n. 4). In fact, she very likely read it in the *Gent. Mag.*, 54 (Mar. 1784), 220, where it was remarked upon by anonymous contributor "L. X.," who went on to comment, "There can consequently be no doubt

poets, and poetesses also, have too often been not of the most exemplary lives, is universally known; but Dr. Johnson never uttered such a sentence as Miss Seward imputes to him. She, indeed, seems doomed to perpetual error; for she mentions a sentence quoted by her anonymous correspondent, p. 1009, from *Warburton*, which she, with all imaginable ease, calls *impious*; when, in truth, that admirable sentence is *not* quoted from Warburton, and was *not* written by Warburton, but by a most distinguished author now alive.[196] Let me ask, also, if it be *fair* in Miss Seward to quote the passage which I have quoted (v. III, p. 547) from bishop Newton, unfavourable to Dr. Johnson, and leave out the apology which I have made for that prelate, namely, "the disgust and peevishness of old age;" as also the general and permanent opinion which bishop Newton entertained of Dr. Johnson, of whom he says, *in the same passage*, that "he respected him not only for his genius and learning, but valued him much more "for the more amiable part of his character, his humanity and charity, his morality and religion."[197]

---

of the authenticity of that record which attests his uttering the same sentiments in speaking of Dr. Watts." The "record" "L. X." is referring to is not known.

196. In her December letter, Seward wrote, "The sentence quoted by my anonymous correspondent from Johnson's *kindred* spirit, Warburton, is impious, pronouncing the decisions of any man sacred, and as unerring as the balance of the sanctuary" (1101). She refers here to a letter contributed by "N. Y." to the Nov. 1793 issue of the *Gent. Mag.*, 1008–9, where it was printed immediately before that of JB's in which he earlier replied to her. "N. Y." says: "Give me leave to produce before your readers what a most distinguished writer, alike eminent for his learning and his philanthropy, has said of *the author of the Rambler*: 'Of literary merit, Johnson, as we all know, was a sagacious, but a most severe, judge. Such was his discernment, that he pierced into the most secret springs of human actions; and such was his integrity, that he always weighed the moral characters of his fellow-creatures *in the balance of the Sanctuary**.'" The footnote in the *Gent. Mag.* attributes this quotation to "Tracts by Warburton, &c. p. 384." "N. Y." also replied to Seward in the *Gent. Mag.* for Jan. 1794 (the same issue in which this present letter of JB's was published) and says, "The concise, but warm and eloquent encomium on Dr. Joh[n]son, which I quoted in his vindication, and which she too rashly styles impious, was not written by Dr. Warburton, though it is to be found in a *collection of certain Tracts which were* written by that illustrious prelate" (7). The "distinguished author now alive" who wrote these lines is SJ's acquaintance Samuel Parr (1747–1825), who edited the volume *Tracts, by Warburton, and a Warburtonian* (1789).

197. Seward quotes (1101)—without remark—a passage that was quoted by JB himself (as he describes; see *Life*, 4:285 n. 3; June 3, 1784) from Dr. Thomas Newton (1704–82), Bishop of Bristol; this passage is from his autobiography, which was published posthumously in his *Works* (1:130–31). Newton was, like SJ and Anna Seward, born in Lichfield; after these comments were published, SJ spoke disparagingly of Newton's achievements (*Life*, 4:285–86).

Miss Seward *dreams* that I have "insinuated *envy* and *selfish prejudice* against her" in my defensive letter; for this, after reading it over again and again, I cannot perceive the smallest foundation. She may make herself quite easy upon that head; for I do not even suspect that my fair antagonist, "herself all the Nine*[198]," envies any human being.

Neither am I at all conscious of "heroical attempts to *injure* a defenceless female," (meaning herself) with which she charges me. "*How canst thou, lovely Nancy, thus cruelly—?*"[199] Is it an *injury* to mention in civil terms that she has been *mis-informed* as to a fact? Is it an *injury* to reprehend with generous warmth her malevolent attacks on "my GUIDE, PHILOSOPHER, and FRIEND?"[200] Would that she were *off*enceless! *def*enceless she is not; as she now avers that she can, at pleasure, put on the masculine attire, and lay about her as a second Drawcansir, armed *cap à pied* in the masked character of *Ben*volio.[201] She modestly wishes that her *strictures*, under that signature, should be "recurred to, and considered *well*." She may rest satisfied that they *have* been *well* and *truly* tried, and that the verdict of *ineffective illnature* will never be set aside. I wonder at her seeming to glory in such effusions.

198. "*See a short Dialogue in verse between her and Mr. Hayley." (BOSWELL)
This refers to Richard Porson, "Dialogue between Miss Seward and Mr. Hayley," *General Evening Post*, Sept. 3, 1787:

Tuneful Poet! Britain's glory!
(Mr. Hayley, that is you)—
Ma'am, you carry all before you,
Trust me, Litchfield Swan, you do.

Ode didactic, epic, sonnet,
Mr. Hayley, you're divine!—
Ma'am, I'll take my oath upon it,
You alone are all the nine!

199. This is the first line of a much-reprinted Scots ballad "Lovely Nancy," which seems to have been first printed in James Oswald's *Curious Scots Tunes*, 2 vols. (1742–44). "How canst thou, lovely Nancy, thus cruelly slight / A swain who is wretched when banished [*sic*] thy sight?"

200. "Guide, Philosopher, and Friend": Pope, *Essay on Man*, epistle 4, line 390. JB quotes this in reference to SJ in the final pages of the *Life* (4:420).

201. In Buckingham's popular comedy *The Rehearsal* (1672), Drawcansir is "a blustering, bragging character . . . , who in the last scene is made to enter a battle and kill all the combatants on both sides" (*OED*). *Cap à pied*: lit. head to foot—i.e., completely covered by armor. The name "Benvolio"—Seward's earlier pseudonym—means well-wisher; there is a character with this name in Shakespeare's *Romeo and Juliet*. Seward uses it in contrast to the "malevolence" of which she accuses SJ.

And now to put an end to all future disputation on the mighty points of the *Duck* and the *Myrtle*, which have been the causes of this *war*,

"————this tumult in a vestal's veins—."[202]

The verses on a Duck, said to be composed by Johnson when he was only three years old, were not made by him, because, from *internal* evidence it is *impossible* they should, without a *miracle*; and because, from *external* evidence, it appears that his mother, and Mrs. Lucy Porter, did not "invent a falsehood," when they credulously told he had made them, so that their veracity is not questioned; his mother heard so from his father, and Mrs. Lucy Porter from his mother. The refutation does not rest on Johnson's recollection of his childhood; but on his telling me, in Mrs. Lucy Porter's presence, that his father had owned to him that he had made them, and wished to pass them for his son's.

The verses on a Sprig of Myrtle, though, perhaps, *afterwards* presented to Mrs. Lucy Porter, were originally written for a friend; because Dr. Johnson himself mentioned the fact, both to Mrs Thrale, and to Mr. Nichols, printer of the Gentleman's Magazine, both of whom have attested it; and because Mr. Hector of Birmingham, Dr. Johnson's schoolfellow and intimate friend through life, has attested that he was the person at whose request they were written. That worthy gentleman, first spontaneously wrote to me on the subject; and, seeing me unavoidably drawn into this aukward and unpleasant squabble with Miss Anna Seward, has again spontaneously favoured me with a letter, which I shall here insert.[203]

To James Boswell, Esq.

"Dear Sir,

I am sorry to see you engaged in altercation with a lady, who seems unwilling to be convinced of her errors. Surely it would be more ingenuous to acknowledge than to persevere.

Lately, in looking over some papers I meant to burn, I found the original manuscript, with the date on it [1731,] which I have enclosed.

The true history (which I could swear to) is as follows. Mr. Morgan Graves, the elder brother of a worthy clergyman near Bath, with whom I was acquainted, waited upon a lady in this neighbourhood, who, at part-

---

202. Pope, "Eloisa to Abelard" (1717), line 4. *Vestal*, i.e., a "vestal virgin": "Resembling a priestess of Vesta in respect of chastity" (*OED*); JB alludes in mockery to Seward's spinsterhood.

203. The *Gent. Mag.* text of this letter is slightly regularized; see *Corres.* 2, 443.

ing, presented him the branch. He shewed it me, and wished much to return the compliment in verse. I applied to Johnson, who was with me, and in about half an hour dictated the verses which I sent to my friend.

I most solemnly declare, at that time Johnson was an entire stranger to the Porter family; and it was almost two years after that I introduced him to the acquaintance of Porter, whom I bought my cloaths of.

If you intend to convince this obstinate woman, and to exhibit to the public the truth of your narrative, you are at liberty to make what use you please of this statement.

I hope you will pardon me for taking up so much of your time. Wishing you *multos et felices annos*,[204] I shall subscribe myself

Your obliged humble servant,

E. HECTOR."

Birmingham, Jan. 9, 1794.

May I not now flatter myself, Mr. Urban, that I shall not have the trouble of any farther altercation with Miss Seward? Let the *duck* be changed into a *swan*, and the *Myrtle* into an *Olive*.[205] Instead of railing, let us have the song. Instead of war, let us have peace. I beg that I may not be reckoned in the number of those "with whom it has been Miss Seward's lot to *contend*."[206] My fair antagonist's fertile fancy has men and things enough to employ itself upon, without vainly aspiring to be the judge of JOHNSON. She will permit me, in perfect good humour, to call to her recollection a verse in very ancient poesy: "I do not exercise myself in great matters, which are too high for me."[207]

Yours, &c.

JAMES BOSWELL.

204. *Ad multos et felices annos*: "Many and happy years" is a traditional new year greeting.

205. In allusion to Shakespeare as the "Swan of Avon," Anna Seward was known as "the Swan of Lichfield"; in biblical and classical tradition, the olive branch is an image for peace.

206. Seward—who, despite her criticisms of SJ, also refers to him as "that wonderful man," "the finest prose-writer in our language"—claimed, "[i]t has been my lot to contend equally with Dr. Johnson's enemies and with his worshipers" (1099).

207. Psalm 131:1 (*AV*).

5

Essays and Letters

"Essays and Letters," as Boswell himself refers to the sort of material in this final section (see the "New Year Address," below), may seem a rather arbitrary generic category and the items here even more of a miscellany than the earlier genre-based chapter, the "Reports and Interviews." But the distinction is clear enough between narrative nonfiction and nonnarrative nonfiction. To describe the latter material in a less negative way, we have only the unemphatic term *essay*, which applies to a literary form so flexible that its characteristics often seem invisible. But if we were to see any of these writings on the "Opinion" pages of a newspaper, which is exactly where they originate, their identity and continuities would be unmistakable.

Like the "Reports and Interviews," these items are occasional, in that they are responses to some topical circumstance in the world outside the mind of the essayist. They are, in this aspect, unlike Boswell's most sustained and deliberate contribution to the genre, the serious and regular "Hypochondriack" essays. In those essays, Boswell is constrained not only by a deadline—no bad thing, for most writers—but also by an obligation to write generally, on general topics. To treat of general topics—marriage, death, riches, war, time, pleasure—obliges a writer of a literary kind to engage in a dialogue with his generic forebears, the previous thinkers on the same topics, and this frequently gives rise, in the work of essayists, to a certain formality and uniformity of voice and a lack of originality of material. Although four "Hypochondriacks" have recently been selected for inclusion in an anthology of *The Great Age of the English Essay*, ed. Denise Gigante (2008), in that volume they stand out as the only one of the nineteen essay series from which selections are given that did not achieve republication in book form in the author's lifetime (or, in the case of Fielding's *Covent-Garden Journal*, shortly after his death, in his collected works). The *Hypochondriack* is bluntly described by Frank Brady as "Boswell's only long work to be a failure" (*Later Years*, 176). Yet, as Brady also observes, "prose was his natural medium," and "the flexibility of the essay accommodated his pleasure in ranging over opinions and events without much regard to organization" (ibid., 177); but the *Hypochondriack* could not be said to be the location of this successful accommodation. It may be that the following collection of short texts gives a far better sense of Boswell's "pleasure in ranging over opinions and events."

Some items are more studied and artful, written in an effort to make some sort of splash: we can detect in the early "Contemplative Walk" and "Original Letter" a voice trying to announce itself, to find a niche in the contemporary clamor for literary reputation. As Brady remarked, "Poems and essays were the favoured try-out genres for contemporary aspirants to authorship" (*Later Years*, 177). Other pieces were written in direct response to some issue that had arisen in either private or public: such as when he writes about high food prices or damage to his books by bookworms or the state trumpeters or (that standby of the "letter to the editor" to the present day) to mock or be grumpy about changes of names and innovations in language and traditional practices. These are all the work of a man whose natural resort when he has a thought is to make it a subject of conversation. They represent a more or less public thinking out loud, as his journals are the repository of a more or less private thinking out loud.

In the 1760s, as the four-page dailies expanded in page size and number of columns (from twelve to sixteen), more material was required to fill them. When, as described in the introduction, newspapers deliberately set out to become venues for opinion as well as news, "the numbers of political letters in the press took off exponentially" (Harris, *Politics and the Rise of the Press*, 38). In the *Public Advertiser*, which explicitly invited the assistance of the public in "feeding the enormous four columns" (*Pub. Adv.*, Apr. 14, 1763), the letters soon achieved "both symbolic and real parity with the paid advertisements, commissioned articles and news that had formed the paper's primary content" (Bertelsen, "Education of Henry Sampson Woodfall," 155). According to Hannah Barker, letters "typically occupied between one and three columns of the paper's space"—which is quite a proportion, given that around half of most papers was advertising (Barker, *Newspapers, Politics, and Public Opinion*, 38). By allowing mere citizens to air their views, often on subjects for which there had never before been a public outlet (other than direct action), the "letters to the editor" contributed to the creation of "an image of widespread political debate ostensibly open to all, irrespective of rank or connection" (Harris, *Politics and the Rise of the Press*, 40). It is certainly consistent with other contemporary changes in British political culture that tended increasingly to bring "the middle and lower ranks within the ambit of national culture" (ibid.).

Unlike essays, letters are not essentially literary and public texts: structurally, they are private communications between two individuals, and their conventional generic markers are the address or salutation at the start and the signed name of the sender at the end. That letters are private means that generic and, to some extent, moral ambiguities and complexities can arise when letters are made public—that is, published. Boswell, who was profoundly alert to all such nuances, knowingly manipulated and exploited these ambiguities by his addressing and self-naming (or not naming) practices and by other means. Typically, letters for publication in the press are addressed (as Boswell's are) "To the Printer"; as Bob Clarke remarks, "the existence of a separate editorial function had yet to be recognised by the public" (*From Grub Street*, 86). Even this is something of a fiction: the printer or editor is addressed only as a matter of politeness—a letter to the public press is really a letter to the readers of the press: the general public. In modern newspapers, the pretense is no longer acknowledged in the body of such letters, but Boswell often addresses the printer in the second person ("your readers"). The use of the heading "Extract of a Letter from XXX," which we have seen a number of times in this book, must also be regarded as a literary device; that there was in all instances a complete letter from which the alleged snippet has been taken must be doubted.

Regarding the signatures, some accommodation was necessary when letters were written for publication, especially in a medium in which writers expected to have anonymity. Letter writers to newspapers dealt with these conflicting requirements by the use of pseudonyms, and in the twenty-eight articles in this section Boswell employs twenty different pseudonyms. (In his total identified periodical output, JB used something like sixty-four different pseudonyms, signed thirty-one items with his own name, and for eleven used the signature "J. B."; see Tankard, "Anonymity and the Press.") Unlike commentators such as "Junius," Boswell apparently had no desire to establish himself as a figure with a consistent point of view, whose pseudonym would eventually gain brand recognition even if his actual identity remained unknown. There is no key to the names he chose—mostly, they suited the particular topic of the letter: so "Medicus Mentis" offers a cure for impotence of mind, "Tantalus" writes about the inadequate provisions at the Lord Mayoral Ball, "A Hungry Correspondent" complains about rising food prices, and "Trumpetarius" writes about the state trumpeters. However, we might observe the number of times that the pseudonym says or implies that the writer is an older person: "Antiquarius," "Vetustus," "Hypodidasculus," "An Old Town Citizen," "Memory," "An Old Courtier"—and there are more such pseudonyms on other articles. Boswell's response to the extension of the discursive franchise, which he might have felt to be an encroachment upon his cherished feudal or other privileges and to offend against the principle of subordination, is to depict himself in the press as a figure still recognizable in the letters columns of newspapers: the older man, perhaps retired to the country or writing from the rooms of his club, who is somewhat removed from active or day-to-day involvement in the affairs of the metropolis, but who has the indisputable authority that comes of having watched the world for many years.

One particular means by which Boswell manipulates the conventions is by what James Caudle has called the "public-private" letter (*Corres. 9*, xl). This is the genre of the earliest book publication in which he is named as author, the Erskine-Boswell *Letters*, and of one item in this chapter, the "Original Letter" to the Earl of Eglinton. We could say that, in many ways, Boswell's great project, in all his writing, was to make the private public: this is his "love of publication," upon which Johnson remarked. Making the private public is the essence of his greatest literary achievement, the *Life of Johnson*, and, while later readers relish the sense of intimacy that Boswell achieves, early critics of the book were disturbed by "the impropriety of reporting private conversation";

and those living persons—such as Burke or Bishop Thomas Percy—who made an appearance in the book were not always enthusiastic about the private becoming public (*Later Years*, 445). One's own privacy is often also the privacy of other people, and the "public-private" letter exposes not only the writer but also the addressee: unless it is anonymous, in which case it does not expose the writer at all, but only the addressee.

A different subgenre again is evident in the two sequential letters of 1763 signed "B" of Westminster. These two items, recently added to the canon of Boswell's journalism by James J. Caudle, are "inventions" of the kind we encountered in earlier chapters. But where we have seen Boswell creating accounts of fictitious events, here we find him creating a fictitious writer. In these cases, Boswell is not simply using a pseudonym, as in other places, in order to present his own true opinions under another name, but he invents a fictitious character and writes in his voice.

We might also notice that there is in this chapter a higher proportion than in the others of Scottish-related subjects. Letters and essays—when they are facts rather than inventions—require a writer to have a sense of his own vantage point, and it is understandable not simply that Boswell should deploy his Scottish identity when an identity is required, but that subjects that confront him as a Scot and a citizen of Edinburgh should be subjects about which he is moved to send a letter to the press. In all his writing to and for the press, Boswell was assuring himself that—whether he was in London or Edinburgh—he was a responsible citizen, someone who belonged.

1758

A Contemplative Walk, at Moffat, on a Summer Night

[Boswell first visited the village of Moffat, in Dumfriesshire—sixty miles southeast of Glasgow and fifty miles southwest of Edinburgh—at the age of eleven, for the sake of its sulfur spring, which was prescribed by doctors for nervous and other complaints. In the Sketch of his early life that he wrote for Rousseau, Boswell records that he was "sent to Moffat, the Spa of Scotland," for a severe cold that had developed into nervous illness and exacerbated his melancholy; later, at sixteen and while at the University of Edinburgh, "a terrible hypochondria seized me," and he returned to Moffat.[1] On both occasions, he seems to have been "cured" less by the waters than by the opportunities for social interaction and physical exercise. (Interestingly, Moffat was in 2009 designated Scotland's first "Walkers Are Welcome" town and hosts an annual Walking Festival.) Boswell also spent time in Moffat when visiting his university friend John Johnston, who was laird of the small estate of Grange, which was nearby.

This essay, which is the earliest piece in this collection and Boswell's earliest published piece of prose, is attributed to him on Pottle's authority (*Lit. Car.*, 216).

1. "Sketch of the Early Life of James Boswell" (a translation by Pottle of a text written by JB in Dec. 1764, to introduce himself to Rousseau); *Earlier Years*, 4.

With its self-conscious literary allusions and conventional piety, it is very much in the character of a schoolboy literary exercise.]

Scots Magazine, 20 (December 1758), 624

A CONTEMPLATIVE WALK,

At MOFFAT, on a summer-night.

A sketch, in imitation of HERVEY's style[2]

————————*propter amorem*

Quod TE imitari aveo.——Lucret.[3]

Wearied with the pleasing toils of a studious day, how delightful is it, in such a night as this, to walk abroad! While I breathe the purest air, and am fanned with the gentle wings of balmy zephyr,

How sweet and solemn is this ev'ning-scene![4]

My eyes are ravished with a most delightful prospect; while the grounds on either side form a sort of noble amphitheatre: On the east, a ridge of gently-rising hills arrayed in vivid green, whose tops catch the sun's departing rays, as if unwilling to be deprived of that glorious luminary, whose benign influence makes all the face of nature wear a cheerful smile. On the west, huge mountains, covered with dusky heath, interspersed with craggy cliffs, serve as a shade and foil to set off the gayer part of the scene. Here and there, a farmhouse adorned with a few trees, diversifies the landscape, and raises the most pleasing images in the mind of the beholder; while the ruins of a once celebrated seat*[5] of a NOBLE

---

2. Rev. James Hervey (1714–58), author of *Meditations among the Tombs* (1746), enlarged and much-reprinted as *Meditations and Contemplations* (1748), a devotional work that JB says "engaged my affections in my early years" and was the delight of his mother, who was the most formative early influence on his religious faith. At Inveraray, he tried unsuccessfully to persuade SJ to appreciate the work (Oct. 24, 1773; *Life*, 5:351). Hervey aimed for a style at once "Majestic, yet familiar" (*Meditations and Contemplations*, 2:xiv); some found it over-elaborate and unconvincing, but his chief works were immensely popular and influential. He died on Christmas Day, in the same month that this piece was published.

3. Lucretius, *De Rerum Natura*, 3.4–5: "[you I follow . . . on the marks you have left I plant my own footsteps firm, not so much desiring to be your rival,] as for love, because I yearn to copy you." Lucretius says this of his master, Epicurus. By capitalizing "te," JB is perhaps emphasizing his devotion to and imitation of Hervey.

4. John Home, *Douglas: A Tragedy* (1756), 5.1.3. Douglas: "How sweet and solemn is this mid-night scene!" For Home, see Chap. 3, n. 21.

5. "* LOCHWOOD, anciently the seat of the family of ANNANDALE, whose melancholy fortune is too well known, too severely felt in that country. I had the curiosity to ride up

FAMILY, adds a grandeur to the prospect, and at the same time reminds me of the transient fate of all sublunary things.

The heavens seem to be one uniform blue expanse of æther; only one little star, as if more eager than the rest to proclaim THE GREAT ORIGINAL,[6] has trimmed its golden lamp, and with a glittering lustre beams through the azure sky: methinks it appears the brightest I ever beheld. And why? Because it alone shines, while the rest lie veiled in a cloudy mantle. A proper monitor this, to dare to be *singularly good*, and while the generality of the world are *meanly* ashamed to appear for the sacred, the amiable truths of virtue and religion, boldly to assert the *glorious* cause. But, lo! a second begins to appear; another, and another, succeed, desirous to imitate their sparkling leader: A beautiful emblem this, of the attractive nature of heaven-born piety, which so sweetly engages the minds of men, and gently leads them to their only *true* and *substantial* happiness.

Let me enforce this, by a passage from the sacred oracles: *Let your light so shine before men*, (says our blessed SAVIOUR), *that others seeing your good works, may glorify your FATHER which is in heaven:*[7] glorify HIM for imparting such grace to men, and glorify HIM by an imitation of the shining examples.

EUGENIO.[8]

---

to the place. There are scarce the remains of a house, only a few venerable old trees, which seemed to mourn their master's fate. I confess I was not a little moved with the gloomy solemnity of the scene." (BOSWELL)

The stone castle of Lochwood, about six miles southwest of Moffat, was built during the fifteenth century for the Johnston(e) clan, the lords of Annandale. Being close to the English-Scottish border, Lochwood Tower was burned in border raids and rebuilt a number of times before being finally abandoned as a family home after an accidental fire, c. 1710, and left to become a ruin. The ancient and majestic oak trees observed by JB are also reported by others; see Honey, *"Gentle" Johnston/es.*

6. That is, the creator, God; Joseph Addison's Ode, based on Psalm 19:1–6, published in *Spectator*, no. 465 (Aug. 23, 1712; 4:144–45) and quoted by Hervey in his final contemplation, "on the Starry Heavens":

The spacious Firmament on high,
With all the blue æthereal Sky,
And spangled Heav'ns, a shining Frame,
Their great Original proclaim. (*Meditations and Contemplations*, 2:130–31)

JB's language and style here is reminiscent of Hervey's.

7. Matthew 5:16, a verse made particularly familiar through its use in the Anglican liturgy for Morning Prayer.

8. *Eugenio*: well-born. As Hannah Barker observes, anonymous contributors to the papers frequently used pseudonyms that purported to be "a description of their social stand-

1761

An Original Letter, from a Gentleman
of Scotland to the Earl of *** in London

[When Boswell ran away from Glasgow in March 1760, to make his first (and frequently overlooked) visit to London at the age of twenty, his father, Lord Auchinleck, asked the Earl of Eglinton—their neighbor in Ayrshire, who was then in London pursuing his political ambitions—if he would seek out the runaway youth and offer him some guidance and support. Boswell's aim in leaving Scotland had been to convert to Catholicism and, perhaps, to enter a monastery, although, while pursuing this scheme, he had also been introduced to London's low-life and carnal pleasures through the agency of Irish grub street writer Samuel Derrick. The earl had him found, gave him funds, took him into his elegant home and circle, and, shrewdly seeing Boswell's fundamental sociability and metropolitan ambitions, introduced him, as Boswell wrote in his "Memoirs," "into the circles of the great, the gay, and the ingenious" (*Lit. Car.*, xxxi). Boswell remained in London for three months, before his father arrived to take him home, relieved that his son's attraction to ascetic religion had dissipated but concerned that the scheme he was now considering of seeking a commission in the Guards would lead only to his living a licentious life in London. The compromise was that Boswell would study the law. But, as Pottle says, "the most significant activity of the [next] two years was not the study of law nor raking: it was scribbling" (*Earlier Years*, 58).]

Scots Magazine, 23 (September 1761), 469–71

AN ORIGINAL LETTER,
From a GENTLEMAN of SCOTLAND to
the EARL of *** in LONDON

Sept. 25. 1761.

MY DEAR LORD,[9]

THE splendid magnificent coronation is now over.[10] How is your Lordship after it? I dare say you are so much out of breath with your great share of the

---

ing and local identity" (*Newspapers, Politics, and Public Opinion*, 39); this applies as well to the following article, from "A Gentleman of Scotland."

9. Alexander Montgomerie, tenth earl of Eglinton (1723–69), politician and landowner, was a wealthy and accomplished socialite and sportsman. He took his feudal responsibilities seriously and worked to advance agricultural reform in Ayrshire, but his political ambitions were frustrated by his more social interests.

10. The coronation of King George III, a great public spectacle, was held at Westminster Abbey on Sept. 22, 1761.

courtly fatigues of the day,[11] that I cannot expect an answer to this letter, for at least a post or two.——Well said, my boy;—I fancy you may think yourself well off, if you are slightly glanced over a month hence.——Undoubtedly you have had a noble show of grandeur. But, if I mistake not, my Lord, you and I have run through more agreeable scenes together, when I had the honour of living under your Lordship's roof and patronage, at London. I say *living*; for at that time, by enjoying, I really knew the value of life. Your Lordship convinced me, that this same existence of ours,—bad as some philosophers and divines may call it,—is yet worth the having; aye and thanking God Almighty for too, if we will but make the most of it. I believe, my Lord, when you and I, after a pleasant drive in the chariot from Ranelaugh,[12] have sat down by ourselves in your dining-room, to an enlivening bottle of Old Hock,[13] and, with all imaginable gaiety, have resumed the adventures of the day—sometimes indeed the former night too, has dropt into the scale—I believe then, my Lord, our sentiments of *all things under the sun* were somewhat different from that illustrious monarch's, who to be sure was a very wise man, but who, for the very reason that he was a man, might chance to fall into a little mistake.[14]——Is not this a lounging length of a sentence? It is so. But, notwithstanding, you must take its appendix, which is but a short one. Only this: Perhaps we may be as sagacious as *Solomon*, when we have got as great a surfeit of pleasure as his Jewish Majesty; but, till that time comes, we must beg leave to differ from him.

Your Lordship is a complete master of the noble science of Happiness. Theory and practice both are not wanting. You have taught me a smattering, for which I thank you. Did you not find me an excellent scholar?—I certainly did pretty well for my time. But I am impatient for a regular course of lectures, and full scope for the exercise of my knowledge; which cannot be, till my propitious

11. Eglinton had recently "been appointed one of the lords of the bedchamber, ... [and] would have played a prominent part on that day of splendour" (*Earlier Years*, 66).

12. Ranelagh Gardens, Chelsea (just outside London at that time), were public pleasure gardens, opened in 1742; they became a fashionable resort for upper-class Londoners; see Chap. 1, n. 65.

13. *Hock*: a British term for any German white wine. Two and a half years after this, on Mar. 15, 1763, JB records spending another such evening with Eglinton as that alluded to here (*Lond. Journ.*, 218).

14. The "illustrious monarch" is Solomon, as proverbial for his wisdom as for his many wives and concubines and traditionally regarded as the writer of the biblical Ecclesiastes, in which "all things under the sun" are repeatedly said to be vain and vexatious to the spirit; see Ecclesiastes 1:4, 2:17, etc.

stars—*Venus* for one,—and, I take it, *Mars* for another,[15]—shall grant us to meet again in the delightful BRITISH METROPOLIS.

The Spectator tells us, that men generally are fonder to *appear* happy, than to be really so.[16] The observation may hold good for most part; but, you know, every rule has its exceptions; and from this, take your humble servant as one: for if that were my opinion, I should at this moment be superlatively blest; being undoubtedly reckoned one of the happiest men alive, especially by every young fellow in this country, who has not got the eyes of a mole, or the perceptions of a burgomaster.[17]

You will now think, I suppose, that I am playing the *sphynx*, and endeavouring to perplex your understanding by a dark and inconceivable enigma.[18] Be it so, my dear Lord.—I will not attempt to beat you out of your conjecture. I might, perhaps, find it as difficult as to persuade a *hypochondriac* that the tower of Babel is not built upon his left shoulder. If a skilful physician was employed to cure a man of this dreadful malady, instead of vainly opposing his disturbed imagination, he would instantly call for workmen, drive the building down about his patient's ears, save him from the ruins, and so deliver him from the terrible apprehension which nodded over his head.[19] This simile may not be entirely applicable to the present case. No matter for that: *Omnis simile claudicat,*

15. Astrologically and in classical mythology, Venus governs love, and Mars, war (the latter is an allusion to JB's anticipated career as a commissioned officer in the army).

16. *Spectator*, no. 261 (Dec. 29, 1711; 2:515): "as I have elsewhere observed, it is one of the most unaccountable Passions of Human Nature, that we are at greater Pains to appear easy and happy to others, than to really make ourselves so." The passage Addison refers to is from *Tatler*, no. 63 (Sept. 3, 1709; 1:435): "[T]here is hardly a Man to be found, who would not rather be in Pain to appear happy, than be really happy and thought miserable."

17. Moles have such limited vision that they are proverbially regarded as blind. For *burgomaster*, see Chap. 1, n. 25. The British had a strong national prejudice against the Dutch, dating from seventeenth-century commercial rivalries between Britain and Holland; they regarded the Dutch as neat and industrious but also proud, overfed, miserly, cowardly unless drunk, frequently drunk, and dull. See Duffy, *Englishman and the Foreigner*, 27–31.

18. Not the Egyptian sphinx, but the monster of Greek mythology, which was said to pose riddles to the Thebans and to devour those who could not solve them.

19. *Hypochondriack* (adj.): "Melancholy; disordered in the imagination" (*SJ Dict.*). JB considered himself a hypochondriac (see *Earlier Years*, 132–33; *Later Years*, 178) and suffered frequent bouts of depression; his preoccupation with the subject surfaces in the essay series *The Hypochondriack*, as well as in the letters (below) on "Impotence of Mind." Here, his advice is to assist the sufferer to combat the supposed delusion, rather than to attempt to persuade him that he is not deluded. The biblical Tower of Babel is the subject of Genesis chap. 11.

as the old churchman said;[20] and why not this? So, my Lord! I will humour your supposition, that I am playing the *sphynx*; but will likewise *double a part*,—as the players say,[21]—and in the character of *Œdipus*, will unravel the wonderful mystery.[22] Like all other discoveries hard to be come at, it is very plain when known. In short, my Lord, the voice of this part of the world has it, that I am just going to be married to an angel of light,—to talk as a poet,—or to give you an expression which you may like better,—to a most beautiful young lady, whom you know very well, and have said a thousand fine things to. You cannot mistake who it is,—the idol of every public place, the toast of every private company.[23] Is not this exaltation enough? Must I not have my own share of envy? The most certain indication of a man's being esteemed fortunate.——However, this is not enough for me. I understand as much of the law, as to know, that the kernel is better than the shell, and that a sagacious man will always prefer substance to shadow.

The last of these I look upon as of the same species with transient fame; the short-liv'd breath,[24] whether sweet or the contrary, of the ignorant world; which, for the most trifling reasons, and frequently for no reasons at all, circulates, with eager rapidity, every thing that fancy suggests.

I have indeed experienced the full extent of this in my own person. Not long ago, they paid me the compliment, forsooth, of *swinging upon Tyburn-tree*,— which, though now dignify'd by *better company*, the want of which *Macheath* regrets so much,[25]—I should not yet be over-fond of. Now the note is chang'd;

20. A proverbial Latin expression, usually found as *omnis comparatio claudicat nisi in punctum comparationis* ("all similes are limp [i.e., are found wanting] except in the point of comparison"); it is often used in a theological context.

21. *Players* are actors; *to double a part* is "to act as the double of or substitute for (another player); to play two parts in the same piece" (*OED*).

22. Oedipus solved the Sphinx's key riddle, and the monster destroyed itself. JB says that he will play the parts of both the Sphinx and Oedipus by answering his own question.

23. As Pottle notes, the young JB "enjoyed playing with ideas of marriage" (*Earlier Years*, 67). Of the young ladies whom he considered as possible amatory partners at this time, Pottle says that the most likely to be "the lucky girl referred to" here was Katherine Colquhoun (1742–1804), daughter of Sir James Colquhoun of Luss.

24. Possibly an allusion to "Transient is fame's immediate breath," a line from the poem "The Temple of Favour" by Robert Lloyd (1733–64).

25. *Tyburn-tree* is the public gallows at Tyburn (see Chap. 2, intro). In John Gay's *The Beggar's Opera*, 3.13, MacHeath sings ("Air LXVII," to the tune of "Greensleeves"):

> Since Laws were made for ev'ry Degree,
> To curb Vice in others, as well as me,
> I wonder we han't better Company,

nothing for it but Bravo!—*Hymen* for ever![26]—A very pretty man!—He deserves her! Would not this, my Lord, have made ONSLOW smile from his chair, during an important debate, could it but have occurred to him?[27] If your Lordship will permit me to use a conceit, this chimerical περιπετεια, (excuse the pedantry of a Greek word;—I love it, and must down with it;—you shall have it in English too), this chimerical *change of fortune* reminds me of a curious expression of some poor, well-meaning, persecuted zealot or another, who used to call the *gallows* the *gate of heaven*:[28]—for from that, it seems, they have transported me to the paradise of Miss——'s arms. Charming project truly for the amiable creature! A pretty sort of a juvenile husband she would have!—How becoming would the volatile pate of *Ranger* look,[29] when wrapp'd up in the matrimonial nightcap!—What a grave prudent master of a family would a flighty young officer of the GUARDS make! Your Lordship's fertile invention may contrive two or three more exclamations of the same kind. In the mean time, let me not forget that you may, by this time, have uttered many an exclamation of impatience at the prodigious extent of this epistle.

Indulge me a little longer: you shall soon get free: I am now near the end of my paper, which is far from being a puny slip.—And what does it contain?—Why, truly, a great deal about my important self.

I am sorry to find myself so remarkable an *Egotist*. But self-sufficiency is so much my style, that I am persuaded, if you will but read a single sentence of

---

Upon Tyburn Tree!
But Gold from Law can take out the Sting;
And if rich Men like us were to swing,
'Twou'd thin the Land, such Numbers to string
Upon Tyburn Tree!

The *better company* by which the gallows was recently dignified was Earl Ferrers, who was hanged while JB was in London (see Chap. 1, n. 33).

26. Hymen was the ancient Greek god of marriage.

27. Arthur Onslow (1691–1768), speaker of the House of Commons, recently retired in Mar. 1761, after a still record speakership of thirty-three years. He "was a rare model of integrity in an age of corruption" (*ODNB*).

28. περιπετεια (peripeteia): a reversal of fortune. JB likely came across the expression "the gate of heaven" (perhaps in his Catholic reading of 1760) in some account of the Catholic martyrs of Tyburn, the 105 religious and lay catholics who, between 1535 and 1681, were executed for treason; there were many accounts of various of these martyrs suffering cheerfully in anticipation of heaven.

29. *Ranger*, a young rake in Benjamin Hoadly's popular comedy *The Suspicious Husband* (1747), was one of JB's favorite characters from the stage. He knew the play from at least Aug. 1761 (*Corres. 9*, 80 and n. 36).

this to *Sir Charles S——*,[30] or any of our common friends, without tipping them the smallest wink, they will tell you who it is from, in the snapping of a hard biscuit. What is *Tristram Shandy* doing? skipping about *alamode de bon vivant?*[31] I wish you great folks would give him as broad a hint to rise in the church, as the *Irishman* once received to go down stairs. He is the best companion I ever knew, and the most taking composer of sermons that I ever read.[32] I shall write to him soon.

Pray be so good as to ask *Lord G——* if he has not forgot me. I lik'd him much, when *Sir Richard*; I hope his peerage has not banished his good humour.[33]

Remember me to all with whose acquaintance I have been honoured through your Lordship's kindness. It would take up the live-long day to name every one of them, from his R——l H——ss, downwards.[34] I must insist that you present my best respects to *Lady M——*, and tell her, that to hear her Ladyship's divine harpsichord, for another forenoon, I would gladly serve her for half a year, as a

30. Sir Charles Sedley (c. 1721–78), politician and champion racehorse owner, whom JB had met through Eglinton in London in 1761 (*Earlier Years*, 48).

31. *Alamode de bon vivant*: usually two separate French expressions; "a la mode" (often hyphenated or as one word; see *SJ Dict.*) for "in the fashion" was used in English from the 1600s, as was "bon vivant" for "one fond of good living."

32. JB alludes rather unsubtly to Laurence Sterne, the fashionable author of the time. Of the hint here that JB was acquainted with Sterne, James J. Caudle concludes that the two never met, pointing out that in his inventions JB tended to make "extravagant claims of friendship with the good and the great" (Caudle, "'Fact' or 'Invention,'" 38; see also *Corres. 9*, 30 n. 1). The first volumes of Sterne's *Tristram Shandy* were published in 1759; while *a la mode* and *bon vivant* describe Sterne's London lifestyle, he was a clergyman and published his sermons as *Sermons by Mr. Yorick* (1760, 1766). According to *Cobbett's Weekly Political Register*, 20, no. 4 (July 27, 1811), cols. 105–6, the story called "John Keale's broad hint" was told in the House of Lords by Charles Stanhope (1753–1816), third Earl Stanhope, who said that he had heard it at Oxford: "There was a man that John Keale did not like; John gave him a hint that he did not like his company: but he would not go away. 'What did you do then?' says one to John. 'Do,' says John Keale, 'why, I kicked him down stairs.' That was a pretty broad hint!!!' (*Laughing*.)" *Taking* (adj.): "That takes the fancy or affection; captivating, engaging, alluring, fascinating, charming, attractive" (*OED*).

33. Sir Richard Grosvenor had been raised to the peerage, as Baron Grosvenor, in Apr. 1761.

34. The most socially significant introduction that JB received in Eglinton's company in 1760 was to the heir presumptive to the throne, his Royal Highness Edward Augustus, Duke of York (1739–67). JB met him at the Newmarket races and dedicated to him his poem *The Cub at Newmarket* (1762). Not long afterward, he confessed to his journal that he no longer relished the connection and thought the duke "not a man of dignity nor of extraordinary genius. He was sunk in debauchery" (Nov. 9, 1763; *Holland*, 62).

downright footman, without any mental reservation whatever.[35]——I remain, with perfect esteem and gratitude, My Dear Lord, your, *&c.*

1763

The Miseries of a Timorous Man

[A vein of invention permeates much of of Boswell's journalism: he used fictitious identities in order to comment on actual contemporary events and reported anonymously on fictitious events. In these two letters, the young Boswell constructs a fictitious persona who reports his own character and doings; generically, they could be the first two installments of an epistolary novel. James J. Caudle, who in 2011 first identified these articles as Boswell's, points out that the alleged narrator, "B." of Westminster, strongly exhibits a Boswellian character and attitude: his "timidity in his youth, his lifelong fear of death, his place-seeking, and perhaps his Restoration-comedy style advances to a 'Lady of great Fortune'" (Caudle, "Three New James Boswell Articles," 25); to which list we might add his love of the theater and his strategy of making familiar and flattering mention of eminent people with whom he might like to become (better) acquainted, such as Garrick, Charles Churchill, and H. S. Woodfall. And, as the notes demonstrate, many of the places mentioned were visited by him. Many of the notes given below have been adapted from James Caudle's extensive annotations, with his permission.]

Public Advertiser, May 23, 1763, 1–2 (leading article)

To the Printer of the PUBLIC ADVERTISER.

SIR,

I AM a Man of a Disposition remarkably timorous; Fear is the predominant Quality, the ruling Principle in my Constitution.[36] I have been told by the good

35. *Lady M*: not identified. Pottle suggests that she may be the "Lady Mirabel" mentioned in JB's journal around this time (Jan. 14, 1763), who is also not identified but who he says might be Lady Mary Coke (1726–1811; *Earlier Years*, 484–85). JB described "Lady Mirabel" as "a Lady of Quality whom I was a little acquainted with, . . . Lady Mirabel is a Widow of middle age, has a jointure sufficient to live genteely upon, altho' not pretty she has a fine air and is very agreable" (*Lond. Journ.*, 142–43). *Downright* (adj.): "Plain, open, apparent, undisguised" (*SJ Dict.*).

36. In the descriptions of himself that he wrote in Dec. 1764 in preparation for meeting Rousseau, JB says that, when he was a child, "The Servants amused me with an infinity of stories of Robbers, of Murderers, of Sorcerers and of Ghosts. Of the kind that

Midwife,[37] who attended my Mother at my Nativity, that I discovered this before I was born; as it was with much Reluctance, that I could be prevailed with to venture into the World.

But if I was frightened at coming into the World, I am much more so at going out of it. Death is to me indeed a King of Terrors: The Horror which I feel from the Thoughts of my Dissolution, throws an incessant Gloom over my Mind, except when I am relieved by little Intervals of social Joy.[38] I am a Sceptic in almost every Point whatever. But let me reason, and twist and turn as I please, I never can get rid of the Certainty of Death.

This Disposition of Mind renders me a very tame and harmless Member of Society, as I studiously shun every Thing that is in the least Degree attended with bodily Hazard. I have refused Places in the Army, the Navy, and the Excise.[39] I would not go to Jamaica, tho' my Uncle there has offered me Five Hundred a Year;[40] and I did not make amorous Advances to a Widow Lady of great Fortune,[41] because I imagined I should interfere with her Butler, a strong Rawbone Irishman; and indeed the Event has justified my Apprehension; for a few Days ago her Ladyship was actually wedd to him, at that genteel Habitation of Holiness—Audley Chapel.[42]

---

my Imagination was continually frightened. I became a being of the most fearful and most contemptible sort"; and that "Until I was eighteen years old I could not be alone at night. . . . I feared cold and everything—a great Poltroon in the streets of Edinburgh" (translation by James Caudle, from the French original in Boswell, *Journal of His German and Swiss Travels*, 356, 364).

37. The name of the midwife who delivered JB is unknown.

38. For death as a *king of terrors*, see Job 18:14: "His confidence shall be rooted out of his tabernacle, and it shall bring him to the king of terrors" (*AV*). JB addresses the subject of fear in *The Hypochondriack*, no. 2; of depressive gloom (or hypochondria, in its eighteenth-century sense) in nos. 5 and 6; and of death in nos. 14–16 (Bailey, 1:111–17, 135–49, 198–220).

39. JB attempted to gain a free commission as an ensign in the (Third or Scots) Foot Guards (or, alternately, the Royal Horse Guards Blue) but succeeded only in gaining Prime Minister Lord Bute's promise of an ensigncy in a regiment of the line (see the letter from Bute to the Earl of Eglinton, Mar. 26, 1763, in *Corres. 9*, 394). JB is not known to have given serious effort to gaining a commission in the navy nor a post in the government office of excise.

40. JB had a distant cousin Charles Boswell (1720–after 1794), who left Scotland "very poor" and returned from Jamaica in 1768 "very rich"; see *Corres. 7*, 150–51 n. 2.

41. This "Widow Lady of great Fortune" resembles the "Lady Mirabel" referred to in JB's journal (see n. 35, above).

42. Presumably, the Grosvenor Chapel, opened in 1731 in South Audley Street, on the Mayfair estate of wealthy landowner Sir Richard Grosvenor. JB attended worship there on

Mobs of every Kind fill me with Dread. When I go into a public Assembly of my Fellow-creatures, I sweat under the Ideas of implacable Resentment, which I may raise by treading upon their Toes. I consider myself as in a Vessel, sailing round the Northern Coast of Scotland, where it is every Moment in Danger of being wrecked on some of the little Islands, which are scattered on all Hands.[43] Mr. Garrick has had many a Compliment payed him; so many indeed, that his most warm Admirers have almost nothing left to give but the *expressive Silence*.[44] I think I can furnish a new Testimony in Favour of our Roscius,[45] by declaring that my Eagerness to be present at his Performances, conquers my strongest natural Passion. On the Nights that he plays, I press into the Pit of Drury-lane; notwithstanding the jostling Multitude, and all the Terrors of Links and Flambeaus and Coaches and Chairs. The last Time that he played Lear,[46] I found myself in a most alarming Situation; Mr. Churchill was immediately before me, as we pressed along the Passage; and as his bodily Strength

---

May 8, 1763: "I went to Audley Chapel, but was still so dissipated, that I could not fix my attention, so I came out after part of the service was over" (*Lond. Journ.*, 254). (Caudle has identified a wedding, on Apr. 28, 1763, involving an Irishman and a widow, which may have taken place there and to which JB may be alluding.)

43. JB actually experienced the horror of almost being shipwrecked in the Scottish seas a decade later, during his tour to the Hebrides with SJ, writing, "I endeavoured to compose my mind. It was not easy to do it; for all the stories that I had heard of the dangerous sailing among the Hebrides, which is proverbial, came full upon my recollection" (*Tour*, Oct. 3, 1774; *Life*, 5:284).

44. Garrick was known for his expert use of dramatic pauses as well as his eloquent speaking of lines. "Garrick experimented with dynamic pacing, even going so far as to insert his own caesuras midsentence, creating dramatic pauses that positively shook the London theatre world"; see Borlik, "'Painting of a sorrow.'" In his memoranda for May 23, the day of this publication, JB wrote, "Break[fast with] Garrick morn[ing] of public [Advertiser]," presumably to show him the article in which he is flatteringly mentioned (Caudle, "Three New James Boswell Articles," 25; Boswell, *London Journal*, ed. Turnbull, 228). JB could have found the term "expressive silence" in the final line of James Thompson's "A Hymn on the Seasons" (1730), usually included with his great work, *The Seasons* (1730). (Caudle gives other earlier occurrences of the expression.)

45. For Garrick as "our Roscius," see Chap. 1, n. 58.

46. JB saw Garrick at Drury Lane theater in the role of Lear eleven days before this publication, on May 12, 1763, and wrote in his journal, "So very high is his reputation, even after playing so long, that the pit was full in ten minutes after four, although the play did not begin till half an hour after six. I kept myself at a distance from all acquaintances, and got into a proper frame. Mr. Garrick gave me the most perfect satisfaction. I was fully moved and I shed abundance of tears" (*Lond. Journ.*, 256–57).

seemed to equal the Vigour of his Mind, I trembled for Fear of irritating that Herculean Bard.[47]

Having now given a pretty clear Notion of my own Character, I shall, in a future Paper, relate some direful Miseries which I have lately suffered.

I am, your humble Servant,

Westminster.   B.[48]

Public Advertiser, June 1, 1763, 1 (leading article)

To the Printer of the PUBLIC ADVERTISER.

SIR,

IN my last I gave a Promise of relating some direful Miseries which have befallen me; and although the Recollection of my Distresses cannot fail to hurt me much, yet will I be a Man of my Word. I shall keep in View the great Example of the pious Æneas, who at the Request of Queen Dido, renewed his sad Calamities, by repeating them.[49] The Hero indeed had the Consolation of receiving the Sympathy of a beautiful Princess,[50] which, without any Disparagement to my good Friend Mr. Woodfall,[51] is more pleasing than that of the best Printer upon Earth. However, I flatter myself that I shall be equal with him in that Respect, as I hope for the tender Compassion of the many fair Ladies in this Metropolis, who are your constant Readers.

47. The poet Churchill was noted for his large and powerful build. JB's only record of being in a theater with him in 1762–63 is on June 20 at the Haymarket, not Garrick's Drury Lane: "I sat by Churchill just at the spikes [i.e., in the front row]. I was vain to be seen talking with that great bard" (*Lond. Journ.*, 281).

48. At the time of this publication and the following, and until July 7, 1763, when he argued with his landlord, JB was living in rooms in Downing Street, Westminster; see *Lond. Journ.*, 295.

49. At the conclusion of book 1 of the *Aeneid*, Dido, queen of Carthage, asks Aeneas to relate his story. In books 2 and 3, Aeneas recounts his life from the time of the Trojan Horse onward to the Fall of Troy and from his escape from the burning city to his arrival in Carthage. Boswell was aware that many referenced the epic without having read it: "People . . . chuse to show that they have either read or heard People talk about the *Aeneid* of Virgil"; see Boswell, "Journal of My Jaunt" (Sept. 14, 1762), 44.

50. Book 4 of the *Aeneid* begins by describing how Dido was moved to love and concern for Aeneas by his account of his bravery and adventures.

51. H. S. Woodfall, editor of the *Pub. Adv.*, and JB were not, as far as we know, good friends at this time. JB was in the habit of referring in print to public figures whom he barely knew as his friends.

It may perhaps appear strange, that a Man of so cool and circumspect a Conduct as I am, should be harrassed with Misfortunes: For I am apt to think, that Calamities, like the Givers of Charity, are seldom at the Trouble to seek out Objects in the Shade of Retirement. They must be met half-way; we must *meet with them*, as the Phrase is:[52] Could a Man extinguish his Passions altogether, and reduce himself to a mere vegetable Existence, he might assuredly pass through the World, without suffering any of the Evils incident to Humanity. Upon this System I in a good Measure proceed; but have not yet arrived at so great Perfection in it, but what vivacious Nature will now and then make me take a sudden Spring out of my serene Path, and make me rashly sport in enchanting, although dangerous, Fields.

Some Nights ago, I spent an Evening at the Somerset Coffee-house with half a Dozen of my old Friends,[53] who went into the Army from a Desire of laced Cloaths, Ease, and Gaiety; but who have been enduring Hunger and Cold, and Fatigue, in Germany and America, for some Years past.[54] Our Conversation turned upon War; in the Course of which I heard such horrid Stories of Dangers, and Wounds, and Death, that I felt the upright Hair, the cold Sweat, and all the other Symptoms of deep Consternation.[55] My Fancy was so much wrought upon with Images of Terror, that when I got home, and went to-bed, it was very long before I could fall asleep; and happy had it been for me, if I had waked all that Night; for before next Day, I endured the most cruel Sufferings.

I thought[56] that I was walking down the Strand about One o'Clock in the Morning; and just at the Corner of Exeter-street,[57] I was attacked by a Man in a Sailor's Habit, who first robbed me, and then most barbarously cut my Throat.[58]

52. This phrase is used in contexts where it suggests to engage with militarily, to contest, or to fight with.

53. JB had been to the Somerset Coffee House for breakfasts on Jan. 19 and June 19, 1763 (*Lond. Journ.*, 153, 280).

54. British combat had, in the Seven Years' War, a "German" theater, focused on defending George II's Electorate of Hanover, and a North American and Caribbean theater.

55. JB recorded in his journal on Nov. 3, 1762, "Upon the road Erskine painted the horrors of a German Campaign very particularly, and very strongly and so frightened both me and Himself" (Boswell, "Journal of My Jaunt," 100).

56. Here "B's" nightmare begins.

57. In London in 1763, Exeter Street and the Strand did not intersect; Exeter Street ended where Bridges Street turned into Catherine Street. "B" presumably meant Exeter Court, near Exeter Exchange; see Hyde, *A to Z of Georgian London*, map 11, grid B/a.

58. On Jan. 5, 1763, JB wrote in his journal of his fear of such robberies: "We stayed till near three. I was really uneasy going home. Robberies in the street are now very frequent" (*Lond. Journ.*, 125).

By a strange inconsistent Combination of Ideas, I was comforting myself that all was now over, and that I needed no longer be distracted with the Torments of Fear; when, on a sudden, I felt myself in a Barge sailing down the Thames, with Intention to land at Whitehall Stairs: But alas! my Watermen were both mortally drunk, and rashly shooting the Bridge, we were instantly plunged to the Bottom of the River. Scarcely was this Shock fully perceived, when methought I was clambering round the Roof of the Cupola of St. Paul's,[59] and looking from that tremendous Height with much Horror; when my Foot slipped, and down I tumbled head-long into the Church-Yard,[60] pitched upon Mr. Newbery's *Bible*, and by the Violence of my Fall, drove his *Sun* from its Sphere.[61] By this last Accident my Skull was fractured in a dismal Manner. I next imagined myself apprehended for robbing on the Highway.[62] I was tried and condemned at the Old Bailey, chained to the Floor in one of the dreary Cells in Newgate,[63] and at last brought to Execution at the fatal Tyburn.[64] The Agonies which then distracted

59. JB attended worship at St. Paul's Cathedral on Christmas Day 1762 (*Lond. Journ.*, 104). During a later visit, as he recorded July 19, 1763, he took an opportunity to explore the church: "I then went up to the roof of the Cupola, and went out upon the leads, and walked around it. I went up to the highest storey of roof. Here I had the immense prospect of London and its environs" (*Lond. Journ.*, 310). The lower gallery around the base of the dome of the Cathedral is the Stone Gallery; the walkway at the top of the dome, encircling the Lantern, is called the Golden Gallery, and is 280 feet from the floor of the Cathedral. From neither of these could a visitor step out upon the lead roof of the dome, although looking immediately down from either gallery the sensation is "of being perched above a great sea of lead, and [. . .] this may have coloured his choice of words" (Joseph Wisdom, Librarian of St. Paul's Cathedral, personal communication, August 15, 2012).

60. From after the reformation, St. Paul's Cathedral Churchyard was the favored site for shops of printers, stationers, and booksellers.

61. John Newbery (1713–67), bookseller, best known for his children's books but also a publisher of serious books, as well as the daily newspaper the *Public Ledger*. "In 1745 he moved to the Bible and Sun (later numbered 65) in St Paul's Churchyard" (*ODNB*). His shop sign consisted of symbols of a Bible and a sun: B's fall breaks these united symbols asunder.

62. For JB's attraction to imaginative representations of highwaymen, see Chap. 2, n. 71. He was actually terrified of being held up by a true-life highwayman, writing in his journal on Nov. 18, 1762: "During our two last stages this night, which we travelled in the dark, I was a good deal afraid of Robbers. A great many horrid ideas filled my mind" (*Lond. Journ.*, 43).

63. JB had visited Newgate Prison on May 3, 1763, a few weeks before this publication. He wrote in his journal: "the cells . . . are surely most dismal places. . . . [I]n these dark mansions are the unhappy criminals confined. I did not go in, but stood in the court, where were a number of strange blackguard beings with sad countenances, most of them being friends and acquaintances of those under sentence of death" (*Lond. Journ.*, 251).

64. For JB's visit to Tyburn on May 4, 1763, a few weeks before this publication, see above, Chap. 2, intro, and *Lond. Journ.*, 250–52. For his identification with dashing convicts, see also his "Original Letter" and n. 25, above.

my Mind are not to be described. However, Despair made me resign myself to my Fate, and I stood in Expectation of the dreadful Moment. But just as the Cart was moving from below me I awoke, and opening my Eyes, perceived the Maid wheeling me up and down my Chamber with great Composure. I had desired her to call me in the Morning. She had spoke to me several times, and found me fast asleep; and being a modest Girl, newly imported from Cumberland, she had taken this Method to break my Repose.[65]

You see then, Mr. *Public*, that your timorous and cautious Correspondent had his Throat cut, his Skull fractured, was drowned in the River Thames, and was within an Ace of being hanged; a Complication of Misery which no Man, while awake, ever endured. I am, Sir,

Your most humble Servant,

Westminster.   B.

The Defects of Polite Conversation

[Boswell wrote and attempted to publish various pieces in the London papers in 1763, some of which he described in his journal as "fanciful little essays" (*Lond. Journ.*, 189). There is no record of him writing or submitting this essay, but it represents some of his views and activities at the time, particularly his deep interest in conversation and sociality, as well as his increasingly good relations with the conductors of the *Public Advertiser*. My notes are indebted to Gordon Turnbull's work on this text and to his advice.]

Public Advertiser, August 4, 1763, 1

For the Public Advertiser *only.*

A PERIODICAL PAPER[66]

Omnes homines qui sese student præstare cæteris Animalibus, summa ope niti debent ne vitam transigent in SILENTIO *veluti pecora quas natura prona & ventri obedientia finxit.*

SALLUST.[67]

65. In his journal for June 6, 1763, JB wrote, "We have now in the house where I lodge, a neat little maid called Nancy, newly imported from Cumberland" (*Lond. Journ.*, 273). The exact match of the phrase "newly imported from Cumberland" in this journal entry and the article greatly strengthens the case for JB's authorship of this article.

66. JB gives the impression that he intended this essay to inaugurate a regular series in the *Public Advertiser*, but no further such essays have been identified. In any case, by the time it was published, he had left England for the continent.

67. The opening words of Sallust's *Bellum Catilinae* [The War with Catiline]: "It behoves all men who wish to excel the other animals to strive with might and main not to

MAN was intended by his Creator, for a sociable Animal. A single human Being can only support his Existence, and indulge himself in Animal Gratifications of the lowest Kind. Mental Felicity cannot be enjoyed but from a reciprocal Communication of Ideas, and Sympathy of Affections.[68] The Conversation of Savages must naturally be coarse and unrestrained: But in the Progress of Civilization, when the Feelings become more delicate, Conversation is gradually polished; we learn to express ourselves with Elegance, and to chuse our Topics with Propriety. Diversity of Ranks and Diversity of Characters are formed, Politeness is cultivated for the sake of Order; and for the sake of mutual Pleasure arising from the Participation of mutual Respect.

Various have been the Opinions of Mankind, with regard to Conversation; and many are the Treatises which have been written upon that Subject. Some have maintained, that Speech should only be used for important purposes, for Religion, Morality, and civil Conduct; others are for exploding these heavy Topics, and will talk of nothing but gay and vivacious Humour; while others (as is the Case in every Dispute) step in between, and chuse to have every Advantage.

But of all Modes of Conversation that human Ingenuity has devised, the reigning Mode of the fashionable Part of this Metropolis is the most incomprehensible. The well-bred People of Rank meet together, in one Room: They bow very stifly, and they simper very aukwardly: They pass many Hours together; during which they neither talk grave Sense, nor lively Nonsense; but resemble a Parcel of Prisoners abroad, who are obliged to converse by dumb Shew. A Gentleman of great Eminence in the Poetical World calls a modern genteel Party, a consensual Obliteration of the human Faculties.[69] In reality, every manly Power is suspended, even the Voice must not be heard; " 'tis so VASTLY loud; no delicate Ear can bear it;"[70] and therefore the few poor Words which they do say, must be mumbled in a half Whisper. I was lately at the Table of a noble Lord,[71]

---

pass through life unheralded, like the beasts, which Nature has fashioned grovelling and slaves to the belly" (*Sallust*, 3).

68. The expression "Sympathy of Affections" is suggestive of Adam Smith's *Theory of Moral Sentiments* (1759), which grew out of a series of lectures that JB heard and admired while a student in Edinburgh.

69. The "gentleman" is JB's friend Erskine, with whom, on Dec. 19, 1762, JB had the conversation he describes about the parties of the polite classes (see *Lond. Jour.*, 96).

70. If this is a quote or allusion, it has not been identified. "Vastly" was a vogue word at the time, as Chesterfield described in *The World* (Dec. 5, 1754).

71. JB attended many social occasions between Dec. 19 and the date of this publication; as Turnbull points out, the standard JB set for conversation rose after he met SJ on May 16, 1763.

where one particular Gentleman struck me so strongly, that I could not help applying to him Virgil's famous Line,

Obstupuit, steteruntque comæ, & vox saucibus hæsit.[72]

Which a comical Wag englished thus: *Obstupuit*, he was very stupid, *steteruntque comæ*, and his Hair was very stifly drest, & *vox saucibus hæsit*, and he spoke below his Breath.

I wish I could be of any use towards remedying this Evil: I am resolved to do my best. Let Doctor Taylor cure the sickly Eyes of my Countrymen;[73] it shall be my Ambition to give them the free Use of their Tongues. I am, Sir,

Your humble Servant,

Inner Temple.[74]

B.

1767

A Recipe Requested for Removing "Rust" from Books

London Chronicle, April 30–May 2, 1767, 423

To the PRINTER *of the* LONDON CHRONICLE.

SIR,

Many of your Readers must have observed in books, certain brown spots, which are nothing else than rust, which gets into the paper and corrodes it very fast,

72. From Virgil's *Aeneid*, 2.774: "I was appalled, my hair stood up and the voice choked in my throat" (trans. Fairclough, 1:369). The speaker is Aeneas, who is giving an account of the fall of Troy. The translation that follows is probably JB's.

73. John Taylor (1703–72), oculist and eye surgeon, was appointed in 1736 oculist to George II. He traveled around the courts of Europe treating eminent people. Although learned in his craft and skilled as a surgeon, he was also a shameless self-promoter and in a stream of publications made extravagant claims about his cures. His three-volume autobiography, *The History of the Travels and Adventures of the Chevalier John Taylor*, was published in 1761–62. On Apr. 24, 1779, SJ described Taylor as "the most ignorant man I ever knew, but sprightly," and Beauclerk told how SJ had described him as "an instance how far impudence could carry ignorance" (*Life*, 3:389–90).

74. The Honourable Society of the Inner Temple is one of the four professional bodies called the Inns of Court, to one of which all barristers practicing in England must belong. JB was not at this stage a barrister (as the address is perhaps intended to imply) but, from July 7, 1763, was living in the chambers in Inner Temple Lane leased by his friend W. J. Temple, who had left London for Cambridge (see *Lond. Journ.*, 295).

and if not prevented, it spreads all around, and will by degrees eat through the whole leaves of the thickest volume.[75] I have found the same thing in old parchments. The only remedy I could yet think of, has been to cut out the infected part; but as this disfigures books and papers, and obliges one to fill up the vacancy with a fresh piece, on which it is necessary to write what words or letters the rust has destroyed: it would be extremely useful, if any method could be fallen upon to prevent the rusting. Perhaps there is such a method which I am ignorant of; if so, I would be very much obliged, if any of your Correspondents would communicate it. It is easy enough, with proper care, to preserve books and parchments from dampness, from moths, and from worms. It is hard if there be a destructive quality against which there is no remedy.[76] I hope to receive some instructions as to this. I am, Sir,

ANTIQUARIUS.[77]

An Essay on Travelling[78]

Public Advertiser, November 20, 1767, 1–2 (leading article); with JB's MS alterations

To the Printer of the Public Advertiser.

SIR,
TRAVELLING is now become so common, that I wonder we have not many more Writers upon that Subject. We have indeed many Books of Travels, but these are nothing else but Catalogues of what is to be seen in different Parts of

---

75. This "rust" is presumably the phenomenon called *foxing*: reddish-brown stains or spots on old paper, which are caused by a combination of factors. Foxed paper contains the rust chemical ferric oxide, which may itself be associated with the processes of a fungoid organism. Although foxing does not "corrode" paper, it thrives in humid conditions, which may also encourage the spread of damaging moulds.

76. JB, his father, Lord Auchinleck, and his sons, Sir Alexander ("Sandy") and James the Younger, were all dedicated bookmen. The family's books were dispersed at various auctions, from 1825 to 1917, and further research is needed to discover which and how many books were owned by JB. A figure between 1,000 and 2,000 is likely. In 1770, JB made a list of 311 works in his library, but he seems not to have made any later or more systematic tally (see "Catalogue of Books").

77. *Antiquarius*: an antiquary is a scholar, collector, or enthusiast of ancient artifacts. The London Society of Antiquaries was established in 1707, and the Scottish, in 1780. I have traced no published replies to this letter.

78. This is the heading that JB has handwritten on his file copy, *Cat. Yale*, P 114(1).

Europe with a few Observations upon the Manners of Foreigners. What I wish
to see is the Effect of Travelling after it is over. Rousseau is of Opinion, that
without Travelling a Man has a very imperfect Education;[79] since he who has
seen only one Nation is like a Botanist, who knows only one Species of Plants.
The sage Lycurgus was of a very different Opinion.[80] He would not allow the
Spartans to travel, because he thought that the different Passions, Fancies, and
Modes, which discriminate Nations, were but inconsiderable Varieties, and were
besides particularly appropriated to their several Governments; so that every
Tincture of Foreign Education was properly a Stain on the original Colour, and
the Spartan Sternness would have been adulterated, had it received any Mixture
of the Elegance of Athens. The King of Prussia thinks with Lycurgus. None of
his Subjects are permitted to travel without special Leave, which is granted with
much Reluctance, and to very few.[81] The ingenious Mr. Hurd hath given us the
Arguments on both Sides in a very just and agreeable Manner.[82] But I think
it is indisputable that the present Inhabitants of Britain are rather Disciples
of the Swiss Philosopher, than of the Lacedemonian Legislator, for I am persuaded that since the Days of the Croisades,[83] this Island hath not sent abroad
such Multitudes. I do not mean those who migrate to the Wastes of America,
elated with prodigious Hopes of territorial Wealth and Dominion; nor those
who embark for the East and West Indies, resolved to leave their Bones behind
them, or come home with Treasures sufficient to dazzle their Countrymen with
all the Splendor of a Table, of Dress, Furniture and Equipage. I mean those less

79. Rousseau's didactic novel *Émile* (1762) presents his views on education. The pro-
tagonist, Émile, in the final stage of his education, is to travel to the European capitals to
experience different societies.

80. Classical historians describe Lycurgus as the lawgiver of seventh-century b.c. Sparta
(or Lacedaemonia) and the author of Sparta's rigid social code and system of military education. According to Plutarch, Lycurgus provided Spartans with examples of good conduct to assist in training them to virtue, and for this reason "he forbade them to travel
abroad, and go about acquainting themselves with foreign rules of morality, the habits of
ill-educated people, and different rules of government" (*Plutarch's Lives*, 1:76).

81. The Prussian king, Frederick the Great, encouraged immigration and internal migration to underdeveloped and sparsely populated areas of the kingdom and restricted external travel by Prussian nationals.

82. Richard Hurd (1720–1808); his *Dialogues on the Uses of Foreign Travel: Considered as a
Part of an English Gentleman's Education, between Lord Shaftesbury and Mr. Locke* (1764) was
in the form of a series of imaginary conversations.

83. That is, the Crusades, the series of western European military campaigns in the
eleventh to thirteenth centuries, mainly against Muslim nations, of which the aim was to
establish Christian rule in the Holy Land.

adventurous Travellers, who visit Foreign Parts with no other Intention than to see and be seen, and of these I can shew such a Train as would have peopled a State in ancient Greece. At the Time when the *Spectator* was published, carrying Boys abroad was a rare Folly, and a fit Subject for the Pen of a masterly Satyrist. Accordingly we have it ridiculed with much Force and Vivacity, in one of the Numbers of that inimitable Collection, in a Letter written by the great Lord Chancellor Hardwick under the Name of Philip Homebred.[84] But now our Striplings are led over the Continent by your travelling Governors, in such Swarms that Custom has vanquished Ridicule; since nothing will appear ridiculous which is done by the Many. Not only are Boys sent upon their Travels, but a Spirit of Restlessness has seized upon all Ranks, and all must sail from Harwich or from Calais;[85] Men, Women and Children, Parsons, Porter-brewers, Common-council-men, and their Wives, nay sometimes whole Families must forsooth make the Tour of Europe. The Consequences of this epidemical Folly are first an incredible Sum of Money squandered away idly among People who laugh at the aukward Dupes; and in the next Place, such an Importation of affected Novelties, that our Principles, our Manners, and our Language are becoming like the Babylonish Confusion.[86] The respectable Character of *True Britons*, which all Nations used to revere, without being able to imitate, is transformed into a motley Compound of Nothings. How few among us can read with a just Emotion the noble Apostrophe of Mr. Samuel Johnson:

> "Illustrious Edward! from the Realms of Day
> The Land of Heroes and of Saints survey;
> Nor hope the British Lineaments to trace,
> The rustic Grandeur, or the surly Grace."

LONDON, a Poem.[87]

---

84. The author of *Spectator*, no. 364 (Apr. 28, 1712), signed "Philip Homebred," was Philip Yorke, first earl of Hardwicke (1690–1764; see also Chap. 1, n. 42). JB reports SJ as saying this essay "was quite vulgar, and had nothing luminous" (Apr. 11, 1776; *Life*, 3:34).

85. Harwich on the Essex coast (from where JB departed for Holland in 1763) and Calais on the coast of France were among the main points of embarkation between England and the Continent.

86. That is, the confusion of tongues resulting from God's punishment on the Babylonians for building the Tower of Babel; see Genesis 11:9.

87. Johnson's poem was published in May 1738. This passage (lines 99–102) refers to King Edward III, whose army defeated the French at Crécy in 1346, and suggests that Edward would not recognize as British the effete and Europeanized young men of present-day England.

It is certainly highly proper, that young Men of Family and Fortune should see the World; but I would have them see it at an Age when their Minds are able to profit by what they see. The common Tour is now so much beaten, that little new can be expected. Of late, indeed, our Countrymen repair to Corsica, where they may behold a Nation in the State in which Cato represents an Individual, as an Object worthy of the Attention of the Gods.[88] No Doubt, that gallant Nation well deserves the Regard of Travellers: But I cannot help observing, that the Corsicans tacitly upbraid the Britons, not only because we do not afford any Assistance to a brave and injured People, but because the Corsicans are in full Possession of that Patriotism, which I am sorry to say is every Year decaying in Britain. Mr. David Hume has with great Justice remarked, that the philosophical Notion of all Countries being alike to the truly wise Man, would destroy the Love of our Country, a Principle more exalted than any of the artificial Sentiments of Metaphysics.[89] In my Opinion, the truly wise Man will never lose the *Amor Patriæ*:[90] But as the indiscriminate Use of Travelling must tend so much to diminish it, I heartily wish that proper Methods were taken, if possible, to correct what is certainly very hurtful.

BRITANNUS.

88. Of course, the most prominent "late" British visitor to Corsica was JB himself. Marcus Porcius Cato, "Cato the Elder" (234–149 B.C.), was a Roman statesman. JB is here, perhaps, confounding two passages. In Seneca's "On Providence" (book 2), it is asserted that acts of human bravery will not "attract the attention of the gods; they are childish and the amusements of human frivolity"; by contrast, "a worthy sight, at which a god who is intent upon his own work, might well look . . . [is] a brave man matched with evil fortune, especially if he has challenged it. I do not see, I say, what more beautiful thing Jupiter could find on earth, if he should turn his attention to it, than to see Cato [the Younger], after his party had more than once been defeated, yet standing upright amidst the ruins of the republic" ("*Tranquillity of Mind*" and "*Providence*"). In the *Nature of the Gods* (book 1), Cicero writes, "men are the objects of the attention of the Gods, and that many benefits are conferred by the immortal Gods on the human race" (*Tusculan Disputations*, 141).

89. In his *Enquiry Concerning Principles of Morals* (1751), Hume wrote: "And as nature has implanted in every one a superior affection to his own country, we never expect any regard to distant nations, where a competition arises. Not to mention, that while every man consults the good of his own community, we are sensible, that the general interest, of mankind is better promoted than by loose indeterminate views to the good of a species, whence no beneficial action could ever result, for want of a duly limited object, on which they could exert themselves" (sec. 5; 93 n.). In his essay "The Sceptic," in his *Essays Moral, Political and Literary* (1741–42)—which JB is perhaps more likely to have read—Hume quotes Fontenelle as saying, "What a poor thing is even the whole globe in comparison of the infinite extent of nature!" (177); to which Hume responds, "This consideration is evidently too distant to ever have any effect; or, if it had any, would it not destroy patriotism, as well as ambition?"

90. *Amor Patriae*: love of one's country.

1772

The "New Town" of Edinburgh

[In 1752, proposals were published to extend Edinburgh beyond the medieval city walls, within which the old town had become increasingly crowded, noisy, and unsanitary. The city boundaries were extended to the north, and work began in 1759 to drain the polluted North Loch. A spacious modern city on a simple grid plan, with wide thoroughfares and open public spaces, was laid out on a ridge overlooking the old town, and construction began in 1767. The wealthy, particularly those newly wealthy and without property rights in the old town, gradually shifted to the northern suburb, building large architect-designed homes in the neoclassical style; see Cosh, *Edinburgh*, chap. 1.]

London Chronicle, September 1, 1772, 216 (Postscript)

Extract of a Letter from Edinburgh.

"Our new town will rival any city of the same size in Europe, for the extensiveness of its prospects, and the elegance of its buildings. Thanks be to Lord Mansfield, who, by his supreme decree, prevented a set of ugly buildings from being erected, merely to put a few paultry pence into the pockets of the Corporation:[91] Our Provost and the rest of 'em now see that it won't do; and, it is said, are most earnest to be let off with some appearance of decency.[92] But the Gentlemen who have built on the faith of the plan, carry it with a proper dignity, and quote the great man's words, that 'for the honour, for the interest of the Corporation, let us hear no more of it.'"[93]

91. JB greatly admired Mansfield; he records hearing him in court for the first time on Mar. 30, 1772 (*Defence*, 83–84). In the case that JB refers to here, a group of gentleman landholders ("feuars") of properties on the south side of Princes Street in the New Town found that their anticipated view of the Old Town was compromised by a set of "mean and irregular" buildings, which they believed to have been erected contrary to the regulations. The feuars took a case to the Court of Session. The Edinburgh local authority, the Town Council, defended the buildings, and the court found for the council. An appeal was made to the House of Lords; JB attended the hearing on Apr. 10, 1772, and wrote in his journal, "I this day heard the appeal between the magistrates of Edinburgh and the feuars in the New Town. Lord Mansfield spoke as well as I could conceive any man to do. It really is a feast to hear him" (ibid., 108). "The House of Lords reversed the decision, and Lord Mansfield forcefully criticized the Corporation as 'misguided.'" See Cosh, *Edinburgh*, 6.

92. The Lord Provost of Edinburgh is the elected head of the Town Council, the equivalent of a Lord Mayor. Gilbert Laurie (1729–1809) of Polmont was Provost for 1766–67 and 1772–73 (Cosh, *Edinburgh*, 928).

93. A text of Mansfield's speech, supposedly taken from contemporaneous notes, was published in *Scots Mag.*, 68 (1806), 255–58; it concludes: "I hope we shall hear no more of the

1773–74

MASQUERADES

[A highly social being such as Boswell, particularly one with an attraction to and a talent for mimicry and preoccupied with questions of character and self-fashioning, was understandably drawn to a form of social amusement popular with the upper classes from early in the century, the masquerade. In 1711, the *Spectator* (nos. 8, 14, and 101) noticed some of the earliest public masquerades or "midnight masques" in England, and first made most of the criticisms that they attracted. The masquerade was clearly a foreign entertainment; the first private masquerades were hosted by the French ambassador the Duke d'Aumont, and the first major public masquerades, with tickets offered for sale, were conducted by a Swiss-born entrepreneur "Count" John James Heidegger. The venues were public pleasure gardens, such as Ranelagh, and the various assembly rooms in the city. Masquerades thrived under Kings George I and II, whose courts were essentially European or, at least, cosmopolitan, but in the reign of George III, who encouraged more British and domestic virtues, they fell into disfavor (see Castle, *Masquerade and Civilization*).

Masquerades were regarded with suspicion by moralists, as providing opportunities for deception and illicit sexual dalliance, and evidence "suggests indeed that this was the object for many men and women" (Langford, *Englishness Identified*, 101). Furthermore, in a highly stratified society, occasions that required people to disguise their identities suggested the worrisome possibility of nobly born folk unknowingly mixing with persons of inferior status. Anonymity would encourage people to behave presumptuously. When Johnson in London read a report of the Edinburgh masquerade, he wrote to Boswell:

> I have heard of your masquerade. What says your Synod to such innovations? I am not studiously scrupulous, nor do I think a masquerade either evil in itself, or very likely to be the occasion of evil; yet as the world thinks it a very licentious relaxation of manners, I would not have been one of the *first* masquers in a country where no masquerade had ever been before. (Feb. 24, 1773; *Letters SJ*, 2:8)

While, as Johnson cheekily suggests, masquerades were predictably, by the Presbyterian clergy, "denounced from the pulpit as 'the encourager of intrigue, of libertinism, of debauchery'" (*Later Years*, 44), more secular or circumspect critics opined that masquerades were not a form of entertainment or socializing that suited the English character. The English, it was argued, were candid and open, not naturally calculating or manipulative; they were frank and plain-speaking and not given to theatrical

---

matter. Let me earnestly recommend to this corporation, to . . . consult with their standing counsel what may be for their honour, what for their interest, neither of which they seem for some time to have understood."

Figure 15. "*Remarkable Characters at Mrs. Cornely's Masquerade,*" *engraved for the* Oxford Magazine, *6 (February 1771), 64. © Trustees of the British Museum.*

behavior. Novelist Samuel Richardson took this position, as well as (in *Sir Charles Grandison*) describing masquerades as obliging one to behave in ways that were fatuous and undignified (Langford, *Englishness Identified*, 100–101). (For an illustration depicting a typical private masquerade, see Figure 15.) In time, the event evolved into the fancy dress ball, diminishing the opportunity for social or sexual transgression but, perhaps, without any appreciable gain in dignity.

Boswell's account of his own attendance as a Corsican chief at the masquerade at the Shakespeare Jubilee in September 1769 is in Chapter 1. The event he reports in the first two articles below and discusses in the essay that follows was held on Friday night, January 15, 1773; although in the second, more matter-of-fact report he says that it was the first of its kind in Scotland, by the time of the essay of 1774, below, he had discovered a seventeenth-century precedent. The hostess was the beautiful Lady Macdonald, whom it pleased Boswell to regard as his kinswoman. In the brief account of the occasion in his journal, Boswell notes that he was feeling ill, went with some reluctance, and came home early; see *Defence*, 152. A number of the people whom Boswell mentions obliquely in his account for Scottish readers, the first more jocular (two-part) piece below, are identified by name in his later more formal report for the London paper. Although in terms of their genre the first two items below belong more properly among the Reports in Chapter 1, I have thought it preferable to cluster all the items on the subject of masquerades together and around the essay.

(Boswell is thought to have contributed in 1792 to the *St. James's Chronicle* one further short paragraph concerning a London masquerade, Mrs. Broadhead's, which is not included here; see *NCBEL*, *1232.)]

Masquerade Intelligence Extraordinary

Caledonian Mercury, January 18, 1773

[MASQUERADE INTELLIGENCE EXTRAORDINARY.]

LOST on Friday night, betwixt twelve and one, a MODESTY-PIECE.[94] Whoever will restore the same to the right owner, will be handsomely rewarded, and no questions asked. N. B. It is of no use to the finder.

FOUND, on Saturday morning, by a boy belonging to the Charity Workhouse, on the cross road betwixt the Potter-row and Bristo-port,[95] some valuable jewels, supposed to belong to a rich SULTANA.[96] If not claimed in a day or two, they will be disposed of, and the money applied for behoof of the Poor's-house,[97] whose funds we are informed, are at present very low.

RUN AWAY, a DANCING BEAR.[98] It is a fierce and dangerous animal; and, if allowed to roam through the streets, may perhaps do as much mischief as the wild beast of France.[99] It is therefore expected, a general warrant will be immediately issued to the constables, sheriff-officers, and city-guard, to apprehend

94. *Modesty-piece*: "a piece of lace, etc., worn over a woman's dress to conceal the bosom" (*OED*).

95. The old Edinburgh Workhouse was opened in 1743, in a large four-story building in an open field west of Bristo Street, to provide employment for the poor. Some of the running costs of this establishment were paid out of local taxes, but it depended upon voluntary contributions (see Grant, 4:235–36).

96. A *sultana*: "The wife (or a concubine) of a sultan" (*OED*). There were two sultanas at the ball: Miss Nancy Ord (whose rich costume is emphasized) and Miss Fletcher; see below, nn. 124, 126. (Further details regarding them and other people alluded to in this essay are given in the notes to the more literal report of the same event, in the *Pub. Adv.*, following.)

97. *Behoof*: "That which behooves; that which is advantageous; profit; advantage" (*OED*).

98. At one point, Sir Alexander Macdonald (see Chap. 3, n. 330) dressed as a showman, leading a dancing bear; see below.

99. The so-called beast of Gévaudan was one or a number of man-eating wolflike animals that were reported to be responsible for over a hundred deaths in south-central France, 1764–67. Over this period, reports of its ravages and attempts to capture it appeared frequently in the British press; see *Lond. Chron.*, Nov. 29, 1764.

and secure the same.—None should venture on this hazardous enterprize, but such as are properly armed.

The WATCHMAN's CLOKE and LANTERN was, on Saturday morning, found by a chairman of this city. It is hoped, the gentleman will be kind enough to allow him to keep them. He promises to furnish him with as good against [the] next occasion.

We are informed, the Two GRAND TURKS, like the two Kings of Brentford, were both smelling at the same NOSE-GAY.[100]

With all our industry, we have not been able to pick up one *bon mot* which passed on this occasion. It was unlucky the Conjurer's *mouth* was shut up. We expect he will be the more busy with the *pen*; *wit being like wind*, &c.[101] The best thing we have heard was the reply made by Lady G. upon being invited to the masquerade: "If, says she, I go there, I will appear as a mendicant nun, asking charity for the highland emigrants from the Isle of S——, in order to carry them to America."[102]

ADVERTISEMENT.[103]

Whereas it was affirmed, that I appeared at the Masquerade on Friday night, with a wheel-barrow, selling fish; I hereby declare, it is a most egregious mistake, as I had nothing to do with either fish or flesh that night. Witness my hand, C. B.[104]

Mr. M. likewise desires to inform the public, that he was not there in *any shape* whatever.[105]

(To be continued.)

Caledonian Mercury, January 20, 1773

100. Mr. Menzies and Mr. Commissioner Brown; see below and n. 129. For the two kings of Brentford, see Chap. 3, n. 124.

101. JB attended as a "dumb conjuror": see below and n. 135. For "wit, like the wind," see *An Hundred Epigrammes* of John Heywood (1550), no. 70: "Of Constancy."

102. From the middle of the eighteenth century, emigration from the Highlands to America became a phenomenon that was remarked upon by writers and politicians and noticed in particular in the *Scots Mag.* "The really sensational departures" were from Skye and the other islands. The emigrants who passed through Edinburgh "became at once an object of interest and compassion, and their unusual appearance and pathetic situation no doubt supplied to Lowland eyes sufficient evidence of distress" (see Adam, "Highland Emigration of 1770," 281, 283). "Lady G." has not been identified.

103. *Advertisement*: "A (written) statement calling attention to anything; a notification, a 'notice'" (*OED*).

104. "C. B." is not identified; perhaps Chief Baron Mure, whose daughter attended the masquerade, but, I can offer no explanation of the joke. Presumably, "C. B." did not dine at all that night, either on meat or—observing the traditional Catholic Friday fast—on fish.

105. "Mr. M." is not identified.

A certain *country man*, we hear, was dressed so much in character, that he had much ado to get admittance.[106]

We are informed a Highland gentleman, on Friday-night, went from home in such a hurry, that he forgot his trowsers, by which means he catched a most severe cold. However, by the able assistance of Dr M. we hear, he is got a good deal better;[107] but is resolved not to go to [the] next masquerade so thinly covered, at this inclement season of the year.

The handsome young *lady* in the riding-clothes was so universally admired, and it is difficult to say who were captivated most; the *ladies*, or the *gentlemen*.[108]

If *Rose*'s eggs are still undisposed of, we are happy to understand she is likely soon to get a *good market* for them.[109]

A *Nun* having advised with two *eminent counsel*, received it as their opinion, that the vow of perpetual virginity is not binding, being contrary to the law of *nature*; upon which she purposes soon to throw off the veil; and it is supposed the example will be followed by several others in the same situation.

A *Shepherdess* being asked, "Where was her sheep?" replied, "Please look around the room; are they not a *goodly flock?*"[110]

The lady who appeared as *Night*, discovered, notwithstanding her disguise, so many shining beauties, that it put us in mind of the poet's *darkness visible*.[111]

We have only heard as yet of one *Patagonian infant* being present;[112] but it is shrewdly suspected there were many more.

Authentic Scottish Masquerade Intelligence

Public Advertiser, January 23, 1773, 3

By a Correspondent at Edinburgh, the Printer is favoured with the following authentic Scottish Masquerade Intelligence:—A Masquerade has been at

106. Lord Elphinstone was dressed as a peasant; see n. 120 and text, below.

107. "Dr M." may be Dr. Alexander Monro (1733–1817), physician and professor of anatomy at Edinburgh, with whom JB was acquainted from 1762; see *Corres. 9*, 240, 242 n. 4.

108. Sir William Cunninghame dressed as an Irish girl; see below and n. 128.

109. Miss Betsy Ord went as a country girl selling eggs; see below and n. 124.

110. Miss Lindsay was dressed as a shepherdess; see below and n. 127.

111. The lady who appeared as Night is not identified. *Discover*: "To disclose or expose to view (anything covered up, hidden, or previously unseen), to reveal, show" (*OED*). *Darkness visible*: see Milton, *Paradise Lost*, 1.62 (where it is a description of hell).

112. For Patagonia, the land of giants, see Chap. 1, n. 54. A "Patagonian infant" seems to have been a standard costume for a masquerade, presumably requiring an adult to dress as an oversized child. See Gunning, *Memoirs of Mary*, 3:98–99: "A little bustle [was] occasioned by a character who had collected many people around him . . . ; the mask was a Patagonian infant, six feet high, and the most noisy brat I ever heard."

all Times decried in this Island of gloomy Gravity. Of late Years however there have been several in England. But to introduce that Entertainment into the City of Edinburgh, was reserved for the beautiful Lady Macdonald, formerly the Admiration of London as Miss Bosville of Yorkshire.[113] This Lady, with her Consort Sir Alexander Macdonald, Baronet,[114] concerted a Scheme for having a Masquerade at their own House for a select invited Party; and altho' much Opposition was made to it by many People, who entertained Notions that every Masquerade was dangerous to Virtue, they compleated their Scheme without the least Injury being done to the most delicate fair one, upon Friday the 15th current, at Duff-house, the Jointure Apartments of the Dowager Countess Fife, where they presently reside by a Lease from her Ladyship.[115]——In order that a proper Decorum might be preserved, several Ladies of Distinction were there unmasked, amongst whom were the Countess Dowager of Moray,[116] Lady Elphinston,[117] and Mrs. Mure, Lady of Mr. Baron Mure, one of the great Favourites of the Earl of Bute.[118] A Number of Dresses, rich, genteel and curious, were exhibited by the Masks. In particular the Earl of Balcarras, a Spaniard;[119] Lord Elphinston, a Scotch Peasant;[120] Lord Kilmares, a running Footman, very elegant;[121] Hon. Capt. Erskine, a Vandych;[122] three Miss Elphinstons in pretty

113. Lady Macdonald, the former Elizabeth Diana Bosville; see Chap. 3, n. 330.

114. For Sir Alexander Macdonald, see Chap. 3, n. 330.

115. Duff House in Banff, completed in 1740, was built for William Duff, first earl of Fife (he never lived there), MP for Banffshire. His widow, Jean Duff (née Grant), Countess Fife (1705–88), was from 1763 the dowager countess. *Jointure*: "The holding of property to the joint use of a husband and wife for life or in tail, as a provision for the latter, in the event of her widowhood" (*OED*).

116. Margaret Stuart (née Wemyss) (d. 1779), widow of the eighth earl of Moray.

117. Clementina Elphinstone (née Fleming), Lady Elphinstone (c. 1719–99).

118. Katherine (née Graham, 1734–1820), wife of William Mure (1718–76), of Caldwell, politician and author. Lord Bute appointed Mure as baron of the Scots exchequer in 1761, after which he was known as Baron Mure.

119. For the Earl of Balcarres, see Chap. 3, n. 414.

120. Charles Elphinstone, tenth Lord Elphinstone (d. 1781); JB dined with him on Feb. 28, 1775 (*Ominous Years*, 71), and his family on Mar. 4, 1780 (*Laird*, 186).

121. James Cunningham, thirteenth earl of Glencairn and Lord Kilmaurs (1749–91), succeeded to the earldom in 1775 and was a representative Scots peer, 1780–84. He was a friend and patron of Robert Burns. The village of Kilmaurs is in East Ayrshire; Glencairn was obliged to sell the estate in 1786. JB saw him socially in Edinburgh and London, 1779–82 (see *Laird*, 117, 134, et seq.).

122. Hon. Andrew Erskine (c. 1740–93), soldier and poet, contemporary and friend of JB since 1761 and co-author of the Erskine–Boswell *Letters*. A customary form of masquerade dress was the style of costume in the portraits of the Flemish-born English court painter Sir Anthony van Dyck (1599–1641)—often called Vandyke dress—which for men consisted

Fancy Dresses;[123] four Miss Ords, Lord Chief Baron's Daughters, Miss Nancy a Sultana, with a Turban quite brilliant with a Profusion of Diamonds; Miss Betsey, a Country Girl selling Eggs; and the other two also in pretty Attire;[124] Hon. Miss Kitty Mackenzie, Sister to the Earl of Seaforth, a Milkmaid;[125] Miss Fletcher, a Sultana;[126] Miss Lindsay, Niece to Lord Mansfield, a Shepherdess;[127] Sir William Cuninghame, an Irish Girl;[128] Mr. Menzies and Mr. Commissioner Brown, two noble Turks;[129] Captain Grant, Oroonoko;[130] Mr. Sinclair,

---

of a plain satin suit, with lace collars and cuffs. In a letter of Feb. 18, 1742, Horace Walpole describes a masquerade, at which he saw "quantities of Vandykes, and all kinds of old pictures walked out of their frame" (*Correspondence*, 17:339).

123. JB saw Lord Elphinstone's daughters socially and mentions in particular Clementina or "Clemie" (1749–1822); see *Laird* (Sept. 8, 1779), 134, and (Mar. 14, 1780), 190. Her sisters were Charlotte (1711–81) and Eleanora (1747–1800).

124. Robert Ord (1700–1778), English politician, appointed in 1755 as chief baron of the Scottish exchequer, had a son and six daughters. On a number of occasions, 1778–83, JB visited various of the daughters, when they were still at home; in addition to Ann ("Nancy") and Elizabeth ("Betsy"), he mentions Margaret in his journals.

125. Catherine Mackenzie (1748–83) was one of six sisters of Lord Seaforth (see Chap. 1, n. 188; also "Rampager," no. 16). JB records calling on sisters of Lord Seaforth in July 1769 and mentions "Kitty" in particular as a correspondent of his wife; see *Search* (July 29, 1769), 258. In Mar. 1773, she married Thomas Griffin Tarpley.

126. Miss Fletcher is not identified; JB dined with her and others at Lord Monboddo's on July 1, 1774 (*Defence*, 229).

127. Presumably Katherine Lindsay (1737–1828), the younger daughter of Sir Alexander Lindsay of Evelick, Perthshire, and his wife Amelia, who was sister of Lord Mansfield. The Lindsays' elder daughter, Margaret (1726–82), eloped in 1752 with painter Allan Ramsay. Katherine was married on Apr. 15, 1773, to JB's friend Alexander Murray, solicitor general from 1775 and later Lord Henderland. In the *Tour*, JB implied that Murray's promotion was a consequence of his marriage (*Life*, 5:50).

128. There are a number of men this could be. William Cuninghame of Caprington succeeded to the baronetcy on the death of his aged father, Sir John, Nov. 30, 1777. At the time of the masquerade, William would have been only twenty years old (JB refers to him as "the young chevalier," *Extremes*, 33, 93, 117). JB breakfasted with Sir William and his mother on Apr. 4, 1784 (*Applause*, 202 and n. 8). Another candidate is Sir William Cuningham (*before* 1705–81), fifth baronet of Robertland, Ayrshire.

129. Archibald Menzies of Culdares (d. 1777) was one of the Scottish commissioners of customs (see App. D, *Life*, 5:573–74); JB and SJ dined with him and Lord Monboddo in Nov. 1773, after they returned from their tour (*Life*, 5:394), and JB was invited by him to a supper party, June 28, 1777, at which there was "Great company . . . [and] Hard drinking" (*Extremes*, 132). George Brown (1722–1806), soldier and commissioner of excise for Scotland (Kay, *Series of Original Portraits and Caricature Etchings*, 1:75); JB dined with him and others on Sept. 25, 1778 (*Laird*, 24).

130. Capt. Lewis Grant (d. 1791), adjutant of the Chelsea Hospital, was born in the manse at Auchinleck; JB records meeting him socially in London, May 29, 1783, and June 26,

an English Nobleman with the white Rod of Office as Lord Chamberlain;[131] Young Mr. Kincaid, Lord Chalkstone, inimitably well kept up;[132] Mr. Digges, as a Dutch Sailor, was very hearty;[133] Mr. Riddell, an Alderman of London;[134] Mr. Boswell, a dumb Conjurer;[135] Mr. Lockhart Macdonald, a wild Man in a very fanciful Dress all covered with Leaves of Ivy;[136] Lady Macdonald, in an elegant Turkish Dress; Sir Alexander, first as a Turk, then as a Baker crying Minced-pies, and repeating Verses in Character; Sir Robert Dabyiel,[137] Colonel Shene,[138] &c. &c. About Ten o'Clock the Company unmasked. There was a good deal of dancing, a Collation,[139] and dancing again, and the Affair went on with more Success than was expected. It may probably break the Ice, and make Way for a Masquerade of pretty general Extent. The Theatre Royal is admirably

---

1785 (*Applause*, 157, 315). In Aphra Behn's novel *Oroonoko* (1688), the title character is a prince, the grandson of an African king.

131. JB knew a number of Sinclairs. This is probably Robert Sinclair (1730–1802) of Stevenston, advocate. JB and W. J. Temple were at college in Edinburgh with him; he became deputy advocate in 1773 and was on the prosecution team against JB in the 1774 trial of John Reid (see Chap. 2); JB later fell out with him (see *Corres. 6*, 11 and n. 10). The Lord Chamberlain is the manager of the royal household; his regalia includes a short white staff.

132. Alexander Kincaid (d. 1777), printer, son of Alexander Kincaid (1710–77), printer, and later—for four months before his sudden death—Lord Provost of Edinburgh. The Boswells were related to and were social friends of the Kincaids (*Defence*, 286), and JB records going with "young Kincaid" to a drunken all-night whist party, Oct. 31, 1775 (*Ominous Years*, 173). On Jan. 28 and Dec. 11, 1777, JB attended the funerals of the father and the son (*Extremes*, 82, 199). Lord Chalkstone, in David Garrick's satirical play *Lethe* (1740), is a dandy; Garrick played the role himself.

133. West Digges (c. 1725–86), actor and theater manager, JB's early role model, with whom he attended the masquerade.

134. Possibly James Riddell or Riddel (d. 1797), of Ardnamurchan and Sunart, Argyllshire, ll.d., later (1778) baronet; see *Corres. 7*, 108–9 and nn. In 1773, he was a widower; his two sons were too young to have attended this event (as were the two brothers Robert and John Riddel of Glenriddel, with whom JB dined, Aug. 8 and 10, 1769; see *Search*, 265–66).

135. Duncan Campbell (c. 1680–1730) was a famous deaf mute in London who advertised his services as a fortune-teller. He is referred to as a "dumb fortune-teller" in *Tatler*, no. 14 (May 12, 1709; 1:121); and *Spectator*, no. 31 (Apr. 5, 1711; 1:127), mentions a "dumb conjuror," as one of the "several Shows that are exhibited in different Quarters of the Town."

136. Charles Lockhart Macdonald (1741–96), of Largie, Argyll, advocate; born Charles Lockhart, he took the surname and arms of his wife's family on his marriage in 1762.

137. Sir Robert Dalyell or Dalziell (1726–91), of Binns, from 1747 fourth Baronet, army officer; he and JB had mutual friends (see *Corres. 7*, 109).

138. *Shene* is a misprint. Robert Skene (see Chap. 1, n. 199) was a colonel at this time. JB met him socially in Edinburgh in 1774–77 (see *Ominous Years*, 43, and *Extremes*, 77, 188).

139. *Collation*: "A repast; a treat less than a feast" (*SJ Dict.*).

contrived for such an Entertainment, and it is said that Mr. Digges will have no Objection to a grand Subscription Masquerade.[140]

An Essay on Masquerade

London Magazine, 43 (February 1774), 80–83

AN ESSAY ON MASQUERADE;
With an Account of one given at EDINBURGH *by*
Lady MACDONALD, *January* 15, 1773.
And VERSES *by Sir* ALEXANDER MACDONALD

THE fertility of human invention hath contrived a great variety of amusements to dispel the gloom of the thoughtful, and exercise the lively activity of the gay. Amongst these, a *masquerade* has in one way or other been practised in most nations, with greater degrees of refinement indeed, as nations became more civilized and more improved in arts and in elegance. To assume feigned characters for a short space of time, under the disguise of suitable dresses, and having the faces of those who assume them concealed under masks, is the sum and substance of a masquerade. In this there is nothing inherently evil; but it has no doubt been often made subservient to licentiousness of manners, those whom modesty restrained, being by means of it set loose from that check of sensation, which in some degree supplies the place of principle. A public masquerade, where an indiscriminate crowd of company is admitted, and where whoever has money may procure a ticket, is therefore a bad thing; but where there is a select invited party, and it is fixed, that before the end of the evening every body is to unmask, there can be no harm: for no one will say or do what is improper in a feigned character, when there is a consciousness, that before the company parts there is to be a full discovery of all the real persons.

In the warmer climates, where there is much sprightliness of fancy among the inhabitants, and an habitual readiness at repartee, a masquerade is a very common and a very suitable entertainment; but it does not seem to be well adapted for the northern region of Great Britain, where the people, though not so extremely remarkable for taciturnity as some foreigners have imagined, are

---

140. The Theatre Royal, Edinburgh (see Chap. 1), was in Shakespeare Square, at the east end of Princes Street. David Ross, who was the first owner, had left for London after the first season, leaving the management in other hands. At this time, West Digges was the manager (*Ominous Years,* 29 n. 3). He held a "grand ridotto" or masked ball at the theater on Mar. 10, 1775, which JB may have attended (ibid., 75).

certainly more distinguished for solidity than for vivacity. Accordingly, although our imitative genius, or our unbounded desire of acquisition, which shews itself in territories, in commerce, in arts, and in amusements and follies, hath added *masquerade* to the catalogue of British customs, we have not seen it fairly naturalized. Although our nation is composed of all kindreds and tongues, there is a tolerable uniformity. Each has lost the peculiar marking characteristic, and cannot be pointed out directly as of a foreign race; but *Masquerade*, if we personify it, has still the outlandish air in a striking degree.[141] *Masquerade* is an *exotic*, which, like the orange-tree, and many others which luxuriantly flourish, and bear rich loads of fruit under a glaring sun; but, when transplanted into our soil, lose their native vigour, and produce only half-formed, green and tasteless, or sour fruit. These observations are applicable even to England, the southern part of our island; and accordingly it will be allowed by all who have been present at the masquerades which that country has exhibited, that, except a few oddities, such as devils, dancing bears, or other grotesque figures, the company have appeared heartily tired of the disagreeable task of attempting what they were unfit to execute.

Let us now turn to a still more unfavourable climate for masquerade.

Scotland, so far as can be gathered either from books or tradition, was very slow of adopting the amusement of masquerade in any regular form. James V had much of the spirit of gallantry, and used to go about as a *jolly beggar*, on which there is an excellent old Scottish song;[142] but neither in his reign, nor in that of the beauteous Queen Mary, tho' she brought with her the gaiety of the court of France;[143] nor when the Duke of York had his residence at Edinburgh, and encouraged many amusements, was a masquerade introduced.[144] It is indeed believed, that there have been but few nations, perhaps none at

141. *Outlandish*: "Not native; foreign" (*SJ Dict.*).

142. The legend, dating to the late sixteenth century, that James V (1512–42), King of Scots, "liked to learn about his subjects by circulating among them incognito" and his post-reformation reputation for being "susceptible to bribes in the form of cash, lands, and nubile young women" (*ODNB*), have led to his name being linked with the Scots song "The Jolly Beggar," which was in circulation from the early 1700s.

143. Mary I, Queen of Scots, was betrothed as a five-year-old to the French Dauphin and lived in France until his death, five months after their marriage, in 1561, when she returned to Scotland.

144. The Duke of York—later King James II (of England) and VII (of Scots) (1633–1701)—lived in Scotland 1679–82, as the king's high commissioner; he spent most of that time in Edinburgh and "kept a splendid court . . . at the Palace of Holyroodhouse." As William Tytler continues, "Balls, plays, and masquerades, were introduced: These last, however, were soon laid aside. The fanaticism of the times could not bear such ungodly innovations. The Masquerade was stiled *promiscuous dancing, in which all sorts of people met together in*

all, amongst which, even in their earliest and rudest state, there have not been frolics of some kind by people disguising themselves. Various instances of this may be found in the accounts which travellers give us. It has been an immemorial custom in Scotland for numbers of young people to go about from house to house, in the evenings of the last days of the old year, and the first of the new one, in fantastical dresses, and from being so *disguised* they have had the name of the *Guisearts*.[145] These have been mostly young people of the lower sort, who in going their rounds proposed to procure a little advantage to themselves. Their practice has been to sing and dance, and sometimes perform some coarse irregular interlude, for which they receive, from every family which they visit, a small gratuity. While popery was the established religion in Scotland, and its numerous holidays were faithfully observed, especially those with which feasting was connected, the *Guisearts* used to proclaim the birth of our Saviour, and the approach of the three kings to worship him in his infancy. Their proclamation was in the French language, owing to the great intercourse which was of old between France and Scotland. It was originally thus:

> *Homme est né,*
> *Trois rois là.*

> The man is born,
> The three kings are there.

But from the corruption, naturally incident to those who pronounce any thing in a language which they do not understand, it has, so far as the memory of any now one alive can reach, run thus:

> *Hogmenay,*
> *Trololay.*[146]

The first attempt in Scotland towards a masquerade, properly so called, was about the year 1696. At that time the Earl of Marchmont had several sons and

---

*disguise. The vulgar gave it the name of the *Horn Order*. This profane entertainment was therefore soon given up" ("On the Fashionable Amusements," 499–500).

145. *Guisard* (chiefly Scots): one who goes about in a fantastic guise or dress; a masquerader, a mummer (*OED*). The traditional activities of guisards—singing at doors in disguise, for money, and performing short plays—are particularly associated with the Scottish celebration of Hogmanay or New Year's Eve.

146. The origin of the term *hogmanay* is disputed and regarded as obscure by lexicographers. In his incomplete MS "Dictionary of the Scots Language," JB gives this same explanation of the origin of the term (Turnbull, "Boswell's 'Dictionary of the Scots Language,'" 40).

daughters, who had all an uncommon degree of gaiety and spirit, and he was prevailed with to have a masquerade at the palace of Holyroodhouse, where he resided.[147] In a strict presbyterian country, where in that age the puritanical gloomy zeal was as strong as it has ever been any where or at any time, the introduction of an amusement supposed to be productive of the utmost licentiousness of manners gave very great offence. The pulpits of Edinburgh resounded with anathemas against it. Kirkton and Meldrum, two very rigid ministers of the city, were particularly violent in their declamation.[148] The masquerade however took place; but the consequence was, that an English captain of dragoons, who was quartered in the neighbourhood, availed himself of that opportunity to carry off one of the Earl of Marchmont's daughters; and this match, which was thought a very unequal one, alarmed the people of fashion so much, that they did not wish for any more masquerades. In the year 1705, when John Duke of Argyll was commissioner to the Scotch parliament,[149] a singular kind of genteel club or coterie, consisting both of ladies and gentlemen, was formed by the Earl of Selkirk, the distinguished *beau* of that age, under the title of *The Horn Order*.[150] Like most institutions of the same kind, it had its origin from mere accidental whim. A horn spoon had been used at some merry meeting, and was assumed as the badge of distinction for the members of this society. They used to have parties of dancing, and sup together; and it is believed by all sensible people of that age, that nothing passed but innocent merriment. A notion however was successfully propagated at the time, that *The Horn Order* was a licentious and debauched society. The characters of several ladies suffered even in the opinion of the better sort; but the mob, who had the most extravagant idea of the profligacy of this order, figured their nocturnal meetings to be like the orgies of Bacchus,[151] and actually believed that they danced naked promiscu-

147. Patrick Hume, Lord Polwarth and from 1697 first earl of Marchmont (1641–1724), leading Scottish politician and trusted supporter of King William III; in 1696, he was made Lord Chancellor of Scotland.

148. James Kirkton (d. 1699) and George Meldrum (c. 1634–1709), both ministers of the Church of Scotland. Kirkton was from 1691 the minister of Edinburgh's Tolbooth parish; Meldrum, from 1692, served at the Tron Kirk of Edinburgh.

149. John Campbell, second duke of Argyll (1680–1743), at the age of only twenty-two, succeeded to the dukedom and his father's seat on the Privy Council, becoming Lord High Commissioner (the sovereign's personal representative) to the Parliament of Scotland in 1705.

150. John Douglas-Hamilton, third earl of Selkirk, first earl of Ruglen (1665–1744); I have not found another mention of his involvement with the Horn Order.

151. *Bacchus*: the Roman name for Dionysius, the Greek god of wine and revelry. His mythological female followers, the Maenads, are alluded to in the following clause.

ously, became exasperated to a degree of fury, and at last attacked, and in a good measure demolished, the house where the order assembled.[152]

We have mentioned this order not as a *masquerade*; for that name will hardly apply to a society of people, supposed to be without any covering at all; but we have mentioned it as a remarkable amusement in Scotland, which may be considered as having come in the place of a masquerade. There was another amusement in the year 1755 at the palace of Holyroodhouse, under the name of a *Ridotto* which was conducted under the patronage of the Duke of Hamilton, father of the present duke,[153] and 'Squire Eccles, an Irish gentleman.[154] This too gave considerable offence without much reason.

To attempt, for the second time to introduce the amusement of masquerade into Scotland was reserved for Lady Macdonald, formerly the beautiful Miss Bosville of Yorkshire. Her husband, Sir Alexander, was pleased with the scheme, and they had a select invited party of very genteel company, on the 15th of January, 1773, at Duff-house, which they then possessed.[155] In order to have the greater security for decorum, several ladies of distinction were there as matrons without masks. Of the masks, there was a rich and fanciful variety. Lady Macdonald, in the character of Flora, was so charming, that if there were any truth in ancient mythology, Jupiter or Pluto must have undoubtedly made part of the company and carried her off.[156] Sir Alexander appeared first in the character of a showman leading a dancing bear, having a stuffed skin of that animal, which he managed with agility and drollery; and next in the character of a macaroni baker,[157]

152. This passage (though not identified as JB's) seems to have been the basis for the account of the Horn Order in Chambers, *Traditions of Edinburgh*, 2:265, and that in Grant, 5:122. See also Tytler, "On the Fashionable Amusements," who confounds the Horn Order with the Duke of York's masquerade.

153. James Hamilton, sixth duke of Hamilton, and his son, Douglas Hamilton, the eighth duke, 1756–99, father and brother of the nominal plantiff in the Douglas Cause (see Chap. 1). A *ridotto* (see also n. 140, above) is "an entertainment or social assembly consisting of music and dancing"; such events were "a marked feature of London social life during the eighteenth century" (*OED*).

154. This may be "Mr. Eccles, an Irish gentleman of fortune, a good ingenious sort of man," whom JB met in London, July 6, 1763; he was an acquaintance of JB's friend the actor Thomas Davies (*Lond. Journ.*, 292 and n. 9). Gordon Turnbull identifies him as Isaac Ambrose Eccles (1737–1809), an author; see Boswell, *London Journal*, ed. Turnbull, 502 n. 13.

155. For Duff House, see n. 115, above; for the Macdonalds, see Chap. 3, n. 330.

156. Flora is the Roman goddess of flowers and the spring. In Roman mythology, the god Jupiter abducted Europa, and Pluto abducted Proserpina.

157. A *macaroni* is "A dandy or fop; *spec.* (in the second half of the 18th cent.) a member of a set of young men who had travelled in Europe and extravagantly imitated Continental tastes and fashions" (*OED*).

squeaking and selling minced pies. In this last character he spoke the following
verses written by himself.

> A macaroni baker, gentlefolks,
> Comes to dispense his wares and crack his jokes.
> Not from his wit aught sterling hope draw:
> Wit only feeds our ears—This*[158] fills our maw.
> Hot from the oven the smoaking morsels come,
> Some minc'd with currants, and with raisins some.
> Ye epicures, whose pamper'd palates smack
> The sav'ry pye at banquet of Almack;[159]
> In streaming coniac drench th' uncovered bait,
> Associate tastes with brandy to create.
> Peace, drunken wretch, some squeamish beldam cries,
> Did ever mortal hear of drams in pyes?
> Marry, quoth I, without or plumbs or suet,
> Some madams clinch the flask, and fairly to it!
> Worship *the twelve apostles* in their closet,[160]
> Secure that not a living creature knows it.
>
> But to my trade—nor envy, sirs, my skill,
> In bringing grist by traffick to my mill.[161]
> To buy or not to buy!—Perchance to steal,[162]
> A pye of beef, or more delicious veal.
> Ay, there's the rub.—For need I here subjoin,
> That pilfering school-boys from these wares purloin,
> Put off the coin from Birmingham's foul forge,
> The trait'rous semblance of the mighty GEORGE.[163]

158. "**A Pye.*" (BOSWELL)

159. Almack's Assembly Rooms, in King Street, St. James, London, opened in 1765 and
offered for subscribers a weekly ball and supper during the London social season.

160. Christ and his twelve apostles were said to be symbolized by the traditional thirteen ingredients (including brandy) used in making plum pudding, which is served at
Christmas. Macdonald's sly jest in this poem is that the matrons (despite their "squeamish"
cries) are hypocritically indulging in liquor (in the alcohol-drenched pudding) and secretly
observing Catholic festivities, disapproved of by the Presbyterian Church of Scotland.

161. *Grist to the mill*: proverbial expression for materials by which, through one's labor,
one may profit.

162. An allusion to Shakespeare, *Hamlet*, 3.1.56 ff.

163. A profile of the king was featured on the obverse of all English coins. Until 1797,
when Matthew Boulton was allowed to make British copper coins at the Soho Mint in

The masquerade began at eight in the evening, and about ten the company unmasked. There was a good deal of dancing, then a collation, and after that dancing again. The company were all dispersed by three next morning. Some animadversions were made upon this experiment by some of the more serious people of Edinburgh, and abundance of ludicrous and satirical witticisms appeared in the newspapers. It was however a very harmless entertainment, nor is there any reason to apprehend that masquerades will become fashionable in Scotland.

1775

Scottish Customs Not Understood in England

[In this piece, Boswell presents himself as an Englishman, resident in Scotland: he writes, "after I came down to Scotland"—so seemingly autobiographical aspects may be unreliable.]

London Chronicle, January 31–February 2, 1775, 109

To the PRINTER *of the* LONDON CHRONICLE.

THE intercourse between England and Scotland is now so great that it were much to be wished that some intelligent Gentleman would publish an account of the peculiar laws and customs of Scotland, for the benefit of Englishmen, many of whom from curiosity, as the celebrated Dr. Samuel Johnson himself; some for profit, as the officers of the revenue and riders from manufacturing towns;[164] and many from necessity, as officers of the army, visit Scotland, or even reside in it for a considerable time. Every body knows that a *Scotch marriage* is a proverb, though that is by no means well understood;[165] for not only does the marriage act not extend to that country, but a man may find himself married there without any ceremony whatever, merely by saying that a woman is his wife, and cohabiting with her in that character, by which he and she are *reckoned*,

---

Handsworth, Birmingham, there had been a severe shortage of government-issued coinage, the gap being filled by copper tokens issued by merchants and by counterfeits, of which a great many were made by illegal "coiners" in Birmingham. See Mayhew, *Sterling*, 104–5.

164. For *riders*, see Chap. 1, n. 52.

165. *Scotch marriage* was an English term for marriage by cohabitation and consent, without any ceremony or license; such marriages were legal in Scotland from medieval times until 1940.

or, as the Scotch call it, *habit and repute*, married persons:[166] so that the most solemn of all contracts, which ought to require the full consent of both parties, is in
this part of the world established, as Harlequin flatters himself, that there must
certainly be a marriage between him and the King's daughter, because *one party*
is agreed?[167] In short, a man may be told to his astonishment in Scotland that he
is married, as the *Mock Doctor* in the farce is told he is a Physician.[168] It behoves
therefore every Englishman, the instant that he gets upon the north side of the
Tweed,[169] to take care that he does not give the designation of *wife* to any female
companion, unless he is resolved to have her for a companion for life, or run the
risk of trusting to her honour, which is but a dangerous experiment. I was told
of a remarkable affair which happened but a few years ago:[170] A young fellow of
good fortune in Ireland was sent by his wise parents, without any tutor, to study
at the university of Glasgow, where the *Roman* law is taught in *English*, or *bonny
Scotch*;[171] and there having fallen in love with a very pretty young woman indeed,
he was assured that he was married to her without the intervention of any Priest
or Clergyman whatever, even a Presbyterian Mess John.[172] Off he went for Ire-

166. The Marriage Act of 1753 was enacted "for the Better Preventing of Clandestine
Marriage" and was the first legislation requiring a formal marriage ceremony. It applied
in England and Wales, but not Scotland. In Scots law, the expression *habit and repute* was
used for a situation recognized and ongoing, such as a cohabiting couple recognized by
their neighbors as man and wife, or a man convicted of theft, who could be sentenced more
severely if he was a thief by "habit and repute."

167. In the play *Les Chinois* (first performed in 1692), by Jean-François Regnard and
Charles de la Rivière Dufresny, it is not Harlequin but Pierrot who thinks his own consent
is sufficient to marry the princess (1.1). JB's error is also made by Voltaire, when quoting
the speech in the article "Reasonable, or Right," in his *Philosophical Dictionary* (1764): "your
marriage resembles that of Harlequin, which was only half performed, as wanting the consent of one of the parties."

168. In Henry Fielding's play *The Mock Doctor; or, The Dumb Lady Cur'd* (1732), adapted
from Molière, the husband, Gregory, pretends to be a doctor, having been talked into doing
so by his wife.

169. That is, the River Tweed, which forms the border between Scotland and England
along part of its route.

170. I have not traced another source for this story.

171. "Roman law," based on Justinian's *Institutes*, was until the late eighteenth century
highly influential in the civil law of most of western Europe. At this time, Glasgow was
the only school of law in Britain with lectures on the Roman law in English. Although
Glasgow was arguably the leading British school of law, it would have been more typical
for an Irishman to go to London to learn the English common law, through the Inns of
Court rather than at a university. *Bonny Scotch* refers to Scots—i.e., the vernacular language
of lowland Scotland—as opposed to Scottish Gaelic (or *Erse*).

172. In Scottish ballad poetry, *Mess John* is a name for a priest, and, colloquially, a parson,
irrespective of denomination; *mess* signifies the priest as celebrant of the mass.

land as fast as post horses and brisk winds could carry him;[173] but Miss brought
a serious action against him in the Court of Session, and I am assured she would
have fixed a marriage, by the law of this country, had not the grave Judges of
that tribunal by a very great majority given judgment, that although the young
Hibernian appeared by an Attorney, yet as he had not received a citation within
their territory, he was not in Court.[174] This was what one may call a *judicial bull*,
to hold that a man might come into Court, or which is the same thing, appear
by his Attorney, and plead that he is not there.[175]

But as I am already a married man, and do not imagine that I have much
chance for being a widower, whatever chance I may have for being *something
else*, my wife being at least twenty years younger than myself,[176] the Caledonian
system of matrimony has not made such an impression upon my mind as another peculiarity in the law of Scotland. You must know, Sir, that after I came
down to Scotland, I for the first time in my life set up a carriage;[177] I had a seal
hanging at my watch, which was given me when at school by my uncle, and
which I was told, had our family arms upon it.[178] These arms I considered to be
a very suitable ornament to my carriage, and gave orders to have them painted
upon it; but luckily for me, I happened to talk of it to a Gentleman of this
country, who asked me whether I could produce *a good title* to these arms, for if
I could not, LION KING OF ARMS had it in his power to seize my carriage and
confiscate it;[179] for that the authority of this Scottish monarch in heraldry, was
such, that he could seize and condemn carriages, and even plate, to any value,

173. *Post-horse*: "A horse kept at a post-house or inn for the use of post-riders, or for hire
by travellers" (*OED*).

174. A *citation* is a summons to appear in court.

175. A *bull* is a self-contradictory proposition; the term is now best known in the expression *Irish bull*.

176. Margaret Boswell was in fact slightly older than JB: by two years, so he said,
though possibly by a little more (*Earlier Years*, 556). The *something else* presumably implies
a cuckold.

177. It was enormously expensive to have one's own carriage.

178. The stamp-like device for impressing one's seal upon wax, etc., could be carried on
a signet ring or on a watch chain, as JB's narrator apparently does. The Boswell family arms
included the hooded hawk and the motto *Vraye Foy* (true faith). JB's uncle, Lord Auchinleck's younger brother, was John Boswell, MD (1710–80); JB seems to have had a warm and
confidential relationship with him (see *Earlier Years*, 21, 41, 109).

179. The Lord Lyon King of Arms is responsible for the regulation of heraldry in Scotland, including the granting and matriculation of coats of arms. The misuse of arms is a
criminal offense in Scotland, and the Lyon Court, unlike its equivalents in England and
other jurisdictions, has the power to confiscate or have destroyed any property bearing
arms that are wrongly assumed. At this time, the Lord Lyon was John Hooke-Campbell
(c. 1733–95).

if they had arms painted or engraved upon them, without an express authority. I was therefore glad to have my cypher only on my carriage, and to put up my uncle's seal till I should get back to England again.

As I have been a constant Reader of the London Chronicle a great many years, and have found in it dissertations upon a variety of subjects, as its motto bears *quicquid agunt homines*,[180] I should wish much to be informed by some of your ingenious correspondents how this affair of armorial bearings is conducted in England, for to tell you the truth I never had occasion to enquire; but I cannot suppose that there is any such power there in the Herald Office as in Scotland; if there were, we should certainly see many instances of the penalty's being inflicted; for in a country of so much wealth and freedom as England, where we so frequently find all laws violated, and the offenders punished, it is not to be believed that the laws of heraldry alone would be obeyed. Indeed I never so much as heard any of my friends or acquaintance mention there having obtained any patent or diploma, or any special permission whatever, for painting what arms they pleased upon their carriages; nor do I imagine that any restraint is laid upon those fancies in the southern parts of this island, where I take it there is the liberty of pencil as much as the liberty of the press.

If I were sure that this is the case, I would endeavour to set a going a spirit among some of our members of parliament to get an act passed for delivering the Scots from the subjection which I have mentioned, not out of pure love to *them*, as you may believe, but because many Englishmen would also participate of the advantage.

I am, Sir, your most humble servant,

A Southern Soul.

"Parliament *Square*": A Foolish Affectation

[The old Parliament House of Scotland—which now houses the Supreme Courts of Scotland—is next to St. Giles' Cathedral, Edinburgh, just off the High Street, in the middle of the Royal Mile. In Boswell's time, both buildings were separated from the tall buildings surrounding them by narrow alleys; this was the Parliament Close (see Figure 16). Also in the Close, clustered around St. Giles, were wooden booths which housed the shops of, in particular, goldsmiths and booksellers. The Court of Session

---

180. "All human activity": part of a quotation from Juvenal, *Quicquid agunt homines, votum, timor, ira, voluptas,/gaudia, discursus, nostri est farrago libelli est* (*Satires*, 1.85–86): "all human activity—prayers, fears, anger, pleasure, joys, hustle and bustle—this is the mishmash of my little book"; this appeared as a motto on the title page of the biannual bound volumes of the *Lond. Chron.*

Figure 16. Parliament Close, Edinburgh. "View from the Cowgate of the build-ings on the south side of the Parliament Close, the highest buildings in Edinburgh," James Grant, Old and New Edinburgh *(London, 1883), 1:168. Courtesy of the University of Otago Library, Special Collections, Dunedin, New Zealand.*

sat in rooms in the Parliament House, and Boswell was frequently there over this period pursuing his professional duties as an advocate (*Ominous Years*, 365).]

Scots Magazine, 37, Appendix, 1775 [i.e., January 1776], 734

CALEDONIAN MERCURY.

Jan. 26. 1776.

SIR,

ALL unnecessary alterations in names of places are idle and inconvenient. One name is just as good as another; and, as Shakespeare says, a rose would smell as sweet with any name as its own.[181] When names of places are changed,

---

181. Shakespeare's Juliet says, "A rose / By any other name would smell as sweet" (*Romeo and Juliet*, 2.2.33–34).

a confusion and perplexity is introduced; and, in future times, the scenes of remarkable events become unknown. Of late, I have observed, in several advertisements, a foolish affectation of calling the *Parliament* CLOSE the *Parliament* SQUARE.[182] Now, Sir, that space, called, *The Parliament Close*, is well known, and has been so for ages. The great fire in the *Parliament-Close*, as a terrible incident,[183] and the poem, intitled, *A Walk at Midnight in the Parliament* CLOSE*[184], as a beautiful composition, will preserve that name for ever. But if this nonsensical innovation shall be encouraged, we shall by and by not know where to find the *Parliament-Close*. Nay, Sir, I would have you look well to your own interest; for we shall not know where to find the *Caledonian Mercury*, which is printed in the *Parliament*-CLOSE.[185] The truth is, that this priggish attempt proceeds from our smattering of English. We are told, or perhaps have seen, that there are *squares* in London; and our little *lanes* in this city are called *closes*. But we have not learnt English enough to know, that a *close* is, in reality, a more proper name for such a place as the Parliament-Close, than a *square*. The celebrated Mr Harris, of the *Close* at Salisbury, would laugh very heartily, if any body should propose to call it a *square*; and as he is the author of so masterly a treatise upon language as *Hermes*, we may rely upon his authority.[186]

182. Examples found in the *Edinburgh Advertiser* from near this time include advertisements for "the best superfine Scots cloth" sold by Hope & Son (Dec. 22, 1775) and for "Spilsbury's Improved Antiscorbic Drops" (Mar. 26, 1776) and "Velnos' Original Vegetable Syrup" (Dec. 3, 1776) sold by Charles Elliot, bookseller; all addresses given as "Parliament Square."

183. The so-called Great Fire of Feb. 1700 burned down the homes of 400 families in crowded buildings up to fifteen stories high in the Close around Parliament House. Although the hall of Parliament escaped destruction, the vaults and cellars underneath were burned down, and the business of the Parliament was temporarily relocated to a tavern (Grant, 1:161–62). When the Close was rebuilt, a twelve-story limit was applied.

184. "* Written by Mr Mickle, the translator of the LUSIAD, and to be found in Donaldson's Collection." (BOSWELL)

JB knew Scots-born poet, dramatist, and translator William Julius Mickle (1735–88) from 1762 in Edinburgh and remained in intermittent contact with him. The poem, "On Passing through the Parliament-Close of Edinburgh at Midnight," of which lines 137–41 treat of the fire, was published in Donaldson's *A Collection of Original Poems*, by Scotch Gentlemen (1762), to which JB himself was a major contributor (*Lit. Car.*, 10–14).

185. From May 1729, when its founder William Rolland died, the *Caledonian Mercury* was "printed for and by Thomas and Walter Ruddiman, and sold at the shop of Alexander Symmers, bookseller, in the Parliament Square"; see *Chambers' Edinburgh Journal*, 3 (1835), 147. See also n. 251, below.

186. James Harris (1709–80), author of *Hermes; or, A Philosophical Inquiry Concerning Universal Grammar* (1751), was born in Salisbury and remained there all his life, as one of

The *Parliament-Close* is the open space, or court-yard, before the Parliament-house; and it is *enclosed* with lofty buildings. A *square* and a *close* in a city may be both of a square form; but the proper distinction between them is, that the former is, comparatively speaking, open, by having several spacious entries to it; whereas the latter has properly but one entry. Now, the Parliament-Close has only one public entry, by the street, from the Cross;[187] for the entries by the two stairs, and the narrow passage from the Council-chamber, do not deserve that name.

Some traders in London who live in the street called the *Poultry*, took it into their heads, not long ago, that because the Mansion-house is situated in that street, they would give it what they thought a *genteeler* or more *magnificent* name, and call it *Mansion-House Street*.[188] But their attempt was altogether ineffectual, and the good old *Poultry* remains as it did.

I have shewn that the *Parliament Close* is the proper designation, even if the matter were now *elective*; but as it has remained for ages, I will also maintain its *indefeasible* right.[189] Let us then, I pray you, Mr Printer, hear no more of the *Parliament* SQUARE.

VETUSTUS.[190]

---

the town's most prominent citizens. He leased Malmesbury House, in the Close. JB met Harris in London, Dec. 7, 1762, and May 9, 1763, at dinners hosted by Lord Eglinton (*Lond. Journ.*, 70, 254). The close around Salisbury Cathedral is an open-lawned area and the largest cathedral close in Britain.

187. The Cross, the city's central meeting place in High Street, was the site of the ancient city cross, called the Mercat Cross, which was demolished in 1756 to make room for increased traffic.

188. The Poultry, located 500 yards east of St. Paul's Cathedral in the city of London, was in Elizabethan times home to London's poulterers; see also Chap. 3, n. 250. The Mansion House, built 1739–52 at the eastern end of the Poultry, is the palatial official residence of the Lord Mayor of the city of London. Despite JB's confidence, "Mansion-house-Street" is found frequently as an address in newspaper advertisements from about 1787. In his *Dictionary of London* (1879), Charles Dickens Jr. remarks, "Many Londoners would deny that such a Street exists, but, in fact, the few houses at the end of the Poultry, facing the Mansion House, and the Mansion House itself, officially stand in Mansion House-street" (s.v. "Mansion House Street").

189. In law, an "*indefeasible* right" is a right that cannot be annulled or made void, as opposed to an *elective* right. Hume asserted that "the principles of *passive obedience*, and *indefeasible right* . . . became the universal doctrine, and were esteemed the true characteristic of a Tory"; see Hume, Essay IX, "On the Parties of Great Britain," *Essays Moral, Political and Literary* (1741–42).

190. *Vetustus*: (Latin) old, ancient, of long standing.

1775–76

IMPOTENCE OF MIND

[In his journal entry for October 16, 1775, Boswell notes beginning this essay "from immediate feeling . . . wishing earnestly to have a cure for it, which perhaps some correspondent had" (*Ominous Years*, 167). A year later, on November 8, 1776, he records finishing the auto-reply and thinking it "a good essay" (*Extremes*, 53).]

London Magazine, 44 (November 1775), 570–71

A Cure requested for occasional IMPOTENCE *of* MIND.

THAT the happiness of man consists in the exercise of his faculties, both of mind and body, will not be denied by any intelligent candid judge of human nature. But I much doubt if to put them in exercise be always in his power. Each man has indeed something peculiar in his frame; but the complaint of *indolence* is so general, that I am convinced I have many fellow sufferers who would be equally thankful with me to know of a remedy which will relieve from uneasiness whenever they apply it. Thomson's *Castle of Indolence* is one of the finest poems in the English language;[191] but it is a masterly picture of an infirmary. We are strongly affected with the distresses of *various* kinds produced by mere mental stagnation; but then we are left without the comfort of seeing how such miseries are to be prevented, or removed. I at this moment am relaxed by indolence of mind. I should not be uneasy, could I acquiesce in a state of incapacity, but at the very time that I am in this state I wish to read, to write, to talk, or at least to think with some activity. I can do neither. I am sensible of what I cannot describe so justly as by an *impotence of mind*. When I know the *cause* of this occasional cessation of mental activity, I have a *cure* ready. If I have exhausted myself by intense application to study, or by excessive enjoyment of sociality; whichever of these has occasioned the malady, the other can be used as a balancing corrective. But the most grievous situation is, when this impotence of mind seizes us we know not how, as a palsy sometimes seizes the body. If reflection were benumbed so as that a man were not conscious of his infirmity, he would not endure positive pain from it: but the misery is, that a man has then as lively ideas of activity as when fully capable to exert it. Friendship glows warmly at his heart, yet time glides for a shorter or longer space, or without his writing a single cordial letter. He is ambitious of fame, he wishes to acquire wealth by honest means; yet although twenty different schemes of successful publication float

191. James Thomson, *The Castle of Indolence* (1748).

in his view, he does not begin upon one of them. While in that situation, the regular progress of periodical works appears amazing; and I myself can declare that I have often been struck with wonder at finding my constant companion, *The London Magazine*, appear without fail on the first day of each month. That from the multiplicity of minds all over Great Britain who contribute towards this monthly miscellany, there should always be enough produced to fill up the stated number of sheets, so far as not supplied with judicious selection from books, is not surprising: but that there should ever be in one person or a few persons exertion enough to arrange and compile, is what strikes me, while I am soothed by a number of the work in which I find an easy amusement.

Perhaps some friendly fellow reader may know of a cure for the complaint which I have mentioned; though to me it seems that there can be none, at least, which a man can administer to himself, for how can a quiescent or sluggish *mind* be capable of beginning or renewing its own activity? The Abbe le Blanc in his letters of the English nation, when treating of vapours, or low spirits, observes that what is imputed to *disease* is often *vice*.[192] I do sincerely believe, that in such instances as I have described, the observation may be reversed; for many a man has been accused of ingratitude and other gross faults, when in reality he should have been pitied, as under a distemper. That a man's friends may assist him, I can very well suppose, as they can rouse him when lethargic, but a man has not always friends near him, and is unwilling to acknowledge his impotence. What I am anxious to know, is a *cure*, which a man himself can have at command, when he wishes for it. Visionary naturalists have indulged hopes of a remedy to prolong human life to a great age; a remedy against its cessation during the time that we breathe, would be equally valuable.

A constant reader of the
London Magazine.[193]

192. Jean-Bernard, abbé Le Blanc (1707–81), in his *Letters on the English and French Nations* (1747)—the author's own translation of the French original—says, "The *spleen* or vapours, and even the consumption, are perhaps nothing else but the *ennui* carried to its highest pitch, and become a dangerous, and sometimes a mortal disease" (1:90). He later devotes a whole letter, no. 27 (1:180–93), to the subject, with the title, "Of that sort of melancholy which proceeds from uneasiness of mind or predominancy of passions: with an application to the hypochondrical disposition of Englishmen." He calls melancholy or "the vapours" a "pretended ill" (182), "an inactivity of soul" caused in the main by laziness (184), "which it is in the power of reason to cure" (189).

193. As a pseudonym or a signoff line ("your constant reader, XX") for letters from anonymous contributors to the literary pages of newspapers, this term seems to have originated in the essay series of the early eighteenth century. It appears at the end of letters in

London Magazine, 45 (November 1776), 594

Consolation under Impotence of Mind, *if not a Cure for it.—*
Being an Answer to an Essay in the Lond. Mag *for* November *last Year*, p. 570.

IT must be acknowledged by a candid inquirer into human nature, who has formed his notions from experience, that the mind of man is indeed liable to fits of what may justly be called *impotence*. I use the term *man* as applicable to the species *in general*; for I believe that there have been, in every age of the world, and still are, *individuals* of mankind whose powers have been uniformly the same, through a long course of existence. I myself have observed a few such men, different however in their constitutions, some being uniformly calm and sedate, some uniformly lively and impetuous. But what shall a man think or do at the time when he is conscious of impotence of mind? I answer that if he is fully convinced that this impotence is real and not imaginary, he should quiet his uneasiness by considering that such temporary feebleness of being, is the common lot of humanity, and he should submit to it with patience, as he would to lameness or any bodily incapacity. He may at the same time soothe himself with the recollection of his former worthy and ingenious exertions, and hope that he shall afterwards be equally happy. Thus far consolation may be had from turning one's thoughts only on this scene of being; but I shall fairly acknowledge that I am so habituated to pious prospects of immortality, that I think the man must be poor and wretched indeed, who is destitute of that noble resource. If the patient has it, let him steadily, or at least earnestly look upon it. If he has it not, let him fervently ask it from our Father in Heaven, from whom cometh every good and every perfect gift.[194]

But I am persuaded that the *impotence of mind*, of which many are too ready to complain, is not a real affliction, but is only a cloudy picture in the imagination. I speak from *experience*; because I have at times *imagined* myself incapable of any exertion, yet as soon as either business, which could not be delayed, or amusement, which happened to please my fancy at the time, came in my way, the springs of life at once resumed their tone, and I was as active as ever. There is nothing more dangerous than to accustom one's self to an acquiescence in defects and faults as irremediable. That there is *power* in the mind of man, I shall ever maintain; and if there be an habitual *will* to do what is right in the small

---

*Tatler*s 118, 132, 146, and 160; *Spectator*s 145, 336, 410, 431, 474, and 613; and in other series thereafter.

194. "Every good and every perfect gift is from above, and cometh down from the Father of lights" (James 1:17; *AV*).

lines of *duty* as well as in the large, the human constitution is rarely such, but that a man *may*. I would advise then every person to accustom himself strictly to do what he thinks right in every particular, and not indolently to indulge himself, by thinking "*I cannot do it*." If he is to read at particular hours, to write at others, and so on in other respects, let him peremptorily do so, notwithstanding any discouraging apprehensions, that he may not be much benefited. The husbandman must plough and sow his lands regularly every spring, though he fears that he shall not have a good crop.

It will occur from what I have already said, that I understand it to be necessary for the cure of *impotence of mind* that a man should live according to a *plan*. I hold this to be absolutely necessary; for that relaxation and sloth which I take to be the causes of the disease, must not be trusted, but be banked up by rules, and spurred on by spirited instigation. Go to the Bank of England, to any of the public offices, or even to any capital merchant's counting house.—Business is carried on there by individuals, all, except some very extraordinary instances, liable to the same frailties, the same cessations of activity, that other men are, yet the planets do not move with more order and constancy than the affairs transacted at those places. Why?—because there is a *plan* which operates with so certain a power as to rouse and bear along even the languid faculties. Go to an army in the field, and observe a more striking example. Observe continued perseverance not only in fatigue but in animation, by individuals of all ages, constitutions and habits of life—all by *discipline*.

If a man has tried a plan and course of discipline, under his own direction, without success, he has reason to be ashamed of his weakness, but that he may not be in a worse state, let him engage himself for a time in a course of study, or business, or exercises, under the direction of some person of known steadiness;[195] and after such a course his mind will probably have acquired so vigorous a tone and such a habit of activity, that he will be able to continue by the power of his own resolution. The course must be of a different degree of rigidness, according to the state of his mind. For my own part, I would rather enlist in a marching regiment, enter on board a man of war, or even indent myself as a bondman in the Plantations,[196] than not be cured of that wretched impotence of which I am

195. JB was strongly attracted to powerfully decisive individuals, men of firm action or philosophy, such as Rousseau, Paoli, or Johnson, from whom he sought advice about practical and psychological self-management. He may also have his own father in mind.

196. A *bondman* is one who contracts for a fixed term of *indentured servitude*, to work, typically in America and the West Indies, not for wages in cash, but in exchange for transportation from Britain and the necessities of life.

treating.[197] It would take a volume should I write of all the various minuter helps, such as books, conversation and amusements. I leave these to every reader's own judgment, and shall be happy if I am of any service to any gentleman.

MEDICUS MENTIS.[198]

1776

On Allegorical Figures in the
Caledonian Mercury

[In the weeks and months before the publication of this letter, there were in the Edinburgh press many contributions of political satire, in the form of dreams, fictitious reports, and parodies. The *Caledonian Mercury* has a letter signed "Pro Patria Semper" ("for my country always"), reporting the forthcoming publication of four satires and announcing that the writer is collecting materials for a "Majestratical Biography, or Curious Anecdotes of city rulers" that will "astonish the public more than whatever has been told of the OLD Fox, or the YOUNG GOAT" (Sept. 14, 4); a poem, "The Political VERMIN-CATCHER: or, The Art of making BRUTES obedient" (Sept. 18); and a parody of scripture, in chapter and verses, called "Les Chroniques Politiques, de———. 1776. Liv. II, Chap. XX," of which the final verse reads, "And the Apostates, the Foxes, the Goats, the Mortars, the Pisspots, the Hammers, and the Heel-tops did sing for joy; and Cersa the scribe was exceeding glad" (Sept. 21, 1). No actual parodic fable has been found.]

Caledonian Mercury, October 5, 1776, 3

To the Printer of the Caledonian Mercury.

SIR,

I AM a country schoolmaster, and am as constantly attentive to do my duty as any of my brethren. I am expert in all that is prescribed in that excellent com-

---

197. On Mar. 19, 1776, JB discussed "constitutional melancholy" with Johnson, who advised that "a man so afflicted . . . must divert distressing thoughts, and not combat with them. . . . Let him take a course of chymistry, or a course of rope-dancing, or a course of any thing to which he is inclined at the time. Let him contrive to have as many retreats for his mind as he can, as many things to which it can fly from itself" (*Life*, 2:440; most of the details of this conversation are not in the journal; see *Ominous Years*, 276).

198. *Medicus Mentis*: physician of the mind. In *London Magazine*, 4 [new series] (Jan. 1785), 63, a correspondent inquired, "Is Medicus Mentis alive, who wrote a short essay in your Magazine, November, 1776, page 594? If so, how can a letter be conveyed to him?" JB does not seem to have taken the opportunity to reply, at least not through the magazine.

position, *Qui mihi discipulus puer es, cupis atque doceri*—In English thus: "O boy, who art my disciple, and desirest to be taught."[199] *The Caledonian* MERCURY is regularly read amongst my boys, that they may be instructed in what is actually passing in the world, while care is taken to store their minds with ancient history. And, indeed, Sir, I find that I can make your paper an excellent text for prelections upon many subjects. You may believe, then, that it is of consequence to me that you should insert nothing but what I can explain; and, in order to [do] this, nothing but what I can understand.

Of late, you have given us a great deal of what had, at first view, the appearance of something like *Æsop's Fables*;[200] and which, if it had been intelligible, would have been very fit for a school. I have observed several allegorical or allusive dissertations concerning *Reynard the Fox*, and concerning a *Kid*;[201] but, after studying all the editions both of *Æsop* and *Phædrus* that are in my possession,[202] I can make out no meaning, and am more puzzled than I would wish to acknowledge under my own name. My wife suggested it to me privately, as her notion, that, as you had lately partridges flying in your city, wild beasts of different sorts might be there now, as well as wild birds formerly.[203] But I checked her for putting so literal a construction on what has, I dare say, much more in it, if we knew its full meaning and import.

199. This is the first line of William Lilye's Latin poem "Carmen de Moribus," a poem that lists the school rules for St. Paul's School in London (of which Lilye was the first master) and gives examples of many rules of Latin grammar; it was included in the composite work known as *Lilye's Grammar* (1548–49), which was used in schools for over 300 years. The translation here appears to be JB's.

200. The ancient Greek fables to which the name of Aesop is attached are mostly "beast-fables"—i.e., stories of anthropomorphized animals. JB uses the device in "Rampager" 8 (Chap. 3).

201. In *Caledonian Mercury*, May 4, 1776, 2–3, there is a report from York, that, "we are assured, is a fact: On the 18th inst., a fox carried off a gosling from a flock belonging to William Maynard, a farmer in the parish of Craike; on the 19th he lamed another, so that it died; and on the 20th, he came again, when the gander seized him by the ear, and beat him so with his wings, that in the morning poor Reynard was found expiring. This gander, we are informed, will fight any dog." (Reynard is the traditional proper name for a fox, from the medieval European trickster figure, Reynard the Fox, best known in England from a version translated and printed by pioneer printer William Caxton in 1481.) The item "concerning a *Kid*" may be a report about Captain Kidd (reported as "Kid") of H. M. Sloop *Princess Anne*, which fell in with a smuggling "dogger" in the Firth of Forth in May 1776 (*Caledonian Mercury*, May 1, 1776, 3).

202. Phædrus was the Roman writer who translated the Latin versions of the fables of Aesop and others.

203. In the *Caledonian Mercury* of Monday, Sept. 9, 1776, an eagle of "prodigious magnitude," weighing 6 st. 9 lb., was reported to have been shot down over Bridlington.

What then I would entreat, Sir, is either that you would illustrate such passages with *notes*, or subjoin a *moral*, as is done in Croxal's Æsop,[204] or publish them in one of your *extraordinary* papers,[205] otherwise you may change the title of your paper, and, instead of *The Caledonian* MERCURY, call it *The Caledonian* SPHYNX.[206]

HYPODIDASCULUS.[207]

Publish the War Casualty Lists

[In his journal for November 8, 1776, Boswell records having read, in the *London Gazette Extraordinary* (actually, an extract published that day in the *Caledonian Mercury*), an account of the capture of New York by the British army under General Howe. He says, "I regretted it. But as there were not many British killed or wounded, there was not an interesting scene" (*Extremes*, 53). Possibly it was thinking about the published list of "eight officers wounded, fourteen men killed, and about seventy men wounded" (*Extremes*, 53 n. 3) that prompted the letter below.]

Public Advertiser, November 18, 1776, 1 (leading article)

To the Printer of the Public Advertiser.

SIR,

SO much has been written upon both Sides in that immense Controversy, "The Justice or Injustice of the present War carried on by Great Britain against her Provinces in America,"[208] that, unless I had something very important to communicate, or were possessed of peculiar Excellence in Expression, I should not willingly intrude upon you and your Readers; but however confined my Abilities may be, I think I can suggest a Hint in the Way of *Humanity*, which I would fain hope may be adopted by those who have the Power of making it effectual.

Upon Occasion of every Battle, we have published by Authority what is called a *List of the Killed and Wounded*: But, Sir, I am to lament the Imperfection of those Lists, in which, indeed, the Names of *the Commissioned Officers* are reg-

---

204. Samuel Croxall's *Fables of Aesop and Others, Newly Done into English, with an Application to Each Fable* (1722).

205. That is, a special issue of the paper, published to announce some major event, such as the outcome of a battle in wartime; see next headnote.

206. In mythology, Mercury was the Roman name for the messenger of the gods; hence, it is often used as a name for newspapers. For the Sphinx, see above, nn. 18, 22.

207. *Hypodidasculus* was a Latin term sometimes used for an usher or under-teacher or private tutor.

208. This seems to signify the name of the controversy in the abstract, not the title of a particular text.

ularly inserted, but *Serjeants*, and *all who serve under them*, are thrown together in a *wretched Blank* as to the *Names*, though the Regiments and the Numbers of Killed and Wounded in each are specified. This, Sir, I cannot help being of Opinion well deserves to be remedied: For in the first Place it would surely be a very noble Incitement to our gallant Soldiers to have their Names recorded in the Annals of their Country. But, 2dly, it is exceedingly distressing to the Relations and Friends of the brave Fellows to be kept so long in the Dark as to their Fate, as they must probably be after every Action, in Comparison of what they would be were the Gazette to give the Names of Non-commissioned Officers and Soldiers, as well as the Officers who are honoured with Commissions.[209] Surely, Mr. Woodfall, there are the same Feelings of Affection and Concern amongst the lower Ranks of Life as amongst the Great; nay, I believe the Feelings of the former are keener and more sincere than those of the latter. How cruel then must it be to the Wife, the Children, the Father, the Brothers or the Sisters of a Soldier, whose Regiment has been engaged in Battle, to have no more particular Information than a Number of *Rank and File* killed and wounded.

I know, Sir, that mentioning the Names of every Man in the Army killed or wounded has been practised in foreign Service; and I myself have in my Possession such a particular List after one of the Engagements in the Civil War in 1715.[210]

It is well known that a most exact *Return* of the Names of every Person killed, wounded, or missing is made in every Regiment. All the Trouble then would be to have those Lists transcribed, transmitted to the Secretary of State, and published in the Gazette;[211] and surely such an additional Trouble is not to be grudged, when it is considered how much Good would be produced by it.

I remember reading in your Paper, after the Action of Bunker's hill, an Extract of a Letter from Chatham,[212] mentioning that there was sad Uneasiness

209. A commission—i.e., the authority that entitles a soldier to officer rank in the armed forces—is issued in the name of the reigning monarch and must therefore be officially proclaimed. The ranks of sergeant and below are noncommissioned and reached by promotion.

210. The "Civil War" is the first Jacobite uprising in 1715. "Foreign service" may be military service overseas, by way of contrast with the civil war, or the service of a tenant beyond the boundary of the lord's estate, with civil war service as an instance (*OED*, with citation from 1607).

211. The *London Gazette* was the official government newspaper, first printed in 1665. The *Gazette* includes news of government appointments, commissions, and promotions in the armed forces, the coming into law of acts of Parliament, royal proclamations, etc. It was perhaps the first, or at least the oldest, continuously published newspaper in England.

212. At Chatham in Kent, there was a large naval dockyard and military barracks, both of which were sites of considerable activity during this period. Extracts from letters from

in a Number of Families there belonging to the Marines, as it was known that many Men of that Corps had fallen: But the poor People were in utter Uncertainty who were particular Sufferers, except the few Officers whose Names were published.

Our most gracious Sovereign, who is so remarkably celebrated for Tenderness of Disposition and domestic Endearments, would, I flatter meself, at once feel the Force of this humble Suggestion; and as I am informed that his Majesty reads the News-papers,[213] it is possible that he may cast his Eye upon these Lines, which I hope many humane Editors will copy; and if they shall have the desired Effect, it will give me a Satisfaction better than what arises from the Vanity of the most admirable of your Correspondents.

A WARM FRIEND OF THE BRAVE.[214]

A Defense of the State Trumpeters

[There are records dating to the early 1700s of trumpeters appointed to the royal household in Scotland having a role in state and judicial ceremonies. Until 1971, trumpeters attended the judges of the High Court of Justiciary when on circuit, in which role Boswell would have often seen them: in May 1767, accompanying his father on his official duties, he passed through Auchinleck village with the trumpeters sounding their call (*Search*, 72). In the *Caledonian Mercury* of Nov. 20, 1776, the first item of news from Edinburgh reported that "his Majesty's proclamation for recalling such seamen as may be employed in foreign service . . . *should have been* read," that the heralds and pursuivants attended in their robes, as did a detachment of the City Guard; "But, lo! Notwithstanding everything being thus prepared and *set in order*, the ceremony itself was obliged to be deferred, by the non-attendance of these necessary beings called *Trumpeters*, without whom, it seems, his Majesty's voice cannot be

---

Chatham appeared frequently in the London press, but I have not found the letter to which JB refers. For the Battle of Bunker Hill, see Chap. 3, nn. 344, 348.

213. Frances Burney, who was a keeper of the robes to Queen Charlotte, reports in her diary a conversation with the king (Dec. 19, 1785): "Some time afterwards, the King said he found by the newspapers, that [actress] Mrs. Clive was dead. Do you read the newspapers? thought I. O, King! you must then have the most unvexing temper in the world, not to run wild." See Burney, *Diary and Letters*, 2:343.

214. The following day, Nov. 19, a reply to this letter appeared in the *Pub. Adv.*; in it, "A Friend to Sinking" says, "Your Correspondent . . . has assigned many good Reasons for publishing the Names of those private Soldiers who fell in Battle, but he forgot that the Ministry have a much better Reason for not doing it, viz. that of concealing their Number." JB filed a copy of this item (*Cat. Yale*, P 114(9)).

heard" (2). This provoked a spirited response from that champion of ceremony and tradition, Boswell.]

Caledonian Mercury, November 23, 1776, 3

To the Printer of the Caledonian Mercury.

SIR,

IN your last paper, I observed a very heavy reflection against *the State Trumpeters*, who, it is said, did not attend as they ought to have done, on which account a Royal Proclamation could not be made.[215] I must set you right as to the *fact*; for the Trumpeters did not get notice to attend upon that day. They are ever ready and willing to do their duty; and, accordingly, upon being properly informed, they were present the day after.

But, Sir, it is not only the *matter*, but the *manner* of your paragraph which I mean to correct; and I must tell you freely, that there is an air of pompous ridicule in it very unsuitable to Trumpeters in general, and to the Trumpeters of this great and free nation in particular. Trumpets have been used to denote dignity and importance in all ages and nations in the world. They have been used in temples, in palaces, and in camps. Heroic poetry abounds with them; and I desire to know, where there is any thing supremely dignified where they are not to be found. They are, indeed, so well understood to be appropriated to what is great, that when a Trumpet was once blown, to advertise a show in this city, a gentleman, eminent for classical learning, exclaimed, with indignation, "What a prostitution of *the ancient* TUBA!"[216] Nay, Sir, that respectable Society, called THE REVOLUTION CLUB, put "our happy security, against Popery, slavery, and arbitrary power," by the succession of the illustrious House of Hanover,[217] upon *the sound of a Trumpet*:[218] Thus,

---

215. The six Scottish state trumpeters still appear at the Mercat Cross in Edinburgh for royal proclamations, and at the Palace of Holyroodhouse and at other places on certain ceremonial occasions (Allison and Riddell, *Royal Encyclopaedia*, s.v. "Trumpeters of Scotland, State"). Since May 1999, the trumpeters' public role has been considerably more noticeable, with their participation in the ceremonial of the Scottish Parliament.

216. The term *tuba* was at this time the Latin word for "the straight bronze war-trumpet of the ancient Romans" (*OED*); the modern tuba was patented in Germany in 1835.

217. An issue of the *Edinburgh Advertiser* for Nov. 1764 announces a meeting of this society, using terms similar to those quoted here by JB. The club celebrated the so-called Glorious Revolution of 1688, which saw King James II and VII overthrown and William of Orange succeed to the British throne as King William III with his wife Queen Mary II. It seems to have been active from at least 1753 to 1788 (see Grant, 5:123).

218. Hebrews 12:19 (*AV*).

Fame, let thy TRUMPET sound;
Tell all the world around,
GREAT GEORGE is KING.[219]

And I hope it will not be considered as too extravagant a metaphor to say, that the subjection of his Majesty's subjects in *America*, to his Majesty's *British Parliament*, does also depend upon a Trumpet; for it depends upon an army clothed in *Red*;[220] and we are told by Mr *Locke*, That a blind man imagined the colour of *scarlet* to be *like the sound of a Trumpet*.[221] If it shall be urged, that much is due to GERMAN auxiliaries,[222] we have, amongst our State Trumpeters, the *Heer* RENEAGLES;[223] and, if the NAVY comes in for a considerable share, we have a MARINE.[224] For the future, then, Mr MERCURY, take care how you meddle with Trumpets, or expect to have your paper assailed with a more violent *blast* than that of John Knox against the *Regimen of Women*.[225]

TRUMPETARIUS.

219. These are the first lines of a song to the tune of "God Save the King," that first appeared in the *Gent. Mag.* for Sept. 1745. The verse continues:

Tell Rome, and France, and Spain
Britannia scorns their chain;
All their vile arts are vain,
Great George is King.

220. From the late 1600s, the coats of British infantry uniforms were red.

221. Locke, *Essay Concerning Human Understanding*, 239.

222. "German auxiliaries" is a general term for the Hessians and other German soldiers who fought for Britain during the American war; see Chap. 3, nn. 322, 359.

223. Joseph Reinagle (c. 1720–75) was a Hungarian-born musician who, having come to Scotland in 1745, was appointed trumpeter to George III in 1762. His son, Joseph the Younger (1762–1825), studied the trumpet and horn with his father. JB went to a benefit concert on Sept. 23, 1780, for Joseph the Younger's brother, Hugh Reinagle (*Laird*, 252–53).

224. James Marine (fl. 1716–86; see Grattan, "Brass Instruments," 51) came from a line of Scottish state trumpeters: his father or grandfather, Francis, is referred to as "Trumpeter Marine" in a ballad from the early 1700s and is mentioned in Scott's *Bride of Lammermoor*, and the son or grandson is mentioned in the author's own note to this passage. See Scott, *Bride of Lammermoor*, n. J, 328–29.

225. A notorious pamphlet by Scottish reformer John Knox, *The First Blast of the Trumpet against the Monstrous Regiment of Women* (1558); *regimen(t)* here means *regime* or *rule* (i.e., of women over men).

1779

Shortage of Provisions at the Mayoral Ball

Public Advertiser, April 8, 1779, 2 (leading article)

To the Printer of the Public Advertiser.

SIR,

I AM by Birth a *North Briton*, as a *Scotchman* must now be called;[226] but like a great many of my Countrymen, love much to come to London; and why not, Sir? as, since the Union of the two Kingdoms, which deprived us of all national Dignity, and all the Advantages of a Vice-Court, and of a Parliament in our own District,[227] London is now the Metropolis of the whole Island, the grand Emporium of every Thing valuable, the strong Center of Attraction for all of us, his Majesty's British Subjects, from the Land's End to Caithness.[228] Full of high Notions of this GREAT CITY, and of its CHIEF MAGISTRATE, the LORD MAYOR in the *Abstract*, without Respect of Persons, (as I am now old enough to know that the Mansion-house is successively inhabited by Men of all Characters,[229] and that *there*, as at *Baldock's Mill*,

> "The Grave and the Gay, the Clown and the Beau
> Without all Distinction promiscuously go,")[230]

226. After the Act of Union in 1707, Scotland was sometimes referred to as North Britain, and Scots, as North Britons, with the implication that Scottish identity and loyalty was or should be of less significance than an allegiance to the United Kingdom. (The title of John Wilkes's paper, the *North Briton*, mocked the Scots.)

227. After 1603, when James VI of Scotland succeeded to the English crown, the court became based in London. From 1603 until the Union of 1707, England and Scotland had the same monarch but separate parliaments and privy councils. The union created a single Parliament of Great Britain; the Privy Council of Scotland was abolished the following year. However, Ireland, which remained a separate kingdom (under the British crown) with its own parliament until 1801, was ruled by the Lord Lieutenant or viceroy, who held court at Dublin Castle; this is likely to be the "vice-court" to which JB refers.

228. Land's End (a headland in Cornwall, England) and Caithness (a former county in Scotland, which includes the village of John o' Groats) are, respectively, the most south-westerly and northeasterly points on the British mainland; the phrase, most frequently *Land's End to John o' Groats*, signifies the whole of Britain.

229. For the Mansion House, see n. 188, above.

230. *Baldock's Mill* is the setting of "the very popular ballad 'The Maid of the Mill,' said to have been written c. 1745 by the then curate of Baldock in Hertfordshire in praise of Mary Ireland, daughter of the miller and inn-keeper of Baldock" (*Laird*, 66 n. 5). The

I went last Night to the Ball at the Mansion-house, and having feasted my Eyes and my Ears for some Time, I desired to have a little Negus to recruit my Animal Spirits.[231] But what was my Astonishment, Sir, when the Waiters told me, "I could not have it; it was all gone; they had no more Wine." Several Ladies and Gentlemen I found were in the same State of Disappointment that I was. Upon which, Sir, I asked an English Friend if this could possibly be countenanced by the Lord Mayor? I was informed he was a Mr. Alderman *Plumb*, but that his Penuriousness was excessive.[232] I was determined, however, that he should not escape quite *impuné*,[233] if he had any *Feeling*, and that I should be, if not a *Thorn*, at least a *Thistle* in his Side.[234] Accordingly away I marched to find his *Lordship*; and pray, Sir, how d'ye think I found him occupied? Upon my Honour (and I can bring fifty Witnesses, with a City Marshal at their Head)[235] I found him standing without his Gown or Chain, in a Bag Wig, and Marone Coat,[236] with his Back leaning against the Stair-case, telling the Company not to go up Stairs, in order that he might get rid of them. Up I went though, in the first Place, to the Egyptian Hall,[237] to see what was doing, and *there* was a Number of Ladies and Gentlemen standing up for a Country Dance; but when they called for Music, they were told the Music were discharged by the Lord Mayor to play any more without fresh Orders,[238] and in a little Time they moved off, amidst the

---

couplet given by JB concludes the first of its four verses. A *clown*: "A rustick; a country fellow" (*SJ Dict.*).

231. Negus is a sweet alcoholic punch, made of wine, spice, and sugar, and drunk warm or hot.

232. Samuel Plumbe (1717–84), sugar refiner, was elected Lord Mayor of London six months earlier, on Sept. 29, 1778. His wife, Frances, was Henry Thrale's sister; he "had a general reputation for stinginess" (*Laird*, 66 n. 6). JB may be punning on *plum* as "soft; yielding" (*OED*), but see also n. 247, below.

233. *Impuné*: the Latin-derived adj. *impune* (obsolete): unpunished (*OED*). (The italics and superfluous accent perhaps signify that JB thought the term was French.)

234. *Thorn in his side*: proverbial expression for a chronic affliction, alluding to 2 Corinthians 12:17; in this case, with a thistle in place of a thorn, for Scotland.

235. A city marshal was first appointed in 1595, in the reign of Elizabeth I, to keep order in the city of London. By 1779, the role required six city marshalmen and an under-marshal. (As the police force expanded, the role has diminished; however, one city marshal still attends the Lord Mayor of London, in a mainly ceremonial capacity.)

236. The gown and chain are the mayor's signs of office; the bagwig was a fashionable type of wig, in which the back hair was enclosed in an ornamental bag. This is a particularly early use of *marone* or *maroon* for a brownish-crimson or claret color (*OED*).

237. The Egyptian Room is a large columned hall that is the main reception room in the Mansion House.

238. The "Music were discharged . . . to play any more": i.e., the musicians were charged not to play any more. An offprint of this letter is in JB's papers (*Cat. Yale*, P 95), in which

Hisses of the Company, who I took it for granted would have instantly broke his Lamps into Shivers with a just Indignation.

But to return to my Negus. *His Lordship* having come up Stairs, stood despondent in one of the Anti-chambers—I went to him, and, with a low Bow, addressed him thus:—"My Lord Mayor, I ask Pardon for giving your Lordship this Trouble; but I beg your Lordship would order me a Glass of Negus, I am afraid your Lordship is ill used by some of your Servants: I asked for Negus, and they told me there was none."

Now, Mr. Woodfall, upon the Word of an honest Man, which *you know* I am, I shall give you literally what passed, without the least Exaggeration. His Lordship, with aukward Surprise and Confusion, said, "Sir, I *wish* you had asked for it sooner."—I would not quit him. "My Lord," said I (putting the Breasts of my Coat in a buttoning Attitude) "I have got a little Cold; if you'll let me have a single Glass, I'll be obliged to you. Here, Sir, (calling one of his Silver-laced Attendants, who approached us) if your Lordship will please to give your Orders to one of your Servants."—"Sir, (replied THE LORD MAYOR of LONDON) I have no Command of the Negus;"—and slunk away.

Now, Sir, are not you Englishmen a Set of pretty Fellows?—You talk with Horror of an Edinburgh Mob committing a few Outrages;[239] and you say not a Word of a London Mob the very Week after breaking half the Windows of your peaceable Citizens.[240] You talk of Scotch Poverty;[241] yet I will venture to

---

JB has marked *discharged* and written "forbid" in the margin. The *Laird* editors say that he intends this "probably as a gloss. 'Discharge' in the sense of 'forbid' was a Scotticism, but in this letter one thinks he would have tended to introduce Scotticisms, not to remove them" (*Laird*, 67 n. 9).

239. In Jan. and Feb. 1779, rioters supporting the Protestant Association in Edinburgh and Glasgow took preemptive action against any attempt to extend to Scotland the provisions of the Catholic Relief Act, which had passed without incident in England the previous May. (See Black, "Tumultuous Petitioners," 183–211.)

240. In London on Saturday, Feb. 20, when the court-martial of naval officer and whig politician Admiral Augustus Keppel (1725–96) was concluded with his acquittal, crowds of his supporters accompanied him home, and the papers reported: "The nocturnal Banditti renewed their Outrages on Saturday Evening; for on the Return of Admiral Keppel from the City about Eleven o'Clock, they broke most of the Windows of Charing-Cross, Pall-Mall, St. James's-Street, Dover-Street, &c. &c." (*St. James's Chron.*, Feb. 23, 1779). When the prosecution of rioters was abandoned a few days later, "infinite windows were broken of those not so much transported by the event as to illuminate their houses" (*Morning Post*, Feb. 23, 1779).

241. In England, the stereotype of Scots as poor and consequently greedy for English wealth was a constant subject for sarcastic remark through the century; it was reinforced by enemies of Lord Bute's administration (see Chap. 3, nn. 17–21), in particular in the satirical essays published in the *North Briton*. The *Middlesex Journal* of Aug. 15, 1772, says of "the old story

say, that at no public Entertainment in the pettiest Borough in Scotland would a Gentleman have been refused a Glass of Negus. The Provost (or Mayor) of little Lord Galloway's little Borough of *Whithorn*, would have lived on Herrings and Water for a Week, rather than have his *Toon* (*Town*) so disgraced.[242] At Edinburgh, *Walter Hamilton*, our worthy LORD PROVOST, would have ordered a DOUBLE BOTTLE, a SCOTCH PINT, a BONUM MAGNUM of excellent CLARET (which by the Way, Harry, you would like very well to see) and would shew that HE "has the Command" of a generous Cellar.[243] But in the *Mansion-House of the City of London* a Glass of Negus is not to be had after One o'Clock in the Morning; and the Lord Mayor, with all the Authority of his Office, has not the Command of a little Wine and Water, and Sugar. So wretchedly inhospitable a House as your Mansion-House last Night I never was in. Let Mr. *Wilkes*, if he can spare Time from his new Employment of *Defender of the Faith*, (as he is always encroaching on *Royal Prerogative*) defend *English* Liberality if he can.[244]

---

of Scotch poverty" that "Wilkes and Churchill made this a reigning topic some years ago in their edifying lucubrations upon Politics." Churchill used the theme in *The Prophecy of Famine: A Scots Pastoral* (1763), dedicated to Wilkes. That the expression was a commonplace is seen in *General Advertiser*, June 29, 1779, in which it is noted, "We have now Scotch Judges, Scotch Counsels, and Scotch poverty—we only want a Scotch K—— to compleat our miseries."

242. Parliamentary representation of the Scottish Royal burgh of Whithorn, in Galloway in the south of Scotland, was controlled by the earls of Galloway. JB met John Stewart, seventh earl of Galloway (1736–1806), in 1762, when, before his succession, he was styled Lord Garlies; he described him as "a little man" of "petulant forwardness" (Journal, quoted in *Laird*, 68 n. 1). The small town of Whithorn had its own provost until the local government reforms of 1975. "Herrings and water" connotes a poor man's food.

243. For the Lord Provost of Edinburgh, see above, n. 92. Walter Hamilton (n.d.) was Lord Provost, 1778–80. The *Scotch pint* was a measure equivalent to approximately three imperial pints; *Bonum Magnum* is a Scottish term for the double-sized wine bottle called a magnum (*OED*). "Harry" is a familiar address for H. S. Woodfall, publisher of the *Pub. Adv.*, known for his conviviality.

244. "Defender of the Faith" is one of the titles of the British monarch. The *Royal Prerogative* is the name for the particular powers belonging exclusively to the monarch. The Bill of Rights, of which John Wilkes was a prominent "Gentleman Supporter," was historically one of the most important limitations on the royal prerogative. On Mar. 10, Wilkes spoke in the House of Commons in support of the bill for the relief of dissenting ministers and schoolmasters from subscription to the Thirty-nine Articles of Religion; in his speech, "Mr. Wilkes proceeded to deny the charge of Atheism having made any Progress in this Island; . . . Pure Deism had indeed made a rapid Progress: But who were the eminent Writers on this Subject? Not dissenting Ministers, but Clergymen of the Established Church—of the Church of England, of which, Sir, I am a Member" (*Pub. Adv.*, Mar. 11, 1779). Wilkes's own mayoralty in 1774–75 was notable for its "liberality" (i.e., extravagance), and there are many contemporary accounts of the lavishness of his April ball.

Why, Sir Whittington's Cat must have starved had she been there.[245] Though indeed I was not a *hungry* Scotchman:[246] I wanted only a Drop of *Liquor*, and I went to the *Fountain Head*. But, alas, it was quite *dry*; there was no *Juice* in the *Plumb*. Yet this Man, I am told, has amassed what you call a *Plumb* by *sweating* and *refining* Gold.[247] A *Sweat*, and a hearty one too, he ought to have. But to *refine* him will be no easy Task.[248] For my own Part, all that I can say is, that be his Wealth ever so great, this PLUMB of yours is in my Opinion at present not worth a FIG.[249]

April 6.   TANTALUS.[250]

1780

New Year's Address

[The *Caledonian Mercury* was a tri-weekly newspaper of six pages, established in 1720. Chambers described it as "the first [newspaper] in Scotland which blended literary criticism with political matter" (*Chambers' Edinburgh Journal*, 3 [1835], 147). In his journal on December 30–31, 1779, Boswell records writing the following piece in the character of the newspaper's editor, "*invita Minerva*" (that is, without inspiration),

245. Richard (Dick) Whittington (c. 1350–1423) was mayor of London for four terms in the late fourteenth and early fifteenth centuries. He is best known for the legend of his coming as a boy to London to make his fortune, accompanied only by his cat.

246. A phrase reminiscent of SJ's reported description of Scots poet and dramatist David Mallet (born "Malloch"; 1705–65), "a hungry Scotchman" to whom Bolingbroke had left a half-crown to publish his impious works after his death (see Murphy, "Essay on the Life," 408). The term "hungry Scotchman" is used in contemporary newspapers in ways that suggest it had a particular resonance at this time, as is also suggested by Churchill's *Prophecy of Famine* (see n. 241, above).

247. *Plum*: "The sum of one hundred thousand pounds" (*OED*). To *sweat* gold or other metal is to fuse it by heat, but *sweating* (in particular) gold coins is criminally to lighten them by friction or other means. JB alludes to Plumbe's membership of the Goldsmiths' Company (*Laird*, 68 n. 5).

248. To *sweat* (a person) was an eighteenth-century medical procedure; *to refine him* refers to Plumb's occupation as a sugar refiner.

249. *Fig*: both a fruit, like the plum, and (in the phrase *not worth a fig*) something "small, valueless and contemptible" (*OED*).

250. In Greek mythology, Tantalus was punished for a hideous crime by being condemned to stand in a pool of water beneath a fruit tree, but, whenever he tried to eat or drink, the branches would rise or the water would recede beyond his reach. Thus his name became proverbial for one who is always tempted and always unsatisfied.

and that he "sent it, careless whether it should be inserted or not." However, when he found it published on January 2, he noted, "Liked it" (*Laird*, 156–57).]

Caledonian Mercury, January 1, 1780, [2]

EDINBURGH.

The PUBLISHER *of the* CALEDONIAN MERCURY *to* READERS.[251]
Truditur dies die,
Novæ que pergunt interire Luneæ. HORAT.[252]

THE first New-year's day after the *accession*, or, to use Mrs *Catharine Macaulay's* phrase, the *elevation*,[253] of the present Publisher to the office of conducting THE CALEDONIAN MERCURY, he took the liberty to offer a particular address to his numerous readers and correspondents.[254] He has not made this an annual custom, as it might have the appearance of intrusion and self-importance; and, to confess the truth, he was afraid of imposing upon himself a task which he might find too difficult. It would, indeed, be easy enough, at the beginning of every year, to besprinkle the first page of his paper with common-place compliments and professions, with about as much variety as we observe in the succession of painted and gilded playthings with which the toy-shops are crowded at this anniversary of *young amusement*.[255] But although THE CALEDONIAN MERCURY is at times the bearer of sportive sallies, and the Publisher can say, in the words of HORACE, *Virginibus puerisque canto*, "I entertain young Ladies and

251. The publisher of the *Caledonian Mercury* was John Robertson, described as "a printer of sufficient learning, and of opulent circumstances," who in May 1772 had purchased "the property of the printing-house, types, and all other materials," as well as "the right of publishing the Caledonian Mercury," from the trustees of Thomas Ruddiman. See Chalmers, *Life of Thomas Ruddiman*, 124 and n. (a). In 1815, Thomas Allen purchased it.

252. "Day treads upon the heel of day,/ and new moons haste to wane" (Horace, *Odes*, 2.18.15–16).

253. JB plays on the title of the long historical work by Catharine Macaulay, *The History of England from the Accession of James I to the Elevation of the House of Hanover*, 8 vols. (1763–83), that was, at this stage, still being published.

254. The *Caledonian Mercury* of Saturday, Jan. 2, 1773, opens with an address from "the Publisher . . . to his Readers."

255. It is not clear if JB is alluding here to anything more specific than Christmas as a time of pleasure for children. Through the 1780s and 1790s, a number of books offered holiday *amusement* to the *young*, such as *Christmas Tales: For the Amusement and Instruction of Young Ladies and Gentlemen in Winter Evenings* (London, [1785?]), by "Solomon Sobersides," of which there was an American edition of 1786, titled *A Pretty New-Year's Gift*.

Gentlemen;"[256] that is but a small and occasional part of his province. He has the honour to communicate information and amusement to the wise, the learned, and the judicious; to those whom he respects too much to attempt to flatter, and to whom he knows flimsy adulation would be disgusting and offensive.

He, however, trusts, that after an interval of several years, during which he has experienced very liberal favour from THE PUBLIC, he shall be allowed the indulgence of an effusion of gratitude, and of a humble solicitation of a continuance of that steady patronage, and those kind communications, by which he has been enabled to keep up the character of this long established, and favourite Scots news-paper.

The period which the present Publisher has occupied, has been a most important and eventful portion of the annals of Great Britain and America. He hopes that, during his gradual accounts of the unhappy contest with our Colonies, his intelligence has been found to be peculiarly authentic, and early, of which particular instances will be recollected by his readers. It has, at the same time, been his study, in the insertion of Essays and Letters upon the subject, to pay a proper deference to the several opinions which have prevailed even on this side of the Tweed. While one of the most learned and respectable societies in Scotland refused to subscribe supplies, or testify their approbation,[257] it would ill have become the Publisher of a news-paper, however clear in his own opinion, to treat all opposition to the measures of Government as factious and unwise. In one article he cannot doubt that all will agree; for all, surely, are averse to the encroaching dominion of France. He means, that all will rejoice at the quarrel between the American army and the French General, who insolently summoned the garrison of Savannah to surrender to His MOST CHRISTIAN MAJESTY, but was repulsed in a manner very ill-suited to his confident Bravado.[258] That quarrel

---

256. "I sing for maidens and boys" (Horace, *Odes*, 3.1.4).

257. It is not known which "learned and respectable society" is referred to here or to what exactly its members had "refused to subscribe supplies, or testify their approbation."

258. In Sept. 1779, French general and admiral Charles Hector, Comte d'Estaing (1729–94), led a joint French–American attempt to retake the British garrison at Savannah, Georgia. Rather than mounting a direct assault, which probably would have succeeded because the British were unprepared, d'Estaing sent an insolent formal demand that the British general surrender "to the arms of his Majesty the King of France," then allowed a 24-hour truce that enabled the British to strengthen their defenses. There were tensions between the allies, with the Americans suspecting that d'Estaing would capture the town and hold it in the name of France. The British refused to surrender, and the city was put under siege. On Oct. 9, the American and French forces began a major assault. On Oct. 19, the last of the besieging forces withdrew, and the British remained in control of Georgia until almost the end of the war. "His Most Christian Majesty" was a title of the king of France.

may dispose the Colonists to renew their applications for conciliation with the Mother Country; and, after what has passed, it is scarcely to be doubted, that there would be a ready acceptance.

The frequent and speedy communication which he has received from Ireland has not been the least valuable part of the Publisher's materials;[259] and the late happy settlement with that island, while it insures a great addition of strength to our common Sovereign, affords a propitious omen of what a generous policy may yet be able to effect with our fellow-subjects on the other side of the Atlantic.[260]

The debates in the British Parliament are always read with eager curiosity; and we of this reign enjoy a liberty of publishing them, which, free as our constitution is, was unknown till of late.[261] To gratify that curiosity in the best manner, a Gentleman has very obligingly engaged to transmit, with expedition, ample and accurate accounts of them for The Caledonian Mercury.[262]

Nor is the Publisher inattentive or negligent in recording what passes in this part of the united kingdom. He knows that the consequence of events is very much in proportion to their nearness. One house being burnt in Edinburgh, will affect a citizen here more than a hundred burnt in London, or than a con-

259. The *Caledonian Mercury* frequently published "extracts" from "A letter from Dublin," as well as Irish parliamentary intelligence.

260. Throughout the 1770s, many British troops stationed in Ireland had left to fight in the American war. In 1779, the Parliament of Ireland under Henry Grattan, with the support of the Irish Volunteer movement, was powerful enough to force the British government to remove most restrictions on Irish trade: this is presumably the "the late happy settlement" to which JB refers.

261. Before 1771, reporting of the proceedings of Parliament was prohibited. Many newspapers employed various means of subverting this, and the prohibition ended as a result of John Wilkes's campaigns for free speech and in particular the popular and judicial protests against the imprisonment of Brass Crosby. Prosecutions ceased, and the publication of the *Parliamentary Register* began in 1775.

262. The *Caledonian Mercury* frequently published long reports from the Houses of Commons and Lords. Robertson was particularly proud of the promptness and quality of his reports; in the *Caledonian Mercury* of Monday, Dec. 13, 1779, he addressed his readers as follows: "The Publisher of the *Caledonian Mercury* begs leave to state a few facts to the Public. The proceedings of the last Session of Parliament being uncommonly interesting, he prevailed with a Gentleman in London to furnish him with the most early intelligence of what passed in both Houses. Possessed of abilities and consequence in every way adequate to this undertaking, this Gentleman has been kind enough to offer his assistance during the present Session. The Publisher, therefore, has the vanity to think, that his Paper, with regard to *Parliamentary Intelligence*, will be greatly superior to any publication in Scotland, and a day at least earlier than any London news-paper" (2). I have not discovered the identity of this Gentleman.

flagration at Constantinople. The loss of a single life by a fatal accident in our neighbourhood, will make a deeper impression than numbers slain in a distant region. During the course of last year, indeed, we have had articles in Scotland but too interesting and very alarming; to resume which would be improper and displeasing. In allusion to one of them, we may quote a passage from the curious notes of Sir David Dalrymple, Lord Hailes, on "Ancient Scottish Poems," p. 229.[263] "Here (says the learned author) let me observe, in passing, that the *origin of news-papers* is probably to be ascribed to the circular letters from the *Pope* to the Clergy, or from the Generals of the different religious orders to their Conventual brethren."[264] Whatever may be in this conjecture as to other news-papers, the Publisher of THE CALEDONIAN MERCURY disclaims all connection with the *Pope*. He defies the keenest Critic to find *Bulls* in his paper. He denounces no *anathemas* upon any sect whatever.[265] Although his *Title* be in the 𝕭𝕷𝕬𝕮𝕶 𝕮𝕳𝕬𝕽𝕬𝕮𝕿𝕰𝕽, he pretends to no conjuration, but exerting his best endeavours to please;[266] and, instead of propagating *legends*, it is his continual study to guard against imposition, and convey only truth. The very name of his paper proves it to be *Pagan* rather than *Popish*.[267] May he be permitted, instead of *Pagan*, to call it *Classical?*

The Publisher shall not trespass longer on the time of his Readers and Correspondents with what so materially concerns himself: But most sincerely wishing them many happy new years, he remains their much obliged humble servant,

THE PUBLISHER.

263. Sir David Dalrymple, Lord Hailes (1726–92), Scottish lawyer and man of letters, was a colleague of JB's father and was an early friend and mentor to JB. He edited *Ancient Scottish Poems, Published from the MS. of George Bannatyne MDLXVIII* (Edinburgh, 1770). In 1568, Bannatyne (1545–1608) collected Scots poems of the fifteenth and sixteenth centuries into a MS book of 800 folio pages. The "alarming" events to which JB alludes are the riots in 1779 in protest against the proposed relaxation of the anti-Catholic penal code (see n. 239, above). JB witnessed the rioting and at one point confronted a mob burning a Catholic chapel (*Laird*, 47 ff.).

264. Hailes's notion of newspapers having originated with papal encyclical letters is not supported in standard histories of the newspaper.

265. JB is punning on *Bull* as a papal edict, from the *bull* or leaden seal attached to it, and *bull*, as in an *Irish bull* (see n. 175, above). In the Catholic Church, a person or group may be condemned and excommunicated by papal *anathema* for disagreement with catholic doctrine.

266. The banner for the *Caledonian Mercury* was in Gothic type (*black letter* or black character: "Old English"), in which these two words are also set. JB plays on the occasional description of printing as "the black art" and the other "black arts" of conjuring.

267. For the Roman ("*Pagan*") god Mercury, see n. 206, above.

1781

Defense of the Edinburgh Town Guard

[The Edinburgh Town Guard was established in 1682 to act as a local police force, to keep order and maintain a kind of curfew in the old town. The Guard, which was paid by the Town Council, originally comprised 120 men in three companies, although when the Guard was reformed in 1737 the number of regular Guardsmen was reduced to seventy-five. Their headquarters was a long, low guardhouse in the middle of the Royal Mile. The men of the Guard were military veterans, mostly from Highland regiments. They were armed with a lethal but antique weapon called a Lochaber axe and, although they had in the past been useful in repressing rowdy behavior and street crime, they were regarded as being rough and ill-disciplined, and the age and rustic ways of the veterans exposed them to intermittent raillery from town gangs. By the 1770s, the Guard was increasingly unable to offer effective protection to the expanding city, and there was pressure, as reported here, for some new arrangements for maintaining civil order. Their Guardhouse was demolished in 1787 for the convenience of traffic; the number of Guards was reduced, and they were given room in the Tolbooth. After a regular police force was established in 1805, the Guard lingered on as a relic of former times before being disbanded in 1817. See Chambers, *Traditions of Edinburgh*, 179–82.]

Caledonian Mercury, February 26, 1781, [3]

For the CALEDONIAN MERCURY.
TOWN GUARD

IT has been remarked, in the history of every country, that no community was ever deprived of any valuable privilege, but under some specious pretext.

I am happy in being the first to sound the alarm to my fellow-citizens, against a proposal which I own astonished me; a proposal to abolish the *Town Guard*.[268]

Edinburgh is the only city in Great Britain that has the honourable privilege of maintaining a constant body of soldiers, with proper officers, neither appointed nor paid by the Crown, but entirely under the command of our City itself.

When, upon occasion of Captain Porteous's act, an attempt was made to disgrace us, by taking away this high and peculiar privilege, not only our own

---

268. JB is responding to a printed broadside, which he preserved and pasted into his file copy of this issue of the *Caledonian Mercury*. Addressed "To the Public" and dated Feb. 21, 1781, it advocates more street lamps, a force of watchmen, and the disbanding of the Town Guard; see *Cat. Yale*, P 114(13).

members of Parliament, but several English members, with a most liberal generosity, exerted themselves in our favour: and the illustrious John Duke of Argyll shook the House of Lords with the thunder of his eloquence against the attempt.[269]

Yet now, because the royalty is extended, and a New Edinburgh is built,[270] and certain gentlemen there wish to have watchmen, as in the new built district upon the south side of the town,[271] which they may have if they will pay for them, it is proposed, that we shall be abject enough at once to renounce our most honourable distinction, and that the abolition of it shall be tacked to a bill for removing the shambles, as if it were a nuisance.[272]

Is it then really supposed, that the old spirit of the citizens of Edinburgh is totally gone; and that we shall quietly submit to be thus humbled?

Let us consider, too, that this is a critical, a mysterious, and an unsettled time; a time when the cry is gone forth of encouragement to Popery and arbitrary power.[273] Let us beware, lest something very important in its consequences be covered under this proposal, that we shall throw away our own arms, and be

269. For the story of Captain Porteous, see Chap. 1, n. 191. The aftermath, to which JB alludes, was that (in the words of Andrew Lang) "In the Lords (February 1737) a Bill was passed for disabling the Provost—one Wilson—for public employment, destroying the Town Charter, abolishing the Town Guard, and throwing down the gate of the Nether Bow. Argyll opposed the Bill; in the Commons all Scottish members were against it; Walpole gave way" (*Short History of Scotland*, chap. 32). For John, second duke of Argyll, see n. 149, above.

270. The *royalty*: the sovereign rule—i.e., of the city of Edinburgh—which was extended to the north in 1767 to take in the area for the proposed New Town (see "The 'New Town' of Edinburgh," above).

271. In the decades before the building of the New Town, development in Edinburgh had mostly taken place to the south of the city. Among the first projects was George Square, laid out by a speculative builder, James Brown, in 1766.

272. *Shambles* is the medieval name for an open-air slaughterhouse and meat market. In 1622, the butchers and fleshers of Edinburgh were banished from a central location at the Lawnmarket, to a site outside the city by the North Loch. This area itself became part of the city when the royalty was extended, and the North Loch shambles was clearly visible from the new North Bridge that connected the Old and New Towns. "In 1780, the Fleshers proposed to erect a shambles, an integrated complex of slaughterhouse booths all built under one roof, and sought the City Council's approval for the development." At the urging of New Town property owners, an act was passed in 1782 forbidding the slaughter of animals within the city. See MacLachlan, "'Greatest and most offensive nuisance.'" JB spoke against this at a meeting of the Faculty of Advocates on Dec. 15, 1781 (*Laird*, 415). (The act was never enforced, and in 1788 the Fleshers Guild was allowed to erect a modern purpose-built shambles on the North Loch site.)

273. In the wake of the anti-Catholic riots of 1779, there were a great many complaints and warnings in the press about "arbitrary power" (and frequently "popery and arbitrary

in the sole mercy of the regulars.[274] Is this a time for the citizens of Edinburgh to surrender their garrison?

Charity, rational Charity, is an interesting motive against this strange proposal. It is rational Charity to aid those who have a claim to our benevolence, while we, at the same time, make them useful. The *Town Guard*, if our rulers conduct it properly, is a comfortable little addition to Chelsea.[275] It is an asylum for veteran soldiers, who, after having fought for their country in distant lands, return home with such certificates of good character, as many of our Scots soldiers deservedly obtain from their officers, and are able to guard the metropolis of their country with fidelity and spirit. Shall we be hard-hearted enough to destroy this resource?

In cases of fire and tumults, the *Town Guard* has ever proved of most essential service.[276] What, indeed, could be done without it? To talk of watchmen is a shallow artifice. Watchmen have no instantaneous effect like soldiers. What are they better than as many of the mob? And we may guess what jobbing there would be in their appointment.[277] Must we be under the necessity, upon any threatening emergency, to repair to the Castle to supplicate aid, which, if granted, would probably come too late, and may be refused?

Were we to have any pecuniary advantage by abolishing the Town Guard; were we to be less taxed in that event, the mean and the sordid might, for a trifle, consent to the loss of our city's honour; but there is not even that paultry argument. Not one shilling is to be abated. Our rulers are still to levy from us the whole tax granted by Parliament for maintaining our Guard, and are to dispose of it according to their good-will and pleasure. They promise us watchmen and additional lamps. What power have we to enforce the promise? Shall we be cajoled out of our old and well-tried establishment, and take our chance of what is not half so good, though we should get it?

Another consideration remains. There is one day in seven called *Sunday*, or *the Lord's day*, which used to be very sacredly kept in this city. Of late years there

---

power"), under which the French were suffering, which the Americans had thrown off, and which—so whiggish propaganda asserted—was encroaching in England.

274. Regular army troops were stationed at Edinburgh Castle and Holyroodhouse, but part of the justification for the Guard was precisely that it was not in the pay of the Crown.

275. The Royal Hospital, Chelsea, in London, was founded in 1682 as a hostel for the accommodation and care of regular soldiers who were no longer fit for service, because of age or injury.

276. One of the Guard's duties was to carry water to the scene of any fires.

277. *Jobbing*: the act or practice of buying and selling goods or stocks in order to profit (*OED*).

has been a wonderful relaxation.[278] But it is, perhaps, prudent not to employ force while there is no direct and open insult. It is a part of the duty of the Town Guard to protect the decency of that day. Some years ago, a riotous company committed public profanation.[279] The Town Guard took them into custody. A prosecution was brought before the High Court of Justiciary. The powers of the Town Guard, to aid our laws and our religion, were confirmed. Is it to be wished that there should be no such aid? Does a majority of the citizens wish it? Here again the cloven foot appears.

Let us, my fellow-citizens, shew, upon this occasion, that we deserve our honourable privilege, because we can maintain it. Let us signify our disapprobation of the proposal to abolish the Town Guard, and it will certainly be laid aside. If it should be obstinately persisted in, let us unite in a petition to Parliament, to be heard by our Counsel against it. We shall find Counsel who will be happy to appear in such a cause without fees; and let us have hope and confidence in the wisdom of the Legislature.

AN OLD TOWN CITIZEN.[280]

278. The strictness of the Presbyterian Sabbath was commented upon by visitors to Edinburgh. Young English journalist Edward Topham (1751–1820), writing in 1775, says, "During the time of Kirk, you scarcely see any body in the streets, or loitering away the time of prayer in wantonness and excess. . . . To be seen on the street after the summons of the bell, or to read any book on a Sunday which has no relation to religion, seems wicked and abominable to the most abandoned." He also remarked on "the extraordinary neatness and simplicity of dress which distinguish them at this time of public prayer"; see *Letters from Edinburgh*, 190–91. Others remarked of being reproved for publicly laughing or humming tunes on the Sabbath; see Cosh, *Edinburgh*, 296, 408. By calling the late supposed *relaxation* "wonderful," JB means it is to be wondered at.

279. On Sunday, June 4, 1758, the Town Guard was dispatched on a verbal order of the Lord Provost, Robert Montgomery, to the house of one John Wightman of Maulsley, where a drunken company was being noisy and obscenely abusing passersby and had attracted a mob. They were taken into custody and roughly conveyed through the streets to the guard house. In August, Wightman took a case to court against the Lord Provost and members of the Guard, alleging that the Guard had violently entered his house without a just cause or proper order. The charge against the Provost was dismissed, it being argued that justices and magistrates had "the power of summary commitment for certain offences, of which *Sabbath-breaking* is one, by parole warrant" (Boyd, *Office, Powers, and Jurisdiction*, 1:460). The corporal of the Guard was found guilty by a jury but later *assoilzied* or absolved of guilt by the court. See also MacLaurin, *Arguments and Decisions in Remarkable Cases*, 188–208; and *Scots Mag.*, 20 (July 1758), 386–87 (App., 1758), 700–703.

280. JB was indeed a citizen of the Old Town. He was born in his father's townhouse, in a building called Blair's Land, on the east side of Parliament Close, behind St. Giles' Church (*Earlier Years*, 12, 14). When Lord Auchinleck sold the house in Jan. 1777, JB noted

A Request for a Recipe against Bookworm

London Chronicle, October 18–20, 1781, 381

SIR,

I Have been a good deal vexed of late, by the apprehensions of getting my books destroyed, by some bookworms, which have got into my library. When I first observed their destructive ravages, I was at great pains to procure some information about them, and for this purpose consulted all the works on Natural History that I could lay my hands on; but my search has been fruitless. Buffon does not treat of insects, and neither Mr. Brookes, the Abbe le Pluche, nor Goldsmith, have taken any notice of the bookworm; which is very strange.[281] In the Tour through the Animal World, I found indeed a plate of the bookworm, and bookspider, with a short account of them, but no direction either how to prevent, or destroy them.[282]

The sum of my own experience is this. I observed at different times several parts of my books cut and damaged, which I did not think were so, when they came into my custody. This led me to be attentive, and to be frequently opening them. In an old copy of Cicero's Offices,[283] I found a small dark-brown insect, something like a bug, which had hollowed out a place for itself, in the inner margin, about the middle of the book. You may believe I did not spare it. I have seen such insects about old wood, and they are winged. Another time I found a small white worm, with a black head, which had encamped about the middle of a French treatise on fortification;[284] and I dare say would have demolished redoubts, if she had not met with a sudden coup de main.[285] As to the insect

---

that he was "a little sorry" (*Extremes*, 76). From 1773 until 1786, he and his family lived in a large apartment in James's Court, north of the Lawnmarket.

281. George-Louis Leclerc, Comte de Buffon, *Histoire naturelle, générale et particulière*, 36 vols. (1749–88); Richard Brookes, *A New and Accurate System of Natural History*, 6 vols. (1763); Noël-Antoine Pluche, *Spectacle de la nature* (1732); Oliver Goldsmith, *An History of the Earth and Animated Nature*, 8 vols. (1774). Only the second of these is recorded as being in JB's library.

282. Denis de Coetlogon, *A Tour through the Animal World* (1746), plates 137–38; see Figure 17.

283. *De Officiis* (On Duties) is an important treatise on the moral life by the Roman statesman and philosopher.

284. Plausible candidates for such a work include Guillaume Le Blond, *Elemens de Fortification a l'Usage des Jeunes Officiers* (Paris, 1742), and Jean Louis Le Cointe, *The Science of Military Posts, for the Use of Regimental Officers Who Frequently Command Detached Parties*, trans. from the French (London, 1761).

285. JB keeps up the theme of fortification: a *redoubt* or *reduit* is "A keep or stronghold into which a garrison may retreat if the outworks are taken, thereby prolonging the defence

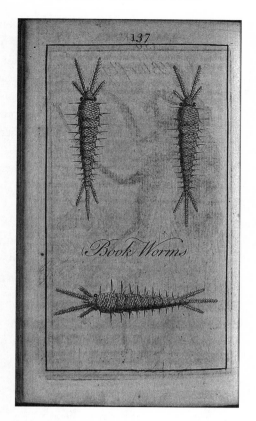

Figure 17. "Book Worms," *Denis Coetlogon,* Tour of the Animal World *(1746), plate 137.*
Courtesy of the Niedersächsische Staats-und Universitätsbibliothek, Göttingen.

which the Writer of the Tour calls the bookworm, it is long, slender, and pearl coloured, has a number of legs, antennæ, and is very swift.[286] I never could find any of these in my books; but I caught one upon a shelf, and put it into a glass vial, with a bit of old paper beside it. Here it lived near six weeks; and as it could have no sustenance, but what it derived from the paper, it is evident that it must have fed on it. However, I could not observe the smallest mark of cutting on the paper.

The precautions I took were these. I carried down all my books in small parcels to a room in which there was fire, to air them, and I looked through them, and beat them together; to drive out dust, and demolish any internal operations that

of the place"; and a *coup de main* (literally, a blow of the hand), in military terms, is "a sudden and vigorous attack, for the purpose of instantaneously capturing a position" (*OED*).

286. Paraphrased from Coetlogon's description of the bookworm (*Tour through the Animal World*, 137–38).

might be going on in them. I was at the pains too, to fill the room where they are kept, several times full of tobacco smoke, which I have heard is mortal to insects.

But as I have never chanced to meet with any person, who had any experience in these matters, I am still uncertain whether these precautions will have any proper effect; and I will hold myself much indebted to any of your Correspondents, who will inform me how these insects may be prevented from getting into a library, how it may be known whether they are there, and how they may be extirpated when they have got in.

I caused a query to this purpose to be inserted in a Northern periodical paper some time ago; but there are few people in Scotland, who dip much into old books; and therefore I never had any answer.[287] I cannot expect any satisfaction, except some of your Correspondents in London, Oxford, or Cambridge, shall take pity on the case of a man, beset by a tribe of horrible banditti, who are daily wasting and destroying his most dear and valuable effects, and whose ravages he knows not how to prevent.[288]

I am, Sir, your's sincerely,
A CONSTANT READER.

1786

A Sentimental Essay on Death

Gentleman's Magazine, 56 (February 1786), 127–28

A SENTIMENTAL ESSAY[289] on
DEATH

"DEATH," says Epicurus, "is nothing to us, because when Death is, we are not, and when we are, Death is not."[290] Such is the true philosophical account

---

287. No such letter in a Scottish newspaper has been discovered.

288. In the *Lond. Chron.* for Oct. 25, a correspondent signing himself "B," from Shaftesbury, wrote briefly to recommend and give directions for the use of camphor against bookworm. In a P.S., he addresses another of JB's queries, saying, "your correspondent may know, '*when they are there*,' by their eating his books."

289. From the middle of the eighteenth century, *sentimental* was something of a vogue word and had a mostly favorable sense, meaning "Characterized by or exhibiting refined and elevated feeling" (*OED*).

290. Epicurus, an ancient Greek philosopher; his Letter to Menoeceus is found in Diogenes Laertius, *Lives and Opinions of Eminent Philosophers* (book 10), 469.

of Death. But the vulgar confound Death with the act of dying, which they consider as an accumulation of the evils of life. Every thing that is called into existence, is subject to the sentence of Death. Fate is inexorable and impartial, and from his court there is no appeal.

"Then die, oh mortal man, for thou wast born!"[291]

"It is impossible," says Swift, "that so universal a thing as Death can be intended as an evil."[292] For many years after the discharge of this opinion he was daily tormented with the terror of death: "my earliest visitation, and my last at even."[293] This is also the confession of Erasmus, at a certain time of his life, in a letter to a friend.[294]

The debt of nature, which is incurred by our grant of the lease of life (which perhaps a wise man would not ask for), must be paid by every body: no merit, no excuses, can avail: "For all is possible to Heaven, but this," says our English Homer.[295] Death is the great leveller of the world;[296] Love and Night, and the crouded streets, being only so for the moment. Education, habit, and constitution, place Death in different points of view—of a friend and an enemy.[297] They are both sometimes unwished-for, and even contemned; though the remark, "that Death and the Sun cannot be steadily looked upon,"[298] is generally true. The instinctive love of life is a great security against our putting an end to it: and few people would die if they could help it. The thought of Lucan is poetical,

291. Matthew Prior, "Solomon on the Vanity of the World: A Poem in Three Books," in *Poems on Several Occasions* (1718), 3.335.

292. "It is impossible that anything so natural, so necessary, and so universal as death, should ever have been designed by Providence as an evil to mankind" (Swift, "Thoughts on Religion," 307).

293. Not found in Swift. But see Milton, *Paradise Lost*, 11.275–76: "My early visitation, and my last / At even" (Adam describing the flowers of Eden, that he will miss after his banishment).

294. This has not been found in the extensive correspondence of humanist scholar and theologian Desiderius Erasmus (1466–1536) of Rotterdam. In his 1770 book list ("Catalogue of Books"), JB listed a 1671 Amsterdam edition of Erasmus's letters.

295. *The Odyssey of Homer*, trans. Alexander Pope (1725), 3.294.

296. "Death is the grand Leveller" (Fuller, *Gnomologia*, 47). *Leveller*: "One who destroys superiority; one who endeavours to bring all things to a state of equality" (*SJ Dict.*); the term acquired a mainly pejorative use from the mid-seventeenth century, for a political movement at the time of the English civil wars.

297. An echo, perhaps, of 1 Corinthians 15:26: "The last enemy that shall be destroyed is death" (*AV*).

298. From the *Maxims* (1665–78) of François, the Duc de La Rochefoucauld, no. 26. In JB's library, there was an edition of 1760, published in Lausanne ("Catalogue of Books," 65).

but not persuasive, "that the gods conceal from men the happiness of death, that they may endure life."[299] No messenger is arrived to announce the situation of the departed, at the place "from whose bourn no traveller returns."[300] Old Hobbes, afraid of Night and of Death, used to call the last, "the leap in the dark."[301] Where the apprehension of Death, prepared to strike, perpetually haunts the imagination, life can afford no happiness. Claudio, in Shakspeare, is enough to make the hair stand an end, when he recites,

> "Ah! but to die, and go we know not where!"[302]

From these distressing images, the poetry of Garth tries to relieve us (himself dying in that faith) which assures, that,

> "To die, is landing on a friendly shore,
> Where billows never beat, or tempests roar;
> Ere we can feel the fatal stroke, 'tis o'er."[303]

It has been often said, and seen, that weeping friends, the tolling bell, the plumed hearse, the opening grave (un-moralized upon only by the hardened sexton) are awful and dramatic terrors.

> *Pompa mortis magis terret, quam mors ipsa.*[304]

Lingering disorders, agonizing pains,

> "Luke's iron crown, and Damien's bed of steel,"[305]

299. Roman poet Lucan, *Civil War*, 4.860–61.

300. From Hamlet's soliloquy, Shakespeare, *Hamlet*, 3.1.79–80.

301. According to the pamphlet *The Last Sayings, or, Dying Legacy of Mr. Thomas Hobbs of Malmesbury*, political philosopher Hobbes (1588–1679) said, "Death, is a Leap into the Dark" (3).

302. Shakespeare, *Measure for Measure*, 3.1.114.

303. "To die, is landing on some silent shore, / Where billows never break, nor tempests roar: / Ere well we feel the friendly stroke, 'tis o'er." Sir Samuel Garth, *Dispensary*, canto 3, lines 225–27.

304. "The pomp of death terrifies us more than death itself"; quoted, without attribution, in Bacon, "Of Death," *Essayes* (1625).

305. From Oliver Goldsmith, *The Traveller* (1764), line 436. Goldsmith has confused the name of Luke with that of his brother, George, who led an insurrection of peasants in Hungary in 1414. George was punished by being made to sit on an iron throne wearing an iron crown; his wrists were slit, and Luke was made to drink his blood. Robert-François Damiens attempted to assassinate the French king, Louis XV, on Jan. 5, 1757. He was hideously tortured before his death, and it was reported that while in prison he was chained to an iron bed.

or morbid melancholy, make us forget the gratifications of sense, afraid of what is to come, wish for a peaceful retreat, and call upon death, to remove the nauseous draught of life from our lips.

> "These are the bugbears of a winter's eve,
> The horrors of the living, not the dead,"

says Young.[306]

But where nature is permitted to wear out by insensible decay, and disease does not immaturely carry us off, as it does at all ages, our departure may resemble the falling asleep, for Death and Sleep are very near relations. Some few are tormented with the personification of Death, as if it were a real, though, like Night, it is only a negative being. And yet Death is no such formidable enemy— Revenge triumphs over it—Love slights it—Honour aspires to it—Grief flies to it—Fear pre-occupies it—says observation and Lord Bacon.[307] Poets, painters, prose and pulpit declaimers, have helped to make Death more terrible, and are more likely to open monasteries, than to prepare men for action and for the field. The Gentoos have a saying that excludes all horror, "that it is better to sit than to walk; to lie down than to sit; to sleep than to wake; and that Death is the best of all."[308] Diversion, hurry, and an active life, are the best preservatives against the dreary opinions of the dissolution of the body. Of the ten thousands who daily walk up and down the streets of London, how few are occupied with the thoughts of mortality! They are more afraid of the apparition of Poverty than of Death. The philosopher used not be alarmed about annihilation, for he knows that matter can only change its form. The Christian considers life as a pilgrimage, and this world as the road to another. Perhaps those who have most reason to be pleased with sublunary things, would not wish their time to come over again. Many who rise from the feast of life, satisfied or cloyed with the length and variety of their entertainment (for life, like wine, must not be tasted to the lees) would consider Death as a smaller evil than a continuation of existence. Scarcely one, says conjecture, how happy soever his life may have been (to express the last idea again), would be willing to return from the verge of the grave, to desire a repetition of pleasure from his sensations or reflections, and to

306. Edward Young, "Night IV," lines 12–13, in *Night-Thoughts*; JB has *horrors* for Young's *terrors*. According to Brady, Young was JB's "favorite poet" (*Later Years*, 102 n. 1).

307. "Revenge triumphs over death; love slights it; honour aspireth to it; grief flieth to it; fear pre-occupateth it" (Bacon, "Of Death," *Essayes*).

308. Found in William Mickle's translation of the Portuguese epic of the discovery of India, *The Lusiad* (book 7), 313 n., where it is said to be a saying of "the Gentoos." *Gentoos*: Hindus, as opposed to Moslems (*OED*). For Mickle, see n. 184, above.

go through precisely the same scenes he has already passed. Human beings are not only made "to look upwards," as Ovid expresses it,[309] but to look forward. Curiosity and hope, those powerful and enlivening principles, establish, beyond refutation, the goodness of our Creator. But, as this world is the best place its inhabitants have been in, very few wish to change their certainty for the prospect of a better. The last scene of the moral and mortal drama few are in haste to perform. To finish it with glory and applause, with public and self-approbation, is the last difficulty. It is more easy to die in hot than in cold blood.

> "Then tell me, frighted reason, what is death?
> Blood only stopp'd, and interrupted breath."[310]

Calm and unruffled must he be who can always cry out, with courage and with truth, "Welcome life, whatever it brings; welcome Death, whatever it is!"[311]

MEMORY.[312]

High Food Prices and High-Living Aldermen

[Supplying the food needs of a rapidly growing metropolis was an increasingly important issue in the late eighteenth century, culminating in the bread riots of the 1790s, which resulted from severe weather and poor harvests, and the rising cost of imports due to war. In 1786, the high prices of meat in particular were investigated by a City of London committee. The City Corporation had limited powers of regulation in this area, but did have jurisdiction over the Billingsgate fish market and the Smithfield sheep and cattle market. The report of this committee was presented by the City Sheriff, Paul Le Mesurier (1755–1805), on March 22, 1787, and found that "the decrease of cattle and sheep brought into Smithfield market, during the years 84 and 85 hath arisen, from the present pernicious system of forestalling in the vicinity of this metropolis" (*The World*, Mar. 24, 1787). "Forestalling was the practice of buying up a commodity, or intercepting it before it reached the open market." (See Brown, "'A Just and Profitable Commerce'," 320–22.)]

Public Advertiser, August 16, 1786, 1

309. Ovid, *Metamorphoses*, 1.84–86: "all other animals are prone, and fix their gaze upon the earth, he [the Creator] gave to man an uplifted face and bade him stand erect and turn his eyes to heaven."

310. Prior, "Solomon" (see n. 291, above), 3.518–19.

311. Henry St. John, first Viscount Bolingbroke, no. xlix of "Fragments, or Minutes of Essays" (*Works*, 5:390). This was first published three years after Bolingbroke's death in 1751 but written some decades before.

312. This pen name was attached to another article in the *Gent. Mag.* a month later, and an editorial note attributed the second article to JB; see *Lit. Car.*, 230.

To the Printer of the Public Advertiser.

SIR,

IT is wonderful how often we meet with such laughable blunders and absurdities in the City of London, as if they should happen in Dublin, would be universally hooted at as true Hibernian.³¹³ A Committee is appointed *to consider of the causes of the present high price of provisions.*³¹⁴ And who pray stand in the front of it? Why, *the Lord-Mayor and all the Aldermen*: Now, Sir, do we not all know, that *rising pale from a city feast*, is *Pope's* celebrated image of *Gluttony.*³¹⁵ Yet the Lord Mayor and all the Aldermen (Mercy on us! ALL) are to *consider* why provisions are so dear.³¹⁶ Alas! Mr. Woodfall, they themselves, while the spirit of high living continues, are undoubtedly the cause. Let each of them lay his hand—not upon his *heart*—but his *belly*, and say in the words of Shakespeare's Othello—

It is the cause, it is the cause, my soul.³¹⁷

But, Sir, the matter does not rest here—it is pleasanter still. This same guzling Committee are also to consider how they may *reduce the price of fish.* Amazing effrontery! Like Swift's fat fellow, who complained of the *press* from a throng in the street,³¹⁸ if they will *take themselves away* we shall soon see a reduction of the price of fish, flesh, fowl, and every thing else that is eatable. If they will but

313. *Hibernia* was the Latin name for Ireland. In this expression of the commonplace anti-Irish prejudice, JB suggests that the present absurdity would be regarded as "Irish" even in Ireland.

314. An announcement from the Guildhall, dated July 21, reads: "The Committee of the Court of Common Council, appointed to consider the causes of the present high price of provisions, and to report their opinion thereon to that Court, and whether it may be expedient to frame any, and what regulations, for better supplying this City with animal and vegetable food, and to grant such bounties for the encouragement of the fisheries carried on from the River Thames, as may tend to encrease the quantities and reduce the prices of the several sorts of fish brought to the London markets" (*Morning Chronicle*, July 24, 1786; frequently reprinted in newspapers over the following month).

315. "How pale, each Worshipful and rev'rend Guest / Rise from a Clergy, or a City, feast!"; from "The Second Satire of the Second Book of Horace," lines 75–76 (Pope, *Imitations of Horace*, 59).

316. Thomas Sainsbury (1730–95), a grocer of Ludgate Hill, was Lord Mayor of London, 1786–87.

317. *Othello*, 5.2.1 (Othello's words).

318. In the preface to *A Tale of a Tub* (1704), Swift tells of "a fat unwieldy fellow, half stifled in the press," who complained, "Lord! what a filthy crowd is here! Pray, good people, give way a little." Another in the crowd asked him, "who . . . helps to make up the crowd half so much as yourself?"

think a moment they must be sensible that *they* would make provisions dear at the land's end, or in Scotland.

But indeed it appears to me that the advertisement of this Committee cannot be serious, but is truly a joke, though a clumsy one. This is plain from some of the persons who are associated in the great business with the Lord Mayor and all the Aldermen. For is there not the following *sequent?*—Imprimis, Mr. *Dornford*, of whom we have read so much. Who follows *him*, holding both his sides, Mr. *Merry*; and who comes next, Mr. *Bullcock*—to proclaim that the whole is a *cock* and a *bull*.[319]

A HUNGRY CORRESPONDENT.

1787

Unholy Trinity in Titles of Newspapers

Public Advertiser, February 9, 1787, 4

A Correspondent says, that so fantastical is the age become, that the old titles of newspapers, the *Evening Posts*, the *Advertisers*, the *Gazetteers* and the *Chronicles* of the times are not sufficient, but we have one called the *Devil*, and another the *World*; and he doubts not but the *Flesh* will follow.[320]

---

319. The names of Dornford, Merry, and Bullcock are listed one after the other among the twenty-nine committeemen in the original notice. In the first place (i.e., "imprimis"), Josiah Dornford (1734–1810), later Sir Josiah, was a councilman for the ward of Billingsgate and for many years a justice of the peace in Deptford. In 1784, he published in the papers and as a pamphlet a series of ten letters under the name "Fidelio," criticizing the management of the city's finances and the administration of the prisons. A committee of inquiry was established to investigate his charges, and Dornford responded frequently in print. JB mentions this in his journal (July 27, 1785; *Applause*, 331–32). See also *Gent. Mag.*, 108 (1810), 389. John Merry (d. 1797), described by John Nichols as "an eminent Stationer" (*Lit. Anec.*, 3:728), was for twenty-seven years councilor for the ward of Bishopsgate. Robert Bullcock (1729–1813), haberdasher and deputy for the ward of Bishopsgate without; see *Gent. Mag.*, 83, no. 1 (May 1813), 494.

320. A newspaper called *The Devil* was published in at least twenty-five issues from Jan. to July 1755 ("*Devil*" headnote, Burney Collection Newspapers). The *World and Fashionable Advertiser*, founded by John Bell and Edward Topham, was first published on Jan. 1, 1787, and continued until June 30, 1794, when it merged with the *Morning Post* (Werkmeister, *London Daily Press*, 154, 217). "The world, the flesh, and the devil" is a familiar expression, from the Litany in the Anglican *Book of Common Prayer*.

1788

CRITICISM OF JOHN HOWARD, PRISON REFORMER

[In the early months of 1787, the columns of the *Public Advertiser* hosted a correspondence between a particular critic of prison reformer John Howard and various
of Howard's supporters. In his first letter (January 17, 1788), "A Traveller" claimed
that Howard—whom "A Traveller" did not name—was visiting prisons in Europe,
where the prisoners were "generally criminals of the most notorious cast—robbers
and murderers—they are not debtors, as in general they are with us." In Britain,
long-term imprisonment was used not as a punishment but for holding prisoners
before trial; once sentenced, convicts were executed, transported, pilloried, or fined,
but not—apart from debtors—imprisoned. (See "Punishments at the Old Bailey,"
Proceedings of the Old Bailey.) The criticism of Howard—the claim (in a second
letter, February 2) that he "communicated nothing but what was well-known before"
and implying that he was profiting from his campaign—attracted defenses from
correspondents calling themselves "Indignation" (January 21 and February 29) and
"More Indignation" (February 14 and March 3). These are the letters to which, under
the name "Domesticus," Boswell replies.]

Public Advertiser, March 12, 1788, 2

To the Printer of the Public Advertiser.

SIR,

YOUR correspondent who *deliberately* subscribes his Letters INDIGNATION,
talks of his *muffin* at breakfast.[321] But I cannot believe that so *crusty* a fellow as
he seems to be ever tastes that *soft* composition, which is cried in our streets
so melodiously with *ho!* as its accompaniment.[322] At least sure I am, that if a
muffin were to get within *Indignation's fiery lips*, it would be baked ten times
more than in the *oven*. It would be made as hard as a sea biscuit at least, if not
burnt to a coal.[323] He disclaims being *another* Indignation, who appeared in your

---

321. In a card signed "Indignation" (*Pub. Adv.*, Feb. 29), a correspondent told "A Traveller" that his third letter (Feb. 23) on the subject of John Howard (see n. 326, below) was
too filthy and brutal to justify continuing the correspondence. To do so, he said, would
"render the Public Advertiser a very unfit companion for the muffin at a decent breakfast
table."

322. The English breakfast muffin is a small round bread that, in the eighteenth century,
was widely sold door to door. "Ho!" was presumably the street cry of the muffin man.

323. Sea biscuit (often known as *hardtack*) is a kind of simple biscuit made with flour,
water, and salt, and double-baked so as to be hard and dry, for use as a nonperishable food
on long sea voyages.

Paper, that is to say, he disclaims being *honest* Indignation—and let him have his will.[324]

But let *me* ask him, who am no irritable man—what in the name of *Common Sense* (which the other of those *indignant Sofias* raged against so violently)[325] shall hinder any writer to express his sentiments freely of any man who has thought proper to make himself as conspicuous as *Prison Howard* has done?[326] Must we all be *compelled* to think one way about this eccentrick genius?[327] To *shackle* the *mind* is I think as hard usage as to put our *feet* in the *stocks*. Let Mr. *Indignation* then compose himself, and I undertake in a future Letter to suggest a few doubts which I have heard very rational men approve, whether or not what Mr. Howard has been endeavouring to effect, be his motives, humane, or ostentatious, or a mixture of both, would not be destructive to the good policy of civilised society, and honest painful industry?

DOMESTICUS.[328]

324. It was in fact the writer of a second reply, signed "More Indignation" (Mar. 3, 1788), to the third letter of "A Traveller," who advised that, despite "the similarity of the signature," the letters of "Indignation" and his own are not "the production of the same person." The correspondent signing as "Honest Indignation" does not appear to have contributed to this correspondence. (All these observations are made by "More Indignation" in his reply to this letter.)

325. No mention of *common sense* is found in any of the letters of the various correspondents named "Indignation." JB may be alluding to a letter concerning a subsidiary issue of this correspondence that was also being pursued separately by other contributors: the controversial English practice of imprisoning debtors. An open letter, signed "The Tradesman" and addressed to MP James Bland Burges, who was campaigning against the practice, claimed that reform of the law regarding the imprisonment of debtors is required by "common sense and sound policy" (*Pub. Adv.*, Mar. 3, 1788; printed immediately above the second letter of "More Indignation"). *Sophia* is a personification of Divine Wisdom.

326. John Howard (1726–90), English philanthropist; in 1773, he took up the cause of prison reform, after an inspection of the Bedford Prison, in his capacity as shire sheriff, moved him to inspect prisons throughout England. He took the issue to Parliament, which commended him for his humanitarianism, and in 1777 he published the first edition of his detailed report, *The State of the Prisons*. He later visited and reported on the prison ships ("hulks," see n. 334, below) and prisons in Ireland and Europe. The first of a number of associations around the world bearing his name and dedicated to prison reform was established in 1867.

327. In the letter signed "A Traveller" (Jan. 17, 1788), which seems to have initiated this correspondence, John Howard is alluded to as an example of the "eccentrick and singular characters" with which "this country abounds." Here, *genius* means "Of persons: Characteristic disposition; inclination; bent, turn or temper of mind" (*OED*).

328. The pen name means "belonging to the house": it is presumably used here in the sense of "domestic" as opposed to "foreign."

[In response to this letter, a third letter signed "More Indignation" appeared (*Pub. Adv.*, Mar. 20). The writer of this letter pointed out that "Domesticus" has confounded the three *Indignations*, reiterated that his criticism of "A Traveller" was not for his opinion of the "expediency or inexpediency" of Howard's activities but for his asserting the "most palpable falsehoods" about him, and congratulated "Domesticus" (ironically) on the impenetrability of his witticisms. In his response and in providing (as his previous letter promised) a more reasoned critique of Howard's proposals, Boswell defends the imprisonment of debtors, a policy that was strongly condemned by "A Traveller," whose first letter began this correspondence.]

Public Advertiser, May 12, 1788, 1 (leading article)

To the Printer of the Public Advertiser.

SIR,

SO it seems we are to understand there are *three* Indignations—*Indignation—More Indignation*—and *Honest Indignation.*—A wonderous triumvirate, surely, equalled only by the three devils, *Io, Mio, Rio*, in *Trapolin's vagaries*.[329] But let this *Cerberus*, this three-headed barker, (for such I hold all this *indignant* correspondence of yours to be—right or wrong in *this*, no great matter) I am no more afraid than *Æneas* was,[330] and without even the precaution of throwing a *sop* into the monster's jaws, shall proceed to investigate a little, with *cool consideration*, the merits of Mr. Howard's prison schemes.

I hold, Sir, the title, *de carceribus*, to be one of the most important subjects of general jurisprudence;[331] for, unquestionably, imprisonment, either for the purpose of civil or criminal effect, has, by the united experience of all nations, been found of essential service.

329. "Eo, Meo, and Areo" are three demons summoned by Mago, the conjuror, in Robert Drury's *The Devil of a Duke: or, Trapolin's Vagaries, a (farcical ballad) opera* (1732), adapted from Nahum Tate's *A Duke and No Duke* (1685).

330. In Greek and Roman mythology, Cerberus is the three-headed dog that guards the entrance to Hades, to prevent the damned from escaping. The beast features in a number of classical works, including Virgil's *Aeneid*, book 6, in which it is put to sleep with a drugged honeycake so that Aeneas can pass in safety. Here, *barker* is also used in the sense of "an auction-room or shop tout; one who 'barks' at a cheap shop or show" (*OED*); JB considers the main issue a sideshow.

331. *De Carceribus*: [the law] of incarceration or imprisonment. Fourteenth-century Italian jurist Baldus de Ubaldis wrote a treatise with this title, in which he states the medieval view that the function of prisons was "not for punishment but for the custody of offenders and debtors": i.e., imprisonment was traditionally regarded as coercive (e.g., to compel debtors to pay) or custodial (for offenders awaiting trial or sentence). See Geltner, *Medieval Prison*, 48.

That it is a misfortune to be imprisoned for any cause whatever, I do not deny. But do not let us vainly endeavour to alter the nature of things, and make that *no* evil which *is* and *ought to be* an evil.

There is a class of prisoners, as to whom I do think a favourable distinction should be made, and that is those who are committed upon *suspicion* in order for *trial*.[332] Yet as the suspicion itself is to a virtuous mind a severe infliction, the accessory pains in consequence of it should be borne with patience, as having a tendency to promote the general principle of more cautious behaviour in future, after deliverance is obtained. I, however, wish that the evil of imprisonment should be alleviated to such, and, if I mistake not, care is taken that it shall be so. But imprisonment must be viewed in other and more extensive lights, which are strangely mistaken by superficial thinkers.

Imprisonment, when it is adjudged by the sentence of a Court as a punishment, will, I hope, be allowed by the most visionary projectors to imply something that the person condemned shall *feel*, and, what is still more useful, that others shall *think* is worse than simple confinement; otherwise to call it a penal infliction, is a mockery of law.

Imprisonment, on account of *debt*, can have no rational meaning, unless it be so disagreeable as to operate in the way of *coercion* upon those whom honesty is insufficient to oblige to act fairly to their creditors. It is by the *squalor carceris*, as it is well expressed,[333] that such debtors are compelled to forego the fraudulent enjoyments of rioting upon the money of other people, in order to be relieved from a situation incompatible with satisfaction. But if prisons are to be rendered commodious and elegant habitations, I desire to know whether a very great part of the community in every country under heaven, would not bless the day which introduced them into such asylums?

Turn then, ye ostentatious boasters of humanity, from prisons, which are the public and salutary, because necessary, evils of all civilized nations;—turn to the humble recesses of private life, where, indeed, you will not have the pompous display of magistrates and gaolers, or the parade of opening iron gates, weighing fetters, and clanking of keys; but where you may have the quiet, heart-felt

332. "Committed upon suspicion in order for trial": i.e., those imprisoned on remand, awaiting a summons to appear in court for a hearing on a later date.

333. Imprisonment for debt was common in medieval Europe and in Britain, until abolished by the Debtors' Act of 1869. Nonpayment of debt was treated as a type of fraud, taking no account of the debtor's capacity or otherwise to pay. In Scots law, the *squalor carceris* (meaning "dirty prison") referred to the strictness of imprisonment, which a creditor was entitled to enforce in order to compel the debtor to pay the debt.

Figure 18. "*The Discovery. Convict Ship lying at Deptford,*" *engraving by E. W. Cooke,*
Sixty-five Plates of Shipping and Craft *(1829–[31]).* © *Trustees of the British Museum.*

satisfaction of relieving wretched cottagers, who, with their families, are worse
lodged, worse clothed, worse fed than those whose situation your impolitic
schemes would improve, so as to make it truly enviable.

This is no fanciful suggestion. Go to the hulks at Woolwich; view the *felons*
there.[334] Go afterwards to the honest labourers in the country around, and say
fairly which of their situations is absolutely the best? Listen also to the faint,
but too just repinings of the latter, *upon this very account*, and *then* retire to your
closets, and resolve to make *vanity* yield to *true charity.*

DOMESTICUS.

334. The "hulks" were ships, unseaworthy but still floating, that were used in Britain
from 1776 (when criminals could no longer be transported to America) until 1856 to accom-
modate the overflow from the crowded prisons; see Figure 18. The first hulks were moored
on the Thames off Woolwich, in southeast London.

1791

To the Man of Fashion

Gentleman's Magazine, 61 (July 1791), 631

To the Man of Fashion

BY an association which may be thought a little extraordinary I pass from the Man of Books to the Man of the World.[335] The transition, however, is not uncommon in real life. The reverse is indeed extraordinary. I would fain unite these two characters; and, having lain-in a fund of scholastic lore, I should like to set it off by the acquisition of a little *ton*;[336] as a preliminary step to which, I should be glad to be informed how I may distinguish the several colours which, in their several seasons, are worn by the fair and fashionable. My taylor is not always at hand; and truly I cannot remember half of them with any degree of accuracy. I have fancied, that as colours are simple ideas, of which a person who has never seen them, or a person who has totally forgotten them, can have no conception, the painter might supply this defect of our knowledge and understanding by depicting some of the most remarkable hues of which the stuffs commonly worn are susceptible. Or, as you are the arbiters of taste and elegance, you might direct the makers of fashionable magazines and memorandum-books to give us, from time to time, a tablet of fashionable colours, with their appropriate epithets. By these means we should not only apprehend the colour itself; but such of us as have not travelled may learn, by reference, the qualities of things and of persons whom we never saw. Our ideas would be multiplied, and we should understand your language though we might not enrich our own.

QUERIST.[337]

---

335. This item was immediately preceded in the *Gent. Mag.* by a similar address, "To the Man of Letters," which, as Pottle says, is "almost a verbal repetition of no. XXVI of [JB's essay series] *The Hypochondriack*" (*Lit. Car.*, 233), published in 1779, and is therefore not reprinted here.

336. *Ton*: the fashion, the vogue, the mode; fashionable air or style (*OED*).

337. "Querist": a person who asks or inquires; a questioner, an interrogator (*OED*).

1793

Presentations at Court

The World, May 16, 1793

To the CONDUCTOR of the WORLD.

SIR,

I have observed, of late, a strange mode in all our News-papers of announcing the presentations at Court, by saying, that one person was presented by another, when in truth, nobody, be his rank what it may, has a right to present any person to the KING, unless the Lord of the Bedchamber in Waiting.[338] Is it not enough then, as was formerly done, to mention the persons who have been presented, the *form* of doing it being well established and well known [?]. The other day we were told that the Earl of CRAWFORD was presented by Colonel SMALL; and numberless other such instances might be pointed out.[339] If you wish to be more full in your accounts of presentations, pray use the word *attended* by whatever friend has come to Court with the *presentee*, and do not continue what is surely an impropriety.[340]

AN OLD COURTIER.

338. Presentations to the king were made at the Royal Levee (see Chap. 3, n. 453), which was originally held in the gallery outside the king's bedchamber. They were accorded a regular column in the newspapers. Gentlemen of the Bedchamber were officers of the royal household, whose duties were to wait upon the king as he arose, dressed, ate privately, etc., and to provide companionship. There were a number of them at any one time.

339. The *St. James's Chron.* (May 7, 1793) and *Lloyd's Evening Post* (May 8) both report that "Yesterday his Majesty had a Levee at St. James's when the following Nobility, &c. were presented, viz. the Earl of Crawford, by Colonel Small." George Lindsay-Crawford, twenty-second earl of Crawford (1758–1808), was colonel of the 63rd Regiment of Foot. John Small (1728–96) was a distinguished army officer, promoted to colonel in 1790.

340. JB's rebuke seems to have had an effect, as subsequent reports of the Royal Levee in the "Court" column in *The World* do in fact mention only the persons presented, using formulae such as "The following Gentlemen were presented . . . ," or "The presentations to the KING at the Levee were . . ."; see *The World*, May 25, May 30, June 1, June 13, 1793, etc.

Attributions and Textual Notes

In the following pages, there is a note for every item in this collection, giving my authority for the attribution to Boswell, textual variants, and other matters of specialist interest. The standard bibliographies of Boswell are both by F. A. Pottle: that is, *The Literary Career of James Boswell, Esq.* (1929) (*Lit. Car.*) and the entry on Boswell that Pottle contributed to *The New Cambridge Bibliography of English Literature*, ed. George Watson, vol. 2 (1971) (*NCBEL*). References below are to page number in *Lit. Car.* and to column number in *NCBEL*. I have included, where necessary, Pottle's own warnings: in both texts an asterisk indicates an attribution made on the basis of internal evidence only, and a question mark is used when the evidence, in Pottle's mind, fell "somewhat short of complete proof" (*Lit. Car.*, 215).

On occasions, Pottle's signs of uncertainty in *Lit. Car.* have disappeared from the later attributions in *NCBEL*, as evidence came to be found through the study of Boswell's manuscript journals or letters. Likewise, items with attributions in *NCBEL* and not *Lit. Car.* have mostly been added to the canon from the evidence of JB's own files, which had not been examined in 1929. Items for which there is an attribution in *Lit. Car.* but not in *NCBEL* are mostly items from the *London Chronicle* for the period 1767–75, for which *NCBEL* provides no detailed listing and refers users to *Lit. Car.* There are other occasional sources of attributions, which are clearly identified. Where the attribution is supported by a cutting or similar in JB's own files, now at the Beinecke Rare Book and Manuscript Library, Yale University, a reference is given with a "P" number (*P* for "Printed matter," in the mostly MS collection), which may be pursued in the Yale Boswell Collection or the three-volume published catalog (*Cat. Yale*). To some of those references are added in quotation marks Pottle's own occasional additional notes on the likelihood of the attribution. Where Boswell has made a note of some kind on his file copy, these are recorded.

For many of these items, there are no textual variants, because there is only one source. Where I have seen another published version, any textual variations are mostly of typographical conventions and other minor matters, which—although they are preserved in the texts here—have no authorial authority. I record where I have corrected occasional typographical errors. Most of the variations recorded below are JB's own MS corrections or additions to his "P" file copies, which I have examined. Throughout the following, these are indicated by the note "*JB.*"

I. REPORTS AND INTERVIEWS

Riot in the Edinburgh Theater
Lit. Car., 238.
Starred in JB's file, indexed, and noted as "Fact."
his friend *Garrick*. Of late] his friend *Garrick, of late Lond. Chron.*
A———n] Aicken *JB*

Two Sailors
Lit. Car., 238.
Starred and indexed in JB's file and noted as "Invention."

Mad Officer Murders Bride
Lit. Car., 239.
Starred and indexed in JB's file and noted as "Invention."

Drunken Capuchin Monk
Lit. Car., 239.
Starred and indexed in JB's file and noted as "Invention."

Canal to Link Dumfries and Ayr
Lit. Car., 239.
Starred and indexed in JB's file and noted as "Invention."
Repr. *St. James's Chron.*, May 26, 1767; *Gazetteer*, May 29, 1767.
Firths] friths *Lond. Chron.*
Dumfries] Drumfies *Lond. Chron.*

Shorthand Reporters, 1: Letter from Edinburgh
Lit. Car., 239.
Both pars. starred and indexed in JB's file and noted as "inventions."

Shorthand Reporters, 2: Letter from Berwick, June 15
Lit. Car., 250; *NCBEL*, 1222.
Repr. *Caledonian Mercury*, June 17 (*Lit. Car.*, 258).

Shorthand Reporters, 3: Letter from Berwick, June 18
Lit. Car., 251; *NCBEL*, 1222.
Repr. *Caledonian Mercury*, June 20; *Lond. Chron.*, Oct. 17–20, 4, abridged (*Lit. Car.*, 259, 241).

Shorthand Reporters, 4: Letter from Berwick, June 25, signed Noel Burridge
Lit. Car., 251; *NCBEL*, 1223.

Repr. *Caledonian Mercury*, June 27 (this text); *Thompson's Newcastle Journal*, June; *Pub. Adv.*, July 8; *Lond. Chron.*, Sept. 3, abridged (see *Lit. Car.*, 251, 259, 264, 255). *Lond. Chron.* abridgement marked by JB in his files.

Shorthand Reporters, 5: Letter from Berwick, July 6, signed Algernon Cust
Lit. Car., 251; *NCBEL*, 1223.
Repr. *Caledonian Mercury*, July 8 (this text).

An Account of the Stratford Jubilee
Lit. Car., 257; *NCBEL*, 1224.
Cutting in JB's files, P 114(4) marked with a star and maniculum and MS corrections. "Written in London."
Repr., lightly revised, *Lon. Mag.*, 38 (Sept. 1769), 451–54 (leading article, immediately before following item, P 92; not all variants noted for reasons of space).
this celebrated Jubilee *Pub. Adv.*] this celebrated Jubilee of genius *Lon. Mag.*
When he sung *Pub. Adv.*] When he sung/There never was seen such a creature, &c. *Lon. Mag.*
I do say it is a Work of superior Merit *Pub. Adv.*] I am sensible of it's defects; but, upon the whole, I think it a work of considerable merit *Lon. Mag.*
wrapped into Wonder and Admiration *Pub. Adv.*] filled with glowing admiration *Lon. Mag.*
the Clouds. Whether *Pub. Adv.*] the Clouds. In this room was lodged Mr. Thomas Becket, of London, grand bookseller to the jubilee. Whether *Lon. Mag.*
Towards the end … with my artichoke] (passage circled in ink in JB's *Pub. Adv.* file copy)
J. B. *Pub. Adv.*] JAMES BOSWELL *London Magazine*

An Account of the Armed Corsican Chief at the Masquerade
Lit. Car., *222; *NCBEL*, *1219.
This item immediately followed the *London Magazine*'s repr. of the Account of the Stratford Jubilee.

Verses in the Character of a Corsican at Shakespeare's Jubilee
Lit. Car., 84, 245; *NCBEL*, 1219.
The verses by themselves first appeared as a broadside (this text, with minor amendments) which JB printed for distribution at the Jubilee (see *Lit. Car.*, 84), and their first periodical publication was in *Lond. Chron.*, Sept. 9–12, 1769, as part of a longer account of the Jubilee.
deeply ting'd with patriot blood *London Magazine, Broadside*] ring'd *Lond. Chron.*
invaders' tenfold *Lond. Chron.*] invaders tenfold *London Magazine, Broadside*
Now when I'm exiled *London Magazine, Lond. Chron.*] (no new par. *Broadside*)
world of harmony——*London Magazine, Lond. Chron.*] world of harmony. *Broadside*
grief should lye *London Magazine, Lond. Chron.*] grief should lie *Broadside*
woman's gentle eye;*] (note added in *London Magazine*)

Verses on Seeing the Print of James Boswell, Esq; in the Corsican Dress
Lit. Car., 245.
Starred in JB's *Lond. Chron.* file at Yale.

An Authentick Account of General Paoli's Tour to Scotland, Autumn 1771
Lit. Car., 222; NCBEL, *1219.

Some Anecdotes of the Late Voyage of Mr. Banks and Dr. Solander in the Northern Seas
NCBEL, *1219.
earliest seats] earliests seats *London Magazine*

Some Account of the very extraordinary Travels of the celebrated Mr. Bruce
Lit. Car., 224; NCBEL, 1219.
Repr. *Lond. Chron.*, Sept. 8, Oct. 4, 1774; *Scots Mag.* (Sept. 1774). (Also notes by "Philo"
    in *Lond. Chron.*, Sept. 20, 1774.)
Lond. Chron. repr. marked in JB's file.
proportion] porportion *London Magazine*

An Account of the Chief of the Mohock Indians, who Lately Visited England
Lit. Car., ?225; NCBEL, 1220.
Repr. *Lond. Chron.*, Aug. 6, 1776; *Caledonian Mercury*, Aug. 12, 1776.

Mutiny in Scotland
NCBEL, 1225.
The first two pieces below were run consecutively in the same issue.
Highlanders] Highlandres *Pub. Adv.*
Sentinals] Centinals *Pub. Adv.*
Highlanders] Highlenders *Pub. Adv.*

Mutiny in Scotland, Fourth Day
NCBEL, 1225.
Highlanders. He read] Highlanders He read *Pub. Adv.*

Burke Installed as Lord Rector of the University of Glasgow
Lit. Car., ?253; NCBEL, *1223.

2. EXECUTION INTELLIGENCE

The Executions of Gibson and Payne
Lit. Car., 256; NCBEL, 1224.
JB's file copy, P 114(3). On his file copy, Boswell has made a number of handwritten
    amendments and noted, "Written in London."
Boswell later reused this letter in "Hypochondriack," no. 68, pub. in the *Pub. Adv.*,
    Apr. 26, 1768, although without incorporating the MS corrections that he made to
    his file copy; see Bailey, 2: 277–82. This text incorporates those MS alterations and
    additions, as noted below, where I also note amendments of substance made in
    the "Hypochondriack" version.
Judgment [. . .] Fancy] Mind *Bailey*
real Ills, or clouded by fanciful ones *JB*] some real Ills, or clouded by some fanciful
    ones. *Pub. Adv.*

this desire] the Desire *Bailey*

we may hug ourselves in Security, and relish more our own Safety and Ease, by comparing ourselves with those who are suffering] they may hug themselves in Security, and relish more their own Safety and Ease, by comparing themselves with those who are suffering *Bailey*

of any lively] of lively *Bailey*

attended] attendeded *Pub. Adv.*

who directs *JB*] who ever directs *Pub. Adv.*, *Bailey*

us all so] us so *Bailey*

heard and known] heard or known *Bailey*

He was helped upon] He was helped up upon *Bailey*

he put on a white nightcap, & gave *JB*] he gave *Pub. Adv.*

It was said [. . .] by *external* acts.] (these two sentences added *JB*; not in *Bailey*. The words "stave off" are a conjectural reading)

miserable Souls] miserable beings *Bailey*

Curious Mr. Boswell on Top of a Hearse at Tyburn
Lit. Car., 245.
Starred in JB's run of the *Lond. Chron.* at Yale.

Verses on Seeing Mr. Boswell on the Top of an Hearse at Tyburn
Lit. Car., 245.
Starred in JB's run of the *Lond. Chron.* at Yale.

John Reid Brought to Edinburgh
NCBEL, 1229 (says Jan. 11, but no such issue).

The Trial of John Reid
Not in *Lit. Car.* nor *NCBEL*. Tentative identification by Brady (*Later Years*, 99).

The Mournful Case of Poor Misfortunate and Unhappy John Reid
NCBEL, 1212.
Composed, as JB noted in his journal, on the evening of Wednesday, Sept. 7, with assistance from Michael Nasmith, a Writer to the Signet, i.e., solicitor (*Defence*, 319–20).
JB's MS and a copy of the broadside are in his Yale files, Lg 24(1) and (2).
The heading on the MS, after Edinburgh, reads, "dated Wednesday night, the 7th of September 1774" (*Defence*, 321). This is the only variation.

A Pardon Urged for John Reid, Condemned to be Hanged for Sheep-Stealing
Lit. Car., 248.
Starred in JB's run of the *Lond. Chron.* See *Defence*, 329–30 and n.

Death of John Reid
Not in *Lit. Car.*
Not marked in JB's file.

Account of the Execution of John Reid
Lit. Car., 248.
Caledonian Mercury and *Edinburgh Evening Courant*, Sept. 21, 1774; this text from
    Lond. Chron., with introductory and final paragraphs added; see *NCBEL*, 1230.
Starred in JB's *Lond. Chron.* files at Yale.
he suffered *JB*] suffered *Lond. Chron.*
circumstantiate *Edinburgh Evening Courant, Lond. Chron.*] circumstantial *Caledonian
    Mercury*

Hackman's Trial for Murder, and His Speech to the Court
Lit. Car., 260; *NCBEL*, 1230.
accessory] accessary *St. James's Chron.*

Reflections on Hackman's Trial
Lit. Car., 260; *NCBEL*, 1230.
Cutting filed by JB, P 119(1). Written at Dilly's, where JB was staying Apr. 16
    (*Laird*, 85).
Grace to restrain] Grace to restain *St. James's Chron.*
worse than yours? No,] worse than yours. No *St. James's Chron.*

Hackman at His Trial: Boswell's Account to Mr. Booth
Lit. Car., *258; *NCBEL*, 1225.
amiable a Man] amiable Man *Pub. Adv.*
Passions are violent, Think ye] Passions are violent. Think ye *Pub. Adv.*

Boswell Did Not Attend Hackman to Tyburn
Lit. Car., *258; *NCBEL*, 1225.

Execution Intelligence, 1
NCBEL, 1225.
Repr. *Morning Chronicle*, July 8; *Lond. Chron.*, July 7, abridged; *General Evening Post*,
    July 5, 1785 (not previously recorded).

Execution Intelligence, 2
NCBEL, *1225.
Hopkins] Hopkius *Pub. Adv.*
fellow convicts] fellow connicts *Pub. Adv.*

3. THE RAMPAGER

These essays are not listed in *Lit. Car.*, having been identified from JB's files after 1929.
Of the twenty here, nineteen are identified in *NCBEL*, 1224; the exception is no. 6 by
the numbering used here (Oct. 26, 1771), which is now added to the canon. JB kept
a file of cuttings of sixteen of these twenty essays, P 152, and made corrections and

alterations in some of them that have been incorporated into the texts; the original published readings are recorded below.

No. 1: Recent Discord in the "Political Orchestra"
JB's file copy, P 152(1). Starred, marked with a maniculum, and annotated "Rampager. Written in Edinburgh" (JB's MS note).
Repr. *Independent Chronicle*, Apr. 13, 1770; *The Repository: or, Treasury of Politics and Literature for MDCCLXX*, vol. 1 (London, 1771), 431–36.
Bell-Ass, ringing] Bell-Ass ringing *Pub. Adv.*

No. 2: The "Political Musicians," Continued
JB's file copy, P 152(2). "Written at Edinburgh" (JB's MS note).
Holles, Dunk, Pynsent] Holles Dunk, Pynsent *Pub. Adv.*
his performance] his peformance *Pub. Adv.*

No. 3: Doctrine of Fatality Avowed by Dissenting Lords in Wilkes Vote
JB's file copy, P 152(3). Starred and marked with a maniculum; "Written at Edinburgh" (JB's MS note).
declaiming JB] declaming *Pub. Adv.*
Macaulay JB] Macauley *Pub. Adv.*
determined to *persevere JB*] determined to persevere *Pub. Adv.*
Endeavours JB] Endeavours *Pub. Adv.*
City JB] ity *Pub. Adv.*
any JB] a y *Pub. Adv.*
that: if they *JB*] that if they *Pub. Adv.*
the *Sheriffs*, neither *JB*] the *Sheriff*, neither *Pub. Adv.*
instead of behaving with calm Resignation *JB*] instead of calm Resignation *Pub. Adv.*
"endeavour" *JB*] endeavour *Pub. Adv.*
are to "persevere" *JB*] are to persevere *Pub. Adv.*
"what the *Fates did decree.*" *JB*] what the *Fates di decree. Pub. Adv.*

No. 4: The "Smelling Medicine," Politically Applied
JB's file copy, P 152(4), is of the repr. in *Caledonian Mercury*, July 16, 1770 (leading article). "Written at Edinburgh Spring 1770, and printed 1st the 7 [*sic*] of July 1770" (JB's MS note).
a prescription Pub. Adv., JB] a *prescription Caledonian Mercury*
Macaulay *Caledonian Mercury*] Macauley *Pub. Adv.*
Body Politic—Thirdly *Pub. Adv., JB*] *Body* Politic——*Thirdly Caledonian Mercury*
wasting away with the *Itch Pub. Adv., JB*] wasting away the Itch *Caledonian Mercury*
Reverse of *Pandora's* box *Pub. Adv., JB*] Reverse of a Pandora's box *Caledonian Mercury*
HIS MAJESTY'S *Pub. Adv., JB*] his MAJESTY'S *Caledonian Mercury*
Townsend] *Townshend Pub. Adv.*; Townsend *Caledonian Mercury*

Buckingham's Pub. Adv.] *Buckingham Caledonian Mercury*

Boar and Sow *Caledonian Mercury*] Bear and Sow *Pub. Adv.*

ORATOR—He *Pub. Adv., JB*] ORATOR—he *Caledonian Mercury*

"the Powers that be who are ordained of God" *JB*] the Powers that be who are ordained of God *Pub. Adv.*; the powers that be who are ordained of God *Caledonian Mercury*

No. 5: The "Touching Medicine": An Old Political Cure

JB's file copy, P 152(5), of the repr. in *Caledonian Mercury*, July 8, 1771 (leading article). "Written at Edinburgh in Autumn 1770 and first printed in *The Public Advertiser* 20 May 1771" (JB's MS note).

I also note below readings from Carte, *General History of England.*

[N.B. In the *Caledonian Mercury*, capitalization conforms to modern practice, but italics persist, although they vary from *Pub. Adv.* These variations will not be noted.]

In my last I treated of *Pub. Adv.*] In my last [see Mercury, 16th July 1770,] I treated of *Caledonian Mercury*

scirrhous *Pub. Adv., Carte*] schirrous *Caledonian Mercury*

Malmsbury observe *Pub. Adv.*] *Malmesbury* observe *Caledonian Mercury; Malmesbury,* observe *Carte*

ceremonial whereof *Caledonian Mercury, Carte*] ceremonial where of *Pub. Adv.*

Relicks of Saint *Marculf, Caledonian Mercury, Carte*] Relicks of Staint *Marculf, Pub. Adv.*

Time of its assembling *Caledonian Mercury, Carte*] Time of it's assembling *Pub. Adv.*

Painted Chamber *Caledonian Mercury*] painted Chamber *Pub. Adv.*; painted chamber *Carte*

sanative *Caledonian Mercury, Carte*] senative *Pub. Adv.*

Opinion of its Merit *Caledonian Mercury*] Opinion of it's Merit *Pub. Adv.*

good Historian. As witness *Pub. Adv.*] good Historian, as witness *Caledonian Mercury*

Cock Lane Pub. Adv.] Cocklane *Caledonian Mercury*

"Lond. Chron. No. 1569" *JB* (added by hand after quotation of lines from "The Guinea")

has its Effect *Caledonian Mercury*] has it's effect *Pub. Adv.*

very well *touched JB*] *very well touched Pub. Adv.*; very well touched *Caledonian Mercury*

No. 6: A Political Parody on Cato, Act V, Sc. 1

Not in *NCBEL.*

No copy in JB's files.

Repr. in *Caledonian Mercury*, Nov. 6, 1771.

No. 7: "Rampageneana," and Other Fruit

JB's file copy, P 152(6). "Written at Edinburgh Autumn 1771" (JB's MS note).

Sunt nobis mitia poma, is his Motto. *JB*] *Sun nobis mitia poma*, his own Motto.
   Pub. Adv.

No. 8: The Public Advertiser *as a Noah's Ark*
No copy in JB's files.
resembles] resemble *Pub. Adv.*

No. 9: On the Feathers Tavern Petitioners
No copy in JB's files; the reply (*Pub. Adv.*, Apr. 23, 1774) to this item is filed by JB,
   P 152(7).
Te Deum, that *Form*] *Te Deum* that *Form Pub. Adv.*

No. 10: Reply, Serious and Otherwise, to "A Feather's Man"
JB's file copy, P 152(8). "Written at Edinburgh in Spring 1774" (JB's MS note).
liberal: but *JB*] liberal, but *Pub. Adv.*
Terms: And *JB*] Terms, and *Pub. Adv.*
Information; one *JB*] Information, as one *Pub. Adv.*
shines;—though perhaps *JB*] shines, though perhaps *Pub. Adv.*
no worse: and *JB*] no worse: And *Pub. Adv.*
Authority of *the Scriptures themselves JB*] Authority of the Scriptures themselves
   Pub. Adv.
by *Edmund Burke*] by *Edmmnd Burke Pub. Adv.*
which the Feathersman says *JB*] which the Featherman says *Pub. Adv.*
The: *Lindesay JB*] the *Lindesay Pub. Adv.*
Metropolis *JB*] Metroplis *Pub. Adv.*
Sheep, for a flock *JB*] *Sheep* for a flock *Pub. Adv.*
humbler Fold, for *Essex House JB*] *humble Fold* for *Essex House Pub. Adv.*
laudi manentem: JB] *laudi manenten Pub. Adv.*
Feather his Nest JB] *Feather hii Nest Pub. Adv.*
I shall say nothing against him *JB*] I shall say nothing against him, ~~I shall say~~
   ~~Nothing against him~~ *Pub. Adv.*, with JB's MS. deletion
my *Flight JB*] my *flight Pub. Adv.*
my *Flight*. It is a wonder *JB*] (i.e., JB inserts par. break)
but *Tarrers JB*] but *Tarers Pub. Adv.*
be thankful *JB*] be the thankful *Pub. Adv.*
a little *Tarring JB*] a little *Taring Pub. Adv.*
Wind of Doctrine," and *JB*] Wind of Doctrine, and *Pub. Adv.*
Shuttle-Cock JB] *Shuttle Cock Pub. Adv.*

No. 11: On the American Tea War: Rhubarb Recommended
JB's file copy, P 152(9). "Rampager Written at Edinburgh in Spring 1775. On the
   American Tea War. Sir A. Dick's Rhubarb recommended to the Americans" (JB's
   MS note).

Salernitona, bona] *Salernitona bona Pub. Adv.*

some Indignation] some Indignationn *Pub. Adv.*

when scattered. In the Epilogue *JB*] when scattered in the Epilogue *Pub. Adv.*

by *Lillo*, I found] by *Lillo*. I found *Pub. Adv.*

No. 12: End the American War by Arming the Jews

JB's file copy, P 152(10). "Written at Edinburgh July 1775" (JB's MS note).

bony Girgashite JB] *bon Girgashite Pub. Adv.*

their Shoutings *JB*] their Shootings *Pub. Adv.*

No. 13: Metaphorical Groupe of Birds

JB's file copy, P 152(11). No marks or corrections. "Rampager Written at Edinburgh in
    Spring 1776. Metaphorical Groupe of Birds" (JB's MS note).

three jolly Pidgeons] three jolly Pideons *Pub. Adv.*

No. 14: John the Painter and John the Peer

JB's file copy, P 152(12). No marks or corrections. "Rampager Written at Edinburgh in
    Spring 1777. John the Painter and John the Peer" (JB's MS note).

Emphasis enough] *Emphasi* enough *Pub. Adv.*

No. 15: American Allusions from a Bookseller's Catalog

JB's file copy, P 152(13). No marks or corrections. "Rampager written at Edinburgh in
    Autumn 1777" (JB's MS note).

No. 16: On the Manchester Regiment

JB's file copy, P 152(14). "Rampager written at Edinburgh Spring 1778. On the Man-
    chester Regiment" (JB's MS note).

Percival draw *Cuts JB*] *Percival* draw Cuts *Pub. Adv.*

No. 17: The Lads at Water Still

No copy in JB's files.

into the Mouths] into the Mouth *Pub. Adv.*

No. 18: On the Parliamentary Inquiry into the War

JB's file copy, P 152(15). "Rampager Written at Edinburgh Summer 1779" (JB's MS
    note).

the *peremptory* Orders *JB*] the peremptory Orders *Pub. Adv.*

much notice has been taken *JB*] much has been taken *Pub. Adv.*

No. 19: On the Duel between Lord Shelburne and Col. Fullarton

JB's file copy, P 152(16). "Rampager on Duel between Lord Shelburne and Col. Ful-
    larton. Written at Edinburgh Autumn 1780" (JB's MS note).

Repr. *Morning Post*, Aug. 24, 1780.

descended, little thought *JB*] descended little thought *Pub. Adv.*

Value of a *Parliamentary Life JB*] Value of a Parliamentary Life *Pub. Adv.*

[a *Commis* or] *JB*] a *Commis* or *Pub. Adv.*

No. 20: On the Change of Ministry
JB's file copy, P 152(17). "Rampager on the Change of Ministry. Parody on General
  Murray's letter on the Surrender of Minorca. Written at Edinburgh Spring 1782"
  (JB's MS note).
ever infected Mortals *JB* (this is the reading of Murray's letter. Ed.)] ever affected
  Mortals *Pub. Adv.*

4. THE LIVES OF JOHNSON

Boswell Honored to Be Recommended as Johnson's Biographer
Lit. Car., 260; *NCBEL*, 1230.
Filed cutting, with JB's MS correction, P 100(1).
Repr. *London Magazine* (Apr. 1785).
am Master of *JB*] were master of *St. James's Chron.*

Boswell Disclaims Authorship of Certain Newspaper Paragraphs
NCBEL, 1225.

Advertisement for the Tour
NCBEL, *1222.

Advertisement for the Life of Johnson
Not in *NCBEL*.
The first paragraph had appeared only in the first edition of the *Tour*. This three-
  paragraph text was reprinted in the third edition of the *Tour* and *A Catalogue of
  Books printed for . . . Charles Dilly* (1787); a leaf with this text has been "apparently
  torn" from the latter and is in JB's papers, P 99. This text is headed "London, May,
  1787."
Preparing for the Press, in one Volume Quarto, Tour] *In the Press, and with all convenient
  Speed will be published, in One Volume, Quarto, Cat. Dilly*
authentick *Tour*] authentic *Cat. Dilly*
authour *Tour*] author *Cat. Dilly*
correspondence *Tour*] correspondence, *Cat. Dilly*

Boswell Denies Suppressing Passage in Second Edition of the Tour
Lit. Car., 261; not in *NCBEL*.
Repr. *Gent. Mag.*, 59 (Apr. 1786), 285; *Lit. Car.*, 231.
without any application from any person *Gent. Mag.*] without any person *Pub. Adv.*

Boswell's Reply to the Postscript of Mrs. Piozzi's Anecdotes
Lit. Car., 263; *NCBEL*, 1233.
First pub. *Gazetteer and New Daily Advertiser*, Apr. 17, 1786; also in *St. James's Chron.*
  and *Pub. Adv.*, Apr. 18, 1786 (this text); repr. *European Magazine, Gent. Mag.,
  Lond. Chron.*, and *Morning Chronicle*.

Piozzian Rhimes
Lit. Car., 266; *NCBEL*, 1222.
Printed the same day in the *Pub. Adv.*; repr. *Morning Herald*, Apr. 21; *St. James's Chron.*, Apr. 27; *An Asylum for Fugitive Pieces: In Prose and Verse, not in any other Collection*, ed. J. Almon, vol. 2 (1786), 288–89.

Boswell's Retort to Mrs. Piozzi Has Upset the Bluestockings
NCBEL, *1225.
Starred, cut out, and filed by JB, P 119(3).
singed *hairs*] singed; *hairs Pub. Adv.*

Mrs. Piozzi, with Her Husband, Will Soon Return to England
Not in *NCBEL*. Attributed in *Experiment*, 62 n. 3.

Johnson's Biographers
NCBEL, 1226.
Starred, cut out, and filed by JB, P 119(15).

Life of Johnson Delayed, Now in Forwardness
Lit. Car., 163; not in *NCBEL* (but noted in MS addition to the Yale Boswell Office copy).
Repr. *Gent. Mag.*, front wrapper (June 1787).
The *Gent. Mag.* version is headed "*London, June, 1787*" and omits the date at the end.

Ode by Dr. Samuel Johnson to Mrs. Thrale, upon Their Supposed Approaching Nuptials
Lit. Car., 131; *NCBEL*, 1214.

Did Johnson Court Mrs. Thrale? Do His Biographers Know?
NCBEL, 1226.
Starred, cut out, and filed by JB, P 116(29).

A Thralian Epigram
NCBEL, 1227.
(Boswell had five items in this issue.) Starred, cut out, and filed by JB, P 116(32).

Life of Johnson *in the Press*
Not in *NCBEL*.
There is no known file of the *Morning Post* for this period; this date is an endorsement by JB. Cut out and filed by JB, P 100(2).
Repr. *English Chronicle*, Jan. 14, 1790; *Diary, or Woodfall's Register*, Jan. 15, 1790; *Gazetteer and New Daily Advertiser*, Jan. 15, 1790; *Pub. Adv.*, Jan. 15, 1790; *Argus*, Jan. 16, 1790; *Lond. Chron.*, Jan. 21, 1790.

Mr. Boswell at the Abbey
NCBEL, 1227.
Starred, cut out, pasted up, and filed by JB, P 117(3).

30th of January] 30t of January *Pub. Adv.*
gravity] graviyt *Pub. Adv.*

Mrs. Piozzi's Terror of Boswell's Life of Johnson
Not in *NCBEL*; but "almost surely written by him" (*Great Biographer*, 40).
Dated, cut out, pasted up, and filed by JB, P 100(4).

Johnson's Monument
NCBEL, 1227.
Starred, cut out, mounted, annotated, and filed by JB, P 117(8).

Mrs. Piozzi's Subscription to Johnson's Monument Defended
NCBEL, 1234.
Starred, dated, cut out, pasted up, and filed by JB, P 117(9).
737£.] 737 1. *Pub. Adv.*

The Brewhouse Entertainment
NCBEL, 1234.
Starred, cut out, pasted up, and filed by JB, P 117(10). The date is assigned by Pottle,
    noting that there is no known file of the *Morning Post* for this time.
left 5£.] left 5 1. *Pub. Adv.*

Mrs. Piozzi's Nerves Shaken by Prospect of Boswell's Book
Not in *NCBEL*; but "almost surely written by him" (*Great Biographer*, 40).
Date is JB's annotation. Cut out, pasted up, annotated, and filed by JB, P 100(5).

Boswell to Spare Mrs. Piozzi
Not in *NCBEL*. In a complete copy of the issue in JB's files, P 101(2), this item is
    crossed and circled in red pencil.

Boswell Will Not Spare Mrs. Piozzi
Not in *NCBEL*.
Date is JB's annotation; precise date unknown. Cut out, pasted, annotated, and filed
    by JB, P 100(3).

Boswell to Send News of Johnson's Life *to the Press*
NCBEL, 1231.
Repr. *Gazetteer*, Oct. 20, 1790.

Advertisement for the Life of Johnson
Not in *NCBEL*.
Repr. *Gent. Mag.*, front wrapper (Apr. 1791) (*NCBEL*, 1220; see *Corres. 4*, 417–18
    and n. 1).

Dr. Johnson's Monument
NCBEL, 1227.
Marked cutting in P 117.

Johnson's Monument Like Mahomet's Coffin
NCBEL, 1227.

Advertisement for Valuable Extracts from the Life of Johnson: *The* Conversation *and*
    Letter
NCBEL, *1227.

Johnson and Burke
NCBEL, 1227.
of superior abilities] of suporior abilities *Pub. Adv.*

Warren Hastings
NCBEL, 1227.
Cut out, pasted up, and starred in P 101.1(2).

The Life of Johnson *a Union of Matter and Spirit*
Not in *NCBEL*; though in the *Pub. Adv.* it follows immediately after the previous item.
Cut out, mounted, dated, and filed by JB, P 101.1(3).

The Engraved Portrait of Dr. Johnson
Not in *NCBEL*.

Literary Property
NCBEL, *1227. See Horne, "Boswell and Literary Property."

Boswell Has Rescued Johnson from Hawkins and Thrale
NCBEL, *1231.
Cut out, mounted, and filed by JB, P 100(16).

Insolvent Debtors
NCBEL, 1227.
Marked cutting, P 100.1(4), with JB's handwritten source note.

Living Twice, through Boswell's Pages
NCBEL, 1227–28.
Marked cutting, P 100(5), with JB's handwritten date. (Misreported in *Great Biographer*, 146, as pub. June 20.)

Portable Soup
NCBEL, 1228.
Starred, cut out, pasted up, and filed by JB, P 101.1(6).

Apology of London Packet *for Infringing Boswell's Copyright*
NCBEL, 1231.
Cut out, mounted, and filed by JB, P 100.1(7), with date and source recorded.
No copies are known of the *London Packet* text; this *St. James's Chron.* version gives
    us the added par. at the start, presumably also JB's. John Nichols gives a text of
    the apology in *Illustrations*, 7:334, which he says is taken from JB's "autograph, in

my possession." Nichols attaches to his text a note from the editor and essayist Alexander Chalmers (1759–1834), recording that the apology was "written in
Dilly's shop."

Earl of Chesterfield] Lord Chesterfield *Illustrations*
Life of Dr. Johnson] life of Dr. Johnson *Illustrations*
Literary Property] literary property *Illustrations*
two articles] two valuable articles *Illustrations*
Stationer's Hall] Stationers' Hall *Illustrations*
which were advertised in some of the news-papers,] which was advertised in some of
    the newspapers; *Illustrations*
escaped us.—We] escaped us. We *Illustrations*
We cannot but be sorry] we are very sorry *Illustrations*

Dilly and Dodsley
NCBEL, 1228.
Starred, cut out, and filed by JB, P 100(22).

Boswell Dining (Out) on Johnson
NCBEL, 1228.
Starred, cut out, and filed by JB, P 100(24).

Sales of the Life
NCBEL, 1231.
Starred, cut out, and filed by JB, P 100(25).

Friendly Patronage, and Two Other Paragraphs
NCBEL, 1228.
Starred, cut out, pasted, and filed by JB, P 100(32).
you may put in] you may pnt in *Illustrations*

Mrs. Piozzi to Reply to Charge of Carelessness
Not in *NCBEL*.
Copy in P 100(14), said to be "probably" by JB.

*Shakespeare's Mulberry Tree: Johnson's Animadversions on the Rev. and Mrs. Gastrell
    Defended*
Lit. Car., 233; *NCBEL*, 1220.

Boswell Recovers from Street Assault
NCBEL, 1232.
Cut out and starred in JB's files, P 124(5).
Under the heading "Literary Intelligence," this par. was followed by two others con-
    cerning Herbert Croft.

Paper-War with Miss Anna Seward: Letter to Gentleman's Magazine *(November
    1793)*
Lit. Car., 234; *NCBEL*, 1220.

Paper-War with Miss Anna Seward: Letter to Gentleman's Magazine *(January 1794)*
Lit. Car., 234; *NCBEL*, 1220.

5. ESSAYS AND LETTERS

A Contemplative Walk, at Moffat, on a summer-night
Lit. Car., ?216; not in *NCBEL*, but Pottle and Bennett say that "it appears to be from
   Boswell's pen" (Boswell, *Journal of a Tour to the Hebrides*, 349). Brooks says that it
   is "almost certainly" his (*James Boswell*, 24).
Wearied with] WEaried with *Scots Mag.*
cheerful smile] chearful smile *Scots Mag.*

An Original Letter, From a Gentleman of Scotland to the Earl of * * * *in London*
Lit. Car., *216; *NCBEL*, 1218.
Repr. *Blackwood's Magazine* (1925), 301; (not from MS) with annotation, in *Corres. 9*,
   104–10.

The Miseries of a Timorous Man
Not in *Lit. Car.* nor *NCBEL*; attributed Caudle, "Three New James Boswell
   Articles."
Midwife] Midmife *Pub. Adv.*
actually wed to him] actually wedd to him *Pub. Adv.*
pious Aeneas] pious Ænæas *Pub. Adv.*
tremendous] tremenduous *Pub. Adv.*

The Defects of Polite Conversation
Not in *Lit. Car.* nor *NCBEL*; attributed Turnbull, "Yale Boswell Edition Notes,"
   19–25. See also *London Journal*, ed. Turnbull, 516.
comæ, and his Hair] *comæ and his Hair Pub. Adv.*

A Recipe Requested for Removing "Rust" from Books
Lit. Car., 239.

An Essay on Travelling
NCBEL, 1224.
Marked leaf in JB's files, P 114(1). The cutting in JB's files has his MS corrections, his
   asterisk and maniculum, the address line and salutation are deleted and replaced
   with "An Essay on Travelling / By James Boswell Esq.," and he has crossed out
   the signature. His amendments are noted below. He adds a note, "Written at
   Auchinlech."
Repr. *Caledonian Mercury*, Nov. 28; *London Magazine*, 36 (Nov., 1767), 582. JB wrote
   this at Auchinleck and sent it, so it seems, to Edward Dilly to forward to Woodfall for the *Pub. Adv.*; see *Corres. 5*, 258 & n. 5.

Travels *JB*] Travel *Pub. Adv.*
Athens *JB*] others *Pub. Adv.*
Prussia thinks with *JB*] Prussia with *Pub. Adv.*
than of *JB*] than that of *Pub. Adv.*
Vivacity,] Vivacity *Pub. Adv.*, vivacisy, *JB*
Collection, in *JB*] Collection in *Pub. Adv.*
Governors, in *JB*] Governors in *Pub. Adv.*
Swarms that Custom *JB*] Swarms, Custom *Pub. Adv.*
them see *JB*] them only see *Pub. Adv.*
Notion *JB*] Principle *Pub. Adv.*
is certainly very hurtful *JB*] appears exceedingly alarming *Pub. Adv.*

The "New Town" of Edinburgh
Lit. Car., 247.

Masquerade Intelligence Extraordinary
Not in *Lit. Car.*; *NCBEL*, 1229.

Authentic Scottish Masquerade Intelligence
Not in *Lit. Car.*; *NCBEL*, *1225.
This article formed the basis of a report in the *Gent. Mag.*, 43 (Jan. 1773), 43.
Balcarras] Balearras *Pub. Adv.*
Lockhart Macdonald] Lockhart; Macdonald *Pub. Adv.*; Lockhart Macdonal *Gent. Mag.*
Dabyiel *Pub. Adv.*] Dalziel *Gent. Mag.*

An Essay on Masquerade
Lit. Car., 223–24; *NCBEL*, 1219.

Scottish Customs Not Understood in England
Lit. Car., 248.
Mess John] Mess. John *Lond. Chron.*

"Parliament Square": A Foolish Affectation
Lit. Car., *219; not in *NCBEL*.
Repr. from the *Caledonian Mercury*, Jan. 27, 1776 (*Lit. Car.*, 259; *NCBEL*, 1230).

A Cure Requested for Occasional Impotence of Mind
NCBEL, 1220.

Consolation under Impotence of Mind, if not a Cure for it
NCBEL, 1220.
Repr. *The North-British Intelligencer; or Constitutional Miscellany*, 3, no. 13 (Dec. 25, 1776), 392–93.

On Allegorical Figures in the Caledonian Mercury
NCBEL, 1230.

Marked cutting in JB's files, P 114(8).

Publish the War Casualty Lists
NCBEL, 1225.
JB confirms his authorship by a note on the reply, in his P 114 file.

A Defense of the State Trumpeters
NCBEL, 1230.
Marked cutting in JB's files, P 114(10).

Shortage of Provisions at the Mayoral Ball
NCBEL, 1225.
JB's file copy, P 95, an offprint, with MS correction.
Repr. *Laird*, 66–68.
its CHIEF] it's CHIEF *Pub. Adv.*
were discharged *Pub. Adv.*] were forbid *JB*

New Year's Address, from the Publisher
Not in *NCBEL*. See *Laird*, 156.

Defense of the Edinburgh Town Guard
NCBEL, 1230.
Copy of this whole number of the *Caledonian Mercury*, P 114(13).

A Request for a Recipe Against Bookworm
Lit. Car., *248–49; *NCBEL*, *1222.

A Sentimental Essay on Death
Lit. Car., 230–31 (Pottle says that it is "patently Boswellian in theme and style,"
    although it is not in *NCBEL*).

High Food Prices and High-Living Aldermen
NCBEL, *1226.
Unmarked cutting in P 119(4).

Unholy Trinity in Titles of Newspapers
Not in *NCBEL*. Cutting, P 119(17).

Criticism of John Howard, Prison Reformer: Letter to Public Advertiser, *March 12, 1788*
NCBEL, 1226.
JB's marked cutting, P 166(25).
and honest painful injury? *JB*] and injurious to painful industry? *Pub. Adv.*

Criticism of John Howard, Prison Reformer: Letter to Public Advertiser, *May 12, 1788*
NCBEL, 1226.
JB's marked cutting, P 166(27).
because necessary, evils] because necessary evils *Pub. Adv.*

To the Man of Fashion
Lit. Car., *232; *NCBEL*, *1220.

Presentations at Court
NCBEL, *1234.
Unmarked cutting in JB's file, P 118(6).
News-papers] New-papers *World*

Chronology of Articles

Bibliography

Adam, Margaret I. "The Highland Emigration of 1770." *Scottish Historical Review* 16, no. 64 (July 1919): 280–93.

Airy, Osmund, ed. *Burnet's History of My Own Time*. Vol. 1. Oxford, 1897.

Allison, Ronald, and Sarah Riddell, ed. *The Royal Encyclopaedia*. London: Macmillan, 1991.

Archenholz, [Johann Wilhelm von]. *A Picture of England: Containing a Description of the Laws, Customs, and Manners of England*. London, 1789.

Armstrong, John. *Miscellanies*. 2 vols. London, 1790.

[Army.] *A List of the General and Field Officers, as They Rank in the Army*. London, 1778.

———. *A List of the General and Field Officers, as They Rank in the Army*. London, 1783.

Aspinall, Arthur. *Politics and the Press, 1780–1850*. London: Home & van Thal, 1949.

Aspromourgos, Tony. *On the Origins of Classical Economics: Distribution and Value from William Petty to Adam Smith*. London: Routledge, 1996.

Bacon, Francis. *The Essayes or Counsels, Civill and Morall*. London, 1625.

Banks, Sir Joseph. *Journal of the Right Hon. Sir Joseph Banks: During Captain Cook's First Voyage in H.M.S.* Endeavour *in 1768–71*. Edited by Joseph Dalton Hooker. 1896. Cambridge: Cambridge University Press, 2011.

Barker, Hannah. *Newspapers, Politics, and Public Opinion in Late Eighteenth-Century England*. Oxford: Clarendon, 1998.

Beattie, J. M. *Crime and the Courts in England, 1660–1800*. Oxford: Clarendon, 1986.

Benedict, Barbara. *Curiosity: A Cultural History of Early Modern Inquiry*. Chicago: University of Chicago Press, 2001.

Bertelsen, Lance. "The Education of Henry Sampson Woodfall, Newspaperman." In *Mentoring in Eighteenth-Century British Literature and Culture*, edited by Anthony W. Lee, 149–69. Farnham: Ashgate, 2009.

Besant, Walter. *London*. London, 1892.

Black, Eugene Charlton. "The Tumultuous Petitioners: The Protestant Association in Scotland, 1778–1780." *Review of Politics* 25, no. 2 (April 1963): 183–211.

Bolingbroke, Henry St. John, Viscount. *The Works of the Late Right Honorable Henry St. John, Lord Viscount Bolingbroke*. Vol. 5. London, 1754.

Bond, Richmond P. *Queen Anne's American Kings*. Oxford: Clarendon, 1952.

Borlik, Todd Andrew. "'Painting of a sorrow': Visual Culture and the Performance of Stasis in David Garrick's Hamlet." *Shakespeare Bulletin* 25, no. 1 (2007): 3–31.

Boswell, James. *An Account of Corsica, The Journal of a Tour to That Island, and Memoirs of Pascal Paoli*. Edited by James T. Boulton and T. O. McLoughlin. Oxford: Oxford University Press, 2006.

———. *James Boswell's "Life of Johnson": An Edition of the Original Manuscript*, vol. 1: *1709–1765*. Edited by Marshall Waingrow. Edinburgh: Edinburgh University Press; New Haven: Yale University Press, 1994.

———. *Journal of a Tour to the Hebrides with Samuel Johnson, LL.D., 1773*. Edited by Frederick A. Pottle and Charles H. Bennett. London: Heinemann, 1963.

———. *The Journal of His German and Swiss Travels, 1764*. Edited by Marlies K. Danziger. Edinburgh: Edinburgh University Press; New Haven: Yale University Press, 2008.

———. "Journal of My Jaunt, Harvest, 1762." In *London Journal, 1762–1763 [Deluxe Edition]: Together with Journal of My Jaunt, Harvest, 1762*, edited by Frederick A. Pottle, 41–111. London: Heinemann, 1951.

———. *Letter to the People of Scotland on the Alarming Attempt to Infringe the Articles of the Union, and Introduce a Most Pernicious Innovation, by Diminishing the Number of the Lords of the Session*. London, 1785.

———. *Letter to the People of Scotland on the Present State of the Nation*. Edinburgh, 1783.

———. *London Journal, 1762–1763*. Edited by Gordon Turnbull. London: Penguin, 2010.

Boyce, George, James Curran, and Pauline Wingate. *Newspaper History: From the Seventeenth Century to the Present Day*. London: Constable; Beverly Hills: Sage, 1978.

Boyd, Robert. *The Office, Powers, and Jurisdiction, of His Majesty's Justices of the Peace*. Vol. 1. Edinburgh, 1787.

Brack, O M, Jr. Introduction to *The Life of Samuel Johnson, LL.D.*, by Sir John Hawkins, xxi–xxxiv. Athens: University of Georgia Press, 2009.

Brack, O M, Jr., and Robert E. Kelley, eds. *The Early Biographies of Samuel Johnson*. Iowa City: University of Iowa Press, 1974.

Bredin, Miles. *The Pale Abyssinian: A Life of James Bruce, African Explorer and Adventurer*. London: HarperCollins, 2000.

Brewer, John. *Party Ideology and Popular Politics at the Accession of George III*. Cambridge: Cambridge University Press, 1976.

————. *A Sentimental Murder: Love and Madness in the Eighteenth Century*. New York: Farrar, Strauss and Giroux, 2004.

Brooks, A. Russell. *James Boswell*. New York: Twayne, 1971.

Brown, Anthony E. *Boswellian Studies: A Bibliography*. 3rd ed. Edinburgh: Edinburgh University Press, 1991.

Brown, Susan E. "'A Just and Profitable Commerce': Moral Economy and the Middle Classes in Eighteenth-Century London." *Journal of British Studies* 32, no. 4 (1993): 305–32.

Brownell, Morris R., and Melita Ann Brownell. "Boswell's Ballads: A Life in Song." In *Boswell in Scotland and Beyond*, edited by Thomas Crawford, 119–45. Glasgow: Association for Scottish Literary Studies, 1997.

Bruce, James. *Travels to Discover the Source of the Nile*. 5 vols. Edinburgh, 1790.

[Buckingham, George Villiers, Duke of.] *The Rehearsal: As it was Acted at the Theatre-Royal*. London, 1672.

Burke, Edmund. *Thoughts on the Cause of the Present Discontents*. London, 1770.

————. *The Writings and Speeches of Edmund Burke*, vol. 2: *Party, Parliament, and the American Crisis, 1766–1774*. Edited by Paul Langford. Oxford: Oxford University Press, 1981.

Burn, W. L. "The General Election of 1761 at Ayr." *English Historical Review* 52 (1937): 103–9.

Burney, Frances. *Diary and Letters of Madame D'Arblay*. Edited by Austin Dobson. Vol. 2. London: Macmillan, 1904.

Burney Collection Newspapers. Gale Cengage Learning. http://find.galegroup.com/bncn

Cadogan, William. *A Dissertation on the Gout, and All Chronic Diseases: Jointly Considered as Proceeding from the Same Causes*. London, 1771.

Campbell, Donald. *Playing for Scotland: A History of the Scottish Stage, 1715–1965*. Edinburgh: Mercat, 1996.

Carey, Harry [Henry]. *The Honest Yorkshireman: A Ballad Farce*. London, 1777.

Carte, Thomas. *A General History of England*. Vol. 1. London, 1747.

Carter, Philip. *Men and the Emergence of Polite Society in Britain, 1660–1800*. London: Longman, 2001.

Cash, Arthur H. *John Wilkes: The Scandalous Father of Civil Liberty*. New Haven: Yale University Press, 2006.

Castle, Terry. *Masquerade and Civilization: The Carnivalesque in Eighteenth-Century English Culture and Fiction*. London: Methuen, 1986.

"A Catalogue of Books Belonging to James Boswell, Esq." 1770. Edited by Eleanor Terry Lincoln. Revised by Su Jing-fen. Typescript, Boswell Editions Office, Yale University, 2010.

Caudle, James J. "'Fact' or 'Invention'?: James Boswell and the Legend of a Boswell—Sterne Meeting." *The Shandean* 22 (Nov. 2011): 30–55.

———. "Three New James Boswell Articles from *The Public Advertiser, 1763.*" *Scottish Literary Review* 3, no. 2 (2011): 19–43.

Chalmers, George. *The Life of Thomas Ruddiman.* London, 1794.

Chambers, Robert. *Traditions of Edinburgh.* Edinburgh, 1825.

Chambers' Edinburgh Journal, 3 (1835).

Christie, Ian R. *The End of North's Ministry, 1780–1782.* London: Macmillan, 1958.

Churchill, Charles. *The Duellist: A Poem.* London, 1764.

———. *The Poetical Works of Charles Churchill.* Edited by Douglas Grant. Oxford: Clarendon, 1956.

Cicero. *De natura deorum; Academica* [On the Nature of the Gods]. Translated by H. Rackham. Loeb Classical Library. London: Heinemann; New York: Putnam, 1933.

Cicero's Tusculan Disputations. Edited by C. D. Yonge. Teddington, Mddx.: Echo Library, 2006.

Clarke, Bob. *From Grub Street to Fleet Street: An Illustrated History of English Newspapers to 1899.* Aldershot: Ashgate, 2004.

Clifford, James L. *Hester Lynch Piozzi (Mrs. Thrale).* 2nd ed. New York: Columbia University Press, 1987.

Clifford, James L., and Donald J. Greene. *Samuel Johnson: A Survey and Bibliography of Critical Studies.* Minneapolis: University of Minnesota Press, [1970].

Cobbett, William. *Paper against Gold: Containing The History and Mystery of the Bank of England.* [London], 1817.

———, ed. *Parliamentary History of England.* Vols. 18 and 19. London, 1813.

Cobbett's Weekly Political Register. Vol. 20. London, 1811.

Cockburn, J. S., ed. *Crime in England, 1550–1800.* Princeton, NJ: Princeton University Press, 1977.

Coetlogon, Denis de. *A Tour through the Animal World, or, an Historical and Accurate Account of near Four Hundred Animals, Birds, Fishes, Serpents, Insects, &c.* London, 1746.

Collier, Jeremy. *Essays upon Several Moral Subjects: Part IV.* London, 1709.

Colman, George. *Prose on Several Occasions; Accompanied with Some Pieces in Verse.* 3 vols. London, 1787.

Cook, Don. *The Long Fuse: How England Lost the American Colonies, 1760–1785.* New York: Atlantic Monthly Press, 1998.

Cosh, Mary. *Edinburgh: The Golden Age.* Edinburgh: John Donald, 2003.

Coxe, William. *Memoirs of the Life and Administration of Sir Robert Walpole, Earl of Orford.* 3 vols. London, 1798.

Craig, Mary Elizabeth. *The Scottish Periodical Press, 1750–1789.* Edinburgh: Oliver and Boyd, 1931.

[Croft, Herbert.] *Love and Madness: A Story Too True: In a Series of Letters between Parties, whose Names would perhaps be Mentioned, were They less Known, or less Lamented.* London, 1780.

Dalrymple, John. *An Argument to Prove, that It is the Indispensible Duty of the Creditors of the Public to Insist, that Government do forthwith Bring forward the Consideration of the State of the Nation; in Order to Ascertain, as Near as May be, the Annual Receipts and Expenditure of the State*. London, 1783.

Davis, Bertram H. *Johnson before Boswell: A Study of Sir John Hawkins' "Life of Samuel Johnson."* 1960. Westport, CT: Greenwood, 1973.

[Dawes, Manasseh.] *The Case and Memoirs of the Late Rev. Mr. James Hackman*. London, 1779.

Deelman, Christian. *The Great Shakespeare Jubilee*. New York: Viking, 1964.

Dibdin, James C. *The Annals of the Edinburgh Stage, with an Account of the Rise and Progress of Dramatic Writing in Scotland*. Edinburgh, 1888.

Dickens, Charles, the Younger. *Dickens's Dictionary of London*. London, 1879. http://www.victorianlondon.org/publications/dictionary.htm.

Dictionary of Canadian Biography Online, general ed. John English. http://www.biographi.ca.

Diogenes Laertius. *The Lives and Opinions of Eminent Philosophers*. Translated by C. D. Yonge. London, 1853.

DuBos, Abbé. *Critical Reflections on Poetry, Painting and Music, with an Inquiry into the Rise and Progress of the Theatrical Entertainments of the Ancients*. Translated by Thomas Nugent. Vol. 1. London, 1748.

Duffy, Michael. *The Englishman and the Foreigner*. Cambridge: Chadwyck-Healey, 1986.

Epstein, William H. *John Cleland: Images of a Life*. New York: Columbia University Press, 1974.

Evelyn, William Glanville. *Memoir and Letters of Captain W. Glanville Evelyn, of the 4th Regiment ("Kings Own"), from North America, 1774–76*. Edited by G. D. Scull. Oxford, 1879.

Farrell, Stephen. "The Practices and Purposes of Party Leadership: Rockingham and the Lords, 1765–82." *Parliamentary History* 22, no. 1 (2003): 13–28.

Finley-Croswhite, Annette. "Henry IV and the Diseased Body Politic." In *Princes and Princely Culture, 1450–1650*, edited by Martin Gosman, Alasdair MacDonald, and Arjo Vanderjagt, 131–46. Vol. 1. Leiden: Brill, 2003.

Fischer, David Hackett. *Washington's Crossing*. Oxford: Oxford University Press, 2004.

Fletcher, Edward G., ed. *The Life of Samuel Johnson LL.D. by James Boswell, with Marginal Comments and Markings from Two Copies Annotated by Hester Lynch Thrale Piozzi*. 3 vols. London: Limited Editions Club, 1938.

Fortescue, J. W. *A History of the 17th Lancers (Duke of Cambridge's Own)*. London, 1895.

Foust, Clifford. "The Society of Arts and Rhubarb." *RSA Journal* (March 1988): 275–78; (April 1988): 350–53; (May 1988): 434–37.

Fry, Michael. "James Boswell, Henry Dundas, and Enlightened Politics." In *Boswell: Citizen of the World, Man of Letters*, edited by Irma S. Lustig, 87–100. Lexington: University Press of Kentucky, 1995.

Fuller, Thomas. *Gnomologia: Adagies and Proverbs; Wise Sentences and Witty Sayings, Ancient and Modern, Foreign and British*. London, 1732.

Garrick, David. *Shakespeare's Garland: Being a Collection of New Songs, Ballads, Roundelays, Catches, Glees, Comic-Serenatas, &c. Performed at the Jubilee at S[t]ratford upon Avon*. London, 1769.

———. *Three Plays by David Garrick*. Edited by E. P. Stein. New York: Rudge, 1926.

Garth, Sir Samuel. *The Dispensary: A Poem*. London, 1699.

Gatrell, V. A. C. *The Hanging Tree: Execution and the English People, 1770–1868*. Oxford: Oxford University Press, 1994.

Geltner, Guy. *The Medieval Prison: A Social History*. Princeton, NJ: Princeton University Press, 2008.

Gowland, John. *An Essay on Cutaneous Diseases, and All Impurities of the Skin*. London, [1792?].

Grafton, Augustus Henry Fitzroy, Duke of. *Autobiography and Political Correspondence of Augustus Henry, Third Duke of Grafton*. Edited by William R. Anson. London, 1898.

———. *Letters between the Duke of Grafton . . . and John Wilkes, Esq*. London, 1769.

Greatheed, Bertie. *The Regent: A Tragedy*. London, 1788.

Griffiths, David N. *The Bibliography of the Book of Common Prayer, 1549–1999*. London: British Library; New Castle, DE: Oak Knoll Press, 2002.

Gunning, Susannah. *The Memoirs of Mary: A Novel*. Vol. 3. London, 1793.

Harris, Bob. *Politics and the Rise of the Press: Britain and France, 1620–1800*. London: Routledge, 1996.

Hathaway, Baxter. "The Lucretian 'Return upon Ourselves' in Eighteenth-Century Theories of Tragedy." *PMLA* 62, no. 3 (September 1947): 672–89.

Hawkins, Sir John. *The Life of Samuel Johnson, LL.D*. Edited by O M Brack, Jr. Athens: University of Georgia Press, 2009.

Hay, John Barras. *Inaugural Addresses by Lords Rectors of the University of Glasgow*. Glasgow, 1839.

Hayward, Abraham, ed. *Autobiography, Letters, and Literary Remains of Mrs. Piozzi (Thrale)*. 2nd ed. Vol. 1. London, 1861.

Herrick, Robert. *Hesperides*. London, 1648.

Hervey, James. *Meditations and Contemplations*. 2 vols. London, 1748.

Heywood, John. *An Hundred Epigrammes*. London, 1550.

A History, Military and Municipal, of the Ancient Borough of the Devizes; and, Subordinately, of the Entire Hundred of Potterne and Cannings, in which It is Included. London and Devizes, 1859.

Hobbes, Thomas. *The Last Sayings, or, Dying Legacy of Mr. Thomas Hobbs of Malmesbury*. London, 1680.

Hogg, James, ed. *The Jacobite Relics of Scotland: Being the Songs, Airs, and Legends, of the Adherents to the House of Stuart.* 2 vols. Edinburgh, 1819–21.

Honey, Russell C. *The "Gentle" Johnston/es: The Story of the Johnston/e Family, from Prehistoric Scotland to Northern Ireland, Australasia, and the New World.* [Colborn, Ont.]: Fallsbrook, 1996.

Horace. *The Odes and Epodes.* Translated by C. E. Bennett. Loeb Classical Library. London: Heinemann; New York: Putnam, 1927.

———. *Odes and Epodes: A Modern English Verse Translation,* by Joseph P. Clancy. Chicago: Chicago University Press, 1960.

———. *Satires, Epistles and Ars poetica.* Translated by H. Rushton Fairclough. Loeb Classical Library. London: Heinemann; New York: Putnam, 1926.

Horn, David Bayne, and Mary Ransome, ed. *English Historical Documents,* vol. 7: *1714–1783.* London: Routledge, 1996.

Horne, Colin J. "Boswell and Literary Property." *Notes and Queries* 195 (1950): 296–98.

———. "Boswell, Burke, and the 'Life of Johnson.'" *Notes and Queries* 195 (1950): 498–99.

Hume, David. *An Enquiry Concerning Principles of Morals.* London, 1751.

———. *Essays: Moral, Political and Literary.* London: Oxford University Press, 1963.

———. *A Treatise of Human Nature: Being an Attempt to Introduce the Experimental Method of Reasoning into Moral Subjects . . . of the Understanding.* 3 vols. London, 1739–40.

Hurd, Richard. *Dialogues on the Uses of Foreign Travel; Considered as a Part of an English Gentleman's Education: between Lord Shaftesbury and Mr. Locke.* London, 1764.

Hyde, Mary. *The Impossible Friendship: Boswell and Mrs. Thrale.* London: Chatto & Windus, 1973.

Hyde, Ralph. *The A to Z of Georgian London.* London: London Topographical Society, 1982.

Jackson, John. *The History of the Scottish Stage.* Edinburgh, 1793.

Johnson, Samuel. *The Idler and The Adventurer.* Edited by W. J. Bate, John M. Bullitt, and L. F. Powell. The Yale Edition of the Works of Samuel Johnson, vol. 2. New Haven: Yale University Press, 1963.

———. *A Journey to the Western Islands of Scotland.* Edited by J. D. Fleeman. Oxford: Clarendon, 1985.

———. *Lives of the English Poets.* Edited by George Birkbeck Hill. 3 vols. Oxford: Clarendon, 1905.

———. *The Lives of the Most Eminent English Poets; with Critical Observations on Their Works.* Edited by Roger Lonsdale. 4 vols. Oxford: Clarendon, 2006.

———. *Poems.* Edited by E. L. McAdam, Jr., with George Milne. The Yale Edition of the Works of Samuel Johnson, vol. 6. New Haven: Yale University Press, 1964.

———. *Political Writings.* Edited by D. J. Greene. The Yale Edition of the Works of Samuel Johnson, vol. 10. New Haven: Yale University Press, 1977.

———. *The Rambler*. Edited by W. J. Bate. The Yale Edition of the Works of Samuel Johnson, vols. 3–5. New Haven: Yale University Press, 1969.

Johnsonian Miscellanies. Edited by George Birkbeck Hill. 2 vols. Oxford, 1897.

Johnsoniana: Anecdotes of the Late Samuel Johnson, LL.D. Edited by Robina Napier. London, 1884.

Junius. *The Letters of Junius: Woodfall's Edition*. Revised and enlarged by John Wade. London: George Bell and Sons, 1902.

Juvenal and Persius. Edited by Susanna Morton Braund. Loeb Classical Library. Cambridge, MA: Harvard University Press, 2004.

Kairoff, Claudia Thomas. *Anna Seward and the End of the Eighteenth Century*. Baltimore, MD: Johns Hopkins University Press, 2012.

Kay, John. *A Series of Original Portraits and Caricature Etchings, with Biographical Sketches and Illustrative Anecdotes*. Vol. 1. Edinburgh, 1877.

Kelsay, Isabel Thompson. *Joseph Brant, 1743–1807: Man of Two Worlds*. Syracuse, NY: Syracuse University Press, 1984.

Lang, Andrew. *A Short History of Scotland*. New York: Dodd, Mead and Co., 1912.

Langford, Paul. *Englishness Identified: Manners and Character, 1650–1850*. Oxford: Oxford University Press, 2000.

———. "William Pitt and Public Opinion, 1757." *English Historical Review* 88, no. 346 (January 1973): 54–80.

The Lark: Containing a Collection of above Four Hundred and Seventy Celebrated English and Scotch Songs. London, 1740.

Larsen, Lyle, ed. *James Boswell: As His Contemporaries Saw Him*. Madison, NJ: Fairleigh Dickinson University Press, 2008.

Lawson, Philip. *George Grenville: A Political Life*. Oxford: Clarendon, 1984.

Le Blanc, Jean-Bernard. *Letters on the English and French Nations*. 2 vols. London, 1747.

Lehmann, Gilly. *The British Housewife: Cookery Books, Cooking and Society in Eighteenth-Century Britain*. Totnes: Prospect, 2003.

Levy, Martin. *Love and Madness: The Murder of Martha Ray, Mistress of the Fourth Earl of Sandwich*. New York: HarperCollins, 2004.

Lillo, George. *Works*. London, 1775.

Linebaugh, Peter. *The London Hanged: Crime and Civil Society in the Eighteenth Century*. 2nd ed. London: Verso, 2006.

———. "The Ordinary of Newgate and His Account." In *Crime in England, 1550–1800*, edited by J. S. Cockburn, 246–69. Princeton, NJ: Princeton University Press, 1977.

Livy. *Ab urbe condita* [History of Rome]. Translated by B. O. Foster et al. 14 vols. Loeb Classical Library. London: Heinemann, 1919–59.

Lock, F. P. *Edmund Burke*, vol. 2: *1784–1797*. Oxford: Oxford University Press, 2006.

Locke, John. *An Essay Concerning Human Understanding*. Edited by A. S. Pringle Pattison. Oxford: Oxford University Press, 1924.

Lucan. *The Civil War* [Pharsalia]. Translated by James D. Duff. Loeb Classical Library. Cambridge, MA: Harvard University Press, 1928.

Lucretius. *De rerum natura.* Translated by W. D. F. Rouse. Revised by Martin Ferguson Smith. Loeb Classical Library. Cambridge, MA: Harvard University Press, 1975.

Lustig, Irma S. "Boswell at Work: The 'Animadversions' on Mrs Piozzi." *Modern Language Review* (1972): 11–30.

McGrattan, Alexander. "Brass Instruments in Masonic Ceremonies: The Building of 'The Athens of the North.'" In *Brass Scholarship in Review: Proceedings of the Historic Brass Society Conference, Cité de la Musique, Paris, 1999*, edited by Stewart Carter, 43–52. Hillsdale, NY: Pendragon Press, 2005.

McIntyre, Ian. *Hester: The Remarkable Life of Dr. Johnson's "Dear Mistress."* London: Constable, 2008.

Macknight, Thomas. *History of the Life and Times of Edmund Burke.* Vol. 3. London, 1860.

MacLachlan, Ian. "'The greatest and most offensive nuisance that ever disgraced the capital of a kingdom': The Slaughterhouses and Shambles of Modern Edinburgh." *Review of Scottish Culture* 17 (2004–5): 57–71.

MacLaurin, John. *Arguments and Decisions in Remarkable Cases, before the High Court of Justiciary, and Other Supreme Courts, in Scotland.* Edinburgh, 1774.

Malcolmson, Robert W. *Popular Recreations in English Society, 1700–1850.* Cambridge: Cambridge University Press, 1973.

Malone, Edmond, ed. *The Plays and Poems of William Shakespeare.* Vol. 1. London, 1790.

Marcus, Harold G. *A History of Ethiopia.* Berkeley: University of California Press, 1994.

Marshall, P. "Manchester and the American Revolution." *Bulletin of the John Rylands University Library of Manchester* 62 (1979–80): 168–86.

Martin, Peter. *A Life of James Boswell.* London: Weidenfeld and Nicolson, 1999.

Mason, William. *An Heroic Epistle to Sir William Chambers, Knight . . . Author of a Late Dissertation on Oriental Gardening.* London, 1773.

Mayhew, Nicholas. *Sterling: The History of a Currency.* London: Penguin, 1999.

Mickle, William Julius, trans. *The Lusiad or, the Discovery of India: An Epic Poem.* Oxford, 1776.

———. "On Passing through the Parliament-Close of Edinburgh at Midnight." In *A Collection of Original Poems*, by Scotch Gentlemen, 137–41. Vol. 2. Edinburgh, 1762.

Miller, Michele L. "J. M. W. Turner's *Ploughing up Turnips, near Slough*: The Cultivation of Cultural Dissent." *Art Bulletin* 77 (1995): 573–83.

Murphy, Arthur. "An Essay on the Life and Genius of Samuel Johnson, LL.D." In *Johnsonian Miscellanies*, edited by George Birkbeck Hill, 353–488. Vol. 1. Oxford, 1897.

Namier, Sir Lewis B. *England in the Age of American Revolution.* 2nd ed. London: Macmillan; New York: St. Martin's Press, 1961.

Namier, Sir Lewis B., and John Brooke. *The History of Parliament: The House of Commons, 1754–1790*, vol. 2: *Members A–J*. London: Her Majesty's Stationery Office for the History of Parliament Trust, 1964.

"A Narrative of the Trial of Laurence Balfe, and Edward Mac Quirk, for Aiding and Abetting in the Murder of Mr. George Clark, at Brentford Election, December 8, 1768." In *The Annals of Newgate; or, Malefactors Register*, 233–38. Vol. 4. London, 1776.

Newman, Donald J., ed. *James Boswell: Psychological Interpretations*. London: Palgrave Macmillan, 1995.

Newton, Thomas. *The Works of the Right Reverend Thomas Newton*. 3 vols. London, 1782.

Nichols, John. *Illustrations of the Literary History of the Eighteenth Century*. Vol. 7. London, 1848.

Nussbaum, Felicity A. "Manly Subjects: Boswell's Journals and *The Life of Johnson*." In *The Autobiographical Subject: Gender and Ideology in Eighteenth-Century England*, 103–26. Baltimore, MD: Johns Hopkins University Press, 1989.

Ovid. *Metamorphoses*. Translated by Frank Justus Miller. Revised by G. P. Goold. 2 vols. Loeb Classical Library. Cambridge, MA: Harvard University Press; London: Heinemann, 1977.

The Parliamentary Register. Vols. 2, 16–17. London, 1797–1802.

Parnell, Thomas. *Collected Poems of Thomas Parnell*. Edited by Claude Rawson and F. P. Lock. Newark: University of Delaware Press, 1989.

Partridge, Eric. *A Dictionary of Slang and Unconventional English*. 8th ed. London: Routledge & Kegan Paul, 1984.

Paulson, Ronald, ed. *Hogarth's Graphic Works: First Complete Edition*. Vol. 1. New Haven: Yale University Press, 1965.

Peters, Marie. *The Elder Pitt*. London: Longman, 1998.

———. "The Myth of William Pitt, Earl of Chatham, Great Imperialist Part II: Chatham and Imperial Reorganization 1763–78." *Journal of Imperial and Commonwealth History* 22, no. 3 (September 1994): 393–431.

Pindar, Peter [John Wolcot]. *A Poetical and Congratulatory Epistle to James Boswell, Esq., on his Journal of a Tour to the Hebrides, with the Celebrated Dr. Johnson*. London, 1786.

Piozzi, Hester Lynch. *Letters to and from the Late Samuel Johnson, LL.D.: To which are Added Some Poems never before Printed, Published from the Original MSS. in Her Possession*. 2 vols. London, 1788.

———. *Thraliana: The Diary of Mrs Hester Lynch Thrale (Later Mrs. Piozzi) 1776–1809*. Edited by Katherine C. Balderston. 2 vols. Oxford: Clarendon, 1951.

Pitt, William. *The Speeches of the Rt. Hon. the Earl of Chatham, in the Houses of Lords & Commons*. London, 1848.

Pliny the Elder. *Pliny's Natural History*. Translation based on Philemon Holland's of 1601. London, 1847–48.

Plutarch's Lives: The Dryden Translation. Edited by Arthur Hugh Clough. 1861. Vol. 1. New York: Modern Library, 2001.

Pope, Alexander. *Imitations of Horace.* Vol. 4 of *The Poems of Alexander Pope.* Edited by John Butt. 2nd ed. London: Methuen; New Haven: Yale University Press, 1953.

Pope, Alexander, and William Warburton, eds. *The Works of Shakespeare.* Vol. 8. London, 1747.

Potter, Harry. *Hanging in Judgment: Religion and the Death Penalty in England.* New York: Continuum, 1993.

Priestley, Joseph. *Institutes of Natural and Revealed Religion.* Vol. 2. London, 1772–74.

Prior, Matthew. *The Literary Works of Matthew Prior.* Edited by H. Bunker Wright and Monroe K. Spears. 2 vols. Oxford: Clarendon, 1959.

The Proceedings of the Old Bailey, 1674–1913. http://www.oldbaileyonline.org.

Ramsay, Allan. *The Tea-Table Miscellany: or, Allan Ramsay's Collection of Scots Sangs.* London, 1730.

Ramsay, James. "Boswell's First Criminal Case: John Reid—Sheep-Stealer." *Juridical Review* (1938): 315–21.

Rauschenberg, Roy A. "The Journals of Joseph Banks's Voyage up Great Britain's West Coast to Iceland and to the Orkney Isles July to October, 1772." *Proceedings of the American Philosophical Society* 117, no. 3 (June 1973): 186–226.

Rawlings, Philip. *Drunks, Whores, and Idle Apprentices: Criminal Biographies of the Eighteenth Century.* London: Routledge, 1992.

Redford, Bruce. "Boswell's Fear of Death." *Studies in Scottish Literature* 21 (1986): 99–118.

Rendle-Short, Morwenna, and John Rendle-Short. *The Father of Child Care: Life of William Cadogan (1711–1797).* Bristol: Wright, 1966.

Rizzo, Betty. "'Innocent Frauds': By Samuel Johnson." *The Library* 6th series, 8, no. 3 (September 1989): 249–64.

Rodger, N. A. M. *The Insatiable Earl: The Life of John Montagu, Fourth Earl of Sandwich, 1718–1792.* New York: Norton, 1994.

Rogers, Ben. *Beef and Liberty.* London: Chatto and Windus, 2003.

Rogers, Pat. "Boswell and the Diurnal." In *Boswell in Scotland and Beyond,* edited by Thomas Crawford, 104–18. Glasgow: Association for Scottish Literary Studies, 1997.

Rounce, Adam. "Charles Churchill's Anti-enlightenment." *History of European Ideas* 31, no. 2 (2005): 227–36.

Rowe, Nicholas. "Some Account of the Life, &c. of William Shakspeare." In *The Plays and Poems of William Shakspeare,* edited by Edmond Malone, 193–541. Vol. 1. London, 1790.

Ruvigny and Raineval, Marquis of. *The Moodie Book: Being an Account of the Families of Melsetter, Muir, Cocklaw, Blairhill, Bryanton, Gilchorn, Pitmuies, Arbekie, Masterton, etc.* [London: privately printed], 1906.

Ruxin, Paul T. "*Dorando* and the Douglas Cause." *Age of Johnson: A Scholarly Annual* 20 (2010): 79–94.

———. "Other People's Books." *Caxtonian* 12, no. 9 (September 2004): 1, 3–7.

Sainsbury, John. *John Wilkes: The Lives of a Libertine*. Aldershot: Ashgate, 2006.

Sale Catalogues of the Libraries of Samuel Johnson, Hester Lynch Thrale (Mrs. Piozzi) and James Boswell. Introduced by Donald D. Eddy. New Castle, DE: Oak Knoll Books, 1993.

Sallust. *Sallust*. Translated by J. C. Rolfe. Loeb Classical Library. London: Heinemann; Cambridge, MA: Harvard University Press, 1931.

Sanborn, Paul J. "James Grant (1720–1806)." In *The American Revolution, 1775–1783: An Encyclopedia*, edited by Richard L. Blanco and Paul J. Sanborn, 665. New York: Garland, 1993.

Saville, Richard. *Bank of Scotland: A History, 1695–1995*. Edinburgh: Edinburgh University Press, 1996.

The School for Satire: Or, A Collection of Modern Satirical Poems. London, 1802.

Schuyler, R. L. "Galloway's Plans for Anglo-American Union." *Political Science Quarterly* 57, no. 2 (June 1942): 281–85.

Scott, Sir Walter. *The Bride of Lammermoor*. Waverley Novels: Centenary Edition. Vol. 8. Edinburgh, 1871.

Seneca. *"Tranquillity of Mind" and "Providence."* Translated by William Bell Langsdorf. New York: Putnam, 1900. [Revised and edited by Michael S. Russo, Sophia Study Editions, http://students.molloy.edu/sophia/seneca/providence.html.]

Shaftesbury, Anthony Ashley Cooper, Earl of. *Characteristics of Men, Manners, Opinions, Times*. Edited by Lawrence E. Klein. Cambridge: Cambridge University Press, 1999.

Shapiro, Fred R., ed. *The Yale Book of Quotations*. New Haven: Yale University Press, 2006.

Sher, Richard B. "'The favourite of the favourite': John Home, Bute and the Politics of Patriotic Poetry." In *Lord Bute: Essays in Re-interpretation*, edited by Karl W. Schweizer, 181–212. [Leicester]: Leicester University Press, 1988.

Shoemaker, R. B. "The Old Bailey Proceedings and the Representation of Crime and Criminal Justice in Eighteenth-Century London." *Journal of British Studies* 47, no. 3 (2008): 559–80.

Smith, Anthony. "The Long Road to Objectivity and Back Again: The Kinds of Truth We Get in Journalism." In *Newspaper History: From the Seventeenth Century to the Present Day*, edited by George Boyce, James Curran, and Pauline Wingate, 153–71. London: Constable; Beverly Hills: Sage, 1978.

Smout, T. C. *A History of the Scottish People, 1560–1830*. London: Collins, 1969.

Sorkin, David. "Geneva's 'Enlightened Orthodoxy': The Middle Way of Jacob Vernet (1698–1789)." *Church History* 74, no. 2 (June 2005): 286–305.

The Spectator. Edited by Donald F. Bond. 5 vols. Oxford: Clarendon, 1965.

Stead, B. L. M. "'Poor distress'd weavers': Conflicting Interpretations of the Raising of the 72nd Regiment, Royal Manchester Volunteers." *British Journal for Eighteenth-Century Studies* 23, no. 2 (2000): 203–32.

Stewart, David. *Sketches of the Character, Manners, and Present State of the Highlanders of Scotland: With Details of the Military Service of the Highland Regiments.* Vol. 2. 3rd ed. Edinburgh, 1825.

Stochholm, Johanne Magdalene. *Garrick's Folly: The Shakespeare Jubilee of 1769 at Stratford and Drury Lane.* New York: Barnes & Noble, 1964.

Swift, Jonathan. Preface to *A Tale of a Tub.* London, 1704.

———. "Thoughts on Religion." In *The Author's Works,* edited by Deane Swift, 303–7. Vol. 12. Dublin, 1765.

Tankard, Paul. "'A Very Agreable Way of Thinking': Devotion and Doctrine in Boswell's Religion." In *Theology and Literature in the Age of Johnson: Resisting Secularism,* edited by Melvyn New and Gerard Reedy, S.J., 237–54. Newark: Univ. of Delaware Press, 2012.

———. "Anonymity and the Press: The Case of Boswell." *Eighteenth-Century Life* (forthcoming).

———. "Boswell, George Steevens, and the Johnsonian Biography Wars." *Age of Johnson: A Scholarly Annual* 22 (2012): 73–95.

The Tatler. Edited by Donald F. Bond. 3 vols. Oxford: Clarendon, 1987.

Thomas, Peter D. G. *John Wilkes: A Friend to Liberty.* Oxford: Clarendon, 1996.

Topham, Edward. *Letters from Edinburgh: Written in the Years 1774 and 1775.* London, 1776.

Trevelyan, George Otto. *George the Third and Charles Fox: The Concluding Part of the American Revolution.* London: Longmans, Green, 1912.

Tungate, Sue. "Matthew Boulton's Mints: Copper to Customer." In *Matthew Boulton: Selling What the World Desires,* edited by Shena Mason, 81–88. New Haven: Birmingham City Council in association with Yale University Press, 2009.

Turnbull, Gordon. "Boswell and Sympathy: The Trial and Execution of John Reid." In *New Light on Boswell: Critical and Historical Essays on the Occasion of the Bicentenary of "The Life of Johnson,"* edited by Greg Clingham, 104–15. Cambridge: Cambridge University Press, 1991.

———. "Boswell's 'Dictionary of the Scots Language.'" *Johnsonian News Letter* 62, no. 2 (September 2011): 37–42.

———. "Yale Boswell Edition Notes." *Johnsonian News Letter* 61, no. 2 (September 2010): 19–25.

Tytler, William. "On the Fashionable Amusements and Entertainments in Edinburgh in the Last Century." *Transactions of the Society of Antiquaries of Scotland* (1812): 499–504.

———. *The Poetical Remains of James the First, King of Scotland.* Edinburgh, 1783.

Villette, John. *The Annals of Newgate: Or, Malefactors Register.* 4 vols. London, 1776.

Virgil. *The Aeneid.* Translated by H. Rushton Fairclough. Loeb Classical Library. Cambridge, MA: Harvard University Press, 1999, 2000.

———. *The Aeneid.* Translated by W. F. Jackson Knight. Harmondsworth: Penguin, 1956.

Vox Senatus: The Speeches at Large which were Made in a Great Assembly, on Wednesday the 27th of November Last. London, 1771.

Walker, Sir Norman. "The Development of Dermatology in Scotland." *British Journal of Dermatology* 45, no. 11 (November 1933): 457–66.

Walpole, Horace. *The Yale Editions of Horace Walpole's Correspondence.* Vols. 17 and 24. Gen. ed. W. S. Lewis. New Haven: Yale University Press, 1954 and 1967.

Warner, Jessica. *John the Painter: Terrorist of the American Revolution.* New York: Four Walls Eight Windows, 2004.

Warton, Joseph. *An Essay on the Writings and Genius of Pope.* London, 1756.

Weintraub, Stanley. *Iron Tears: America's Battle for Freedom, Britain's Quagmire, 1775–1783.* New York: Free Press, 2005.

Werkmeister, Lucyle. *Jemmie Boswell and the London Daily Press, 1785–1795.* New York: New York Public Library, 1963.

———. *The London Daily Press, 1772–1792.* Lincoln: University of Nebraska Press, 1963.

Whitefield, George. *Eighteen Sermons.* London, 1771.

Wilkes, John. *The Controversial Letters of John Wilkes, Esq., the Rev. John Horne, and Their Principal Adherents.* London, 1771.

Williams, Gordon. *A Dictionary of Sexual Language and Imagery in Shakespearean and Stuart Literature.* London: Continuum, 1994.

Woolley, James D. "Johnson as Despot: Anna Seward's Rejected Contribution to Boswell's *Life.*" *Modern Philology* 70, no. 2 (November 1972): 140–45.

Yonge, Charles Duke. *The Constitutional History of England.* London, 1882.

Young, Edward. *The Complaint: Or, Night-Thoughts on Life, Death, and Immortality.* London, 1742–46.

Yung, Kai Kin. *Samuel Johnson, 1709–1784.* London: Herbert Press, 1984.

Index

Abercorn, James Hamilton, eighth earl of, 36 & nn. 104 & 106, 267 & n. 131

Abercrombie, James, 195–96 & n. 344

Abercromby, Patrick, *The Martial Achievements of the Scots Nation*, 193, 195

Abingdon, Willoughby Bertie, fourth earl of, 204 & n. 383

Abyssinia, 47–55 & nn.

Adair, James, 186 n. 306; *The History of the American-Indians*, 186 & n. 306

Adam, Agnes, 75

Adam, Margaret, 75

Adams, William, 230 & n. 10, 250 n. 73

Addison, Joseph, 79 n. 5, 170 & n. 244, 176 & n. 260; *Cato*, 104–5 & n. 90, 153–56. See also *Spectator*

Aesop's Fables, 163 n. 212, 341 & n. 200, 342

Aickin, James, 5 & n. 6

Ailred, 145 & n. 138

Aitken, James, 190–93 & nn.

Akerman, Richard, 105

allegories: allegorical figures in the *Caledonian Mercury*, 340–42; of the Douglas Cause, xxviii, 11; political, 114–28, 128–31, 136–44, 144–53, 201

Allen, Robert, xxxix

America: and Britain, 60 & n. 184, 183, 190 & n. 325, 195, 196 & n. 348, 197, 354; boycotts of British goods in, 179, 181 & n. 284; customs and duties, 164, 179, 196; First Continental Congress, 6 n. 8, 179, 181 n. 284; "olive branch" petition, 189 & n. 324; Second Continental Congress, 183, 189 n. 324. *See also* American War, Mohock Indians, taxation (of the American colonies)

American War (of Independence), 115, 179, 189–90 & nn., 213 n. 423, 216–18 & nn., 251 n. 82, 353–54 & n. 258; arming the Jews to end the, 111, 183–86 & nn.; Battle of Bunker Hill, 183, 195 n. 344, 196 n. 348, 343–44; Battle of Concord, 183, 197 & n. 350; Battle of Lexington, 183, 197 n. 350; Battle of Philadelphia, 197 n. 348, 207; Battle of Saratoga, 197 n. 348, 199, 202 n. 372, 204–6 & nn., 207, 211 n. 415, 216; British casualties and casualty lists in the, 183, 196 & n. 345, 199 n. 359, 342–44; French entry into the, 62 n. 189, 216; German auxiliaries in the, 189 & n. 322, 199 n. 359, 346 & n. 222; JB's response to the, 4 n. 1, 109, 111, 112, 182, 183–84, 189–90, 193–99 & nn.; Manchester Regiment, 199–204 & nn.; Parliamentary Enquiry into the, 207–11 & nn.; Tea War, 178–83 & nn.; 17th

Stuart, Maj. Charles, 197 & n. 352

Stuart, Peter, xxxix

Stuart, Prince Charles Edward ("Bonnie
Prince Charlie"), 8 n. 17, 12 n. 32, 15 n. 48,
37 n. 108, 197 n. 352, 229 & n. 7

Stuart, Rev. John, 59 & n. 180, 60 n. 186

Swift, Jonathan, 58 n. 179; *Gulliver's Travels*,
199 & n. 358; *Tale of a Tub*, 367 & n. 318;
"Thoughts on Religion," 363 & n. 292

Syene, 55 & n. 171

Tacitus, *Germania*, 33 & n. 95

tar-water, 178 & n. 270

Tatler, 58 n. 179, 297 n. 16, 322 n. 135, 337
n. 193

taxation, in Britain, xxxvii, 149 n. 157, 182,
251, cider tax, 121 n. 24, 123 nn. 30 & 33,
129 n. 60; of the American colonies, 111,
115, 118 n. 12, 178–79, 196 n. 346, stamp
tax, 4 n. 1, 123 n. 31, 124 n. 36, sugar tax,
127 n. 51, tea duty, 178–79

Taylor, Elizabeth, 75, 105 & n. 94, 106 &
nn. 99 & 101

Taylor, John, 309 & n. 73

Taylor, Martin, 75, 105 & n. 94, 106 & nn.
99 & 101

Taylor, Rev. Dr. John, 230 & n. 10

Taylor, Stephen, 149 n. 156

tea, 180; American Tea War, 178–83, 183–84;
rue tea, 181 & n. 283, 183–84

Tekle Haimanot II, emperor of Abyssinia,
50 n. 154

Temple, Richard Grenville, second Earl,
130 & n. 70, 155

Temple, William Johnson, xxix, 13 n. 36,
110, 113, 309 n. 74, 322 n. 131; *An Essay on
the Clergy*, 173 & nn. 248 & 250

theater, xxv, 4, 6 n. 10, 253, 301, 303 n. 46,
304 n. 47

Theyendanegea, *see* Brant (Joseph)

Thomas, Nathaniel, xxxviii, 94

Thomas, Sir Noah, 185 & n. 303

Thompson, Capt. Edward, 31 & n. 89

Thomson, James, 35 n. 102; *Alfred*, 204
n. 382; *Castle of Indolence*, 35 & n. 102,

336 & n. 191; "Hymn on the Seasons,"
303 n. 44

Thornton, Bonnell, xxxi, xxxviii

Thrale, Henry, 233 n. 15, 237, 242, 244 &
n. 53, 253; Thrale's entire, 245, 246 &
n. 60, 253, 256

Thrale, Hester. *See* Piozzi (Hester Lynch)

Thurlow, Edward, first Baron, 221 & n. 461

Tice, Capt. Gilbert, 3, 58, 59 & n. 183, 60

Timur Lenk (or Tamerlane), 221 & n. 462

Tiyanoga/Theyanoguin (or King Hendrick), 58 n. 178, 59 n. 181

Tonson, Jacob, 236 & n. 23

Tooker, William, 145 & n. 141, 146–47

Topham, Edward, xxxix, 359 n. 278, 368
n. 320

touching medicine, 141 n. 116, 144–53 & nn.

Townsend, James, 142 & n. 123

Townshend, Charles, 164

Townshend, George, first marquess, 127
n. 53, 196 n. 345, 218–19 & n. 452

Tracy, John, 14 n. 42

Tracy family, 14 & n. 41

"Tradesman," 370 n. 325

Traill, Robert, 37–38 & n. 114

"Traveller," 369 & n. 321, 370 nn. 324 & 327,
371

travelling, 46, 310–13 & nn.

Trotz, Christian Heinrich, 9 & n. 24

Trumpeters, State, 290, 344–46 & nn.

trumpets, 128 & n. 56, 345–46 & n. 216

truth, 170, 174 & n. 251

Turnbull, Gordon, xxv n. 2, xxvii n. 3, 110,
307, 327 n. 154

Tyburn, 72, 74, 76, 80, 217 & n. 443, 298 &
n. 25, 299 n. 281, 306 & n. 64

Tyers, Thomas, 240 & n. 43; "Biographical
Sketch of Dr. Samuel Johnson," 223, 228
nn. 2 & 3, 240 n. 43

Tytler, William, 324 n. 144, 327 n. 152

Union, 66 n. 203, 182 n. 288, 347 & nn. 226
& 227

universality, 135 & n. 93

Utrecht, xxvii, 9–10 & nn.